W9-DJL-033

UNITED STATES HISTORY and GOVERNMENT

BRIGGS / FISH PETERSEN

SAVVAS

LEARNING COMPANY

ISBN-13: 978-1-4188-3519-4
ISBN-10: 1-4188-3519-6

3 22

Table of Contents

New York State Framework

Topic 1   Colonial Foundations (1607–1763) 1

11.1a, 11.1b, 11.1c

Topic 2   Constitutional Foundations (1763–1824) 35

11.2a, 11.2b, 11.2c, 11.2d

Topic 3   Expansion, Nationalism, and Sectionalism (1800–1865) 83

11.3a, 11.3b, 11.3c

Table of Contents

Table of Contents

About This Book

This book has been written to help you, the student, review your United States History and Government course in order to take the New York State Regents Examination for that course. The purpose of this book is to

- help you focus on the key facts, unifying themes, and social studies practices tested on the Regents Examination.
- familiarize you with the format of the Regents Examination.
- provide you with the test-taking skills and strategies you need to succeed on the Regents Examination.

Review of Content and Concepts
To help you master the content and skills required for this course

- This book is organized chronologically into eleven topics, just like the new New York State United States History and Government Grade 11 Framework.
- Brief Review United States History and Government focuses on the key concepts and content of each topic on the new Grade 11 Framework.
- The *Key Concept, topic* and *Section Overview,* and the *Unifying Themes* at the beginning of each section organize the content at a glance.
- The charts, maps, cartoons, timelines, graphic organizers, and other stimulus-based documents, such as letters, speeches, and laws, in each topic will help reinforce your understanding of the content and concepts of United States History and Government and their historical context across time.

Test-Taking Skills
Brief Review United States History and Government provides multiple opportunities to practice your test-taking skills in preparation for stimulus-based questions that make up the new Regents Examination.

- *Multiple-Choice Stimulus-Based Questions, Short Essay Questions,* and *Civic Literacy Essay* tasks are included with every topic.
- Every topic contains activities for practice of test-taking skills under headings such as *Preparing for the Regents, Social Studies Practices, Unifying Themes,* and *Analyzing Documents.*
- Each topic highlights the key people, terms, and events on which to focus.
- An extensive *Test-Taking Strategies* section reviews the skills and strategies you need for the exam.
- *Preparing for the Regents* notes in the margins help reinforce test-taking strategies.
- The *Reference Section* provides charts updated to reflect the new Framework, including
  - Presidents of the United States
  - Landmark Supreme Court Cases
  - Important People in United States History
  - Thirteen Basic Constitutional Principles—a guide to the Civic Literacy Essay
  - Expanded Glossary
  - Expansive Index

Bonnie-Anne Briggs

Bonnie-Anne Briggs is a graduate of Nazareth College of Rochester and the State University of New York at Brockport. She is retired from her position as teacher and Teacher-in-Charge of Social Studies (department head) at Gates Chili High School in suburban Rochester. She was an adjunct professor in social studies education at the State University of New York at Brockport for seventeen years. Miss Briggs is a past president of the Rochester Area Council for the Social Studies. She is also a past officer of both the New York State Social Studies Supervisory Association and the New York State Council for the Social Studies. Miss Briggs is a recipient of the Rochester Area Council Distinguished Educator Award, the New York State Social Studies Supervisory Association Supervisor of the Year Award, the New York State Council for the Social Studies Distinguished Educator Award, and the Outstanding Alumni Award from Nazareth College of Rochester. She has been inducted into the Gates Chili High School Alumni Hall of Fame, and in 1993, she was a semifinalist for the New York State Teacher of the Year Award. Miss Briggs is a docent at the Susan B. Anthony House in Rochester, New York.

Catherine Fish Petersen

Catherine Fish Petersen is a graduate of Wellesley College, Harvard University, and the State University of New York at Stony Brook. Ms. Petersen was the consultant to the New York State Education Department on the *Social Studies Resource Guide* and their social studies consultant for the New York State Academy for Teaching and Learning. She also was an editor of the State publication, *Social Studies Instructional Strategies & Resources Pre K-Grade Six*. Before retirement, she chaired the Department of Humanities (Social Studies and English) in the East Islip School District on Long Island. Ms. Petersen is a past president of the New York State Social Studies Supervisory Association. She is also a past president, treasurer, and executive secretary of the Long Island Council for the Social Studies. She served on the Board of Directors of the New York State Council for the Social Studies. Ms. Petersen is a recipient of the Long Island Council for the Social Studies Presidential Leadership Award and its Gus Swift Outstanding Service to Social Studies Education Award, the New York State Social Studies Supervisory Association Supervisor of the Year Award and that organization's Special Service Award, as well as the Distinguished Social Studies Service Award from the New York State Council for the Social Studies.

Standard 1:
History of the United States and New York

Students will use a variety of intellectual skills to demonstrate their understanding of major ideas, eras, themes, developments, and turning points in the history of the United States and New York.

Standard 2:
World History

Students will use a variety of intellectual skills to demonstrate their understanding of major ideas, eras, themes, developments, and turning points in world history and examine the broad sweep of history from a variety of perspectives.

Standard 3:
Geography

Students will use a variety of intellectual skills to demonstrate their understanding of the geography of the interdependent world in which we live—local, national, and global—including the distribution of people, places, and environments over Earth's surface.

Standard 4:
Economics

Students will use a variety of intellectual skills to demonstrate their understanding of how the United States and other societies develop economic systems and associated institutions to allocate scarce resources, how major decision-making units function in the United States and other national economies, and how an economy solves the scarcity problem through market and nonmarket mechanisms.

Standard 5:
Civics, Citizenship, and Government

Students will use a variety of intellectual skills to demonstrate their understanding of the necessity for establishing governments; the governmental systems of the United States and other nations; the United States Constitution; the basic civic values of American constitutional democracy; and the roles, rights, and responsibilities of citizenship, including avenues of participation.

Social Studies Unifying Themes With Context

These ten unifying Social Studies themes represent different lenses that can be applied to learning the Key Ideas and Conceptual Understandings in U.S. History and Government. The Unifying Themes specific to each topic of this text are identified at the beginning of the topic.

1. Individual Development and Cultural Identity (ID)
- Role of social, political, and cultural interactions in the development of identity
- Personal identity as a function of an individual's culture, time, place, geography, interaction with groups, influences from institutions, and lived experiences

2. Development, Movement, and Interaction of Cultures (MOV)
- Role of diversity within and among cultures
- Aspects of culture such as belief systems, religious faith, or political ideals as influences on other parts of a culture, such as its institutions or literature, music, and art
- Cultural diffusion and change over time as facilitating different ideas and beliefs

3. Time, Continuity, and Change (TCC)
- History as a formal study that applies research methods
- Reading, reconstructing, and interpreting events
- Analyzing causes and consequences of events and developments
- Considering competing interpretations of events

4. Geography, Humans, and the Environment (GEO)
- Relationship between human populations and the physical world (people, places, and environments)
- Effect of human activities on the environment
- Interactions between regions, locations, places, people, and environments
- Spatial patterns of place and location

5. Development and Transformation of Social Structures (SOC)
- Role of social class, systems of stratification, social groups, and institutions
- Role of gender, race, ethnicity, education, class, age, and religion in defining social structures within a culture
- Social and political inequalities
- Expansion and access of rights through concepts of justice and human rights

6. Power, Authority, and Governance (GOV)
- Purposes, characteristics, and functions of various governance systems as they are practiced
- Individual rights and responsibilities as protected and challenged within the context of majority rule
- Fundamental principles and values of constitutional democracy
- Origins, uses, and abuses of power
- Conflict, diplomacy, and war

7. Civic Ideals and Practices (CIV)

- Basic freedoms and rights and responsibilities of citizens in a democratic republic
- Role of the citizen in the community and nation and as a member of the global community
- Civic participation and engagement
- Respect for diversity
- Civic ideals and practices in countries other than our democratic republic
- Struggle for rights, access to citizenship rights, and universal human rights

8. Creation, Expansion, and Interaction of Economic Systems (ECO)

- Production, distribution, and consumption
- Scarcity of resources and the challenges of meeting wants and needs
- Supply/demand and the coordination of individual choices
- Economic systems
- Trade, interdependence, and globalization
- Role of government in the economy
- Personal finance

9. Science, Technology, and Innovation (TECH)

- Scientific and intellectual theories, findings, discoveries, and philosophies
- Applications of science and innovations in transportation, communication, military technology, navigation, agriculture, and industrialization
- Relationship between science, technology, and innovation and social, cultural, and economic change

10. Global Connections and Exchange (EXCH)

- Past, current, and likely future global connections and interactions
- Cultural diffusion; the spread of ideas, beliefs, technology, and goods
- Role of technology
- Benefits/consequences of global interdependence (social, political, economic)
- Causes and patterns of migration
- Tension between national interests and global priorities

Social Studies Practices

The Social Studies Practices are the social science and historical thinking skills that help you to gather, organize, use, and present information.

A. Gathering, Interpreting, and Using Evidence

1. Define and frame questions about events and the world in which we live, form hypotheses as potential answers to these questions, use evidence to answer these questions, and consider and analyze counter-hypotheses.

2. Identify, describe, and evaluate evidence about events from diverse sources (including written documents, works of art, photographs, charts and graphs, artifacts, oral traditions, and other primary and secondary sources).

3. Analyze evidence in terms of content, authorship, point of view, bias, purpose, format, and audience.

4. Describe, analyze, and evaluate arguments of others.

5. Make inferences and draw conclusions from evidence.

6. Deconstruct and construct plausible and persuasive arguments, using evidence.

7. Create meaningful and persuasive understandings of the past by fusing disparate and relevant evidence from primary and secondary sources and drawing connections to the present.

B. Chronological Reasoning and Causation

1. Articulate how events are related chronologically to one another in time and explain the ways in which earlier ideas and events may influence subsequent ideas and events.

2. Identify causes and effects using examples from different time periods and courses of study across several grade levels.

3. Identify, analyze, and evaluate the relationship between multiple causes and effects.

4. Distinguish between long-term and immediate causes and multiple effects (time, continuity, and change).

5. Recognize, analyze, and evaluate dynamics of historical continuity and change over periods of time and investigate factors that caused those changes over time.

6. Recognize that choice of specific periodization favors or advantages one narrative, region, or group over another narrative, region, or group.

7. Relate patterns of continuity and change to larger historical processes and themes.

8. Describe, analyze, evaluate, and construct models of historical periodization that historians use to categorize events.

C. Comparison and Contextualization

1. Identify similarities and differences between geographic regions across historical time periods, and relate differences in geography to different historical events and outcomes.

2. Identify, compare, and evaluate multiple perspectives on a given historical experience.

3. Identify and compare similarities and differences between historical developments over time and in different geographical and cultural contexts.

4. Describe, compare, and evaluate multiple historical developments (within societies; across and between societies; in various chronological and geographical contexts).

5. Recognize the relationship between geography, economics, and history as a context for events and movements and as a matrix of time and place.

6. Connect historical developments to specific circumstances of time and place and to broader regional, national, or global processes and draw connections to the present (where appropriate).

D. Geographic Reasoning

1. Ask geographic questions about where places are located, why their locations are important, and how their locations are related to the locations of other places and people.

2. Identify, describe, and evaluate the relationships between people, places, regions, and environments by using geographic tools to place them in a spatial context.

3. Identify, analyze, and evaluate the relationship between the environment and human activities, how the physical environment is modified by human activities, and how human activities are also influenced by Earth's physical features and processes.

4. Recognize and interpret (at different scales) the relationships between patterns and processes.

5. Recognize and analyze how place and region influence the social, cultural, and economic characteristics of civilizations.

6. Characterize and analyze changing connections between places and regions.

E. Economics and Economics Systems

2. Analyze the ways in which incentives influence what is produced and distributed in a market system.

3. Evaluate the extent to which competition between sellers and between buyers exists in specific markets.

F. Civic Participation

1. Demonstrate respect for the rights of others in discussions and classroom debates; respectfully disagree with other viewpoints and provide evidence for a counter-argument.

2. Participate in activities that focus on a classroom, school, community, state, or national issue or problem. . . .

6. Identify situations in which social actions are required and determine an appropriate course of action.

Social Studies Framework Grade 11
U.S. History and Government

The Grade 11 Regents Examination tests the new Social Studies Framework Grade 11: United States History and Government, printed below. For you to see how critical the Content Understandings are to provide focus and direction to the new curriculum, we have shown the text that makes up the Framework Key Idea 11.1 in its entirety. Brief Review United States History and Government addresses every line in the new Framework. Space limitations, however, prevent including all the Content Specifications portions of the Grade 11 Framework below.

Please note that after Key Idea 11.1 only the Key Ideas and Conceptual Understandings of the New York State Framework for United States History and Government are listed. For a copy of the full text of the Framework, please visit the Office of Assessment website at http://www.p12.nysed.gov/assessment/ss/framework-ushistory.html.

Social Studies Framework Grade 11: United States History and Government

Grade 11 begins with the colonial and constitutional foundations of the United States and explores the government structure and functions written in the Constitution. The development of the nation and the political, social, and economic factors that led to the challenges our nation faced in the Civil War are addressed. Industrialization, urbanization, and the accompanying problems are examined, along with America's emergence as a world power, the two world wars of the 20th century, and the Cold War. Students explore the expansion of the federal government, the threat of terrorism, and the place of the United States in an increasingly globalized and interconnected world.

11.1 COLONIAL FOUNDATIONS (1607–1763): European colonization in North America prompted cultural contact and exchange between diverse peoples; cultural differences and misunderstandings at times led to conflict. A variety of factors contributed to the development of regional differences, including social and racial hierarchies, in colonial America.
(Standards: 1, 2, 3, 4, 5; Themes: MOV, TCC, GEO, GOV, ECO, EXCH)

11.1a Contact between Native American* groups and Europeans occurred through cultural exchanges, resistance efforts, and conflict.

• Students will trace European contact with Native Americans, including the Dutch, the English, the French and the Spanish.

• Students will examine the impacts of European colonization on Native Americans, who eventually lost much of their land and experienced a drastic decline in population through disease and armed conflict.

11.1b A number of factors influenced colonial economic development, social structures, and labor systems, causing variation by region.

• Students will examine the impacts of geographic factors on patterns of settlement and the development of colonial economic systems.

• Students will examine the factors influencing variations in colonial social structures and labor systems.

---

*For this document the term "Native American" is used with the understanding that it could say "American Indian."

- Students will analyze slavery as a deeply established component of the colonial economic system and social structure, indentured servitude vs. slavery, the increased concentration of slaves in the South, and the development of slavery as a racial institution.

11.1c Colonial political developments were influenced by British political traditions, Enlightenment ideas, and the colonial experience. Self-governing structures were common, and yet varied across the colonies.

- Students will examine colonial political institutions to determine how they were influenced by Enlightenment ideas, British traditions such as the Magna Carta, and the colonial experience.
- Students will examine colonial democratic principles by studying documents such as the Mayflower Compact and the Maryland Toleration Act of 1649, colonial governmental structures such as New England town meetings and the Virginia House of Burgesses, and the practice of the right of petition in New Netherland.

11.2 CONSTITUTIONAL FOUNDATIONS (1763–1824): Growing political and economic tensions led the American colonists to declare their independence from Great Britain. Once independent, the new nation confronted the challenge of creating a stable federal republic.
(Standards: 1, 5; Themes: TCC, GOV, CIV, ECO)

11.2a Following the French and Indian War, the British government attempted to gain greater political and economic control over the colonies. Colonists resisted these efforts, leading to increasing tensions between the colonists and the British government.

11.2b Failed attempts to mitigate the conflicts between the British government and the colonists led the colonists to declare independence, which they eventually won through the Revolutionary War, which affected individuals in different ways.

11.2c Weaknesses of the Articles of Confederation led to a convention whose purpose was to revise the Articles of Confederation but instead resulted in the writing of a new Constitution. The ratification debate over the proposed Constitution led the Federalists to agree to add a bill of rights to the Constitution.

11.2d Under the new Constitution, the young nation sought to achieve national security and political stability, as the three branches of government established their relationships with each other and the states.

11.3 EXPANSION, NATIONALISM, AND SECTIONALISM (1800–1865): As the nation expanded, growing sectional tensions, especially over slavery, resulted in political and constitutional crises that culminated in the Civil War.
(Standards: 1, 3, 4, 5; Themes: TCC, GEO, GOV, ECO, TECH)

11.3a American nationalism was both strengthened and challenged by territorial expansion and economic growth.

11.3b Different perspectives concerning constitutional, political, economic, and social issues contributed to the growth of sectionalism.

11.3c Long-standing disputes over States rights and slavery and the secession of Southern states from the Union, sparked by the election of Abraham Lincoln, led to the Civil War. After the issuance of the Emancipation Proclamation, freeing the slaves became a major Union goal. The Civil War resulted in tremendous human loss and physical destruction.

11.4 POST–CIVIL WAR ERA (1865–1900): Reconstruction resulted in political reunion and expanded constitutional rights. However, those rights were undermined, and issues of inequality continued for African Americans, women, Native Americans, Mexican Americans, and Chinese immigrants.
(Standards: 1, 4, 5; Themes: ID, TCC, CIV, ECO)

11.4a Between 1865 and 1900, constitutional rights were extended to African Americans. However, their ability to exercise these rights was undermined by individuals, groups, and government institutions.

11.4b The 14th and 15th amendments failed to address the rights of women.

11.4c Federal policies regarding westward expansion had positive effects on the national economy but negative consequences for Native Americans.

11.4d Racial and economic motives contributed to long-standing discrimination against Mexican Americans and opposition to Chinese immigration.

11.5 INDUSTRIALIZATION AND URBANIZATION (1870–1920): The United States was transformed from an agrarian to an increasingly industrial and urbanized society. Although this transformation created new economic opportunities, it also created societal problems that were addressed by a variety of reform efforts.
(Standards: 1, 3, 4, 5; Themes: TCC, GEO, SOC, CIV, TECH)

11.5a New technologies and economic models created rapid industrial growth and transformed the United States.

11.5b Rapid industrialization and urbanization created significant challenges and societal problems that were addressed by a variety of reform efforts.

11.6 THE RISE OF AMERICAN POWER (1890–1920): Numerous factors contributed to the rise of the United States as a world power. Debates over the United States' role in world affairs increased in response to overseas expansion and involvement in World War I. United States participation in the war had important effects on American society.
(Standards: 1, 2, 3, 4: Themes: GEO, SOC, GOV, ECO)

11.6a In the late 1800s, various strategic and economic factors led to a greater focus on foreign affairs and debates over the United States' role in the world.

11.6b While the United States attempted to follow its traditional policy of neutrality at the beginning of World War I, the nation eventually became involved in the war. President Woodrow Wilson led the nation into war with the hope of reforming the international order through his Fourteen Points.

11.6c World War I had important social, political, and economic effects on American society.

11.7 PROSPERITY AND DEPRESSION (1920–1939): The 1920s and 1930s were a time of cultural and economic changes in the nation. During this period, the nation faced significant domestic challenges, including the Great Depression. (Standards: 1, 4; Themes: ID, TCC, SOC, CIV)

11.7a The 1920s was a time of cultural change in the country, characterized by clashes between modern and traditional values.

11.7b African Americans continued to struggle for social and economic equality while expanding their own thriving and unique culture. African American cultural achievements were increasingly integrated into national culture.

11.7c For many Americans, the 1920s was a time of prosperity. However, underlying economic problems, reflected in the stock market crash of 1929, led to the Great Depression. President Franklin D. Roosevelt's responses to the Great Depression increased the role of the federal government.

11.8. WORLD WAR II (1935–1945): The participation of the United States in World War II was a transformative event for the nation and its role in the world. (Standards: 1, 2; Themes: TCC, GOV, CIV, TECH)

11.8a As situations overseas deteriorated, President Roosevelt's leadership helped to move the nation from a policy of neutrality to a pro-Allied position and, ultimately, direct involvement in the war.

11.8b United States entry into World War II had a significant impact on American society.

11.8c In response to World War II and the Holocaust, the United States played a major role in efforts to prevent such human suffering in the future.

11.9 COLD WAR (1945–1990): In the period following World War II, the United States entered into an extended era of international conflict called the Cold War which influenced foreign and domestic policy for more than 40 years. (Standards: 1, 2, 3; Themes: TCC, GOV, ECON)

11.9a After World War II, ideological differences led to political tensions between the United States and the Soviet Union. In an attempt to halt the spread of Soviet influence, the United States pursued a policy of containment.

11.9b The United States and the Soviet Union engaged in a nuclear arms race that eventually led to agreements that limited the arms buildup and improved United States-Soviet relations.

11.9c American strategic interests in the Middle East grew with the Cold War, the creation of the State of Israel, and the increased United States dependence on Middle Eastern oil. The continuing nature of the Arab-Israeli dispute has helped to define the contours of American policy in the Middle East.

11.9d A combination of factors contributed to the end of the Cold War, including American policies and Soviet economic and political problems that led to the loss of Soviet control over Eastern Europe.

11.10 SOCIAL AND ECONOMIC CHANGE/DOMESTIC ISSUES (1945–present): Racial, gender, and socioeconomic inequalities were addressed by individuals, groups, and organizations. Varying political philosophies prompted debates over the role of the federal government in regulating the economy and providing a social safety net.
(Standards: 1, 4, 5; Themes: ID, TCC, SOC, GOV, CIV, ECO)

11.10a After World War II, long-term demands for equality by African Americans led to the civil rights movement. The efforts of individuals, groups, and institutions helped to redefine African American civil rights, though numerous issues remain unresolved.

11.10b Individuals, diverse groups, and organizations have sought to bring about change in American society through a variety of methods.

11.10c Varying political philosophies prompted debates over the role of the federal government in regulating the economy and providing a social safety net.

11.11 THE UNITED STATES IN A CHANGING WORLD (1990–present): The United States' political and economic status in the world has faced external and internal challenges related to international conflicts, economic competition, and globalization. Throughout this time period, the nation has continued to debate and define its role in the world.
(Standards: 1, 2, 4, 5; Themes: TCC, GOV, CIV, TECH, EXCH)

11.11a The United States created a coalition to defeat Iraq in the Persian Gulf War (1991), but was reluctant to commit American military power through the rest of the decade.

11.11b In response to the terrorist attacks of September 11, 2001, the United States launched the War on Terror, which involved controversial foreign and domestic policies.

11.11c Globalization and advances in technology have affected the United States economy and society.

Structure of the Regents Examination

You will have three hours to complete the United States History and Government Regents Examination. The test is divided into three parts that are made up of different types of questions and have different point allocations.

Part I: Stimulus-Based Multiple-Choice Questions	Consists of 28 questions based on stimuli; usually two questions per stimulus; each question has a value of one point	Total of 28 points 54% of exam grade
Part II: Stimulus-Based Short Essay Questions	Consists of two sets of paired documents; two short-answer questions for each pair of sources; each set has a value of five points, determined by a 5-point rubric	Total of 10 points 17% of exam grade
Part III: Civic Literacy Essay	Consists of six documents of which at least one must be non-text; each document or document set question is worth one point and the essay has a value of five points, determined by a 5-point rubric	Total of 11 points 29% of exam grade

Stimulus-Based Multiple-Choice Questions

Part I is made up of stimulus-based multiple-choice questions that will account for 54 percent of the points to be earned. There will be 28 questions, based on different stimuli, such as text, maps, graphs, political cartoons, charts, and photographs. Usually each stimulus will have two questions. Four possible choices will be provided for each question, only one of which is correct.

Such document-based questions often ask for the main idea of a passage or cartoon. Sometimes they will ask you to identify an accurate statement or the statement best supported by the data. They may also ask you to choose a valid conclusion drawn from the document. These types of questions often require both skills in interpreting documents and factual knowledge of United States History and Government.

In June 2019, the New York State Education Department released a prototype (sample) of the 2020 United States History and Government Regents Exam. Some of those multiple-choice questions are used in the appropriate category in this test-taking section. Those questions are identified as being from the prototype. Most of the other questions in this section are from previous Regents Exams.

Stimulus-Based Short Essay Questions

There will be two sets of paired documents, each with a short essay question, in this portion of the exam, which makes up Part II. The format of these questions will be similar on each Regents Examination. Clear and definite directions will be provided to guide you in answering these short essay questions. This section will have a total point value of 10 and will account for 17 percent of the final score.

Civic Literacy Essay

In Part III of the exam, there will be a single extended essay about a civic or constitutional issue, based on the reading and interpretation of six documents or document sets. Outside information from the study of United States History and Government is expected in the writing of the essay. The format of the civic literacy essay question on ALL Regents Examinations will always be the same. The essay will be scored on a 5-point rubric, and each question that accompanies each document or document set will have a value of one point each. Part III will account for 29 percent of the exam's total point value.

Understanding Causes and Impacts

The Regents Examination will require that you understand the cause-and-effect links between events. As you review major events and turning points, make sure that you understand the factors and conditions that caused them. Then make sure that you can explain the impacts that these events had on later developments.

Practice in Analyzing Documents

This review book provides you with many historical documents, including written documents, maps, tables, charts, graphs, and political cartoons. ALL three sections of the Regents Examination will require you to analyze a variety of different types of documents. You will be expected to take into account both the source of each document and the historical thinking skills that are essential for interpretation and analysis, such as purpose, audience, point of view, bias, and reliability.

Developing Your Writing Skills

You will earn a higher score on the test if you practice and improve your ability to communicate through writing. Essay-writing skills are required for the Part III essay. It is most important to write an essay that demonstrates a logical plan of organization and includes a strong introduction and conclusion.

How to Succeed on the Regents Exam in United States History and Government

This section of the book is intended to help you prepare to take the Regents Examination itself. Other parts of the book review the contents of the course you have studied. This section includes hints about preparing for and actually taking the examination based on test-taking skills you have probably been developing for years in social studies classes. Read and think carefully about all parts of this section as you prepare for the examination.

Practical Suggestions for Preparing to Take the Regents Examination

1. **Attend review sessions.** If review sessions are offered by your teacher or school, attend them. You will probably be reminded of something you studied earlier in the year and have not thought of since then. Review sessions also help you bring together the main ideas of the whole course.
2. **Find a study partner.** Two heads can be better than one. Try to review with a friend or a family member who can give you the chance to explain various parts of this course. You will have a better chance of remembering details if you have already explained them correctly to someone else. It has been said that the best way to learn something is to teach it to someone else.

3. **Do not "overstudy."** As important as it is to review carefully and over a period of time for your exams, do not make the mistake of "overstudying" or cramming at the last minute. This could leave you exhausted and unable to think clearly during the exam itself. This exam is important enough for you to ask your employer for time off right before the test.

4. **Eat a good meal.** Eat something before the exam so your energy level stays high.

5. **Know the exam site.** Be sure you know the correct time and place of the examination. Arriving half an hour late can make the difference between passing and failing. Be sure someone else at your house has a schedule of your exams.

6. **Be prepared**. Bring several dark ink pens and pencils.

7. **Wear a watch, if possible.** You will need to pay close attention to the time during the exam, and you might be seated where you cannot see a clock. You will not be allowed to have your cell phone with you or near you during the Regents exam.

Suggestions for Actually Taking the Regents Examination

1. **Arrive on time.** Use a reliable method of getting to school so you can arrive early in the exam room. This will allow you to get your mind on the task at hand.

2. **Select a seat.** If you are allowed to select your own seat, be sure to choose one with the least distraction. Choose one away from doors or windows.

3. **Dress comfortably.** You will be sitting in one place for a long period of time, so be sure you are comfortably dressed.

4. **Listen to instructions.** Pay full attention to all instructions given by the proctor(s).

5. **Read directions carefully.** Read all directions written on the test booklet as you take the exam. If you have reviewed well, you will be familiar with the terms *discuss, explain, show,* and *describe.* Nonetheless, take the time to read carefully the instructions given to you on the test.

6. **Be an active test-taker.** Become a participant in the exam, not a spectator. You may write on the exam. Underline key ideas. You may write in the margins as you think about the questions. The idea is for you to interact with the exam. Other hints are given as you review the multiple-choice questions from the practice examination.

7. **DON'T leave blanks.** No credit can be given for a blank on either multiple-choice or essay questions. Write something. Write anything, but never leave an answer blank.

8. **Stay for the full allotted time.** Come to the exam prepared to stay for the full three-hour examination period. Do not tell someone to pick you up in two hours—you will need all the time allowed. Don't sacrifice a year's worth of work to get outside faster on a nice day.

Part I: Stimulus-Based Multiple-Choice Questions

Part I of the Regents Examination will be made up of 28 multiple-choice questions. These questions will be based on 14 documents related to U.S. history and government. The documents may be selections from primary or secondary sources, maps, graphs, charts, photographs, timelines, and cartoons. These documents will provide information about a specific time period, event, or person or persons. You will need to know some social studies background beyond what is given in the document to be able to answer the multiple-choice questions.

More than half the points to be earned on the Regents Examination (54 percent) are earned by answering multiple-choice questions. You will therefore want to get the highest possible score in this section.

Strategies for Multiple-Choice Questions

Keep several points in mind when you are answering the stimulus-based multiple-choice questions on the Regents Examination. These are as follows:

1. Read the entire question carefully. Read the document(s), and apply the analytical skills that you have learned for each type of stimulus.
2. Read all the choices before you make a decision.
3. Eliminate any choices that you are sure are not true, crossing them out in the test booklet.
4. Remember that in the Regents Examination, there is no penalty for guessing. Therefore, you should make your best guess at an answer to every question.
5. Look for a key word or phrase that signals what you should be looking for in the question. Not all questions have such phrases. However, you should be aware of certain signal words and phrases. Some examples are *claim, evidence, turning point, cause, effect, similarity, difference, inference*, and *conclusion*.

You will be faced with a variety of different types of stimuli in the multiple-choice question portion of the exam. Therefore, it is important that you develop the skills that are necessary to allow you to analyze and interpret the material successfully. The strategies contained on the next several pages will help you in this effort.

Interpreting Data

A **table of information** is a set of facts arranged in rows and columns. It is made up of different categories of information. **Graphs** and **charts** are visual representations of data in the form of points, lines, bars, and pie slices. Types of graphs and charts include line graphs, bar graphs, and circle charts.

A **line graph** or **line chart** is a graphical display of information that changes continuously over time. Within a line graph, there are points connecting the data to show a continuous change. The lines in a line graph can descend and ascend based on the data. A line graph can be used to compare different events, situations, and information.

A **bar chart** or **bar graph** presents data with rectangular bars with heights or lengths proportional to the values that they represent.

A **pie** or **circle chart** is a circular statistical graphic that is divided into slices to illustrate numerical proportion. In a pie chart, the width of each slice is proportional to the quantity it represents. Pie charts are used to show comparison. Different types of graphs and charts display data in different ways, and some are better suited than others for different uses.

To interpret a graph or chart, read the title and the labels and look at the key, if one is included. Then, study the graph to understand what it shows, and draw conclusions based on the data. You can reach conclusions faster with graphs than you can using a data table or a written description of the data. Often, a line graph will reveal a pattern or trend. If several events or actions are compared in the graph, the trend shown in each line can provide a clearer idea if there is an overall trend.

Example:

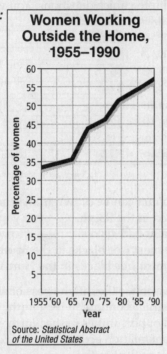

Women Working Outside the Home, 1955–1990

Source: *Statistical Abstract of the United States*

The trend shown in the graph was mainly the result of
1. increases in immigration
2. demands for more schoolteachers
3. a buildup in the defense industry
4. new social attitudes

Answer: The correct answer is 4. The graph indicates a steady increase in the number of women working outside the home between 1955 and 1990. You must draw upon your knowledge of U.S. history to provide the reason for this trend. The questions in the new Regents Examination will require you to think beyond the content of the question's stimulus.

Tables Some questions require you to draw conclusions from information provided in tables. Be very careful to base your conclusions on the information in the table and your knowledge of social studies. Be sure to note the title, the source, and date or dates of the information given in the table. The following table and questions come from the prototype exam provided by the New York State Education Department.

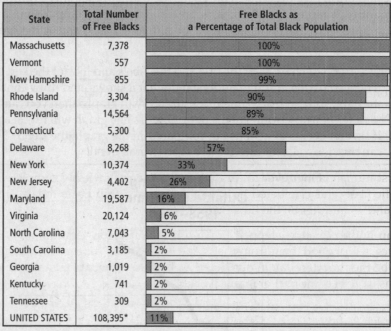

Number and Percentage of Free Blacks, by State, 1800

State	Total Number of Free Blacks	Free Blacks as a Percentage of Total Black Population
Massachusetts	7,378	100%
Vermont	557	100%
New Hampshire	855	99%
Rhode Island	3,304	90%
Pennsylvania	14,564	89%
Connecticut	5,300	85%
Delaware	8,268	57%
New York	10,374	33%
New Jersey	4,402	26%
Maryland	19,587	16%
Virginia	20,124	6%
North Carolina	7,043	5%
South Carolina	3,185	2%
Georgia	1,019	2%
Kentucky	741	2%
Tennessee	309	2%
UNITED STATES	108,395*	11%

*Total includes figures from the District of Columbia, Mississippi Territory, and Northwest Territory. These areas are not shown on the chart.

1. What is one conclusion that can be drawn from this table?
   1. No free blacks lived in the South.
   2. Most Northern states had slaves.
   3. Kentucky had the most free blacks in the South.
   4. Vermont had the most free blacks in the North.

2. What is the primary reason for the differences shown in this chart?
   1. failure of an industrial economy in the North
   2. fewer educational opportunities in the North
   3. development of a plantation economy in the South
   4. growth of railroads in the South

Answers: The correct answer for question 1 is 2. This question tests your ability to read the table as well as use your knowledge of social studies to interpret the information in order to draw a conclusion. To answer a question such as this, eliminate all possible answers that do not have information related in any way to the table. In this case, there is a lot of information provided, so make sure you understand all the information as you interpret the data, as this will help you choose the correct answer. The correct answer for question 2 is 3. To answer a question such as this, you need to be able to not only understand the information on the table but also draw on your social studies knowledge in order to be able to identify the central cause of the circumstances illustrated by information on the table.

Identifying Turning Points

A turning point is a major event, idea, or historical development that brings about significant change. It can be local, national, or global. Turning points should be major occurrences that changed the course of history. A turning point need not

center on a specific event, such as the 9/11 attack on the World Trade Center in New York City, but may refer to a major change, such as the Industrial Revolution. The concept of a turning point may be tested on the Regents in both the multiple-choice and essay sections.

Document 1

> That's one small step for a man, one giant leap for mankind.

Source: Neil A. Armstrong, as he stepped on the Moon, July 20, 1969

Document 2

> The first human beings ever to set foot on the Moon flawlessly completed their scientific tasks and clambered back into their space ship Eagle today after two hours and 13 minutes on the lunar surface. . . .
>
> Only an hour after they stepped down, President Nixon, emotion apparent in his voice, telephoned them from the White House that "for every American this has to be the proudest day in our lives. . . . Because of what you have done, the heavens have become part of man's world."

Source: Sanders Lamont, "Man Walks on Moon: Neil, Buzz Prepare for Return Trip," *The Democrat Chronicle*, July 21, 1969

1. The event noted in the documents would be best paired with which era in United States history?
    1. Progressive Era
    2. Space Race
    3. Women's Rights Movement
    4. Arms Race

2. Why could this event be considered a turning point in both world history and the history of the United States?
    1. It showed that the United States could catch up to the Soviet Union's success in the race to the moon.
    2. Although a great achievement, the event was not followed by similar progress in travel in space research.
    3. Other world nations stopped research and development in this scientific field.
    4. American presidents were overly concerned for possible loss of life in explorations of this type.

Answers: The correct answer for question 1 is 2, and the correct answer for question 2 is 1. The sources both relate to the space race between the United States and the Soviet Union during the Cold War. Questions such as these test your knowledge of history and your ability to recognize how specific events are connected and have influenced changes over time.

Identifying Cause and Effect and Understanding Chronology

Causation and **chronological reasoning** are important historical thinking skills that will be tested on the Regents in both the Multiple-Choice and Short Essay sections. In order to understand and explain historical events, historians attempt to determine their causes and effects. Most events do not have a single, central cause or a single, central effect. There may be many variables that contribute to an event, sometimes referred to as *long-term causes* and *short-term causes*. Similarly, some effects may be short term and others long term. When you analyze information by identifying cause-and-effect relationships, you find how one event leads to the next. It is important to find evidence that one event caused another. If one event happened earlier than another, it did not necessarily cause the later event. It is critical that you determine whether there is a connection between events, and if, indeed, one event caused another to occur.

The following excerpt and questions come from the prototype exam provided by the New York State Education Department.

> We admit, as all must admit, that the powers of the Government are limited, and that its limits are not to be transcended. But we think the sound construction of the Constitution must allow to the national legislature that discretion with respect to the means by which the powers it confers are to be carried into execution which will enable that body to perform the high duties assigned to it in the manner most beneficial to the people. Let the end be legitimate, let it be within the scope of the Constitution, and all means which are appropriate, which are plainly adapted to that end, which are not prohibited, but consist with the letter and spirit of the Constitution, are Constitutional.

Source: Chief Justice John Marshall, majority opinion, *McCulloch* v. *Maryland* (1819)

1. Critics feared that this decision would result in
    1. a stronger federal government that would limit state powers
    2. states being able to nullify federal laws
    3. elimination of the amendment process
    4. congressional actions that would limit the federal courts

2. The precedent set in this case was later used by Congress to
    1. declare war against Spain in 1898
    2. reject the Treaty of Versailles following World War II
    3. establish New Deal programs during the Great Depression
    4. confirm the appointment of Earl Warren to the Supreme Court

Answers: The correct answer for question 1 is 1. In this example, you are being tested on your ability to connect the content of an excerpt to an immediate effect. The correct answer for question 2 is 3. In this case, the question is asking you to identify how an event or action can have an impact years later. Both questions require you to not only understand the content of the excerpt but look beyond the stimulus and draw from your knowledge of U.S. history in order to select the correct answer.

Political Cartoons

Some questions ask you to analyze and interpret a political cartoon. Political cartoons address social and political issues and often express strongly held viewpoints about those issues. They are visual commentaries about events or people. In order to understand a political cartoon, you need to examine its major parts carefully.

When analyzing a political cartoon, follow these steps:

- Study the caption.
- Look for a date.
- Read all words in the cartoon. Look closely for any small print written on figures or objects in the cartoon. Determine what and why words or phrases seem to be the most significant.
- Identify the symbolism used by the cartoonist.
- Identify the historical context of the cartoon, what is the cartoonist's point of view, and who is the cartoonist's audience.

Example:

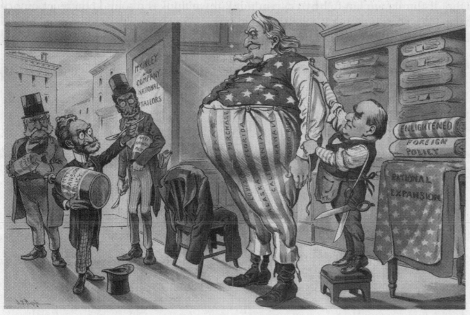

Declined with Thanks

The Antis—"Here take a dose of this anti-fat and get thin again!"
Uncle Sam—"No, Sonny! I never did take any of that stuff, and I'm too old to begin."

Source: J.S. Pugh, *Puck*, September 5, 1900 (adapted)

Which foreign policy is the main issue of this cartoon?
1. containment
2. imperialism
3. internationalism
4. neutrality

Answer: The correct answer is 2, imperialism. When analyzing this cartoon, be sure to look very carefully at all parts of the cartoon: the caption under the figures in the cartoon, the writing on the large figure representing Uncle Sam, the writing on the tailor (McKinley) and the material behind him, and the writing on the containers that the men at the door are carrying. The date of the cartoon (1900) is also an important hint about the answer.

Maps

The first task in map interpretation is to identify the title and the region shown. Second, you always need to read the map's key or legend because it tells you the meaning of the symbols or patterns used in the map as they represent specific information. **Political maps** are used to display artificial boundaries, such as state or national borders, as well as cities. **Physical maps** show the physical features of a place, such as mountains, plains, rivers, and oceans. **Special purpose maps** show specific content, such as economic data, geographic patterns, and population. Maps may be *contemporary* or *historical*. Some combine features; for example, a political map may also show geographic features.

As you study a map, ask If it is a historical map, how does it compare to a current map of the same place? Why do you think the map was made? Is there a point of view? Who do you think is the map's audience? What other documents or historical evidence can you use to help you understand the event or topic shown on the map?

Example:

Seesaw in Korea

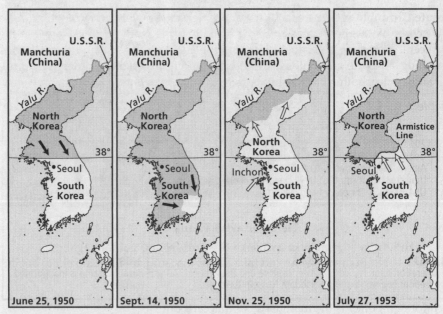

Source: Thomas A. Bailey, *A Diplomatic History of the American People*, 1980

What conclusion can be drawn from a study of this map of Korea?
1. Once North Korea conquered territory in 1950, it never lost that territory.
2. The cease fire line of July 1953 split Korea at the 38th parallel of latitude.
3. After more than three years of fighting, South Korea agreed to form one nation with North Korea.
4. Soviet aid to South Korea impacted the final outcome of the war.

Answer: The correct answer is 2. The line is shown on the map and the word *Armistice* is printed, illustrating the separation of the two areas. Choice 1 is wrong, as the map shows the changes in North Korean territory. Choice 3 is wrong because the separation line shows that North and South Korea remained divided, and choice 4 is wrong because the Soviet government never helped South Korea.

Timelines

A timeline is a graphic way of showing relationships among events over time. Questions dealing with timelines often ask you to draw a conclusion about a series of events. When answering timeline questions, be careful to focus on the time period shown; do not jump to a different era to answer the question.

Sequence means "order." Placing events in the correct chronological order is very important in the study of history. When studying history, you need to analyze the information by sequencing significant events, individuals, and time periods in order to understand them. The impact of time and place affect why an event occurred. Often, these relationships are graphically represented by a timeline.

Relative chronology is used to describe events in time in general terms. It does not include dates but rather simply lists what came first, what came second, and so on. An era is a time period that holds similar people, places, and events, such as the Progressive Era. Relative chronology is placing events in the order in which they happened relative to one another. You do not necessarily have to know specific dates, but you should be able to use associations to figure out how to place eras and events in relative chronological order.

Absolute Chronology is the exact time and date that an event occurred. Similar to relative chronology, these dates are also placed in order from the latest event to the most recent. However, you must know the specific dates of eras and events when establishing absolute chronology. Putting events in an absolute order is helpful, and it shows clearly the relationship and succession of events.

Example:

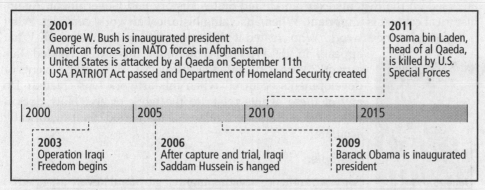

Which best describes a cause-and-effect relationship between the events shown on the timeline?

1. President Obama was the expected successor to the presidency when President Bush completed his two terms.
2. Saddam Hussein was blamed for the 2001 terrorist attacks on the United States.
3. The creation of the Department of Homeland Security was a direct result of the events of September 11th.
4. The purpose of Operation Iraqi Freedom was to cause the death of Osama Bin Laden.

Answer: The correct answer is Choice 3. This new department developed a variety of anti-terrorism protections for Americans, especially at airports and American international borders. Choice 1 is wrong, as these presidents had little connection and are of different political parties. Choice 2 is wrong because Hussein was a dictator in Iraq and not connected to the attacks. Choice 4 is wrong because Operation Iraqi Freedom was to find and destroy weapons of mass destruction that the Bush administration claimed Iraq had in its possession.

Images

Visual documents often record history. A **poster** is a "public" piece of paper conveying information through text (words) and/or graphic images (symbols or pictures). Its main target audience are people walking by. Often, posters are used for the purpose of propaganda, which is the spreading of information to influence thoughts, beliefs, feelings, and actions.

When you analyze a poster, you should answer the following questions: In what time and place was the poster created? What do you see? List the people, objects, places, and activities in the poster. Are words used in the poster? If so, what words? Is the message in the poster mostly found in words, pictures, or both? Who most likely created the visual? Why was it created? Who was the intended audience?

Photographs can be used as documents to understand historical events and societal values. In order to understand the meaning of a photograph, it is important to know the historical and social context. In your analysis, you should consider the following questions: What people and objects do you see? Describe exactly what you see in the photograph. What is the setting and season? Is it posed or candid? What was happening at the time in history during which the photo was taken? Why might the photographer have taken it?

Historical artwork, such as **paintings, sketches,** and **sculpture,** are documents that are used on the Regents exam in United States History and Government. Again, historical context is important. When analyzing historical artwork, consider: What is the name of the artwork? Who created it? When and where was it created? What appears in it? Why do you think this artist created this artwork? Who is the intended audience? What major events or developments occurred when this artwork was created? Do any of these events relate to the work of art? How does it reflect the attitude and values of the period? Is it historically accurate?

Source: Paul Revere, colored engraving of the Boston Massacre, 1770

Example:

For what audience was this engraving by Paul Revere intended?

1. King George III
2. American colonists
3. Parliament
4. American Tories

Answer: The correct answer is 2. Created by Paul Revere, a proponent of American independence, this image was a piece of propaganda aimed at American colonists in order to gain their support for American independence from British rule. Although some American Tories may have been swayed by the image, for the most part, the engraving would have had little effect on King George III, Parliament, or most American Tories.

Sources and References

Some questions test your ability to identify a valid source of information. A primary source is one written or told by someone who was present at an event. These sources can be biased, but they can also give a special insight into an event. Secondary sources, such as textbooks, are those that are written after an event.

Questions Using Information From Social Scientists

Some questions may ask about the opinions and research of certain types of social scientists.

These might include the following:

- *Historian:* a person who studies the past and makes judgments about why events happened and how they affected other events
- *Economist:* a person who studies the monetary systems of countries or cultures. The work of economists is important to our understanding of events such as the Great Depression.
- *Political scientist:* a person who studies the workings of government and politics. For example, political scientists analyze the results of elections to determine trends in voting patterns.
- *Geographer:* a person who studies the physical, biological, and cultural features of the Earth and how they may affect each other
- *Sociologist:* a person who studies people and how they act within society and with other people or groups

Gathering, Interpreting, and Using Evidence

In order to do well on the exam, it is important that you master the Social Studies Practices skill of Gathering, Interpreting, and Using Evidence. To master this skill, you need to be able to

- develop and frame questions about events and the world in which we live
- identify, describe, and evaluate evidence about events from diverse sources
- describe, analyze, and evaluate arguments
- analyze evidence in terms of content, authorship, point of view, bias, purpose, and audience

Evidence Evidence refers to information or details from a source that can be used for a specific purpose, such as drawing a conclusion or formulating an argument. Determining evidence from a source

- Is based on the interpretation of the source(s)
- Is based on the examination/questioning of sources to determine/judge/ interpret if a source is authentic, if it is biased, if it is accurate, and therefore if it is reliable

Sourcing For historians, primary sources are materials from the time period being studied. These original documents offer the freshness that comes from direct personal observation but lack the benefit that comes only from hindsight. These materials include letters, speeches, diaries, newspaper articles, oral history interviews, documents, photographs, and artifacts. They can also include less obvious sources, such as songs, plays, poems, advertisements, survey data, legal documents, and financial documents, as long as they come directly from the time period in question and provide relevant historical evidence.

For historians, secondary sources are works of synthesis, analysis, and interpretation based on primary sources as well as on the work of other authors. Some examples are textbooks, history books, scholarly journal articles, biographies, and encyclopedias. Secondary sources are interpretive works created or written after the time period being studied and have the benefit of hindsight but lack the benefit of immediacy.

Both sources are useful, but it is important to differentiate between valid primary and secondary sources. There are numerous factors that influence the intention of the author of a source and whether the source can be used as historical evidence.

Point of View is an opinion. Historians use point of view differently than English teachers, who define point of view as first person, second person, and third person.

Difference Between Point of View and Bias Point of view and bias exist on a range between objectivity and subjectivity. An author may express an objective point of view on an issue in a balanced way or may express an opinion that shows bias by providing unreasoned or poorly supported beliefs and/or strong personal feelings.

Bias refers to one-sidedness. It always implies the opposite of objectivity. Instead of presenting facts in a neutral way, without inserting one's particular opinion, bias is usually expressed in one of several ways:

- Through the use of "loaded" language, including appeals to emotion, exaggeration, or propaganda designed to frame a person, event, group, or institution in an overly positive or overly negative manner.
- Through the deliberate inclusion or deliberate exclusion of certain facts to support a particular interpretation, including a lack of balance or an argument in which only one side is presented and specific details are overemphasized, downplayed, or omitted
- Through character attacks and slurs, including subjective statements against a particular race, nation, or group within a society

An author may have a reason for being one-sided. Bias may result from limited access to information, unquestioned traditions, and/or life experiences. Unreasoned judgment or a prejudiced outlook can produce bias. Bias may be indicated by knowledge about the background of the author, who may have a specific point of view: political, economic, social, religious, or moral. Being biased does not limit the value of a source; however, it does affect how evidence from the biased source is used.

Purpose refers to the reason a record, document, or source was produced. When thinking about purpose, ask yourself: Why does this work/document exist? Why did the author create this work/document? What is the intent of this work/document?

Audience refers to the group for whom a given document or source was produced or intended. When thinking about audience, ask yourself: Why does this work/document exist? Who was the author thinking would receive this work/document? Does the author of the work/document indicate who the intended audience is?

Analyzing Texts

Reading and understanding text documents is critical in all three sections of the Regents exam. A text document—primary or secondary—is used as a stimulus to your understanding of the events, topic, and so on. To this end, it is important in your analysis of text selections that you begin by finding the main idea.

A main idea is the most important point of the selection. Identifying the main idea will help you remember details and descriptions, such as names, dates, and events, which should support the main idea, and increase your grasp of the passage. It is necessary for you to then apply your prior knowledge of American history and government to the content of the text passage in order to draw inferences and conclusions. You are then ready to either answer the Multiple-Choice Questions and the Short Essay Questions or use the information in the writing of the Civic Literacy Essay.

The following are examples of text sources, primary as well as secondary, with multiple-choice questions written in a variety of styles that are likely to appear on the exam. These text excerpts and questions are from the prototype exam provided by the New York State Education Department.

- Be sure to look for dates, or other historical references to help you. Who wrote the document? When? What is the title of the document? What type of document is it? A letter, legal opinion, law, speech?
- What is the main idea of the document?
- What is each of the two multiple-choice questions asking you about the document or based on the document?
- What opinions are expressed in the document? The questions often require you to recognize and evaluate an opinion expressed in the document.
- Are there words you are unsure of in the selection? Try to find a root word you know.
- You may write notes in the margin near the selection.

Primary Source: Personal Letter

For myself, I was escorted through Packingtown by a young lawyer who was brought up in the district, had worked as a boy in Armour's plant, and knew more or less intimately every foreman, "spotter," and watchman about the place. I saw with my own eyes hams, which had spoiled in pickle, being pumped full of chemicals to destroy the odor. I saw waste ends of smoked beef stored in barrels in a cellar, in a condition of filth which I could not describe in a letter. I saw rooms in which sausage meat was stored, with poisoned rats lying about, and the dung of rats covering them. I saw hogs which had died of cholera in shipment, being loaded into box cars to be taken to a place called Globe, in Indiana, to be rendered into lard. Finally, I found a physician, Dr. William K. Jaques, 4316 Woodland Avenue, Chicago, who holds the chair of bacteriology in the Illinois State University, and was in charge of the city inspection of meat during 1902–3, who told me he had seen beef carcasses, bearing the inspectors' tags of condemnation, left upon open platforms and carted away at night, to be sold in the city.

Source: Upton Sinclair, letter to President Theodore Roosevelt, March 10, 1906

1. Upton Sinclair wrote this letter to President Theodore Roosevelt to inform the president about
    1. excessive federal regulation of meatpacking plants
    2. unhealthy practices in the meatpacking plants
    3. raising wages for meatpacking workers
    4. state laws regulating the meatpacking industry

2. What was one action taken by the federal government to deal with the issues described in this letter?
   1. closing the Armour Meat Packing plant
   2. increasing federal aid for medical research
   3. passing the Meat Inspection Act
   4. limiting freedom of expression

3. Historians would most often use Sinclair's letter to study the
   1. Reconstruction Era
   2. suffrage movement
   3. Progressive movement
   4. civil rights era

Answers: The answer to question 1 is 2. This type of question is testing your ability to identify the purpose of the document, which often requires you to know more than just what is included in the document. In this case, you need to know who Upton Sinclair is and what he is known for trying to accomplish. The answer to question 2 is 3. This type of question requires you to use your knowledge of history to identify an action that was taken by an individual, group, or government as a result of the events described in the stimulus. The answer to question 3 is 3. In this type of question, you need to use your knowledge and skills to evaluate how this stimulus is connected to specific developments in time and place.

Secondary Source: Nonfiction Book by a Historian

Yet in the year after that June day in 1948—long after the postwar parades had passed, after the ticker tape had been swept away, after all the heroes had supposedly been minted—it was these unlikely men who improvised and stumbled their way into inventing a uniquely American approach to the world that married the nation's military and moral might. . . .

Their story has powerful resonance for our own time. In confronting the Berlin blockade, America went to battle against a destructive ideology that threatened free people around the world. In a country we invaded and occupied that had never had a stable democracy, we brought freedom and turned their people's hatred of America into love for this country, its people, and its ideals. Never before—or since—would America be so admired around the world and stand so solidly on the side of light.

Source: Andrei Cherny, *The Candy Bombers*, 2009

1. What was the "destructive ideology" referred to by the author?
   1. colonialism
   2. nativism
   3. communism
   4. capitalism

2. What action turned the German people's hostility toward the United States into respect for its ideals?
   1. the division of Germany by the Allied powers
   2. the trial of war criminals at Nuremberg
   3. the airlift of supplies into Berlin
   4. the construction of a wall to divide Berlin

3. This passage is most closely associated with which United States foreign policy?
 1. mercantilism
 2. isolationism
 3. détente
 4. containment

Answers: The answer to question 1 is 3. This type of question is testing your ability to identify the context, or the circumstances or setting of an event, surrounding the document. You need to know what was going on at the time of the events described, which, in this case, is the ideological conflict between the democratic United States and communist Soviet Union. The answer to question 2 is 3. This type of question requires you to use your knowledge of history to identify the significance of an event as it relates to the content of the passage. In this case, you need to know that in response to the events described in the passage, the United States took action to help the Germans during the Berlin blockade. The answer to question 3 is 4. In this type of question, you are being tested on your ability to recognize a similarity among historical developments or events. In this case, you need to recognize the connection between the American actions during the Berlin blockade and the American containment policy.

Part II: Short Essay Questions

In Part II of the Regents Examination, you will be presented with two sets of two documents, which could be either primary or secondary, followed by two questions for each set. Each set is graded on a 5-point rubric. The content-specific rubric provided by the New York State Education Department follows each essay question. These short essays do not require an introduction or a conclusion paragraph, but it is expected that your response should be at least two or three paragraphs in length.

Set #1 will always focus on the relationship between the two documents in the set. Your first task is to identify the historical context surrounding the two documents. Your second task is to identify and explain the relationship—cause and effect, similarity or difference, or turning point—between the two documents. Definitions for *describe, historical context, identify,* and *explain* as well as the *types of relationships* will always be included in the student instructions for this set.

Set #2 will always focus on sourcing—who created the document, why was it created—and reliability—how accurate and useful the information found in the document is for a specific purpose. Like in Set #1, your first task is to identify the historical context surrounding the two documents. However, your second task is to analyze one of the documents and explain how audience, purpose, bias, or point of view affects the reliability of the document. The exam will tell you on which document you need to focus this second task, but you choose whether to focus on audience, purpose, bias, or point of view. The student instructions for this set include definitions for *describe, historical context, analyze, explain,* and *reliability.* However, the instructions do not include the definitions for *audience, purpose, bias,* or *point of view,* so make sure you are familiar with the definitions of these terms (see p. xxxii in this book).

The following Short Essay Question sets are from the prototype provided by the New York State Education Department.

STIMULUS BASED SHORT ESSAY QUESTION–SET # 1

This Short Essay Question is based on the accompanying documents and is designed to test your ability to work with historical documents. Each Short Essay Question set will consist of two documents. Some of these documents have been edited for the purposes of this question. Keep in mind that the language and images used in a document may reflect the historical context of the time in which it was created.

Task: Read and analyze the following documents, applying your social studies knowledge and skills to write a short essay of two or three paragraphs in which you:

> - Describe the historical context surrounding these documents
> - Identify and explain the *relationship* between the events and/or ideas found in these documents (Cause and Effect, *or* Similarity/Difference, *or* Turning Point)

In developing your short essay answer of two or three paragraphs, be sure to keep these explanations in mind:

Describe means "to illustrate something in words or tell about it"

Historical Context refers to "the relevant historical circumstances surrounding or connecting the events, ideas, or developments in these documents"

Identify means "to put a name to or to name"

Explain means "to make plain or understandable; to give reasons for or causes of; to show the logical development or relationship of"

<u>Types of Relationships:</u>

Cause refers to "something that contributes to the occurrence of an event, the rise of an idea, or the bringing about of a development"

Effect refers to "what happens as a consequence (result, impact, outcome) of an event, an idea, or a development"

Similarity tells how "something is alike or the same as something else"

Difference tells how "something is not alike or not the same as something else"

Turning Point is "a major event, idea, or historical development that brings about significant change. It can be local, regional, national, or global"

Document 1

Reporter: Mr. President, would you mind commenting on the strategic importance of Indochina for the free world? I think there has been, across the country, some lack of understanding on just what it means to us.

The President: You have, of course, both the specific and the general when you talk about such things. First of all, you have the specific value of a locality in its production of materials that the world needs. Then you have the possibility that many human beings pass under a dictatorship that is inimical [hostile] to the free world. Finally, you have broader considerations that might follow what you would call the "falling domino" principle. You have a row of dominoes set up, you knock over the first one, and what will happen to the last one is the certainty that it will go over very quickly. So you could have a beginning of a disintegration that would have the most profound influences.

Source: President Dwight D. Eisenhower, press conference, April 7, 1954

Document 2

Joint Resolution

To promote the maintenance of international peace and security in southeast Asia.

  Whereas naval units of the Communist regime in Vietnam, in violation of the principles of the Charter of the United Nations and of international law, have deliberately and repeatedly attacked United States naval vessels lawfully present in international waters, and have thereby created a serious threat to international peace; and

  Whereas these attackers are part of deliberate and systematic campaign of aggression that the Communist regime in North Vietnam has been waging against its neighbors and the nations joined with them in the collective defense of their freedom; and

  Whereas the United States is assisting the peoples of southeast Asia to protest their freedom and has no territorial, military or political ambitions in that area, but desires only that these people should be left in peace to work out their destinies in their own way: Now, therefore be it

  Resolved by the Senate and House of Representatives of the United States of America in Congress assembled, That the Congress approves and supports the determination of the President, as Commander in Chief, to take all necessary measures to repel any armed attack against the forces of the United States and to prevent further aggression.

Source: Tonkin Gulf Resolution, August 7, 1964

DRAFT RUBRIC FOR PART II
SHORT ESSAY QUESTION—SET 1

Read and analyze the following documents, applying your social studies knowledge and skills to write a short essay of two or three paragraphs in which you:

- Describe the historical context surrounding these documents
- Identify and explain the *relationship* between the events and/or ideas found in these documents (Cause and Effect, *or* Similarity/Difference, *or* Turning Point)

Document 1

> **Reporter:** Mr. President, would you mind commenting on the strategic importance of Indochina for the free world? I think there has been, across the country, some lack of understanding on just what it means to us.
>
> **The President:** You have, of course, both the specific and the general when you talk about such things. First of all, you have the specific value of a locality in its production of materials that the world needs.
>
> Then you have the possibility that many human beings pass under a dictatorship that is inimical [hostile] to the free world.
>
> Finally, you have broader considerations that might follow what you would call the "falling domino" principle. You have a row of dominoes set up, you knock over the first one, and what will happen to the last one is the certainty that it will go over very quickly. So you could have a beginning of a disintegration that would have the most profound influences. . . .

Source: Press Conference with President Dwight Eisenhower,
April 7, 1954

Document 2

> Joint Resolution
>
> To promote the maintenance of international peace and security in southeast Asia.
>
> Whereas naval units of the Communist regime in Vietnam, in violation of the principles of the Charter of the United Nations and of international law, have deliberately and repeatedly attacked United States naval vessels lawfully present in international waters, and have thereby created a serious threat to international peace; and
>
> Whereas these attackers are part of deliberate and systematic campaign of aggression that the Communist regime in North Vietnam has been waging against its neighbors and the nations joined with them in the collective defense of their freedom; and
>
> Whereas the United States is assisting the peoples of southeast Asia to protest their freedom and has no territorial, military or political ambitions in that area, but desires only that these people should be left in peace to work out their destinies in their own way: Now, therefore be it
>
> *Resolved by the Senate and House of Representatives of the United States of America in Congress assembled,* That the Congress approves and supports the determination of the President, as Commander in Chief, to take all necessary measures to repel any armed attack against the forces of the United States and to prevent further aggression. . . .

Source: Tonkin Gulf Resolution in Congress, August 7, 1964

Content-Specific Rubric
Short Essay Question–Set 1

Scoring Notes:

1. This short essay question has ***two*** components (describing the historical context surrounding these two documents and identifying and explaining the ***relationship*** between the events *and/or* ideas found in these documents).
2. The description of historical context and the relationship between the events and/or ideas may focus on immediate or long-term circumstances or on immediate or long-term effects.
3. Only ***one*** relationship between the events and/or ideas needs to be discussed; however, the response may refer to a second relationship as part of the discussion.
4. The relationship between events and/or ideas in the documents may be discussed from any perspective as long as the relationship is supported by relevant information.

Score of 5:

- Thoroughly develops ***both*** aspects of the task in depth by discussing the historical context surrounding these documents and explaining the relationship between the events and/or ideas found in these documents
- Is more analytical than descriptive (analyzes and/or evaluates information), e.g., (*Historical Context:* discusses how during Cold War the United States policy of containment extended into Asia and included Vietnam after the defeat of the French by Ho Chi Minh's communist forces; *Cause-and-Effect:* connects President Eisenhower's domino theory which convinced Americans of the importance of defending Indochina to the 1964 congressional resolution supporting any measure President Johnson needed to take to prevent further North Vietnamese aggression against United States Armed Forces; *Similarity:* President Eisenhower's domino theory and the Tonkin Gulf Resolution both supported presidential action against North Vietnam and were used by war hawks to justify United States involvement in a long, costly, and divisive war)
- Integrates relevant outside information (See Relevant Outside Information chart)
- Supports the theme with many relevant facts and/or examples from the documents (See Key Ideas From Documents chart)

Test-Taking Strategies

Score of 4:
- Develops *both* aspects of the task in depth *or* may do so somewhat unevenly by thoroughly developing *one* aspect of the task in depth while developing the other aspect of the task in *some* depth
- Is both descriptive and analytical (applies, analyzes and/or evaluates information), e.g., (*Historical Context:* discusses how United States containment policy was applied to Vietnam to support France after communists took over North Vietnam; *Cause-and-Effect:* explains how President Eisenhower's domino theory led Congress to pass a resolution granting President Johnson the power to fight the North Vietnamese; *Turning Point:* explains how the domino theory and Gulf of Tonkin Resolution became the basis for United States intervention in Vietnam which greatly impacted American society and Southeast Asia)
- Includes relevant outside information
- Supports the theme with relevant facts and/or examples

Score of 3:
- Develops *both* aspects of the task in some depth
- Is more descriptive than analytical (applies and may analyze information)
- Includes some relevant outside information
- Includes some relevant facts and/or examples from the documents; may include some minor inaccuracies

Note: If only *one* aspect of the task is thoroughly developed in depth and if the response meets most of the other Level 5 criteria, the response may be a Level 3 paper.

Score of 2:
- Minimally develops *both* aspects of the task *or* develops *one* aspect of the task in some depth
- Is primarily descriptive; may include faulty analysis
- Includes little relevant outside information
- Includes a few relevant facts and/or examples from the documents; may include some inaccuracies

Score of 1:
- Minimally addresses the task
- Is descriptive; may lack understanding or application
- Includes minimal or no relevant outside information
- Includes a few relevant facts and/or examples from the documents; may make only vague, unclear references to the documents; may include inaccuracies

Score of 0:
Fails to develop the task; *OR* includes no relevant facts and/or examples; *OR* includes only entire documents copied from the test booklet; *OR* is illegible; *OR* is a blank paper

Key Ideas From Documents
(This list is not all inclusive.)

Document 1—Lack of understanding of Indochina's strategic importance
A locality has a specific value in terms of its production of materials the world needs
There was a possibility that dictatorships would emerge that are hostile to the free world
The domino theory means if one country falls others are likely to fall
There was a possibility that the "falling domino" principle is the beginning of disintegration [of non-communist nations]

Document 2—North Vietnam violated the United Nations charter and international law by attacking United States naval vessels in international waters
The attack was part of a communist campaign of aggression against neighbors and their allies
The United States is assisting Southeast Asians freedom and peace without territorial, military, or political ambition in the region
Congress approves and supports the president's right to take all necessary measures to repel any armed attack against United States forces and prevent further aggression

Relevant Outside Information
(This list is not all inclusive.)

Application of containment policies to East Asia (Korean War, 1950–1953) and Southeast Asia (Vietnam War, 1950–1975)
French efforts against Ho Chi Minh were unsuccessful (Dien Bien Phu)
Division of Vietnam at the 17th parallel
Formation of Southeast Asia Treaty Organization (collective security)
Increasing economic aid and military advisors to South Vietnam (Eisenhower, Kennedy)
Alleged attack on United States destroyers in Gulf of Tonkin
Gulf of Tonkin Resolution was a "blank check" given by Congress to President Johnson to defend United States forces and support South Vietnamese, 1964–1973 (undeclared war; President Johnson's escalation of troop strength; expanded war powers of commander in chief; vastly increased military spending; sparked a national debate over involvement in this war)
Television coverage of the war increased opposition to it
Impact of war (increased support for the 26th amendment; credibility gap)
Anti-war protests (hawks versus doves; Kent State University; response to returning soldiers/Vietnam veterans; Vietnam Syndrome)

SHORT ESSAY QUESTION–SET # 2

This Short Essay Question is based on the accompanying documents and is designed to test your ability to work with historical documents. Each Short Essay Question set will consist of two documents. Some of these documents have been edited for the purposes of this question. Keep in mind that the language and images used in a document may reflect the historical context of the time in which it was created.

Task: Read and analyze the following documents, applying your social studies knowledge and skills to write a short essay of two or three paragraphs in which you:

- Describe the historical context surrounding documents 1 and 2
- Analyze **Document 2** and explain how *audience*, **or** *purpose*, **or** *bias*, **or** *point of view* affects this document's use as a reliable source of evidence

In developing your short essay answer of two or three paragraphs, be sure to keep these explanations in mind:

Describe means "to illustrate something in words or tell about it"

Historical Context refers to "the relevant historical circumstances surrounding or connecting the events, ideas, or developments in these documents"

Analyze means "to examine a document and determine its elements and its relationships"

Explain means "to make plain or understandable; to give reasons for or causes of; to show the logical development or relationship of"

Reliability is determined by how accurate and useful the information found in a source is for a specific purpose

Document 1

> ... On the 4th March next, this party (the Republican Party) will take possession of the Government. It has announced, that the South shall be excluded from the common [national] Territory; that the Judicial Tribunals shall be made sectional, and that a war must be waged against slavery until it shall cease throughout the United States.
>
> The Guaranties of the Constitution will then no longer exist; the equal rights of the States will be lost. The slaveholding States will no longer have the power of selfgovernment, or self-protection, and the Federal Government will have become their enemy. . . .
>
> We, therefore, the people of South Carolina, by our delegates, in Convention assembled, appealing to the Supreme Judge of the world for the rectitude of our intentions, have solemnly declared that the Union heretofore existing between this State and the other States of North America, is dissolved, and that the State of South Carolina has resumed her position among the nations of the world, as a separate and independent State; with full power to levy war, conclude peace, contract alliances, establish commerce, and to do all other acts and things which independent States may of right do.

Source: South Carolina Ordinance of Secession, December 1860

Document 2

> . . . Plainly, the central idea of secession, is the essence of anarchy. A majority, held in restraint by constitutional checks, and limitations, and always changing easily, with deliberate changes of popular opinions and sentiments, is the only true sovereign of a free people. Whoever rejects it, does, of necessity, fly to anarchy or to despotism. Unanimity is impossible; the rule of a minority, as a permanent arrangement, is wholly inadmissable; so that, rejecting the majority principle, anarchy, or despotism in some form, is all that is left. . . .
>
> Why should there not be a patient confidence in the ultimate justice of the people? Is there any better, or equal hope, in the world? In our present differences, is either party without faith of being in the right? If the Almighty Ruler of nations, with his eternal truth and justice, be on your side of the North, or on yours of the South, that truth, and that justice, will surely prevail, by the judgment of this great tribunal, the American people. . . .
>
> In *your* hands, my dissatisfied fellow countrymen, and not in *mine*, is the momentous issue of civil war. The government will not assail you. You can have no conflict, without being yourselves the aggressors. You have no oath registered in Heaven to destroy the government, while I shall have the most solemn one to "preserve, protect and defend" it. . . .

Source: Collected Works of Abraham Lincoln Volume 4 (adapted)

DRAFT RUBRIC FOR PART II
SHORT ESSAY QUESTION—SET 2

Task: Read and analyze the following documents, applying your social studies knowledge and skills to write a short essay of two or three paragraphs in which you:

- Describe the historical context surrounding documents 1 and 2
- Analyze **Document 2** and explain how *audience*, **or** *purpose*, **or** *bias*, **or** *point of view* affects this document's use as a reliable source of evidence

Document 1

. . . On the 4th March next, this party (the Republican Party) will take possession of the Government. It has announced, that the South shall be excluded from the common [national] Territory; that the Judicial Tribunals shall be made sectional, and that a war must be waged against slavery until it shall cease throughout the United States.

The Guaranties of the Constitution will then no longer exist; the equal rights of the States will be lost. The slaveholding States will no longer have the power of selfgovernment, or self-protection, and the Federal Government will have become their enemy. . . .

We, therefore, the people of South Carolina, by our delegates, in Convention assembled, appealing to the Supreme Judge of the world for the rectitude of our intentions, have solemnly declared that the Union heretofore existing between this State and the other States of North America, is dissolved, and that the State of South Carolina has resumed her position among the nations of the world, as a separate and independent State; with full power to levy war, conclude peace, contract alliances, establish commerce, and to do all other acts and things which independent States may of right do.

Source: South Carolina Ordinance of Secession, December 1860

Document 2

Abraham Lincoln First Inaugural Address, March 4, 1861

. . . Plainly, the central idea of secession, is the essence of anarchy. A majority, held in restraint by constitutional checks, and limitations, and always changing easily, with deliberate changes of popular opinions and sentiments, is the only true sovereign of a free people. Whoever rejects it, does, of necessity, fly to anarchy or to despotism. Unanimity is impossible; the rule of a minority, as a permanent arrangement, is wholly inadmissable; so that, rejecting the majority principle, anarchy, or despotism in some form, is all that is left. . . .

Why should there not be a patient confidence in the ultimate justice of the people? Is there any better, or equal hope, in the world? In our present differences, is either party without faith of being in the right? If the Almighty Ruler of nations, with his eternal truth and justice, be on your side of the North, or on yours of the South, that truth, and that justice, will surely prevail, by the judgment of this great tribunal, the American people. . . .

In *your* hands, my dissatisfied fellow countrymen, and not in *mine*, is the momentous issue of civil war. The government will not assail *you*. You can have no conflict, without being yourselves the aggressors. *You* have no oath registered in Heaven to destroy the government, while *I* shall have the most solemn one to "preserve, protect and defend" it. . . .

Source: Collected Works of Abraham Lincoln Volume 4 (adapted)

Content-Specific Rubric
Short Essay Question—Set 2

Scoring Notes:

1. This short essay question has *two* components (describing the historical context surrounding these two documents and analyzing and explaining how *audience*, **or** *purpose*, **or** *bias*, **or** *point of view* affects the use of **Document 2** as a reliable source of evidence).
2. The description of historical context of both documents may focus on immediate or long-term circumstances or on immediate or long-term effects.
3. The discussion of reliability must focus on Document 2 although information from Document 1 may be included in the discussion.
4. The analysis of reliability of Document 2 may be considered from any perspective as long as it is supported by relevant information.

Score of 5:

- Thoroughly develops *both* aspects of the task in depth by discussing the historical context surrounding these documents and explaining how *audience,* **or** *purpose,* **or** *bias*, **or** *point of view* affects the use of Document 2 as a reliable source of evidence
- Is more analytical than descriptive (analyzes and/or evaluates information), e.g., *Historical Context:* discusses how the Republican Party's 1860 platform pledged to end the expansion of slavery and Abraham Lincoln's victory without a single electoral vote from the South prompted the secession of South Carolina; *Audience:* connects how President Lincoln's conciliatory inaugural address aimed at both a Northern and a Southern audience promising no interference with existing slavery or no initiation of civil war against the South was reliable because it was consistent with his position before and during the 1860 campaign; *Point of View*: connects Lincoln's strong belief that secession is not a legitimate option to his pledge to preserve, protect, and defend the Union, making his inaugural address a reliable document of the president's core beliefs
- Integrates relevant outside information (see Relevant Outside Information chart)
- Supports the theme with many relevant facts and/or examples from the documents (see Key Ideas From Documents chart)

Score of 4:
- Develops **both** aspects of the task in depth *or* may do so somewhat unevenly by thoroughly developing *one* aspect of the task in depth while developing the other aspect of the task in *some* depth
- Is both descriptive and analytical (applies, analyzes, and/or evaluates information), e.g., *Historical Context:* describes how Abraham Lincoln ran for president in 1860 on a platform to stop the spread of slavery and won without any Southern support, causing South Carolina to secede from the Union; *Purpose:* Lincoln's speech was an attempt to reassure Southern citizens that the federal government would not be the aggressor and his pledge is reliable because the Civil War began when South Carolina fired on federal troops; *Point of View:* Lincoln's address promises that the Union would not be the aggressor against the South but that as president he would preserve, protect, and defend the Union, making the address an accurate reflection of what he actually did and therefore a reliable document
- Includes relevant outside information
- Supports the theme with relevant facts and/or examples from the documents

Score of 3:
- Develops **both** aspects of the task in some depth
- Is more descriptive than analytical (applies and may analyze information)
- Includes some relevant outside information
- Includes some relevant facts and/or examples from the documents; may include some minor inaccuracies

Note: If only one aspect of the task is thoroughly developed in depth and if the response meets most of the other Score Level 5 criteria, the response may be a Score Level 3 paper.

Score of 2:
- Minimally develops **both** aspects of the task *or* develops **one** aspect of the task in some depth
- Is primarily descriptive; may include faulty analysis
- Includes little relevant outside information
- Includes a few relevant facts and/or examples from the documents; may include some inaccuracies

Score of 1:
- Minimally addresses the task
- Is descriptive; may lack understanding or application
- Includes minimal or no relevant outside information
- Includes few or no relevant facts and/or examples from the documents; may make only vague, unclear references to the documents; may include inaccuracies

Score of 0:
Fails to develop the task; *OR* includes no relevant facts or examples; *OR* includes only entire documents copied from the test booklet; *OR* is illegible; *OR* is a blank paper

Key Ideas From Documents
(This list is not all inclusive.)

Document 1—In a few months the Republican Party will take possession of the federal government

South Carolina believes that the South will be excluded from the common national territory and a war against slavery will begin

The equal rights and self-government of the states will be lost

The federal government will become the enemy

The convention declared that the union between South Carolina and the other states is dissolved

The state of South Carolina resumed its position as a separate and independent state; South Carolina could levy war, conclude peace, make alliances, and establish commerce

Document 2—Secession is anarchy

The only true sovereign of a free people is the majority that is restrained by checks and balances and can be changed according to popular opinion

Be patient with the ultimate justice of the people and truth and justice will prevail

The issue of civil war is in the hands of dissatisfied Southerners

There will be no conflict unless the South is the aggressor

Lincoln took an oath to preserve, protect, and defend the Union

Relevant Outside Information
(This list is not all inclusive.)

Southern support for States rights doctrine

Westward expansion of slavery

Dred Scott decision (1857)

Lincoln-Douglas debates (1858)

Several states seceded by March 1861

Lincoln pledged to keep control of remaining federal property such as forts

Any use of force against the Union would be considered a rebellion and met with force

Southern attack on Fort Sumter (April 1861)

Reliability of Document 2
(This list is not all inclusive.)

Reliable—*Audience:* Lincoln's speech reassuring the South that the federal government would not be the aggressor against them is reliable because the South Carolina Ordinance of Secession claimed that the state had the full power to wage war and South Carolina ended up being the aggressor when it attacked Fort Sumter

Bias: Lincoln's First Inaugural Address is a reliable source of his core beliefs about the legality of secession and importance of preserving the Union

Unreliable—*Bias:* While Lincoln attempted to be conciliatory to the South, his strong personal opposition to slavery influenced his policy of not allowing slavery to expand which weakens the reliability of the source for evidence about the secession crisis

Part III: Civic Literacy Essay

There will be one Civic Literacy Essay on the examination. The score on this essay question ranges from 0 to 5 points, using a generic scoring rubric. You should become familiar with this rubric as you prepare for the exam, because it will help you learn how to write the most effective essay possible.

The Civic Literacy Essay has two important parts. First, each document or set of documents is followed by a question in which you examine the document individually and complete a short-answer question. Second, there are three tasks associated with the final essay question in which you draw upon your analysis of the documents and your knowledge of U.S. history and government to write the essay. The three tasks are as follows:

- You will need to describe the historical circumstances surrounding a constitutional or civic issue discussed in the six documents.
- You will need to explain efforts by individuals, groups, and or government to address this constitutional or civic issue.
- You will need to discuss the extent to which the efforts were successful OR discuss the impact of the efforts on the United States and/or American society.

Read and Understand the Tasks

Read this part carefully to be sure that you complete all parts. Underline any parts of the test that you do not want to forget or overlook. Do not leave any questions that accompany each document or document set unanswered because each question is worth one point. Any blanks you leave will cause you to lose points automatically. Keep track of main ideas/block your essay. As you work through the questions, write down the main idea or ideas of each document on your scrap paper. Briefly listing the main ideas of each document will help you organize your thoughts so that you can successfully support your viewpoint in the essay. You may choose to organize the main ideas by creating a simple chart.

Blocking Essay Answers

Blocking an essay will help you organize your ideas before you write your answer. Organizing your thoughts before writing will help you earn more points on the essay and avoid leaving out parts of the essay. Experts in helping students prepare for tests know that the more involved you become with a test, the better you will do on it.

Steps in Blocking an Essay

1. Underline the words that tell you what you need to do: *discuss, describe, explain,* and so on.
2. Study the directions next to each bulleted point (•).
3. Use those directions to form headings for your block.
4. Under each section of your block, write facts to help you answer that part of the question.
5. Review to see if you have completed all parts of the Task.
6. Check to see that your introduction and conclusion show thought and are not just a repetition of the ones you are given in the question.

7. When you have arranged all your facts in the section of the block, check to be sure you have not left any blocks empty.

Guidelines:
In your essay, be sure to
- Develop all aspects of the task
- Incorporate information from *at least four* documents
- Incorporate relevant outside information
- Support your answer with relevant facts, examples, and details
- Use a logical and clear plan of organization, including an introduction and a conclusion that are beyond a restatement of the theme

The Civic Literacy Essay example that follows on the next several pages is from the prototype provided by the New York State Education Department.

Part III
CIVIC LITERACY ESSAY (Questions 31–37)

This Civic Literacy Essay Question is based on the accompanying documents. The question is designed to test your ability to work with historical documents. Some of these documents have been edited for the purpose of this question. As you analyze the documents, take into account the source of each document and any point of view that may be presented in the document. Keep in mind that the language and images used in a document may reflect the historical context of the time in which it was created.

Historical Context: Imperialism in the 1890s

> Throughout United States history, many constitutional and civic issues have been debated by Americans. These debates have resulted in efforts by individuals, groups, and governments to address these issues. These efforts have achieved varying degrees of success. One of these constitutional and civic issues is *imperialism in the 1890s*.

Task: Read and analyze the documents. Using information from the documents and your knowledge of United States history, answer the questions that follow each document in Part A. Your answers to the questions will help you write the Part B essay in which you will be asked to

> - Describe the historical circumstances surrounding this constitutional or civic issue
> - Explain efforts by individuals, groups, and/or governments to address this constitutional or civic issue
> - Discuss the extent to which the efforts were successful

In developing your answers to Part III, be sure to keep these general definitions in mind:

(a) <u>describe</u> means "to illustrate something in words or tell about it"
(b) <u>explain</u> means "to make plain or understandable; to give reasons for or causes of; to show the logical development or relationships of"
(c) <u>discuss</u> means "to make observations about something using facts, reasoning, and argument; to present in some detail"

Civic Literacy Essay
Part A
Short-Answer Questions (31–36)

Directions: Analyze the documents and answer the questions that follow each document in the space provided.

Document 1

> . . . By the 1890s any U.S. interest in the actual annexation of territory had given way to "informal empire," or commercial penetration that led either to economic dominance without direct political controls or to the acquisition of colonies having no prospect of statehood. The expansionist mood was not national, partly because of the lack of coherence in the political parties, and partly because of the general fragmentation still evident from the Civil War. Anti-imperialist feelings ran strong, especially among Americans who recognized their nation's limitations outside the hemisphere, but also among those who feared the incorporation of non-white peoples and worried about the negative effects of imperialism on democratic institutions. But the economic hard times of the decade dictated a search for new commercial outlets, not so much for acquiring raw materials as for securing markets capable of absorbing the United States's excess stock of manufactured goods. Although business and government did not jointly orchestrate a push toward expansion, commercial interests often had the Washington government's tacit support in searching for investment fields and foreign markets that would promote the good of the economy and hence safeguard the national interest. . . .

Source: Howard Jones, *Crucible of Power: A History of American Foreign Relations to 1913*, Scholarly Resources, Inc., 2002

31 According to Howard Jones, what is *one* historical circumstance that led to support for United States expansion overseas in the 1890s? [1]

_____

_____

Document 2

"A LESSON FOR ANTI-EXPANSIONISTS."
"Showing how Uncle Sam has been an expansionist first, last, and all the time."

Source: Victor Gillam, *Judge,* 1899 (adapted)

32 Based on this document, state *one* historical circumstance that supports American expansion in the 1890s. [1]

_____

_____

Document 3

While running for the United States Senate in 1898, Albert Beveridge argued in favor of American expansion.

> ... In Cuba, alone, there are 15,000,000 acres of forest unacquainted with the ax, exhaustless mines of iron, priceless deposits of manganese, millions of dollars' worth of which we must buy, today, from the Black Sea districts. There are millions of acres yet unexplored.
>
> The resources of Porto Rico have only been trifled with. The riches of the Philippines have hardly been touched by the fingertips of modern methods. And they produce what we consume, and consume what we produce—the very predestination of reciprocity—a reciprocity "not made with hands, eternal in the heavens." They sell hemp, sugar, cocoanuts, fruits of the tropics, timber of price like mahogany; they buy flour, clothing, tools, implements, machinery and all that we can raise and make. Their trade will be ours in time. Do you indorse [endorse] that policy with your vote?
>
> American merchants, manufacturers, farmers, have as good right as those of Germany or France or Russia or England; Asia, whose commerce with the United Kingdom amounts to hundreds of millions of dollars every year; Asia, to whom Germany looks to take her surplus products; Asia, whose doors must not be shut against American trade. . . .

Source: Albert Beveridge, "The March of the Flag" speech, September 16, 1898

33 According to Albert Beveridge, what is *one* reason to support American expansion overseas? [1]

_____

_____

Document 4a

Platform of the American Anti-Imperialist League

We hold that the policy known as imperialism is hostile to liberty and tends toward militarism, an evil from which it has been our glory to be free. We regret that it has become necessary in the land of Washington and Lincoln to reaffirm that all men, of whatever race or color, are entitled to life, liberty and the pursuit of happiness. We maintain that governments derive their just powers from the consent of the governed. We insist that the subjugation of any people is "criminal aggression" and open disloyalty to the distinctive principles of our Government. . . .

We demand the immediate cessation of the war against liberty, begun by Spain and continued by us. We urge that Congress be promptly convened to announce to the Filipinos our purpose to concede to them the independence for which they have so long fought and which of right is theirs.

The United States have always protested against the doctrine of international law which permits the subjugation of the weak by the strong. A self-governing state cannot accept sovereignty over an unwilling people. The United States cannot act upon the ancient heresy that might makes right. . . .

Source: Carl Schurz, Address at the Anti-Imperialistic Conference in Chicago, October 17, 1899

Document 4b

Democratic Party Platform

. . . We hold that the Constitution follows the flag, and denounce the doctrine that an Executive or Congress deriving their existence and their powers from the Constitution can exercise lawful authority beyond it or in violation of it. We assert that no nation can long endure half republic and half empire, and we warn the American people that imperialism abroad will lead quickly and inevitably to despotism at home. . . .

The greedy commercialism which dictated the Philippine policy of the Republican administration attempts to justify it with the plea that it will pay; but even this sordid [greedy] and unworthy plea fails when brought to the test of facts. The war of "criminal aggression" against the Filipinos, entailing an annual expense of many millions, has already cost more than any possible profit that could accrue from the entire Philippine trade for years to come. Furthermore, when trade is extended at the expense of liberty, the price is always too high. . . .

Source: Democratic Party Platform, July 4, 1900

34 Based on these documents, what was *one* reason for opposition to American imperialism? [1]

_____

_____

Document 5

Republican Party Platform

. . . In accepting by the Treaty of Paris the just responsibility of our victories in the Spanish war, the President [McKinley] and the Senate won the undoubted approval of the American people. No other course was possible than to destroy Spain's sovereignty throughout the West Indies and in the Philippine Islands. That course created our responsibility before the world, and with the unorganized population whom our intervention had freed from Spain, to provide for the maintenance of law and order, and for the establishment of good government and for the performance of international obligations. Our authority could not be less than our responsibility; and wherever sovereign rights were extended it became the high duty of the Government to maintain its authority, to put down armed insurrection and to confer the blessings of liberty and civilization upon all the rescued peoples. . . .

Source: Republican Party Platform, June 19, 1900

35 Based on this document, what was *one* reason the Republican Party supported American imperialism? [1]

_____

_____

Document 6a

Permission to use this
third-party content has not been granted to Pearson.
View content at
nysedregents.org.

Document 6b

> . . . Those who first pushed the United States toward global military power—the expansionists of 1898—may also claim a measure of vindication. They believed that taking Cuba, the Philippines, and other island nations would be the first steps toward a world largely dominated by American power. That world emerged much as they imagined. Entire regions fell under the formal or informal control of the United States. This gave Americans almost unlimited access to the world's markets and resources. In the space of just a few generations, the United States reached levels of national wealth unmatched in human history. This prosperity helped propel Americans to victory in two world wars and the Cold War. Henry Cabot Lodge was right when he predicted that overseas expansion would bring "enormous material benefits to our trade, our industry, and our labor."
>
> Imperialists believed that American influence would benefit the whole world. This, they argued, would happen in two ways. First, Americans who intervened in foreign countries would bring the material blessings of civilization: good schools, orderly systems of justice, modern transport networks, new jobs, control of tropical diseases. Second, even in places where such tangible benefits did not take hold, rising American power would be good for everyone simply because it meant strengthening the world's most beneficent [generous] nation. . . .

Source: Stephen Kinzer, *The True Flag: Theodore Roosevelt, Mark Twain and the Birth of an American Empire*, 2017

36 Based on these documents, what was *one* result of American expansion in the late 1800s? [1]

_____

_____

Part B
Civic Literacy Essay Question (37)

Directions: Write a well-organized essay that includes an introduction, several paragraphs, and a conclusion. Use evidence from *at least **four*** documents in the body of the essay. Support your response with relevant facts, examples, and details. Include additional outside information.

Historical Context: Imperialism in the 1890s

Throughout United States history, many constitutional and civic issues have been debated by Americans. These debates have resulted in efforts by individuals, groups, and governments to address these issues. These efforts have achieved varying degrees of success. One of these constitutional and civic issues is *imperialism in the 1890s*.

Task: Using information from the documents and your knowledge of United States history, write an essay in which you

> * Describe the historical circumstances surrounding this constitutional or civic issue
> * Explain efforts by individuals, groups, and/or governments to address this constitutional or civic issue
> * Discuss the extent to which the efforts were successful

Guidelines:

In your essay, be sure to
* Develop all aspects of the task
* Explain *at least **two*** efforts to address this issue
* Incorporate information from *at least **four*** documents
* Incorporate relevant outside information
* Support the theme with relevant facts, examples, and details
* Use a logical and clear plan of organization, including an introduction and conclusion that are beyond a restatement of the theme

CIVIC LITERACY ESSAY QUESTION
SAMPLE RATING GUIDE
Imperialism in the 1890s

Part IIIA
Question-Specific Rubric
(Questions 31–36)

31 **According to Howard Jones, what is** *one* **historical circumstance that led to support for United States expansion overseas in the 1890s?**

Score of 1:

- States a historical circumstance that led to support for United States expansion overseas in the 1890s according to Howard Jones

    Examples: need for investment fields and foreign markets that would promote the good of the economy/safeguard national interest; economic hard times of the decade dictated a search for new commercial outlets; need to find places to sell excess stock of manufactured goods; desire for commercial penetration that would lead to economic dominance; tacit support for commercial interests from government in Washington

Score of 0:

- Incorrect response

    Examples: lack of coherence of political parties; negative effects of imperialism on democratic institutions; fear of incorporation of non-white peoples; presence of strong anti-imperialist feelings among Americans, who recognized nation's limitations outside of hemisphere

- No response

Test-Taking Strategies

32 Based on this document, state *one* historical circumstance that supports American expansion in the 1890s.

Score of 1:

- States a historical circumstance that supports American expansion in the 1890s based on this document
    - *Examples:* United States has been an expansionist nation since its birth; United States has been constantly growing; tradition of expansion, such as annexation of Texas by the United States in 1845; United States grew to over 3 million square miles by the 1890s; possession of valuable colonies in Cuba/Philippines/Puerto Rico; several acquisitions were made to expand the United States; foreign nations were extending a welcoming hand to the United States/wanted to be on friendly terms with Uncle Sam

Score of 0:

- Incorrect response
    - *Examples:* lesson for anti-imperialists; in 1861 the Union consisted of 34 states; Germany/Russia/Italy/Austria/Japan/England/France/China helped the United States expand; just kept getting bigger
- No response

---

33 According to Albert Beveridge, what is *one* reason to support American expansion overseas?

Score of 1:

- States a reason to support American expansion overseas according to Albert Beveridge
    - *Examples:* territories will benefit from American expansion; for economic growth; to control other territories; for world power; Cuba/Puerto Rico/Philippines have resources we need; we have the right to increase our commerce in Asia; Cuba/Puerto Rico/Philippines produce what we consume and consume what we produce; American merchants/manufacturers/farmers have the same rights to foreign markets/natural resources as those of Germany/France/Russia/England

Score of 0:

- Incorrect response
    - *Examples:* resources have been trifled with; it would touch fingertips of modern methods; America can raise and make our own goods; Asia must be closed to American trade; the Black Sea districts are in Cuba; Germany has surplus products
- No response

34 Based on these documents, what was *one* reason for opposition to American imperialism?

Score of 1:
- States a reason for opposition to American imperialism based on these documents
    - *Examples:* it is hostile to liberty; it tends toward militarism; subjugation of any people is criminal aggression/open disloyalty to the distinctive principles of our government; a self-governing state cannot accept sovereignty over an unwilling people; United States cannot act upon the ancient heresy that might makes right; that all men, of whatever race or color, are entitled to life/liberty/pursuit of happiness; the Filipinos have fought for/have the right to their independence; to reaffirm that governments derive their just powers from the consent of the governed; idea that might makes right is an ancient heresy; no nation can long endure half republic and half empire; the President/Congress cannot exercise lawful authority beyond/in violation of the Constitution; imperialism abroad will lead quickly/inevitably to despotism at home; war against the Filipinos has cost more than any profit that could accrue from trade; belief that in the land of Washington and Lincoln, all men of any race or color are entitled to life, liberty, and the pursuit of happiness

Score of 0:
- Incorrect response
    - *Examples:* imperialism is an important United States policy; it is in the platform; in the land of Washington and Lincoln; belief in subjugation of people
- No response

---

35 Based on this document, what was *one* reason the Republican Party supported American imperialism?

Score of 1:
- States a reason the Republican Party supported American imperialism based on this document
    - *Examples:* with the acceptance of the Treaty of Paris it had the approval of the American people; destruction of Spain's sovereignty in the West Indies/the Philippines created American responsibility before the world; it would provide for the performance of international obligations; United States authority could not be less than our responsibility; it was the duty of the United States government to maintain its authority/to put down insurrection/to confer the blessings of liberty and civilization upon all rescued peoples

Score of 0:
- Incorrect response
    - *Examples:* the defeat of the Treaty of Paris by the American people; the war gave Spain control of the West Indies/the Philippine Islands; the Spanish government ended resurrection; population was unorganized
- No response

36 Based on these documents, what was *one* result of American expansion in the late 1800s?

Score of 1:
- States a result of American expansion in the late 1800s based on these documents
    - *Examples:* large number of trade routes developed across Pacific Ocean; many islands became United States possessions; United States empire grew in the Pacific; United States became a world power; Alaska acquired in 1867; American trade increased; United States expanded; United States emerged as world power/global military power; Americans got almost unlimited access to world's markets/resources; United States reached levels of national wealth unmatched in human history; prosperity helped propel Americans to victory in two world wars/Cold War; overseas expansion brought enormous material benefits to our trade/industry/labor; entire regions fell under formal/informal control of United States; Americans who intervened in foreign countries would bring material blessings of civilization/good schools/orderly system of justice/modern transport networks/new jobs/control of tropical diseases

Score of 0:
- Incorrect response
    - *Examples:* Australia became a United States possession; the United States ruled the world; New Guinea became part of the United States; access to world markets was reduced
- No response

Part IIIB
Content-Specific Rubric
(Question 37)

Historical Context: Imperialism in the 1890s

Throughout United States history, many constitutional and civic issues have been debated by Americans. These debates have resulted in efforts by individuals, groups, and governments to address these issues. These efforts have achieved varying degrees of success. One of these constitutional and civic issues is *imperialism in the 1890s*.

Task:
- Describe the historical circumstances surrounding this constitutional or civic issue
- Explain efforts by individuals, groups, and/or governments to address this constitutional or civic issue
- Discuss the extent to which the efforts were successful

Scoring Notes:

1. This civic literacy essay has a minimum of *four* components (describing the historical circumstances surrounding imperialism in the 1890s, explaining *at least two* efforts to address the issue by individuals, groups, and/or governments, and discussing the extent to which the efforts were successful).
2. The efforts to address the issue of imperialism in the 1890s may focus on efforts by individuals, groups, governments, or any combination of these.
3. Individuals, groups, and/or governments do not need to be specifically identified as long as they are implied in the discussion.
4. The efforts to address the issue of imperialism in the 1890s may be from the perspective of supporters or opponents of imperialism.
5. The same or similar information may be used to address more than one aspect of the task as long as the information is relevant to the aspect of the task being addressed, e.g., "consent of the governed" may be discussed as both part of the historical circumstances and part of the position of opponents in the debate over imperialism.
6. The explanation of efforts to address the issue of imperialism in the 1890s may be included in the discussion of the extent to which the efforts were successful.
7. The description of historical circumstances and the extent to which the efforts were successful may focus on either immediate or long-term circumstances or immediate or long-term results.
8. The response may discuss efforts to address the issue and the extent to which the efforts were successful from different perspectives as long as the position taken is supported by accurate historical facts and examples.
9. For the purpose of meeting the criteria of using *at least four* documents in the response, documents 4a, 4b, 6a, and 6b may be considered separate documents *if* the response uses specific information from *each* selected document.

Test-Taking Strategies

Score of 5:

- Thoroughly develops *all* aspects of the task evenly and in depth by describing the historical circumstances surrounding imperialism in the 1890s, explaining *at least two* efforts to address the issue of imperialism in the 1890s by individuals, groups, and/or governments, and discussing the extent to which the efforts were successful
- Is more analytical than descriptive (analyzes, evaluates, and/or creates* information), e.g., connects the long tradition of American expansion and the interest in expanding trade opportunities as a result of the post–Civil War industrial and commercial developments to the national, political, and constitutional debates over annexation of the Philippines and the Filipino-American War to the commercial and strategic military opportunities gained from territorial acquisitions after the Spanish-American War as well as the increased responsibilities of becoming a colonial/world power
- Incorporates relevant information from *at least four* documents (see Key Ideas From Documents chart)
- Incorporates substantial relevant outside information (see Relevant Outside Information chart)
- Richly supports the theme with many relevant facts, examples, and details, e.g., Spanish-American War; Social Darwinism; gained Guam, Puerto Rico, Cuba, and Philippines; "consent of the governed"; Platt Amendment; Emilio Aguinaldo; "benevolent assimilation"; Open Door policy; Roosevelt Corollary; Panama Canal
- Demonstrates a logical and clear plan of organization; includes an introduction and a conclusion that are beyond a restatement of the theme

Score of 4:

- Develops *all* aspects of the task but may do so somewhat unevenly by discussing one aspect of the task less thoroughly than the other aspects of the task
- Is both descriptive and analytical (applies, analyzes, evaluates, and/or creates* information), e.g. discusses the interest in expanding trade opportunities as a result of post–Civil War industrial and commercial development and reasons for the national debate over annexation of the Philippines and the commercial opportunities and world-power status achieved through territories acquired after the Spanish-American War
- Incorporates relevant information from *at least four* documents
- Incorporates relevant outside information
- Supports the theme with relevant facts, examples, and details
- Demonstrates a logical and clear plan of organization; includes an introduction and a conclusion that are beyond a restatement of the theme

Score of 3:

- Develops *all* aspects of the task with little depth *or* develops *at least three* aspects of the task in some depth
- Is more descriptive than analytical (applies, may analyze and/or evaluate information)
- Incorporates some relevant information from some of the documents
- Incorporates limited relevant outside information
- Includes some relevant facts, examples, and details; may include some minor inaccuracies
- Demonstrates a satisfactory plan of organization, includes an introduction and a conclusion that may be a restatement of the theme

Score of 2:

- Minimally develops **all** aspects of the task *or* develops *at least two* aspects of the task in some depth
- Is primarily descriptive; may include faulty, weak, or isolated application or analysis
- Incorporates limited relevant information from the documents *or* consists primarily of relevant information copied from the documents
- Presents little or no relevant outside information
- Includes few relevant facts, examples, and details; may include some inaccuracies
- Demonstrates a general plan of organization; may lack focus; may contain digressions; may not clearly identify which aspect of the task is being addressed; may lack an introduction and/or a conclusion

Score of 1

- Minimally develops some aspects of the task
- Is descriptive; may lack understanding, application, or analysis
- Makes vague, unclear references to the documents or consists primarily of relevant and irrelevant information copied from the documents
- Presents no relevant outside information
- Includes few relevant facts, examples, or details; may include inaccuracies
- May demonstrate a weakness in organization; may lack focus; may contain digressions; may not clearly identify which aspect of the task is being addressed; may lack an introduction and/or a conclusion

Score of 0:

Fails to develop the task or may only refer to the theme in a general way; *OR* includes no relevant facts, examples, or details; *OR* includes only the historical context and/or task as copied from the test booklet; *OR* includes only entire documents copied from the test booklet; *OR* is illegible; *OR* is a blank paper

*The term *create* as used by Anderson/Krathwohl, et al. in their 2001 revision of Bloom's *Taxonomy of Educational Objectives* refers to the highest level of the cognitive domain. This usage of *create* is similar to Bloom's use of the term *synthesis*. Creating implies an insightful reorganization of information into a new pattern or whole. While a Level 5 paper will contain analysis and/or evaluation of information, a very strong paper may also include examples of creating information as defined by Anderson and Krathwohl.

Imperialism in the 1890s

Key Ideas From Documents

Historical Circumstances

Doc 1—By 1890s no interest in actual annexation of territory (economic dominance without direct political controls; acquisition of colonies having no prospect of statehood)

Expansionist mood not national (lack of coherence in political parties; general fragmentation evident from Civil War)

Presence of strong anti-imperialist feelings (recognition of America's limitations outside of hemisphere; fear of incorporation of non-white peoples; worry about negative effects of imperialism on democratic institutions)

Search for new commercial outlets as result of economic hard times of decade (need for markets capable of absorbing United States excess stock of manufactured goods)

Tacit support of federal government in searching for investment fields and foreign markets (to promote the good of the economy; safeguard the national interest)

Doc 2—History of United States is one of expansion (Louisiana ceded by France in 1803; Florida ceded by Spain in 1819; Texas annexed in 1845; Hawaii annexed in 1898; Cuba, Philippines, and Puerto Rico added in 1899)

Efforts by political cartoonists to gain support for idea that United States has always been expansionist

Efforts to Address Imperialism

Doc 3—Supporters of expansionism in 1898—Albert Beveridge's "March of the Flag" speech when running for United States Senate (15,000,000 acres of forest, exhaustless mines of iron, priceless deposits of manganese, millions of unexplored acres in Cuba; riches of Puerto Rico hardly touched; claim that "they produce what we consume, and consume what we produce"; equal access of American merchants, manufacturers, farmers to those of Germany, France, Russia, or England; access to United Kingdom's commerce with Asian markets which should not be shut to American trade)

Doc 4—Platform of American Anti-Imperialist League opposing imperialism (hostile to liberty and tends toward militarism; all men of whatever race or color entitled to life, liberty, and pursuit of happiness; subjugation of any people is "criminal aggression" and open disloyalty to principles of United States government; independence for Cuba and Philippines because they have fought long and hard and it is their right; history of protest by United States against international law which permits subjugation of weak by strong; sovereignty over unwilling people cannot be accepted by self-governing state; ancient heresy "might does not make right" cannot be acted upon by United States)

Democratic Party Platform opposing imperialism (belief that Constitution follows the flag; existence and powers of president and Congress from Constitution meant they cannot exercise lawful authority beyond it or violate it; no nation can long endure half republic and half empire; belief that imperialism will lead quickly and inevitably to despotism at home; cost of "criminal aggression" against Filipinos; more than any possible profit from trade for years to come; trade to be at expense of liberty for Filipinos)

Doc 5—Support of Republican Party for imperialism (responsibility of United States government to provide for maintenance of law and order and for establishment of good government and performance of international obligations; duty of United States government to maintain authority, put down armed insurrection, and confer blessings of liberty and civilization on all rescued peoples)

Key Ideas From Documents (continued)

Extent to Which the Efforts Were Successful

Doc 2—Many nations anxious to be friendly with United States in 1899 (Russia, Germany, Italy, Austria, Japan, England, France, China)

Doc 5—Treaty of peace with Spain ratified in Treaty of Paris on February 6, 1899 ending Spanish-American War

Doc 6—American acquisitions in 1898 and after (Philippine Islands, 1898; Guam, 1898; Hawaiian Islands, 1898; Palmyra Island, 1898; Puerto Rico, 1898; American Samoa, 1899; Wake Island, 1899; Panama Canal Zone, 1903; naval base leased in Cuba, 1903)

Push by expansionists toward global military power as taking Cuba, the Philippines, and other island nations first steps toward a world largely dominated by American power

Almost unlimited access gained to world's markets and resources as entire regions fell under formal or informal control of United States

Prosperity of United States a reason for American victories in two world wars and Cold War

Henry Cabot Lodge correct in his prediction that overseas expansion would bring "enormous material benefits to our trade, our industry, and our labor"

Belief of imperialists that American influence would benefit the whole world: material blessings of civilization brought by Americans who intervened in foreign countries (good schools; orderly system of justice; modern transportation networks; new jobs; control of tropical diseases); in places where tangible benefits did not happen then rising American power good for everyone because it would mean strengthening generosity of America

---

Test-Taking Strategies

Imperialism in the 1890s

Relevant Outside Information
(This list is not all-inclusive.)

Historical Circumstances
National feeling of "New Manifest Destiny" (United States interest in Caribbean, Pacific, and Asia)
Turning of United States interests toward distant shores with advances of post–Civil War era (industrial; technological; commercial)
Influence of missionaries and investors in overseas territories (Hawaii, Cuba)
Duty to advance American ideals of democracy and republican government (Josiah Strong's *Our Country*; Social Darwinism; Rudyard Kipling's *White Man's Burden*)
Appeal of new challenges with temporary resolution of domestic issues (Reconstruction; Native Americans)
Search for new economic opportunities with close of frontier, 1890 (Industrial Revolution)
Diversion from domestic problems (Depression, 1890s; labor violence; agrarian unrest)
Establishment of colonies by Europeans for centuries (competition)
Political and military competition (Mahan's *The Influence of Sea Power on History*; strategic bases)
Details about Spanish-American War

Efforts to Address Imperialism
Rebellion against Hawaiian royal rule by planters and businessmen
Rejection of Hawaiian annexation by President Grover Cleveland
Details about divisive national debate over Treaty of Paris, 1898
President McKinley's decision to annex Philippines
Three-year guerilla war with Philippines (role of Emilio Aguinaldo)
American protectorate established over Cuba (Teller Amendment v. Platt Amendment)
Complicated legal issues with annexation of Puerto Rico ("Does the Constitution follow the flag?"; *Insular Cases*)
Theodore Roosevelt's speeches and writings about benefits of expansion
Speeches of Democratic presidential candidate William Jennings Bryan opposing imperialism

Extent to Which the Efforts Were Successful
Increasing responsibility for policing Western Hemisphere (Roosevelt Corollary; Big Stick Policy)
Acquisition of bases to accommodate expanding navy (Manila; Pearl Harbor)
Power in the Far East for United States (John Hay's Open Door policy; complications regarding Japanese expansion pre–World War II)
Theodore Roosevelt's mediation of Russo-Japanese War
Growth of public interest for an isthmian canal
Offer for military and diplomatic support to businessmen in Caribbean (Dollar Diplomacy)
Details about Puerto Rico (commonwealth; citizenship; current status; migration)
Continued United States presence in Cuba (Guantanamo)
Return of canal to Panama under Carter (current status of Panama Canal)

Document 1b

Although 1890 to 2000 is a relatively short span of time, these eleven decades comprise a critical period in American history. The collapse of Reconstruction after the Civil War led to the establishment of white supremacy in the Southern states, a system of domination and exploitation that most whites, in the North as well as the South, expected to last indefinitely. In 1900, despite the nation's formal commitment to racial equality as expressed in the Fourteenth and Fifteenth Amendments, racial discrimination remained a basic organizing principle of American society. In the South, racial discrimination, reinforced by racial segregation, became official state policy. In the North discrimination and segregation also became widely sanctioned customs that amounted to, in effect, semiofficial policy. The federal government practiced racial segregation in the armed services, discriminated against blacks in the civil service, and generally condoned, by its actions if not its words, white supremacy.

Source: Adam Fairclough, *Better Day Coming: Blacks and Equality 1890–2000*, 2002

1. Based on these documents, state *one* way the end of Reconstruction affected African Americans. [1]

_____

_____

Document 2

By 1905 those African Americans who stayed in the former Confederacy found themselves virtually banished from local elections, but that didn't mean that they weren't political actors. In his famous 1895 Atlanta Exposition speech, Tuskegee College president Booker T. Washington recommended vocational training rather than classical education for African Americans. The former slave implied that black southerners would not seek social integration, but he did demand that southern factories hire black people: "The opportunity to earn a dollar in a factory just now is worth infinitely more than the opportunity to spend a dollar in an opera-house." He looked forward to the near future when the African American third of the southern population would produce and share in one-third of its industrial bounty. . . .

The northern-born black sociologist W. E. B. Du Bois positioned himself as Washington's nemesis [opponent]. A graduate of Tennessee's Fisk University, Du Bois was the first African American to earn a Harvard Ph.D. He believed that Washington had conceded too much and said so in his 1903 book *The Souls of Black Folk*. Any man, he insisted, should be able to have a classical education. Moreover, accepting segregation meant abdicating all civil rights by acknowledging that black people were not equal to whites. "The problem of the Twentieth Century is the problem of the color line." Du Bois warned. In 1905 he founded the Niagara Movement, the forerunner of the National Association for the Advancement of Colored People (NAACP), which was begun in 1909 to fight for political and civil rights.

Source: Glenda Elizabeth Gilmore and Thomas J. Sugrue, *These United States: A Nation in the Making 1890 to the Present*, 2015

2. According to this document, what is *one* way Booker T. Washington and W. E. B. Du Bois disagreed about how African Americans should achieve equality? [1]

_____

_____

Document 3

In 1950 Reverend Oliver Brown of Topeka, Kansas, was incensed that his young daughters could not attend the Sumner Elementary School, an all-white public school close to their home. Instead, they had to walk nearly a mile through a dangerous railroad switchyard to reach a bus that would take them to an inferior all-black school.

In the early 1950s, this sort of school segregation was commonplace in the South and certain border states. By law, all-black schools (and other segregated public facilities) were supposed to be as well-funded as whites'—but they rarely were. States typically spent twice as much money per student in white schools. Classrooms in black schools were overcrowded and dilapidated.

In 1951 NAACP lead counsel Thurgood Marshall filed suit on behalf of Oliver Brown. By fall 1952, the Brown case and four other school desegregation cases had made their way to the U.S. Supreme Court, all under the case name *Brown* v. *Board of Education of Topeka*. Marshall argued that the Supreme Court should overturn the "separate but equal" ruling of *Plessy* v. *Ferguson* (1896), which had legitimized segregation. Marshall believed that even if states spent an equal amount of money on black schools, the segregated system would still be unfair because the stigma of segregation damaged black students psychologically.

Source: Beth Bailey, et al., *The Fifties Chronicle*, 2008

3. According to this document, what is *one* reason Thurgood Marshall argued that the "separate but equal" ruling of *Plessy* v. *Ferguson* should be overturned? [1]

_____

_____

Document 4a

Sit-in at Woolworth's lunch counter in Greensboro, North Carolina

Document 4b

At lunch counters in other cities, protesters encountered hostile reactions from outraged white patrons. Sit-in demonstrators were assaulted with verbal abuse, hot coffee, lit cigarettes, and worse. Invariably, it was the young protesters who ended up arrested for "creating a disturbance." Nevertheless, by fall 1961 the movement could claim substantial victories among many targeted cities.

Source: David Farber, et al., *The Sixties Chronicles*, 2004

4. Based on these documents, state *one* result of the sit-in at the Greensboro Woolworth. [1]

_____

_____

Document 5

The direct action protests of the 1960s paid dividends. In 1964 and 1965, the Johnson administration orchestrated the passing of the two most significant civil rights bills since Reconstruction. The Birmingham protests and the March on Washington had convinced President Kennedy to forge ahead with a civil rights bill in 1963. But his assassination on November 22, 1963, left the passage of the bill in question. President Johnson, who to that point had an unfavorable record concerning civil rights, had come to believe in the importance of federal protection for African Americans and deftly tied the civil rights bill to the memory of Kennedy. . . .

Despite passage of this far-reaching bill, African Americans still faced barriers to their right to vote. While the Civil Rights Act of 1964 addressed voting rights, it did not eliminate many of the tactics recalcitrant [stubborn] southerners used to keep blacks from the polls, such as violence, economic intimidation, and literacy tests. But the Freedom Summer protests in Mississippi and the Selma-to-Montgomery march the following year led to the passage of the Voting Rights Act of 1965. Johnson had already begun work on a bill before the Selma march, and he again urged Congress to pass it. On March 15, 1965, he addressed both houses of Congress.

Source: Henry Louis Gates, Jr., *Life Upon These Shores: Looking at African American History 1513–2008*, 2011

5. According to Henry Louis Gates, Jr., what was *one* result of the 1960s civil rights protests? [1]

_____

_____

Document 6

When the clock ticked off the last minute of 1969 and African Americans took stock of the last few years, they thought not only about the changes they had witnessed but also about the ones they still hoped to see. They knew they were the caretakers of King's dream of living in a nation where character was more important than color. And they knew they had to take charge of their community. After all, the civil rights and Black Power eras had forged change through community action. Although many blacks may have sensed that all progress was tempered by the social, economic, and political realities of a government and a white public often resistant to change, they could not ignore the power of their own past actions. America in 1969 was not the America of 1960 or 1965. At the end of the decade, a chorus could be heard rising from the black community proclaiming, "We changed the world."

Source: Robin D. G. Kelley and Earl Lewis, eds., *To Make Our World Anew: A History of African Americans,* 2000

6. Based on this document, state *one* impact of the civil rights movement of the 1960s. [1]

_____

_____

Answers: The following are examples of answers for each question: 1. African Americans faced restrictions on their civil rights at the end of Reconstruction even though their rights were guaranteed by the 14th and 15th amendments. 2. Booker T. Washington accepted segregation, believing that economic and political equality would eventually occur, but W. E. B. Du Bois felt that accepting it would ensure that African Americans would never be considered equal. 3. Thurgood Marshall felt that the ruling should be overturned because it legitimized segregation. 4. The sit-in in Greensboro led to the growth in public support for African American rights. 5. The 1960s protests resulted in the federal government enacting several major civil rights laws. 6. The civil rights movement of the 1960s empowered African Americans socially and politically. Your essay should provide support for your answers to all three tasks, include evidence from at least four documents as well as outside information, include an introduction and conclusion, and be well thought out and well written.

Colonial Foundations (1607–1763)

Topic Overview

Over thousands of years the indigenous people of the Americas developed many different societies. These Native Americans adapted to and transformed the environment of North America. European colonization in North America prompted cultural contact and exchange between diverse peoples; cultural differences and misunderstandings at times led to conflict. European contact with Native Americans began with the Spanish followed by the French, Dutch, and English. Native Americans lost much of their land and many lives.

Geography and other factors led to different settlement patterns, economic systems, social structures, and labor systems in the thirteen English colonies. Slavery became a deeply established component of the colonial economic system and social structure, particularly in the South. By 1700, slavery had developed into a racial institution.

The development of the colonial political systems was influenced by British political traditions such as the Magna Carta, Enlightenment ideas, and the colonial experience. The Mayflower Compact, a major colonial document, expresses colonial democratic principles. Self-government in various forms was common. The Virginia House of Burgesses was the first democratic institution established in the English colonies.

European Contacts and Colonization Impact Native Americans

Key Concept

11.1a Contact between Native American groups and Europeans occurred through cultural exchanges, resistance efforts, and conflict.

Lesson Overview

The history of the United States begins with the native people of North America who, for thousands of years, were its only inhabitants. The geography and environment of North America affected the migration patterns of the Native Americans as well as the diverse societies that they developed.

Beginning in the late fifteenth century, Europeans, including the Spanish, French, Dutch, and English, came to the continent. Europeans and Native American groups came in contact through cultural exchange and trade. However, cultural differences and misunderstandings also led to resistance efforts and conflict. Eventually the impact of European colonization resulted in Native Americans losing much of their land and suffering a catastrophic loss of life through diseases and armed conflict.

Unifying Themes

As you review this lesson take special note of the following themes:

- **Development, Movement, and Interaction of Cultures** What were the causes of the early cultural contact and exchanges, resistance efforts, and conflicts between Europeans and Native Americans?

- **Time, Continuity, and Change** What were the consequences of European contact with Native Americans? In what ways is the cause-effect pattern of European contact with Native Americans similar and different for the Spanish, French, Dutch, and English?

- **Geography, Humans, and the Environment** What is the setting in which the Native Americans and the Europeans meet? How did that setting affect the relationship between the diverse Native American societies and the European explorers and colonizers? How did the activities of Native Americans and the Europeans affect the environment?

- **Global Connections and Exchange** How did the patterns of migration to and within North America affect both the Native Americans and the Europeans? What were the effects of the cultural exchanges between Native Americans and Europeans?

Key People

Christopher Columbus   Henry Hudson

Key Terms and Events

Bering Strait land bridge	New Spain	New Netherland
Paleo-Indians	*conquistadores*	Fort Orange
indigenous	encomienda system	New Amsterdam
capitalism	Pueblo Revolt	transatlantic slave trade
nation-states	Northwest Passage	Jamestown
commerce	New France	Powhatan Confederacy
mercantilism	French and Iroquois	Plymouth Colony
missionary	Wars	King Philip's War
balance of power	Iroquois Confederacy	Columbian Exchange

The Peopling and Geography of North America

The settling of the Americas began long before the arrival of European explorers. The region's geography influenced how ancient people arrived, where they settled, and how they lived.

The Bering Strait Land Bridge

Geographers believe that during the Ice Ages much of the earth's water was frozen into glaciers. As a result, ocean levels dropped, exposing a flat bridge of land between Alaska and eastern Asia where the Bering Strait is today. It is believed that nomadic hunters from East Asia crossed this **Bering Strait land bridge** and gradually spread out over the Americas.

Recent scientific findings have led scientists to propose that some migrants also came to the Americas in canoes by following the Pacific coastline. These **Paleo-Indians,** who are the ancestors of all Native American peoples, are the **indigenous,** or original, people in the Americas.

Migration to the Americas

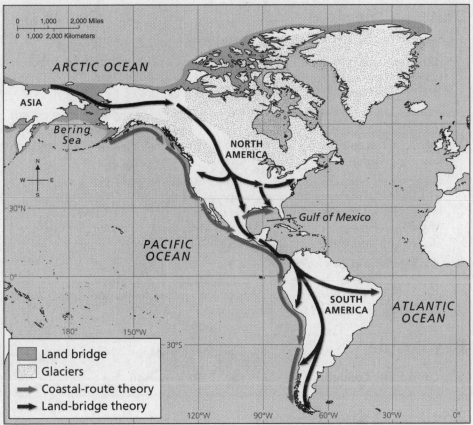

Native Americans in Pre-Columbian North America

In the late 1400s, Native Americans in North America numbered as many as 15 million. There were more than 300 different native groups speaking more than 200 often unrelated languages. Their way of life was heavily influenced by the environment in which they lived by adapting to or altering that environment. They created many societies with different governmental, social, economic, and cultural practices.

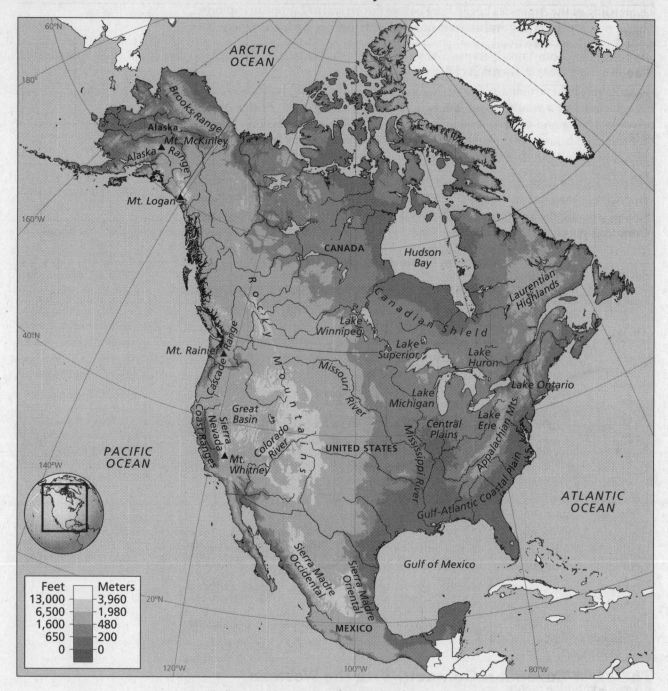

The Physical Geography of North America

Examine the physical map of North America above for an understanding of the similarities and also extreme differences in the geographic regions of North America. This fact is critical to understanding the history of this nation.

Landforms, water bodies, vegetation, and climate are some of the physical characteristics that a region shares. North America's terrain was shaped in part by glacial movement. The continent benefits from many rivers, sounds, bays, and lakes offering access and an abundance of natural resources.

Geographic Regions of the United States	
Gulf-Atlantic Coastal Plain	on the East Coast, a low region with rich soil, mild climate, and deep water harbors
Appalachian Mountain Range	old mountains to the west of the coastal plain, running 2,000 miles from Canada to Alabama
Central Plains	west of the Appalachians and east of the Great Plains, containing the rich flat lands of the Mississippi River valley
Great Plains	a 3,000-miles long area of high plateau with mostly treeless semiarid grasslands or prairie, west of the Central Plains and east of the Rocky Mountains
Rocky Mountain Range	part of the North American Cordillera, a related set of parallel mountain ranges stretching from northern Alaska to Mexico; west of the Great Plains and east of the Great Basin and the Coastal mountain ranges
Great Basin	a vast arid (dry) region between the Rockies and the Coastal ranges made up of many bowl-shaped basins; water within it has no outlet to the sea
Pacific Coastal Ranges	series of younger, rugged mountain ranges along the Pacific coast from northwest Canada into central Mexico that form part of the North American Cordillera

Geography's Influence on the Lives of Early Native Americans

The regions in which Native Americans chose to live greatly affected their way of life. A region with ample resources allowed groups to become more settled, while regions with limited resources caused groups to have a more nomadic existence.

- The Native American lifestyle in present-day northeastern and southeastern United States was agricultural, as well as dependent on hunting and fishing. Permanent villages were often built next to rivers.

- The Native Americans living in arid areas such as the Great Basin and the westernmost Great Plains were nomadic hunters. The introduction of European horses and guns radically altered their culture and their lives.

- In the Pacific Northwest and along the California coast, most of the native peoples led a hunter-gatherer life, but some settled on the coast and created a culture based on resources from the sea.

- In parts of the present-day southwestern United States the Pueblos built an economic system that involved irrigated and terraced farms.

- In Mexico, the Aztecs maintained the wealthiest, most complex and advanced civilization in North America.

The First European Contacts With the Western Hemisphere

Historians acknowledge that the Norse (Vikings) from Norway were the first Europeans to reach the Americas by 1000 A.D. Nearly 500 years later the two continents were explored and settled by other Europeans, who left a more permanent mark in the Americas.

Social Studies Practices
Geographic Reasoning

- Using the geographic description in the table and the map of North America, compare the positive and negative geographic features of a region.

- Determine how these features would affect people attempting to survive there.

- How did geography affect the policies of the European nations in the 1400s?
- How did economics affect the policies of these nations?
- Identify two examples of how geography and economics led to European exploration and contacts.

Motives for European Exploration and Colonization

The 1400s and the 1500s were a period of major changes in Europe. Nation-states were replacing feudal states. The **Renaissance** placed the focus on the individual and the secular at a time when the **Reformation** provoked bitter disputes and wars between Catholics and Protestants. Trade increased and expanded. **Capitalism** was changing the economic systems. This was the context in the early 1400s in which the era of exploration and colonization began. During this time, Europe

- was changing politically into unified **nation-states** with centralized power and financial resources to support exploration.
- transitioned to an economic system based on **commerce**—buying and selling of products on a large scale. Commerce encouraged the growth of cities and a middle class. It also spurred interest in more trade and in finding better, more direct trade routes.
- promoted **mercantilism**, or the regulation of a nation's economy for the purpose of increasing a nation's wealth. A nation's power and wealth were measured by how much gold and silver it accumulated. Colonial economies were controlled to benefit the mother country.
- developed new technologies in navigation and shipbuilding that allowed for longer sea voyages.
- searched for a direct all-water route to Asia to obtain directly the highly desirable goods available there.
- extended its economic, religious, and political rivalries among nations to the Americas, often enlisting Native Americans in its conflicts.
- considered it its mission to convert non-Christians to Catholicism and other Christian religions. Protestant and Catholic nations competed for conversions as part of the larger worldwide conflict.

In turn, Portugal, Spain, France, the Netherlands, and England sent explorers, soldiers, **missionaries** (clergy), traders, merchants, and family units to the Americas. This led to the interaction of diverse cultures within and between both Hemispheres. The result was significant global changes in the ways of life and **balance of power** of nations, societies, families, and individuals. The Native Americans suffered the most, permanently and catastrophically.

The Portuguese

Beginning in the early 1400s, the Portuguese led Europe in competition for new transoceanic trade routes. Encouraged by their king and aided by new technology, explorers for Portugal were the first to sail along the African coast and then beyond the tip of Africa to reach India by sea. In the 1440s, Portugal became the first European nation to engage in the slave trade. Slave trade had existed in Africa for hundreds of years, but Portugal rapidly expanded it, creating a system of large-scale farming dependent on slave labor on islands off the coast of West Africa. When colonization followed the voyages of Columbus, the Portuguese slave labor system became a model for parts of North and South America, particularly in the Caribbean as well as in Brazil, which had been claimed by Portugal in 1500.

Spanish Contacts With Native Americans and Their Impact

Spain was the first European nation to explore and colonize in the Western Hemisphere and the first to reap the riches it offered at the expense of the Native Americans. In the late 1400s, Spain challenged Portugal for control of the trade routes and colonies in the Americas. Spain hired **Christopher Columbus,** an Italian, to attempt to reach Asia by sailing west. Other explorers extended and solidified Spanish claims. Colonization followed.

Social Studies Practices
Cause and Effect

"God, Gold, and Glory" is how historians summarize the Spanish motivations in the Americas.

- For each of the three motivators identify an example of how the Spanish carried out that objective and explain its effect.

Spain's primary colonization goal was to make Spain an even more powerful European and world power. They would extract gold and silver from the Americas, exploit other resources, and further stimulate the Spanish mercantilist economy by maintaining a positive balance of trade. Their missionaries would convert Native Americans to Christianity.

The Spanish Empire, or **New Spain,** in the Americas spread to include most of South America, Mexico, Mesoamerica, and large sections of what is today the United States. For a time, Spain was enriched by the gold and silver that their explorers, known as *conquistadores,* took from the Aztecs in Mexico and the Incas in Peru. Both the Aztec and Inca civilizations were virtually destroyed as a result of Spain's exploitation of their people and resources.

Spain used its **encomienda system** to control the indigenous people, create a labor system, and reward the *conquistadores.* This system forced the native people to work in the fields and the mines and to pay tributes in return for protection. Eventually, with the native population decimated by disease and enforced labor, African enslaved people replaced them as a source of labor. Spain exercised power and authority through the Catholic Church, the military, and a rigid social structure.

Spain's increased wealth and power provoked challenges from France, the Netherlands, and England. In 1565, Spain established **Saint Augustine** in Florida as a fort to protect its trading routes to the Caribbean islands and to defend Florida against the French. From 1540 to 1542, Spanish explorers claimed parts of southwest United States, waging war against native people in present-day New Mexico. In 1598, to protect Mexico, Spain began to colonize New Mexico. In about 1609, Santa Fe was founded as its capital the second permanent city in the United States.

From 1539 until 1542, Hernando De Soto explored and claimed for Spain the southeastern present-day states of Florida, Georgia, the Carolinas, Tennessee, Alabama, Mississippi, Arkansas, Oklahoma, Louisiana, and Texas. He killed or captured and enslaved Native Americans, left villages without food, encouraged conflicts among Native American groups, and spread disease.

In 1542, Spanish explorers first claimed California. Not until 1769, led by Father Junípero Serra, did Spanish priests begin founding missions along the California coast. Thousands of the native people were converted to Christianity. They found that the demands of mission life made it difficult to retain their own culture.

Case Study: The Pueblo Revolt in New Mexico

In addition to protecting Mexico, converting the Pueblos to Catholicism and establishing an economically successful colony were the Spanish objectives in New Mexico. While the missionaries successfully made converts, the Pueblos objected to being forced to give up their own religious customs and resented the inhumane treatment they received if they maintained their native religious practices. The Pueblos were also required to provide the Spanish with food and labor. They endured years of starvation due to drought and disease.

In 1680, the Pueblos unified in a successful attempt to reclaim their land, culture, and religious practices. About 8,000 Native Americans from almost every Pueblo group within 300 miles of Santa Fe and even Apaches joined in the **Pueblo Revolt,** also known as Po'pay's (Popé's) Rebellion. Priests, soldiers, and settlers were killed and the Catholic churches torn down. Although Spain retook New Mexico in 1692, the Pueblo Revolt is recognized as one of the most successful Native American actions against the Europeans. After they regained control, the Spanish softened their demands for food and labor from the Pueblos and moved away from the encomienda system.

Po'pay statue in National Statuary Hall, U.S. Capitol

Analyzing Documents
Point of View

I learned that one of the Indians who was leading them was from the villa and had gone to join them. . . . I asked him how it was that he had gone crazy too—being an Indian who spoke our language, was so intelligent, and had lived all his life in the villa among the Spaniards, where I had placed such confidence in him—and was now coming as a leader of the Indian rebels.

—Governor Don Antonio de Otermín, letter on the Pueblo Revolt, 1680

- What in these remarks tells us that the governor fails to understand why the Pueblos have rebelled?

Native American Population in North America, 1492–1900

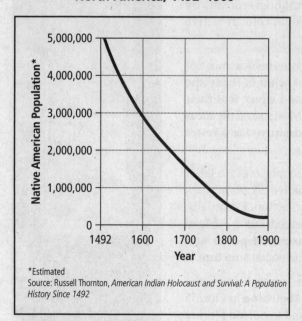

*Estimated
Source: Russell Thornton, *American Indian Holocaust and Survival: A Population History Since 1492*

Social Studies Practices
Compare and Contrast

• Compare and contrast the effects of Spanish versus French contacts on Native Americans.

• Identify reasons for the similarities and for the differences.

French Contacts With the Native Americans and Their Impact

French explorers made their claims to portions of the northern section of North America.

• In 1534, France, wanting a share of the precious metals in the Americas and seeking a **Northwest Passage,** sent Jacques Cartier to North America. While failing to achieve these two goals, Cartier established French land claims in eastern Canada based on his exploration of the Gulf of Saint Lawrence and the Saint Lawrence River.

• Between 1604 and 1615, Samuel de Champlain explored **New France,** founded Quebec, encouraged French settlements, and supported the fur trade. He looked for a water route to Asia. Champlain advocated for peaceful relations with Native Americans, recognizing their pivotal role in building a profitable fur trade in beaver pelts. Montréal, founded in 1642, was the hub of trade in New France.

• In 1669, René Robert Cavalier de La Salle explored the Ohio River valley resulting in later French claims to the area. In 1682, he traveled down the Mississippi to the Gulf of Mexico and declared that the river and all of its tributaries belonged to France. He named the immense region Louisiana.

The beaver trade brought wealth to France. Products were sent back to France down the Mississippi through the port of New Orleans. In addition to the St. Lawrence River, the French established forts and trading posts along the Mississippi, Ohio, and other rivers and lakes. Jesuit missionaries worked to convert Native Americans.

But New France grew more slowly than Spanish and English colonies. Like Spain, the French colonizers were mostly men. The focus was on fur trade rather than on farming. French traders and political leaders were concerned with establishing peaceful relations with the native people. Marriage of a French man to a native woman was seen as one way to establish an alliance. New France was a royal province; the colonists had no political rights, while the Church exercised influence over daily life. French Protestants called Huguenots were banned from emigration to New France.

Case Study: French and Iroquois Wars

The **French and Iroquois Wars** were fought off and on from 1642 to 1698. They are considered some of the most brutal and bloody wars fought in North America. As the beaver population declined due to increasing use of guns, the Iroquois moved to expand their territory north and west and to take control of the fur trade between France and its Native American allies. The armed conflicts at first involved Iroquois versus Algonquin but soon included both the French and British, who were bitter rivals for territory in North America and enemies in Europe as well. The wars ended in 1701 when the Iroquois adopted a policy of neutrality toward both France and England.

The Iroquois Confederacy

The most powerful government of the Eastern Woodlands Native Americans was the **Iroquois Confederacy,** formed in 1570, and made up of first five and then six Iroquois nations located in central and western New York. The Confederacy made it possible for the Iroquois to hold onto their lands against European pressure for almost two centuries, playing the English and French against each other.

Dutch Contacts With the Native Americans and Their Impact

The Netherlands reached its peak as the world's leading trading and naval state during the 17th century. The Dutch used powerful companies to trade and colonize. In 1621, the Dutch West India Company was chartered to trade and colonize in the Americas based on the explorations of **Henry Hudson.** In 1609, working for the East India Company, Hudson sailed up the river now named for him hoping it was the Northwest Passage through North America. It was not but Hudson claimed the land for the Netherlands. Like the French, Dutch **New Netherland** developed a fur trade based on maintaining good relations with the Native-American nations that controlled the hunting grounds and routes. Also like the French, the Dutch upset the power balance among the Native American tribes each of whom wanted a monopoly of the trade in beaver, guns, and other European goods.

In 1624, the Dutch West India Company built a fort and a trading post at present-day Albany, naming it **Fort Orange,** and in 1626, settled **New Amsterdam,** now New York City, which functioned as an international fur trade center. The company, in the interests of being commercially successful, accepted people from many different ethnic origins and religions. It offered large plots of land along the Hudson River to those who would colonize it. The colony expanded from the Hudson River onto Long Island and into New Jersey and south to the Delaware River.

In the end, the company, failing to attract large numbers of settlers and dissatisfied with the profits from fur, looked for commercial gain on its sugar cane plantations in the Caribbean and through the **transatlantic slave trade.** It was the Dutch who in 1619 brought the first African enslaved labor to Virginia. In the 17th century, England and the Dutch fought a series of three naval wars for control of colonies and trade. In 1664, during the Second Anglo-Dutch War, the English took control of New Netherland and renamed it **New York.**

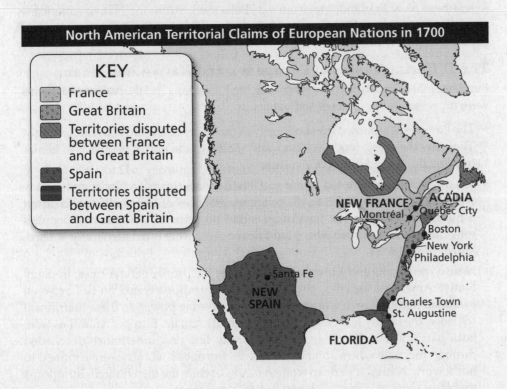

North American Territorial Claims of European Nations in 1700

KEY
France
Great Britain
Territories disputed between France and Great Britain
Spain
Territories disputed between Spain and Great Britain

NEW FRANCE
Montréal
ACADIA
Québec City
Boston
New York
Philadelphia
Santa Fe
NEW SPAIN
Charles Town
St. Augustine
FLORIDA

The Impact of English Contacts With the Native Americans

Relations between colonists and Native Americans centered around trade and exchange, alliances, or warfare. The survival of **Jamestown,** founded in 1607 as the first permanent English settlement in North America, is credited in part to the food supplied, in return for weapons, by the Algonquin tribes that made up the Powhatan Confederacy. Native Americans also offered food to the **Plymouth Colony,** settled in 1620, in order to gain the colony as an ally against other tribes.

Interactions between Native Americans and the settlers led to outbreaks of diseases, such as measles and smallpox, which decimated the Native American population. The indigenous people lacked immunity to European diseases. As the Native Americans became increasingly dependent on European products, their traditional culture weakened.

Case Study: War in the English Colonies

In the 1600s, English settlers and Native Americans engaged in wars caused by the expansion of English settlements and fears of Native Americans for the survival of their culture. In tidewater Virginia, profitable tobacco farming led settlers to move westward into Native American lands. By 1646, after two wars, the **Powhatan Confederacy** was close to destruction, unable to hold back the settlers' movement.

I am now grown old, and must soon die; . . . Why should you take by force that from us which you can have by love? Why should you destroy us, who have provided you with food? . . . What is the cause of your jealousy? You see us unarmed, and willing to supply your wants, if you come in a friendly manner, not with swords and guns, as to invade an enemy.

—Chief Powhatan, c. 1609

In 1675, in New England, an alliance of Native American tribes launched **King Philip's War** (Metacom's Rebellion). They were reacting to the increasingly rapid loss of their lands and growing dependency on English guns and food. Some of the tribes sided with the English. The colonists eliminated most Native Americans in southern New England. Metacom was beheaded. Surviving Native Americans were sold into slavery. However, the damage from this bitter fight slowed colonial expansion in New England for the next 50 years.

The Differing Values of Europeans and Native Americans

Fundamental cultural differences between the Europeans and the Native Americans were expressed in their views and values.

- The Europeans assumed the superiority of their way of life and acted accordingly. They saw the dress, foods, religion, and shelter of the native people as evidence of a less developed or inferior culture.

- The Europeans attempted to convert Native Americans to Christianity. They wanted converts to abandon the religious practices of their culture and adopt a European lifestyle. The missionaries had no respect for the native people's religious customs. Those who would not convert were often physically abused, killed, or enslaved.

- Native Americans and Europeans differed on the proper gender roles. In many Native American societies, strong social organizations rested on ties between extended families, with women in positions of some power. In these matrilineal societies, the family line descended through the female. European families were both patrilineal and patriarchal. The family line and inheritance descended through the male who also held the power. European women were confined to housework. Native American women farmed, while the men hunted. Europeans saw farm work as a man's job and hunting as a sport.

Preparing for the Regents

Stimulus-Based Questions: Speech

- Answer Powhatan's question, "What is the cause of your jealousy?"

- Cite specific textual evidence of the impact of European colonization on Native Americans.

- Examine wars fought between Europeans and Native Americans in the 15th–18th centuries. What are the similarities and differences?

- Native Americans looked at wealth as something to share. They did not understand or agree with the importance of accumulation of goods that was driving trade and commerce in Europe. Trade was a valued part of the Native American economic system. It was centered on the practice of both giving and receiving. The French and the Dutch involved the native people as allies in the fur trade. That resulted in inter-tribal wars and European and Native American alliances fighting each other.

- Possession of the land was at the center of conflict between Native Americans and colonists, particularly the English settlers. The land had a spiritual importance to the indigenous people. They had no concept of land ownership, of selling land, or giving it up in treaties or exchanges. Earth and its resources were for all to share. Native Americans held land in common and believed it should be used for the good of all. Ancestral lands were sacred. The English valued individual ownership and property rights. Many English settlers believed land in the colonies could just be taken not bought.

The Columbian Exchange

One way to better understand the short- and long-term impact of European colonization on Native Americans is to examine the effects of the Columbian Exchange. The **Columbian Exchange** refers to the plants, crops, technology, diseases, animals, people, and culture that were transferred by Europeans from Europe, Asia, and Africa to the Americas and vice versa. These exchanges resulted in changes throughout the world. There were permanent benefits and immeasurable losses. There were predictable and unpredictable consequences. By examining the effects of the Columbian Exchange one better understands the impact of European colonization on Native Americans—why and how they lost much of their lands and their lives.

The Columbian Exchange

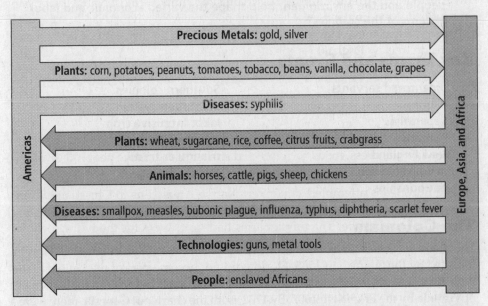

The Columbian Exchange was a transfer or intermingling among Europe, Asia, Africa, and North and South America of food and other crops, animals, metals, diseases, people, technologies, and cultures. The chart lists some examples.

Regional Factors Influence the Development of the Thirteen Colonies

Key Concept

11.1b A number of factors influenced colonial economic development, social structures, and labor systems, causing variation by region.

Lesson Overview

Beginning in the seventeenth century, one hundred years after Columbus' voyages, England founded thirteen colonies along the North American Atlantic coast. The settlers were primarily English but included other Europeans, as well as Africans brought as slaves.

A number of factors influenced the economic development, social structures, and labor systems of the English colonies that caused variation by region. Geography impacted the patterns of settlement and the diversity of economic systems among the New England, middle Atlantic, and southern colonies.

By 1700, slavery as a racial institution had replaced indentured servitude as a deeply established component of the colonial economic system and social structure. Slavery existed in all of the colonies but was concentrated in the South.

Unifying Themes

As you review this lesson take special note of the following themes:

- **Development, Movement, and Interaction of Cultures** What factors, from its earliest history, indicate that America was a nation of diverse cultures?

- **Time, Continuity, and Change** How and why, over time, did indentured servitude in the English colonies develop into slavery as a racial institution?

- **Geography, Humans, and the Environment** How did interaction between people and the environment help shape the varied economic and labor systems of the colonies?

Key Terms and Events

indentured servants	Southern colonies
Pilgrims	plantation system
Separatists	labor-intensive crop
Puritans	two-way trade
New England	triangular trade
middle colonies	Middle Passage
patroonships	

The Colonists

The oldest settlement in what is now the United States is Saint Augustine, Florida, founded by the Spanish in 1565. Florida did not become part of the United States until 1819. Instead, what was to become the United States began with the settlement of Virginia by the English in 1607. By 1732, with the charter of Georgia, there were a total of 13 British colonies spread along the Atlantic coast of North America.

Who Came to the English Colonies

From its origins, present-day United States was a multicultural and multiethnic society. Although they were primarily English, Protestant, and from northern and western Europe, the immigrants to the English colonies were a diverse group. They included Scots-Irish from northern Ireland, Germans, Portuguese, Swedes, Dutch, French, Welsh, Irish, Scots, Belgians, and Swiss. Africans arrived first as indentured servants, but most were enslaved people brought against their will from West Africa or the West Indies. In the colonial period, a large number of young, poor European immigrants came as **indentured servants** who contracted to work as many as seven years to repay the cost of their passage.

Most of each colony's population, however, was English. The first census of the population of the United States, taken in 1790, reported the ethnic makeup of the new nation as English 49%, African 19%, Scots-Irish 8%, Scottish 7%, German 7%, Dutch 4%, French 3%, other 3%.

Why They Came

Just as the European colonists represented many ethnic backgrounds, their motivations for coming to the colonies also varied. Yet they all wanted to make a better life than they could have in Europe. Some wanted religious freedom at least for themselves and the economic security made possible by the abundance of land in the colonies. Some hoped to escape the rigid class structures of Europe.

Religious Reasons Some colonies were founded for religious reasons, but the colonists practiced different religions and had different motivations. Massachusetts, for example, was founded by **Pilgrims,** or **Separatists,** who had left the Church of England, and **Puritans** who wanted to reform it. In a great migration during the 1630s more than 20,000 Puritans came to the colonies to escape persecution by Charles I. Colonies controlled by the Puritans allowed no religious freedom. Rhode Island, on the other hand, permitted all religions, including Judaism. Pennsylvania was founded as a refuge for Quakers. William Penn, the proprietor of Pennsylvania, also welcomed Huguenots (French Protestants), Mennonites, Amish, and Lutherans. Maryland began as a refuge for Roman Catholics.

Economic Reasons Economic motives were a major factor in the founding of Virginia, Delaware, and New Netherland (later New York and parts of other colonies), as well as North and South Carolina. Organized as joint-stock companies, the shareholders hoped to profit from their investment. In most cases they were disappointed. Settlers in all colonies were drawn by the availability of land and the opportunity to own it.

The Colonial Experience, 1607–1732

Preparing for the Regents

Stimulus-Based Questions: Timeline

- How many years were there between the settling of the first and the last of the 13 English colonies?

- What was the impact on the colonial experience of the political events shown on the timeline?

Colonial Settlement by Ethnic Group in 1770

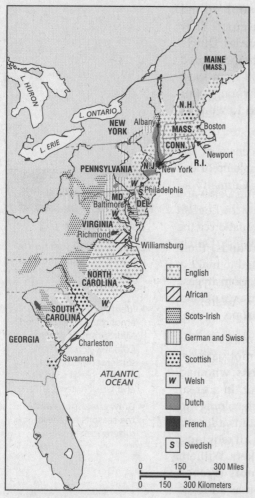

Legend:
- English
- African
- Scots-Irish
- German and Swiss
- Scottish
- W Welsh
- Dutch
- French
- S Swedish

0   150   300 Miles
0   150   300 Kilometers

Social Studies Practices

Geographic Reasoning

Examine the map above then answer the following questions.

- By 1776, two thirds of the population of the English colonies lived no more than 50 miles from the ocean. Why?

- Which ethnic groups had the largest settlements in 1770? Which had the smallest settlements?

- Which natural harbors in the thirteen colonies contributed to the development of commerce, or trade, between cities, states, and nations?

Political Reasons Political events in seventeenth-century England influenced patterns of migration. Separatists and Puritans came to North America after having fallen into political disfavor because of their objections to the established Church of England and the king who headed it. After the monarchy was restored in 1660, colonies that included New Jersey and the Carolinas were founded on land granted by the king to his loyal supporters. Quakers, Catholics, French Huguenots, and Jews came to escape governmental persecution as well as religious intolerance. Georgia was founded for the poor and for Protestants who wanted to escape intolerance. But the major motivation was to create a buffer to protect South Carolina and other Southern colonies from the Spanish, French, and their Native Americans allies to the South and West.

What Influenced Their Experiences

Geography was a primary influence on colonial settlement patterns and economic systems. So were the practices colonists brought from their homelands. Ethnic groups tended to settle together as did people of the same religion. Large distances and difficult transportation encouraged continuing family patterns, gender roles, and farming methods brought from Europe, although these were sometimes modified by the new environment. Native American and African cultures also influenced changes in colonial lifestyles.

Geography Affects Colonial Social and Economic Structures

The geography and natural resources along the Atlantic coast influenced the development of regional differences among the English colonies.

The New England Colonies

New England earned its name as it is the location of some of the earliest colonies, Massachusetts, Rhode Island, and Connecticut, and later New Hampshire, Vermont, and Maine. The cold climate, short growing season, hills and mountains, and poor rocky soil of New England challenged Puritan farmers, who grew crops mostly for their own families' consumption. They were only successful at commercial farming when they reached the Connecticut River Valley with its richer soil.

Although farming remained the most common occupation, New England turned to its forests, harbors, rivers, and ocean to develop a diversified economy. It became the center of colonial shipping, with major ports at Boston and Salem. Commercial fishing and shipbuilding were among the related industries. Merchants and professionals made up the wealthiest social class. The middle class included lawyers, doctors, ministers, and skilled craftsmen.

Puritans migrated largely as family units and the population grew rapidly in cool, healthy New England. Family farms were clustered around towns that were clearly and deliberately kept separate from the Native Americans villages. The farm family worked as a unit to live off and improve the land. Without a commercial crop these small farms did not need a large labor supply. In the North, enslaved workers worked mostly in cities. They were servants in the homes of the wealthy, seaman, dockworkers, laborers, carpenters, and other craftsmen.

In the early colonial period, every aspect of New England life was influenced by religion. Church membership was a requirement for participation in government. Strict moral codes were enforced. To question the religion was to question the government. The penalty included banishment from the colony. Roger Williams founded Rhode Island after he was banished from the Massachusetts Bay Colony.

Education was considered essential. In 1636, the Massachusetts Bay Colony founded Harvard College to train ministers. It was believed that a child must be taught to read the Bible as well as the laws of the colony. Parents were thus required to teach their children to read and write. A 1647 law called for towns to establish and maintain schools, although many towns found it cheaper to pay the penalty than to obey the law.

The Middle Colonies

The **middle colonies** included New York, New Jersey, Pennsylvania, and Delaware. Parts of these colonies were originally New Netherland until taken by the English from the Dutch in 1664. The middle colonies had the most varied population of the English colonies. Immigrants, in addition to being English included, Welsh, Dutch, Swedes, Finns, Danes, Germans, and Scots-Irish.

The middle colonies shared part of the fertile coastal plain with the South. Three long and wide rivers with protected harbors, the Susquehanna, the Delaware, and the Hudson, aided in trading furs and shipping grains to overseas markets. The economy was based on corn and wheat exports. This trade helped build New York City and Philadelphia. Iron ore, lumber, some textiles, and furs were also exported. Shipbuilding was an important industry.

The middle colonies were the most socially and religiously tolerant of the three colonial regions, in large part due to the diversity of the population and the influence of the Dutch guarantee of freedom of conscience in their private beliefs. The Quaker culture in Pennsylvania also encouraged an accepting climate that attracted immigrants. There was no tax-supported religion. All religions were permitted to worship. Although small farmers predominated, and a middle class prospered, a wealthy landowner class continued to control huge tracts of lands along the Delaware and the Hudson rivers. Called **patroonships** by the Dutch and estates by the English, these parcels were not broken up until the revolutionary war and later. Large numbers of tenant farmers—who rented rather than owned the land—lived in the Hudson River Valley of New York and in New Jersey and continued to pay rent into the 19th century.

The Southern Colonies

Virginia and Maryland are called the Chesapeake colonies because of their location on Chesapeake Bay. Jamestown, Virginia, was the first permanent English colony of the thirteen. The three other **Southern colonies** were North Carolina, South Carolina, and Georgia. In the Southern colonies, a warmer climate, rich soil, a coastal plain, multiple tidal rivers, wetlands, and a long growing season led to the development of the **plantation system.** This agricultural, single-crop economy was initially based on tobacco and then also on rice, indigo, and cotton crops.

Colonies charted as corporate colonies sought a crop that would be a commercial success. In about 1616, Virginia found that successful crop in tobacco. Tobacco is a **labor-intensive crop.** It requires constant care at all stages from preparing the fields to preparing the product for market. Many workers were needed and needed over a long period of time. Virginia tobacco farming marked the beginning of a Southern single-crop plantation economy dependent on **slavery as a racial institution.** Large tracts of land were cultivated first by indentured servants and then by enslaved Africans and African Americans.

Preparing for the Regents

Using Evidence

Examine the information in the text, including the map as well as the chart (on the next page).

• Identify the differences among the New England, Middle, and Southern Colonies in pattern of settlement, economic systems, social systems, and labor systems.

• Draw conclusions as to the reasons for these differences.

The tobacco planters became the wealthiest social and governing class in the Chesapeake colonies. This pattern repeated itself in the Carolinas and Georgia where the rice, indigo, and cotton planter class dominated the social and political structure. The planters eventually owned most of the fertile tidewater lands as well as the wetlands in which rice was grown. Smaller farms settled by Scots-Irish and Germans were located farther up the rivers in the backcountry of Virginia, the Carolinas, and Georgia. The plantation system contributed to the rural and more isolated nature of the social life in the South. As slavery became more established in the region, the social, economic, and political structure became more rigid with a larger gap between the upper and lower classes. And the central role of plantation agriculture led to a growing dependence on slavery to support the economic, social, and political systems of the Southern colonies.

Comparing the Thirteen Colonies 1607–1760

	New England Colonies MA, RI, CT, NH	Middle Colonies NY, NJ, PA, DE	Southern Colonies VA, MD, NC, SC, GA
Geography	cold winters, rocky soil, short growing season, mountains, forests, rivers, natural harbors	less severe winters, fertile soil, rivers, natural harbors	mild climate, long growing season, fertile lowlands, tidal rivers, wide coastal plain
Early Colonists	English Pilgrims, mostly English Puritans, Africans	Dutch, English, Welsh, Germans, Scots-Irish, Irish, Swedes, French, Africans	English, enslaved Africans
Economy 17th to Mid-18th Centuries	diverse economy included small-scale farming, fishing, fur trade, shipbuilding, lumbering, trade and commerce, crafts, and industry. Major City: Boston, MA	economy included medium-scale farming for cash crops of wheat, corn, and flax, as well as fur trade, commerce, crafts, and industry. Major Cities: New York, NY; Philadelphia, PA	highly agricultural economy included large plantations, which used indentured servants or enslaved persons to produce cash crops of tobacco, rice, and indigo. Major City: Charleston, SC
Lifestyle	high literacy level, Protestant work ethic, town meetings; Colonial colleges: Harvard (the oldest), Yale, College of RI (Brown), Dartmouth	most regional diversity in religion and nationalities; Colonial colleges: College of NJ (Princeton), College of Philadelphia (Univ PA), King's (Columbia), Queen's (Rutgers)	self-sufficient plantation life, few cities, least populated and developed region, small farmers largest social group; Colonial college: William and Mary
Colonial Political Developments	1620: Mayflower Compact (MA) 1639: Fundamental Orders of CT	1649: Right of Petition in New Netherland 1683: NY Chapter of Liberties	1619: House of Burgesses (VA) 1649: MD Act of Toleration

Slavery in the Colonies

By 1700, the institution of slavery—primarily involving Africans—already served to highlight the regional differences in the colonies.

Origins of the Atlantic Slave Trade

As you have read, the first enslaved people in the Americas were Native Americans. In the 1500s, the Spanish and Portuguese forced them to work in mines and on sugar plantations. After the Native American population declined as a result of European diseases, the Spanish, Portuguese, and French began enslaving West Africans. With the growth of tobacco, indigo, and rice plantations, the British colonies also started to participate in the slave trade. By the 1730s and 1740s, England controlled the Atlantic slave trade. It was embedded in the British economy from 1640 until 1807.

Under mercantilism there was a **two-way trade** between England and the colonies for goods such as grains, fish, fur, wood products, tobacco, indigo, and rice, which the colonies exchanged for English manufactured goods. The slave trade, however, was a **triangular trade.** New England merchants traded rum for enslaved people in West Africa. The enslaved people were sold in the West Indies for molasses or sugar, which was shipped to New England to make more rum. Boston was a major port in the triangular trade as were New York and Philadelphia. Between 1709 and 1807, about 100,000 enslaved Africans were transported to the Americas on ships based in Newport and Bristol, Rhode Island.

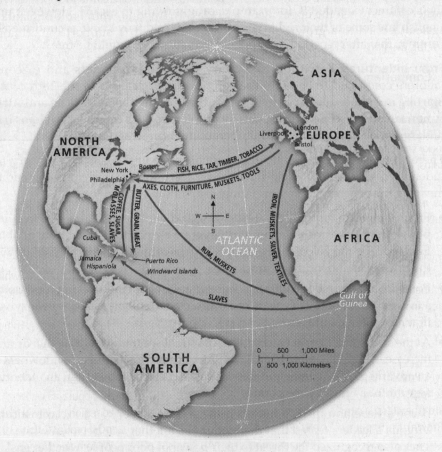

Social Studies Practices

Geographic Reasoning

Use the routes illustrated on the globe to:

• Identify a trade pattern that is an example of mercantilism.

• Identify an example of the triangular trade.

Development of Slavery in the Colonies

The first African enslaved people in English North America were brought to Virginia in 1619. At the time, most African arrivals were considered indentured servants. They often worked with indentured white servants. Neither group was paid for their work and both groups were considered free when their contracts ended. But, in the course of the 17th century in the English colonies (1607–1700) profound changes in practice and in law developed slavery into a racial institution.

The Rise in Indentured Servitude After 1616 when tobacco profits began to boom, Jamestown needed cheap labor. The number of Native Americans was depleted by European diseases and escape from enforced labor proved easy in land that they knew so well. The Virginia Company introduced the system of **indentured servitude** in the English colonies. The Company offered poor, young, white, primarily men a contract to provide passage, food, clothing, and shelter and some type of "freedom dues" in return for four to seven years of work without pay. "Freedom dues" typically included basic supplies such as corn, a gun, tools, and perhaps money.

In the early 1600s, England suffered from overpopulation and economic depression. This encouraged poor and sometimes homeless farmers without land, unemployed craftsmen, and laborers as well as ex-convicts to agree to the terms of indenture. An indentured servant was gambling that he or she would survive the high mortality rate caused by the ocean voyage, the hard fieldwork, hot and humid climate, and brutal treatment by the contract holder, and live to receive freedom dues and resume life as a free person. Most of those who served out their contracts joined the colony's economic and social system as members of the working class. Indentured servants could have their contract bought and sold, be punished physically, have their contract extended if, for example, caught trying to escape. However, under English law some of their rights were protected. And they knew, as confirmed by a contract, that after a period of four to seven years they would be free.

From Indentured Servitude to Slavery Indentured servants and ex-convict laborers continued to come to the colonies through most of the 18th century. Starting in the last quarter of the 17th century, the number of African and African American enslaved people, especially in colonies with economic systems based on large-scale plantations, outnumbered indentured servants.

There were several reasons for the gradual move in the late 17th century from indentured servant to lifelong slavery to slavery for you and your descendants, meaning the generations of your family that follow you.

- From the 1650s through the 1680s, England experienced a sharp drop in its population. As a result, more employment opportunities were available in England. For the colonies, the supply of indentured servants decreased while the price of an indenture contract rose.

- Potential indentured servants had learned more about the working conditions on a tobacco plantation. They were more attracted to colonies such as Pennsylvania that now offered land and other work opportunities.

- At the same time Britain entered the Atlantic slave trade resulting in a dramatic increase in the availability of enslaved Africans at a lower price. Landowners saw an advantage in obtaining permanent enslaved labor rather than an indentured servant for a limited time period.

- Bacon's Rebellion in 1676 hastened the shift to slavery as a racial institution. Virginia's leaders feared that there might be another war between white elites. They also recognized the threat to their power of poor people, whether enslaved persons or indentured servants, again uniting against the ruling class.

The Development of Slavery as a Racial Institution

By 1705, a **race-based definition of a slave** that included restrictions and punishments, was written into law in Virginia. It became a model for other colonies. A system of permanent slavery was in place. It was a legal system that both discriminated against and exploited the Africans and African Americans. Slavery became central to the economic system of the South. It influenced not only the economy but also the social and political systems, affecting southerners of both races.

Virginia was the first colony to develop and codify laws to restrict the rights and freedom of Africans and African Americans by institutionalizing slavery. Through a series of laws passed between 1640 and 1705, the General Assembly of Virginia

- removed rights from Africans and African Americans while placing limits and restrictions on their freedom to move about and to gather together with others.

Preparing for the Regents

Analyzing Documents

Their Servants, they distinguish by the Names of Slaves for Life, and Servants for a time. Slaves are the Negroes, and their Posterity [children], following the condition of the Mother. . . . They are call'd Slaves, in Respect of the Time of their Servitude, because it is for Life. Servants are those which serve only for a few Years, according to the time of their Indenture or the Custom of the Country.

—Robert Beverley, *The History and Present State of Virginia*, 1705

- To the writer, what is the basis of the difference between "slaves" and "servants"?

- created two different and unequal legal systems for treating whites and Africans and African Americans. Defining those of African descent as property was codified into law as was the right to use physical force against them.
- worded laws to legally connect race with enslavement.
- made slavery not only for life but also hereditary.

Examples of 18th Century Virginia Laws on Slavery	
1639/40 All people except Africans and African Americans must be armed.	**1661** A child's status is dependent on the mother not the father as in English common law. An enslaved woman's child is also a slave. This hereditary system removed any legal responsibilities from the father. Slavery was for life, passed down from generation to generation.
1667 Becoming a Christian as a means to claim freedom was outlawed.	**1680** To prevent insurrections by slaves, written permission was required to leave a plantation, while visiting time on another plantation is limited to four hours. It was unlawful to carry any type of weapon or to gather in large numbers.
1691 Marriage between a white man or woman and an African American was prohibited.	**1705** The Virginia Slave Code codified, or organized, the slave laws. All slaves were "to be held as real estate." They were property that could be bought and sold or willed or used in payment.

Examples of Slavery in the Colonies

Massachusetts in 1641 was the first colony to allow slavery. Slavery existed in every colony. However, the diverse economy, cooler climate, and smaller farms in the middle and northern colonies meant slavery there was less common. At the end of the colonial period on the eve of the American Revolution, there were 50,000 enslaved people in the North compared with 400,000 in the South. While most enslaved people in the North, like those in the South, worked in agriculture, enslaved people in northern cities were often skilled.

The legalization of slavery in Virginia coincided with an increased market for tobacco and a decrease in the availability of indentured servants. In Virginia the makeup of the population shifted. One source indicates that in just thirty years—from 1680 to 1710—the African population of the colony jumped from 7 to 28 percent with half of the colony being enslaved people.

Slavery in South Carolina was based on that of the Caribbean rice and sugar cane plantation system. Many of these settlers came from English colonies in the West Indies, bringing with them their slaves and their slave code. South Carolina's slave code, based on that of Barbados, was the strictest in the colonies. Africans were brought to South Carolina to work on huge rice plantations.

When founded in 1732–1733, Georgia banned slavery. Land parcels were limited to 500 acres. Under pressure from settlers, many from South Carolina, Georgia legalized slavery in 1751. Georgia's economy was anchored in a plantation system based on rice, indigo, and later cotton dependent on slave labor.

Beginning in the 1800s, the lower Mississippi Valley contained the largest number of plantations, with 100 or more enslaved people. Cotton profits related directly to the amount of land cultivated, encouraging the slave system to increase in numbers and to expand in territory.

Social Studies Practices
Interpreting Evidence

But is not the slave trade entirely a war with the heart of man? And surely that which is begun, by breaking down the barriers of virtue, involves in its continuance destruction to every principle, and buries all sentiments in ruin!

—Olaudah Equiano, *The Interesting Narrative of the Life of Olaudah Equiano,* 1794

The writer was an enslaved person who bought his freedom.

- Is there evidence that the writer's opinion has validity?
- What does the first sentence mean? What is the "war"?
- What does the second sentence tell us about the writer's view of slavery?

Organizing Information

Many enslaved Africans found both peaceful and violent ways to resist their enslavement.

What are two peaceful ways that slaves resisted?

1.

2.

What are two violent ways that they resisted?

1.

2.

What are two 19th century examples of these patterns of resistance?

1.

2.

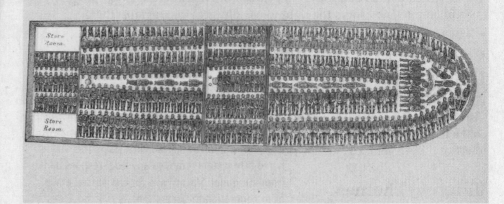

A drawing of a typical slave ship showing the cramped conditions endured by enslaved Africans

Slave Resistance

From the beginning of the West African slave trade in the 1400s those captured fought back. For that reason, the Portuguese followed a system used by African and Arab Muslim traders of separating captives from others of their family or tribe. Throughout the period in which slavery was legal, Africans and African Americans continued to resist their enslavement. On the slave ships during the voyage from Africa to America, called the **Middle Passage,** some staged revolts. Others chose starvation or drowning rather than enslavement.

Once in the Americas or the Caribbean, even in the face of severe punishment, some enslaved Africans attempted escape. Small communities of escaped enslaved people formed in Spanish Florida, South Carolina, Georgia, and Virginia. Other enslaved people offered more subtle resistance, such as slowing down at work, pretending illness, or damaging tools and crops.

In colonial America, open rebellion was not very common. Two notable colonial revolts took place in New York City in 1712 and at the Stono River near Charleston, South Carolina, in 1739. Both rebellions were put down by local militia. Most of the enslaved people who survived were later executed.

The Influence of African Culture

The Africans forcibly brought to the colonies in the 17th and 18th centuries were from West Africa. However, they came from many different cultures with a variety of traditions, religious practices, and languages. With succeeding generations, slaves lost some of their ethnic identity but many elements of their West African traditions became the basis of African American culture. Particularly important was maintenance of an extended family network that provided some stability in their lives. Some African words found their way into the English language, as did certain farming methods, foods, folk literature, and folk art. African building traditions of multiple small dwellings, front porches, and decorative ironwork influenced southern colonial architecture. Some African musical styles and instruments, such as the banjo, continued to be incorporated into religious music and work songs. African musical traditions later influenced many forms of American music.

Colonial Political Institutions and Democratic Principles

Lesson Overview

Between 1607 and 1763, the English colonies created self-governing political institutions and political documents that supported democratic principles. The colonial governments were influenced by British political traditions, Enlightenment ideas, and the colonial experience.

Unifying Themes

As you review this lesson take special note of the following themes:

- **Time, Continuity, and Change** In what ways did the colonial governments reflect, modify, and further develop British political traditions, law, and Enlightenment ideas?

- **Power, Authority, and Governance** In what ways did the principles and values of constitutional democracy influence colonial governments? What individual liberties were most valued and protected in British tradition and colonial practices? What rights were more limited than they are in the United States today?

Key People

John Locke

Baron de Montesquieu

Jean-Jacques Rousseau

Voltaire

William Penn

John Peter Zenger

Key Terms and Events

democracy

direct democracy

republican government

representative
  democracy

common law

Magna Carta

constitutional principles

Petition of Right

writ of *habeas corpus*

English Bill of Rights

representative
  government

rule of law

Enlightenment

natural rights

social contract

separation of powers

charter

joint-stock company

proprietary colony

royal colony

representative
  legislature

suffrage

seditious libel

Mayflower Compact

majority rule

Fundamental Orders of
  Connecticut

Maryland Toleration Act
  of 1649

Virginia House of
  Burgesses

town meeting

right of petition

Key Concept

11.1c Colonial political developments were influenced by British political traditions, Enlightenment ideas, and the colonial experience. Self-governing structures were common, and yet varied across the colonies.

Unifying Themes
Power, Authority, and Governance

American political rights and governmental institutions had three major sources:

1. British constitutional, political, and historical traditions
2. Seventeenth- and eighteenth-century Enlightenment ideas
3. American colonial experience

What is an example of how each source influenced the political rights and governmental institutions in the United States?

Analyzing Documents

No free man shall be seized or imprisoned, or stripped of his rights or possessions, or outlawed or exiled, or deprived of his standing in any way, nor will we proceed with force against him, or send others to do so, except by the lawful judgment of his equals or by the law of the land.

—Magna Carta, Clause 39, 1215

- What fundamental protection is stated in Clause 39 of the Magna Carta?
- Identify examples of this principle in a colonial document and in the U.S. Constitution.

Major Historical Influences on Colonial Political Development

The colonial period in American history extended from the first settlers landing at Jamestown in 1607 to the decision for independence in 1776. Just as the American colonial economy and society grew and changed during this time period so did the colonial governments. The governments of each of the 13 colonies reflected ideas that came from the heritage of Western civilization. Those ideas were then modified by centuries of English thought and practice and by the lengthy colonial experience in a growing, changing environment thousands of miles from Britain.

Ideas from Ancient Greece and Rome

The concept of **democracy,** or government by the people, began in the city-state of Athens (in what is now Greece) between 750 B.C. and 550 B.C. Athens had a **direct democracy,** one in which all eligible citizens participated in government.

The concept of **republican government** was established by the ancient Romans. In a republic, voters elect representatives who speak and act for other citizens in the business of government. These representatives are supposed to work for the common good. This form of government is sometimes called **representative democracy.** In the United States today representative democracy is practiced at the local, state, and national levels.

The Influence of English Documents and Political Traditions

Several basic principles of government and the **common law** were established in England during the middle ages. The common law system developed in England from customs and traditions based on precedents, meaning previous court decisions. Because England applied its common law system in places it colonized, the common law is the basis of the legal system of most of the United States. Louisiana, colonized first by the French, is one exception.

Magna Carta In 1215, English noblemen forced King John of England to agree to the **Magna Carta,** or Great Charter, a document that placed limits on his power to rule. King John did not honor the Magna Carta. But for 800 years the Great Charter has been the foundational document for individual liberties. It became part of the common law that the King must follow the rule of law and that justice could not be denied nor delayed nor require a bribe. Eventually reinterpretation over the centuries led to a guarantee of trial by jury of one's peers, or equals.

During the political turmoil of the 1600s several other major **constitutional principles** were agreed to by the English monarchy. The Magna Carta expressed the fundamental principle of limits on a government—government under the rule of law rather than rule by arbitrary, absolute power—that shaped future democracies including that of the United States.

Petition of Right In 1628, Parliament enacted and King Charles I signed the **Petition of Right.** It put in writing certain basic rights and legal traditions first expressed in the Magna Carta such as guarantee of a writ of *habeas corpus.* In Latin, *habeas corpus* means "You shall have the body." A **writ of *habeas corpus*** is a court order requiring that a person be brought before a court and the court shown evidence why the person should be held for trial. It prevents arrest and imprisonment without a trial. It is referenced in Article I Section 9 of the United States Constitution. The Petition also required that Parliament consent to taxation. This right evolved from Clause 12 of the Magna Carta. Taxation and the meaning of representation became a critical issue in the debates that led to the American Revolution.

The English Bill of Rights In 1689, the Glorious Revolution ended a decades-long power struggle between the English Parliament and the monarchy. Parliament overthrew James II and replaced him with William and Mary, who were required to agree to the **English Bill of Rights.** This document established in law the principles that **representative government** and the **rule of law** outweighed the authority of any monarch. In England power had shifted from the monarchy to Parliament—from absolute to constitutional monarchy.

Foundations of American Rights

Rights	Sources of Rights			
	Magna Carta (1215)	English Bill of Rights (1689)	Virginia Declaration of Rights (1776)	Bill of Rights (1791)
Trial by jury	✔	✔		✔
Due process	✔	✔		✔
Private property	✔			✔
No unreasonable searches or seizures			✔	✔
No cruel punishment		✔	✔	✔
No excessive bail or fines		✔		✔
Right to bear arms		✔		✔
Right to petition		✔		✔
Freedom of speech			✔	✔
Freedom of the press			✔	✔
Freedom of religion			✔	✔

Preparing for the Regents

Stimulus-Based Questions: Table

Review the table above, then answer the following questions.

- Which two rights guaranteed in the U.S. Constitution can be traced directly to the English Bill of Rights?

- Why is the writ of *habeas corpus* called the "Great Writ of Liberty"?

The Influence of Enlightenment Thought on Colonial Government

The **Enlightenment** was a European intellectual movement that held that reliance on reason, knowledge, and experience would lead to social progress. From the mid-1600s to the end of the 18th century, the Age of Reason applied Enlightenment thinking to politics, science, religion, culture, and philosophy. Enlightenment problem solving, experimentation, questioning, and logic laid a groundwork for a modern age of more individualism, greater liberties, new ideas, and necessary reforms.

People in colonial America were influenced by Enlightenment thinking, especially in the fields of religion and politics. Benjamin Franklin and Thomas Jefferson were two of our nation's founders whose Enlightenment ideas are seen in the Declaration of Independence and the Constitution.

Locke, Montesquieu, Rousseau, and Voltaire are four of the philosophers of the Enlightenment. Some of their ideas about politics and government are reflected in the beliefs, actions, institutions, and documents of the thirteen colonies and the new nation.

John Locke (1632–1704) Englishman **John Locke** was a professor at Oxford University. He defended natural rights, majority rule, property rights, the separation of the executive and legislature, and the right to revolution. He wrote *Two Treatises on Government* in 1690 to justify the Glorious Revolution. Locke's ideas in the *Treatises*, such as his **contract theory of government**, influenced

Men being, . . . by Nature, all free, equal, and independent, no one can be. . . subjected to the Political Power of another, without his own Consent. . . . For when any number of Men have, by the consent of every individual, made a Community, they have thereby made that community one Body, with a Power to Act as one Body, which is only by the will and determination of the majority.

—John Locke, *Two Treatises on Government,* 1690

• Compare Locke's statement to the Mayflower Compact and to the Declaration of Independence.

• The democratic principle of the consent of the governed is expressed in all three documents. Does it have the same meaning in each document?

the Declaration of Independence, state constitutions, and the United States Constitution.

• Locke believed that people were born free with certain **natural rights,** including the rights to life, liberty, and property.

• Such rights predate any government and exist in the "state of nature."

• Locke stated that when people agree to form a state and grant to its government the powers necessary to protect their natural rights, a **social contract** is formed between the people and their government. Therefore, governments exist only with the consent of the governed.

• When a government fails to protect these rights, the contract has been broken and the people are free to change or even to replace or overthrow that government.

Baron de Montesquieu (1689–1755) Charles-Louis de Secondat, baron de La Brède et de Montesquieu, was a French philosopher known as the **Baron de Montesquieu.** He believed that the British political system was successful because the power to govern was divided among the monarch and the two houses of Parliament. This division helped balance political power among the branches in order to protect individual liberties. Colonial governments as well as the United States Constitution adopted this principle of **separation of powers.**

Jean-Jacques Rousseau (1712–1778) Another French philosopher, Swiss-born **Jean-Jacques Rousseau,** developed further the idea of a social contract. His arguments in support of government by the consent of the governed influenced the Declaration of Independence.

Voltaire (1694–1778) A third important French philosopher, **Voltaire,** wrote *Philosophical Letters,* praising British institutions and rights. He wrote also against religious intolerance and persecution.

The Influence of the Colonial Experience on Government

During the colonial period, three important forces helped shape a uniquely American way of life:

• Political ideas based on the English political experience and traditions

• Political ideas based on Enlightenment thinking

• The colonists' experience living thousands of miles from their home country

The English colonists were a people united by a common law, common language, and a common history. They were proud of England at a time when it was becoming a global naval and commercial power and building a worldwide empire. Even in the 1600s, when political and religious conflicts at home pushed many people to emigrate, the English colonists at all levels of society came to America with what they felt were their rights as English people. The beliefs that colonists held about the proper role of government shaped the way they structured their governments.

Shared political principles included:

• Individual rights

• Rule of law

• Self-government

• Limited government

- Right to vote
- Participation in government
- Separation of powers

Differences in the ethnicity, race, politics, geography, economy, wealth, and culture of the colonies affected the way in which their colonial governments developed. These factors also affected the way in which and the degree to which the colonists understood these political principles. The physical separation of the colonies from England and the real possibility of social mobility due to the availability of land also shaped the thinking and behaviors of the settlers.

Colonial Charters and Self-Government

During the colonial period self-governing institutions were common, yet they varied across the colonies. Twelve of the thirteen original colonies were founded based on charters issued by the British government. A **charter** provided legal authority to companies or individuals to start a colony. Virginia is an example of a colony founded by a company. **Joint-stock companies** such as the Virginia Company financed and managed a colony. Few made a profit for their stockholders. The Plymouth colony and the Massachusetts Bay Colony were also corporate colonies. Their Pilgrim and Puritan founders financed their colonies themselves.

Maryland held the first charter issued to a **proprietary colony,** one that is owned, managed, and governed by an individual. Pennsylvania was also a proprietary colony. It offered religious freedom to Quakers and others but **William Penn,** the colony's proprietor, also hoped to profit from trade. He died virtually penniless.

Most of the colonies were originally self-governing private enterprises, but by the 1770s eight had become **royal colonies,** directly under the control of the king. Even after England centralized control, the colonies remained largely self-governing and independent. A **representative legislature** was considered an important factor to attract colonists to a colony. Most colonial legislatures were bicameral, meaning made up of two houses. In some colonies, the second legislative body was the Governor's Council. The Council was more often appointed than elected.

Separation of Powers A system of separation of powers developed in the colonies. Colonial charters divided government into three branches—the legislative, the executive, and the judicial. However, since colonial governors were usually appointed by the king and the judges by the governors, it was primarily through the colonial legislatures, who were elected by the people, that the colonists received their training in self-government. Many of the debates centered on taxation, a major power of the legislatures.

Limits on Government The colonists believed that the power of government should be limited, in accordance with English laws and traditions. The colonists wrote laws based on the principle that government existed to protect people's natural rights. The rights to life, liberty, and protection of property were most often mentioned. As early as 1641 in Massachusetts, the right to own property and protect it from being illegally seized by the government was written into law. **Suffrage,** or the right to vote, helped to protect property rights.

Voting Rights and Participation in Government In the 17th century, Massachusetts Bay Colony required membership in the church in order to vote. At that time only a relatively small percentage of Puritans were allowed to become church members. Voting requirements at the local town meetings were broader. Voting rights were extended to white male property holders as was usual at all levels of government in most of the 13 colonies. Because there were more opportunities to own property in the colonies, proportionately many more could vote than in England in the same time period. A smaller number was eligible to hold office because property and religious qualifications were stricter.

Freedom of the Press In 17th- and 18th-century England and its colonies, freedom of expression in speech and in writing was not yet an established principle in English common law except for members of Parliament. **Seditious libel** was a crime. It was illegal to criticize the government in print or in speech. Colonists believed that there should be legal limits on government attempts to control what is written. In 1735, **John Peter Zenger,** a German immigrant to New York, was tried for seditious libel for accusing the governor of the colony of wrongdoing. Zenger's lawyer argued that no crime was committed when what Zenger had printed was true. The jury found Zenger not guilty even though the law stated that the truth was not a defense for seditious libel. The Zenger case helped establish the principle of freedom of the press in the United States.

Colonial Documents, Institutions, and Democratic Principles

Some of the democratic principles that are at the heart of American democracy were reflected in early colonial governmental documents.

Mayflower Compact The Separatists, or Pilgrims, who sailed to North America in 1620 came with a contract from the Virginia Company to settle at the mouth of the Hudson River. They anchored instead at present-day Cape Cod. Finding themselves well outside of the area of existing English authority and facing unrest from the non-Separatists aboard, the Pilgrims wrote and signed the **Mayflower Compact.**

- It was a contract in which the colonists consented to be governed by a government that they created.
- They stated their loyalty to the king.
- It was the first plan for self-government and **majority rule** in the colonies.
- The colonists would make their own laws and elect their own leaders.
- Only adult males signed the document.
- The Compact was based on the model for church self-government that the Pilgrims used in England and Holland.

Social Studies Practices

Interpreting Evidence

From the context of the paragraph about the Zenger case:

- What is meant by seditious libel?

- In 1735, the English libel law held that the "The greater the truth, the greater the libel." Evaluate the two sides of the arguments in the Zenger trial.

Jean Leon Gerome's 19th century painting of the signing of the Mayflower Compact

"We whose names are underwritten . . . covenant and combine ourselves together into a civil body politic, for our better ordering and preservation and furtherance of the ends aforesaid; and by virtue hereof to enact, constitute, and frame such just and equal laws, ordinances, acts, constitutions, and offices from time to time, as shall be thought most meet and convenient for the general good of the colony, unto which we promise all due submission and obedience."

—Mayflower Compact, 1620

Social Studies Practices
Interpreting Evidence

- What words indicate that this is a contract or a compact?
- What textual evidence is there that the intent is to establish a limited government?

Fundamental Orders of Connecticut Another example of a colonial compact or basis of self-government is the **Fundamental Orders of Connecticut,** which was adopted in 1639. It was an early model of a constitution. Voting was not limited to members of the Puritan church as, for example, in the Massachusetts Bay Colony.

Maryland Toleration Act Maryland was founded in 1633 by the Calvert family as a refuge for Catholics. By 1649, however, the majority of the Maryland population was Protestant. Although Lord Baltimore, as the proprietor, had the right to make laws for the colony, he had permitted the creation of a legislature in order to recruit settlers. That assembly approved the **Maryland Toleration Act.** It protected all men and women who belonged to those Christian religions that believed in the doctrine of the trinity. The Toleration Act was a first step toward freedom of religion. Although it failed to protect all religions or all Christians, Maryland offered greater religious tolerance than many other colonies.

But after the Glorious Revolution established a Protestant line of monarchs, the Calvert family was removed from power, and for a time Maryland became a royal colony. In 1702, the Protestant Church of England was made the official established church, financially supported by all members of the colony. Catholics could no longer hold office and, while still allowed to settle in Maryland, in 1718 they lost the right to vote. The Maryland Toleration Act is an example of the complicated and slow way in which a democratic principle becomes a legally protected practice.

Examples of Self-Government: Colonial Assemblies and Local Governments

Participation in government by representatives of the people is seen in the colonial assemblies established in each colony. As early as 1619, Virginia colonists took the first step toward republican government when they instituted the colonies' first representative lawmaking body, the **House of Burgesses.**

Colonists also recognized the need for local governments. The county was the center of local government in most of the colonies. The difficulties and expense of travel to the colonial capitol also increased interest and involvement in local government. In New England, local government was at the town level, where the New England **town meeting** allowed all male property holders to govern themselves through direct democracy. The small size of the New England towns and villages made possible public discussion and voting by majority rule.

The **right of petition** was practiced in New Netherland. Self-government there was limited compared to the colonies founded by the English. In 1647, Governor Peter Stuyvesant allowed the election of a board to advise him. In 1649, the Nine Men advisory board sent documents called the Petition and Remonstrance directly to the government in the Netherlands. The papers spelled out conditions in the colony and proposed solutions. Finally, in 1652, New Netherland was granted a more representative government.

Base your answers to questions 1 through 3 on the passage below and on your knowledge of social studies.

> THIS Indenture Witnesseth, that John Reid of freedhold in the County of Monnmouth Jersey by and with the Consent of his father John Riad of Said place hath put himself, and by these Presents doth voluntarily, and of his own free Will and Accord put himself an Apprentice to Robert Livingston Junior of New York with him to live, and (after the Manner of an Apprentice) to Serve from the first Day of November: *Anno Domini*, One Thousand Seven Hundred and Forty two till the full Term of five years be complete and ended. During all which Term the said Apprentice his said Master faithfully shall serve, his Secrets keep, his lawful Commands gladly every where obey.

Source: John Reid, contract, 1742

1 This contract is an example of

(1) mercantilism

(2) indentured servitude

(3) early colonial democracy

(4) salutary neglect

2 What is the primary motivation for the labor system described in this document?

(1) a desire for a cheap and renewable labor source

(2) the establishment of the mercantile system by Parliament

(3) a reduction in the availability of Chinese labor

(4) the onset of the American Revolution

3 The labor system described in this document was eventually replaced with

(1) convict labor

(2) mercenaries from Germany

(3) members of the planter class

(4) enslaved people from Africa

Base your answers to questions 4 and 5 on the passage below and on your knowledge of social studies.

> Be it Therefore . . . enacted . . . that no person or persons whatsoever within this Province, or the Islands, Ports, Harbors, Creeks, or havens thereunto belonging professing to believe in Jesus Christ, shall from henceforth be anyways troubled, Molested or discountenanced for or in respect of his or her religion nor in the free exercise thereof within this Province or the Islands thereunto belonging nor any way compelled to the belief or exercise of any other Religion against his or her consent. . . .

Source: Maryland Toleration Act of 1649

4 What key American democratic right is promoted by this document?

(1) People are endowed with natural rights that cannot be taken away.

(2) People should be guaranteed the right of freedom of religion.

(3) People have the right to life, liberty, and the pursuit of happiness.

(4) People give authority to a government through popular sovereignty.

5 Why would this Act encourage immigrants to settle in the Maryland colony?

(1) Some immigrants came to the colonies to avoid paying taxes in their homeland.

(2) Some immigrants came to the colonies to be able to own their own land.

(3) Some immigrants came to the colonies to find economic security.

(4) Some immigrants came to the colonies to escape religious persecution.

Base your answers to questions 6 through 8 on the two passages below and on your knowledge of social studies.

The whole number of people belonging to the Nottoway town, if you include women and children, amount to about two hundred. These are the only Indians of any consequence now remaining within the limits of Virginia. The rest are either removed, or dwindled to a very inconsiderable number, either by destroying one another, or else by the small-pox and other diseases. . . . And here I must lament the bad success Mr. Boyle's charity has hitherto had towards converting any of these poor heathens to Christianity. Many children of our neighbouring Indians have been brought up in the college of William and Mary. They have been taught to read and write, and have been carefully instructed in the principles of the Christian religion, till they came to be men. Yet after they returned home, instead of civilizing and converting the rest, they have immediately relapsed into infidelity [paganism] and barbarism themselves.

Source: William Byrd, *The History of the Dividing Line Run in the Year of Our Lord 1728*, written in 1728, published in 1841

We were told that two ministers and an Indian had been lately here—probably it was the Presbyterian [David] Brainerd, and his interpreter Tatami. He had assembled the Delawares in Shikellmy's house, and (as Shikellmy's people told us) informed them that on Sundays they should assemble as the whites do, and pray as they do. Hence he would build a house for that purpose, and stay with them two years. . . . To this Shikellmy said: "We are Indians, and don't wish to be transformed into white men. The English are our Brethren [brothers], but we never promised to become what they are. As little as we desire the preacher to become Indian, so little ought he to desire the Indians to become preachers. He should not build a house here; they don't want one."

Source: Oneida leader Shickellamy, as recounted by a missionary, 1745

6   These documents are similar in that they both

   (1) provide proof of the success of Native American assimilation

   (2) offer sentiments on converting Native Americans to Christianity

   (3) refer to the dwindling Native American populations

   (4) advocate for peace between settlers and Native Americans

7   Shickellamy and William Byrd would agree that

   (1) most Native Americans and the English shared religious beliefs

   (2) most Native Americans are as well educated as the English settlers

   (3) many Native Americans wish to convert the English to their religion

   (4) many Native Americans want to keep their tribal rituals and practices

8   The enduring nature of the clash of views expressed by Shickellamy was reflected in the 1800s by the

   (1) passage of the Indian Removal Act by Congress

   (2) forced assimilation of Native Americans in boarding schools

   (3) nativist opposition to the American Indian Movement

   (4) conversion of Native Americans during the Great Awakening

Base your answers to questions 9 and 10 on the map below and on your knowledge of social studies.

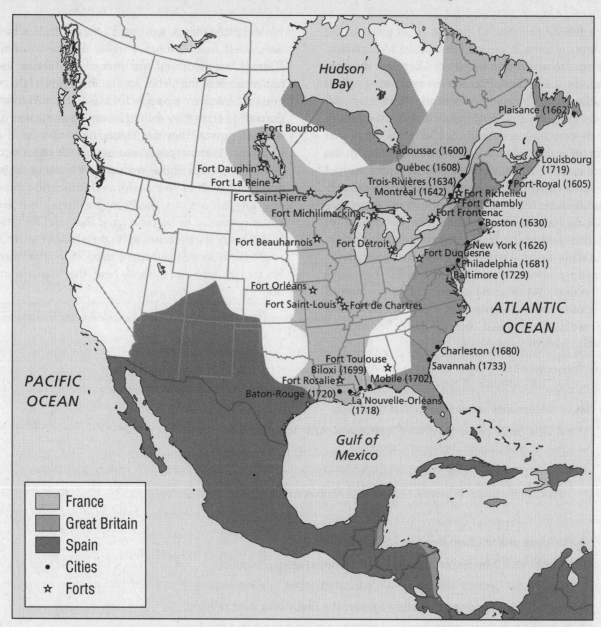

9   Which conclusion can be drawn from this map?

(1) Most European nations established colonies in the Americas.

(2) The British colonial economy was based mainly on the fur trade.

(3) Most colonial cities were established near strategic waterways.

(4) Many French forts were built as a direct result of conflict with Spain.

10   What is the best title for this map?

(1) Early Settlement Patterns in North America

(2) The Settlement of the Thirteen Colonies

(3) The Practice of Mercantilism in North America

(4) Outcome of the French and Indian War

Base your answers to questions 11 and 12 on the passage below and on your knowledge of social studies.

> When some Englishmen entered slave trading directly, it became clear that many of the English public had misgivings about slave-trading and re-creating slavery on English soil. It was an era when the ideals of equality, justice, democracy, and human rights were becoming dominant features of Western political philosophy. Those involved in the trade rationalized their actions by arguing that the Africans were heathens after all, and it was a Christian duty to save their souls. By the early part of the 18th century, the institution was fully established for Africans and their descendants. Large numbers of slaves flooded the southern colonies and even some northern ones. Sometimes they outnumbered whites, and the laws governing slavery became increasingly harsher.

Source: Audrey Smedley, "Origin of the Idea of Race," 1997, PBS, *RACE—The Power of an Illusion*

11 As a result of the circumstances described in this document,

(1) the slave trade was regarded as inhumane and outlawed in the northern colonies

(2) conversion to Christianity became a factor in the forced assimilation of enslaved Africans

(3) slavery became an established element of the colonial economic system

(4) the ideas of Enlightenment philosophers influenced the labor system in the colonies

12 The impact of the practice described in this excerpt is best exemplified by

(1) Jim Crow laws

(2) muckraking

(3) the Red Scare

(4) populism

Base your answers to questions 13 and 14 on the passage below and on your knowledge of social studies.

> There is no liberty if the power of judging be not separated from the legislative and executive powers. Were it joined with the legislative, the life and liberty of the subject would be exposed to arbitrary control; for the judge would then be the legislator. Were it joined to the executive power, the judge might behave with all the violence of an oppressor.

Source: Baron de Montesquieu, *The Spirit of the Laws*, 1748

13 How did this political principle advocated by Montesquieu influence colonial government?

(1) The colonies created a two-tiered structure for their judicial branches.

(2) The colonies based their governments on the social contract theory.

(3) The colonies separated powers among their branches of government.

(4) The colonies incorporated the natural rights of individuals into their charters.

14 What document was shaped, in part, by the Founders' belief in this governmental principle?

(1) Mayflower Compact

(2) United States Constitution

(3) Magna Carta

(4) English Bill of Rights

Short Essay Questions

Task: Read and analyze the following documents, applying your social studies knowledge and skills to write a short essay of two or three paragraphs in which you:

- Describe the historical context surrounding these documents
- Identify and explain the *relationship* between the events and/or ideas found in these documents (Cause and Effect, *or* Similarity/Difference, *or* Turning Point)

Types of Relationships:

Cause refers to "something that contributes to the occurrence of an event, the rise of an idea, or the bringing about of a development"

Effect refers to "what happens as a consequence (result, impact, outcome) of an event, an idea, or a development"

Similarity tells how "something is alike or the same as something else"

Difference tells how "something is not alike or not the same as something else"

Turning Point is "a major event, idea, or historical development that brings about significant change. It can be local, regional, national, or global"

Document 1

Major Economic Activities of the 13 Colonies

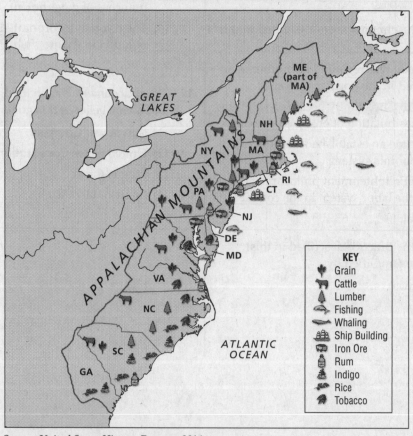

Source: United States History, Pearson, 2016

Document 2

Estimated Population of the American Colonies				
	1680		1760	
	White	Black	White	Black
New England				
Connecticut	17,196	50	138,687	3,783
Massachusetts	39,582	170	197,734	4,866
New Hampshire	1,972	75	38,493	600
Rhode Island	2,842	175	42,003	3,468
Sub-total:	61,592	470	416,917	12,717
Middle Colonies				
Delaware	950	55	31,517	1,733
New Jersey	3,200	200	87,246	6,567
New York	8,630	1,200	100,798	16,340
Pennsylvania	655	25	179,294	4,409
Sub-total:	13,435	1,480	398,855	29,049
Southern Colonies				
Georgia			6,000	3,578
Maryland	16,293	1,611	113,263	49,004
North Carolina	5,220	210	76,888	33,554
South Carolina	1,000	200	36,740	57,334
Virginia	40,596	3,000	199,156	140,570
Sub-total:	63,109	5,021	432,047	284,040

Source: Historical Statistics of the United States, U.S. Census Bureau

Document Analysis for Civic Literacy Essay

Historical Context: Property Rights

Throughout United States history, many constitutional and civic issues have been debated by Americans. These debates have resulted in efforts by individuals, groups, and governments to address these issues. These efforts have achieved varying degrees of success. One of these constitutional and civic issues is property rights.

Task: Read and analyze the document. Using information from the document and your knowledge of United States history, write an essay in which you

- Describe the historical circumstances surrounding this constitutional or civic issue
- Explain efforts to address this constitutional or civic issue by individuals, groups, and/or governments
- Discuss the extent to which these efforts were successful

Describe means "to illustrate something in words or tell about it"

Explain means "to make plain or understandable; to give reasons for or causes of; to show the logical development or relationship of"

Discuss means "to make observations about something using facts, reasoning, and argument; to present in some detail"

Document 1

Solomon Stoddard was a Puritan minister and prominent religious leader in the Massachusetts Bay Colony. In his 1722 pamphlet, he expressed his opinions about a variety of ethical issues pertaining to colonial life.

Q[uestion] VIII. DID we any wrong to the Indians in buying their Land at a small price?

A[nswer]. 1. THERE was some part of the Land that was not purchased, neither was there need that it should; it was *vacuum domicilium* [uninhabited and free to settle] and so might be possessed by virtue of GOD's grant to Mankind. . . .

2. THE Indians were well contented that we should sit down [settle] by them. And it would have been for great Advantage, both for this World and the Other; if they had been wise enough to make use of their Opportunities. . . .

3. THO' we gave but a small Price for what we bought, we gave them their demands. We came to their Market and gave them their price, and, indeed, it was worth but little and had it continued in their hands, it would have been of little value. It is our dwelling on it and our Improvements that have made it to be of Worth.

Source: Reverend Solomon Stoddard, *An Answer to Some Cases of Conscience Respecting the Country*, Boston, 1722

1. How does Reverend Stoddard defend the way in which land was acquired by the colonists?

Document 2

Minavavana was a Chippewa chief who sided with the French against the British during the French and Indian War. The victorious British did not include Native Americans in the treaty process.

Englishman!—It is to you that I speak, and I demand your attention! . . .

Englishman!—Although you have conquered the French, you have not yet conquered us! We are not your slaves. These lakes, these woods and mountains, were left to us by our ancestors. They are our inheritance, and we will part with them to none. Your nation supposes that we, like the white people, cannot live without bread, and pork, and beef! But, you ought to know, that He, —the Great Spirit and Master of Life,—has provided food for us, in these broad lakes, and on these woody mountains.

Source: Chief Minavavana, statement to English fur trader Alexander Henry, 1761

2. What is Chief Minavavana's viewpoint on the control and ownership of land?

Constitutional Foundations

(1763–1824)

Topic Overview

The Treaty of Paris of 1763 ended almost 100 years of war between England and France. In North America the colonists fought with the British in each of the four wars. At the end of the French and Indian War, called the Seven Years War elsewhere in the world, Britain changed its policy of salutary neglect. It began to enforce its economic policy of mercantilism and attempted to strengthen its control over the 13 colonies.

From 1763 until 1775, political and economic tensions grew between the colonies and the British Parliament. During this time of turmoil, the colonies further developed their beliefs about government, governing, representation, self-government, liberty, and individual rights.

In 1775, war began in Massachusetts. In July 1776, the American colonists issued the Declaration of Independence. It declared their independence from Great Britain. In 1781, the American and French victory at Yorktown, Virginia ended the war. The Treaty of Paris of 1783 determined the boundaries of the new United States. The new nation stretched to the Mississippi River. The war impacted many different groups and individuals.

The United States struggled to create an effective government for the newly united nation. The Articles of Confederation proved to be too weak. Our Constitution was written to replace it. The ratification debate over the proposed Constitution led the Federalists to agree to add a bill of rights to the Constitution. The new nation confronted the challenge of creating a stable federal republic.

Decisions for Revolution and Independence

Key Concepts

11.2a Following the French and Indian War, the British government attempted to gain greater political and economic control over the colonies. Colonists resisted these efforts, leading to increasing tensions between the colonists and the British government.

11.2b Failed attempts to resolve the conflicts between the British government and the colonists led the colonists to declare independence, which they eventually won through the Revolutionary War, which affected individuals in different ways.

Lesson Overview

British efforts to gain greater political and economic control over the colonies, such as in the Proclamation of 1763, the Stamp Act, the Townshend Acts, the Tea Act, and the Coercive Acts, resulted in colonial reactions to these efforts and then to the American Revolution. The purpose of and the ideas contained in the Declaration of Independence affected the development of the new nation. Both the American Revolution and the Declaration of Independence had long-term impacts on the people living in the colonies, our nation as a whole, and the rest of the world.

Unifying Themes

As you review this lesson take special note of the following themes:

- **Time, Continuity, and Change** What were the causes and effects of the American Revolution? Why did the British government and the colonists have such different views of events?

- **Power, Authority, and Governance** What did the colonists see as British abuses of its power to govern them? What were the fundamental principles of government that the colonies and later the new nation valued? Who in the early years of the new nation benefited from the ideals of the American Revolution and who did not?

- **Civic Ideals and Practices** What were the different responses and reactions of individuals and groups to the events in what is now the United States between 1763 and 1783?

- **Creation, Expansion, and Interaction of Economic Systems** How did mercantilism influence the events that led to the American Revolution?

Key People

Samuel Adams
Paul Revere
John Adams
Thomas Paine
Richard Henry Lee

Thomas Jefferson
Benjamin Franklin
John Locke
George Washington
John Jay

Key Terms and Events

salutary neglect
confederacy
French and Indian War
Treaty of Paris of 1763
Proclamation of 1763
Navigation Acts
writ of assistance
Sugar Act
Stamp Act
Committees of
 Correspondence

Stamp Act Congress
Quartering Act
Declaratory Act
Townshend Acts
Boston Massacre
Tea Act
Coercive Acts
"Intolerable Acts"
Quebec Act
natural rights
tyranny

Olive Branch Petition
First Continental
 Congress
Second Continental
 Congress
Common Sense
social contract theory
Declaration of
 Independence
Treaty of Paris of 1783

The Historical Context of the American Revolution

For almost a century before the outbreak of the American Revolution in 1775, England and France competed for world power, fighting four wars for control in Europe, Asia, and North America. Preoccupied with France and concerned with protecting its growing empire, England governed the colonies under an unofficial policy known as **salutary neglect**— weak enforcement of British trade laws with the colonies. This policy resulted in the colonists gaining more independence in their trade practices and Great Britain benefiting from the colonies' economic prosperity. The colonies also became used to exercising a large degree of self-government.

Before the American Revolution, colonists saw themselves as British subjects and as New Yorkers, or Rhode Islanders, or Virginians. In 1754, Benjamin Franklin tried to get the colonies to join together to better protect themselves against the French. His **Albany Plan of Union**, a **confederacy** like that of the Iroquois, was rejected by the colonies because each feared loss of power and independence.

The French and Indian War

The **French and Indian War** (1754–63) began when the English challenged the French for control of the Ohio River Valley, land that now includes Ohio and western Pennsylvania. The war pitted the British army and colonists against the French and their Native American allies. Because the French entered regions to trade furs, building forts rather than settlements, Native Americans tended to support them rather than the British who settled and farmed the land. Toward the end of the war, the Iroquois, influenced by an earlier conflict with the French over trade, ended their neutrality and supported the British.

The **Treaty of Paris of 1763** marked Great Britain's victory over France in the French and Indian War, or the Seven Years War, as it was called in Europe and India. By the terms of the treaty:

- France lost all its land claims on the North American continent.
- France kept only its valuable sugar cane islands in the West Indies.
- France turned its land claims west of the Mississippi River including New Orleans over to its ally, Spain.
- Spain gave up Florida to the British, while the British returned Cuba to Spain.

The treaty made it clear that Great Britain was now the major force in North America as well as the world's greatest naval power. It also shifted the way power was distributed in North America. With French land in North America now in British hands, Native Americans could no longer benefit from balancing French and English interests against one another. The colonists felt their war efforts earned them the right to move into the newly acquired lands and saw less need for the protection of the British government. However, with the French threat ended, England changed its imperial policy toward the colonies.

The **Proclamation of 1763** was an early sign of the tensions between the British and the colonists over post–1763 British policies, which resulted in the American Revolution. The Proclamation prohibited permanent colonial expansion west of the ridge of the Appalachian Mountains. The British aim was to maintain a peaceful relationship with the Native Americans by avoiding conflicts between them and the colonists. Britain was in part influenced by Chief Pontiac, an Ottawa leader who led a confederacy of tribes from 1763–1766 in a war called **Pontiac's Rebellion.** The colonists deeply resented the Proclamation and often ignored it.

Analyzing Documents

Ben Franklin published this political cartoon in 1754.

- Why?
- What point of view does he express?
- How was his message received?
- What was the response to this cartoon in 1765 when the Stamp Act was issued?

Social Studies Practices
Turning Point

- Why is the Treaty of Paris of 1763 considered a turning point in history?

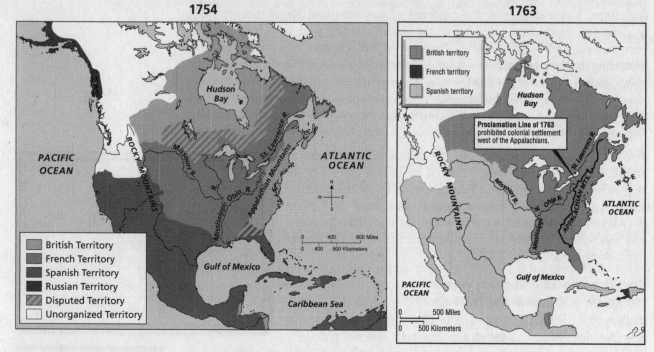

Land Claims of European Nations Before and After the French and Indian War

1754

British Territory
French Territory
Spanish Territory
Russian Territory
Disputed Territory
Unorganized Territory

1763

British territory
French territory
Spanish territory

Proclamation Line of 1763 prohibited colonial settlement west of the Appalachians.

Preparing for the Regents

Stimulus-Based Questions: Maps

- Compare the 1754 map to the 1763 map and identify any evidence to support the Proclamation of 1763.

- Trace the changes in Spanish holdings from 1754 to 1763 to 1803 to 1819 to 1848 and examine the reasons for British and then United States concern with this territory.

Unifying Themes
Change

- What caused the changes in British imperial policy after 1763?

- Why did the colonists resist those changes?

- What was the result of that resistance?

England Attempts to Gain Greater Control Over the Colonies

The four wars with France in the colonies as well as across the globe left the British government with a huge war debt. Britain also had to pay the costs of maintaining a military force in the colonies to defend against any new French threat. The British Parliament, needing money and believing that the colonies had also benefited from these two expenses, began to again enforce its policy of mercantilism, an economic system practiced by European trading nations in the 16th, 17th, and 18th centuries.

Mercantilism held that a nation's power was based on how much gold and silver it accumulated. A major goal was to increase the nation's wealth. To that end, a nation sought a favorable balance of trade by protecting manufacturing and promoting exports while limiting imports. Colonial economies were controlled to benefit the mother country. Colonies were to supply raw materials and serve as markets while restrictions limited their manufacturing and commerce.

For example, the **Navigation Acts** (1650–1673) required that most colonial trade occur only within the British empire and that certain goods could be shipped only to Great Britain. In some ways these mercantilist acts helped the colonies. Virginia tobacco

Events Leading to the American Revolution

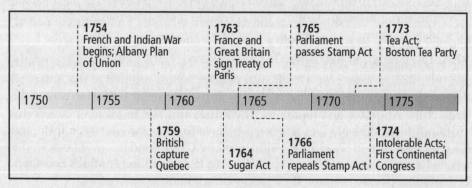

1754 French and Indian War begins; Albany Plan of Union

1763 France and Great Britain sign Treaty of Paris

1765 Parliament passes Stamp Act

1773 Tea Act; Boston Tea Party

1750   1755   1760   1765   1770   1775

1759 British capture Quebec

1764 Sugar Act

1766 Parliament repeals Stamp Act

1774 Intolerable Acts; First Continental Congress

planters, for example, knew that England would buy their entire tobacco crop. Most importantly, until 1763, Britain only lightly enforced the Navigation Acts, while the colonists routinely ignored or avoided them. While often evading the Navigation Acts, the colonists had accepted the right of England to regulate trade.

Parliament Acts and the Colonies React

Beginning in 1763, Parliament acted to increase its economic and political control over the thirteen colonies. Its actions were each followed by a negative colonial reaction. Parliament would often further arouse opposition by trying even harder to enforce the new law. Eventually Parliament would back down and repeal the act to which the colonists objected. In time, Parliament would make another attempt to control the colonies and to collect taxes from them. In 1775, this pattern of act and react led to the first shots of the Revolution fired at Lexington and Concord.

1763: The Proclamation of 1763 is announced.

1763: The English Prime Minister ordered rigid enforcement of the Navigation Acts. **Writs of assistance**—open-ended, transferable search warrants—were issued to look for smuggled goods in merchants' ships, warehouses, and homes. The U.S. Constitution's Bill of Rights' protection against unreasonable search and seizure reflects the colonists' anger against the writs of assistance.

1764: Parliament passed the **Sugar Act** to raise money. It lowered the duty on molasses but took steps to make sure that the money was collected. Accused smugglers would be tried in admiralty courts that lacked the two basic English rights of trial by jury and innocence until proven guilty.

1765: Parliament passed the **Stamp Act,** the first **direct tax** on the colonists, requiring a tax stamp on printed material from newspapers to wills; from deeds to diplomas. The taxes would be used to pay for the British army stationed in the colonies. The Stamp Act most affected colonial merchants, printers, and lawyers, most of whom were already active in colonial politics.

Protests against the Stamp Act were widespread and took many forms, passive and violent. The rallying cry was "Liberty." New York organized **nonimportation agreements** or **boycotts** of British goods. Other colonies soon participated. **Samuel Adams,** a Boston political organizer and journalist, helped create the Sons of Liberty and the Massachusetts Committee of Correspondence. Between 1765 and 1774, **Committees of Correspondence** met throughout the colonies to develop communication systems within and between the colonies. It was through the efforts of the Committees of Correspondence that the **Stamp Act Congress** met in New York. Nine colonies sent representatives to the Congress, the first time the colonies showed unity at the legislative level in reaction to British policies.

The secret **Sons of Liberty** also spread throughout the colonies. It both organized protests and tried to control riots and other acts of violence. The stamp tax collectors were pressured to resign. Only Georgia failed to make sure that no stamp could be sold in a colony.

1765: The **Quartering Act** required that the colonies house in public buildings and provide food to British troops being sent to protect the colonies. When the New York assembly would not vote for the supplies, Britain dissolved it.

1766: The Stamp Act was repealed. The **Declaratory Act** was issued stating that Parliament had the right and authority to make laws for the colonies "in all cases whatsoever."

Social Studies Practices
Interpreting Evidence

In May 1765, Patrick Henry voiced his opposition to the Stamp Act with a speech to the Virginia House of Burgesses. In that speech, he said:

Caesar had his Brutus; Charles the First, his Cromwell; and George the Third . . . may profit by their example. If this be treason, make the most of it.

(**Note:** Brutus assassinated Caesar, and Cromwell defeated Charles I and had him beheaded.)

• What is Patrick Henry's message or point of view?

• What might Patrick Henry have been implying but would not say?

• What textual evidence makes Patrick Henry's message quite clear?

1767: The **Townshend Acts** taxed imports such as glass, lead, tea, paper and paint, but again, producing revenue, not regulating trade, was the objective. The money raised would be used to pay some of the English officials in the colonies. Colonial legislatures believed this action undermined their power to exert control over English officials by withholding their salaries. The colonists reacted to the new taxes with petitions, boycotts, and other more violent protests. The Sons of Liberty reorganized. All of the import duties, except that on tea, were repealed.

1770: The **Boston Massacre** occurred as a result of the presence of British troops sent to Boston in 1768 to enforce the Townshend Acts. The troops, who made up 20 percent of the city's population, were often the targets of demonstrations. A mob of sixty citizens attacked ten soldiers with sticks, snowballs, and rocks. The soldiers opened fire, killing five and wounding other protestors. **Paul Revere** and Samuel Adams used the massacre as a means of stirring up anti-British sentiment. **John Adams** defended the soldiers at their trial.

1773: Parliament passed the **Tea Act.** The Act gave the British East India Company a monopoly on the American tea trade at a price less expensive than tea imported by colonial tea merchants. Colonists saw the Tea Act as another British attempt to tax them without representation. In Boston members of the Sons of Liberty staged the **Boston Tea Party,** dumping three shiploads of East India Company tea into Boston Harbor.

1774: The British government punished Massachusetts with the **Coercive Acts.** Labeled the **"Intolerable Acts"** by the colonists, the acts closed the port of Boston, forbid town meetings, reduced the powers of the legislature, and sent more British troops to the colony to enforce the acts. The colonies responded with support for Boston and unity in opposition.

1774: The **Quebec Act** added the land all the way to the Ohio River to Quebec province, land for which the colonists had fought and which they were already settling. The French Catholics were given legal toleration, further arousing fears of colonial Protestants for their own religious and political liberties.

Causes of the American Revolution

The fundamental cause of the Revolution was Britain's belief that, after more than a century of salutary neglect of its North American colonies, it could bring them under centralized control to take their place as English subjects of the British empire. Leaders in Great Britain failed to understand that

- separation by 3,000 miles of ocean had led, over generations, to a sense of self-sufficiency and independence in the colonies.

- the colonies had developed their own self-governing bodies based on English traditions and Enlightenment views.

- because of the abundance of land in the colonies, about 70 percent of the white male population held enough land to qualify them for the right to vote, involving them directly in political issues. At the time, only 10 percent of white males in Britain could vote.

- colonial actions were grounded in the colonists' belief in their **natural rights** as English citizens. Colonists viewed these new taxes as a threat to their liberties, including the right to property.

Social Studies Practices
Cause and Effect

Identify examples of actions between 1763 and 1775 that support the details listed under the "Causes of the American Revolution."

- the colonists valued the **republican principles** of limited government grounded in representation of the people and the consent of the governed supported by the **civic virtue** of men with property who put the public good over their own self-interest.

- the colonists feared power. They saw it as dangerous to their rights and liberties. The colonists came to believe that the actions of both King George III and Parliament were a deliberate plan to force tyranny on the colonies. **Tyranny** means abuse of power and the rule of law by an oppressive government, ruler, or dictator.

- because they had no representation in Parliament, colonists claimed that taxation could come only from the colonial legislatures. They saw the new laws as **taxation without representation.** Great Britain insisted that the colonists had "virtual representation" because Parliament acted for all of its subjects.

- **The Great Awakening,** a religious movement, had encouraged people to question authority and increased a sense of equality among people.

War and Independence

Tensions between the colonists and Parliament continued to mount. Although efforts to prevent war were made, war proved to be inevitable.

Attempts to Avoid War

In 1774 and 1775, Congress attempted to avoid war with Britain. The First Continental Congress (September–October 1774) approved the Petition of the Grand American Continental Congress, to the King's Most Excellent Majesty. It listed colonial grievances but emphasized loyalty to the king. The Petition was rejected.

In May 1775, in the Conciliatory Proposition, Parliament reached out to the colonies. Parliament would continue to pass laws to govern the colonies but tax laws would be only to regulate trade. The money raised would go to the colonies who would agree to take on additional defense responsibilities. It was an offer too little and too late. In April fighting had started in Massachusetts.

In July 1775 the Second Continental Congress (1775–81) approved the **Olive Branch Petition**. It was one last effort to avoid war against Britain. The king would not even read this petition. In August 1775, he proclaimed that the colonies had "proceeded to open and avowed rebellion" and in October declared an official state of war against the colonies.

The American Revolution and the Declaration of Independence, 1775–1783

```
1775                    1777                                        1783
Second Continental      Battle of                                   Treaty of Paris
Congress; Battles of    Saratoga
Lexington and Concord

1775          1777              1779              1781              1783

      1776                                  1781
      Common Sense published;              Cornwallis
      Declaration of                       surrenders
      Independence signed                  at Yorktown
```

Preparing for the Regents

Stimulus-Based Questions: Letter

But what do We mean by the American Revolution? Do We mean the American War? The Revolution was effected before the War commenced. The Revolution was in the Minds and Hearts of the People.

—From John Adams' letter to Hezekiah Niles, February 13, 1818

- Why is it important to consider the writer when reading this excerpt?

- To the writer, what is the difference between American Revolution and American War?

Resistance Leads to Crisis and War

In the late summer of 1774, twelve of the colonies sent representatives to Philadelphia to plan a response to the British actions. This meeting became known as the **First Continental Congress.** After the start of the American Revolution in 1775 at **Lexington and Concord,** a **Second Continental Congress** met and took charge of the war effort.

While the colonies moved toward war and demands for independence, colonists were divided. Those known as **Tories,** or **Loyalists,** about 16 to 20 percent of the white colonial population, supported the king and obedience to English laws. Loyalists tended to be upper class and from the middle and most southern colonies. Opposing independence, 20,000 to 80,000 went to Canada and Great Britain during the war. Some returned after the fighting ended. Many thousands more left the United States at the end of the Revolution, including large numbers from New York. Over 20,000 Loyalists fought in the British army against the Patriots and others joined local Loyalist militias. The revolution pitted Americans against each other.

Decision for Independence

The decision to declare independence was made over a year after the American Revolution began. **Thomas Paine,** in his pamphlet, *Common Sense,* was influential in persuading the colonists to end their relationship with Great Britain.

"We have boasted the protection of Great Britain, without considering that her motive was interest not attachment; and that she did not protect us from our enemies on our account; but from her enemies on her own account. . . . A government of our own is our natural right: and . . . it is infinitely wiser and safer to form a constitution of our own, in a cool deliberate manner, while we have it in our power, than to trust such an interesting event to time and chance."

—Thomas Paine, *Common Sense*, 1776

In June 1776, **Richard Henry Lee** of Virginia presented a resolution to the Second Continental Congress calling for independence from Great Britain. The Congress appointed a committee (including **Thomas Jefferson, Benjamin Franklin,** and John Adams) to draft a formal declaration. The resulting Declaration of Independence was almost entirely the work of Thomas Jefferson. In writing the Declaration, Jefferson relied heavily on **John Locke's** Enlightenment ideas of **social contract theory** and belief in natural rights. The delegates adopted the **Declaration of Independence** on July 4, which marks the birth of the United States of America.

Preparing for the Regents

Stimulus-Based Questions: Primary Source

- What is common sense to Paine?
- What textual evidence communicates Paine's central idea?

The Declaration of Independence

The PURPOSE of the Declaration:	The Declaration's KEY IDEAS OF GOVERNMENT:
• To explain and justify the reasons that the united colonies had decided to become the United States of America • To persuade European nations to support their cause • To announce to the world that the colonies were now a new independent nation	• "All men are created equal"; they are created with natural rights including the rights to "life, liberty and the pursuit of happiness." • Legitimate governments receive their power to govern "from the consent of the governed"; that power is for the purpose of protecting the people's natural rights. • When a government fails to protect and instead abuses those rights, it is the "right of the people to alter or abolish" that government.
The FOUR PARTS of the Declaration:	
• A preamble stating why it was written • A new theory of government • A list of grievances against the King • A formal resolution declaring independence	

The Long-Term Impact of the Declaration of Independence

The ideals of the Declaration of Independence are still a goal for our nation. In 1791, the Bill of Rights reemphasized the importance of individual liberties and limits on government power first stated in the Declaration of Independence. Other American documents that were influenced by the Declaration of Independence include Elizabeth Cady Stanton's "Declaration of Sentiments," Abraham Lincoln's "Gettysburg Address," and Martin Luther King's "I Have A Dream" speech.

Those ideals have also served to inspire people in other nations and at other times, such as during the French Revolution of the late 1700s, the South American independence movement in the early 1800s, and twentieth-century independence movements in Africa and Asia. The Universal Declaration of Human Rights approved by the United Nations in 1948 states that "All human beings are born free and equal in dignity and rights."

There was a fundamental contradiction between slavery and the Declaration's ideals of freedom and liberty. Locke's contract theory stated that no person may rule another without the consent of the other person. The colonists protested their treatment by England and chose liberty. The grievance that blamed the king for the slave trade was one of the statements removed from the Declaration. South Carolina and Georgia raised objections as did some northern colonies in which the transatlantic slave trade was active. Virginians Jefferson and James Madison as well as Bostonian John Hancock were just three of the signers who owned enslaved people.

Fighting the Revolutionary War

During the American Revolution, the **Second Continental Congress** served as the national government. The Congress had no constitutional basis in law. It was extralegal; the Congress was created in a crisis and supported by the colonial and later state governments and popular opinion. The Second Congress governed until 1781 when the Articles of Confederation went into effect.

The American Revolution pitted Great Britain, then the world's most powerful nation, against thirteen former colonies that lacked financial resources and a regular army. The make-shift American navy consisted mostly of privateers against a Royal Navy that controlled the seas. The British army was larger in number, better trained, and aided by the Creek, Cherokee, and Shawnee in the South and most Iroquois in the North. The British were disadvantaged by their use of European military techniques in America and by the behavior of their troops, which alienated many colonists. British troops included Hessian mercenaries. These were German soldiers hired to fight the American army.

Assembling and training the Continental Army (the colonists' army) was the achievement of **George Washington,** the colonial commander in chief. The Continental Army was reinforced as it moved from region to region by an untrained and unreliable **militia** of volunteers defending their homes.

The Death of General Warren at the Battle of Bunker Hill, June 1775

In 1778, the colonists were aided by two alliances with France, one commercial and one military, negotiated by Benjamin Franklin. The French were motivated by its ongoing rivalry with Great Britain and a desire for revenge. These French alliances were critical to the American victory. France provided the colonists with military supplies including much needed firearms, troops, and naval support. France, along with her ally Spain, also engaged Great Britain in war elsewhere in the world.

Preparing for the Regents

Turning Point

• Why is the Battle of Saratoga a turning point in the war?

The American victory at the **Battle of Saratoga** helped bring the French into the war. France saw that the colonists might possibly win the war. The win at Saratoga also prevented the British from isolating New England from the rest of the colonies by taking control of the Hudson River Valley and the area north of it to Canada.

The American Revolution lasted from 1775 to the surrender of the British at the **Battle of Yorktown** in Virginia, in 1781. A peace treaty, the **Treaty of Paris of 1783,** was negotiated by John Adams, **John Jay,** and Benjamin Franklin. Under its terms Great Britain recognized the independence of the United States. The treaty set the new nation's boundaries at Canada to the north, Spanish Florida to the south, and the Mississippi River to the west.

Some Effects of the American Revolution

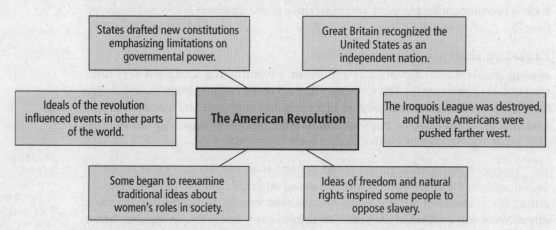

The Revolution had important consequences for many groups of people.

The Revolution's Impact on the People in North America

After the success of the American Revolution, the ideas that were at its center affected the everyday lives of the people living in the colonies. For some the impact was positive; for others less so.

American Workers

Yeoman farmers and craftsmen and artisans working in cities were two large and influential groups supporting the Revolution. They in turn benefited from its ideals. The revolutionary cry for liberty resulted in questioning the new nation's political practices and institutions. Workers, artisans, and farmers involved themselves in discussions of political issues of the day. In the name of democracy, they called for more equality. Eligibility to vote was made easier and qualifications for holding political office were lowered. Many more white men could vote. Some states gave the right to vote to property-owning African Americans and Native Americans. Voting was becoming a political right.

The so-called "common man" also was elected to local and state governments. Between 1776 and 1787, eleven of the thirteen states adopted new constitutions. These constitutions were based on republican principles and the democratic influence of new voters. The constitutions placed most of the authority to govern in the hands of the legislature whose members were usually elected every year. Special state conventions were called so that the constitutions could be written by the people. When complete, they were ratified, or approved, by the voters.

The New York Constitution of 1777, which even included the text of the Declaration of Independence, gave most of the power to the legislature, rather than to a single person, such as a governor. In New York, as in most states, the legislature remained bicameral, rather than unicameral. State constitutions, including the New York State Constitution, protected some individual rights, such as the right to religious freedom. In addition, the State government could not give money to any religion. This was part of a national movement to disestablish churches, which meant the end of government endorsement and financial support of any single religious group.

Indentured servitude and apprenticeships were ended and replaced in the North with those working for pay. The availability of land ceded by Britain after the Revolution presented new opportunities to American citizens. The United States was no longer bound by English common law. Virginia, for example, eliminated the law of primogeniture that required passing the family land solely to the eldest son. This change was a move toward equality and away from a hereditary upper class. Workers, artisans, and farmers as well as merchants and professionals gained social mobility as the colonial hierarchy of each in a fixed position became more flexible.

Enslaved Africans and African Americans

Although African Americans fought on both sides during the American Revolution, more fought on the British side because of British promises of freedom from slavery. After first hesitating, Washington and the Continental Congress recruited African Americans, as did state militias.

During the Revolution, some enslaved Africans in the South successfully escaped. Others were freed in return for military service. Some left the country with the British army, while others settled in northern cities and became part of a growing free African American population.

The revolutionary ideals resulted in the beginnings of an antislavery movement in the North. An antislavery movement led by Quakers started in the North before the Revolution. By 1804 every northern state had passed laws that immediately or gradually abolished slavery. The Northwest Ordinance prohibited slavery in that Trans-Appalachian territory. In Virginia and Maryland where tobacco was now less profitable, some slaves were freed but slavery in the rice-growing regions of Georgia and South Carolina remained strong. Although free, African Americans in the North still faced discrimination. Except in New England, many were not allowed to vote. There was segregation in public places, housing, and transportation.

In 1774, several northern states stopped their transatlantic slave trade. The new United States Constitution ratified in 1788 prohibited the importation of enslaved people as of 1808.

Analyzing Documents

[We] *have in common with all other men a natural and inalienable right to that freedom, which the Great Parent of the Universe hath bestowed equally on all mankind, and which they have never forfeited by any compact or agreement whatsoever.*

—From a petition of a group of enslaved people to the Massachusetts legislature, 1777

• Cite the specific textual evidence that the writers knew about Enlightenment ideas and the Declaration of Independence.

Native Americans

Because of concern that their land and their way of life faced a bigger threat from Americans than the English, most Indian nations who were not neutral supported the British side. Shawnees, Cherokees, and Creeks allied with the Great Britain. In the North, the Revolution divided and then dissolved the **Iroquois Confederacy,** or Haudenosaunee (People of the Longhouse). Four of the Six Nations supported the British, their traditional allies, but the Oneida and Tuscarora fought on the side of the Americans.

In the Treaty of Paris of 1783, however, Great Britain turned over all of the land—Native American land—from Canada to Florida, from the Appalachians to the Mississippi River to the new United States. Both Britain and the United States acted without any Native American representation nor consideration of the position, British, American, or neutral, that the native tribes had taken during the war. The United States did not consider Native Americans to be citizens, and therefore treated them as nations to be dealt with through treaties. The new nation took the position that in defeating the British it had also defeated the Native Americans.

The government planned to sell plots of this huge bloc of land to raise desperately needed money. The land would also be given to soldiers to whom the government owed back pay or pensions. The ordinary citizens were already on the move across the Appalachians. Native nations continued to fight for their land, but after the Revolution, those living east of the Mississippi were doomed to lose their land and their culture.

Women

During the prerevolutionary period, women had participated in protests and were key to the effectiveness of boycotts of British products. During the war, a few were soldiers and some were spies. Many women ran the farm or the shop while their husbands were away fighting.

When the war ended, white women were still denied equal citizenship with white men. The revolutionary spirit praised women for their efforts in support of independence, but their legal position remained unchanged. One exception was New Jersey, where in 1776 its first Constitution allowed women and free African Americans who met the property and residency requirements to vote. Single women did exercise their right until 1807 when the law was changed. Under English common law, a married woman existed legally only through her husband. In addition, any property or money she might have owned now belonged to him.

Abigail Adams was an early advocate for women's rights in education and property ownership

For white women who were well off and living in the North, especially in New England and in cities, more educational opportunities were available. Educated mothers were the teachers of the young citizens of the new republic. Female academies were founded in the 1790s. Higher education and entry into the professions were not offered. Education did lead to a more equal relationship between husband and wife socially and culturally but not legally.

Writing and Ratifying the U.S. Constitution

Lesson Overview

While the successes of government under the Articles of Confederation were important, its weaknesses resulted in the Critical Period. A convention was called for the purpose of revising the Articles of Confederation. Instead, the Founders attending the Constitutional Convention wrote a new Constitution.

The new Constitution was written during months of major debates and their resolutions, which included compromises over representation, taxation, and slavery. The structure, power, and function of the federal government as created by the Constitution was based on key constitutional principles such as the division of power between federal and state government, the separation of powers at the federal level, the creation of checks and balances, the sovereignty of the people, and judicial independence.

The key points of debate expressed in the *Federalist Papers* and the *Antifederalist Papers,* focused on the protection of individual rights and the proper size for a republic. After the ratification the Bill of Rights was added. It listed rights and protections of the people from the federal government. Today, these rights and protections have been extended and expanded.

Key Concept

11.2c Weaknesses of the Articles of Confederation led to a convention whose purpose was to revise the Articles of Confederation but instead resulted in the writing of a new Constitution. The ratification debate over the proposed Constitution led the Federalists to agree to add a bill of rights to the Constitution.

Unifying Themes

As you review this lesson take special note of the following themes:

- **Time, Continuity, and Change** Why did the Framers first write a weak constitution and then replace it with our present Constitution? What were the consequences of each action? What were the Federalists and the Anti-Federalists competing interpretations of government?

- **Power, Authority, and Governance** What is the structure, power, and function of the federal government as created by the Constitution? What is the importance of each fundamental principle and value of our government as expressed in the Constitution? Why were they thought to be important when the Constitution was written? Why have they remained critical issues throughout United States history?

- **Civic Ideals and Practices** What basic freedoms and rights and responsibilities of citizens in a democratic republic are protected in the Constitution and its Bill of Rights? What are some examples of citizen participation during the writing and ratification of the Constitution?

- **Creation, Expansion, and Interaction of Economic Systems** What evidence is there that economic concerns influenced the writing of our Constitution? What was the role of government in the economy according to Federalists compared to Anti-Federalists?

Key People

George Washington

James Madison

Alexander Hamilton

George Mason

Edmund Randolph

John Jay

Key Terms and Events

constitution	Three-Fifths Compromise	federalism
Articles of Confederation	Commerce Compromise	separation of powers
ratify	Fugitive Slave Clause	legislative branch
confederation	Presidency Compromise	executive branch
Constitutional Convention	Federalists	judicial branch
Virginia Plan	Anti-Federalists	checks and balances
bicameral legislature	popular sovereignty	judicial independence
New Jersey Plan	limited government	judicial review
unicameral legislature	rule of law	amendment
Great Compromise	Supremacy Clause	Bill of Rights

The Articles of Confederation, 1781–1789

The first **constitution**, or basic framework of a national government of the United States, was the **Articles of Confederation**. This constitution, proposed by the Second Continental Congress in 1777, went into effect in 1781 after all 13 states had **ratified**, or approved, it. The Articles set up a confederation among the 13 states. A **confederation** is an alliance of independent states in which the states give as much power as they choose to the central government, while keeping the greater part of the power and remaining **sovereign**. The Articles were more like a treaty among the states than a plan of centralized government.

The Articles of Confederation, 1781–1789

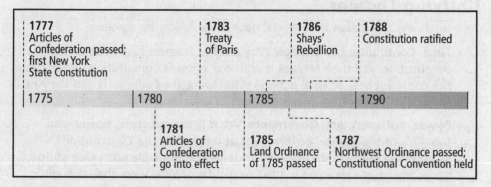

| **1777** Articles of Confederation passed; first New York State Constitution | **1783** Treaty of Paris | **1786** Shays' Rebellion | **1788** Constitution ratified |

| 1775 | 1780 | 1785 | 1790 |

| | **1781** Articles of Confederation go into effect | **1785** Land Ordinance of 1785 passed | **1787** Northwest Ordinance passed; Constitutional Convention held |

Successes of the Confederation Government

The government under the Articles of Confederation had the power to make treaties, declare war, and receive ambassadors. The Confederation Congress is credited with several notable achievements

1. Successful conclusion of the American Revolution.

2. Negotiation of the Treaty of Paris of 1783, ending the war and setting U.S. borders at Canada, the Mississippi River, and Florida.

3. Passage of the **Land Ordinance of 1785** and the **Northwest Ordinance of 1787** that

   - set the pattern and procedure for settlement of the Northwest Territory

   - provided the guidelines by which new states would join the nation on a basis of equality with the thirteen original states. This policy was applied as the nation expanded west.

   - guaranteed equality of citizenship to those settling in the new territory.

- contained a bill of rights protecting religious freedom, the right to a writ of *habeas corpus*, trial by jury, and other rights.
- prohibited slavery in the Northwest Territory
- allowed for the return of fugitive slaves

Northwest Territory, 1787

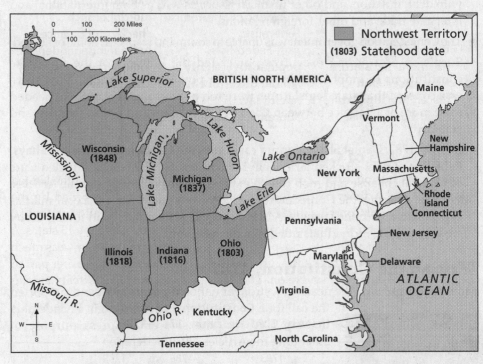

Analyzing Documents

Sec. 13. And, for extending the fundamental principles of civil and religious liberty . . . to fix and establish those principles as the basis of all laws, constitutions, and governments, which forever hereafter shall be formed in the said territory: to provide also for the establishment of States, and permanent government therein, and for their admission to a share in the federal councils on an equal footing with the original States. . . .

—Northwest Ordinance, July 13, 1787

- What words are evidence that the Northwest Ordinance is a turning point in history?
- How did this law affect the development of the rest of our nation?

Weaknesses of the Confederation Government

The Confederation government proved unable to deal with the nation's problems during the **Critical Period** of the 1780s. The Articles of Confederation reflected the colonists' fear of a strong government and the desire of the individual states to protect their powers. Limited powers to govern were given to a legislature. It was unicameral, with each state, no matter its population, having one vote. Nine votes were required to pass any important legislation. Amendments to the Articles had to pass unanimously.

Remembering the conflicts with royal governors and British-controlled courts before the Revolution, the Articles deliberately lacked a president to direct operations and a national judiciary. There was no single national currency, because the states could also coin money. The Congress could not tax the people directly but had to ask the states for funds. Congress could raise an army only by requesting troops from the states.

The new nation had borrowed heavily to finance the Revolution. With no power to tax, the government and the nation faced severe economic problems. No longer a part of the British empire, new trading partners had to be found. Foreign imports undercut the prices of the products of urban artisans and craftsmen. States acted independently; some printed their own paper money while others taxed imported goods. The British still occupied forts in the frontier regions of the nation. Spain blocked use of the port at New Orleans. The Articles were not working, but it was nearly impossible to strengthen them. All 13 states had to agree before the Articles could be amended.

Preparing for the Regents

- Why are the years 1781–1789 under the Articles of Confederation called the "Critical Period"?

Calling for a Constitutional Convention

By the mid-1780s, it was clear that the fear of too much power in the hands of the government expressed in the Articles of Confederation had created a government unable to function.

- Lacking power, the Confederation government had increasing difficulty dealing with debt, inflation, and other financial issues as well as both international and interstate trade and other foreign relations.

- The Confederation government was unable to command respect at home or abroad.

- Suspicion of a strong executive power led the Framers of the first state constitutions to emphasize limitations on power of governors. Now there was concern that state legislatures were too powerful and that there needed to be more of a balance between liberty and freedom and order, security, and stability.

- In 1786–1787, Daniel Shays, former captain in the Continental army led **Shays' Rebellion** of debt-stricken farmers in Massachusetts. The rebellion fueled fears of national collapse and mob rule. It exposed basic weaknesses of the Articles. Without an army, the Confederation government could not act. Local militias sympathized with the farmers. A Massachusetts state militia paid for in part by wealthy private individuals put down the rebellion.

Writing the Constitution, 1787

More Americans saw the need for a stronger national government and supported the call for a **Constitutional Convention** in Philadelphia in May 1787 for "the sole and express purpose of amending the Articles of Confederation."

Members of the Constitutional Convention signing the United States Constitution

The Framers of the Constitution

Fifty-five delegates, representing all the states except Rhode Island, met in the Pennsylvania State House (now known as Independence Hall) in Philadelphia in May 1787 at the Constitutional Convention. The delegates were prominent lawyers, planters, and merchants at a time when most of the population were small farmers. They were among the wealthiest, most educated, and most socially and politically influential men of their time. Many hated slavery, including some of the 25 who owned slaves. Their average age was 42. Over half of the delegates were college graduates. They had years of political experience. The Framers included eight men who had signed the Declaration of Independence. Some had been members of the Continental Congress and/or Confederation Congress. Of the 55 men, 39 would sign the final Constitution.

The most famous and respected delegate was **George Washington,** who was elected president of the Constitutional Convention. Another well-known figure was **James Madison,** the Father of the Constitution, whose Virginia Plan of government had the most influence on the Constitution. Also attending were **Benjamin Franklin,** the oldest delegate, and **Alexander Hamilton,** a strong nationalist from New York. Some famous Americans from the Revolution were noticeably absent. Thomas Jefferson and John Adams were serving the country as diplomats in Europe.

Analyzing Documents

- Identify evidence in the painting that supports the description of who attended the Convention.

A few patriots, such as Patrick Henry who announced, "I smell a rat," refused to attend. They suspected that the convention would try to create a strong national government which they viewed as a return to government tyranny. In addition, no women, Native Americans, African Americans or poor white men attended the Constitutional Convention. At that time, these groups had either no or only limited political and legal rights.

The Major Compromises at the Constitutional Convention

The delegates decided not to revise the Articles of Confederation, but to write a new constitution instead. They also agreed that discussions and any written records would be kept secret in order to debate freely without outside pressure. Much of what we know about the Convention comes to us from James Madison's *Notes of the Debates of the Federal Convention of 1787.*

The delegates' task was to create a government with enough authority to govern effectively while protecting individual liberties as a way to unite the thirteen diverse and divided states into a nation. To achieve this goal the founders wrote a constitution containing a contradiction to fundamental national beliefs. Without ever mentioning the words "slavery" or "slaves" the founders agreed to compromises that allowed the continued existence of slavery in the new nation. Many historians argue that the "bundle of compromises" related to slavery kept Southern states from leaving the convention therefore making the United States Constitution possible.

The Great Compromise The Virginia Plan served as the basis for much of the new Constitution. The first issue to be resolved was the design of the legislature and congressional representation within it. The Virginia Plan called for a **bicameral** (two house) **legislature**. A state's representation in each house would be based on its population. Larger states supported this plan. The smaller states favored the **New Jersey Plan.** This plan called for a **unicameral** (one house) **legislature** in which each state had equal representation.

Social Studies Practices
Compare and Contrast

- What evidence is there that the writers of the Articles of Confederation had different objectives than the writers of the Constitution?
- What evidence indicates that historical context influenced the writers of each document?
- What evidence is there of continuity between the two documents?

Unifying Themes
Governance

At the Constitutional Convention, four major compromises were achieved.

- For each issue, how did the compromise satisfy each side?
- Why were the compromises necessary?
- How was slavery an issue in each compromise?

Governments of the United States: 1781 and 1789

How the Weaknesses of the Articles of Confederation Were Corrected by the Constitution	
Articles of Confederation	**Constitution of the United States**
• Confederacy: State governments, not the national government, have most of the power.	• Federal system: Power to govern is divided between national and state government.
• No executive officer to carry out the laws of Congress.	• The Constitution and acts of Congress take supremacy.
• No national courts. Only state courts exist.	• A president heads the executive branch.
• Congress is responsible to the states.	• Both federal and state courts exist.
• The states are sovereign.	• Congress is responsible to the people.
• Laws must be approved by 9 of 13 states.	• Legislature is bicameral with one house's representation based on population.
• Legislature is unicameral with one vote per state no matter its population.	• Laws require a majority vote in both houses of Congress.
• Congress has no power to tax.	• Congress has the power to levy and collect taxes.
• Congress cannot raise and maintain an army. It has to ask states for troops.	• Congress can raise and maintain military forces.
• Congress cannot regulate trade among the states nor the nation's foreign trade.	• Congress is given sole control over interstate and foreign trade.
• Congress can make foreign treaties but not involving trade. Each state managed its own interstate and international trade.	• Only national government has the power to coin money.
• Congress could coin money, but so did many states.	• Amendment process does not require a unanimous vote and involves both Congress and state governments.
• All 13 states must agree to any amendment of the Articles.	

The matter of representation had to be settled by what is known as the **Great Compromise,** or the Connecticut Plan, which created the **Congress,** a bicameral legislature. The states had equal representation in the upper house, or the **Senate.** In the lower house, or the **House of Representatives,** representation was based on population. In addition, all bills dealing with money would have to start in the House, but would also need the approval of the Senate. The Great Compromise also affected a state's vote in the Electoral College.

The Three-Fifths Compromise resolved one issue in the bitter debate over slavery, representation, and power. Even though Southern laws classified the enslaved as property not people, Southerners wanted their enslaved population to be counted when determining representation in the House but not for determining taxes. The **Three-Fifths Compromise** permitted three fifths of the enslaved African Americans in a state to be counted for purposes of both **congressional representation** and taxation. No direct taxation law was ever passed. **Tariffs** and **excise taxes,** not direct taxation, were the primary source of income for the federal government until the passage of the income tax amendment in 1913. But for 70 years the Three-Fifths clause gave slave holding states additional voting power in the House of Representatives and in the Electoral College.

The Commerce Compromise Northerners proposed that the government regulate both interstate and foreign trade and by a majority not a two-thirds vote. Southerners, however, feared that the importing of enslaved Africans would be prohibited and that their agricultural exports would be taxed. New Englanders with commercial and manufacturing interests also opposed export taxes. Southern delegates supported the Northerners' two proposals. Under the Commerce Compromise it was agreed that no export duties could be passed by Congress and that Congress could not prohibit the overseas slave trade for 20 years (1808). But the government could tax the slave trade because, in this case, slaves were classified as goods or property, not people. In 1808, Congress ended slave importation. The buying and selling of enslaved people within the United States, however, continued until the Civil War.

The controversial **Fugitive Slave Clause**, considered by some historians to be part of the Commerce Compromise, required all states to aid in the return of an enslaved person to his or her owner. The Northwest Ordinance of 1787 had prohibited slavery in that territory but included a fugitive slave law. In 1793 Congress passed a law to put the new Fugitive Slave Law into effect. The rights of states opposed to slavery and the procedure for the return of a fugitive slave were just two of the enforcement problems. In 1850 the reaction to a third Fugitive Slave Law moved the nation closer to civil war.

The Presidency or Electoral College Compromise The delegates agreed on the indirect election of the president through the Electoral College system to serve a renewable four-year term. Each state legislature would decide how its electors were chosen. This compromise settled a debate over how to balance the delegates' fear of an all-powerful and/or corrupt ruler versus the need for an executive to enforce the laws and conduct foreign policy. Election of the president by Congress was recognized as a danger to separation of powers. Direct election by the voters raised concerns of mob rule. Limited power, checks and balances, the desire to be reelected, and the threat of impeachment were seen as constitutional ways to control presidential overreach.

Major Compromises of the Constitutional Convention

Compromise	Issue	Solution
Connecticut Plan, or Great Compromise	Equal or proportionate representation in Congress: The larger states wanted representation based on population. The smaller states wanted equal representation.	With a bicameral legislature, a state would have equal representation in the Senate, while representation in the House would depend on a state's population.
Three-Fifths Compromise	Counting enslaved people within population to determine representation but not counting them when determining taxation	Three fifths of the enslaved people in a state would be counted for the purpose of determining both representation and taxation.
Commerce Compromise	Granting Congress the power to regulate foreign and interstate trade	Congress was forbidden to tax a state's exports or to take action against the overseas slave trade for 20 years (1808).
Presidency Compromise or the Electoral College Compromise	Length of president's term of office and method of election	President would serve a four-year term and be elected by the Electoral College rather than popular vote, or selection by Congress, or state legislatures.

Preparing for the Regents

Point of View

- What do the sections on slavery in the Constitution tell us about the Founders views on the topic?
- Are these compromises or an attempt to protect the institution of slavery?

Preparing for the Regents

Point of View

Analyze the chart on Major Compromises of the Constitutional Convention and determine

- Which groups stood in opposition to each other on the major issues at the Constitutional Convention?
- Why did they take their particular positions?
- How has each of the Constitutional compromises experienced change and/or continuity across time?

Signing the Constitution

After four months of debate in Philadelphia, delegates approved the Constitution of the United States. On September 17, 1787, thirty-nine of the delegates remaining in Philadelphia signed the Constitution. A few had left early due to business or family commitments or ill health. Several left early because they opposed the lack of a Bill of Rights or objected to other parts of the document. The fact that three of those who remained refused to sign it gave an indication of the coming debate. The three were **George Mason,** author of the Virginia Declaration of Rights, Elbridge Gerry of Massachusetts, and Edmund Randolph, the governor of Virginia.

The Great Debate and Ratification of the Constitution

In each state people took sides with the **Federalists,** who favored ratification, or the **Anti-Federalists,** who opposed it. In the views of historians today and political leaders then, ratification of the Constitution was very much in doubt. A majority vote of the population would most likely have been against it.

Both the Federalists and the Anti-Federalists included patriots from revolutionary days, ex-soldiers, men who had written the major governing documents of their states and nation, and those who had served in state and national governments. But among these men there was a deep division about the proper role of government, a division formed in part by how they viewed the Revolutionary era. One side trusted local and state governments and wanted a national government lacking the ability to exercise power. The other side attempted to create an effective but limited government with safeguards such as separation of powers and checks and balances so as to achieve a balance between stability and liberty.

Federalists tended to be wealthier, better educated, and more influential. Most lived along the coast and in cities. Seeking a sound economic foundation for the nation, craftsmen, artisans, and merchants tended to support the Federalists as did almost all of the nation's newspapers. Anti-Federalists included most but not all farmers, supporters of state governments, the lower working class, and debtors. Many lived in the less settled western and/or northern regions of each state.

The Federalists were nationalists in their thinking. These Founders, aware that ratification would meet with opposition from many states, carefully organized. They had already ensured in Article VII of the Constitution that only nine of the thirteen states must approve the Constitution for it to go into effect. Anti-Federalists thought this anti-republican, but the Federalists knew that Rhode Island was a "no" vote.

Article VII assured that approval of the Constitution would be done through special conventions called in each state rather than through the state legislatures. Federalists championed like-minded nationalists for election to each state's ratification convention. Their greatest concern was that the new nation would end in anarchy. Their most serious error was their failure to include a Bill of Rights in the Constitution.

Anti-Federalists wanted authority and sovereignty to remain with local and state governments. Their greatest fear was that the new nation would return to the tyranny and corruption of the colonial governments under Britain but this time under a too powerful federal government. Their most persuasive argument was that Constitution lacked a Bill of Rights.

The Great Debate About Ratification of the United States Constitution

The Federalist Arguments	The Anti-Federalist Arguments
Wanted a strong national government.	Wanted a weak national government.
Believed an effective national government was essential to provide order and protect the rights of the people.	Believed that a strong national government threatened the rights of the people and the powers of the states.
Wanted stronger national government than that of the Articles of Confederation. Saw need to write a new constitution.	Wanted to keep the Articles of Confederation or make only minor changes to strengthen it.
Wanted a central government with more power and states with less power. Believed that new bicameral Congress adequately represents the states' interests.	Wanted power to remain with local and state government in order to maintain government by the people.
Created an independent executive and judiciary to share power with the legislature.	Feared power of executive and judiciary, trusted only legislative branch controlled by consent of the governed.
Set terms of office longer than one year in order to provide a stable government.	Saw longer terms of office as a dangerous attempt to seize and control the government.
Believed a large republic was the best size for a nation to be able to protect individuals' rights and liberties.	Believed a small republic was the best size for a nation to be able to protect individuals' rights and liberties.
Wanted government capable of managing the nation's economic and financial policies and problems such as the large debt.	Believed states should control their own finances. Opposed taxation.
Feared mob rule and anarchy without a stronger government.	Feared loss of liberty and return to tyranny and corruption under the Constitution.
Feared power in a government but sought to control it through federalism, separation of powers, and checks and balances.	Saw themselves as representing the ideals of the Revolution. Feared power in government, especially large, distant one.
Claimed that a bill of rights was unnecessary because the new government's powers were limited by the Constitution.	Demanded a bill of rights be added to the Constitution to protect the people against abuses of power by the federal government.

. . . the smaller the number of individuals composing a majority, and the smaller the compass within which they are placed, the more easily will they concert and execute their plans of oppression. Extend the sphere, and you take in a greater variety of parties and interests; you make it less probable that a majority of the whole will have a common motive to invade the rights of other citizens. —James Madison, *The Federalist Papers*, No. 10, November 22, 1787	History furnishes no example of a free republic, any thing like the extent of the United States. The Grecian republics were of small extent; so also was that of the Romans. Both of these, it is true, in process of time, extended their conquests over large territories of country; and the consequence was, that their governments were changed from that of free governments to those of the most tyrannical that ever existed in the world. . . . In a republic of such vast extent as the United States, the legislature cannot attend to the various concerns and wants of its different parts. It cannot be sufficiently numerous to be acquainted with the local condition and wants of the different districts, and if it could, it is impossible it should have sufficient time to attend to and provide for all the variety of cases of this nature, that would be continually arising. —Robert Yates, *The Anti-Federalist Papers*, October 18, 1787

The major weakness in the Anti-Federalists arguments was the lack of a proposal for a government other than the discredited Articles of Confederation. For example, **Edmund Randolph,** one of three who would not sign the Constitution in Philadelphia, switched his vote in the Virginia convention. He explained, "The accession of eight states reduced our deliberations to the single question of Union or no Union."

The Federalist Papers were 85 essays written by James Madison, Alexander Hamilton and John Jay working together under the alias Publius to persuade delegates to vote for ratification. *The Anti-Federalist Papers*, written by independent and anonymous writers, never received the same amount of attention. North Carolina did not ratify the Constitution until 1789 and Rhode Island not until 1790. But the new government took office in 1789. Congress acted in response to concerns of the Anti-Federalists about the need for a **Bill of Rights** to be in the Constitution. James Madison prepared the first draft of these first ten amendments. By 1791 the states had ratified them.

Key Constitutional Principles in the U.S. Constitution

The Constitution of the United States includes important basic principles of our government, which are listed below.

Popular Sovereignty: The Sovereignty of the People

The Preamble states the principle of **popular sovereignty,** meaning that the source of all power or authority to govern is the people. *Popular* means "of or by the people." *Sovereignty* means "supreme power." In this way the Constitution creates a democracy, or government by the consent of the governed as stated in the Declaration of Independence.

Limited Government and the Rule of Law

Governmental powers are defined by the Constitution. In this way, our government is limited by law. The U.S. Constitution, as well as state constitutions, establishes a **limited government** by placing restrictions on the powers of state and national governments and on governmental officials as well. Under this principle of the **rule of law**, no person is considered above the law.

Federalism: The Division of Power Between Federal and State Government

The Constitution divides the power to govern between the states and the national government. This division of power between these two levels of government

Preparing for the Regents

Stimulus-Based Questions: Primary Sources

• Using the chart above, summarize the argument of each side on the proper size of a republic.

• What evidence supports your opinion?

Analyzing Documents

We the People of the United States . . . do ordain and establish this Constitution for the United States.

—Preamble to the U.S. Constitution

• According to the Preamble, who is creating this Constitution?

• In what other documents have we seen a concept that is restated here?

System of Federalism

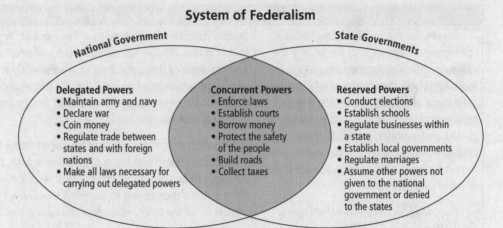

National Government   State Governments

Delegated Powers
- Maintain army and navy
- Declare war
- Coin money
- Regulate trade between states and with foreign nations
- Make all laws necessary for carrying out delegated powers

Concurrent Powers
- Enforce laws
- Establish courts
- Borrow money
- Protect the safety of the people
- Build roads
- Collect taxes

Reserved Powers
- Conduct elections
- Establish schools
- Regulate businesses within a state
- Establish local governments
- Regulate marriages
- Assume other powers not given to the national government or denied to the states

creates a federal system of government. Disputes between the national and state governments are settled by the courts, but the **Supremacy Clause** of Article VI of the Constitution makes the Constitution, federal laws, and treaties superior to state laws.

The principle of **federalism** is illustrated in the U.S. Constitution in the various powers allocated or not allocated to the states and the national government.

Delegated Powers Certain powers of the national government are spelled out in the Constitution. Most of these **delegated powers** are listed in Article I, Section 8. One example is the power of the national government to declare war.

Implied Powers Certain powers of the national government are not stated in writing. Their existence is implied by the elastic clause. One example of an **implied power** is the regulation of child labor; this power is implied by the delegated power to regulate interstate commerce.

Denied Powers Certain powers are denied to the national government, for example, the power to pass an export tax is a **denied power.** Other powers are denied to the states, for example, the power to print money. Still other powers are denied to both national and state governments. An example is the power to deny the right to vote because of race or sex, which was accomplished by the 15th and the 19th amendments.

Concurrent Powers Certain powers belong to both national and state governments. One example of such a **concurrent power** is the power to tax.

Reserved Powers The **reserved powers** are neither delegated to the national government nor denied to the states. One example is the power to make divorce laws.

The Separation of Powers Within the National Government

The Constitution establishes the **separation of powers,** meaning that power to govern is divided among the **legislative, executive,** and **judiciary branches** to ensure that no single branch can dominate the government. Each branch takes its power directly from the Constitution, not from another branch.

Checks and Balances

In addition to separation of powers among the three branches of government, the Constitution includes a system of **checks and balances**. Each branch of the national government has ways to check, or control, the other branches. This prevents one branch from gaining too much power. It helps to maintain the rule of law.

The Check and Balances System

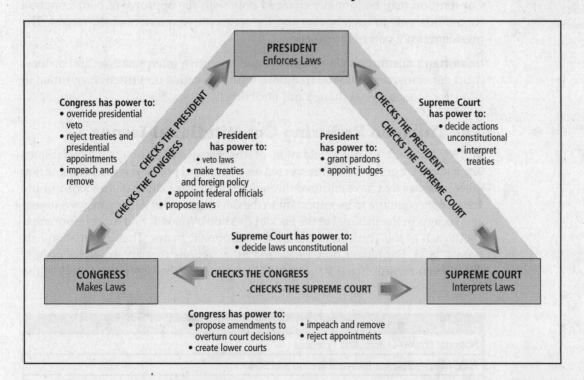

PRESIDENT
Enforces Laws

CHECKS THE PRESIDENT

CHECKS THE CONGRESS

CHECKS THE PRESIDENT

CHECKS THE SUPREME COURT

Congress has power to:
- override presidential veto
- reject treaties and presidential appointments
- impeach and remove

President has power to:
- veto laws
- make treaties and foreign policy
- appoint federal officials
- propose laws

President has power to:
- grant pardons
- appoint judges

Supreme Court has power to:
- decide actions unconstitutional
- interpret treaties

Supreme Court has power to:
- decide laws unconstitutional

CONGRESS
Makes Laws

CHECKS THE CONGRESS

CHECKS THE SUPREME COURT

SUPREME COURT
Interprets Laws

Congress has power to:
- propose amendments to overturn court decisions
- create lower courts
- impeach and remove
- reject appointments

In *The Federalist Papers* No. 51, James Madison addresses how federalism, separation of powers, checks and balances, and a large republic with more groups opposing each other work to prevent tyranny.

Ambition must be made to counteract ambition . . . If men were angels, no government would be necessary. If angels were to govern men, neither external nor internal controls on government would be necessary. In framing a government which is to be administered by men over men, the great difficulty lies in this: you must first enable the government to control the governed; and in the next place oblige it to control itself.

—James Madison, *The Federalist Papers* No. 51

Judicial Independence

The Constitution tries to make sure that the national judicial system is independent by removing judges from political influence. To ensure **judicial independence**, federal judges are appointed rather than elected and they serve for a lifetime. This process is another way the Constitution is designed to protect the rule of law. The Supreme Court and lower federal courts review cases that involve possible conflicts with the Constitution and federal laws. This means the courts have the power to interpret local, state, and federal laws, as well as executive actions and to decide if the law in question is constitutional.

Flexibility

The Constitution's flexibility allows it to meet changing conditions in three important ways.

The Elastic Clause Article I, Section 8, Clause 18, known as the **elastic clause**, states that Congress can make all laws "necessary and proper" for carrying out the tasks listed in the Constitution.

Analyzing Documents

- Based on this quote, what was James Madison's view of the relationship between human nature and good government?

- Anti-Federalists opposed ratification because the Constitution shifted the balance of power between the national and state governments. How would Madison respond to this concern?

The Amendment Process In keeping with the principle of federalism, the Constitution may be formally changed only with the approval of both Congress (two-thirds vote in each house) and the states (three-quarters of the states). The president is not part of the process.

Unwritten Constitution Congressional and executive interpretations and actions, court decisions, customs, and traditions form a so-called unwritten constitution to allow for constitutional change and flexibility.

The Thirteen Enduring Constitutional Issues

In 1987, as part of the celebration of the bicentennial of the United States Constitution, a group of well-respected historians and political scientists identified thirteen issues that have endured through the 200-year history of the Constitution. Today they continue to be important to the development of American government and society. In the material at the back of this book you will find more information about each of the Thirteen Enduring Constitutional Issues. That information lists events, laws, Supreme Court cases, and other actions that are examples of how the thirteen constitutional issues have been recurring themes in the history of the United States.

The Thirteen Enduring Constitutional Principles
National Power—Limits and Potential
Federalism—Balance Between Nation and State
The Judiciary—Interpreter of the Constitution or Shaper of Public Policy
Civil Liberties—Protecting Individual Liberties from Government Abuses; the Balance Between Government and the Individual
Criminal Procedures—The Balance Between the Rights of the Accused and the Protection of the Community and Victims
Equality—Its Historic and Present Meaning as a Constitutional Value
The Rights of Women Under the Constitution
The Rights of Ethnic and Racial Minority Groups Under the Constitution
Presidential Power in Wartime and in Foreign Affairs
The Separation of Powers and the Effectiveness of Government
Avenues of Representation
Property Rights and Economic Policy
Constitutional Change and Flexibility

The Structure, Power, and Functions of the Federal Government

The United States Constitution is a fundamental plan, or framework, clearly defining and limiting the powers of government.

Preamble to the Constitution

In the **Preamble,** or introduction, to the Constitution, the Framers defined their reasons for writing the document:

- To create a better, stronger national government
- To ensure a system of justice
- To provide for peace at home

- To provide for the defense of the nation
- To promote the well-being of the people
- To secure liberty to the people and to future generations

The first three articles that follow the Preamble describe and define the powers of the legislative, executive, and judicial branches of the national government. These articles detail the separation of powers, while showing how each branch can check and balance the others.

Federal Officeholders

Office	Number	Term	Selection	Requirements
Representative	at least 1 per state; based on state population	2 years	elected by voters of congressional district	• age 25 or over • citizen for 7 years • resident of state in which elected
Senator	2 per state	6 years	original Constitution-elected by state legislature Amendment 17-elected by voters	• age 30 or over • citizen for 9 years • resident of state in which elected
President and Vice President	1	4 years	elected by Electoral College	• age 35 or over • natural-born citizen • resident of U.S. for 14 years
Supreme Court Justice	9	Life	appointed by president with approval of the Senate	• no requirements in Constitution

Preparing for the Regents

Stimulus-Based Questions: Chart

Some questions in the exam will require you to read and interpret charts. Use data from the chart on Federal Officeholders to answer the questions below.

- Why do the terms of Supreme Court justices and federal judges differ from those of other federal officeholders?

- In the original Constitution which officials were selected in the most democratic manner?

Article I: The Legislative Branch

Article I establishes the United States Congress with its two houses—the Senate and the House of Representatives. Congress is the legislative, or lawmaking, branch of government. Article I gives the qualifications for election to Congress, the rights and privileges of members of Congress, and some basic operating procedures of both houses. Article I also lists the powers delegated to Congress. These include the **"necessary and proper,"** or **elastic clause**, which enables the government to adapt to changing times. Each house of Congress also has special duties that it alone can perform.

Article I briefly outlines how a bill becomes a federal law. The complex process requires the approval of each house and of the president. A presidential **veto,** or rejection, of a bill can be overridden by a two-thirds vote of each house.

Special Powers of the House and Senate

House	Senate
• To select the president if no candidate receives a majority of the electoral vote with each state casting one vote	• To select the vice president if no candidate has a majority of the electoral vote with each senator casting one vote
• To bring impeachment charges by majority vote	• To act as jury in cases of impeachment with two-thirds vote needed for conviction
• To originate all revenue (money) bills	• To ratify treaties (by a two-thirds vote)
	• To approve presidential appointments, including Supreme Court justices and federal judges (by a majority vote)

Due to its size, debate in the House is limited. The Senate usually permits unlimited debate on a bill. At times, a minority of senators **filibuster,** or keep talking, in an attempt to force a Senate majority to amend or even drop a bill. On major bills in the Senate, **cloture,** meaning the votes of sixty senators, is required to end a filibuster or a filibuster threat and force a vote on a bill. Senate rules changed in 2013 and 2017 to allow approval of executive nominations, including all federal judges and United States Supreme Court justices, by a simple majority vote.

Article II: The Executive Branch

Article II outlines the workings of the executive branch, beginning with the method of electing the president and vice president and including the powers and duties of the office. The framers made the the legislature the subject of Article I of the Constitution because they saw it as the most important government branch. However, in the 20th and 21st centuries the United States presidency has become the most powerful position not only in our government but in the world.

Electing the President A key compromise at the Constitutional Convention created the Electoral College system, an indirect method of electing the president and vice president. The presidency has been amended by the Twelfth, Twentieth, Twenty-second, Twenty-third, and Twenty-fifth Amendments. Today the voters, not the state legislatures, select the electors but the Electoral College process remains fundamentally the same.

While only the names of the presidential candidates are on the ballot, voters are selecting the group of electors who will vote for the candidate that the voter supports. The group of electors representing the winner of each state's popular vote then casts that state's electoral votes for president and vice president. The candidate with a majority (270 of 538) of the electoral votes nationally becomes the president.

Each state has as many presidential electors as it has senators (2 per state = 100) plus representatives. In 1929 the number of representatives in the House was set at 435. The number of seats per state is reallocated or reset after each census. The 23rd Amendment gave 3 electoral votes to Washington, D.C. bringing the total number of electoral votes to 538 of which 270 is a majority.

The Constitution requires that a **census,** or counting of the population, be taken every ten years. Changes to reflect shifts in population are then made in the number of representatives per state, which in turn affects the electoral vote. Census data is also used to make decisions about other national needs.

Presidential Roles and Powers Article II describes the powers and duties of the president of the United States. In carrying out the duties of office, the president fills several different roles including:

- **Chief Executive** The president has the power to enforce or put laws into effect, administer the huge federal bureaucracy, issue executive orders that have the effect of laws, appoint judges, diplomats, and other high government officials, some with Senate approval and others without, and remove appointed government officials within the executive branch.

- **Chief Diplomat** The president has the power to make treaties with the advice and consent of the Senate, make executive agreements with nations without Senate approval, and extend or withdraw diplomatic recognition to a nation.

- **Commander in Chief** The president has broad military powers that are shared with Congress. In times of war, these powers are even stronger.

Social Studies Practices
Cause and Effect

The U.S. Constitution requires that a census of the population be taken every 10 years. The census is used to determine how many representatives each state will send to the House.

- What impact does the census have on the Electoral College?

- How have the 2020 census results affected each of the following states in the House of Representatives and in the Electoral College? Texas, Florida, Colorado California, New York, West Virginia

- What is the pattern of these population shifts?

- What are the major causes of this changing population pattern?

- **Chief Legislator** The president has the power to recommend legislation to Congress and to veto potential laws.
- **Chief of State** In addition to being head of the government, the president is also chief of state, the ceremonial head of government, and the symbolic leader of all the people of the nation.
- **Judicial Powers** The president can grant reprieves, pardons, and amnesties to individuals in cases of federal crimes.
- **Head of the Party** The president is also the leader of the political party in power. The duties of this role are not mentioned in the Constitution because the party system developed through custom, making it part of the unwritten constitution.

Growth of Presidential Power Power in the executive branch is centered in one individual making the president the single focus of attention while allowing him/her to act swiftly in times of war and national crisis. Presidential domination in foreign affairs, command of the huge executive branch of the government, and the ability to promote the power of the office using modern communication methods to influence public opinion help to explain the power of the presidency.

The Vice Presidency The Constitution assigns two roles to the vice president of the United States: to become president upon the death, assassination, or resignation of the president and to serve as the president of the Senate voting only to break a tie vote. Constitutional amendments Twelve, Twenty, Twenty-two and Twenty-five affect the vice presidency. For example, the Twenty-Fifth Amendment details how to fill a vice-presidential vacancy. Fifteen vice presidents have become president.

The Federal Bureaucracy consists of the administrative agencies and staff that put the decisions or policies of the government into effect. Such a bureaucracy has developed through legislation, executive action, and custom.

Article III: The Judicial Branch

Article III of the Constitution creates the Supreme Court and gives Congress the power to create lower federal courts. The role of this judicial branch is to interpret the law. In addition to this national court system, each of the 50 states has its own court system.

Jurisdiction With two court systems—federal and state—the Constitution had to define the **jurisdiction,** or authority, of the federal courts in order to make clear which cases go to federal courts and which to state courts. A federal court has the authority to hear cases involving federal laws, treaties, maritime law, and interpretation of the Constitution. Federal courts also have jurisdiction if cases involve certain parties or participants, such as a state or a foreign government.

The Constitution states that in some types of cases, the Supreme Court will have original jurisdiction. This means the Supreme Court will hear the case first and make a decision. In most cases, the Supreme Court has appellate jurisdiction. This means that, in a lower court, if the losing side believes a judge made a mistake in applying the law in a case, that case may be appealed to a higher court. A Supreme Court decision is usually issued after both sides present their cases in person, justices confer, and issue a signed decision that includes their legal explanations. In recent years the Court has issued more "emergency orders." Critics object to these unsigned and often unexplained decisions when they deal with issues of national concern such as Covid restrictions or climate change.

Analyzing Documents
Impeachment

"The President, Vice President and all Civil Officers of the United States, shall be removed from Office on Impeachment for, and Conviction of, Treason, Bribery, or other high Crimes and Misdemeanors."

— **U.S. Constitution, Article II, Section 4**

- **What is the punishment if a civil officer is found guilty of Impeachment?**
- **What role does Congress have in Impeachment?**

Judicial Review The most important power of the federal courts is the right of **judicial review.** This power enables the courts to hear cases involving the application and interpretation of law and to declare state laws and acts of Congress and of the executive branch unconstitutional and void if judged not in keeping with the Constitution's intent. The Supreme Court is the final voice in interpreting the Constitution. The right of judicial review strengthened the judiciary against the other two branches of government. Chief Justice John Marshall first applied the doctrine of judicial review in *Marbury* v. *Madison* **(1803)**, voiding parts of the 1789 Judiciary Act.

Articles IV through VII

Article IV: Federalism Federalism is expressed in this Article's guarantee to each state of a republican form of government and protection against invasion and domestic violence.

Social Studies Practices
Using Evidence

• The process of amending the Constitution is an excellent example of federalism in practice. Why?

Article V: Amending the Constitution Article V describes methods of amending, or formally changing, the Constitution. The purpose of an amendment process is to ensure that the government meets the nation's changing needs. In accordance with the principle of federalism, both national and state governments are involved in the amendment process. In the most common method of **amendment,** Congress approves a proposed amendment by a two-thirds vote in each house. The amendment then goes to the state legislatures. If three quarters of them ratify it, the amendment becomes part of the Constitution. Twenty-six of the constitutional amendments have been adopted by this method. To date, only the Twenty-first Amendment has been ratified by special conventions called in the states.

Article VI: Supreme Law of the Land This Article states that the Constitution, the laws of the United States, and all treaties made under the authority of the United States are considered to be the "supreme Law of the Land."

Article VII: Ratification The new Constitution must first be approved, or ratified, by conventions of nine of the states.

The Formal Amendment Process (Four Methods)

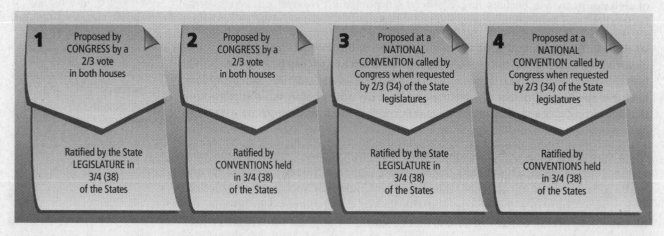

1 Proposed by CONGRESS by a 2/3 vote in both houses	2 Proposed by CONGRESS by a 2/3 vote in both houses	3 Proposed at a NATIONAL CONVENTION called by Congress when requested by 2/3 (34) of the State legislatures	4 Proposed at a NATIONAL CONVENTION called by Congress when requested by 2/3 (34) of the State legislatures
Ratified by the State LEGISLATURE in 3/4 (38) of the States	Ratified by CONVENTIONS held in 3/4 (38) of the States	Ratified by the State LEGISLATURE in 3/4 (38) of the States	Ratified by CONVENTIONS held in 3/4 (38) of the States

It has been several times truly remarked, that bills of rights are, in their origin, stipulations between kings and their subjects. . . . Such was Magna Carta, obtained by the Barons, sword in hand, from King John . . . It is evident, therefore, that according to their primitive signification, they have no application to constitutions professedly founded upon the power of the people, and executed by their immediate representatives and servants. Here, in strictness, the people surrender nothing, and as they retain every thing, they have no need of particular reservations. . . .

On the subject of the liberty of the press, as much as has been said, I cannot forbear adding a remark or two: in the first place, I observe, that there is not a syllable concerning it in the constitution of this State; in the next, I contend, that whatever has been said about it in that of any other State, amounts to nothing. What signifies a declaration, that "the liberty of the press shall be inviolably preserved"? What is the liberty of the press? Who can give it any definition which would not leave the utmost latitude for evasion? I hold it to be impracticable; and from this I infer, that its security, whatever fine declarations may be inserted in any constitution respecting it, must altogether depend on public opinion, and on the general spirit of the people and of the government. And here, after all, as is intimated upon another occasion, must we seek for the only solid basis of all our rights.

—Alexander Hamilton, *The Federalist Papers,* No. 84, July 16–August 9, 1788

Here is a revolution as radical as that which separated us from Great Britain. It is radical in this transition; our rights and privileges are endangered, and the sovereignty of the states will be relinquished: And cannot we plainly see that this is actually the case? The rights of conscience, trial by jury, liberty of the press, all your immunities and franchises, all pretensions to human rights and privileges, are rendered insecure, if not lost, by this change, so loudly talked of by some, and inconsiderately by others….You are not to inquire how your trade may be increased, nor how you are to become a great and powerful people, but how your liberties can be secured; for liberty ought to be the direct end of your Government.

—Patrick Henry, speech, June 5, 1788

The Bill of Rights

The **Bill of Rights** is the name given to the first ten amendments to the Constitution adopted in 1791. Five states ratified the Constitution with recommendations that included the addition of specific protections of rights and liberties. In the months of debate many Federalists had come to support the proposal on which Anti-Federalists had insisted.

Originally these ten amendments guaranteed certain basic or fundamental rights of the people against the power of the federal government. James Madison wrote the Bill of Rights working with over 200 recommendations for amendments. Because the Constitution had been ratified, Madison dismissed any proposals that would alter the structure of the government under the Constitution. Instead, he concentrated on protecting individual rights from the federal government. Madison consulted George Mason's Virginia Declaration of Rights approved by Virginia in 1776. Beliefs and rights expressed in English documents such as the Magna Carta, the Petition of Right, the English Bill of Rights, are also reflected in the United States Bill of Rights.

Extending Constitutional Protections of the Bill of Rights

In the more than 200 years since the Bill of Rights was added to the Constitution, the civil and political rights of the people have been expanded by court decisions, additional amendments, and even by presidential actions. The **Fourteenth Amendment,** added to the Constitution in 1868, contains the **equal protection**

Preparing for the Regents

Stimulus-Based Questions: Primary Sources

- Using the chart, summarize the argument of each side on the protection of individual rights.

- What evidence supports your opinion?

The Bill of Rights

Amendment	Subject
1st	Guarantees freedom of religion, of speech, and of the press; the right to assemble peacefully; and the right to petition the government.
2nd	Protects the right to possess firearms.
3rd	Declares that the government may not require people to house soldiers during peacetime.
4th	Protects people from unreasonable searches and seizures.
5th	Includes protection against self incrimination and double jeopardy; guarantees due process of law.
6th	Guarantees the right to a speedy, public trial, to confront witnesses, and to legal counsel.
7th	Guarantees the right to trial by jury in most civil cases.
8th	Prohibits excessive bail, fines, and "cruel and unusual" punishments.
9th	Declares that rights not mentioned in the Constitution belong to the people.
10th	Declares that powers not given to the national government belong to the states or to the people.

Analyzing Documents

"I may detest what you say, but will defend to the death your right to say it."

—Voltaire

• What basic civil liberty is Voltaire defending?

clause and the **due process clause.** Supreme Court interpretations have held that through these clauses the Fourteenth Amendment extends the protections of most of the Bill of Rights against state and local governments as well as the national government. The due process clause is the only clause that is in the Constitution more than once. It is a right named in both the Fifth and Fourteenth amendments.

The courts have held that civil rights (as defined in the Bill of Rights and other amendments) are relative, not absolute. The courts have thus tried to balance an individual's rights against the rights of society and other individuals. In recent years, Bill of Rights issues such as privacy versus national security have been debated. Sometimes basic civil rights conflict with each other. For example, the Sixth Amendment right of the accused to confront witnesses might clash with a reporter's First Amendment, the right of freedom of the press to protect news sources. In such conflicts, the courts often must decide the issue. Below and in the Landmark Supreme Court Cases listed at the end of this book, you will find information about legal interpretations of the Bill of Rights.

• *Schenck* v. *United States* (1919), 1st Amendment, "clear and present danger"
• *Gideon* v. *Wainwright* (1963), 6th Amendment, right to a lawyer
• *New York Times* v. *Sullivan* (1964), 1st Amendment, freedom of the press, libel
• *Tinker* v. *Des Moines* (1969), 1st Amendment, freedom of speech, students

Additional Constitutional Amendments

Between 1795 and 1992, an additional 17 amendments have been added to the Constitution. Note that the Thirteenth, Fourteenth, and Fifteenth amendments were passed after the Civil War to prohibit slavery and to define citizenship and guarantee it and the right to vote to the formerly enslaved. However, the right to vote applied only to African American men. It took women over fifty years more (1920) to secure the right to vote. Five amendments—the Fifteenth, Nineteenth, Twenty-third, Twenty-fourth and Twenty-sixth—have expanded the right to vote.

Amendments 11–27

Amendment	Year Ratified	Subject
11th	1795	Grants states immunity from certain lawsuits
12th	1804	Separates voting for president and vice president
13th	1865	Abolishes slavery
14th	1868	Defines citizenship; prohibits states from denying people due process and equal protection of the law
15th	1870	Grants voting rights for African American men
16th	1913	Gives Congress power to tax incomes
17th	1913	Requires election of U.S. Senators by people of a state, not the state legislature
18th	1919	Prohibits manufacture, sale, and transportation of alcoholic beverages
19th	1920	Grants voting rights for women
20th	1933	Shortens amount of time between election of a president and of Congress and start of their term of office
21st	1933	Repeals Eighteenth Amendment
22nd	1951	Limits president to two terms
23rd	1961	Grants electoral votes and right to vote in presidential elections for the District of Columbia
24th	1964	Abolishes poll taxes as qualification for voting in federal elections
25th	1967	Sets procedure for determining presidential disability and succession, and for filling a vice-presidential vacancy
26th	1971	Lowers voting age to 18
27th	1992	Bans mid-term congressional pay raises

Extending the Right to Vote

Year	People Allowed to Vote
1789	White men over age 21 who meet property requirements (state laws)
Early 1800s–1850s	All white men over age 21 (state laws)
1870	African American men (15th Amendment)
1920	Women (19th Amendment)
1961	Citizens in the District of Columbia in presidential elections (23rd Amendment)
1964	Citizens previously denied right to vote because they could not afford to pay a tax (24th Amendment)
1971	Citizens age 18 or over (26th Amendment)

Preparing for the Regents

Stimulus-Based Question: Chart

- Based on the chart what has been the most common way of extending the right to vote to more people?

New York State Government Compared to the Federal Government

The government of New York has many similarities to the federal government. New York has a constitution and a Bill of Rights. The New York government has three branches. The executive branch is headed by the governor. The bicameral legislature has a Senate and an Assembly. The highest court in the judicial branch is the Court of Appeals.

National Security and Political Stability Under the U.S. Constitution

Key Concept

11.2d Under the new Constitution, the young nation sought to achieve national security and political stability, as the three branches of government established their relationships with each other and the states.

Lesson Overview

The new nation under the leadership of George Washington began the challenge of creating a federal republic. The three branches of government implemented their powers under the Constitution while creating an unwritten Constitution through interpretation, traditions, and customs. Presidential actions and precedents established by George Washington are part of an unwritten constitution that guides the United States government today. Washington was a nationalist who supported Alexander Hamilton's economic plan. The debate surrounding the plan and its impacts led to the development of political parties, the Federalists and the Democratic-Republicans.

The three branches of government worked to establish their relationships with each other and the states. Congress passed laws to create a national judiciary and executive offices such as the Department of State. Congressional and judicial practices are also a part of the unwritten constitution. Under the leadership of Chief Justice John Marshall, the judicial branch strengthened the powers of the federal government and the power of the Court in several landmark Supreme Court cases.

A tradition of a peaceful transfer of power began with the presidential election of 1800 and continues today as seen in the presidential election of 2000. Other branches had roles in these elections, namely, the Electoral College and Congress in 1800 and the Electoral College and the Supreme Court in 2000.

Unifying Themes

As you review this lesson take special note of the following themes:

- **Time, Continuity, and Change** What are the similarities and the differences in the issues facing the Founders in 1776, 1787, and 1789?

- **Power, Authority, and Governance** How did the new nation go about putting its constitution into effect? What conflicting opinions about government were discussed and debated in those early years?

- **Creation, Expansion, and Interaction of Economic Systems** What is the role of government in the economy according to Hamilton? to Jefferson?

Key People

George Washington   John Marshall
Alexander Hamilton

Key Terms and Events

cabinet	Twenty-second	judicial restraint
"necessary and proper"	Amendment	third parties
clause	neutrality	election of 1800
elastic clause	Farewell Address	Twelfth Amendment
strict constructionists	Judiciary Act of 1789	election of 2000
loose constructionists	judicial review	Electoral College
Whiskey Rebellion	judicial activism	

Key Supreme Court Cases

As you review this lesson be sure you understand the significance of these key Supreme Court cases:

Marbury v. *Madison* (1803)
McCulloch v. *Maryland* (1819)
Gibbons v. *Ogden* (1824)
Bush v. *Gore* (2000)
Citizens United v. *FEC* (2010)

Shaping Government Under the Constitution

The United States Constitution was implemented, or put into effect, on April 30, 1789 in New York City, when our first president, **George Washington,** took office. Washington, the only president elected unanimously by the Electoral College, led the first presidential administration for two terms, leaving office on March 4, 1797. John Adams was our first vice president and second president.

Our leaders first needed to

- create economic stability through a sound financial foundation for the new nation.
- establish a solid political system to ensure political stability.
- provide national security through foreign policy decisions.

Not all the actions that shaped our government in its early years grew directly out of the plan set down in the Constitution. From the time of our first president an unwritten constitution developed in response to changing times and circumstances. This unwritten constitution resulted from a combination of:

- executive interpretations and actions.
- congressional interpretations and actions.
- court decisions, especially judicial review.
- customs and traditions.
- the actions of political parties.

First Years of the New Government, 1789–1820

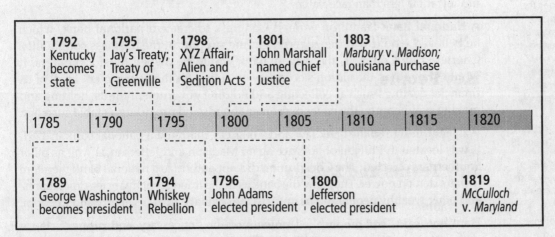

1792 Kentucky becomes state	**1795** Jay's Treaty; Treaty of Greenville	**1798** XYZ Affair; Alien and Sedition Acts	**1801** John Marshall named Chief Justice	**1803** *Marbury* v. *Madison;* Louisiana Purchase

1785	1790	1795	1800	1805	1810	1815	1820

1789 George Washington becomes president	**1794** Whiskey Rebellion	**1796** John Adams elected president	**1800** Jefferson elected president	**1819** *McCulloch* v. *Maryland*

Executive Interpretation, Action, and Custom

Under President Washington's leadership, the executive branch developed processes and procedures. It also set precedents followed by future presidents.

Political Stability: Executive Decision-Making

When developing policy, presidents follow several precedents started by George Washington. They are considered part of the **unwritten constitution**. For example, they seek advice from the heads of the executive departments who are called the president's cabinet. Appointed with Senate approval, cabinet members can be fired without it. Today, the White House staff plays a major role in the presidential advisory process. President Washington also issued executive orders and claimed executive privilege, powers not specifically named in the Constitution.

The early presidents also consulted with congressional leaders when developing policies. Such **"advise and consent"** consultation is an informal procedure. Today, the Senate's official role often seems more "to consent" than "to advise" on presidential decisions. This method of advising the president has become custom.

Economic Stability: Developing a Financial Plan

With Washington's confidence and support, **Alexander Hamilton,** the first secretary of the treasury, set out to put the government on a sound economic footing. Hamilton's financial plan included four key elements:

Funding and Assumption Hamilton wanted the national government to pay off American Revolution war debts run up by the Continental Congress as well as the wartime debts of the states. In this **assumption plan,** payment would be made at full face values even though some of the debt was in near worthless paper money. New bonds that paid interest would be issued to cover the cost of the assumption plan. Hamilton believed that this assumption of debt would establish the credit of the nation while building public respect for the government. By buying the bonds, citizens would become personally invested and involved in the success of the new nation.

Congress approved this plan over objections from James Madison and Thomas Jefferson. They argued that the assumption plan would financially reward states that had not paid their war debt and speculators who had bought up the paper money at far less than face value.

A National Bank Hamilton wanted Congress to create a **national bank,** which he believed would win the government the support of the business community. Chartered by Congress, the private bank would be owned by stockholders. It would strengthen the nation's economy by acting for the government in all of its financial dealings such as collecting and holding government funds, holding and making payments on the new government bonds and providing a stable currency.

Washington signed the bank law and Congress chartered a national bank in 1791. It was located in Philadelphia. Once again Madison and Jefferson as well as other Southerners objected. The Constitution did not authorize a national bank therefore it was a denied power. They saw the bank as in the interests of financiers, merchants, and other wealthy people and harmful to the ordinary citizen's liberty and freedom.

Hamilton said that the implied powers of the **"necessary and proper" clause** authorized creating a national bank. The Constitution gave Congress financial powers including collecting taxes, duties, and excises, coining and borrowing money, and paying debts. The "necessary and proper clause," also called the **elastic clause,** gave Congress the power to create a bank in order to implement (carry out) its financial powers.

Alexander Hamilton

Thomas Jefferson

Analyzing Documents

[The Congress shall have the power] to make all laws which shall be necessary and proper for carrying into execution the foregoing powers, and all other powers vested by this Constitution in the government of the United States, or in any department or officer thereof.

—U.S. Constitution, Article I, Section 8, Clause 18

- Was Hamilton justified in using the "necessary and proper" clause to create a national bank?

- How does the Supreme Court decision on the bank explain why it supported Hamilton's argument?

The lines between the Jeffersonian strict constructionists and the Hamiltonian loose constructionists had been drawn. **Strict constructionists** favor a narrow interpretation of the Constitution, holding that government can do only those things the document specifically spells out. **Loose constructionists** favor a broader reading of the Constitution so that the government is more able to respond as the nation grows and circumstances change.

An Excise Tax Hamilton proposed that the government raise operating revenues through an **excise tax** on whiskey.

Protective Tariff Hamilton called for a **protective tariff** to shield products of the nation's infant industries from foreign competition. Hamilton believed the future of the United States was as an economy based on manufacturing. The objections came mainly from the South, the most agricultural region with the least to gain from manufacturing. Congress rejected the protective tariff but passed other tariffs to generate income for the government.

The Hamilton plan raised controversy, but it put the new nation on a sound financial footing. It also encouraged the wealthy to support the government and built a solid foundation for the nation's future as an industrial power. Congressional passage of the Financial Plan was the result of an understanding between Jefferson and Hamilton. Southerners would vote for the Plan if northerners would agree to the location of the nation's permanent capital on the Potomac River between Virginia and Maryland.

The Whiskey Rebellion

In 1794, western Pennsylvania farmers refused to pay an excise tax on the whiskey they made from grain. Washington called out state militias and put down this **"Whiskey Rebellion."** There is debate today over how serious a threat this rebellion really was, but Washington's actions demonstrated that the new government intended to enforce federal law—the supreme law of the land.

The Two-Term Presidency

Washington rejected a third term as president. In doing so, he established a tradition that was not broken until 1940 and 1944, when Franklin D. Roosevelt won a third and then a fourth term. Unhappiness over Roosevelt's break with tradition led to the passage of the **Twenty-second Amendment** that limits a president to two terms or no more than ten years in office.

Washington's Foreign Policy

From 1789 to 1815, the French Revolution and the European wars that grew out of it put many pressures on the young nation. President Washington believed that the safest policy for the United States as a new nation was **neutrality.**

Washington's **Farewell Address** in 1796 is considered one of this nation's founding documents. It was the work first of James Madison and later Alexander Hamilton. Washington wrote the final draft. President Washington:

- warned of the danger of permanent alliances with other nations. He recommended a foreign policy of neutrality, and "friendly" commercial relations: *Observe good faith and justice towards all nations; cultivate peace and harmony with all.*

- praised the benefits of the new government and the importance of unity to preserve liberty: *Your union ought to be considered as a main prop of your liberty, and . . . the love of the one ought to endear to you the preservation of the other.*

- Expressed concern that geographical or regional differences would lead to the formation of political factions and political parties: *The name of American . . . must*

Unifying Themes
Governance

- What impact did Franklin D. Roosevelt's decision to run for a third and fourth term eventually have on the U.S. Constitution?

Analyzing Documents

It is our true policy to steer clear of permanent alliances with any portion of the foreign world. . . .

—Washington's Farewell Address, September 17, 1796

- Why did Washington make this foreign policy?

- How did geography make it possible for the United States to follow Washington's policy for over a hundred years?

always exalt the just pride of patriotism more than any appellation [name] derived from local discriminations.

- Considered political parties a danger to the nation: *However [political parties] may now and then answer popular ends, they are likely. . . to become potent engines, by which cunning, ambitious, and unprincipled men will be enabled to subvert the power of the people and to usurp for themselves the reins of government, destroying afterwards the very engines which have lifted them to unjust dominion.*

Congressional Interpretation, Action, and Custom

The executive branch was not alone in establishing the new government. During these early years, the legislative branch began to create its policies and procedures under the Constitution.

Creating Structures of Government

The Constitution supplied few details of how the machinery of government would operate, so early congressional actions helped set up that machinery. For example, the Constitution established only a Supreme Court. Congress, therefore, passed the **Judiciary Act of 1789,** creating the rest of the federal court system. Congress also created the first five executive departments—State, Treasury, War (Defense), Attorney General (Justice), and Postmaster General. Today, there are 15 departments and more than 200 independent agencies.

In 1789, Congress began the custom of assigning bills to committees. This developed into today's **committee system**, in which standing committees review all bills before sending them on to the full House or Senate. Congressional committees can also operate as investigative committees, gathering information in order to determine the need for new laws or to examine how current laws are working.

Lobbying

Custom has led to **lobbying** by people representing special-interest groups who act to influence legislation and elect people who support the lobby group's views. Lobbying is protected by the First Amendment's right to petition but also regulated by federal law. The National Rifle Association and the National Association of Realtors are two examples of over 4,600 political action committees **(PACs)** funded by lobby groups to seek access and influence.

Judicial Interpretation of the Constitution

Under Chief Justice **John Marshall** (1801–1835), a series of Supreme Court decisions strengthened the power of the national government and the authority of the judicial branch of government.

The John Marshall Court

First, and most critically, Marshall led the Court in the 1803 decision in *Marbury v. Madison.* This decision established the Court's most significant right—that of **judicial review,** the power to rule on the constitutionality of a law.

The decision in *McCulloch v. Maryland,* in 1819, upheld the creation of a national bank. The decision strengthened federal supremacy over state law, the use of the elastic clause, and national economic interests.

Similarly, in 1824, the Marshall Court verdict in *Gibbons v. Ogden* expanded the powers of the national government in the area of commerce through a broad interpretation of the congressional power to regulate interstate commerce (Article I, Section 8).

Preparing for the Regents

- What types of PACs are involved in election campaigns and what methods do they use to elect their candidates?
- How does federal law attempt to limit PACs?
- How has the Supreme Court decision in *Citizens United v. FEC* affected presidential election campaigns?

Social Studies Practices
Cause and Effect

Supreme Court decisions have affected the separation of powers in the federal system.

- How did *Marbury v. Madison* (1803) affect the separation of powers?

Activism vs. Restraint and the Supreme Court

In our history, the Court has been activist and restrained, irrespective of whether the Court was considered conservative or liberal. The Court has also been influenced by changes in the nation's social and political climate. Those favoring **judicial activism** believe the Court should use this power to help make public policy. Those favoring **judicial restraint** believe that this power should be used only when there is an obvious violation of a particular clause of the Constitution, opposing a policy-making role for the Court.

Actions of Political Parties

Political parties developed through custom and tradition. The debate between Federalists and Anti-Federalists over ratification revealed the existence of differences of opinion on government. Divisions deepened in Washington's administration and exploded under President John Adams. These differences led to the formation of the first two political parties—the **Federalists** and the **Democratic-Republicans,** also known as the Republicans.

The formation of political parties has led to constitutional changes in the method of electing the president. Party politics also gave rise to nominating conventions and the pledging of electoral votes to a presidential candidate. Today, due to the trend toward state primaries, the presidential candidate has usually been selected before the delegates attend the nominating convention. In the first half of the 1800s, many more men had the right to vote, and the campaign techniques and organization of political parties changed to appeal to this broader electorate.

While major political parties have changed infrequently, the nation has seen many influential **third parties.** Such parties have offered criticisms and suggested reforms later adopted by the major parties when in power.

The First Political Parties

Federalists	Democratic-Republicans
1. Led by Alexander Hamilton, John Adams	1. Led by Thomas Jefferson, James Madison
2. Wealthy and well-educated should lead nation	2. Believed people should hold the political power
3. Believed in strong federal government	3. Believed in smaller government and strong states' rights
4. Favored order and unity	4. Favored individual rights
5. Favored economy based on manufacturing, shipping, and trade	5. Favored economy based on agriculture
6. Favored loose interpretation of Constitution	6. Favored strict interpretation of Constitution
7. Were pro-British, but pro-neutrality	7. Pro-French, but pro-neutrality
8. Favored national bank	8. Opposed national bank
9. Favored protective tariff	9. Opposed protective tariff

Today, political parties play a major role in elections at the local, state, and national levels. The presidential election is considered the most important contest. The party works with the nominee's campaign committee to raise money, monitor the campaign using polls, and in general promote the election of the party candidate. The chart, The Path to the Presidency, on the next page traces today's presidential election process.

Unifying Themes
Power

- In *McCulloch* v. *Maryland* (1819), the Court rejected the right of Maryland to tax the national bank. Chief Justice Marshall wrote, "The power to tax is the power to destroy." What did he mean?

Preparing for the Regents

Stimulus-Based Question: Secondary Sources

- Use the text and the chart, "The Path to the Presidency," to determine what steps to the presidency are part of the Constitution and which have developed from custom.

The Path to the Presidency

First Step in a Presidential Campaign: Announcing Intention to Run

- Announces candidacy in person, or via television, video, phone call, or social media over a year before election.

The Campaign for Delegates Begins

- Today the permanent campaign is part of U.S. presidential politics, raising concern that the line between a president campaigning and governing is now blurred. Aiming to win state party delegates to the national nominating convention, the pace and intensity of endless campaigning expands to include multiple intra-party primary debates, over 50 primaries and caucuses, and the search for even more donations.
- Most states now hold primary elections to select some or all of each party's delegates but in the 2020 election four states still held caucuses. Population and party loyalty in previous elections determine the number of delegates allotted to each state. Many states want a "frontloaded" primary schedule. By voting early a state has more influence in the selection of the candidate. Again in 2020 party rules allowed only four states to hold February primaries while 14 states held their primaries on Super Tuesday, the first Tuesday in March.

Raising Money for the Primaries and General Election

- In 5 of the last 6 presidential elections the candidate spending the most money has won. The 2020 presidential election was the most expensive in U.S. history costing about 5.7 billion dollars, more than double the 2.4 billion dollars spent in 2016. Donations from small donors (gave $200 or less) online soared as did those from millionaires and billionaires.
- In 2010, *Citizens United* v. *FEC* ruled that the 1st Amendment allowed corporations, unions, and individuals (Also see *Buckley* v. *Valeo*; also *SpeechNOW.org* v. *FEC*) to spend unlimited amounts of money on candidates if these "independent expenditures" do not go directly to and are not coordinated with the candidate or political party. Super PACs formed that were required to disclose donors and finances to FEC. Other Super PACS were created as nonprofit "social welfare" organizations not "primarily engaged" in election activity and exempt from naming their so-called "dark money" donors. In 2020, the top 100 donors contributed 1.6 billion dollars to Super PACs.

The National Convention: Selecting the Party Nominees

- National party conventions are held the summer before the election. Having won a majority of delegate votes in the primaries, the nominee is usually already known.
- Party conventions, no longer decision-making gatherings, introduce and celebrate the candidate and the vice-presidential running mate he/she has selected. In 2020, due to Covid, both conventions were largely virtual events.

The Presidential Campaign

- In 2020 due to the global pandemic the candidates held more virtual and fewer in-person campaign events, focusing time, money, and media attention on "contested" rather than "safe" states. As in 2016, in 2020 candidates increased use of targeted digital communication to reach voters.
- The 2010 census mirrored the 2000 census pattern moving another 12 House seats from Eastern and Midwestern states to Western and Southern states in a population trend that also shifts electoral votes.
- The global pandemic changed the way people voted with 100 million people voting early by mail or in person.

Voters Choose the Electors Who Elect the President

- Voters cast ballots for president on the Tuesday following first Monday in November in years divisible by four. They decide which party's electors in each state will vote for its presidential slate. The Electoral Count Act of 1887 sets the Monday following the second Wednesday in December as the date electors, meeting in each state, cast their votes for president. At least six days earlier each State certifies the election results, making them official.
- Each state sends its electoral votes (Certificates of Vote) to the President of the Senate (the U.S. vice president) and the Archivist of the United States. On January 6, in a joint session of the newly elected Congress chaired by the President of the Senate each state's electoral vote is formally opened and counted. Congress then certifies the election results.
- Voter turnout in 2020 was 7% higher than in 2016. Both candidates set new popular vote records. Joe Biden won both the popular vote and the electoral vote.
- The new President is sworn in (inaugurated) on January 20.

Presidential Elections and the Rule of Law: The Peaceful Transfer of Power

The transition from one presidential administration to another is a time of uncertainty even in a democracy and particularly as our government has become ever larger, increasingly politicized, and more complex. Tensions are further heightened when the presidency is changing from one party to another. In 2021 Congress' certification of the 2020 election and Joseph Biden's inauguration took place as scheduled by law in the face of an attack on the Capitol and other threats to the completion of the transfer of presidential power.

The peaceful transfer of power is a pattern set in the **election of 1800**. Thomas Jefferson of Virginia and Aaron Burr of New York were the presidential and vice-presidential candidates for the Democratic Republicans. The Federalists nominated President John Adams of Massachusetts for a second term running with Charles C. Pinckney from South Carolina. Jefferson beat Adams 73 electoral votes to 65. However, due to a flaw in the Constitution's wording about the Electoral College, the electors' ballots were not identified as a vote for president and a separate vote for vice president. As a result, Jefferson and Burr tied with 73 votes each.

The Constitution calls for a tied election to be decided by the House of Representatives with each state casting one vote. In 1801, the newly elected Republican House was not yet seated. The winner would be decided by the old Federalist House. If a delegation does not have a majority for a candidate its vote is left blank. A majority vote of the states, at the time 9 of 16, was needed. Jefferson was elected president on the 36th ballot when Federalist delegates in Vermont and Maryland switched their votes.

Ratified in 1804, the **Twelfth Amendment** was added to the Constitution. It requires that electors cast separate ballots for president and vice president.

The **election of 2000** was another time in the history of the presidency that a peaceful transfer of power under the rule of law took place. The 2000 election crisis involved the popular vote versus the electoral vote and hinged on counting the popular vote in Florida. The then Vice President Al Gore of Tennessee was the Democratic Party candidate running against Republican George W. Bush from Texas.

In Florida, the problems with counting votes, contested ballots, and recounts led to lawsuits. The Florida Supreme Court ordered a recount of the ballots in some counties but not statewide. In **Bush v. Gore** (2000), with Bush leading by 537 out of almost 6 million votes, the U.S. Supreme Court in a 5–4 vote stopped the recount. The Court cited the equal protection clause of the 14th Amendment, ruling that the right to vote was being violated because of the unequal treatment of votes once they had been cast. Gore had a popular vote win of 543,895 (0.5%) while Bush won the Electoral College 271–266.

In conceding the election, Gore stated:

Now the U.S. Supreme Court has spoken. . . . while I strongly disagree with the court's decision, I accept it. . . . for the sake of our unity as a people and the strength of our democracy, I offer my concession. . . . in one of God's unforeseen paths, this belatedly broken impasse can point us all to a new common ground, for its very closeness can serve to remind us that we are one people with a shared history and a shared destiny.

—Al Gore, concession speech, December 13, 2000

Analyzing Documents

The orderly transfer of authority as called for in the Constitution routinely takes place, as it has for almost two centuries, and few of us stop to think how unique we really are. In the eyes of many in the world, this every 4-year ceremony we accept as normal is nothing less than a miracle.

—Ronald Reagan, First Inaugural Address January 20, 1981

What does President Reagan describe as "normal," unique, and a "miracle"?

Analyzing Documents

Upon due consideration of the difficulties identified to this point, it is obvious that the recount cannot be conducted in compliance with the requirements of equal protection and due process without substantial additional work.

—From Supreme Court ruling in *Bush v. Gore*, 2000

Although we may never know with complete certainty the identity of the winner of this year's Presidential election, the identity of the loser is perfectly clear. It is the Nation's confidence in the judge as an impartial guardian of the rule of law.

—Justice John Paul Stevens, dissenting opinion, *Bush v. Gore*, 2000

Point of View

Identify the point of view of each quote and place it in its historical setting.

Debating the Electoral College System

From the days of the Constitutional Convention, Americans have argued about the Electoral College System as the method of electing the president and vice president.

Reasons to Change the System

1. The major argument against the Electoral College system is that it is undemocratic, a leftover from a different time that fails to reflect the "will of the people." The president and vice president should be directly elected by the people just as they elect members of Congress and most state and local officials.

2. Five presidents who lost the popular vote (in 1824, 1876, 1888, 2000, and 2016) were elected because they won a majority or 270 electoral votes. This occurs because, except for Maine and Nebraska, the states use a "winner-take-all" system. The candidate with the most popular votes in the state gets all the state's electoral votes, no matter how close that popular vote.

3. Because every state is guaranteed two electors for its two senators no matter its population, and at least one member in the House, the less-populated states have more electoral votes per person than the more populated states. For example, California, the largest state, has one electoral vote per 712,000 people, while Wyoming, the least populous state, has one electoral vote per 195,000 residents.

4. The presidential campaign is focused on putting together 270 electoral votes. Therefore, the campaign concentrates its resources on the six to twelve "swing" states where the vote could go to either political party, while the rest of the states receive little attention. One effect is to lower the turnout in the majority of states because people feel that their vote will not count in the election results.

5. In seventeen states, the electors for the candidate who wins that state's popular vote have no legal requirements on how they cast their electoral vote.

6. Two proposals for change would not need a constitutional amendment. One is the National Popular Vote Interstate Compact (NPV). It would most likely be challenged as unconstitutional. The other is the congressional district method now used by Maine and Nebraska. Critics fear it would encourage more extreme gerrymandering of congressional districts.

Reasons to Keep the System

Despite such criticisms, the Electoral College system continues to be the way in which the United States elects its president and vice president.

1. A Constitutional amendment to change the electoral college system would be extremely difficult to pass. Approval by two-thirds of each house of Congress and ratification by three-fourths of the states is required to amend the Constitution. Small states oppose presidential election by popular vote because they would lose their over-representation in the Electoral College.

2. The Electoral College system was never designed to express the popular vote. To reach the 270 electoral vote majority, a candidate must build a coalition of states with diverse interests across different geographic parts of the country. One result is greater national unity. The system also protects the interests of smaller states while preventing a highly populated region or urban areas to dominate an election.

3. The requirement of a majority of electoral votes ensures that a president enters office with a clear majority, no matter the popular vote. An election by popular vote could lead to turmoil if a multi-state or a nationwide recount is required.

4. A move to a popular vote might threaten the two-party political system. We do not have a multi-party system because a presidential candidate needs a majority of the Electoral College vote. While third parties have influenced the outcome of some presidential elections, no third-party candidate has won the presidency.

Preparing for the Regents

Using Evidence

Why were 96% of the 2020 presidential campaign events held in twelve states?

Why is the Electoral College System considered federalism in practice?

A tie vote or other dispute about the presidential electoral vote can be settled in the House by a majority vote with each state having one vote.

Why might this power influence reapportioning and gerrymandering congressional districts?

Base your answers to questions 1 through 3 on the letter below and on your knowledge of social studies.

There is a violent spirit of opposition raised on the Continent against the execution of the Stamp Act, the mob in Boston have carried it very high against Mr. Oliver . . . for his acceptance of an office in consequence of that act. They have even proceeded to some violence, and burnt him in Effigy &c. They threaten to pull down & burn the Stamp Office row building, and that they will hold every man as Infamous that shall presume to carry the Stamp Act into Execution; so that it is thought Mr. Oliver will resign. I don't find any such turbulent spirit to prevail among us, if it should, the means are in our Hands to prevent any tumults or Insults; what the consequences may be in the Colonies who have no military force to keep the rabble in order, I cannot pretend to say.

Source: Archibald Hinshelwood, letter to Joshua Mauger, 1765

1 The protests described by Hinshelwood were primarily motivated by the

(1) passing of taxes by Parliament without colonial representation

(2) British practice of salutary neglect of the colonies

(3) firing upon the citizens of Boston by British soldiers

(4) rejection of the Olive Branch Petition by King George III

2 The British Parliament reacted to these protests by

(1) sending the Royal Navy to New York

(2) quartering soldiers in colonists' homes

(3) repealing the Stamp Act

(4) closing the Port of Boston

3 The views expressed by Hinshelwood illustrate those of

(1) a member of the Sons of Liberty

(2) an American colonist

(3) a British loyalist

(4) a member of Parliament

Base your answers to questions 4 and 5 on the passages below and on your knowledge of social studies.

All legislative Powers herein granted shall be vested in a Congress of the United States, which shall consist of a Senate and House of Representatives.

—U.S. Constitution, Article I, Section 1

The senate shall consist of fifty members, except as hereinafter provided. The senators elected in the year one thousand eight hundred and ninety-five shall hold their offices for three years, and their successors shall be chosen for two years. The assembly shall consist of one hundred and fifty members. The assembly members elected in the year one thousand nine hundred and thirty-eight, and their successors, shall be chosen for two years.

—New York State Constitution, Article III, Section 2

4 What government structure is provided for by both of these Articles?

(1) bicameral legislature

(2) president

(3) independent judiciary

(4) elected assembly

5 Which constitutional principle is demonstrated by the existence of both of these governmental documents in the United States?

(1) popular sovereignty

(2) limited government

(3) federalism

(4) republicanism

Base your answers to questions 6 and 7 on the map below and on your knowledge of social studies.

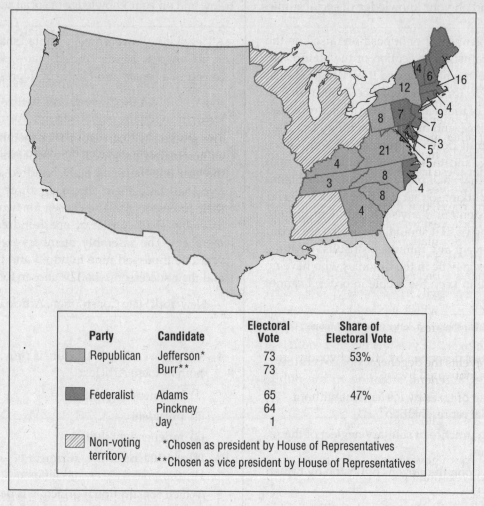

Party	Candidate	Electoral Vote	Share of Electoral Vote
Republican	Jefferson*	73	53%
	Burr**	73	
Federalist	Adams	65	47%
	Pinckney	64	
	Jay	1	
Non-voting territory			

*Chosen as president by House of Representatives

**Chosen as vice president by House of Representatives

6   The election of 1800 is significant because it

(1) represents the first peaceful transfer of power from one political party to another

(2) proved that one could win the presidency without winning the popular vote

(3) showed the need to extend the right to vote to more citizens

(4) was the first election in which the winner received a clear majority of the electoral vote

7   The rules of the selection process that created the tie between Jefferson and Burr would eventually be settled by

(1) a Supreme Court decision

(2) a constitutional amendment

(3) the abolition of the Electoral College

(4) the rewriting of the Articles of Confederation

Base your answers to questions 8 through 10 on the letters below and on your knowledge of social studies.

Societies exist under three forms sufficiently distinguishable. 1. Without government, as among our Indians. 2. Under governments wherein the will of every one has a just influence, as is the case in England in a slight degree, and in our states in a great one. 3. Under governments of force: as is the case in all other monarchies and in most of the other republics. To have an idea of the curse of existence under these last, they must be seen. It is a government of wolves over sheep. It is a problem, not clear in my mind, that the first condition is not the best. But I believe it to be inconsistent with any great degree of population. The second state has a great deal of good in it. The mass of mankind under that enjoys a precious degree of liberty and happiness. It has its evils too: the principal of which is the turbulence to which it is subject. But weigh this against the oppressions of monarchy, and it becomes nothing. . . . Even this evil is productive of good. It prevents the degeneracy of government, and nourishes a general attention to the public affairs.

Source: Thomas Jefferson, letter to James Madison, January 30, 1787

We stand, I conceive, in a ridiculous point of view in the eyes of the Nations of the Earth; with whom we are attempting to enter into Commercial Treaties without means of carrying them into effect and who must see, & feel, that the Union, or the States individually, are Sovereigns, as it best suits their purposes. In a word that we are one Nation today, & thirteen tomorrow—Who will treat with us on such terms?

Source: George Washington, letter to James McHenry, August 22, 1785

8 For what type of government is Thomas Jefferson advocating?

(1) autocracy

(2) monarchy

(3) democracy

(4) oligarchy

9 According to George Washington, what problem exists under the Articles of Confederation?

(1) The central government has been granted too much power.

(2) The states are unable to freely manage their international trade.

(3) The central government lacks an executive to lead the nation.

(4) The states can undermine the central government's authority.

10 What is the main disagreement between George Washington and Thomas Jefferson?

(1) Washington advocates for a stronger central government compared to Jefferson.

(2) Washington wants a more expansionary foreign policy compared to Jefferson.

(3) Washington does not trust the people in power, while Jefferson does.

(4) Washington supports sovereign states, while Jefferson does not.

Base your answers to questions 11 and 12 on the map below and on your knowledge of social studies.

Land Claims of Royal Proclamation of 1763

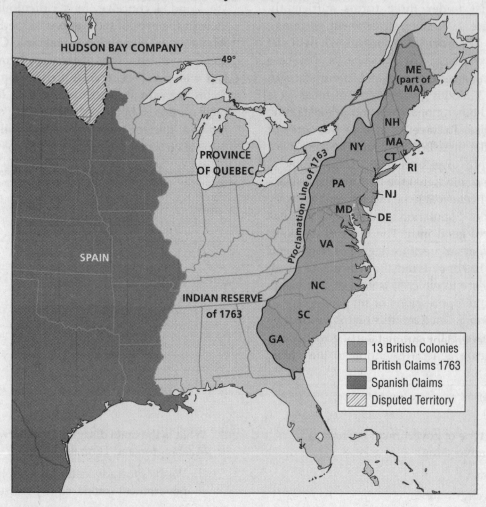

11 Using the map, what can be inferred was a goal of the Proclamation of 1763?

(1) prevent conflict between the colonists and Native Americans

(2) put an end to the French and Indian War

(3) keep France from expanding into the Great Lakes region

(4) create a system for the admittance of territories as new states

12 Why were colonists angered by the Proclamation of 1763?

(1) Colonists did not believe the Proclamation adequately defended them from the Spanish.

(2) Colonists argued for a larger allotment of land for their Native American allies.

(3) Colonists hoped to take over the fertile land in the Indian territory.

(4) Colonists could not gain access to the Hudson Bay Company.

Base your answers to questions 13 and 14 on the chart below and on your knowledge of social studies.

Three Branches of U.S. Government

Legislative	Executive	Judicial
Senate **House of Representatives**	**President** **Vice President**	**Supreme Court** **Federal Courts**
Makes laws	**Enforces laws and treaties**	**Explains and interprets laws**
• Overrides presidential vetoes • Approves presidential appointments • Approves treaties • Taxes to provide services • Provides for defense, declares war • Regulates money and trade • Impeaches officials	• Can veto laws • Appoints high officials • Conducts foreign policy • Enforces laws and treaties • Commander in chief of the military • Recommends bills to Congress • Reports the state of the Union to Congress	• Settles legal disputes between states • Settles State and federal disputes • Settles disputes between States and foreign countries • Hears cases with ambassadors of foreign governments • Settles disputes between individuals and Federal Government

Source: U.S. Department of Justice

13 What system did the Constitution establish by creating three branches of government, as shown in this chart?

(1) a system defined by the supremacy clause

(2) an independent national judicial system

(3) a system of federalism

(4) a checks and balances system

14 Which Enlightenment thinker was most influential in the structure described in this chart?

(1) John Locke

(2) Voltaire

(3) Baron de Montesquieu

(4) Denis Diderot

Short Essay Questions

Task: Read and analyze the following documents, applying your social studies knowledge and skills to write a short essay of two or three paragraphs in which you:

- Describe the historical context surrounding documents 1 and 2
- Analyze **Document 2** and explain how *audience,* **or** *purpose,* **or** *bias,* **or** *point of view* affects this document's use as a reliable source of evidence

In developing your short essay answer of two or three paragraphs, be sure to keep these explanations in mind:

Describe means "to illustrate something in words or tell about"

Historical Context refers to "the relevant historical circumstances surrounding or connecting the events, ideas, or developments in these documents"

Analyze means "to examine a document and determine its elements and its relationships"

Explain means "to make plain or understandable; to give reasons for or causes of; to show the logical development or relationship of"

Reliability is determined by how accurate and useful the information found in a source is for a specific purpose

Document 1

We hold these truths to be self-evident, that all men are created equal, that they are endowed by their Creator with certain unalienable Rights, that among these are Life, Liberty and the pursuit of Happiness.—That to secure these rights, Governments are instituted among Men, deriving their just powers from the consent of the governed,—That whenever any Form of Government becomes destructive of these ends, it is the Right of the People to alter or to abolish it, and to institute new Government, laying its foundation on such principles and organizing its powers in such form, as to them shall seem most likely to effect their Safety and Happiness. Prudence, indeed, will dictate that Governments long established should not be changed for light and transient causes; and accordingly all experience hath shewn, that mankind are more disposed to suffer, while evils are sufferable, than to right themselves by abolishing the forms to which they are accustomed. But when a long train of abuses and usurpations, pursuing invariably the same Object evinces a design to reduce them under absolute Despotism, it is their right, it is their duty, to throw off such Government, and to provide new Guards for their future security.—Such has been the patient sufferance of these Colonies; and such is now the necessity which constrains them to alter their former Systems of Government. The history of the present King of Great Britain is a history of repeated injuries and usurpations, all having in direct object the establishment of an absolute Tyranny over these States. To prove this, let Facts be submitted to a candid world.

Source: Declaration of Independence, 1776

Document 2

General Colin Powell was the former head of the Joint Chiefs of Staff and the first African American secretary of state, a position he held from 2001–2005. The following excerpt is from an interview conducted for a public television series called *Africans in America*.

> *Interviewer:* The Declaration of Independence is unprecedented, a watershed moment in the nation. How did it apply to black people?
>
> *Powell:* The Declaration of Independence is one of the most remarkable documents in the world, and certainly in the English language or in Christendom. And in just a few words, it captures the essence. You know, "inalienable rights", rights not given to you by the state but given to you by God, so they can't be taken away. And the purpose of the state is to secure these rights, not to give them to you or to tell you what you're supposed to do with them, but to secure those rights for you.
>
> What are those rights? Life, liberty, and the pursuit of happiness. "We hold these truths to be self-evident." In other words, you don't have to prove them. It's self-evident. Why is it self-evident? Came from God. They're inalienable. Government secures them. Remarkable document. It didn't apply to black folks.

Source: Colin Powell, *Africans in America*, PBS, 1998

Historical Context: Individual Rights

Throughout United States history, many constitutional and civic issues have been debated by Americans. These debates have resulted in efforts by individuals, groups, and governments to address these issues. These efforts have achieved varying degrees of success. One of these constitutional and civic issues is individual rights.

Task: Read and analyze the documents. Using information from the documents and your knowledge of United States history, write an essay in which you

- Describe the historical circumstances surrounding this constitutional or civic issue
- Explain efforts to address this constitutional or civic issue by individuals, groups, and/or governments
- Discuss the extent to which these efforts were successful

Describe means "to illustrate something in words or tell about it"

Explain means "to make plain or understandable; to give reasons for or causes of; to show the logical development or relationship of"

Discuss means "to make observations about something using facts, reasoning, and argument; to present in some detail"

Document 1

For the security of liberty it has been declared, "that excessive bail should not be required, nor excessive fines imposed, nor cruel or unusual punishments inflicted—that all warrants, without oath or affirmation, to search suspected places, or seize any person, his papers or property, are grievous and oppressive."

These provisions are as necessary under the general government as under that of the individual states; for the power of the former is as complete to the purpose of requiring bail, imposing fines, inflicting punishments, granting search warrants, and seizing persons, papers, or property, in certain cases, as the other.

For the purpose of securing the property of the citizens, it is declared by all the states, "that in all controversies at law, respecting property, the ancient mode of trial by jury is one of the best securities of the rights of the people, and ought to remain sacred and inviolable."

Source: Antifederalist essay No. 2, Brutus, *New York Journal*, November 1, 1787

1. What is one individual right that the author believes should be protected under the new Constitution?

Document 2

The reason assigned for the omission of a bill of rights, securing the liberty of the press, and other invaluable personal rights, is an insult on the understanding of the people. . . .

[In] the new plan . . . there is no declaration, . . . in the free exercise of religious worship: that the trial by jury in civil cases as well as criminal, and the modes prescribed by the common law for safety of life in criminal prosecutions shall be held sacred; that the requiring of excessive bail, imposing of excessive fines and cruel and unusual punishments be forbidden; that monopolies in trade or arts, other than to authors of books or inventors of useful arts, for a reasonable time, ought not to be suffered; that the right of the people to assemble peaceably for the purpose of consulting about public matters, and petitioning or remonstrating to the federal legislature ought not to be prevented; that the liberty of the press be held sacred; that the people have a right to hold themselves, their houses, papers and possessions free from search or seizure.

Source: Antifederalist essay No. 2, Centinel, *The Freedmen's Journal*, October 24, 1787

2. Which of the rights listed by Centinel are included in the First Amendment of the U.S. Constitution?

Expansion, Nationalism, and Sectionalism (1800–1865)

Topic Overview

In 1789, President George Washington took on the task of achieving security and stability for the new nation just as the French Revolution began. War enveloped Europe until 1815.

American nationalism was both strengthened and challenged by foreign policy, territorial expansion, and economic growth. The Louisiana Purchase doubled the nation's size. The market revolution resulted in economic and cultural changes. The North began industrializing. In the South, cotton became the dominant crop, and slavery became more firmly rooted in law. Andrew Jackson's presidency strengthened presidential powers and challenged constitutional principles.

Differing views on constitutional, political, economic, and social issues contributed to a growing sectionalism. In a new age of mass politics and reform, tensions grew, pulling the nation apart. Westward expansion led to more controversy over slavery spreading and strengthened the abolitionist movement. A women's rights movement developed.

The Southern states saw their power and influence decreasing while the disputes on states' rights and slavery became louder and opinions became more rigid. When Abraham Lincoln was elected president, southern states began to secede. The Emancipation Proclamation made freeing the slaves a major Union goal. The question of federal supremacy versus states' rights was settled with Lee's surrender in April 1865.

Foreign Policy, Territorial Expansion, Economic Growth Affect Nationalism

Key Concept

11.3a American nationalism was both strengthened and challenged by territorial expansion and economic growth.

Lesson Overview

American nationalism was strengthened by the Louisiana Purchase, the War of 1812, and the Monroe Doctrine. It was strengthened as well as challenged by economic growth and territorial expansion. From 1790 to 1860, the Market Revolution affected how people interacted economically. It influenced the development of transportation networks, the growth of domestic industries, the increased demands for free and enslaved labor, the changing role of women, and the rise of political democracy.

Andrew Jackson was the first president to be elected from a state west of the Appalachian Mountains. In 1828, he became president at a time of the rise of mass politics. Jackson's presidency strengthened presidential power but challenged constitutional principles as in the Supreme Court case of *Worcester* v. *Georgia* (1832) and the Indian Removal Act that followed.

Unifying Themes

As you review this lesson take special note of the following themes:

- **Time, Continuity, and Change** In what ways is the United States' foreign policy from 1789 to 1823 seen as a pattern of continuity? Of change?

- **Power, Authority, and Governance** Did Andrew Jackson strengthen constitutional democracy or abuse presidential power?

- **Creation, Expansion, and Interaction of Economic Systems** What were the similarities and differences in the economic systems of the North, South, and West? How were nationalism and sectionalism influenced by the economic systems in each region?

- **Science, Technology, and Innovation** What are key examples of the relationship between the technology and innovations of the market revolution and social, cultural, and economic change?

Key People

George Washington	Andrew Jackson	Henry Clay
John Adams	William Henry Harrison	John C. Calhoun
Thomas Jefferson	James Monroe	
James Madison	John Quincy Adams	

Key Terms and Events

nationalism	Monroe Doctrine	urbanization
neutrality	Market Revolution	nativism
Alien and Sedition Acts	industrialization	"Know Nothings"
Virginia and Kentucky Resolutions	specialization	spoils system
Louisiana Purchase	factory system	Second Bank of the United States
Embargo Act of 1807	transportation revolution	Indian Removal Act
War of 1812	Erie Canal	Trail of Tears

Key Supreme Court Cases

As you review this lesson be sure you understand the significance of this key Supreme Court case:

Worcester v. Georgia (1832)

U.S. Foreign Policy Strengthens and Challenges American Nationalism

Events in Europe from 1789 to 1815 influenced domestic and foreign policies of the United States. As the nation grew in territory, a sense of American **nationalism,** or loyalty and devotion to one's nation, developed across the expanding country.

Foreign Policy from 1789 to 1800

Wars in Europe placed pressure on the young United States. The nation's leadership determined that a policy of neutrality would be best for the new nation.

Washington's Foreign Policy The French Revolution began in 1789, the same year that the first administration under our new Constitution took office. The revolution was followed by the Napoleonic Wars, which ended in 1815 with Napoleon's defeat. **George Washington** recognized that maintaining the security of the young United States was a necessity. To protect the new nation Washington set the precedent of **neutrality** as U.S. foreign policy, when in 1793 he issued a **Proclamation of Neutrality.** In 1795, Washington supported the unpopular **Jay's Treaty,** an agreement designed to resolve conflicts with Great Britain and keep the United States from going to war. In 1796, when Washington was about to leave office, his **Farewell Address** included a warning against "permanent alliances."

Adam's Foreign Policy Our second president and a leading Federalist, **John Adams,** also understood the importance of keeping the nation out of war. An undeclared naval war with France was fought at sea from 1798 to 1800. Adams chose to settle rather than expand the war. By putting the country before his party, Adams' actions divided his own Federalist Party, contributing to his failure to win a second term. But Adams, in resisting internal and external pressures for war, maintained the nation's neutrality and security.

Conflict Among the Major Parties The French Revolution and wars divided more than united the nation. Many **Democratic Republicans,** including the party leaders Jefferson and Madison, supported the French and their revolution. The **Federalists** favored the British. In 1793, France and Spain had declared war on Britain and Holland. The Democratic Republicans objected to Washington's neutrality policy and to Jay's Treaty as too pro-British. Protesting what he correctly saw as Washington favoring Federalist policies, **Thomas Jefferson** resigned as our first secretary of state.

Reacting to Dissent Taking advantage of the emotions stirred up by the French Revolution, the Federalists passed the **Alien and Sedition Acts** (1798), four acts designed to strengthen the Federalist Party and weaken the Democratic Republican opposition. The **Alien Acts** made it more difficult to become a citizen and easier to arrest and deport any noncitizens thought to endanger national security. The **Sedition Act** made it easier to arrest a person for criticizing the government. The Alien and Sedition Acts were in part politically motivated. However, Federalists feared that the new republic would be destroyed by the spread to our nation of the radical behavior being displayed in the French Revolution.

Writing anonymously, **James Madison** and Thomas Jefferson in the **Virginia and Kentucky Resolutions** opposed the Acts. The resolutions declared the Alien and Sedition Acts a threat to First Amendment rights of freedom of speech and of the press and a danger to representative government. They charged that the federal government had exceeded its authority and claimed that each state had the right to interpret the constitutionality of a federal law. Jefferson, in the Kentucky Resolution, implied that a state could nullify a federal law.

Foreign Policy from 1800 to 1815

As a new century began, events in Europe continued to influence domestic and foreign policies of the United States.

The Louisiana Purchase In 1803, facing war with Great Britain, Napoleon offered to sell Louisiana to the United States. For Jefferson and other Democrat Republicans to support the purchase meant rejecting their strict interpretation of the Constitution. They overcame their reluctance and agreed to the purchase citing the Constitution's "necessary and proper" clause. For $15 million, President Jefferson doubled the size of the nation. Most immediately, the **Louisiana Purchase** gave the United States control of the Mississippi River and its vital port of New Orleans. This opened up a water route for Ohio River Valley farmers and others to ship their products to market. Jefferson chose the national interest over strict interpretation of the Constitution and strengthened American nationalism.

Embargo Act of 1807 With the Atlantic Ocean providing a 3,000-mile buffer, presidents were aided in maintaining a foreign policy of American neutrality. During the Napoleonic wars the United States tried to balance neutrality with its right and need as a sovereign nation to trade with European nations. Great Britain had blockaded French ports. Americans were outraged by Britain seizing American merchant ships trying to reach France. Jefferson, in an

The Louisiana Purchase, 1803

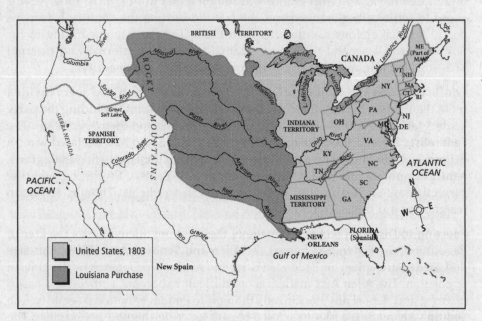

attempt to avoid war and to force Great Britain and France to lift their blockades, had Congress pass the **Embargo Act of 1807.** An embargo is a government ban on trade with a particular nation. The Embargo Act prohibited the export of goods from the United States. New England, with its trade-based economy, was hit the hardest. Major port cities were paralyzed. Western and southern farmers could not ship their products overseas. In 1809, protests due to the economic impact of the law led to its repeal. These regional dissensions and divisions challenged American nationalism.

War of 1812 Great Britain continued to violate American freedom of the seas, seizing

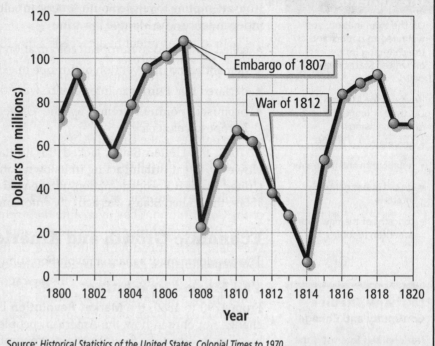

United States Exports, 1800–1820

Source: *Historical Statistics of the United States, Colonial Times to 1970*

American ships and **impressing** or forcing American sailors to serve in the British navy. Napoleon had agreed to stop taking hold of American ships. Meanwhile, western and southern "War Hawks," who wanted to expand into British Canada and Spanish Florida, urged war. In 1812, Congress declared war on Great Britain. The **War of 1812,** however, was not supported by all Americans and provoked disputes among different sections of the nation. In 1814 at the **Hartford Convention,** New Englanders objected to the war and proposed changes in the Constitution.

Although the war ended in a draw in 1814, it produced some significant long-term results.

- The war reinforced the American belief that a policy of neutrality regarding European affairs was justified.
- Native American tribes in the West lost their ally, Great Britain, and were much less able to stand up to American expansion.
- American manufacturing grew, particularly in New England, when the war cut the United States off from European imports.
- Opposing the war in the face of a growing sense of nationalism, weakened the Federalist Party, which soon ceased to be a major factor in national politics.
- In **Andrew Jackson** and **William Henry Harrison,** the nation gained new war heroes. "The Star-Spangled Banner" was inspired by the bombarding of Fort McHenry.

The Monroe Doctrine: Foreign Policy After the War of 1812

Under President **James Monroe,** Secretary of State **John Quincy Adams** settled the border between the United States and Canada. He acquired Florida from Spain and reached an agreement with that nation on the southern boundary of the Louisiana Purchase. Adams was also Monroe's chief advisor for the Monroe Doctrine.

Preparing for the Regents

On the examination, you will need to understand the changing influences on United States foreign policy.

How was the Monroe Doctrine influenced by each of the following?

- geography
- isolationism and neutrality
- United States national interests
- concerns of the new Latin American republics

The 1823 **Monroe Doctrine** became the foundation of the United States' foreign policy in the Western Hemisphere. It was issued to prevent former colonial powers from attempting to regain South American colonies that had recently declared their independence. The Monroe Doctrine

- called for an end to European colonization in the Western Hemisphere.
- demanded no intervention by Europe in existing nations in this hemisphere.
- declared that European interference was "dangerous to our peace and safety."
- promised noninterference by the United States in European affairs and European colonies.

In 1823, the United States lacked the military might to enforce this doctrine. However, Great Britain, acting in its own national interest, agreed to support the United States if European nations challenged the new doctrine. By the end of the 1800s, the United States was actively enforcing the policy on its own.

Economic Growth and American Nationalism

The development of a market revolution stimulated economic growth nationwide.

The Market Revolution

From 1790 to 1860, the **Market Revolution** brought about a basic and complex change not only in how the American people acted and interacted economically but also in how they thought about economics and economic growth. Its effects on social, cultural, and economic aspects of American life were revolutionary. The "market" determined fundamental questions such as what to make, what to grow, where to sell your product and for how much money.

A Nationwide Market The development of a **market economy** stimulated economic growth nationwide. The market became national, not local and regional. Southern and western crops were exchanged for northern manufactured goods. Southern cotton was spun on power looms in New England cities. The market influenced the development of transportation networks that linked the nation. Products could be shipped faster and at lower costs. Canals, roads, steamboats, and later, railroads, also encouraged expansion west. The market revolution linked the settlers to the land and their farm products to distant markets.

Unifying Themes
Continuity and Change

National self-interest is the prime motivation behind a nation's foreign policy.

- Did the motives behind American foreign policy change after the War of 1812? Why or why not?

The market encouraged a movement from self-sufficient farming to larger scale cash crop farming. Technology such as the steel plow and the reaper led to the growth of this new **commercial farming** and increased demands for both free and enslaved labor. In the South, a single commercial crop based on enslaved labor was made possible by the cotton gin.

Industrialization and Specialization In the North, technological improvements in industry encouraged the creation of domestic industries and increased demands for free labor. The new opportunities in transportation and **industrialization** affected both the size and number of American cities. **Specialization** was possible because people could now purchase what they did not make or grow. Specialization was also regional with the North becoming more industrial, the West concentrating on grain and livestock production, and the South growing cotton for export.

A National Economy The market economy was reinforced by banks that expanded to provide the capital for investment and the funds needed for exchange of goods and services. **Limited liability corporations** formed. Now an investor could lose no more than the value of the company stock he owned. Decisions of the **John Marshall Supreme Court** helped to promote national unity and encourage a national economy by expanding interstate commerce and protecting the validity of contracts.

Market changes led to swings in the economy as did land speculation. There were times of growth and great profits. There were also slow times of financial losses or depressions, called panics. The **Panic of 1819** and the **Panic of 1837** were two severe financial crises that became depressions. Bankruptcies, bank failures, and unemployment were particularly hard on the wage-earning class.

Comparing Household and Market Economies

	Household Economy	Market Economy
Producers	Household	Industries
Labor	Members of the household produce a variety of goods at home.	Workers specialize in producing a certain product outside the home. They exchange their labor for cash.
Goods	Goods are made primarily to be used by the household.	Goods are sold on the open market for a profit.

Preparing for the Regents

Stimulus-Based Questions: Chart

Based on the chart at left and your knowledge of American history, answer the following questions.

• How were workers affected by the change to a market economy?

• How did the shift to a market economy promote nationalism?

The American System Supports a National Economy

Senator **Henry Clay,** supported by John Quincy Adams, designed a legislative program called the **"American System."** The program's objective was to unify the nation by benefiting the North, the South, and the West. This would be accomplished by:

• establishing a better national transportation system to aid trade and national defense.

• setting the first protective tariff to encourage American manufacturing and provide funds for improved national transportation networks.

• creating a second national bank to promote the necessary financial support by extending credit to farmers and industrialists.

While the second national bank was created and a protective tariff passed, the American System was never completely successful. Southerners opposed the higher tariffs. They did not see the need for a national transportation network because they could sell their cotton overseas. Others opposed federal funding of roads, bridges, and canals as unconstitutional as well as an effort to increase the power of the national government. Andrew Jackson, a nationalist, originally backed the American System but as president turned against it. He vetoed internal improvement bills and opposed tariffs. Jackson had personal and political differences with Clay, John Quincy Adams, and his vice president, **John C. Calhoun.**

Technology Changes Industrial Patterns in the North

By the early 1800s, the new technologies that gave rise to the Industrial Revolution in Great Britain reached the United States. Technology such as steam engines and machines to spin thread and weave cloth led to the **First American Industrial Revolution.** Factory builders flocked to the North, particularly New England, because of its abundant supplies of iron, coal, and swiftly flowing rivers used for water power to operate machinery.

By 1860, Northern factories had entered a worldwide competition for markets. While agriculture, especially in its westernmost states, continued to be a major part of its economy, the North began to take on a new identity as an urban manufacturing and commercial area. About 70 percent of national manufacturing was located in the North.

The Factory System

By 1850, most American manufacturing was no longer done in homes and small workshops, but instead in impersonal factories by workers using machines. This was called the **factory system.** The first mills were in New England. The "model" **Lowell mill** employed white, teenage farm girls as its labor force, offering them an opportunity for financial independence. The girls lived at the mill in a highly regulated and supervised environment. It was these young women workers at the Lowell mill who, in 1834 and 1836, organized the first work protests and strikes against wage cuts.

Technology Creates a National Transportation Network

A **transportation revolution** brought about the development of internal transportation systems. Canals, steam transport, and then railroads connected northern markets to western farmlands and westward migration accelerated. In 1825, New York completed the building of the **Erie Canal.** It linked the Atlantic Ocean at New York City through the Great Lakes to the vast interior of the United States. As a result, shipping costs dropped sharply. Population in upstate New York as well as in New York City increased rapidly. Industry grew and commerce boomed. Railroads later connected New York to other major cities and to the West. By 1840, New York City was the nation's major port as well as its financial, commercial, and industrial center.

Major Inventions of the Early 1800s

Invention	Year	Inventor	Effect
Power Loom	1784	Edmund Cartwright	Factory-produced cloth
Cotton Gin	1793	Eli Whitney	Mass produced cotton; dependence on slave labor
Interchangeable Parts	1798	Eli Whitney	Mass production of muskets, a type of firearm replaced by rifles
Cotton Spinning Machine	1798	Samuel Slater	Factory-produced cotton fiber
Steamboat	1807	Robert Fulton	Cut travel and shipping times and costs
Iron-Bladed Plow	1819	Jethro Wood	Plowing fields was faster and easier
Horse Streetcar	1820	John Stephenson	Improved public urban transportation
Steam Locomotive	1830	Peter Cooper	Faster travel and shipping; networks connected the nation
McCormick Reaper	1831	Cyrus McCormick	Harvested grain faster and more easily; grain mass produced
Steel-Bladed Plow	1837	John Deere	Plowed sod in Great Plains without breaking; migration west increases
Telegraph	1844	Samuel Morse	Supported business activities; connected nation
Sewing Machine	1846	Elias Howe	Clothing and shoes made faster, cheaper in factories; increased productivity in textile industry

The Transportation Revolution

Steam Power

- In 1807, Robert Fulton's *Clermont* steamed up the Hudson River.
- Steamships helped farmers ship their goods to markets around the world.

Canals

- Erie Canal connected Lake Erie to New York City in 1825.
- By 1840, 3,000 miles of canals are in use.

Changes in Transportation

Roads

- By 1833, the Cumberland Road ran from Maryland to Ohio.
- New roads of stone and gravel helped Americans move west.

Railroads

- In 1828, the B & O railroad line became nation's first railroad.
- By 1840, United States had more miles of railroad track than any other country in the world.

The Market Revolution Leads to the Growth of Cities

By 1860, nine of the ten largest cities in the nation were in the North. Population in the older cities doubled. After 1840, immigrants made up the majority of the population in some cities. The gap between rich and poor widened, as a distinctive rich upper class and a poor working class developed in the cities. Private companies provided sanitation and water only to those who could afford to pay for these services. Cities were unsafe, and police forces did not begin to appear until the mid-1830s.

Urban and Rural Populations, 1800–1850

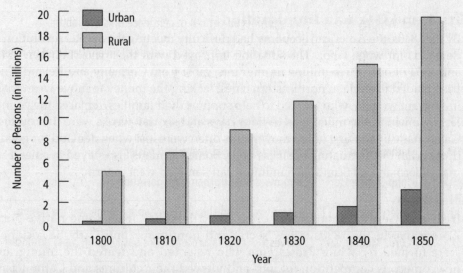

Both urban and rural populations grew rapidly in the early 1800s. By 1850, 12 percent of the total population lived in urban areas

Unifying Themes
Change

Cities grew tremendously during the first half of the 19th century. The population of New York City (Manhattan only), for example, soared from about 33,000 in 1790 to 124,000 in 1820 to about 516,000 by 1850.

The Effects of the Increased Demand for Free Labor in the North

As a result of industrialization, the manner in which people earned a living changed in the North. The demand for workers in Northern factories increased immigration to the region, which led to distrust and discrimination.

Working-Class Life

Industrialization and **urbanization** changed family life and gender roles. Previously, families worked together at home and on the farm, taking on different tasks according to gender. After industrialization, both working-class men and women worked for wages, and their jobs also differed depending on their gender. Uncertainty was a part of life since jobs depended on market fluctuations. More women worked as servants, more men in factories. Working-class children under age ten often worked in the factories.

Middle-Class Life

The lives of middle-class men were often centered in the new business world. One of the few jobs considered proper for a single middle-class woman was teaching. After marriage middle-class women were housewives and mothers, their lives defined by the home where they had some influence. By the 1830s there were more educational opportunities for women. Families had fewer children. Working-class children had to make economic contributions to the family, but middle-class children did not. Childhood, as a specific stage in life, received new attention. Middle-class parents supported the growing movement for public schools.

Life for Free African Americans

Free African Americans in the North continued to face racism and legal restrictions. Public places remained segregated. African Americans also faced discrimination in hiring. Free African American women were more likely than free African American men to find permanent work, most often as household helpers.

Irish and German Immigration

By the 1840s, the American economy had difficulty meeting the market revolution's demands for wage labor. The situation improved with the arrival between 1845 and 1854 of over three million immigrants, most from Germany and Ireland. The Irish tended to settle in northeastern cities, lacking the money to move west. Irish immigrant women, who worked to help support their families, replaced the young farm women in the mills. Twelve-hour days and six-day weeks were the routine. Gains made by the first union movements often were lost when demand for goods dropped in the fluctuating business cycle. Some Germans also stayed in cities, but many German and Scandinavian immigrants moved west to farm.

Nativism

Irish and German immigrants often faced hostility from some native-born Americans. In the 1830s, a few secret anti-immigrant, anti-Catholic societies were formed by white Protestants who resented and feared the immigrant newcomers as competition for jobs and viewed their cultures and Catholicism as a threat to American values. Most successful was the nativist, xenophobic, and anti-Catholic **American Party**, called the **"Know Nothings."** Between 1849 and the mid-1850s the "Know Nothings" elected thousands to local, state, and national office by calling for restrictions on immigration while limiting the right to vote and to hold office to native-born Americans.

Unifying Themes
Continuity and Change

• How did the European immigrants of the first half of the nineteenth century differ from earlier U.S. immigrants?

• What reaction did these new immigrants face from some native-born Americans?

Technology Results in Increased Demands for Enslaved Labor in the South

Technological advancements in agriculture led Southern planters to focus on cotton, a highly profitable crop. However, it was also highly labor intensive, increasing the South's bond to a slave-based economy.

Technological Innovations and the Growth of a Cotton Economy

In contrast to the North, in the first half of the 19th century, the South remained largely agricultural. Its climate and topography favored the plantation system of agriculture. With its economy dependent on cotton, Southern wealth continued to be invested in land and in the enslaved people who cultivated the cotton crop grown on it.

In the 18th century, rice, tobacco, and indigo were grown. By the end of that century, tobacco farming methods had worn out the land. In 1793, **Eli Whitney's** invention of the **cotton gin,** a machine that removed the seeds from cotton, had transformed cotton into a successful commercial crop. The opportunity for wealth afforded by cotton stimulated the growth of **slavery,** linking cotton and slavery inseparably to the Southern economy. As a result of this bond

- Between the 1830s and the 1850s, the price of both land and enslaved labor doubled. A pattern of borrowing money to buy more land and more enslaved labor in order to grow more cotton to make more money to compete with other growers meant living with risk, pressure, profit, and failure.

- Planters with their enslaved labor joined the westward migration looking for new land on which to grow cotton. Methods of growing cotton exhausted the soil, making it necessary to move into the southern Mississippi River Valley and then beyond.

- Cotton became central to the national economy, making up half of all the nation's exports. The South remained economically linked to the North, both as a market for its crops and as a source of manufactured goods. Both the New England and British textile mills were dependent on Southern cotton for their economic growth. New Orleans, Charleston, and Norfolk grew as important port cities through which to ship cotton.

The Growth of "King Cotton"

South has good conditions for farming. → South develops economy based on farming and enslaved labor.

Invention of cotton gin makes cotton manufacturing more profitable.

Industrial Revolution leads to growing textile industry which needs cotton to make cloth.

Cotton becomes the most valuable product in the South.

Rich landowners create huge plantations, relying on enslaved labor to grow cotton.

In the early 1800s, cotton became the South's most important crop.

Preparing for the Regents

Stimulus-Based Question: Graphic Organizer

Examine the graphic organizer at left.

- Why did the South become increasingly dependent on enslaved labor in the first half of the nineteenth century?

Life of Slaveowners on Farms and Plantations

Although they were a minority of the Southern free white population, slaveholding men with huge plantations and many enslaved workers dominated political, economic, and social life in the South. Planters' wives and daughters were responsible for the domestic sphere. They managed the care, feeding, and clothing of their families and the enslaved families as well.

Life of Enslaved People on Farms and Plantations

Daily life for those enslaved was very difficult. They had no control over their own lives or their children's lives, and they were at the mercy of the slaveholders and overseers. The enslaved who worked as field hands often toiled from dawn to sunset, while those who were house servants often worked long past sunset. They were physically and even sexually abused. However, the enslaved were also a financial investment, and this placed some limits on physical mistreatment. The enslaved continued to practice nonviolent resistance. Some practices were to slow down the pace of work, cause a problem on purpose through "carelessness," fake illness, or pretend not to understand.

After the Nat Turner Rebellion in 1831, more restrictive **slave** laws limited movement and quality of life. For example, it was now illegal to teach enslaved people to read and write. The enslaved could not legally marry, but families remained central to the African American community. Parents instilled the importance of family in their children, while preparing them to cope with a life of **slavery.** Children began work as young as eight years old. There was a constant fear of being "sold down the river," meaning enslaved families were broken up as planters moved west toward and then across the Mississippi. The religious practices of enslaved people blended Protestant Christian and African elements. Music was an important part of worship services.

Social Studies Practices
Gathering Evidence

- What were some of the effects of the expansion of slavery?

Andrew Jackson and the Rise of Mass Politics

Andrew Jackson was twice elected president of the United States, serving from 1829 to 1837. He was the first president elected from a state other than one of the 13 original states. In 1824, Jackson ran unsuccessfully for president. When none of four presidential candidates received a majority of the electoral votes the House of Representatives, as required by the Constitution's 12th Amendment, selected the president from the three candidates with the most electoral votes. Although Jackson had the most popular votes and the most electoral votes, the House, with each state casting one vote, chose John Quincy Adams as the president.

By the mid-1820s, most states had dropped their property qualifications for voting. In 1828, the number of voters was three times larger than it had been in 1824. Andrew Jackson, a popular hero of the War of 1812, a wealthy slaveholder, an Indian fighter, and a nationalist who opposed tariffs and pressed for cheap land for farmers, appealed to these new voters and won both the electoral and the popular vote.

Preparing for the Regents

Constitutional Issue

- What is the difference between the popular and the electoral vote?
- Examine how each of the presidential elections of 1800, 1824, 1876, 2000, and 2016 was resolved.

Andrew Jackson and the National Two-Party System

In 1832, selecting a presidential candidate became more democratic. For the first time, candidates were chosen by a national nominating convention, rather than a few party leaders. Rallies, slogans, and often vicious written attacks marked the advent of mass politics. Jackson's party, the Democrats, got its support from urban workers and middle-class and small farmers from the South and the West.

Both the first and second two-party systems helped to unify the United States in part because they were national, not sectional, parties. The first two-party system consisted of the **Federalists** and the **Democratic-Republicans** (formed from the Federalists and Anti-Federalists) parties that offered different political philosophies and proposals for action, disagreeing over interpretation of the Constitution. The **second two-party system** developed in 1834, when an anti-Jackson national party, the **Whigs**, was formed. Jackson is credited with turning the **Democratic Party** into an organized and unified political force from the local to the national level. Both parties ran campaigns that attracted interest and increased the numbers of those who voted and were involved in national issues. To maintain unity within each party, addressing slavery as a national issue was avoided.

The Spoils System

Andrew Jackson, insisting that it was a reform measure, instituted the **spoils system.** It gave government jobs to people who had worked to help Jackson and the Democratic Party win the 1828 election. This method of selecting government employees was called the spoils system because a Democratic senator defended the system by saying, "to the victor belong the spoils of the enemy." The spoils system was not replaced until 1883.

The National Bank Issue—The Bank War

Whether to renew the charter of the Second Bank of the United States provoked sectional differences and the opposition of President Jackson. Southerners and Westerners, who wanted a greater supply of money in circulation, distrusted the **Second Bank of the United States** and resented the bank's control over state banking. Most knowledgeable citizens recognized the bank's role in providing financial security.

In 1832, President Jackson vetoed a bill to re-charter the bank. He called the bank unconstitutional and a symbol of privilege and source of power of special northern interests. Jackson then withdrew federal money from the bank, effectively killing it. He placed the federal funds in largely unregulated state banks. Jackson ignored congressional protests. His actions provoked outrage. State banks used their newfound federal funds to engage in land speculation. That action ended in the Panic of 1837. It turned into a depression that lasted into the 1840s.

Andrew Jackson's Native American Policies

As American settlers moved westward in the 1800s, conflict continued with the Native Americans who lived in these territories. Under President Jackson, the government forced Native Americans in the Southeast to move off their homelands to allow for European American settlement.

Native American Cultural Survival Strategies

By the 1820s, there were few Native Americans in the northeast United States. In the Southeast, Cherokees, Chickasaws, Choctaws, and Creeks continued to live on large tracts of tribal lands. As American settlers moved ever westward, Native Americans tried a variety of strategies to cope and retain their land and culture.

- In the early 1800s, two Shawnee brothers, Prophet and Tecumseh, tried to build a **Pan-Indian Movement** in the Old Northwest, but this movement died with Tecumseh in 1811, when William Henry Harrison defeated him at Tippecanoe Creek.

- Meanwhile, a Seneca named Handsome Lake, urged the Iroquois to adopt a lifestyle based on temperance, education, farming, and peace. This lifestyle became known as **cultural revitalization.**

Analyzing Documents

Surrounded by the whites with their arts of civilization, which by destroying the resources of the savage doom him to weakness and decay, the fate of the Mohegan, the Narragansett, and the Delaware is fast overtaking the Choctaw, the Cherokee, and the Creek. That this fate surely awaits them if they remain within the limits of the States does not admit of a doubt. Humanity and national honor demand that every effort should be made to avert such a calamity.

—President Andrew Jackson, 1st Annual Message to Congress, December 1828

- What does this quote reveal about Jackson's attitude toward Native Americans?

- In 1813, Creeks attacked settlers in Georgia and Alabama in a series of raids, but in 1814, they were defeated by Andrew Jackson at Horseshoe Bend, Alabama. The Mississippi Territory was then opened to settlement.

- The Cherokees attempted to survive and retain their culture through **cultural adaptation,** combining elements of Native American and European culture, including a written constitution and an agricultural lifestyle. This strategy, however, did not save them.

States vs. Federal Policy: Who Has Final Legal Authority Over Native Americans?

Andrew Jackson became president at a time when Georgia, Alabama, and Mississippi were maintaining that they, the states, not the federal government, had legal authority over Native American nations. Jackson had long supported that position. In fact, the first treaty between the United States and a tribe was negotiated by the Continental Congress and approved in 1778. The Supreme Court upheld decades of precedent and ruled for the Native American nations. The federal government used a combination of treaties and force to move Native Americans to lands west of the Mississippi River. The treaties were worthless, however, because Native Americans were pressured repeatedly to give up their tribal land even though ownership was guaranteed by treaty.

The Indian Removal Act

In 1830, President Andrew Jackson succeeded in persuading Congress to pass the **Indian Removal Act.** It provided funds for all Native Americans to move west of the Mississippi to new lands given to them by the government. In 1832, the Cherokee went to court to prevent Georgia from taking their land. In *Worcester* v. *Georgia,* Chief Justice John Marshall ruled that Georgia had no authority over Cherokee territory, but Georgia simply ignored the ruling. Jackson personally entered the first negotiations, giving the tribes a choice of moving west or coming under state control. Most Cherokees refused to move so that in 1838 the U.S. Army rounded up the Cherokee and moved them west in a forced march known as the **Trail of Tears.**

The Seminole of Florida were also faced with removal. A group fought the effort in the Second Seminole War. Many remained in Florida. By the 1840s, however, only scattered groups of Native Americans still lived in the East.

Analyzing Documents

We wish to remain on the land of our fathers. We have a perfect and original right to remain without interruption. . . .

—Cherokee public appeal, July 17, 1830

- What does this quote reveal about how the Cherokee viewed their possession of the land?

Social Studies Practices
Constitutional Issues

- Examine evidence to determine whether or not President Andrew Jackson abused his constitutional powers.

Preparing for the Regents

Stimulus-Based Question: Map

Compare the map at right with the Territorial Expansion map on page 105.

- How does the map at right relate to the territorial expansion of the United States?

Native American Land Transfer Before 1850

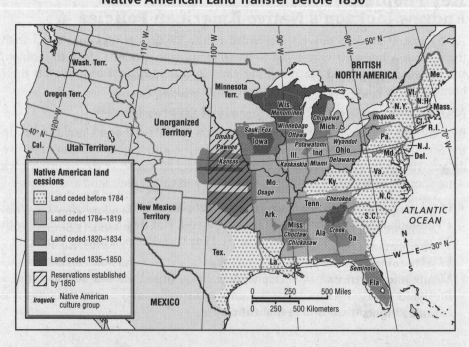

Differing Views Contribute to the Growth of Sectionalism

Lesson Overview

Different perspectives concerning constitutional, political, economic, and social issues contributed to the growth of sectionalism. As a new age of mass politics and reform dominated the 1830s and 1840s, tensions grew among the regions, pulling the North and the South apart. The Nullification Crisis, centered on tariffs, brought into the open the different perspectives of North and South on economics and federalism.

The Age of Reform's developing anti-slavery and abolitionist movements resulted in public discussion and debate about slavery. A reform movement for women's rights developed from the abolitionist movement. Immigration and territorial expansion produced growth and change. As more people moved west, the issue of the expansion of slavery became increasingly controversial, and sectional tensions increased.

Key Concept

11.3b Different perspectives concerning constitutional, political, economic, and social issues contributed to the growth of sectionalism.

Unifying Themes

As you review this lesson take special note of the following themes:

- **Time, Continuity, and Change** What were the causes and consequences of American nationalism in the first half of the 19th century? What were the causes and consequences of American sectionalism in the first half of the 19th century?

- **Geography, Humans, and the Environment** How did westward expansion intensify sectional differences?

- **Power, Authority, and Governance** How did both the North and South reconcile their positions on states' rights and on slavery with the Constitution?

Key People

John C. Calhoun	Angelina and Sarah Grimké
Andrew Jackson	Elizabeth Cady Stanton
Nat Turner	Lucretia Mott
William Lloyd Garrison	Harriet Tubman
Frederick Douglass	Abraham Lincoln
Sojourner Truth	Stephen A. Douglas
Harriet Beecher Stowe	John Brown

Key Terms and Events

nationalism	abolitionist movement	Texas Revolution
sectionalism	*The Liberator*	Mexican-American War
nullification	*Uncle Tom's Cabin*	Missouri Compromise
Nullification Crisis	Women's Rights	Compromise of 1850
state compact theory	Convention	popular sovereignty
supreme law of the	Declaration of	Kansas-Nebraska Act
land	Sentiments	
states' rights	Manifest Destiny	

Key Supreme Court Cases

As you review this lesson be sure you understand the significance of these key Supreme Court cases:

Marbury v. *Madison* (1803)
McCulloch v. *Maryland* (1819)
Dred Scott v. *Sanford* (1857)

Growing Sectionalism: States' Rights vs. Federal Supremacy

While American **nationalism** strengthened during the first half of the 19th century, **sectionalism** developed, as constitutional, social, economic, and political differences pulled the North and South in opposite directions. Debate raged over how the balance of power between the states and the federal government should be achieved. From 1828 to 1833, this debate focused on **protective tariffs** and **nullification.** An early danger sign for the nation was the constitutional and economic issues raised by the **Nullification Crisis.**

Sectionalism and the Tariff Issue

Southern states opposed protective tariffs. The agricultural South saw northern industries as the chief beneficiaries of such tariffs. They saw the federal government supporting the North at the South's expense. The tariff made British imports more expensive so that Southerners were forced to buy northern manufactured goods.

With passage of the high **Tariff of 1828,** called the **Tariff of Abominations** in the South, tensions increased. Vice President **John C. Calhoun** of South Carolina wrote the **South Carolina Exposition and Protest,** in which he argued the **state compact theory.** Calhoun stated that states, having created the federal government by ratification of the Constitution, had the right to **nullify,** or declare void, any federal law that a state considered harmful to its survival as a sovereign entity. Moreover, a state also had the right to **secede,** meaning to leave the compact into which it had entered.

Unionists opposing the state compact theory pointed out that the Preamble to the Constitution says that the people of the United States, not of the states, created the government of this nation. Furthermore, the Constitution is the **supreme law of the land** because it was ratified by the people in special conventions, not by votes in state legislatures. This pro-Federalism position is reinforced by Supreme Court decisions. As early as 1803 in *Marbury* v. *Madison,* the Supreme Court established its right of **judicial review.** Only the federal courts, not a state, could declare a federal law unconstitutional. Chief Justice John Marshall in *McCulloch* v. *Maryland* (1819) declared that in the United States the people are constitutionally sovereign. He wrote: "The government of the Union, then, . . . is, emphatically, and truly, a government of the people. In form and in substance it emanates from them. Its powers are granted by them, and are to be exercised directly on them, and for their benefit."

In 1798 in the **Virginia and Kentucky Resolutions,** Madison and Jefferson had cited the state compact theory in a similar argument regarding a state's right to interpret federal laws. They were arguing against the **Alien and Sedition Acts** that they believed challenged constitutionally protected first amendment civil liberties. They were making a political statement while attempting to unite the states in a common action. Only Jefferson, in the Kentucky Resolutions, defended the right of nullification. In 1832, other Southern states did not support South Carolina's nullification of the tariff.

Social Studies Practices
Economics

• What is a protective tariff?

• Why did the South believe that the North benefited from a protective tariff while the South did not?

• How did this debate increase sectional conflict?

In response to a slightly lower 1832 tariff, South Carolina enacted an **Ordinance of Nullification,** voiding both the 1828 and 1832 tariffs in the state. The state also threatened to secede if force was used to collect the tariffs. President **Andrew Jackson**

President Andrew Jackson

- defended federal supremacy and denounced nullification as treasonous.
- requested a **Force Bill** to use federal troops in South Carolina to enforce the law by collecting the tariffs.
- supported the **Compromise Tariff of 1833**, proposed by **Henry Clay**, that gradually lowered tariffs.

Jackson's solution resolved the immediate crisis. South Carolina withdrew its tariff nullification but then nullified the Force Bill. The fundamental issue remained unresolved. Calhoun, who had resigned as vice president in order to lead the nullification effort, continued his promotion of **states' rights** as a U.S. senator from South Carolina.

Social Studies Practices
Constitutional Issues

What is an example of a conflict in the pre–Civil War period involving each concept below?

- supremacy clause
- states' rights
- sectionalism
- nationalism
- federalism
- nullification
- secession

Origins of the American Reform Tradition

In the early 1800s, changes such as the First Industrial Revolution, urbanization, new waves of immigrants, westward expansion, and the slave-based southern cotton economy created opportunities as well as serious problems for the United States. The Enlightenment and the American Revolutionary tradition of the belief in reason and the ability of people to bring about change were important factors for reform.

Still another motivator of reform was the **Second Great Awakening,** a religious revival movement. It emphasized self-reliance and one's ability to affect one's future and to improve the world. The Second Great Awakening called for self-improvement, human perfectibility, and fighting forces of evil. The religious feelings that drove reform were reinforced by the Republican political belief in civic virtue—that a good citizen acts for the common good.

A newly expanded middle class in cities and small towns had the time and financial resources to engage in reform. They also saw firsthand the negative effects of urbanization. Educated women played an important organizational role in the various reform movements. Other participants were Quakers and Unitarians. Reformers used the new technology in printing and transportation to spread their message of reform. The work of reform was done primarily by voluntary organizations started at local and, sometimes, regional levels. Some became national organizations, but growing sectional differences often worked against organized national efforts.

Examples of Early Reform Movements

Reformers pushed for the creation of prisons, hospitals, orphanages, and institutions to care for physically disabled people. In addition, a strong temperance movement was organized to eliminate alcohol consumption. Education and care of the mentally ill were two other areas of American life that inspired reform movements.

Public Schools Reformers recognized that if the people were to govern, they needed to be educated. Under the leadership of **Horace Mann,** Massachusetts led the nineteenth-century drive for public education. Mann believed that every human being had the right to an education, and he developed an educational system with grade levels and teacher training. His ideas spread rapidly. By 1860, most people had at least an elementary education in all regions but the South. Educational opportunities for girls and young women also expanded.

Care of the Mentally Ill In the early 1800s, most mentally ill people were kept locked up in prisons. In the 1840s, a Massachusetts reformer named **Dorothea Dix** studied the poor treatment of the mentally ill and reported her findings to the state legislature, which authorized funds for mental hospitals. Dix later worked with several other states, helping them to follow the Massachusetts model.

The Development of the Abolitionist Movement

In the 1820s, the **abolitionist movement,** or the effort to end slavery, grew as cotton production became more profitable and slavery grew in numbers and spread west. The antislavery movement was part of the larger American reform tradition. In the Revolutionary Era, Philadelphia Quakers opposed slavery and Northern states began to abolish it. Under the Articles of Confederation, slavery was banned in the Northwest Territory. To create our present government, the Founders agreed to constitutional compromises on slavery. In 1820, the debate was over whether enslaved people and the institution of slavery should move west with settlers of new territories. The issue was temporarily settled with the Missouri Compromise.

Nat Turner's Rebellion

Southerners lived with a sense of insecurity. Their society was increasingly anchored in violence. Every day enslaved people faced the threat, stated or unstated, of physical abuse, even death, while the possibility of a revolt of the enslaved or free African Americans instilled constant fear within the white slaveholding society.

In the first decades of the 19th century, there were several notable slave revolts. None succeeded. In 1800, **Gabriel Prosser's** Conspiracy in Virginia, led by urban skilled workers, was discovered. In 1822, **Denmark Vesey's** plans to lead a South Carolina revolt were uncovered. In 1831, **Nat Turner** launched a revolt in southern Virginia. Turner was an enslaved preacher who considered himself a religious prophet. He led his five followers, a number that grew to 60, from one plantation to another, killing over 50 white men, women, and children. The state military and vigilante groups put down the rebellion, killing over 200 African Americans, many not involved in the revolt. Trials and executions followed.

Southern lawmakers, having seen their worst fears verified, passed increasingly strict laws to control the enslaved. All forms of emancipation (set free) were made illegal. Gathering in groups was further restricted. Teaching an enslaved person to read and write was made illegal. The South became more defensive and hostile to what it saw as threats to its way of life.

Garrison Founds the American Antislavery Society

In the North, Nat Turner's Rebellion led some of those already against slavery or uncomfortable about the issue to reconsider their approach to slavery. At the time, the conventional antislavery position favored gradual emancipation, compensation for slaveholders, and colonization, meaning removal of African Americans to Africa. This was the position of the **American Colonization Society,** organized in 1817.

In 1831 in Boston, **William Lloyd Garrison** started the **New England Anti-Slavery Society** and *The Liberator,* an abolitionist newspaper. **Abolitionism** was controversial at the time, and Garrison's view of abolitionism was considered radical. In his first issue, he wrote

On this subject, I do not wish to think, or speak, or write, with moderation. No! no! Tell a man whose house is on fire, to give a moderate alarm; . . . tell the mother to gradually extricate [pull out] her babe from the fire into which it has fallen;—but urge me not to use moderation in a cause like the present. I am in earnest . . .—I will not retreat a single inch—AND I WILL BE HEARD.

—William Lloyd Garrison, *The Liberator,* 1831

In 1833, Garrison and others founded the **American Anti-Slavery Society,** formed to develop and support a plan for immediate rather than gradual abolition of slavery. Members were from upstate New York, northern cities, and those western states with large northeastern populations. The movement attracted a wide variety of activists—men, women, religious leaders, freed slaves, wealthy and poor—including Frederick Douglass, Sojourner Truth, and Harriet Beecher Stowe.

Frederick Douglass: Abolitionist Leader and Social Reformer

Frederick Douglass was the leading African American abolitionist. He was a slave, a runaway slave, and then a free African American. He was famous as a social reformer, abolitionist, speaker, editor, and author. In 1841, he began speaking against slavery for the American Anti-Slavery Society, relating his slave experience to abolitionism. In 1845, Douglass wrote his autobiography, *Narrative of the Life of Frederick Douglass, An American Slave, Written by Himself,* first published in *The Liberator.* From 1847 to 1851, Douglass published his own abolitionist newspaper, *The North Star,* in Rochester, New York. It continued in circulation as *Frederick Douglass' Paper.*

Douglass broke with Garrison when the antislavery movement divided over Garrison's radical positions. Garrison charged that because the Constitution protected slavery, a new one had to be written. Douglass instead agreed with those who believed the Founders thought the constitutional compromises would not be permanent. Slavery would end. He continued his work with those who advocated political action against slavery, convinced that Congress had the authority to abolish slavery.

Sojourner Truth

Sojourner Truth was born into slavery in upstate New York but escaped. She became a free African American who devoted her life to social reform and civil rights. A religious speaker, like many in the reform movement she campaigned for several causes, including temperance, women's rights, and abolition.

Harriet Beecher Stowe Writes *Uncle Tom's Cabin*

Harriet Beecher Stowe wrote ***Uncle Tom's Cabin*** to urge active opposition to the **Fugitive Slave Law** passed by Congress as part of the **Compromise of 1850.** Published in 1852, *Uncle Tom's Cabin* was the bestselling book of the nineteenth century, with 300,000 copies sold in the first year alone. Its vivid portrayal of the horrors of slavery influenced many in the United States and in Europe to reconsider their perspectives on the South as well as on slavery and its expansion west. Southerners protested by writing novels praising the life of enslaved people. Harriet Beecher Stowe was an abolitionist raised in a family of reformers. She spoke about her book in the United States and abroad, advocating abolition.

Frederick Douglass

The Abolitionist Impact in the North

Some Northerners were angered by Garrison's strong anti-Constitution position and unrelenting refusal to consider other points of view. In 1834 and 1835, there were incidents of anti-abolitionist mob protests, riots, and death threats in Boston, New York, and Philadelphia. Economic considerations influenced some northern merchants, who feared that the abolition movement would further sour relations between the North and the South and harm trade. White workers feared competition from escaped or freed slaves willing to work for lower wages. But Garrison succeeded in bringing the antislavery cause out into open debate. By 1840, the abolitionist movement had over 1,000 chapters in the North.

The South Opposes the Abolitionist Movement

The beginning of the abolitionist movement, occurring at the same time as Nat Turner's Rebellion and the Nullification Crisis, aroused Southern hostility. By 1860, all aspects of southern life and culture, such as religion, literature, the arts, and politics, were based on a defense of slavery. Slavery was called a "positive good." It was said to be condoned in the Bible.

In 1835, Southerners, with the support of President Jackson, were able to stop delivery of abolitionist mailings to religious and political leaders in the South. Anti-abolitionist mobs or the postmasters were allowed to continue destroying United States mail. In 1836, southern members of Congress succeeded in passing the so-called **gag rule,** which prohibited any antislavery petitions from being taken up in the House. The gag rule stayed in place for eight years. Abolitionists pointed out that the gag rule was an example of how slavery threatened the rights of all Americans.

The Women's Rights Movement

Women were deeply involved in a variety of reform efforts. Some soon recognized that their own rights were a cause for which it was worth fighting.

The Women's Rights Movement Emerges From the Abolitionist Movement

Reform-minded women were actively involved in local and national movements for change. These middle-class, educated women were often active in their churches, which motivated involvement in temperance and antislavery efforts. In the 1830s and 1840s, after experiencing discrimination within reform organizations, some women shifted their focus to women's rights while maintaining their efforts for abolition and temperance. Frederick Douglass, William Lloyd Garrison, and Sojourner Truth were among the many well-known abolitionists who also actively worked for women's rights.

Sisters from a prominent slaveholding family in South Carolina, **Sarah and Angelina Grimké** were early activists speaking and writing for the abolition of slavery, racial equality, and women's rights. Hating slavery, they moved to Philadelphia in the 1820s and became Quakers. In the 1830s, William Lloyd Garrison recruited them, as former slaveholders, to the abolitionist cause. The Grimké sisters' efforts on behalf of women's rights developed from the objections, insults, and threats they faced at a time when women speaking publicly, especially to audiences of both sexes, was not only unacceptable but also outrageous behavior.

The roots of the 70-year-long organized campaign for women's rights can be traced to Elizabeth Cady Stanton and Lucretia Mott. Women delegates selected to attend the 1840 World Anti-Slavery Convention in London, they were barred because of their sex from participation in the convention. At the same time, back in the United States, the American Anti-Slavery Society was splitting, in part, over a similar issue, whether women's participation in the abolitionist movement hurt the cause.

The Start of the Women's Rights Movement at Seneca Falls

The women's rights movement began officially in 1848, when Stanton and Mott organized the **Women's Rights Convention** in Seneca Falls, New York. **Elizabeth Cady Stanton** is celebrated as the intellectual and philosophical leader of the drive for women's legal rights, especially for suffrage, meaning the right to vote. **Lucretia Mott**, a Quaker, was well known for her work as an abolitionist. Over 300 people attended the Seneca Falls Convention, including 40 men, of whom Frederick Douglass was the most famous.

At the meeting, Stanton read her **Declaration of Sentiments.** The first goal of this chiefly middle-class movement was to end legal inequalities faced by married women. New York that year had passed a Married Women's Property Act, but in most states in 1848, a husband had the legal right to control his wife's property, earnings, and children. A married woman existed legally only through her husband. The convention attendees approved all of the demands of the Declaration unanimously except the call for women to have the right to vote. Aided by outspoken support from Douglass, it too passed, but not unanimously. One hundred of the 300 attending the convention signed the Declaration of Sentiments.

Much of the newspaper coverage of the convention was negative, but the publicity brought the issue to the public's attention. It helped launch a national movement, a movement with its objectives clearly defined in the natural rights language of the Declaration of Independence.

Territorial Expansion and the Spread of Slavery

Between 1783 and 1853, the United States expanded to its present continental boundaries.

Manifest Destiny Spurs Territorial Expansion

In 1845, a New York journalist is said to have come up with the term **Manifest Destiny** while writing to urge Texas annexation. John L. O'Sullivan had given a name to a belief long held by many Americans. Manifest Destiny was motivated by nationalism as well as the faith in human perfectibility we have seen in the religious and other reforms of the 1830s and 1840s. Manifest Destiny is the conviction that the United States had a clear, inevitable, and divine mission

- to expand westward to the Pacific Ocean and even to possess the entire North American continent.
- to spread the American ideals of freedom, liberty, and democracy.

What Americans saw as Manifest Destiny was viewed quite differently by the Native American and Mexican peoples, who possessed these western lands. Expansion increased national pride, but by raising serious questions about slavery, it also contributed to growing sectional tensions.

Elizabeth Cady Stanton

Preparing for the Regents

Stimulus-Based Question: Primary Source

We hold these truths to be self-evident: that all men and women are created equal. . . . The history of mankind is a history of repeated injuries and usurpations [seizures of power] on the part of man toward woman, . . . [to establish] absolute tyranny over her. . . . He has never permitted her to exercise her inalienable right to the elective franchise. . . . He has made her, if married, in the eye of the law, civilly dead. He has taken from her all right in property, even to the wages she earns.

—Elizabeth Cady Stanton, Declaration of Sentiments, 1848

- Cite textual evidence to analyze how this document is structured and why.
- Evaluate the demands made in the Declaration of Sentiments.

Motives to Move West

Often using river systems, the first Americans to move westward beyond the Mississippi River were explorers, naturalists, trappers, traders, and missionaries. They were followed by trailblazers and settlers who traveled along routes such as the Santa Fe and Oregon trails. In 1846, Mormons, led by **Brigham Young**, settled at the Great Salt Lake. In order to escape religious persecution, they selected a spot which placed them far from others.

Discovery of gold and silver in California and other western territories accelerated settlement in those regions. Most settlers chose more prosperous lands in the far West, leaving the flat but dry and treeless Great Plains to be settled after the Civil War. Cotton planters with their enslaved workers moved steadily west across the Appalachians, seeking new, larger, and richer farmland. Native Americans were resettled in the west only to be moved again as the wave of settlers reached them.

Lands Acquired Between 1783–1853

The Treaty of Paris of 1783 set the western border of the United States at the Mississippi River. By 1853, the continental United States had expanded to the boundaries we recognize today.

Louisiana Purchase (1803) Stretching from the Rocky Mountains to the Mississippi River and including the Great Plains, this territory was bought from France for $15 million. In 1803, President Thomas Jefferson sent **Meriwether Lewis** and **William Clark** to seek a water route to the Pacific Ocean, to locate economic resources, and to strengthen United States control of the territory. Their data and maps contributed to the nation's expansion by increasing understanding of the vast area.

Florida (1819) This territory was acquired by treaty from Spain, satisfying southern expansionists. In the **Adams-Onís Treaty,** Spain also gave up its claims to the Pacific Northwest in return for the United States giving up its claims to Texas.

Texas (1845) The United States acquired Texas and what is now parts of New Mexico, Oklahoma, Colorado, Wyoming, and Kansas from Mexico by **annexation.** After Mexico declared its independence from Spain in 1821, southern slaveholders and other American settlers moved into Texas. In 1836, in the **Texas Revolution,** the Americans declared independence from Mexico. After defeating the Mexican army, they created the Republic of Texas.

In 1837, Texas requested admission to the Union. However, President Andrew Jackson and later President **Martin Van Buren** were concerned about the political effects of admitting another slave state as well as the diplomatic effects of making land still claimed by Mexico a part of the United States.

In 1845, after nine years of controversy, Texas was admitted to the Union as a slave state during the administration of President John Tyler and days before the inauguration of President **James K. Polk.** The territory that the United States acquired from Mexico was by annexation not by treaty. A treaty is an agreement between nations, while annexation adds territory to a country by the action of only one nation. While a treaty requires a two-thirds vote of the Senate, annexation by a **joint resolution** needs only a majority of each house of Congress.

Preparing for the Regents

• Why were Texas and Hawaii each annexed by joint resolution instead of by treaty?

Territorial Expansion of the United States and Other Acquisitions

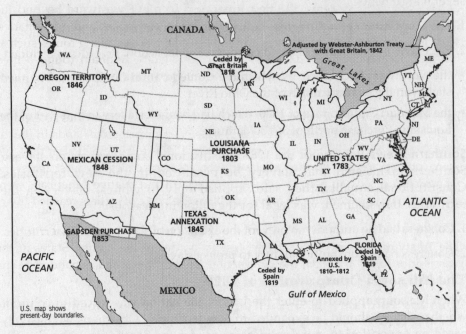

Preparing for the Regents

Stimulus-Based Questions: Map

Using the map at left and the map on page 96, answer the following questions.

- What was the effect of the Appalachian Mountains and Rocky Mountains on settlement?
- Why was the Great Plains the last region to be settled?
- How did the arid conditions affect the settlement of parts of the Mexican Cession?

Oregon Country (1846) What is now Oregon, Washington, Idaho, and parts of Montana and Wyoming was gained from Great Britain in a compromise that continued the northern border set at the 49th parallel all the way to the Pacific coast.

Mexican Cession (1848) What is now California, Nevada, Utah, Arizona, and parts of New Mexico, Colorado, and Wyoming became part of the United States by the Treaty of Guadalupe Hidalgo, which ended the **Mexican-American War** (1846–1848). The United States paid $15 million to Mexico. Mexico strongly objected to the Texas annexation. Tensions increased when it became clear that President James Polk wanted to acquire California. Polk sent an envoy to Mexico with an offer to buy California and at the same time moved federal troops into the Rio Grande area that was at the center of a border dispute between the United States and Mexico. When fighting occurred there, war was declared. National opinion was divided. Expansionists welcomed an opportunity to acquire more land. Northerners feared the future addition of more slave states. Some, such as Abraham Lincoln, saw it as a "war of conquest," others saw it as fulfilling "Manifest Destiny." The **Wilmot Proviso** was never approved but it brought the slavery issue into open national debate.

Gadsden Purchase (1853) This piece of land in southern Arizona and New Mexico was purchased from Mexico as a possible railroad route.

The Expansion of Slavery and the Threat of Civil War

The issue of expansion of slavery into new territories between the North and South threatened the existence of the nation. It involved moral questions about the very existence of slavery as well as fundamental constitutional issues. The expansion of American territory in the West inflamed the controversy over whether these new territories should allow slavery or not. At stake was the power to control Congress and elect a president.

Constitutional Debates: Viewpoints on the Extension of Slavery

With the expansion of the United States in the West, controversy brewed over whether slavery should be allowed in these new territories.

Analyzing Documents

. . . as an express and fundamental condition to the acquisition of any territory from . . . Mexico, . . . neither slavery nor involuntary servitude shall ever exist in any part of said territory. . . .

—The Wilmot Proviso, 1846

- Why did the Wilmot Proviso create controversy?
- From the wording, what was the writer's position on slavery?

Social Studies Practices

Chronological Reasoning

Below are eight events that led to the Civil War.

- Place them in chronological order
- Identify how the events are related to each other chronologically.

Compromise of 1850

Confederacy formed

Dred Scott v. *Sanford* decision

John Brown's raid

Kansas-Nebraska Act

Lincoln elected president

Missouri Compromise

South Carolina secedes

Social Studies Practices

Civic Issues

Compromise is essential to democratic government.

- How did the Missouri Compromise postpone the clash between the North and the South?
- Why did the Compromise of 1850 satisfy neither side?

Northern Views Northerners who sought to stop the spread of slavery had several arguments:

1. The Constitution gave Congress jurisdiction, or power, over the territories.

2. Precedent, or previous acts, justified congressional action. Precedents included

- the Northwest Ordinance, by which the Confederation Congress had banned slavery in the territory north of the Ohio River.
- the Missouri Compromise of 1820, which had banned slavery in that part of the Louisiana Purchase north of 36° 30′ latitude.

Southern Views Because of the 1787 constitutional compromises on slavery, Southerners insisted that slavery be permitted in the new territories. Constitutional equality, they said, applied only to whites. Slavery in the territories, they claimed, was legal for the following reasons:

1. Congress had no authority to prevent the extension of slavery into the territories.

2. Congress had a constitutional duty to protect slavery.

The Missouri Compromise of 1820

When Missouri applied to enter the Union, the nation was forced to confront whether slavery should be expanded to new territories. Objections were largely based on opposition to more political power for the South rather than on the morality of slavery. As a way to keep the balance of slave and free states in the Senate, the Missouri Compromise admitted Missouri as a slave state and Maine as a free state. Slavery in the Louisiana Purchase north of the southern boundary of Missouri was banned. The crisis faded away for a time.

The Compromise of 1850

Until 1850, with an equal number of slave and free states in the Union, the South maintained a balance of power in the Senate. That year, this balance was threatened when California, its rapid growth aided by the Gold Rush, applied to become a free state. Again, the question of slavery in the new territories was settled for a brief time. The **Compromise of 1850** included four key laws

1. California entered the Union as a free state.

2. A stricter **Fugitive Slave Law** required that escaped slaves be returned.

3. Slave trade, but not slavery, was prohibited in Washington, D.C.

4. **Popular sovereignty,** or a vote of the people living in the territory, would determine whether a territory in the Mexican Cession was to be slave or free.

The Compromise of 1850 pleased no one. Some Northerners engaged in **civil disobedience** against the Fugitive Slave Law by protesting the return of runaway slaves and aiding slaves trying to reach the safety of Canada. Abolitionists had earlier organized the **Underground Railroad,** a series of safe houses where escaping slaves could rest safely as they made their way north and into Canada. They were reenergized in their efforts. **Harriet Tubman,** who made 19 trips to escort runaways, was a leader of the Underground Railroad. Southern defenders of states' rights supported the authority of federal government officials to locate and return slaves who might be fugitives without following due process.

The popular sovereignty provision was unclear. Would the vote to make a territory slave or free be held at the time the territory was settled or when it applied to become a state? This uncertainty led to further conflict and to violence.

The Kansas-Nebraska Act of 1854

In 1820, the Missouri Compromise had prohibited slavery in the lands that made up Kansas and Nebraska. The **Kansas-Nebraska Act of 1854** overturned the Missouri Compromise by allowing those two territories, both north of 36° 30', to decide the question of slavery in their state by popular sovereignty.

Violence erupted when pro- and antislavery people rushed into Kansas to vote on the slave or free state issue. The territory was called **Bleeding Kansas** after a pro-slavery mob destroyed homes, stores, and offices in anti-slavery Lawrence, and John Brown's group killed pro-slavery settlers at Pottawatomie Creek. Violence extended to the U.S. Senate when, angered at a speech made by abolitionist Senator Charles Sumner, Southern congressman Preston Brooks assaulted Sumner on the Senate floor. Sumner was so badly injured that he could not return to the Senate for three years.

Rise of the Republican Party

Reactions to the Kansas-Nebraska Act led to a reorganization of the national political party system. One major party, the **Whigs,** split into northern and southern wings and soon died out. By 1854, the Democrats were seriously weakened in the North and in 1860 divided into Northern and Southern parties. In 1854, the **Republican Party** was founded to oppose the spread of slavery, not to abolish it. It was a sectional rather than a national party, made up of former Free Soilers, anti-immigrant and antislavery Know-Nothings, northern Whigs, and northern antislavery Democrats.

The Dred Scott Case

In 1857 in ***Dred Scott* v. *Sanford,*** the Supreme Court ruled that Dred Scott remained enslaved although he had lived in a free state and free territory because

- African Americans were not citizens and therefore had no right to sue in federal court or seek constitutional protection.

- Congress could not deprive citizens of their right to their property (enslaved people) by banning slavery in any territory. The Missouri Compromise was unconstitutional.

The *Dred Scott* decision further inflamed sectional divisions. In the North, the Supreme Court lost all credibility. The basis of the Republican platform, halting the spread of slavery, was now constitutionally invalid.

The Lincoln-Douglas Debates

In Illinois in 1858, **Abraham Lincoln,** a Republican, challenged the well-known Senator **Stephen A. Douglas,** author of the Kansas-Nebraska Act, in the campaign for U.S. Senate. A series of debates was held, then the Illinois legislature reelected Douglas to the Senate. The Lincoln-Douglas debates weakened Douglas in the South while making Lincoln a national political figure unacceptable to the South because of his position against the extension of slavery. Lincoln had accepted the Republican Senate nomination with a speech that included the famous lines:

"A house divided against itself cannot stand. I believe this government cannot endure, permanently half slave and half free. I do not expect the Union to be dissolved—I do not expect the house to fall—but I do expect it will cease to be divided. It will become all one thing or all the other."

John Brown's Raid at Harpers Ferry

In 1859, **John Brown** led a small group in a raid against a federal arsenal in what is now West Virginia. His plan was to seize weapons and organize a slave uprising. Brown was unsuccessful and was later executed for treason. In the North, Brown became a hero. In the South, distrust of the North increased.

Analyzing Documents

It is the opinion of the Court that the Act of Congress which prohibited a citizen from holding and owning property of this kind in the territory of the United States north of the line . . . is not warranted by the Constitution, and is therefore void. . . .

—Dred Scott v. Sanford, 1857

- What is meant by "property of this kind"?

- What were the Supreme Court's reasons for declaring the Missouri Compromise unconstitutional?

- What role did the Northwest Ordinance play in the *Dred Scott* decision?

Preparing for the Regents

- Why did the "House Divided" speech hurt Lincoln in his Senate race but help him to be elected president?

Disputes Over States' Rights and Slavery Lead to Civil War

Key Concept

11.3c Long-standing disputes over States' rights and slavery and the secession of Southern states from the Union, sparked by the election of Abraham Lincoln, led to the Civil War. After the issuance of the Emancipation Proclamation, freeing the enslaved became a major Union goal. The Civil War resulted in tremendous human loss and physical destruction.

Lesson Overview

The Southern states saw their power and influence decreasing while the disputes on states' rights and slavery became louder and opinions became more rigid. In 1860, when Abraham Lincoln was elected president, Southern states began to secede from the Union. The first state to secede was South Carolina, and there, in Charleston harbor, the Civil War began. Lincoln's primary goal was to save the nation from division.

The relative strengths of the Union and the Confederacy in terms of industrial capacity, transportation facilities, and military leadership contributed to a long and devastating war. After the issuance of the Emancipation Proclamation, freeing the enslaved became a major Union goal. The constitutional question of federal supremacy versus states' rights was settled, at a great cost in lives, on the battlefields of Antietam and Gettysburg. The North won, but the war had a lasting effect on the United States.

Unifying Themes

As you review this lesson take special note of the following themes::

- **Time, Continuity, and Change** Why did the Union and the Confederacy interpret slavery, secession, federalism, states' rights, and freedom differently? How did those different interpretations affect how each side conducted the war?

- **Geography, Humans, and the Environment** What were the positive and negative effects of the Civil War on the physical environment of the South?

- **Power, Authority, and Governance** What fundamental principles and values of a constitutional democracy were challenged during the Civil War?

- **Creation, Expansion, and Interaction of Economic Systems** What effect did the economic systems of the Union and the Confederacy have on the outcome of the Civil War?

- **Science, Technology, and Innovation** What are examples in the North of technology and innovation both helping the war effort and accelerating industrial growth?

Key People

Abraham Lincoln

Jefferson Davis

Robert E. Lee

Ulysses S. Grant

Key Terms and Events

secede

Confederate States of America

border states

writ of *habeas corpus*

martial law

Emancipation Proclamation

Thirteenth Amendment

Gettysburg Address

The Election of 1860

The election of 1860 showed clearly how divided the United States had become. The only remaining national party, the Democratic Party, split between the North and the South, with each wing running a candidate. Their candidates were **Stephen A. Douglas,** who ran as a Northern Democrat opposed to the extension of slavery, and **John Breckinridge,** who ran as a Southern Democrat favoring the extension of slavery but not secession. **Abraham Lincoln,** the first **Republican** to be elected president, received only 39 percent of the popular vote but a clear majority of the electoral vote. A group of Unionists organized the Constitutional Union party with **John Bell** as their candidate. Bell won in Virginia, Kentucky, and Tennessee. Breckinridge took the cotton-producing states. The Republicans were a sectional party. Lincoln was not even on the ballot in the South. His vote came entirely from the North and the Northwest.

Election of 1860

Presidential Candidate	Political Party	Popular Vote		Electoral Vote	
Abraham Lincoln	Republican	1,865,908	39.8%	180	59.4%
John Breckenridge	Southern Democrat	848,019	18.1%	72	23.8%
John Bell	Constitutional Union	590,901	12.6%	39	12.9%
Stephen A. Douglas	Democratic	1,380,202	29.5%	12	3.9%

The Secession Crisis

The election of a Northern Republican who opposed the extension of slavery motivated some Southerners to threaten secession and others to act on it. To prevent secession, Senator John Crittenden of Kentucky proposed the **Crittenden Compromise,** which would have designated slave versus free territory all the way to California, along the line of the Missouri Compromise. Lincoln opposed the plan. He refused to change his position against the extension of slavery, stating, "If we surrender, it is the end of us and the end of the government."

Lincoln's election was the immediate cause of secession. Lincoln would not be inaugurated until March 4, 1861, yet, in December 1860, South Carolina announced it was **seceding** from, or leaving, the Union. By February 1861, six more Southern states seceded and, with South Carolina, formed the **Confederate States of America.** Not until June 1861 did Tennessee become the last of the eleven states to secede. These Southerners had decided that under Lincoln and the Republicans they would no longer have political control of the nation's government.

President **James Buchanan** took no action to stop the secessionist states. He stated that neither he nor Congress had the right to preserve the Union by use of force because it "rests upon public opinion and can never be cemented by the blood of its citizens shed in war." Lincoln disagreed and denied that states could secede. In his **First Inaugural Address** in March 1861, Lincoln stated that "in view of the Constitution and the law, the Union is unbroken."

Constitutional Issue: Preservation of the Union Once a state had entered the United States, did it have the right to leave? From the Southern view, the South had the right to secede because the United States had not protected Southern rights. In this case, only the rights of the white population were being considered. Lincoln took the position that states could not leave the Union. No minority could act to destroy the nation and its government.

Preparing for the Regents

Stimulus-Based Questions: Chart and Map

Review the chart on page 112 and the map on this page.

- What advantages did the South have at the beginning of the Civil War? What advantages did the North have?

- How did industrial capacity and transportation facilities affect the outcome of the war?

- How can the differences between the two areas best be explained?

- Why does the map show the five border states differently? With which side did these states align?

The Union and the Confederacy, 1861

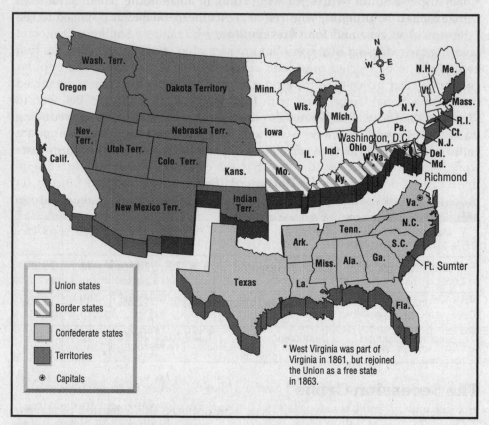

Union states
Border states
Confederate states
Territories
⊛ Capitals

* West Virginia was part of Virginia in 1861, but rejoined the Union as a free state in 1863.

The Civil War Begins

Lincoln's policy was to oppose secession but to take no military action until the South fired against Union forces. The South, not the Union, would have to start any military conflict. In April 1861, the South bombarded and seized Fort Sumter in Charleston Harbor, South Carolina. Lincoln called for troops to put down the rebellion. Four more Southern states, including Virginia, seceded. The Civil War had begun.

Lincoln's Aims and Actions in the Civil War

From the beginning of the secession crisis, Lincoln's goal was to preserve the Union. In 1862, Lincoln wrote: "My paramount object in this struggle is to save the Union and is not either to save or to destroy slavery. If I could save the Union without freeing any slave I would do it, and if I could save it by freeing all the slaves I would do it; and if I could save it by freeing some and leaving others alone I would also do that."

Lincoln took bold executive action to achieve this aim.

- He called out state militias, increased the size of the navy, ordered a naval blockade of the South, and approved funds for military expenses while Congress was not in session. Congress later approved these actions.

- He worked to keep the **border states** of Maryland, Delaware, Kentucky, Missouri, and later West Virginia in the Union, recognizing how their population, industries, and geographic locations benefited the Union and would aid the Confederacy.

Unifying Themes

Power, Authority, and Governance

Historically, presidential powers increase in times of war.

- In what ways did Lincoln increase presidential power during the Civil War?

- Name three other examples of increased presidential powers during wartime.

- Historically, how has the increase of presidential power during wartime been a threat to civil liberties?

- What arguments have been used to defend presidential wartime powers?

- He ordered the arrest of Southern sympathizers in Maryland and Delaware to prevent secession of those states. Failure to act might have meant the encircling of the capital by Confederate states.

- He suspended the **writ of *habeas corpus*** in areas not in rebellion. Lincoln maintained that as president he had the right to suspend the Great Writ. Congress approved his action in 1863, two years later.

- He declared **martial law,** which led to the arrests of thousands for suspected disloyalty.

- He censored newspapers and arrested publishers and editors.

Constitutional Issue: Presidential Power in War Lincoln's actions broadened the power of the executive. They also raised troubling questions: Were such actions constitutional? Did they fall within the scope of the president's war powers, or were they dictatorial? Did the fact that some Northerners sympathized with the rebelling South justify the limiting of their civil rights? Did Lincoln set precedents for expanded executive action that later presidents might use in more questionable circumstances?

The Emancipation Proclamation

In July 1862, Lincoln informed his cabinet that, using his power as commander in chief during a war, he was issuing an Emancipation Proclamation. He waited until the Union victory at Antietam in September to make his announcement. If the Confederacy had not ended their fight by January 1, 1863, Lincoln would end slavery in the states in rebellion. On that date, Lincoln's Emancipation Proclamation, a military order, went into effect. In addition to a war to restore the Union, the Civil War had become a fight to end slavery.

The **Emancipation Proclamation** decreed that all slaves in those areas still in rebellion against the Union "shall be then, thenceforward, and forever free." Because the proclamation exempted 750,000 slaves in the border states and in sections of the South that were under Union control, some saw it as largely symbolic. In fact, the Proclamation aided the war effort. It was a logical application of the total war strategy.

- It undermined the economic foundation of the Confederacy by accelerating the number of ex-slaves leaving the plantations and their work behind the military lines.

- It helped to satisfy Northern abolitionists and ensure their support.

- It averted, or stopped, British recognition of the Confederacy.

- It provided for African Americans to enlist in the Union army. With 185,000 to 200,000 African American enlistments, mostly from Southern states, Northern manpower increased.

- It added a moral cause to the war aims in addition to the constitutional and patriotic cause of Union Forever.

Permanent emancipation depended on a final military victory and on a constitutional amendment. Lincoln wanted to make sure that, at the end of the war, a court could not rule that those freed could be again enslaved because the slaveholders had lost their "property" without due process of law. On January 31, 1865, the House of Representatives followed the Senate and approved the **Thirteenth Amendment.**

President Abraham Lincoln

Social Studies Practices
Constitutional Issue

The privilege of the writ of habeas corpus shall not be suspended, unless when in cases of rebellion or invasion the public safety may require it.

—U.S. Constitution, Article I, Section 9

- Trace the history of the writ of *habeas corpus* in the United States to determine why it is included in the Constitution.

On April 8th, the war ended. A week later, Lincoln was killed. In December 1865, final state ratification of the amendment abolished slavery in the United States. Lincoln had called the proclamation "an act of justice." Some of his critics said it was unconstitutional. Others declared it a political act, an attempt to win reelection.

The Union and the Confederacy: A Comparison

The Union had overwhelming advantages in terms of population, industrial capacity, and transportation facilities. In time, properly mobilized and utilized, these factors would heavily influence the outcome of the war.

Comparison of the Economies of the Union and Confederacy, 1860

Category	North	South
Population	71%	29%
Factories	86%	14%
Factory Production	91%	9%
Bank Deposits	81%	19%
Firearms	97%	3%
Railroad Tracks	72%	28%
Pig Iron	93%	7%
Food Crops	72%	28%
Cotton	0.1%	99.9%
Horses	72%	28%
Cloth	94%	6%
Boots and Shoes	90%	10%

Population

The Union had a population of 21.5 million people compared to 9 million in the Confederacy. Of the 9 million in the South, over 3.5 million were enslaved people. Their work on the farms and plantations as well as aiding the Confederate army behind the lines was crucial. It explains why the United States designated enslaved people fleeing to freedom as contraband of war. **Contraband** refers to goods that an army takes from the enemy during a war. The formerly enslaved, living contraband, often became paid workers for the Union army. In 1863, the Emancipation Proclamation allowed former slaves and other African Americans to enlist in the Union army. **Jefferson Davis,** president of the Confederacy, and the Confederate Congress debated organizing military units of enslaved men, but approval was not given until March 1865.

Industrial Capacity

Continued rapid industrialization in the North and availability of farm lands in the West contributed to the Union's larger source of manpower. Except for the border states, free labor prevailed. Even as the Southern slave system collapsed, production throughout the Union increased. Mechanized farm machinery meant more food could be produced while freeing men to join the military. Technology continued to alter products.

When the Civil War began, the South had limited industrial capacity and the Confederacy was kept supplied with imported munitions. By 1863, the military industrial capacity included armories and foundries. But over time, the slave-based, labor-intensive cotton-growing agricultural system in the South was hurt by the war. The war was being fought almost exclusively in the South. Capture or destruction of land, railroad lines, and factories made organized mobilization of war resources difficult. In 1863, increased loss of enslaved workers, the main labor source, to the Union side further crippled the Southern war effort. Eventually, Northern shipyards built more ships, and the Northern blockade became effective. This led to shortages of food as well as military supplies. In 1864, inflation soared to 7,000% compared to 182% in the North. Furthermore, the Confederate government met opposition when attempting to collect food for the army or asking that some cotton-growing fields be shifted to producing much-needed food crops.

Transportation Facilities

When the war began, the Confederacy contained 9,000 miles of railroad track compared to the 21,700 miles of track in the Union. The South had a capacity to feed its army but had difficulty delivering food and other supplies to its troops. The new but limited railroad system deteriorated as the war progressed. Much was destroyed by Union forces. Confederacy philosophy of states' rights and limited government meant that the rail system remained under private control until February 1865. Most of the free labor that built, ran, and maintained the system went back to the North at the start of the war. Finally, the South did not have the industrial capability to build or maintain the rail system.

In contrast, during the war, the United States improved and increased the size of its rail system. Early in the war, Congress gave the federal government temporary control of moving the military by rail. The work was headed by railroad experts rather than by professional officers. As war continued, Union armies moved by rail further into the south and west while efficiently extending their supply lines. Railroad centers were targets of both sides.

Military Leadership

Because almost all of the nation's military academies were in the South, the Confederacy began the Civil War with a larger group of officers. Soon these officers were leading men in a defensive war on home territory, a particularly favorable position in nineteenth-century warfare.

A Virginian, **Robert E. Lee,** headed the Confederate Army of Northern Virginia. He led and inspired the most important Confederate army through major battles in the east until his surrender at Appomattox Court House in April 1865. In February 1865, he was given command of all Confederate forces. Two of Lee's generals in the Army of Northern Virginia, James Longstreet and Thomas J. (Stonewall) Jackson, are often singled out for outstanding military leadership. Some military historians have said that the Confederacy lacked strong military leadership in the West, such as at Vicksburg. There, they believe, is where the South lost the war.

Abraham Lincoln was the leader of all aspects of the Civil War for the Union. Early in the war, he knew what the Union must do in order to win. Not until March 1864 did **Ulysses S. Grant** become commander of the Army with the rank of Lieutenant General, a rank previously held only by George Washington. George G. Meade, William T. Sherman, and Winfield Scott Hancock rank high among the Union's generals.

The End of the War

Both sides settled on specific strategies that they believed would help their side win the war. By the war's end in April 1865, over half a million Americans were dead. The Union had won but at a great cost.

Military Strategies

The Confederate war strategy was to maintain its defensive position with bursts of attacks north against the Union army. The objective was to repeatedly inflict casualties and wear down the Union army until it lost the will to fight. The Confederacy hoped to gain aid and diplomatic recognition from Great Britain and France, two nations that relied on Southern cotton. Neither strategy was successful. The Emancipation Proclamation in particular prevented Britain from allying itself with a slave society. The **Battle of Gettysburg** was the turning point in the war. It was the last time that the South attempted to invade the North. From then on, Lee fought a defensive war.

The Union relied on its superior resources and technology. Union ships blockaded Southern ports to cut off overseas markets from both imports and exports. By late in the war, the navy achieved this objective and was able to prevent the Confederacy from importing food and military supplies. In 1863, General Grant accomplished another war aim. He led the Union forces at Vicksburg, Mississippi, to victory, giving the North control of the Mississippi River and dividing the South. Lincoln realized that the Union could not win the war by the traditional method of taking control of territory and occupying it, nor by capturing cities.

In 1864, Grant, the new commander, worked with Lincoln to implement a strategy of total war. The objective was to bring together in one coordinated effort all the nation's military, economic, industrial, financial, and diplomatic resources to destroy not only the Confederate army but also all that supported the Confederate war effort, including its labor system and its infrastructure.

Lincoln, Grant, and other leaders believed that improved leadership and a better strategy combined with the North's wealth of resources, including its manpower, would bring a final victory. General William T. Sherman's campaign through Georgia from Atlanta to Savannah destroyed Southern infrastructure such as railroad lines, plantations, and industry. It is a vivid example of the intensity of the last years of the war.

United States Military War Deaths

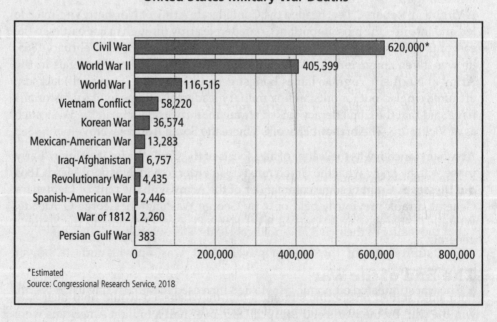

*Estimated

Source: Congressional Research Service, 2018

The Human Cost

The Civil War was the bloodiest war the United States has ever fought. Over 600,000 Americans lost their lives as new military technologies and old diseases struck down soldiers and civilians. Families along the border between the Union and the Confederacy were particularly devastated, as family members fought on opposite sides. The dead included President Abraham Lincoln himself, assassinated within days of the war's end.

The Robert Gould Shaw and the Massachusetts 54th Volunteer Infantry Regiment Memorial in Boston honors the first African American regiment to fight in the Civil War.

The worst single day of the war occurred in 1862 at the **Battle of Antietam** in Maryland, where the Southern commander General Robert E. Lee attempted to invade Maryland. Some 5,000 soldiers died and more than 17,000 were wounded. In 1863, the three-day Battle of Gettysburg in Pennsylvania was the most costly battle of the war, leaving more than 50,000 dead and wounded on both sides.

The Gettysburg Address

In November 1863, Lincoln dedicated the Union military cemetery at Gettysburg. His short speech summarized the meaning of the Civil War. The **Gettysburg Address** expresses Lincoln's view of America's past and his vision of its future. He defines democracy. Looking ahead, Lincoln uses the word *nation* several times in the 272-word speech.

Four score and seven years ago our fathers brought forth on this continent, a new nation, conceived in Liberty, and dedicated to the proposition that all men are created equal. Now we are engaged in a great civil war, testing whether that nation, or any nation so conceived and so dedicated, can long endure. . . . that we here highly resolve that these dead shall not have died in vain . . . and that government of the people, by the people, for the people, shall not perish from the earth.

—Abraham Lincoln, The Gettysburg Address, November 1863

Major Impacts of the Civil War

- The issue of secession was settled and the Union preserved, but a legacy of resentment, bitterness, and divisiveness remained.
- With the passage of the Thirteenth Amendment, the enslaved people were freed, but the reality of their civil and political rights was unresolved.
- The supremacy of the federal government was upheld and its power strengthened.
- The war stimulated economic growth and increased manufacturing in the North.
- The South was economically and financially devastated.

Preparing for the Regents

Stimulus-Based Question: Speech

- For what event did Lincoln make the Gettysburg Address?
- Why did Lincoln refer back to the founding of the United States?
- In Lincoln's view, what was the purpose of the Civil War?
- What are the long-term effects of the ideas expressed in the Gettysburg Address?

Multiple-Choice Questions for Regents Practice

Base your answers to questions 1 and 2 on the passage below and on your knowledge of social studies.

> Texas is now ours. . . . Her star and her stripe may already be said to have taken their place in the glorious blazon [display] of our common nationality; and the sweep of our eagle's wing already includes within its circuit the wide extent of her fair and fertile land. She is no longer to us a mere geographical space. . . . She is no longer to us a mere country on the map. She comes within the dear and sacred designation of Our Country. . . . [O]ther nations have undertaken to intrude themselves . . . in a spirit of hostile interference against us, . . . limiting our greatness and checking the fulfillment of our manifest destiny to overspread the continent allotted by Providence for the free development of our yearly multiplying millions.

Source: John L. O'Sullivan, *United States Magazine and Democratic Review*, 1845

1 What occurred as a result of the belief expressed in this document?

  (1) Texas joined the United States as a free state and upset the balance of power in the Senate.

  (2) Immigration to America led to overpopulation and a need to expand westward.

  (3) Oregon gained its independence from Great Britain and became a republic.

  (4) Texas statehood led to war with Mexico and U.S. expansion to the Pacific Ocean.

2 What bias is communicated by O'Sullivan?

  (1) American virtues and ideologies were superior to others.

  (2) American expansion is justified by its belief in imperialism.

  (3) American unity can only be maintained through Christian beliefs.

  (4) American society is slowly being destroyed by immigrants.

Base your answers to questions 3 and 4 on the speech below and on your knowledge of social studies.

> We owe it, therefore, to candor [openness] and to the amicable [friendly] relations existing between the United States and those [European] powers to declare that we should consider any attempt on their part to extend their system to any portion of this hemisphere as dangerous to our peace and safety. With the existing colonies or dependencies of any European power we have not interfered and shall not interfere. But with the Governments who have declared their independence and maintain it, and whose independence we have, on great consideration and on just principles, acknowledged, we could not view any interposition [interference] for the purpose of oppressing them, or controlling in any other manner their destiny, by any European power in any other light than as the manifestation of an unfriendly disposition toward the United States.

Source: President James Monroe, annual message to Congress, December 2, 1823

3 Which best describes President Monroe's foreign policy message to European nations?

  (1) The United States will not interfere in Latin American affairs.

  (2) The United States seeks to end human rights abuses in Latin America.

  (3) European nations must assist in preventing the spread of communism in Latin America.

  (4) European nations are no longer to see Latin America as a place for colonial expansion.

4 The Louisiana Purchase, the War of 1812, and the Monroe Doctrine were similar in that they strengthened

  (1) sectionalism

  (2) territorial expansion

  (3) nationalism

  (4) the market revolution

Base your answers to questions 5 and 6 on the cartoon below and on your knowledge of social studies.

BORN TO COMMAND.

KING ANDREW THE FIRST.

Source: Library of Congress, Artist Unknown, c. 1833

5 What is the point of view of the cartoonist?

(1) Andrew Jackson is abusing the presidential veto power to maintain the spoils system.

(2) Andrew Jackson is overstepping the presidential powers delegated by the Constitution.

(3) Andrew Jackson is weakening a basic constitutional principle by challenging the vote of the Electoral College.

(4) Andrew Jackson is turning the presidency into a monarchy through nullification.

6 Andrew Jackson gained the reputation shown in this cartoon when he

(1) ordered the removal of federal funds from the National Bank

(2) led the Battle of New Orleans during the War of 1812

(3) supported nullification of the Tariff of 1830

(4) called for term limits for members of Congress and the Supreme Court

Base your answers to questions 7 and 8 on the map below and on your knowledge of social studies.

Forced Migration of Native Americans, 1830–1838

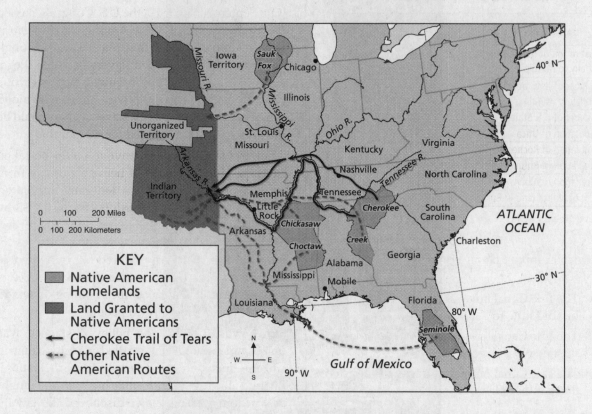

7   What was the immediate cause of the forced migration shown in this map?

(1) the Homestead Act

(2) the Indian Removal Act

(3) the annexation of Florida

(4) the Dawes Act

8   President Andrew Jackson called for this forced migration in order to

(1) enforce the Supreme Court's decision in *Worcester* v. *Georgia*

(2) provide land for Americans to settle east of the Mississippi

(3) reduce the growing conflicts among colonial groups

(4) return their homelands to displaced Native Americans

Base your answers to questions 9 and 10 on the chart below and on your knowledge of social studies.

The Effects of the Erie Canal

Category	Before Erie Canal c. 1820	c. 1850
Cost of ton of freight from Albany to Buffalo	$100	$10
Number of days travel Albany to Buffalo	14	6
Number of U.S. States	23	31
Population of Utica	2,972	17,565
Population of Rochester	1,502	36,403
Population of Buffalo	2,095	42,261
Population of Albany	12,630	50,736
Cost of plot of land in Buffalo	$250	$20,000

Source: Erie Canalway National Heritage Corridor, 2019

9   Which claim can be supported by the evidence in this chart?

(1) The Erie Canal made shipping costs cheaper but did little to cut travel time.

(2) The Erie Canal led to the growth of cities in upstate New York.

(3) The Erie Canal improved trade in the eastern and southern United States.

(4) The Erie Canal made travel difficult between eastern and western New York.

10   Which statement reflects the economic impact the Erie Canal had on the nation?

(1) Transportation costs for goods from the West led to price increases for consumers in the East.

(2) Linking the Great Lakes to the Atlantic Coast encouraged the rise of a consumer economy from the Midwest to New York City.

(3) Albany became the major commercial hub for goods transported between the Midwest and the East Coast.

(4) The construction of railroads in the mid-1800s increased the importance of the Erie Canal.

Base your answers to questions 11 and 12 on the passage below and on your knowledge of social studies.

[O]n September 18, 1850, the U.S. Congress passed the Compromise of 1850. Among its provisions was creation of the Fugitive Slave Law. Although helping those who escaped slavery had been illegal since 1793, the new law required that everyone . . . help catch alleged fugitives. Those who aided escapees or refused to assist slave-catchers could be fined up to $1,000 and jailed for six months.

After the law's passage, anyone could be taken from the street, accused of being a fugitive from slavery, and taken before a federally appointed commissioner. The commissioner received $5 by ruling the suspected fugitive person was free, and $10 for ruling the person was "property" of an enslaver. The law clearly favored returning people to slavery. Free blacks and anti-slavery groups argued that the new law bribed commissioners to unjustly enslave kidnapped people.

Stowe was furious. She believed slavery was unjust and immoral, and bristled at a law requiring citizen—including her—complicity [participation]. Living in Brunswick, ME while her husband taught at Bowdoin College, Stowe disobeyed the law by hiding John Andrew Jackson, who was traveling north from enslavement in South Carolina.

Source: Harriet Beecher Stowe Center, "A Moral Battle Cry for Freedom," 2019

11   Both the Fugitive Slave Law and the writings of Harriet Beecher Stowe were considered

(1) effects of westward expansion

(2) causes of the Civil War

(3) results of the election of Abraham Lincoln

(4) turning points for the U.S. economy

12   Stowe's actions in response to the law

(1) reflected support for the abolitionist movement

(2) were championed by Anti-Federalists

(3) helped to repeal the Kansas-Nebraska Act

(4) assisted in the passage of the 19th Amendment

Short Essay Questions

Task: Read and analyze the following documents, applying your social studies knowledge and skills to write a short essay of two or three paragraphs in which you:

- Describe the historical context surrounding documents 1 and 2
- Analyze **Document 1** and explain how *audience*, **or** *purpose*, **or** *bias*, **or** *point of view* affects this document's use as a reliable source of evidence

In developing your short essay answer of two or three paragraphs, be sure to keep these explanations in mind:

Describe means "to illustrate something in words or tell about"

Historical Context refers to "the relevant historical circumstances surrounding or connecting the events, ideas, or developments in these documents"

Analyze means "to examine a document and determine its elements and its relationships"

Explain means "to make plain or understandable; to give reasons for or causes of; to show the logical development or relationship of"

Reliability is determined by how accurate and useful the information found in a source is for a specific purpose

Document 1

The words "people of the United States" and "citizens" are synonymous terms, and mean the same thing. They both describe the political body who, according to our republican institutions, form the sovereignty and who hold the power and conduct the Government through their representatives. They are what we familiarly call the "sovereign people," and every citizen is one of this people, and a constituent member of this sovereignty. The question before us is whether the class of persons described in the plea in abatement compose a portion of this people, and are constituent members of this sovereignty? We think they are not, and that they are not included, and were not intended to be included, under the word "citizens" in the Constitution, and can therefore claim none of the rights and privileges which that instrument provides for and secures to citizens of the United States. On the contrary, they were at that time considered as a subordinate and inferior class of beings, who had been subjugated by the dominant race, and, whether emancipated or not, yet remained subject to their authority, and had no rights or privileges but such as those who held the power and the Government might choose to grant them.

Source: Chief Justice Robert B. Taney, majority opinion, *Dred Scott* v. *Sanford*, March 6, 1857

Document 2

I have said, in substance, that the Dred Scott decision was, in part, based on assumed historical facts which were not really true; and I ought not to leave the subject without giving some reasons for saying this. I therefore give an instance or two, which I think fully sustain me. Chief Justice Taney, in delivering the opinion of the majority of the Court, insists at great length that negroes were no part of the people who made, or for whom was made, the Declaration of Independence, or the Constitution of the United States.

On the contrary, Judge Curtis, in his dissenting opinion, shows that in five of the then thirteen States, to wit: New Hampshire, Massachusetts, New York, New Jersey and North Carolina, free negroes were voters; and, in proportion to their numbers, had the same part in making the Constitution that the white people had.

Source: Abraham Lincoln, speech in Springfield, Illinois, June 26, 1857

Document Analysis for Civic Literacy Essay

Historical Context: Presidential Power in Wartime

Throughout United States history, many constitutional and civic issues have been debated by Americans. These debates have resulted in efforts by individuals, groups, and governments to address these issues. These efforts have achieved varying degrees of success. One of these constitutional and civic issues is presidential power during times of war.

Task: Read and analyze the documents. Using information from the documents and your knowledge of United States history, write an essay in which you

- Describe the historical circumstances surrounding this constitutional or civic issue
- Explain efforts to address this constitutional or civic issue by individuals, groups, and/or governments
- Discuss the extent to which these efforts were successful

Describe means "to illustrate something in words or tell about it"

Explain means "to make plain or understandable; to give reasons for or causes of; to show the logical development or relationship of"

Discuss means "to make observations about something using facts, reasoning, and argument; to present in some detail"

Document 1

You ask . . . whether I really claim that I may override all the guaranteed rights of individuals, on the plea of conserving the public safety—when I may choose to say the public safety requires it. This question, divested of the phraseology [wording] calculated to represent me as struggling for an arbitrary personal prerogative [claim], is either simply a question *who* shall decide, or an affirmation that *nobody* shall decide, what the public safety does require, in cases of rebellion or invasion. The Constitution contemplates the question as likely to occur for decision, but it does not expressly declare who is to decide it. By necessary implication, when rebellion or invasion comes, the decision is to be made, from time to time; and I think the man whom, for the time, the people have, under the Constitution, made the Commander-in-Chief of their Army and Navy, is the man who holds the power.

Source: President Abraham Lincoln, letter to Ohio Democrats, June 29, 1863

1. According to Lincoln, what authority does the president hold that allows him to suspend civil liberties?

Document 2

The Constitution of the United States is a law for rulers and people, equally in war and in peace, and covers with the shield of its protection all classes of men, at all times and under all circumstances. No doctrine, involving more pernicious [evil] consequences was ever invented by the wit of man than that any of its provisions can be suspended during any of the great exigencies [emergencies] of government. Such a doctrine leads directly to anarchy or despotism, but the theory of necessity on which it is based is false, for the government, within the Constitution, has all the powers granted to it, which are necessary to preserve its existence, as has been happily proved by the result of the great effort to throw off its just authority.

Source: Supreme Court Justice David Davis, majority opinion, *Ex parte Milligan*, 1866

2. According to Justice Davis, what happens if the provisions of the U.S. Constitution are suspended during wartime?

Post–Civil War Era (1865–1900)

Topic Overview

With the Union victory came the task of putting the nation back together. President Lincoln's assassination increased existing hostilities. The Radical Republicans who controlled Congress sought ways to additionally punish the former Confederate states.

Reconstruction resulted in political reunion but very difficult economic times for the war-torn South. The South needed to work to rebuild a devastated economy while coping with thousands of freed and homeless slaves. Three new constitutional amendments expanded civil rights for some African Americans. However, new laws in the South made it almost impossible for them to experience these rights.

American women who had worked for abolition could now refocus their goals on suffrage for women. Susan B. Anthony and Elizabeth Cady Stanton and others began to organize women across the United States.

Westward migration increased after the war. The idea of Manifest Destiny attracted people from across the nation and around the world. As settlers moved west, they encroached on Native American lands, leading to a cultural clash that nearly eliminated Native American cultures.

Issues of inequality continued for African Americans, women, Native Americans, Mexican Americans, and some immigrant groups, such as the Chinese throughout the century.

Reconstruction and the Rights of African Americans

Key Concept

11.4a Between 1865 and 1900, constitutional rights were extended to African Americans. However, their ability to exercise these rights was undermined by individuals, groups, and government institutions.

Lesson Overview

After the Civil War, the nation faced the immense task of restoring the Union. Conflicting plans for Reconstruction produced bitter political battles including one that led to the impeachment of a president. Radical Republicans tried to increase the rights of African Americans while limiting those of former Southern leaders. The 13th, 14th, and 15th Amendments extended constitutional rights to African Americans. However, their new political gains were gradually rolled back in the South by individuals, groups, and government institutions. During the late 1800s a number of restrictions were placed on African American rights, particularly in the South. The election of 1876 and the compromise of 1877 were historic events, especially for African Americans.

Unifying Themes

As you review this lesson take special note of the following themes:

- **Individual Development and Cultural Identity** How did the end of slavery cause Americans to interact with people of different cultural backgrounds in both positive and negative ways?

- **Civic Ideals and Practices** In what ways did the Civil War era amendments attempt to increase civic participation?

Key People

Abraham Lincoln

Andrew Johnson

Ulysses S. Grant

Samuel Tilden

Rutherford B. Hayes

Key Terms and Events

Reconstruction

Radical Republicans

Radical Reconstruction

Thirteenth Amendment

Fourteenth Amendment

Fifteenth Amendment

election of 1876

Compromise of 1877

black codes

Ku Klux Klan

poll taxes

literacy tests

Freedmen's Bureau

grandfather clauses

segregation

Jim Crow laws

Key Supreme Court Cases

As you review this lesson be sure you understand the significance of these key Supreme Court cases:

Civil Rights Cases (1883)

Plessy v. *Ferguson* (1896)

Brown v. *Board of Education of Topeka, Kansas* (1954)

After the Civil War ended, the effort to rebuild the Southern states and to restore the Union was known as **Reconstruction**. This period lasted from 1865 to 1877. Reconstruction required the rebuilding of the nation's economy as well as its government. With so much at stake, rival political factions—with competing plans for the future—waged bitter battles in Washington.

Plans of Reconstruction

Several different plans for Reconstruction emerged during and after the Civil War. Much debate about differing plans centered on who would control Reconstruction—the president or Congress.

Lincoln's Plan

President **Abraham Lincoln** had begun planning for the restoration of the South long before the end of the war. His plan of Reconstruction was based on the idea that the Southern states had never legally left the Union. It featured the following elements

- pardons to Southerners who swore oaths of loyalty to the United States
- recognition of new Southern state governments when 10 percent of those who had voted in the 1860 election took these oaths and when the states adopted new constitutions abolishing slavery
- concern that healing the nation's wounds quickly was essential

Lincoln was open to suggestions from Congress for changes in his plan. Unexpectedly, President Lincoln was assassinated in April 1865, which meant he would never be able to carry out his plan for Reconstruction.

Johnson's Plan

Vice President **Andrew Johnson** became president after Lincoln's death. He intended to follow the broad outlines of Lincoln's plan. Johnson recognized four Southern state governments and prepared to readmit the others. These states would participate fully in Congress.

Radical Republicans, who wanted to punish the South, controlled Congress. They wanted harsher terms for Reconstruction. Johnson's failure to consider congressional views on Reconstruction and his efforts to block radical plans finally led Republicans in Congress to attempt to impeach him. In 1868, the House charged the president with "high crimes and misdemeanors"—specifically, for violating the Tenure of Office Act. This act was passed in 1867 and required the President to get Senate approval to remove certain officials from office. For example, Johnson tried to remove his own Secretary of War, Edwin Stanton, from his position but could not. When the Senate voted on impeachment, it fell one vote short of the two-thirds vote required by the Constitution to remove a president from office. Although Johnson was acquitted (found not guilty), his political power was gone.

Radical Reconstruction

The Republican-controlled Congress dictated the terms of Reconstruction. The chief features of this **Radical Reconstruction** included

- the division of the South into five military districts controlled by the U.S. Army, while new state constitutions and governments were being set up.
- the requirement of the new state governments to grant African American males the right to vote.

Social Studies Practices
Turning Point

- Why is President Lincoln's assassination considered a turning point in history?

Social Studies Practices
Gathering Evidence

- Why did Congress impeach President Johnson?

Social Studies Practices
Compare and Contrast

During Radical Reconstruction, some groups of people exerted great power over the terms of Reconstruction, while others had very little power.

- Which groups had the largest roles in the Radical Reconstruction?
- Which had the smallest roles?

Unifying Themes
Power, Authority, and Governance

- Which plan limited the voting rights of former Confederate officers?

Unifying Themes
Governance

During Reconstruction, three new amendments to the Constitution were ratified. In the space below, name these three amendments and provide the major provisions of each.

1.

2.

3.

- the requirement of Southern states to ratify the Fourteenth Amendment. In addition to addressing several fundamental civil rights issues, the amendment prohibited many former Confederate government officials from holding office.

State Governments During Reconstruction

Immediately after the Civil War ended, white Southerners who had served in leadership positions before and during the Civil War tried to reassert their control of state and local governments. They were especially concerned with limiting the freedom and movement of former slaves.

When the radical plan of Reconstruction took effect, most of the former Confederate leaders—largely Democrats—were barred from holding office and voting. Republicans headed the new state governments that emerged, and they were overwhelmingly supported by African Americans, who had recently won the right to vote. In many cases, African Americans themselves won election to office. Between 1870 and 1877, there were two African American Senators elected in the South and fourteen Congressmen. (Note that there were no African Americans elected to either house in the North until the 20th century.) Early in Reconstruction it was easier for African American men to register to vote, to actually vote, and then to be elected to office. Remember that many white southern men had served in various positions in the Confederacy and were disqualified from voting or serving in government.

Many white Southerners deeply resented the federal government's imposition of Radical Reconstruction. They also resented the new Reconstruction governments and the role of African Americans in them. They branded the few white Southerners active in those governments as **scalawags** and the Republican Northerners who came to the South to take part in Reconstruction as **carpetbaggers.** White southerners sometimes used terror and violence in efforts to keep African Americans from taking part in government.

New Constitutional Amendments

During the Reconstruction period, the states ratified three amendments to the Constitution:

- **Thirteenth Amendment** (1865)—abolished slavery in the United States
- **Fourteenth Amendment** (1868)—(1) declared that all native-born or naturalized people, including African Americans, were citizens; (2) forbade states to make laws that "abridge the privileges . . . of citizens" or that "deprive any person of life, liberty, or property, without due process of law" or that "deny to any person . . . the equal protection of the laws"; (3) limited the rights of former Confederate officers and government officials; and (4) promised to pay Civil War debts owed by the federal government but declared Confederate debts to be void
- **Fifteenth Amendment** (1870)—declared that states could not keep citizens from voting because of "race, color, or previous condition of servitude" (slavery)

President Grant

The first presidential election after the Civil War took place in 1868. Union war hero General **Ulysses S. Grant** ran as a Republican and won. Grant's strengths, however, were those of a military leader, not those of a politician or government leader. Scandals and corruption damaged Grant's administration, as business owners in the booming postwar economy offered bribes to politicians who would do favors for them. Among the most notorious scandals were the following

- *Crédit Mobilier Scandal:* Railroad officials impoverished the railroad, then bribed members of Congress to block any investigation.

- *"Salary Grab"*: Congress voted itself a 50 percent pay raise and added two years of "back pay." Public outcry forced repeal of this act.
- *"Whiskey Ring"*: Whiskey distillers paid graft to federal tax collectors rather than pay tax on their liquor.

The End of Reconstruction

Corruption in the Grant administration weakened the political strength of the Republican party. In addition, by the early 1870s, all but a handful of former Confederates could vote again. Most of these white Southern males now voted Democratic in reaction to Radical Republican Reconstruction. For most of the next century, the Democratic party would dominate voting in the South, giving rise to the term **solid South.**

While nearly dying out in the South, the Republican Party remained strong in the North and the Midwest. It focused on issues of interest to businessmen and farmers, such as keeping the money supply tight and tariffs on imports high.

The Election of 1876

The emergence of the solid South gave the Democrats greater power in politics at the national level. In the **election of 1876,** Democrats nominated **Samuel Tilden,** the governor of New York, to run for president against **Rutherford B. Hayes,** the Republican governor of Ohio.

Tilden clearly won the popular vote, but the electoral vote was contested. Four states sent in disputed election returns. Which votes were counted would determine the outcome of the election. A special electoral commission was named to count the votes. The Republican majority on the commission gave all the electoral votes in question to Hayes, thus guaranteeing his victory.

In the **Compromise of 1877,** Democrats agreed to go along with the commission's decision in return for promises by Hayes to

- withdraw remaining federal troops from the Southern states, thus ending the Reconstruction period.
- name a Southerner to his cabinet.
- support federal spending on internal improvements in the South.

The Compromise of 1877 effectively weakened the North's political victory in the Civil War, restoring to power many of the Southern families who, 16 years before, had formed the Confederacy and led it into war.

Social Studies Practices

Geographic Reasoning

- How did voting patterns in the South affect the presidential election of 1876?

Preparing for the Regents

On the examination, you will need to identify the significance of an event and its effects.

- Why do you think the Democrats agreed to support the Compromise of 1877?
- What resulted from this decision?

Preparing for the Regents

Stimulus-Based Questions: Timeline

Examine the timeline, then answer these questions.

- How many years passed between the end of the Civil War and the states' ratification of the Fifteenth Amendment?
- In what ways did the Fifteenth Amendment affect the lives of African Americans in the South?

The Reconstructed Nation, 1865–1876

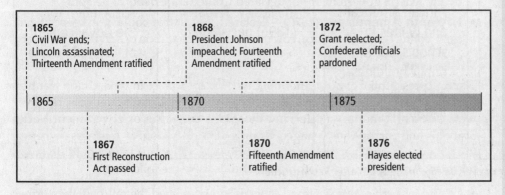

1865
Civil War ends;
Lincoln assassinated;
Thirteenth Amendment ratified

1868
President Johnson impeached; Fourteenth Amendment ratified

1872
Grant reelected; Confederate officials pardoned

1865   1870   1875

1867
First Reconstruction Act passed

1870
Fifteenth Amendment ratified

1876
Hayes elected president

White Control in the South

The withdrawal of federal troops enabled white Southerners to eliminate any political advances African Americans had made during Reconstruction. Various methods were used to curb the rights of African Americans, and by 1900, their civil rights had been sharply limited.

Black Codes Passed in most Southern states immediately after the Civil War, **black codes** were based on old slave codes and aimed at keeping African Americans in conditions close to slavery. The black codes produced an angry reaction in the North that helped passage of the Radical Reconstruction program. Reconstruction governments in the South overturned these codes.

Secret Societies White Southerners originally formed groups like the **Ku Klux Klan** to try to frighten African Americans and their supporters out of taking part in Reconstruction governments. The lawlessness and brutality demonstrated by these groups led the federal government to use the army against the societies. With the end of Reconstruction and the growth of white political power, the Klan and other similar groups played a less active role in the South. Such organizations, however, remain in existence to this day.

Poll Taxes Southern states imposed a tax on every voter. Those who were too poor to pay **poll taxes**—including many African Americans—could not vote.

Literacy Tests Some states required citizens to demonstrate that they could read and write before they voted. Often **literacy tests** involved interpreting a difficult part of the Constitution. Few African Americans could pass these tests because they had received little schooling. While the **Freedmen's Bureau,** created by Congress in 1865 to aid former slaves, established many schools for young African Americans, the bureau lasted only a few years. Thereafter, state laws forced African American children to attend separate schools that were poorly equipped and funded.

Unifying Themes
Development and Transformation of Social Structures

• Why did some white Southerners form secret societies such as the Ku Klux Klan?

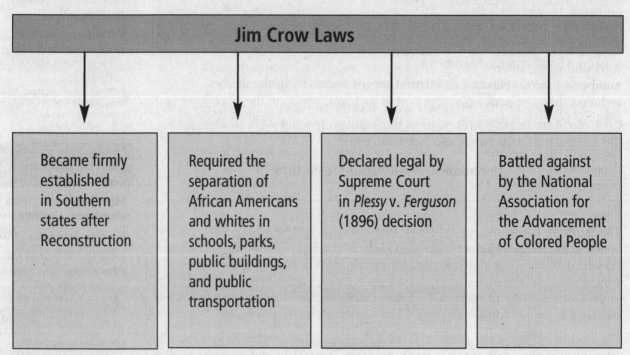

Jim Crow Laws

| Became firmly established in Southern states after Reconstruction | Required the separation of African Americans and whites in schools, parks, public buildings, and public transportation | Declared legal by Supreme Court in *Plessy* v. *Ferguson* (1896) decision | Battled against by the National Association for the Advancement of Colored People |

Jim Crow laws were a part of everyday life in the South after Reconstruction.

The Freedmen's Bureau was able to represent African Americans in court, which set a precedent for African Americans to be recognized in court cases in later years. During this time the Bureau, often working with Northern religious or civic groups, was able to establish schools, orphanages and hospitals for African Americans.

Grandfather Clauses Poll taxes and literacy tests would have kept poor and uneducated whites from voting. To prevent this, Southern states added **grandfather clauses** to their constitutions. These clauses allowed the son or grandson of a man eligible to vote in 1866 or 1867 to vote himself even if he could neither pay the tax nor pass the test. Since few African Americans could vote in 1867, the clause benefited whites almost exclusively.

Jim Crow Laws Southern states also passed laws establishing social as well as legal **segregation,** or the separation of people on the basis of race. Such **Jim Crow laws** forbade African Americans from sharing facilities with whites, such as railroad cars or water fountains. The passage of Jim Crow laws in the South after Reconstruction was aided in part by a narrow interpretation of the Fourteenth Amendment by the United States Supreme Court.

Economic Developments in the South

The Civil War ruined the South's economy. The Civil War Era Amendments (13, 14, 15) ended slavery and with it the plantation system on which southern wealth was based. During the fighting, plantations were burned, railroads ripped up, and the region's few factories destroyed. Many former plantation owners had to sell some of their land to pay off debts or to start over. These landowners often found themselves in debt to banks or merchants. Yet, Southern farmers again began to produce cotton and tobacco.

Some Southern leaders, however, believed that the South's economy should not rest simply on agriculture. They began to create a **New South,** with rebuilt railroads, new textile and steel mills, and, later, new industries, such as oil and coal production.

Despite these changes, the South lagged behind the North in economic growth. Agriculture still offered the most jobs, and many southerners, including large numbers of former slaves, farmed land owned by others. These landless farmers included sharecroppers, who gave part of each year's crop to the landowner and received the rest as payment. Sharecropping was a way to provide a labor supply to plantation owners. Tenant farmers paid cash to rent land. A negative effect of the sharecropping system was that it kept formerly enslaved persons economically dependent. Beginning in the 1880s, African Americans began a migration to the North in search of better jobs. This migration accelerated during and after World War I.

The Supreme Court's Response

The Supreme Court did not interfere with efforts to restore white control in the South. In the 1883 **Civil Rights Cases,** the Court ruled that the Thirteenth Amendment abolished slavery but did not prohibit discrimination and that the Fourteenth Amendment prohibited discrimination by government but not by individuals. Later, in the landmark case of **Plessy v. Ferguson** (1896), the Court ruled that segregation was legal as long as African Americans had access to "equal but separate" facilities.

The Court's ruling in the *Plessy* case set a precedent that justified segregation in all public facilities—schools, hospitals, passenger terminals, and more—until the 1950s. It was not until the pivotal case of **Brown v. Board of Education of Topeka, Kansas** (1954) that the Supreme Court reversed the finding in *Plessy* v. *Ferguson*. The *Brown* decision stated that educational facilities separated solely on the basis of race were by their nature unequal.

Social Studies Practices
Gathering Evidence

- Reread the section entitled "White Control in the South." What were five major ways in which white Southerners reasserted their control in the South after Reconstruction?

Themes and Concepts
Individuals, Groups, Institutions

As the southern economy grew after the Civil War, some groups lagged behind others.

- Who were the sharecroppers?
- How did sharecroppers differ from tenant farmers?

Unifying Themes
Civic Ideals and Practices

The following three cases deal with segregation and Jim Crow laws:

Civil Rights Cases (1883) ruled that slavery was abolished but that discrimination by individuals was not prohibited by the Constitution.

Plessy v. *Ferguson* (1896) established segregation to be legal as long as "equal but separate" facilities were available to African Americans.

Brown v. *Board of Education of Topeka, Kansas* (1954) established that facilities separated by race were unequal.

- How did these three cases influence laws concerning segregation?

The Post–Civil War Struggle for Women's Rights

Key Concept

11.4b The 14th and 15th amendments failed to address the rights of women.

Lesson Overview

The Seneca Falls (New York) convention in 1848 was the first major organized effort by women to obtain political, social, and economic rights in the United States. The Civil War interrupted these efforts. The years immediately after the Civil War improved the rights of men but not of women. This encouraged women to increase their efforts to improve their political and economic situation.

Unifying Themes

As you review this lesson take special note of the following themes:

- **Time, Continuity, and Change** In what ways did the goals of the Seneca Falls Convention continue and expand throughout the 19th century?

- **Civic Ideals and Practices** Why did women in the post–Civil War era struggle with the fact that they were citizens but unable to practice a basic right of citizenship?

Key People

Elizabeth Cady Stanton   Carrie Chapman Catt
Susan B. Anthony

Key Terms and Events

Women's Rights Convention   grassroots
suffrage   Nineteenth Amendment

You will recall from Topic 3 that the women's rights movement began officially in 1848, when **Elizabeth Cady Stanton** organized the **Women's Rights Convention** in Seneca Falls, New York. In the early 1850s, before the Civil War, **Susan B. Anthony,** from Rochester, New York, joined Stanton in the drive for women's rights. The women's rights movement began focusing on winning the vote for women. Anthony strongly believed that once women earned the right to vote they would be able to solve many other issues at the ballot box.

Women Respond to the Civil War Amendments

As you have read, the political rights of African Americans were improved at least in writing by the three new amendments added to the Constitution at the end of the Civil War. Freedom was granted by the 13th, citizenship by the 14th, and **suffrage,** the right to vote, was given to African American males by the 15th.

Many women were angered that African American males, both former slaves and free black men, were granted the right to vote and women were not. As a result, Susan B. Anthony and several other women in Rochester and around the country decided to "test" the amendments. Anthony voted in the presidential election of 1872 and was arrested for doing so. Her trial for committing a federal crime was conducted in 1873 in Canandaigua, New York. She was found guilty and fined $100.00 (a very large sum at that time), which she refused to pay.

The Road to Winning the Vote

Later, Elizabeth Cady Stanton and Susan B. Anthony provided the driving leadership for the National Woman Suffrage Association. The more conservative American Woman Suffrage Organization was headed by Lucy Stone, Henry Blackwell, and Julia Ward Howe. In 1890, the groups united to form the National American Woman Suffrage Association (NAWSA) with Stanton as president.

Anthony traveled the United States speaking and meeting with large groups to promote women's suffrage and other rights for women, including the right to own property. She regularly spoke before Congress and met with American presidents to advocate for women.

Elizabeth Cady Stanton died in 1902. When Susan B. Anthony died in 1906 at 86 years old, four states, Wyoming, Utah, Idaho and Colorado had granted women the right to vote.

The Progressive spirit in the early 1900s gave the movement a new surge. The leadership of NAWSA and the campaign passed to **Carrie Chapman Catt,** who devised the strategy that was to secure women the vote. She concentrated on achieving the vote

Susan B. Anthony

for women by a constitutional amendment while coordinating the national effort with a state-by-state movement to put more pressure on Congress and build **grassroots,** or public support for ratification when the time came. NAWSA swelled to two million members.

During World War I, women demonstrated in front of the White House, questioning American efforts to preserve democracy in Europe. They said that American women did not have democratic rights in the United States. The **Nineteenth Amendment** granting women the right to vote was finally passed in 1920.

A group of suffragists picket the White House in 1917 in an effort to pressure President Wilson to support their cause

Westward Expansion Impacts the Economy and Native Americans

Key Concept

11.4c Federal policies regarding westward expansion had positive effects on the national economy but negative consequences for Native Americans.

Lesson Overview

Federal policies regarding westward expansion encouraged the settlement of the western frontier. Land grants allowed many Americans to own their own land. The transcontinental railway made it easier to travel as well as transport goods, making settlement of the West possible and profitable. The American economy boomed. Western expansion was beneficial to many Americans. However, Native Americans suffered greatly as a result.

Unifying Themes

As you review this lesson take special note of the following themes:

- **Development, Movement, and Interaction of Cultures** What economic and cultural effects resulted from American settlement of the West?

- **Power, Authority, and Governance** In what ways did the federal government's policies on western expansion affect Native Americans?

- **Creation, Expansion and Interaction of Economic Systems** Why did the 19th century westward movement create a new demand for goods and services?

Key Terms and Events

Great Plains	westward expansion
transcontinental railroad	reservations
Homestead Act	Dawes Act of 1887
Morrill Land Grant Act	Carlisle Indian School
Pacific Railway Act of 1862	forced assimilation

Preparing for the Regents

On the examination, you will need to identify and explain a central effect of an issue or an event.

- What is the transcontinental railroad?
- How did it contribute to economic growth?

The Government Encourages Westward Growth

Prior to the end of the Civil War, in 1862, Congress passed three major acts to facilitate economic growth after the war ended, primarily by encouraging development of the **Great Plains** and far west. Congress

- passed the Pacific Railway Act, authorizing the building of the **transcontinental railroad,** financed with public land grants and cash loans.

- passed the **Homestead Act,** providing for the settlement of western land

- approved the **Morrill Land Grant Act,** which gave public lands to states and territories to found agriculture, mechanical arts, and military science colleges.

Completion of the transcontinental railroad, authorized by the **Pacific Railway Act of 1862,** opened new markets in the West and brought products of western farms and mines to the East. The federal government encouraged the building of the transcontinental railroads by giving land to the railroad companies who in turn sometimes sold the land at a profit. Economic growth attracted new waves of immigrants to the United States. Some sought farms on the Great Plains and farther west.

The American West, 1862–1896

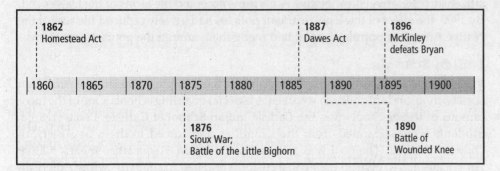

```
1862              1887        1896
Homestead Act     Dawes Act   McKinley
                              defeats Bryan

|——————|——————|——————|——————|——————|——————|——————|——————|——————|
1860   1865   1870   1875   1880   1885   1890   1895   1900

                  1876                    1890
                  Sioux War;              Battle of
                  Battle of the Little Bighorn   Wounded Knee
```

Preparing for the Regents

Stimulus-Based Questions: Timeline

Examine the timeline, then answer the following questions.

- How many years passed between the Homestead Act and the Battle of Wounded Knee?

- What is the relationship between the Dawes Act and the Battle of Wounded Knee?

Native Americans and Westward Expansion

The **westward expansion** of the late 1800s continued to create problems for the Native Americans who stood in its path. By the 1840s, only scattered groups of Native Americans still lived in the East. Most lived west of the Mississippi on lands that few whites wanted. The California gold rush, the building of the transcontinental railroad, and the discovery of rich farmland in the Great Plains changed this situation. Now white people began to move onto Native American lands in the West.

Indian Wars

The Native Americans fought back. From the 1850s to 1890, a series of wars raged in the West. Gradually the Native Americans were forced to accept treaties that crowded them into smaller and smaller areas of land called **reservations.** Native American resistance was weakened by the greater numbers of whites with superior technology and divisions among Native American peoples that did not permit a unified resistance. The defeat of the Sioux at Wounded Knee, South Dakota, in 1890, is usually considered the end of the Indian wars.

Sitting Bull

The Sioux Wars

1865	Federal government decides to build a road through Sioux territory. Sioux warriors resist violently, sparking Red Cloud's War.
1867	Red Cloud's War ends. Sioux agree to live on reservation in Dakota Territory.
1875	Federal government allows miners to search for gold on Sioux reservation. Second Sioux War begins. Chief Sitting Bull leads many Sioux off the reservation.
1876	At the Battle of the Little Bighorn, Sitting Bull's warriors destroy General Custer's army. In response, federal government sends more troops to the region. Most Sioux agree to move to reservations.
1890	At the Massacre of Wounded Knee, American soldiers open fire on unarmed Sioux, killing 200.

Preparing for the Regents

Stimulus-Based Questions: Table

American expansion westward led to many wars and the near destruction of western Native American nations. The table (left) outlines the struggle experienced by one tribe, the Sioux.

- What caused the first Sioux War in 1865?

- How did the federal government respond to Sitting Bull's defeat of General Custer?

- What resulted from Native American resistance to the settling of the West?

Changing Government Policies

In victory, the federal government continued to display little understanding or respect for Native American cultures and values. Native Americans were given reservation land that rarely could produce adequate crops or support game for the people living on it. Reservations were located in sparsely populated areas of the West. Further, in 1887, Congress passed the **Dawes Act,** aimed at Americanizing Native Americans. It proposed to break up tribes and reservations and to grant land directly to Native Americans as individuals and families. Native Americans

Unifying Themes
Power, Authority, and Governance

The Dawes Act was aimed at breaking up Native American tribes and reservations. It offered Native Americans who gave up tribal ways the deeds to their land and U.S. citizenship after 25 years.

- Was the Dawes Act fair to Native Americans?
- Did Native Americans support it?

Social Studies Practices
Turning Point

Why can the decline of the Plains Indians be traced to the following events?

- the Homestead Act
- the mass killing of buffalo
- the transcontinental railroad

Social Studies Practices
Geographic Reasoning

- How was the economy of the West influenced by each of the following?

Rocky Mountains

Great Plains

railroads

Homestead Act

who abandoned tribal ways would be granted deeds to their land and United States citizenship. Relatively few Native Americans accepted the terms of the Dawes Act. By 1900, the effect of these government policies had greatly reduced the size of the Native American population and had made them among the poorest Americans.

Indian Schools

In an effort to force Native Americans to adopt the lifestyle and culture of American society, thousands of children were sent to special boarding schools. One of the most famous of these schools was the **Carlisle Indian School** at Carlisle, Pennsylvania. Students were separated from their families and forced to dress as American children dressed. The goal was a **forced assimilation.** *Assimilation* means Native Americans had to give up their tribal customs and had to adapt to "white American ways" of the time period. These schools were primarily scattered throughout the western states to be near the Native American centers of population.

The Economy of the West

In 1893, Frederick Jackson Turner wrote in his paper "The Significance of the Frontier in American History" that the frontier, "and the advance of American settlement westward, explain American development." Turner claimed life in the West had given rise to inventiveness, independence, and unique American customs. (While other historians would argue instead that other factors, such as the nation's European heritage or economic abundance, were the key influences, Turner's thesis has had lasting influence.) In 1890, the government had announced that the West was closed. Industrialization had aided the settling of the West.

Technological Advances

An **Agricultural Revolution** with new technologies helped people who moved onto Native American lands exploit the wealth of the West. Railroads brought people and carried western crops and products to eastern markets. Barbed wire aided the growth of both farming and ranching. Steel plows cut tough prairie soil. Windmills pulled water to the surface of dry western lands. Mechanical reapers and farm tools allowed a smaller number of workers to plant and harvest larger crops.

Vast Natural Resources

The riches of the West, like the land itself, took many forms. In the Rocky Mountains, miners dug up millions of dollars in gold, silver, copper, lead, and zinc ore. In the Great Plains, ranchers turned cattle raising into big business, as cowhands moved huge herds across the open ranges to rail lines. Farmers, too, were attracted to the Great Plains because of its rich topsoil and overcame heat, blizzards, droughts, insects, and occasional conflicts with ranchers to raise crops. Many settled lands claimed under the Homestead Act and later built huge farms. (Through the Homestead Act, as well as in government land grants and other aid to large railroad companies, the federal government played a significant role in encouraging development of the resources of the West.)

By the late 1800s, American farmers were raising enough to feed the nation and still export wheat and other crops. Mechanization of agriculture caused an increase in production. Spurred by the expansion of mining, ranching, and farming, cities like Omaha, Denver, and San Francisco became some of the fastest growing in the nation.

19th Century Discrimination Against Mexicans and Chinese

Lesson Overview

In addition to Native Americans, other groups experienced discrimination and prejudice as Americans settled the West. Mexicans faced injustices as a result of Mexico's defeat in the Mexican-American War. Chinese immigrants encountered legal discrimination and nativism as a consequence of the federal government's response to Americans' growing distrust of immigrants coming into the United States.

Unifying Themes

As you review this lesson take special note of the following themes:

- **Individual Development and Cultural Identity** How did Mexicans and Chinese immigrants struggle to maintain their cultures while learning to live in the United States?

- **Creation, Expansion, and Interaction of Economic Systems** In what ways did Mexicans and Chinese immigrants contribute to the economic growth of the American West?

Key Terms and Events

Treaty of Guadalupe Hidalgo

Gadsden Purchase

Manifest Destiny

discrimination

nativism

Chinese Exclusion Act of 1882

Key Concept

11.4d Racial and economic motives contributed to long-standing discrimination against Mexican Americans and opposition to Chinese immigration.

The Treaty of Guadalupe Hidalgo

As you read in Topic 3, by the end of the Mexican War (1846–1847), the Mexicans had been badly defeated by the larger, more powerful, and better-supplied American army. American troops had captured Mexico City before the country surrendered. In February 1848, with the signing of the **Treaty of Guadalupe Hidalgo,** Mexico was forced to surrender approximately the northern third of their country to the United States. The new border between Texas and Mexico was the Rio Grande River.

More than one million square miles of Mexican territory were ceded as well as land in New Mexico and California. The United States agreed to pay Mexico $15,000,000 for this very large land acquisition. Five years later, for the purpose of building a railroad, the United States encouraged Mexico to enter the **Gadsden Purchase,** which included 29,640 acres of land in New Mexico and Arizona. The states of Nevada, Utah, Arizona and one half of Colorado were formed from all of this combined land.

Although the Treaty of Guadalupe Hidalgo clearly stated that Mexicans residing in the areas ceded to the United States would retain their land and become citizens, the reality was very different. Families often lost their ancestral land to challenges made by American settlers in the federal courts. Their citizenship was also challenged and many Mexican Americans found that their rights were no longer protected as a result. American mining companies consumed large quantities of water in their operations and this became a serious conflict with Mexican Americans who depended on water for farming in arid sections of the United States. American settlers to the area continued the American concept of **Manifest Destiny,** implying that their culture was superior to others in their path. Mexicans resented the results of the treaty for generations to come.

Immigration from China

As the United States developed westward, the building of the transcontinental railroad was essential to its growth. The actual construction required large crews of laborers working from both the west coast and the east across the Great Plains and through the Rocky Mountains. The work was dangerous and difficult but thousands of immigrant men seized the opportunity to work and save money to bring their families to America. The rough physical labor was avoided by most American men but immigrants from Ireland especially and other European countries risked their lives on the enormous project. Injury or illness that forced a worker to be unemployed immediately gave an opportunity to the next immigrant in line.

Chinese immigrants, entering through California since the 1850s, had already found jobs in farming, small manufacturing, laundries, and tailoring. Later thousands found the construction of the railroad to be a major source of employment. These Chinese workers not only worked on the railroad directly but also supplied services to the project ranging from being cooks at work camps to doing laundry and providing other services.

Discrimination against these individuals, who looked and spoke differently, became commonplace. At these worksites, it was not unusual for it to be said that there was nothing lower than an Irishman but a Chinese. The Chinese especially were discriminated against for their different appearance, language, clothing, customs, and religion. Just as European immigrants tended to settle in groups of their own background either in cities or in rural areas, so too did the Chinese who formed Chinatowns. These Chinatowns were frequently the site of violence by Americans who feared the growth of the Chinese culture in their neighborhoods.

European and Chinese immigrants gold mining in California

These acts of discrimination, known as **nativism,** or a belief in the superiority of one nation's people over another's, were the foundation of the **Chinese Exclusion Act of 1882.** The state of California for several years prior to this Act had begun to limit Chinese immigration and to discriminate legally against Chinese people living in California. Some native-born American citizens labeled immigration from Asia as the "yellow peril." This Act sharply limited Chinese immigration to the United States. It continued for many years into the 20th century and had a negative impact on relations between China and the United States.

Base your answers to questions 1 and 2 on the graph below and on your knowledge of social studies.

American Territorial Growth
(As a percentage of present United States territory)

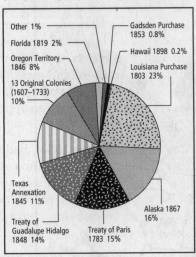

Other 1%
Florida 1819 2%
Oregon Territory 1846 8%
13 Original Colonies (1607–1733) 10%
Texas Annexation 1845 11%
Treaty of Guadalupe Hidalgo 1848 14%
Treaty of Paris 1783 15%
Alaska 1867 16%
Gadsden Purchase 1853 0.8%
Hawaii 1898 0.2%
Louisiana Purchase 1803 23%

1 Which policy is best illustrated by the chart?

(1) isolationism

(2) manifest destiny

(3) containment

(4) globalization

2 Which effect was a direct result of the information on this chart?

(1) The United States became a global superpower.

(2) Native Americans' way of life was nearly destroyed.

(3) Mexican Americans' trust in the U.S. government grew.

(4) The U.S. economy converted from agriculture to industry.

Base your answers to questions 3 and 4 on the speech below and on your knowledge of social studies.

These men [buffalo hunters] have done more in the last two years, and will do more in the next year, to settle the vexed [troublesome] Indian question, than the entire regular Army has done in the last thirty years. They are destroying the Indians' commissary [store of supplies]; and it is a well-known fact that an army losing its base of supplies is placed at a great disadvantage. Send them powder and lead, if you will; but, for the sake of a lasting peace, let them kill, skin, and sell until the buffaloes are exterminated. Then your prairies can be covered with speckled cattle, and the festive cowboy, who follows the hunter as a second forerunner of an advanced civilization.

—General Philip Sheridan, speech to the Texas legislature, 1873

3 The success of the actions described by General Sheridan is supported by the fact that the

(1) damage to Native American homelands was so great that many were forced to accept grants of land through the Homestead Act

(2) destabilization of the Native American economic base was so severe that it made living on a reservation even more attractive

(3) access to ammunition and weapons was so limited that Native Americans could not defend themselves against American troops

(4) reduction of their main source for food and materials was so significant that Native Americans were forced off their homelands

4 Around the same time this statement was made, what other groups in the American West faced similar attitudes as those expressed by Sheridan?

(1) English and Irish

(2) Mexicans and Chinese

(3) Germans and Norwegians

(4) French and Puerto Ricans

Base your answers to questions 5 and 6 on the map below and on your knowledge of social studies.

Woman's Suffrage Before 1920

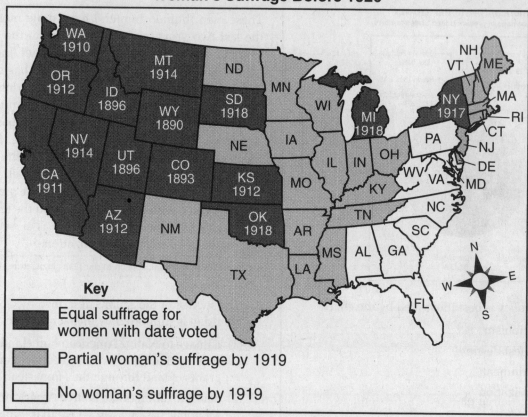

Key

Equal suffrage for women with date voted

Partial woman's suffrage by 1919

No woman's suffrage by 1919

Source: Sandra Opdycke, *The Routledge Historical Atlas of Women in America,* Routledge
(adapted)

5   This map would be best used to support the claim that the women's movement

   (1) had made significant progress in achieving its goals by 1919
   (2) had limited support for women's suffrage even by 1919
   (3) had a relatively easy time promoting its cause in the state legislatures
   (4) had its greatest support in the Solid South

6   Which leader had the greatest influence on the developments shown in the map?

   (1) Jane Addams
   (2) Margaret Sanger
   (3) Susan B. Anthony
   (4) Ida B. Wells-Barnett

Base your answers to questions 7 and 8 on the image below and on your knowledge of social studies.

7   What legislation passed by the federal government brought about the way of life shown in the photograph?

(1) Dawes Act

(2) Fourteenth Amendment

(3) Morrill Land Grant Act

(4) Homestead Act

8   How did the settling of the American West lead to the growth of the nation's economy?

(1) It encouraged new and innovative uses for the vast natural resources that were now available.

(2) It opened new markets where goods could be bought and sold across the nation.

(3) It reduced the need to import manufactured goods from outside the United States.

(4) It decreased the growing nativism faced by newly arrived immigrants from Europe and Asia.

Task: Read and analyze the following documents, applying your social studies knowledge and skills to write a short essay of two or three paragraphs in which you:

- Describe the historical context surrounding documents 1 and 2
- Analyze **Document 1** and explain how *audience*, **or** *purpose*, **or** *bias*, **or** *point of view* affects this document's use as a reliable source of evidence

In developing your short essay answer of two or three paragraphs, be sure to keep these explanations in mind:

Describe means "to illustrate something in words or tell about"

Historical Context refers to "the relevant historical circumstances surrounding or connecting the events, ideas, or developments in these documents"

Analyze means "to examine a document and determine its elements and its relationships"

Explain means "to make plain or understandable; to give reasons for or causes of; to show the logical development or relationship of"

Reliability is determined by how accurate and useful the information found in a source is for a specific purpose

Document 1

After the Battle of Wounded Knee, which occurred in 1890, Thomas Jefferson Morgan wrote *The Present Phase of the Indian Question*. Morgan was the Commissioner of Indian Affairs and made recommendations about how the United States could avoid future conflicts with Native Americans.

...Fifth.—The only possible solution of our Indian troubles lies in the suitable education of the rising generation. So long as the Indians remain among us aliens, speaking foreign languages, unable to communicate with us except through the uncertain and often misleading medium of interpreters, so long as they are ignorant of our ways, are superstitious and fanatical, they will remain handicapped in the struggle for existence, will be an easy prey to the medicine man and the false prophet, and will be easily induced, by reason of real or imaginary wrongs, to go upon the war-path. An education that will give them the mastery of the English language, train their hands to useful industries, awaken within them ambition for civilized ways, and develop a consciousness of power to achieve honorable places for themselves, and that arouses within them an earnest and abiding patriotism, will make of them American citizens, and render future conflicts between them and the Government impossible.

Source: Thomas Jefferson Morgan, *The Present Phase of the Indian Question*, 1891

Document 2

A group of Native Americans are pictured when they arrived at the Carlisle Indian School (left) in Pennsylvania and several months later (right).

Apache children on their first day at the Carlisle Indian School, 1886

Apache children at the Carlisle Indian School, four months later

Document Analysis for Civic Literacy Essay

Historical Context: African American Rights

Throughout United States history, many constitutional and civic issues have been debated by Americans. These debates have resulted in efforts by individuals, groups, and governments to address these issues. These efforts have achieved varying degrees of success. One of these constitutional and civic issues is African American rights.

Task: Read and analyze the document. Using information from the document and your knowledge of United States history, write an essay in which you

- Describe the historical circumstances surrounding this constitutional or civic issue
- Explain efforts to address this constitutional or civic issue by individuals, groups, and/or governments
- Discuss the extent to which these efforts were successful

Describe means "to illustrate something in words or tell about it"

Explain means "to make plain or understandable; to give reasons for or causes of; to show the logical development or relationship of"

Discuss means "to make observations about something using facts, reasoning, and argument; to present in some detail"

Fifteenth Amendment to the Constitution of the United States (Ratified on February 3, 1870)

Section 1.
The right of citizens of the United States to vote shall not be denied or abridged by the United States or by any State on account of race, color, or previous condition of servitude.

Section 2
The Congress shall have power to enforce this article by appropriate legislation.

Source: The United States Constitution

1. What right was guaranteed by this Amendment?

Industrialization and Urbanization (1870–1920)

Topic Overview

The United States was transformed during this time period from an agrarian (rural, farming) society to an increasingly industrial and urbanized society. This change created many new economic opportunities for those who were able to take advantage of them. The government began to take on a new role as some industries grew so large as to cause a need for legislative controls.

Industrialization and urbanization also created problems as people tried to adapt to changing lifestyles. There were a variety of reform movements that developed out of a need to improve conditions for many Americans.

New Technology and Business Organizations Transform the Nation

Key Concept

11.5a New technologies and economic models created rapid industrial growth and transformed the United States.

Lesson Overview

From Reconstruction through World War I, the United States developed a prosperous industrial economy that revolutionized American society. New machines made possible the mass production of goods. Industrial growth led to a new type of business, the corporation, headed by a rising class of enterprising industrialists, such as Henry Ford, John D. Rockefeller, and others.

With little government interference, these corporate giants created new business structures, some legal and some not, that brought them fabulous wealth. They used their riches both to benefit society and to increase their power. Industries attracted a new type of laborer, the factory worker, who often worked long hours in hazardous conditions.

Unifying Themes

As you review this lesson take special note of the following themes:

- **Time, Continuity, and Change** How would you describe the consequences of the growth of big business during this time period?

- **Geography, Humans, and the Environment** Which inventions brought changes to the ways people lived in urban areas?

- **Development and Transformation of Social Structures** What was happening during these years that caused the gap between rich and poor Americans to grow larger? How did business organizations change and become more profitable for their owners?

- **Civic Ideals and Practices** What role did the government begin to play in protecting consumers?

- **Science, Technology, and Innovation** How did new inventions bring changes to both business and consumers during this time period?

Key People

Andrew Carnegie   Henry Ford
John D. Rockefeller   Theodore Roosevelt
J.P. Morgan

Key Terms and Events

urbanization	trust	conspicuous
capital	holding company	consumption
corporation	entrepreneur	philanthropist
monopoly	laissez faire	Interstate Commerce
conglomerate	free enterprise system	Act
merger	Social Darwinism	Sherman Antitrust Act
pool	robber baron	trust-busting

Key Supreme Court Cases

As you review this lesson be sure you understand the significance of these key Supreme Court cases:

Munn v. *Illinois* (1877)
Wabash, St. Louis & Pacific R.R. v. *Illinois* (1886)
Northern Securities Co. v. *United States* (1904)

New Technologies

Urbanization was aided and improved by new technologies in transportation, architecture, utilities, and sanitation. In addition, cities offered new cultural opportunities. Builders turned to new technologies to meet the challenge posed by huge numbers of people living together. Subways, elevated trains, and streetcars provided mass transportation. Steel girders and elevators made possible high-rise skyscrapers. Gas and electric lights brightened city streets and made them safer. Growing health problems forced officials to design and build new water and sewage systems.

Many innovations enabled businesses to market their products more effectively. In urban areas, new department stores offered customers a wide variety of goods under one roof. For rural areas, retailers developed mail-order catalogs that saved customers a trip to faraway stores. The items offered in these stores and catalogs expanded as well, thanks to new inventions, such as the vacuum cleaner, telephone, electric light bulb, electric iron, and safety razor.

Business Developments

Before the Civil War, sole proprietors, or single owners, and partnerships had controlled most American businesses. The mills and factories that came with industrialization, however, usually required greater **capital,** or money for investment, than one person or a few partners could raise.

Some 19th Century Inventions That Changed American Life

Date	Invention	Impact on Culture
1857	passenger elevator	multistory buildings could be built, and by 1885, the first skyscraper was built in Chicago; escalators followed in 1891
1867	barbed wire	allowed farmers to fence in the formerly open prairies
1873	Levi Strauss created blue jeans, known as "Levi's"	heavy duty farm clothing was quickly successful and continued into the twenty-first century as a fashion garment as well
1874	first structural steel bridge	steel from Carnegie Mills, used in a triple arch design that spanned the Mississippi River at St. Louis, opened the way for other bridges
1876	telephone	increased speed and ease of communication for business, political, and social needs; aided in organization for farm groups and others
1879	earliest incandescent lights	before the end of the century, offices, homes, factories and farms were affected by availability of longer hours of light
1892	first gas-powered car and first gas-powered tractor	earliest efforts at "horseless carriages" and farm equipment without animals helped spur further growth

Unifying Themes
Economy and Business

- What do you call a business in which many investors own shares?

- Name two kinds of businesses that speeded the growth of American industry.

- What do you call a company that has complete control over a particular kind of business? Name two examples.

- What do you call the merger of a group of unrelated companies? Name an example.

- What effect did these different business structures have on the American economy?

To raise capital for expansion, many businesses became corporations. A **corporation** is a business in which many investors own shares, usually called stocks. In exchange for their investment, each stockholder receives a dividend, or part of the corporation's profits. Besides paying dividends, the corporations also limited investor losses. If a corporation failed, an investor lost only his or her investment and was not responsible for the corporation's debts. The money raised by corporations speeded the growth of American industry. Among the fastest growing industries were transportation (railroads, urban transportation, and, later, automobiles), building materials (steel), energy (coal, oil, and electricity), and communications (telegraph and telephone).

As the nation's economy boomed and industries grew larger in the late 1800s, other ways of organizing business appeared. Often the aim of such business organizations was to eliminate competition and dominate a particular area of the economy.

Monopoly A company or small group of companies that has complete control over a particular field of business is a **monopoly**. One example of a monopoly in the late 1800s was the E. C. Knight Sugar Company. Having a monopoly in a field often allowed a company to raise prices to almost any level it desired. Such abuses led to federal legislation aimed at curbing monopolies. Some monopolies are permitted today. Public utility companies that provide gas, water, and electricity are examples of private companies that often have monopolies in their fields. Government agencies closely monitor the operations of such utilities.

Conglomerate A corporation that owns a group of unrelated companies is a **conglomerate.** Such conglomerates are usually formed by **merger,** the process by which one company acquires legal control over another. Mergers and conglomerates are both legal and common today. General Electric, for example, is a conglomerate that has acquired many different divisions through mergers.

Pool Sometimes competing companies in one field entered into agreements to fix prices and divide business. Such an agreement was a **pool.** Railroad companies in the late 1800s formed such pools, which were later outlawed.

Trust A group of corporations in the same or related fields sometimes agreed to combine under a single board of trustees that controlled the actions of all the member corporations. This was a **trust.** Shareholders in the corporations received dividends from the trust but lost any say in its operation. The Standard Oil Trust was one example of such a combination. Trusts were later made illegal. Both trusts and pools were used by big business in an effort to limit competition.

Holding Company To get around the outlawing of trusts, corporations formed holding companies. The **holding company** bought controlling amounts of stock in different corporations rather than take operations over directly as a trust did.

Unifying Themes
Economics

Vertical trusts controlled all aspects of production, from beginning to sale. Horizontal trusts grouped related industries for maximum profits.

- Give an example of each type of trust.

Social Studies Practices
Gathering Evidence

In the space below, name four key entrepreneurs of the late 1800s and early 1900s and the industries each operated.

1.

2.

3.

4.

Entrepreneurs

These new forms of business organization and innovative ideas from inventors helped American industry grow in the late 1800s and early 1900s. Yet without the business knowledge and daring of certain individuals, that growth would have been much slower.

These individuals were **entrepreneurs**, people who take responsibility for the organization and operation of a new business venture. Entrepreneurs often risk large sums of venture capital in hopes of making enormous profits.

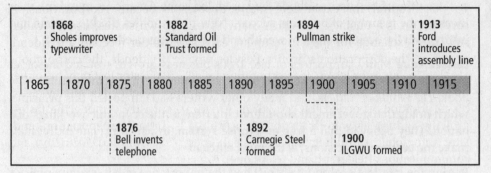

Innovations and Business Developments, 1868–1913

| 1868 Sholes improves typewriter | 1882 Standard Oil Trust formed | 1894 Pullman strike | 1913 Ford introduces assembly line |

| 1865 | 1870 | 1875 | 1880 | 1885 | 1890 | 1895 | 1900 | 1905 | 1910 | 1915 |

1876 Bell invents telephone   1892 Carnegie Steel formed   1900 ILGWU formed

Preparing for the Regents

Stimulus-Based Questions: Timeline

Examine the timeline, then answer these questions.

- How many years passed between the formation of Standard Oil Trust and the formation of Carnegie Steel?

- How do you think the invention of the telephone encouraged the growth of other companies?

The business decisions made by turn-of-the-century entrepreneurs had a great impact on the lives of most Americans. Some of the key entrepreneurs of the late 1800s and early 1900s are discussed below.

Andrew Carnegie An immigrant from Scotland, **Andrew Carnegie** started work in a textile factory at age 12. He worked his way up through a variety of jobs and invested his money shrewdly. At age 38, Carnegie entered the steel industry, which was booming because of the growth of railroads. Carnegie sought to control all aspects of steelmaking and built his company into the world's largest steelmaker.

Carnegie sold his company in 1901 for a quarter billion dollars. He believed the wealthy had a duty to society and gave hundreds of millions to charities. He also underwrote the founding of free public libraries all across the country. Many of those libraries still stand and can be found in many cities and small towns.

John D. Rockefeller Industrialist **John D. Rockefeller** entered the oil-refining business during the Civil War. He believed competition was wasteful and used ruthless methods to eliminate competitors. By 1882, his Standard Oil Company controlled over 90 percent of American oil refining. In 1882, he formed the Standard Oil Trust to control more aspects of oil production. Rockefeller also gave away hundreds of millions of dollars to charity.

J. Pierpont Morgan Trained as a banker, **J. P. Morgan** profited by making loans to growing businesses. He took control of many bankrupt railroads in the late 1800s, reorganized them, and made a huge profit. His critics and competitors said he "ReMorganized" those businesses. He also controlled electrical, insurance, and shipping companies. Morgan bought Carnegie Steel in 1901, merged it with other companies, and created the United States Steel Corporation, the world's largest.

Henry Ford Entrepreneur **Henry Ford** revolutionized automaking in 1913 by using a moving assembly line that permitted the mass production of cars, significantly lowering the cost of production. Ford also paid workers higher wages and set a standard that enabled laborers to afford such purchases.

Attitudes Toward Business

Industrialization and the changes associated with it caused American attitudes toward business to alter in the late 1800s. Traditional attitudes, of course, still existed. They could be found in books by the popular writer Horatio Alger. Alger's novels describe poor boys who become rich through hard work and luck. Alger's novels illustrate what is known as the **Puritan work ethic**. This is the belief, brought with the Puritans to colonial New England and embodied in the preaching of Puritan minister Cotton Mather, that hard work builds character and is its own reward.

Andrew Carnegie

J. Pierpont Morgan

Unifying Themes

Technology and Innovation

New production techniques increased efficiency in many industries, such as in steel and automotive production.

- Explain how one of these techniques worked to increase efficiency.

The tremendous wealth some entrepreneurs gained during the late 1800s, as well as the cutthroat business methods they used, led some Americans to rethink their ideas on the meaning of business success. New philosophies tried to explain and justify both the accumulation of wealth and the practices used to achieve it.

Laissez Faire Many supporters of late 1800s business growth restated the older principle of **laissez faire**, or noninterference. Economist Adam Smith, in his 1776 book, *The Wealth of Nations*, and many other writers had supported this principle, which holds that government should not interfere in the economic workings of a nation. They believed that a **free enterprise system,** in which private individuals make the economic decisions, is the most efficient.

During the late 1800s, economists restated the importance of laissez-faire policies to economic growth. Government interference with business was minimal for much of this period, and entrepreneurs expanded their businesses and earned great wealth. Businesses in the eastern part of the United States profited from large farms in the west.

Social Darwinism Laissez-faire capitalists found justification for their beliefs in new scientific theories being developed at that time. Naturalist Charles Darwin had developed a theory of evolution that described how animal species live or die by a process of natural selection. Other writers simplified Darwin's theories and created a philosophy called **Social Darwinism**.

Social Darwinists held that life was a struggle for the "survival of the fittest." Unregulated business competition would see weak businesses fail and healthy businesses thrive. Government action regulating business practices would interfere with the process of natural selection. Likewise, any government programs to aid the poor or workers would also violate "natural laws."

Robber Barons or Philanthropists? The philosophies described above and the growing gulf between rich and poor led some Americans to criticize laissez-faire policies and those who profited from them. Critics condemned the wealthy entrepreneurs as, **robber barons**, those who gained their wealth by ruthless methods in their dealings with competitors at the expense of the poor and the working class. The lavish lifestyles of the wealthy at this time fed such criticism.

During this so-called Gilded Age, the rich spent freely to show off their wealth, a practice known as **conspicuous consumption.** Public criticism and a sense of social responsibility led entrepreneurs to use a part of their wealth to aid society. People like Carnegie and Rockefeller became **philanthropists**, donating vast sums of money to charities and institutions such as schools, museums, libraries, and orchestras.

Government Policies Toward Business

The federal government generally held a laissez-faire attitude toward business for much of this period. Expanding industries and growing foreign trade seemed to justify such an attitude. In addition, many business leaders made financial contributions, legal and illegal, to the politicians who set federal policies.

A number of government policies were designed to aid the growth of business. These included loans and land grants to large railroad companies, high tariffs that discouraged competition from foreign manufacturers, tight limits on the amount of money in circulation, and few limits on immigration.

Steps Toward Government Regulation

Several factors led the government to take the first steps in the late 1800s toward regulating business

- periodic downturns in the national economy
- growing criticism of practices that saw big business profit at the expense of the poor and working class
- increasing grassroots political pressure for change

Although government intervention at this time had limited impact, it did set the course for more federal actions in years to come.

Some Supreme Court Decisions During the late 1800s, railroads developed a number of policies that discriminated against farmers and small shippers. These groups pressured some states to pass laws regulating railroad practices. The railroads sued to have such laws overturned.

In the 1877 case **Munn v. Illinois**, the Supreme Court upheld an Illinois law controlling grain elevator rates. The Court ruled that the Constitution recognized a state's right to a "police power" that permitted regulation of private property "affected with a public interest."

In the 1886 case **Wabash, St. Louis & Pacific R.R. v. Illinois**, however, the Court ruled that states could not regulate railroad rates on portions of interstate routes that lay within their borders. Under the Constitution, only the federal government can regulate **interstate trade**. This decision meant that states could do little to regulate the railroads.

Interstate Commerce Commission In 1887, public pressure for reform of railroad policies led Congress to pass the **Interstate Commerce Act.** The act set up the Interstate Commerce Commission (ICC), an agency charged with ending such railroad abuses as pools and rebates, discounts available only to special customers. Although court decisions kept the commission ineffective for several years, its establishment set a precedent for federal regulation of interstate commerce.

Sherman Antitrust Act By the late 1800s, some large corporations and trusts had eliminated most competition and won almost total monopolies in their fields. Politicians heeded the public protests over the ensuing abuses. One result was the **Sherman Antitrust Act** of 1890. The act prohibited monopolies by declaring illegal any business combination or trust "in restraint of trade or commerce."

Yet when the federal government tried to enforce the act, the Supreme Court, in *United States* v. *E. C. Knight Company* (1895), ruled that many businesses were exempt from the new law. In addition, some other corporations circumvented the act by forming holding companies rather than trusts. Once again, the precedent set by the act proved more important than the act itself.

Theodore Roosevelt and the Square Deal

The first three presidents of this century—Theodore Roosevelt, William Howard Taft, and Woodrow Wilson—are known as the Progressive Presidents. **Theodore Roosevelt**, elected vice president in 1900, became president when President William McKinley was assassinated in 1901. He was elected in his own right in 1904.

Roosevelt saw his job as one of stewardship—leading the nation in the public interest, like a manager or supervisor. He believed that the president had any powers not specifically denied to the executive in the Constitution. Roosevelt's administration is often known as the **Square Deal** because of the many reforms made during his presidency.

Social Studies Practices
Gathering Evidence

- What factors led the government toward regulating business in the late 1800s?

Unifying Themes
Power and Authority

Two landmark Supreme Court cases dealt with railroad regulation: *Munn v. Illinois* (1877) and *Wabash, St. Louis and Pacific R.R.* v. *Illinois* (1886).

- How did these two cases influence railroad regulation?

Unifying Themes
Power

The Sherman Antitrust Act was an attempt to reduce the power of business owners in an effort to protect individual workers and consumers.

Unifying Themes
Power and Authority

We must see that each is given a square deal, because he is entitled to no more and should receive no less.

—Theodore Roosevelt, 1903

- What did Theodore Roosevelt mean by the Square Deal?
- What was meant by the stewardship theory of government?

Trust-Busting Roosevelt saw a difference between "good trusts," which were to be subject only to regulation, and "bad trusts," which were to be dissolved. The actions he took against big business earned him a reputation as someone who would do **trust-busting**. In 1903, Roosevelt convinced Congress to form the Bureau of Corporations within the Department of Commerce and Labor. He used the bureau to pressure corporations through investigations and publicity about their activities.

The Northern Securities Case By the end of the 1800s, the Northern Securities Company controlled the railroad system in the Pacific Northwest. In 1901, the Justice Department began prosecution of Northern Securities under the Sherman Antitrust Act. The case was eventually appealed to the Supreme Court. In its ruling in ***Northern Securities Co. v. United States*** (1904), the Supreme Court upheld the judgment against the company and ordered the company to be dissolved.

The "Beef Trust" Another government action using the Sherman Antitrust Act was directed against a group of meatpackers known as the "beef trust." This prosecution, too, was upheld by the Supreme Court, in *Swift & Co.* v. *United States* (1905). This decision gave the government broader powers under the Constitution's interstate commerce clause than the Court's ruling did in the landmark case, *United States* v. *E. C. Knight Company* (1895).

Industrialization, Immigration, and Labor

Lesson Overview

Immigration and urbanization changed the United States dramatically. Industrialization and new building technologies triggered an explosion of urban growth that brought social changes, both good and bad. A prosperous middle class emerged, while urban crowding and disease took a heavy toll on the working poor, many of whom were immigrants.

New arrivals came in waves, first from western Europe and Africa, then from eastern Europe and Asia. Despite widespread discrimination, many immigrants prospered. A growing United States population and a demand for new lands and resources lured Americans westward, which resulted in reducing the Native American population and forcing them into ever-shrinking parcels of land. Western land was gobbled up by miners, ranchers, and a growing political force: farmers.

Key Concept

11.5b Rapid industrialization and urbanization created significant challenges and societal problems that were addressed by a variety of reform efforts.

Unifying Themes

As you review this lesson take special note of the following themes:

- **Time, Continuity, and Change** What effects did industrialization and urbanization have on American culture, work life, and family life?

- **Geography, Humans, and Environment** How did patterns of immigration change from colonial times through the early 1900s? What types of land, resources, and economic opportunities caused Americans to move farther and farther westward?

Key People

Jane Addams

William Jennings Bryan

William McKinley

Terence Powderly

Samuel Gompers

Key Terms and Events

tenement	strike	Homestead Steel Strike
settlement house movement	American Federation of Labor	American Railway Union
push-pull factors	International Ladies Garment Workers' Union	Pullman Strike
nativism		Industrial Workers of the World
The Grange	boycott	Lawrence Textile Strike
Granger Movement	Great Railway Strike	
Populist Party	Haymarket Riot	
Knights of Labor		

Social Studies Practices
Cause and Effect

- How was industrialization related to urbanization?
- Did one process lead to the other, or were these processes interdependent?

Social Studies Practices
Chronological Reasoning

The growth of cities had both positive and negative effects. Some of the negative effects included crowded and unsanitary living conditions for workers.

- How might these conditions change over time?
- How might they stay the same?

Industrialization and Urbanization

Cities offered the best and the worst of life for newcomers from the countryside and from abroad. The dazzling skyscrapers and bustling streets were symbols of the new opportunities for prosperity in America. Yet behind the dazzle grew a darker side of city life.

Industrialization and urbanization, or the growth of cities, went hand in hand. Cities offered large numbers of workers for new factories. Cities provided transportation for raw materials and finished goods. As more plants were built, more workers moved to cities seeking jobs. In 1880, about 25 percent of Americans lived in cities. By 1900, roughly 40 percent did. By 1920, more than half of all Americans lived in cities. This shift from rural to urban life had both positive and negative effects.

Negative Effects of City Growth

Some of the negative effects of urbanization included crowded, unsanitary living conditions for workers, as well as corrupt city politics.

Housing Construction of decent housing often lagged behind the growth of city populations. Much city housing consisted of multifamily buildings called **tenements.** Immigrant and working-class families, who could pay little for rent, crowded into such buildings. These poorly maintained tenements deteriorated, and whole neighborhoods became slums. Crime flourished in such poor, congested neighborhoods.

Health Urban crowding helped spread disease. Water and sanitation facilities were often inadequate. Poor families could not afford proper diets and lacked knowledge of basic health procedures.

Politics Many city governments were taken over by **political machines,** who were providing help to the growing number of poor immigrant voters and thereby gaining their support. Corruption increased, and money that could have been spent on public works often ended up in private pockets.

Positive Effects of City Growth

Urbanization was aided and improved by new technologies in transportation, architecture, utilities, and sanitation. In addition, cities offered new cultural opportunities.

A public school in Washington, D.C., in 1899

Cultural Advances Public and private money funded new museums, concert halls, theaters, and parks. New printing presses turned out mass-circulation newspapers, magazines, and popular novels by authors such as Mark Twain and Horatio Alger. Public schools educated more students than ever before. Reformers, including the philosopher and educator John Dewey, improved the quality of teaching.

Community Improvement Other reformers founded groups intended to correct the problems of society. In Chicago, **Jane Addams** started **Hull House**, a model project that led a **settlement house movement** to provide education and services to the poor. Political reformers sought to unseat corrupt political machines and see that public money was spent on improved services, such as police and fire departments and new hospitals, rather than on graft.

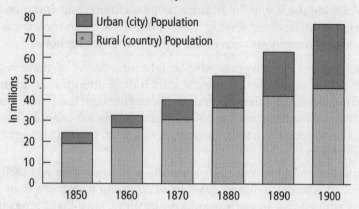

Urban and Rural Populations, 1850–1900

Preparing for the Regents

Stimulus-Based Questions: Chart

Some examination questions require you to read and interpret charts. Study the chart and answer these questions.

- Approximately how much did the urban (city) population in the United States grow between 1860 and 1900?
- Did the rural population increase or decrease between 1870 and 1890?
- What factors caused this to happen?

The Urban Mixture

The people who lived and worked in these growing cities generally could be divided into three broad groups.

Workers and the Poor The largest group contained the workers and the poor. Most immigrants belonged to this group, whose members lived in slums and poorer neighborhoods. (Living conditions generally were better in the **company towns**, which were built and owned by a single employer, but workers in these towns were dependent on their employer for everything from housing to food to police protection.) Often workers lacked the time and money to go to theaters or museums or use other resources that cities provided.

The Middle Class As a result of industrialization, doctors, lawyers, office workers, and skilled laborers made up a growing middle class. Middle-class neighborhoods offered more spacious, better-maintained housing. The middle-class people had both money and leisure time. Their homes contained the new consumer goods becoming available, such as sewing machines and phonographs. They could afford to go to concerts, attend increasingly popular football, basketball, or baseball games, and save money for their children's higher education.

The Wealthy Entrepreneurs and wealthy business people usually made the city their chief residence, although they often had summer estates outside it. The rich made up the smallest segment of urban society. They lived in large mansions or elegant apartment buildings. They often contributed to charities and cultural institutions, such as opera companies and libraries. They could enjoy the broadest range of benefits of city life.

Changes for Women, Families, and Workers

Industrialization and urbanization brought changes to the lives of women in all the classes. Many Americans had long held the view that the ideal woman devoted herself to home and family, instilling in her husband and children high moral values. In fact, usually only wealthy women could dedicate themselves full time to such tasks.

Social Studies Practices
Interpreting Evidence

Into which three groups can the urban population of the late 1800s be divided?

- Which group was the largest?
- Which group was the smallest?
- What might be the effects of this divided society?

Unifying Themes
Change

In the late 1800s, more women began to seek paid employment outside the home.

- What reasons led to this change?
- What kinds of new jobs did women seek outside the home?

Social Studies Practices
Gathering and Interpreting Evidence

- How much did the number of working women grow between 1880 and 1910?

- What challenges did women face in the workplace?

- How did some women address those challenges? How successful were these efforts?

Unifying Themes
Transformation of Social Structures

- What other groups of workers also began working in the late 1800s? What kinds of conditions did they face?

Social Studies Practices
Gathering Evidence

- Think about your family's history. Select a relative who immigrated to the United States. Find out why the person came and decide if the reason was a push factor or a pull factor.

Unifying Themes
Movement

During the colonial period, a huge number of immigrants arrived in the United States. People from England, Germany, and Sweden, for example, made up a large number of these immigrants, but people from other countries came as well.

- What motivated immigrants in the colonial period to come to the United States?

In the late 1800s, more women began taking jobs outside the home, some out of economic necessity and others out of a desire for a larger role in society. These jobs provided added income and personal fulfillment but sometimes produced added stress for family members. For example, women who worked outside the home were also expected to continue performing most of the jobs in the home, and children often had to be cared for by relatives or neighbors during the day.

New Employment Opportunities for Women Working-class women often had to hold jobs outside the home. In addition to jobs women had traditionally filled, such as household services, sewing, or laundering, women took some new jobs created by recent inventions such as the typewriter and telephone.

Middle- and upper-class women also sought jobs. Many of these women had long been active in reform movements, including abolition and temperance, and had attended college in increasing numbers through the 1800s. They sought to apply their educations and social concerns in the job market. Women took jobs as teachers, social workers, doctors, and lawyers, often struggling against public disapproval.

Women thus became an ever-larger part of the workforce. Between 1880 and 1910, the number of working women grew from 2.6 million to more than 7 million. Conditions women met in the workplace—hostility, laws that barred them from certain jobs, unequal pay—led more women to seek legal remedies. To gain the political power to force change, however, women first needed to win the right to vote, called **suffrage**. The women's suffrage movement grew more active.

Other Groups of Workers Groups besides women faced problems in the workplace. Employers regularly discriminated against African American workers and workers who were older or disabled, refusing to hire them or keeping them in low-paying jobs.

Nor did laws protect children from dangerous and unhealthful work, such as in mines and factories. Nevertheless, many families were forced to send their children to work rather than to school in order to help make ends meet.

Immigration

Immigration is sometimes discussed with a phrase called the **push-pull factors**. Push factors of immigration are those factors that cause people to want to leave their homelands for another place. Push factors include such possibilities as natural disasters, forms of oppressive government, lack of religious freedoms, and others. Pull factors are those conditions that attract people to another place, such as opportunities for employment, better living conditions, political freedom, and others.

The United States has always been a nation of immigrants. After the Civil War, however, industrialization drew an even greater flood of immigrants. From 1865 to 1900, some 13.5 million people arrived from abroad. During much of the nineteenth century, there were few restrictions on immigration as the growing numbers of factories provided job opportunities for cheap labor. Not until the 1920s would the numbers begin to dwindle. Immigration to the United States can be divided into three stages.

Colonial Immigration

This period lasted from the arrival of the first people from England through the writing of the Declaration of Independence. The following features characterize this period of immigration.

Colonial Immigrants People from England made up the largest part of these immigrants. However, Scotch-Irish, German, Swedish, and Dutch also came in significant numbers. Large numbers of Africans were also part of the colonial immigration.

Reasons for Immigration Some came seeking political and religious freedom. Others sought to improve their economic standing and their way of life. Most of the Africans came unwillingly, as slaves.

Areas of Settlement English settlement spread along the Atlantic Coast from Maine to Georgia and inland to the Appalachians. Within this area, other ethnic groups became concentrated in certain regions. For example, many Dutch settled in New York and New Jersey, many Germans in Pennsylvania, and many Scotch-Irish in the hill and mountain country areas of the Carolinas. Most Africans were brought at first to the Chesapeake region, then spread through the South and occasionally to the North.

Difficulties They Faced Immigrants came into conflict with the Native Americans. They also had to overcome the challenge of building homes, farms, and a new way of life in an unfamiliar region.

Contributions The immigrants succeeded in establishing a culture much like the one they had left in Europe, yet were heavily influenced by the geographic factors they encountered in North America. In addition to their language, people coming from England brought forms of government, religions, family and cultural traditions, and economic patterns from their home country. Other groups contributed customs from their home country. All worked to build a successful economy in North America.

Old Immigration

The Old Immigration period covered the years from the establishment of the United States until around 1850. Most immigrants came from northern and western Europe, especially from Ireland, Germany, and Scandinavia.

Reasons for Immigration Massive famine caused by the failure of the potato crop drove millions of Irish immigrants to seek opportunity in the United States. Revolution in Germany caused many immigrants to seek peace and stability in America. Many people continued to arrive in search of better economic opportunity.

Areas of Settlement The Irish largely settled in cities in the Northeast. Some Germans also stayed in cities, but many moved west to start farms, as did a large number of Scandinavian immigrants.

Difficulties They Faced Irish Catholic and German Catholic immigrants often faced hostility on their arrival in the United States. Some Americans feared economic competition from the newcomers. Since at this time the nation was predominantly Protestant, resentment toward Catholics and Jews was also strong.

Contributions Irish workers helped build railroads and canals and labored in factories. Germans and Scandinavians brought, among other things, advanced farming techniques and new ideas on education, such as kindergarten. They were also often skilled craftsmen in woodworking. When the opportunity existed, the Irish and Germans especially demonstrated their musical talents.

Social Studies Practices
Geographical Context

During the colonial period, in what areas did most English immigrants settle? List two other examples of immigrant groups and the areas in which they settled.

1.

2.

• Why might they have chosen to settle in these areas?

Unifying Themes
Movement

"Old immigration" took place during the first half of the nineteenth century. People from northern and western Europe, Ireland, and Scandinavia, for example, made up a large number of these immigrants, but people came from other countries as well.

• What motivated immigrants in the post-colonial period to come to the United States?

Social Studies Practices
Geographical and Historical Context

• Where did most Irish and German immigrants settle?

• What difficulties did these immigrant groups face?

Immigrants

Where they came from 1840–1860

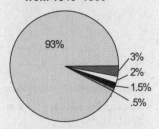

93%

3%
2%
1.5%
.5%

Where they came from 1880–1900

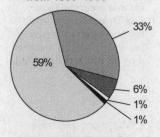

33%
59%
6%
1%
1%

☐ Northern and Western Europe

▨ Eastern and Southern Europe

■ Americas

☐ Asia

■ All others

Source: Historical Statistics of the United States

Preparing for the Regents

Stimulus-Based Questions: Pie Charts

Examine the pie charts, then answer the following questions.

- What percentage of immigrants between 1840 and 1860 came from northern and western Europe?

- How much did the percentage of immigrants from eastern and southern Europe increase from the period 1840 to 1860 to the period 1880 to 1900?

- What may have caused this increase?

New Immigration

The New Immigration period covered the time from roughly 1870 to 1924. This period was marked by a shift in the origins of immigration to southern and eastern Europe, especially from the nations of Italy, Poland, and Russia. In addition, substantial numbers of Japanese and Chinese arrived.

Reasons for Immigration Hope of greater economic opportunity prompted many of these immigrants to come to America. Some also came seeking political freedom. Other groups, such as Russian Jews, sought religious freedom.

Areas of Settlement Most of the new immigrants settled in cities, especially in industrial centers and ports, and often were concentrated in ghettos, or urban areas (usually poor), that were dominated by a single ethnic group. Asian immigrants tended to settle on the west coast, usually in California.

Difficulties They Faced Adjusting to life in the United States could cause strains in immigrant families. At school, immigrant children learned not only English but also American tastes and customs. Immigrant parents often feared that their children were losing their religious and cultural heritage.

In addition, the growing numbers of new immigrants produced reactions of fear and hostility among many native-born Americans whose ancestors had come from very different backgrounds. Newcomers faced discrimination in jobs and housing. As low-wage workers, they also competed against other minority groups, such as African Americans. Popular pressure to limit immigration increased.

Political party bosses often arranged assistance for newly arriving immigrants and in return expected those immigrants to show their gratitude by supporting that political party in elections.

Contributions The new immigrants found an abundance of jobs in the nation's expanding industries. Yet the steady stream of incoming workers to fill such jobs kept wages low. Young Italian and Jewish girls worked in the sweatshops of the garment industry. Poles and Slavs labored in the coal mines and steel mills of Pennsylvania and the Midwest. Chinese workers helped build the transcontinental railroad. These immigrants aided America's economic expansion and contributed to the nation's rich cultural diversity.

Reaction Against Immigration

The flood of immigration in the late 1800s brought with it a new wave of **nativism**. This was the belief that native-born Americans and their ways of life were superior to immigrants and their ways of life. In the late 1800s, descendants of the old immigrants were often among the nativists protesting the arrival of new immigrants.

Nativists believed that immigrant languages, religions, and traditions would have a negative impact on American society. Nativist workers believed that the many new immigrants competing for jobs kept wages low. A series of downturns in the economy added to fears that immigrants would take jobs from native-born Americans.

These immigrants were generally unskilled laborers. Immigrants thus often met with prejudice and discrimination. Jokes and stereotypes about the newcomers were common. Nativists also tried to influence legislation against immigrants. Key developments in this area are included in the chart on the next page.

Reaction Against Immigration

- **Know-Nothing Party:** The party's members worked during the 1850s to limit the voting strength of immigrants, keep Catholics out of public office, and require a lengthy residence before citizenship. Also known as the American party, the Know-Nothing party achieved none of these goals and died out by the late 1850s.

- **Chinese Exclusion Act of 1882:** Some native-born Americans labelled immigration from Asia a "yellow peril." Under pressure from California, which had already barred the Chinese from owning property or working at certain jobs, Congress passed this law sharply limiting Chinese immigration.

- **"Gentlemen's Agreement":** In 1907 President Roosevelt reached an informal agreement with Japan under which that nation nearly halted the emigration of its people to the United States.

- **Literacy Tests:** In 1917 Congress enacted a law barring any immigrant who could not read or write.

- **Emergency Quota Act of 1921:** This law sharply limited the number of immigrants to the United States each year to about 350,000.

- **National Origins Act of 1924:** This law further reduced immigration and biased it in favor of those from northern and western Europe.

Immigrants and American Society

Over the years, sociologists and others who studied immigration developed different theories on how immigrants were absorbed into the larger society.

"Melting Pot" Theory According to this theory, people from various cultures have met in the United States to form a new American culture. The contributions of individual groups are not easily distinguished. The resulting culture is more important than its parts.

Assimilation/Americanization According to this theory, immigrants disappeared into an already established American culture. They gave up older languages and customs and became Americanized, adopting the appearances and attitudes of the larger society in order to be accepted. Immigrants from Africa and Asia, who looked least like Americans of European ancestry, had the hardest time becoming assimilated.

Farmers, Populists, and Politics

As you read in Topic 4, new technologies in farming and transportation led to a surge in settlement in the Great Plains and farther westward. Farms and ranches dotted the region. Agriculture became a key component of the American economy. In time, farmers banded together to overcome challenges as well as to increase their political influence. Farmers gained influence and power through two organizations: the Grange and the Populist Party.

The Grange

Many farmers facing the hardships and isolation of rural life joined the **Grange**. This organization, founded in 1867, was originally meant to develop social ties. However, poor economic conditions made farmers aware that railroad companies, which often stored farmers' crops and carried them to market, had great control over their livelihoods. To win back some of this control, the **Granger Movement** began to press for political changes to limit the power of the railroads. Pressure from the Grange and other groups led to the state laws regulating railroads that were upheld in *Munn* v. *Illinois* (1877) and to the federal law creating the Interstate Commerce Commission.

The Populist Party

Farmers and many factory workers realized that the best hope of winning more reforms was the formation of a new political party. In 1891, they founded the **Populist Party**, which had among its goals a graduated income tax, direct election of United States senators, an eight-hour workday, and government ownership of railroads, telegraphs, and telephones.

Unifying Themes
Economics

The overproduction of staple products caused low prices for agricultural products, which hurt farmers during this period.

- What economic principle is illustrated by this cause-and-effect relationship?

Unifying Themes
Civic Ideals and Practices

Many workers, both farm and factory, joined the Populist Party, which had strong support from the people rather than from powerful politicians. List three goals of the Populist Party.

1.

2.

3.

- Why would these goals appeal to both farm and factory workers?

The new party had strong grassroots support—support directly from the people rather than from established political figures. Populist candidates soon made strong showings in elections for state legislatures and for the United States Congress. Many of the ideas and goals of the Populists eventually became laws.

The Election of 1896

The Populists made their strongest showing in the election of 1896, the first election to follow an economic depression that had begun in 1893. The chief Populist issue in the campaign was **free silver**. The free coinage of silver would produce cheap money, or currency inflated in value, that would make it easier for farmers to pay off debts. **William Jennings Bryan**, who ran on both the Populist and Democratic tickets, argued tirelessly for this idea. Republican candidate **William McKinley** had the support of big business, which contributed heavily to his campaign. McKinley claimed the nation's economy was sound and opposed free silver.

McKinley won the election by a fair margin. The nation's economy meanwhile improved, and the Populists disappeared as a political party. Yet, as has happened with other minor parties in American history, some of the Populists' ideas were later adopted by the other political parties. The defeat of the Populists symbolized the great changes that had swept the nation since the Civil War. The economy had changed from agrarian to industrial. The United States was becoming a nation of cities rather than farms and villages. The West was closing and its influence coming to end. New immigrants were creating a new, complex, pluralistic culture in America. By 1900, the United States was entering both a new century and a modern age.

Labor Organizations

Business growth in the late 1800s brought generally higher wages to American workers. Yet periodic unemployment and poor working conditions remained a fact of life for workers. In addition, employers held enormous power over the lives of their workers and could lower wages and fire employees at will.

The Growth of Unions

To improve conditions, increasing numbers of American workers formed labor unions beginning in the 1820s. As working conditions changed with industrialization, many more workers became interested in unions. "Eight hours for work, eight hours for sleep, eight hours for what we will" was a popular slogan that promoted a major goal of labor unions.

Americans had long understood the values of cooperation and association, and labor unions provided a means to put these values into action. In **collective bargaining**, union members representing workers negotiated labor issues with management. Instead of each worker trying to achieve individual aims, a united group would put pressure on management. Several early unions helped advance the cause of labor.

Knights of Labor Under the direction of **Terence Powderly**, the **Knights of Labor**, formed in 1869, welcomed skilled and unskilled workers as well as women and African Americans. The Knights fought for broad social reforms such as an eight-hour day for workers, an end to child labor, and equal opportunities and wages for women. As a rule, the union opposed **strikes**, or work stoppages, but a successful strike against railroads in 1885 brought in many new members. However, an antilabor feeling swept the nation after the Haymarket Riot in late 1886. The Knights declined in influence due to a series of unsuccessful strikes and competition from the American Federation of Labor.

Social Studies Practices
Interpreting Evidence

• What changes did the outcome of the election of 1896 symbolize in the United States?

William McKinley

William Jennings Bryan

Unifying Themes
Power and Authority

• What do you call the process through which union members represent workers in labor negotiations with management?

• Why would this method of negotiation be more productive than others?

American Federation of Labor In 1886, **Samuel Gompers** formed the **American Federation of Labor (AFL)**. The AFL was a collection of many different craft unions, unions of skilled workers in similar trades. In contrast to the Knights of Labor, the AFL fought for immediate goals such as better wages, hours, and working conditions. This policy was known as *bread-and-butter unionism*. AFL membership reached about a million by 1900, making the AFL the most powerful union in the nation. Nevertheless, groups such as women, immigrants, and African Americans generally were not welcome. The AFL specifically focused on the needs of skilled workers.

International Ladies' Garment Workers' Union Women made up the majority of workers in the garment industries. In 1900, the **International Ladies' Garment Workers' Union (ILGWU)** was formed to represent the laborers who toiled in sweatshops. After a successful strike in 1910, the ILGWU soon became an important part of the AFL. In March 1911, a horrific fire at the Triangle Shirtwaist Company in New York City caused the deaths of almost 150 people, mostly young immigrant women. Dozens leapt to their deaths from upper stories to escape the burning building due to locked exits and inadequate fire escapes. This event gave further impetus to the work of the ILGWU.

Labor Conflict

If collective bargaining failed, labor unions sometimes used **boycotts** against the employer or resorted to strikes to achieve their aims. Boycotts are still used today. They are an organized refusal to buy or use a product or service or to deal with a company or a group of companies. This type of protest is used as a means of forcing action by a company. Strikes sometimes ended in union victories; often, however, they led to violence as business owners sought state and even federal support to end walkouts. The strikes and labor-associated violence described below sometimes advanced the cause of labor and sometimes set it back.

During the late 1800s, when most efforts at collective bargaining failed, big business often used court injunctions against labor unions to force workers back to work. Other tactics used by big business were blacklists and yellow dog contracts. If a worker's name was put on a **blacklist**, it meant that the name was circulated to other companies or employers so that the person would not be hired because of his or her actions or beliefs. Big business also used **yellow dog contracts**, which forced workers to sign agreements stating that they would never join a labor union.

Great Railway Strike In 1877, a series of pay cuts for railroad workers led to a strike that spread across several states. At the request of state governors, President Rutherford B. Hayes sent federal troops to help end the strike. The workers gained little benefit from the strike, and owners took a harder position against unions.

Haymarket Riot A labor rally called by Chicago anarchists in 1886 ended with a bomb blast and riot that left many people dead, including seven police officers. Although the Knights of Labor had no responsibility for the violence, some public opinion blamed them.

Homestead Steel Strike In 1892, union members at the Carnegie steel plant in Homestead, Pennsylvania, went on strike to protest a wage cut. Management brought in security guards to protect the plant. In the violence that followed, 16 people were killed. The National Guard finally ended the fighting and the strike. Fewer than 25 percent of the striking workers got their jobs back. The strike halted the union movement in the steel industry for 20 years.

Social Studies Practices
Gathering Evidence

American workers began to form a number of labor unions in the 1800s. In the space below, name three different labor unions and describe the workers who joined each of them.

1.

2.

3.

Preparing for the Regents

For the examination, you will need to understand the history of labor conflict in the United States.

Identify the outcome of each of the following strikes:

- Great Railway Strike (1877)
- Haymarket Riot (1886)
- Homestead Steel Strike (1892)
- Pullman Strike (1894)
- Lawrence Textile Strike (1912)

The U.S. Calvary escorting a train during the Pullman Strike

The American Railway Union and the Pullman Strike In 1893 the **American Railway Union (ARU)** was organized. It was briefly one of the largest and one of the first industrial unions. It brought together railway workers of all types and skills. It was organized by Eugene V. Debs, who went on to years of involvement in union and labor causes.

In 1894, a strike by railway-car makers in Illinois spread and tied up other rail lines. President Grover Cleveland sent in federal troops to end the strike. Union leader Debs was jailed for his involvement. The Supreme Court, in the 1895 case *In re Debs*, ruled that the president had the right to deploy the troops, even over the objection of the governor of Illinois. Cleveland's action confirmed the belief of many that government favored the interests of business over those of labor. Both the Homestead Steel Strike and the **Pullman Strike** ended sooner than expected as a result of direct government intervention.

The Lawrence Textile Strike In 1905, the **Industrial Workers of the World (IWW)**, a radical union of skilled and unskilled laborers, was formed. It was a new type of union as it allowed and encouraged membership of unskilled workers. Due to this, it attracted women, immigrants, and unskilled African Americans. In 1912, the IWW led a huge strike against the textile mills in Lawrence, Massachusetts. The **Lawrence Textile Strike** proved one of the greatest successes of that era, and workers won most of their demands.

The IWW continued its efforts in the pre–World War I years but became increasingly militant against owners and managers of large businesses. It was divided internally between those who favored a socialist approach going forward and those who favored anarchy, or violence and strikes. By 1917, involvement with the IWW was frequently condemned as traitorous and could lead to deportation. The membership went from 100,000 to fewer than 30,000. Near the end of the war, over 100 members were jailed for antiwar activities. The union still exists today with a very small membership.

An Era of Strikes, Late 1800s

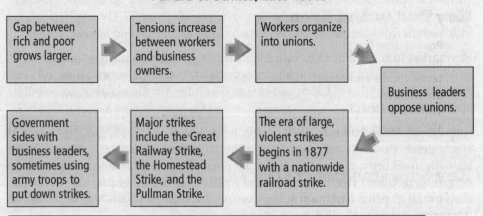

Gap between rich and poor grows larger.	→ Tensions increase between workers and business owners. → Workers organize into unions. →
	Business leaders oppose unions.
Government sides with business leaders, sometimes using army troops to put down strikes.	← Major strikes include the Great Railway Strike, the Homestead Strike, and the Pullman Strike. ← The era of large, violent strikes begins in 1877 with a nationwide railroad strike. ←

Increasing tensions between workers and employers led to large, often violent strikes

Challenges of Urbanization Lead to Reform Efforts

Lesson Overview

Between the end of the Civil War and the turn of the twentieth century, the United States became a more industrialized and urban nation. These changes brought many benefits to society, but they created problems as well. Americans responded to domestic change in the years from 1900 to 1920 in several ways. This period is called the Progressive Era. The term comes from the word *progress* and indicates that Americans were reacting to problems by working for reform.

Key Concept

11.5b Rapid industrialization and urbanization created significant challenges and societal problems that were addressed by a variety of reform efforts.

Unifying Themes

As you review this lesson take special note of the following themes:

- **Time, Continuity, and Change** What specific changes occurred during the Progressive Era? Were these changes good or bad for Americans? Use examples to support your answer.

- **Geography, Humans, and the Environment** What is urbanization? Do you live in an urban or a rural area? How is your area similar to or different from the same area described at the early 20th century?

- **Development and Transformation of Social Structures** Who were the Progressives? What did they hope to accomplish? Why did the change in lifestyles for Americans impact government?

- **Science, Technology, and Innovation** What technological developments can you identify that changed American society in the Progressive Era?

Key People

Ida Tarbell	Alice Paul	Ida B. Wells-Barnett
Upton Sinclair	Margaret Sanger	Robert M. La Follette
Jacob Riis	Booker T. Washington	Theodore Roosevelt
Jane Addams	W.E.B. Du Bois	William Howard Taft
Carrie Chapman Catt	Marcus Garvey	Woodrow Wilson

Key Terms and Events

Progressive Era	NAACP	recall
muckraker	spoils system	direct primary
temperance movement	Pendleton Act	17th Amendment
prohibition	secret ballot	conservation
18th Amendment	initiative	16th Amendment
19th Amendment	referendum	Federal Reserve System

Key Supreme Court Cases

As you review this lesson be sure you understand the significance of these key Supreme Court cases:

Lochner v. New York (1905)
Muller v. Oregon (1908)

Social Studies Practices

Compare and Contrast

Identify the similarities and differences among the five periods of American reform movements listed below.

- Birth of reform tradition in first half of 19th century.
- The Granger Movement and the Populist Party in the late 19th century.
- Progressive movement in the early 20th century.
- New Deal reforms of the 1930s.
- Civil Rights movements of the 1960s.

Preparing for the Regents

Stimulus-Based Questions: Timeline

Using the information in this section and in the timeline, answer the following questions.

- During whose presidency was the Supreme Court case *Lochner* v. *New York* (1905) decided?
- Which event on the timeline involved the creation of an organization that worked for the rights of African Americans?
- How did Sinclair's *The Jungle* lead to reform?

Pressures for Progressive Reform

By 1900, the United States was a rich and powerful nation. Industrialization, urbanization, and immigration had transformed the nation into a major world economy. The changes in American life, however, also brought problems. The Progressives' call for reform, which led to a period of time known as the **Progressive Era**, was a reaction to

- powerful monopolies restricting competition and controlling prices.
- labor unrest and violence.
- unhealthy and unsafe living and working conditions.
- increasing gap between living standards of the rich and the poor.
- urban poverty, crime, congestion, and poor sanitation.
- political corruption and lack of government responsiveness.
- abuse of the nation's natural resources.

Reform During the Progressive Era, 1901–1920

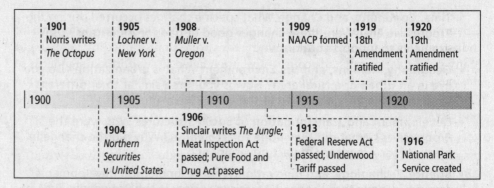

Effects of Business Practices

The corporate world grew increasingly wealthy and more powerful. Industrial leaders believed that economic success demonstrated fitness to lead, that Social Darwinism explained why some were rich and others were poor. Those who succeeded earned their position, and those who failed deserved their failure. Social Darwinists believed that the government should not intervene in this process, a belief consistent with the ideas of laissez-faire economics.

Conditions for Industrial Workers

Working conditions for factory workers were harsh. Many laborers worked 60-hour weeks on machinery, often in unsafe, unhealthy conditions. Getting hurt on the job often resulted in the worker being fired. Workers earned low wages, and women and children were paid even less than male workers. Workers had little security because their employers could fire them at any time. Soon, workers grew less tolerant of these terrible working conditions. Some tried to organize labor unions, but employers often fired those who did. Strikes were met with armed attacks from factory security guards and sometimes even from federal troops.

Life for the Urban Poor

The gap between living standards of the rich and the poor increased widely during this period. This gap was most apparent in the cities. As the rich grew richer, building lavish townhouses in relatively safe and clean neighborhoods, the poor grew even poorer. They lived in urban slums characterized by poverty, crime, congestion, and poor sanitation. Housing in the cities was segregated by social and economic status, by race, and often by ethnic background.

The first elevated train in New York City

Mixed Response of Government at All Levels

Government at all levels remained relatively unresponsive to the impact of industrialization and urbanization. Industries were unrestrained by federal and many state governments; the courts most often failed to support fair standards of business. The laissez-faire philosophy prevailed and so did political corruption at all levels of government. The public received little help from its elected representatives.

Several United States Supreme Court rulings provide examples of the mixed response of the federal government in the struggle for improved working conditions:

- In *Lochner v. New York* (1905), the Supreme Court ruled that a New York law limiting bakers' hours was unconstitutional because it interfered with the contract between employer and employee.
- In *Muller v. Oregon* (1908), the Court let stand an Oregon law limiting women to a ten-hour workday, ruling that the law was justified because it protected women's health. The effect of laws like this, however, was to keep women out of better paying jobs.

Who Were the Progressives?

The Progressives set out to tackle the problems of their era. They did not form one single group. The Progressive movement was made up of many different movements, and the Progressives included many different kinds of Americans. Their commitment and their success varied from person to person and from cause to cause. They did have some things in common, however.

Characteristics of Progressives

The Progressives were influenced by the Populists but differed from them. While the Populists lived in rural areas or in small towns, the Progressives were largely city dwellers. Most of the Populists were farmers, who focused on farm problems. The Progressives tended to be educated professionals—doctors, lawyers, social workers, clergy, and teachers—with a wide range of concerns. The Progressive movement demonstrated the rising power and influence of America's middle class.

Social Studies Practices
Geographic Reasoning

Some urban problems persist over time, while others arise as society develops. Evaluate the relationship between human activities and the environment.

- Consider concerns in urban areas, such as waste disposal, water and air pollution, energy usage, and congestion.
- Consider which urban problems at the beginning of the 20th century continue to be problems today.
- Consider what new urban problems exist in the 21st century.

Preparing for the Regents

Two landmark Supreme Court cases that dealt with state laws limiting the number of working hours were *Lochner* v. *New York* (1905) and *Muller* v. *Oregon* (1908).

There is no reasonable ground for interfering with the liberty of a person or the right of free contract by determining the hours of labor. . . . Clean and wholesome bread does not depend upon whether the baker works but ten hours per day or only sixty hours per week.

—*Lochner v. New York* (1905)

- What seems to be the position of the Court on Progressive reform?
- How do the decisions in *Lochner* and in *Miller* differ?
- How does the Court's action compare with the Court's decisions during the New Deal?

Social Studies
Practices
**Geographical and
Historical Context**

Throughout history, the middle class has developed with the growth of cities built around trade, commerce, and industry.

• Collect evidence to evaluate the geographic, historic, and economic role of the middle class in America's history.

Social Studies
Practices
Gathering Evidence

• Identify the major reform movements of the Progressive Era.
• Compare and contrast the characteristics of each reform movement using the categories below.

Causes:
Goals:
Leadership:
Influence:
Degree of success achieved:

Unifying Themes
**Time, Continuity, and
Change**

Media has played an investigative role at various times in United States history. Newspaper, radio, and television journalists provide a different view in order to balance that of governments, corporations, and other sources of power.

The muckraking tradition continued long after the Progressive Era. The publication by *The New York Times* of the Pentagon Papers and the reporting of the Watergate scandal by Bob Woodward and Carl Bernstein in *The Washington Post* are two late twentieth-century examples of the muckraking tradition.

Beliefs and Goals

Like all reformers, the Progressives were optimists. They believed that abuses of power by government and business could be ended. They believed that new developments in technology and science could be used to improve the basic institutions of American society—business, government, education, and family life. Progressives believed in capitalism and were concerned about the growth of socialism as a more radical reaction to the effects of industrialization. Progressives wanted to bypass party politics, which they saw as corrupt, but they had faith that a strong government could and should correct abuses and protect rights.

Not all Americans were Progressives or agreed with Progressive goals. Many business and political leaders opposed business regulation. They accepted the Social Darwinists' view that the vast differences in wealth and power in American society were the result of scientific forces that could not be changed. Many workers and farmers did not benefit from Progressive reform, nor did most African Americans, Asian immigrants, and Native Americans.

Factors Aiding the Movement

Many Progressives worked with national voluntary organizations, which grew rapidly in the 1890s. The movement was centered in cities at a time when more of the population was living in cities. This helped communication among Progressives, as did the expanding telephone and telegraph systems. The availability of inexpensive mass-circulation magazines and newspapers also helped spread Progressive ideas. Finally, the Progressives were aided by an improved economy. The first decade of the twentieth century brought prosperity. Industrial profits, wages, and employment all rose; farmers thrived. The result was an optimistic climate and the financial resources to support reform.

Progress Toward Social and Economic Reform and Consumer Protection

A wide variety of reform movements developed from the 1890s to the 1920s.

The Muckrakers and Reform

Muckrakers helped bring reform issues to the attention of the public. Most were journalists and writers, but others were artists and photographers. **Muckrakers** investigated and exposed corruption and injustice through articles in mass-circulation magazines. They also wrote novels dramatizing situations that demanded reform. For example, **Ida Tarbell** wrote a series of articles on the Standard Oil Company monopoly in *McClure's Magazine* starting in 1902 that were eventually published as a book in 1904 entitled *The History of the Standard Oil Company*. Tarbell's detailed account of the company's unfair business practices led to the breakup of the company's monopoly and the passage of key legislation regulating commerce.

In 1906, the work of the muckrakers resulted in the passage of the Pure Food and Drug Act and the Meat Inspection Act—the first two acts of consumer protection legislation. The federal government passed these laws after it became clear that the unsanitary conditions exposed by the novel *The Jungle* by **Upton Sinclair** were based on fact.

As time passed, the muckrakers' influence declined, partly because readers tired of its sensationalism. Nevertheless, their tradition has continued to the present day.

Progressive Era Muckrakers

Muckraker	Book/Article	Subject of Exposé
Frank Norris	*The Octopus* (1901)	monopolistic railroad practices in California
Ida Tarbell	*History of the Standard Oil Company* (1904)	ruthless practices of Standard Oil Company
Lincoln Steffens	*The Shame of the Cities* (1906)	political corruption in city government
Jacob Riis	*How the Other Half Lives* (1890)	conditions of the poor in New York's tenements
Upton Sinclair	*The Jungle* (1906)	dangerous and unsanitary conditions in meatpacking industry

Other Areas of Concern

Other people and groups also worked to bring Progressive reforms to American society.

Problems of Poverty Attempts to end the poverty, crowding, and disease in American cities began before 1900. Once the germ theory of disease was accepted, cities put more effort into improving water and sewage systems. A well-known urban reformer was **Jacob Riis**, who used writings and photographs to show the need for better housing for the poor. Some Protestant church leaders became part of the Social Gospel movement, which worked to help poor city dwellers. One goal of urban reformers was to establish building codes that would require safer, better-lighted, better-ventilated, and more sanitary tenements.

Social Settlement Movement One early group of Progressive urban reformers was the settlement-house workers. Settlement houses, located in working-class slums, offered people—especially immigrants—education, child care, social activities, and help in finding jobs. Well-known settlement houses included Hull House in Chicago, founded by **Jane Addams**, and the Henry Street Settlement in New York City, founded by **Lillian Wald**.

The Peace Movement Addams and Wald were among the Americans who led peace groups, such as the Woman's Peace Party, in the period before and during World War I. Support of pacifism—the policy of opposition to war and fighting—weakened with America's entry into World War I in 1917 but was later revived. Pacifist Jeannette Rankin, the first woman elected to Congress (1916), voted against the entry of the United States into World War I and World War II, as well. For her pacifist efforts, Jane Addams won the Nobel Peace Prize in 1931.

Temperance and Prohibition The **temperance movement**, which opposed the use of alcoholic beverages, began in the 1820s. Over the years, its chief goal became **prohibition**—outlawing the manufacture and sale of alcoholic beverages. Under the leadership of **Frances Willard**, the **Woman's Christian Temperance Union (WCTU)**, founded in 1874, was a strong advocate of prohibition. Its members included many Populists and Progressives. It joined with the Anti-Saloon League, and the two groups sought moral reform through prohibition. They believed that consuming alcohol was damaging to society and that through prohibition, problems of poverty and disease could be eased, family life improved, and the national economy made more productive. The temperance crusade led to national prohibition with the adoption of the **Eighteenth Amendment**, which banned the manufacture, sale, and transportation of alcoholic beverages in the United States as of 1920.

Child Labor The National Child Labor Committee was formed in 1904 to rouse public opinion against child labor. The committee recognized the courts' opposition to child labor legislation as expressed in the Supreme Court's "freedom to contract" verdict in *Lochner* v. *New York* (1905) but successfully lobbied the federal

Preparing for the Regents

- What are some current examples of investigative reporting on government or corporations using television or the Internet?
- What is the difference between investigative reporting and sensationalism in the media?
- What has been the effect of the Internet and 24-hour cable news on journalism?

Social Studies Practices
Cause and Effect

Use the text and the chart to answer this question.

- What effect did the work of each muckraker have on Progressive reform?

government to create a Federal Children's Bureau (1912) to investigate child labor and pressured most states to set minimum wages and maximum hours for children. By 1920, as a result of state laws and compulsory school attendance, 11.3 percent of children ages 10 to 15 were working, down from 18.2 percent in 1900.

Women's Rights

Women were involved in all aspects of social reform, but **suffrage** for women continued to be the main goal of the women's rights movement in the Progressive Era. Women who had experienced success in other reform activities wanted to be able to vote. Furthermore, many suffragists thought that the women's vote would serve to correct various social problems. (Review Topic 4 Section 2 for a more detailed history of this topic. Also see Topic 10 Section 2 for more recent events related to the struggle for women's rights.)

Women's Suffrage Before 1920

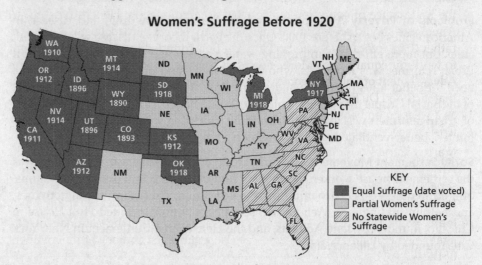

After Susan B. Anthony's retirement in 1900, **Carrie Chapman Catt** became the president of National American Woman Suffrage Association (NAWSA) and successfully led the last years of the struggle. **Alice Paul** led the more militant Congressional Union until she was expelled from the NAWSA. She then formed the National Woman's Party. Paul alienated many women by her use of militant tactics and her campaigning against Woodrow Wilson for reelection in 1916. In the end, it was the highly visible activity of women during World War I that brought them the final public support needed. In 1920, the **Nineteenth Amendment** was ratified, giving women the right to vote.

Education for Women Another sign of women's progress was the growth of educational opportunities. Among women's colleges founded in the late 1800s were Vassar (1861), Wellesley (1870), and Smith (1871). State universities set up under the Morrill Act of 1862 were coeducational. By the early 1900s, one third of those attending college were women.

The Fight for Birth Control The women's movement also included a campaign for family planning through birth control. This campaign was led by **Margaret Sanger**, who began her work as a nurse caring for poor immigrant women in New York City. The American Birth Control League founded by Sanger later became the Planned Parenthood Federation. Sanger's movement was very controversial. She was arrested several times for sending information about contraception through the mail.

Preparing for the Regents

Stimulus-Based Questions: Map

• Why is it significant that this map is dated 1920?

• In what region of the nation did women first receive the right to vote?

• In what regions did they have partial suffrage?

• What relationship is there between the pattern of suffrage and the pattern of migration and settlement of the states?

• What might explain that pattern?

Unifying Themes
Civic Ideals

The right of citizens of the United States to vote shall not be denied or abridged by the United States or by any state on account of sex.

—Section 1, Nineteenth Amendment

• Whose rights does this amendment protect?

• What are the other important steps in U.S. history in the extension of the right to vote?

The Rights of African Americans

The decades following the Civil War were a difficult time for African Americans. Laws prevented them from exercising their right to vote. In *Plessy* v. *Ferguson* (1896), the Supreme Court upheld the Jim Crow laws, which required segregated— "separate but equal"—public facilities for African Americans and whites. Lynchings by white mobs killed hundreds of African Americans. Some of the key African American leaders who worked to secure African American rights are described below.

- **Booker T. Washington**, a former slave and founder of Tuskegee Institute, urged African Americans to get vocational training in order to establish themselves economically. This strategy, he believed, would increase their self-esteem and earn them respect from white society. Washington's policy, called accommodation, was expressed in an 1895 speech known as the Atlanta Compromise.

- **W.E.B. Du Bois**, a Harvard-educated professor, shared Washington's view of the importance of education but rejected accommodation. He felt that African Americans should protest unfair treatment and receive a broad, liberal education, rather than a vocational one. In 1905, Du Bois founded the Niagara Movement to work for equal rights. More successful was the **National Association for the Advancement of Colored People (NAACP)**, started in 1909 by a group of reformers that included Du Bois and Jane Addams. The NAACP successfully used lawsuits as a weapon on behalf of civil rights. Du Bois, with the NAACP, published *The Crisis* magazine and was a leader in the Silent Protest March in 1917.

- **Marcus Garvey** founded the Universal Negro Improvement Association, an African American nationalist and separatist group, in 1914. The group wanted a separate African American economy and urged African Americans to emigrate to Africa. Garvey's ideas influenced the Black Power Movement of the 1960s.

- **Ida B. Wells-Barnett** was a journalist who launched a lifelong national crusade against lynching in the 1890s. She was also a suffragist and one of the founders of the NAACP.

Rights of Others Facing Discrimination

In 1913, a group of American Jews established the Anti-Defamation League, an agency of the Jewish service organization B'nai B'rith ("Sons of the Covenant"), which had been founded in 1843. The Anti-Defamation League worked mainly to combat defamation, or libel and slander, directed against Jews. Later, its program was broadened to aim at securing the civil liberties of all Americans.

Progressivism and Government Action

During the Progressive Era, political reform took place at all levels of government—city, state, and national.

The Spoils System and Civil Service Reform

The **spoils system**, which dates from the presidency of Andrew Jackson, gave government jobs to people who had worked to help their political party win the election. This method was called the spoils system because of the saying "To the victor belong the spoils [rewards]." In 1881, a party worker who had failed to get a government job killed President James Garfield. At that point, people began to demand reform, and the new president, Chester Arthur, supported it. The **Pendleton Act** of 1883 marked the beginning of **civil service reform**. The Act

- provided that competitive exams be used to hire some government workers.
- set up a commission to administer the tests.
- banned the common practice of forcing government employees to give money to political parties.

Social Studies Practices

Gathering and Interpreting Evidence

To help you understand the various reforms at the city, state, and federal levels:

- Create a chart that outlines the major reforms made at each level.
- Find evidence to identify the most influential factors for and against reform at each governmental level.

Unifying Themes

Civic Ideals and Practices

- Which do you consider the most important of the changes to increase citizen participation in government? Why?
- Has direct election stopped undue influence on U.S. senators?
- How have initiative and referendum been used by a special interest group?
- How has the direct primary changed the way in which we select a president?

Reform of City Government

Given the Progressives' urban, middle-class roots, it is not surprising that they first concentrated their efforts on the governments of the cities in which they lived and in which they were influential citizens. They attacked political machines that controlled government at the city and state levels, condemning practices such as accepting bribes in return for favors. In the 1890s, Americans interested in good government worked to elect reformist mayors. Success in doing so, however, did not always ensure permanent improvement. Progressives had to change not only the leader, but also the way city government worked.

Two new types of city government plans are associated with the Progressive movement. They were popular in small and medium-sized cities. In the city commissioner plan, the city is run by a group of commissioners, rather than by a mayor and city council. In the city manager plan, the city council hires a professional city manager to run the various municipal departments.

Progressives Respond to Urban Problems

While some Progressives concentrated not only on making city governments more efficient and less corrupt, Progressive architects and city planners tried to improve the appearance of cities by constructing large, elaborate libraries, museums, and other public buildings. Progressive engineers recognized that the sudden and rapid growth of cities called for redesigning and improving needed city services, such as sanitation, street lighting, and a water system. Still others worked to regulate these and other utilities or even to turn them into publicly owned facilities.

Reform of State Government

Progressives also acted to limit the power of boss-controlled political machines and powerful business interests at the state level. Progressives recognized that states exercised control over many of their cities. Extension of reform to the state, and even to the national level, was seen as necessary to protect any gains made at the municipal level.

Progressive reforms often proved difficult to enforce, meeting opposition from business interests and the courts. Thus, changes in the way state governments worked were also part of the Progressive program. These reforms, aimed at increasing citizen control of their government, included the following:

- The **secret ballot,** or **Australian ballot,** lessens the chance of intimidation because it prevents party bosses (and anyone else) from knowing how people vote.
- The **initiative** is a system that allows voters to petition the legislature to consider a proposed law.
- In a **referendum**, voters, not the legislature, decide whether a given bill or constitutional amendment should be passed.
- **Recall** is a form of petition used by voters to force elected officials out of office.
- A **direct primary** allows voters, rather than party leaders, to select the candidates who will run for office. In recent years, the number of state convention delegates elected by a direct primary has increased to the point that the party's presidential nominee is known well before the national convention is held.
- Ratified in 1913, the **Seventeenth Amendment** replaced election of U.S. senators by state legislatures with direct election of senators by the people of each state. Progressives had labeled the Senate the Millionaires' Club, serving the business and political interests who controlled state legislatures.

Remember that the secret ballot, initiative, referendum, and direct election of senators were all parts of the Populist Party program. Adoption of these reforms offers an example of how third parties can influence major parties.

State Social, Economic and Environmental Reforms

Wisconsin, under Governor **Robert M. La Follette**, was the model for Progressive reform. The State passed laws to regulate railroads, lobbying, and banking. It also started civil service reforms, shifted more of the tax burden to the wealthy and to corporations, required employers to compensate workers injured on the job, and provided for factory inspections.

Several other states passed laws like those of Wisconsin. In 1912, Massachusetts became the first state to pass a minimum wage law. Leading Progressive governors included Hiram Johnson of California, who reformed the railroad industry, and Theodore Roosevelt of New York. As governor of New York (1899–1900), **Theodore Roosevelt**, a friend of Jacob Riis and other Progressives, was concerned about social and economic reform. He supported the creation of the New York State Tenement Commission to investigate New York City tenements. He also worked to eliminate sweatshop factory conditions, which forced women and children to work long hours for very low pay in dangerous conditions.

Theodore Roosevelt and Labor

Although basically a conservative, once elected president, Roosevelt did not hesitate to use his presidential power to deal directly with social and economic problems. In the process, he achieved important reforms in working conditions.

The Anthracite Coal Strike In 1902, when Pennsylvania coal mine owners refused to negotiate with striking workers, Roosevelt threatened to send the army to take over the mines. The mine owners then agreed to arbitration, and the United Mine Workers, under John Mitchell, won shorter hours and higher wages but not recognition of their union. For the first time in a labor dispute, the federal government did not intervene solely on the side of management.

Employers' Liability One Progressive goal was to make employers assume more liability, or responsibility, for their workers. The Employers' Liability Act of 1906 provided accident insurance for workers on interstate railroads and in Washington, D.C.

Working Hours Another Progressive goal was to limit workers' hours on the job. As you read above, in *Lochner* v. *New York* (1905) and *Muller* v. *Oregon* (1908), there were inconsistent results in conflicts between the rights of individuals and the rights of businesses.

The Presidents of the Progressive Era

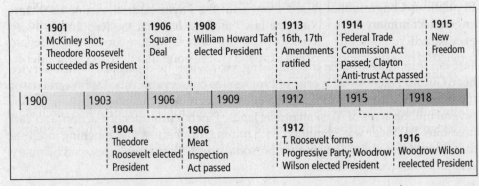

Unifying Themes
Geography, Humans, and the Environment

- How did Roosevelt's land policy differ from that of earlier presidents?
- What was the end result of Roosevelt's land policy by the time he left office?

Roosevelt and Conservation

As a naturalist, Theodore Roosevelt was interested in **conservation**, or protecting the nation's environment and its wilderness lands. His policies were influenced by the conservationists Gifford Pinchot and John Muir.

Before Roosevelt, the government's land policy put land in the private hands of homesteaders, railroads, and colleges. Roosevelt shifted this policy and kept some land under federal government protection. This was the philosophy of **John Muir**, a founder of the Sierra Club, who was also instrumental in the creation of Yosemite National Park.

- Roosevelt used the Forest Reserve Act of 1891 to place national forests under the control of the U.S. Forest Service, headed by conservationist **Gifford Pinchot**. A total of about 150 million acres of public lands was placed under the protection of the federal government. When Roosevelt left office, he had tripled the amount of land set aside for the public as national forests, national parks, wildlife refuges, and national monuments.

- The National (Newlands) Reclamation Act of 1902 set aside money from the sale of public lands to build dams and irrigation systems in the West.

- In 1908, Roosevelt called a national Conservation Congress, attended by hundreds of naturalists and conservationists as well as by 44 governors.

Progressivism Under Taft

After Roosevelt declined to run for a third term, **William Howard Taft** succeeded him in 1909. Taft began his presidency with the support of Roosevelt and the Progressive wing of the Republican Party.

Reforms Under Taft

Under Taft, the Justice Department brought twice as many suits against big business as it had under Roosevelt. One of the most important cases involved the Supreme Court's ruling in *Standard Oil Co. of New Jersey* v. *United States* (1911) in which it held that the monopoly should be dissolved. But it also applied the so-called "rule of reason" to the Sherman Antitrust Act. There was a difference, said the Court, between "reasonable" and "unreasonable" business combinations. Size alone did not mean that a company was "unreasonable."

The Taft era witnessed other reforms, too. The Mann-Elkins Act of 1910 gave the Interstate Commerce Commission the power to regulate communication by telephone and telegraph.

Problems for Taft

Taft, who was not as politically able as Roosevelt, soon ran into problems that split the Republican Party into a Taft faction and a Progressive faction. Like other Progressives, Taft wanted to lower tariffs, but he was unable to stand up to the Republican Congress that raised them with the Payne-Aldrich Act of 1909. Taft angered Progressives by calling the law "the best bill that the Republican Party ever passed."

Taft ran into more trouble the following year when he dismissed Forest Service head Gifford Pinchot—a favorite of Progressive conservationists. Taft's secretary of the interior, Richard A. Ballinger, had allowed a group of business people to obtain several million acres of Alaskan public lands. Pinchot protested the action, and Taft fired him. Ballinger was identified with mining, lumbering, and ranching interests that wanted to develop the land for personal profit. They were supported by many senators from western states.

Woodrow Wilson and the New Freedom

In 1912, Theodore Roosevelt challenged Taft for the Republican presidential nomination. When the nomination went to Taft, Roosevelt ran as the candidate of a third party, the Progressive or Bull Moose Party. **Woodrow Wilson** was the Democratic candidate, and Eugene Debs ran on the Socialist ticket.

Roosevelt offered what he called the **New Nationalism**, while Wilson called his program the **New Freedom**. Both were Progressive philosophies. Roosevelt, however, accepted social legislation and business regulation. The more traditional Wilson aimed for a return to competition in the marketplace with enforcement of antitrust laws. Wilson won the election of 1912 by a landslide of electoral votes, although he received only 41 percent of the popular vote. In 1916, he was reelected into office in an even closer race.

Two Major Financial Reforms

In 1913, Wilson secured passage of the Underwood Tariff Act, which lowered tariffs for the first time since the Civil War. The law, a reaction to unequal distribution of income, included a progressive or **graduated income tax**—one that taxed larger incomes at a higher rate (6 percent) than it did lower ones (1 percent). Ratification of the **Sixteenth Amendment** in 1913 made this new income tax possible.

Also in 1913, the **Federal Reserve System** was created to provide economic stability by strengthening federal control over the money supply. This national banking system is divided into 12 districts, each with a Federal Reserve bank. The government could now (1) issue a new, sound currency—Federal Reserve notes; (2) control the amount of money in circulation and set interest rates; and (3) shift money from one bank to another as needed. The Federal Reserve Board lowers interest rates to stimulate consumer spending in times of recession or raises interest rates to control inflation.

Business Regulation

Wilson also achieved two important business regulations. The **Federal Trade Commission Act of 1914** aimed to prevent unfair competition. It created a commission to investigate such practices as false advertising and mislabeling.

The **Clayton Antitrust Act of 1914** strengthened the government's power to control business practices that threatened competition. Among other things, the act prohibited companies from price fixing and from buying stocks in competing firms. The Clayton Antitrust Act tried to end the practice of using antitrust laws against unions, but later Supreme Court decisions undercut this provision. Later in the twentieth century, federal prosecutions of alleged violations of antitrust laws continued against corporations such as AT&T and Microsoft.

Other Reforms Under Wilson

- The Adamson Act (1916) set an eight-hour day for workers on railroads in interstate commerce.
- The Federal Farm Loan Act (1916) made low-interest loans available to farmers.
- Ratification of the Nineteenth Amendment in 1920 gave women the right to vote.

End of the Progressive Era

The Progressive Era came to an end when the United States entered World War I. During the war, American priorities shifted to the war effort, and in the 1920s, the trend shifted away from reform and toward acceptance of society as it was.

Multiple-Choice Questions for Regents Practice

Base your answers to questions 1 and 2 on the passage below and on your knowledge of social studies.

> Suppose we look into one [a tenement]? Be a little careful, please! The hall is dark and you might stumble over the children pitching pennies back there. . . . Here where the hall turns and dives into utter darkness is a step. . . . You can feel your way, if you cannot see it. . . . All the fresh air that ever enters these stairs comes from the hall-door that is forever slamming. . . . The sinks are in the hallway, that all the tenants may have access—and all be poisoned alike by their summer stenches. . . . Listen! That short hacking cough, that tiny helpless wail—what do they mean? . . . Oh! a sadly familiar story. . . . The child is dying with measles. With half a chance it might have lived; but it had none. That dark bedroom killed it.

Source: Jacob A. Riis, *How the Other Half Lives*, 1890

1 The circumstances described in this document are a direct result of

(1) unionization

(2) the temperance movement

(3) urbanization

(4) the Granger movement

2 Which action was taken in response to the conditions exposed in Jacob Riis's book?

(1) Jane Addams established Hull House, the first settlement house in Chicago.

(2) Governor Theodore Roosevelt created the New York Tenement House Commission.

(3) President Chester Arthur approved the Pendleton Act to reform the civil service.

(4) Terence Powderly formed the Knights of Labor, a union that included unskilled workers.

Base your answers to questions 3 and 4 on the passage below and on your knowledge of social studies.

Emma Goldman was a political activist and radical who fiercely supported workers' rights. The document below comes from her autobiography, in which she remembers her reaction to the Homestead steel strike.

> The steel-workers declared that they were ready to take up the challenge of Frick: they would insist on their right to organize and to deal collectively with their employers. Their tone was manly, ringing with the spirit of their rebellious forebears of the Revolutionary War. . . . [T]he news was flashed across the country of the slaughter of steel-workers by Pinkertons. Frick had fortified the Homestead mills, built a high fence around them. Then, in the dead of night, a barge packed with strike-breakers under protection of heavily armed Pinkerton thugs, quietly stole up the Monongahela River. The steel-men had learned of Frick's move. They stationed themselves along the shore, determined to drive back Frick's hirelings. When the barge got within range, the Pinkertons had opened fire, without warning, killing a number of Homestead men on the shore, among them a little boy, and wounding scores of others.

Source: Emma Goldman, *Living My Life*, 1931

3 The author of this document would most likely support

(1) legislation to protect the rights of workers to organize

(2) the use of military to end strikes in American factories

(3) longer work days and lower wages

(4) consumer protections in the steel industry

4 Which industrialist would be most closely associated with the events described in this passage?

(1) J. P. Morgan

(2) Cornelius Vanderbilt

(3) Andrew Carnegie

(4) John D. Rockefeller

Base your answers to questions 5 through 7 on the cartoon below and on your knowledge of social studies.

Woman's Holy War:
Grand Charge on the Enemy's Works

Source: Currier & Ives, circa 1874

5 The movement most closely associated with this cartoon was known as

(1) the populist movement

(2) the temperance movement

(3) the women's rights movement

(4) the civil rights movement

6 What was the goal of the "Holy War" depicted in this cartoon?

(1) reduce the use of alcohol

(2) repeal the 18th Amendment

(3) promote women's suffrage

(4) recruit female soldiers

7 The period that followed the success of the movement shown was known as

(1) the Progressive Era

(2) Prohibition

(3) the Great Depression

(4) the Cold War

Base your answers to questions 8 and 9 on the charts below and on your knowledge of social studies.

Rural and Urban Populations in the United States, 1870–1920

Year	Rural	Urban
1870	28,656,010	9,902,361
1880	36,059,474	14,129,735
1890	40,873,501	22,106,265
1900	45,997,336	30,214,832
1910	50,164,495	42,064,001
1920	51,768,255	54,253,282

Source: U.S. Census Bureau

Population of Major U.S. Cities, 1880–1920

City	1880	1900	1920
New York	1,206,299	3,437,202	5,620,048
Philadelphia	847,170	1,293,697	1,823,779
Chicago	503,185	1,698,575	2,701,705
Boston	362,839	560,892	748,060
St. Louis	350,518	575,238	772,897
Baltimore	332,313	508,957	733,826

Source: U.S. Census Bureau

8 Which claim is best supported by these two charts?

(1) The rural population of the United States outnumbered the urban population by the 1900s.

(2) Anti-immigration laws began to show an impact on the American population by 1880.

(3) The population of the United States began a declining trend after 1900.

(4) Immigrants coming to America at the turn of the 20th century most likely settled in cities.

9 What is the best explanation for the population changes seen in these charts?

(1) industrialization

(2) imperialism

(3) populism

(4) xenophobia

Base your answers to questions 10 and 11 on the passage below and on your knowledge of social studies.

> This, then, is held to be the duty of the man of Wealth: First, to set an example of modest, unostentatious [simple or not showy] living, shunning display or extravagance; to provide moderately for the legitimate wants of those dependent upon him; and after doing so to consider all surplus revenues which come to him simply as trust funds, which he is called upon to administer, and strictly bound as a matter of duty to administer in the manner which, in his judgment, is best calculated to produce the most beneficial result for the community—the man of wealth thus becoming the mere agent and trustee for his poorer brethren [brothers], bringing to their service his superior wisdom, experience, and ability to administer, doing for them better than they would or could do for themselves.

Source: Andrew Carnegie, "Wealth," *North American Review*, June 1889

10 In this article, Andrew Carnegie is advocating for the wealthy to engage in

(1) trust busting

(2) philanthropy

(3) forming monopolies

(4) conspicuous consumption

11 Which is the best example of an industrialist following the advice of Andrew Carnegie?

(1) Cornelius Vanderbilt built Grand Central Terminal in New York City.

(2) Cornelius Vanderbilt consolidated New York Central and the Hudson River Railroad.

(3) John D. Rockefeller joined the Southern Improvement Co. in return for shipping rebates.

(4) John D. Rockefeller funded the General Education Board to promote education.

Base your answers to questions 12 and 13 on the speech below and on your knowledge of social studies.

> If they dare to come out in the open field and defend the gold standard as a good thing, we shall fight them to the uttermost, having behind us the producing masses of the nation and the world. Having behind us the commercial interests and the laboring interests and all the toiling masses, we shall answer their demands for a gold standard by saying to them, you shall not press down upon the brow of labor this crown of thorns. You shall not crucify mankind upon a cross of gold.

Source: William Jennings Bryan, "Cross of Gold" speech at the Democratic National Convention, July 9, 1896

12 In this speech, William Jennings Bryan is advocating for

(1) policies to cut inflation

(2) the free unlimited coinage of silver

(3) a policy of open immigration

(4) freedom of religion

13 What group of Americans would most likely be leaders in the support of William Jennings Bryan's comments?

(1) immigrants

(2) farmers

(3) women

(4) environmentalists

Short Essay Questions

Task: Read and analyze the following documents, applying your social studies knowledge and skills to write a short essay of two or three paragraphs in which you:

- Describe the historical context surrounding documents 1 and 2
- Analyze **Document 2** and explain how *audience*, **or** *purpose*, **or** bias, **or** *point of view* affects this document's use as a reliable source of evidence

In developing your short essay answer of two or three paragraphs, be sure to keep these explanations in mind:

Describe means "to illustrate something in words or tell about"

Historical Context refers to "the relevant historical circumstances surrounding or connecting the events, ideas, or developments in these documents"

Analyze means "to examine a document and determine its elements and its relationships"

Explain means "to make plain or understandable; to give reasons for or causes of; to show the logical development or relationship of"

Reliability is determined by how accurate and useful the information found in a source is for a specific purpose

Document 1

Our greatest danger is that in the great leap from slavery to freedom we may overlook the fact that the masses of us are to live by the productions of our hands, and fail to keep in mind that we shall prosper in proportion as we learn to dignify and glorify common labour, and put brains and skill into the common occupations of life; shall prosper in proportion as we learn to draw the line between the superficial and the substantial, the ornamental gewgaws [trinkets] of life and the useful. No race can prosper till it learns that there is as much dignity in tilling a field as in writing a poem. It is at the bottom of life we must begin, and not at the top. Nor should we permit our grievances to overshadow our opportunities.

Source: Booker T. Washington, speech at the Atlanta Exposition, 1895

Document 2

I am an earnest advocate of manual training and trade teaching for black boys, and for white boys, too. I believe that next to the founding of Negro colleges the most valuable addition to Negro education since the war, has been industrial training for black boys. Nevertheless, I insist that the object of all true education is not to make men carpenters, it is to make carpenters men; there are two means of making the carpenter a man, each equally important: the first is to give the group and community in which he works, liberally trained teachers and leaders to teach him and his family what life means; the second is to give him sufficient intelligence and technical skill to make him an efficient workman; the first object demands the Negro college and college-bred men . . . to inspire the masses, to raise the Talented Tenth to leadership; the second object demands a good system of common schools, well-taught, conventionally located and properly equipped.

Source: W.E.B. Du Bois, "The Talented Tenth," *The Negro Problem: A Series of Articles by Representative American Negroes of Today*, 1903

Historical Context: Economic Protest

Throughout United States history, many constitutional and civic issues have been debated by Americans. These debates have resulted in efforts by individuals, groups, and governments to address these issues. These efforts have achieved varying degrees of success. One of these constitutional and civic issues is protesting.

Task: Read and analyze the document. Using information from the document and your knowledge of United States history, write an essay in which you

- Describe the historical circumstances surrounding this constitutional or civic issue
- Explain efforts to address this constitutional or civic issue by individuals, groups, and/or governments
- Discuss the extent to which these efforts were successful

Describe means "to illustrate something in words or tell about it"

Explain means "to make plain or understandable; to give reasons for or causes of; to show the logical development or relationship of"

Discuss means "to make observations about something using facts, reasoning, and argument; to present in some detail"

The Uprising of the Twenty Thousands
(Dedicated to the Waistmakers [shirt makers] of 1909)

In the black of the winter of nineteen nine,
When we froze and bled on the picket line,
We showed the world that women could fight
And we rose and won with women's might.

Chorus:
Hail the waistmakers of nineteen nine,
Making their stand on the picket line,
Breaking the power of those who reign,
Pointing the way, smashing the chain.

And we gave new courage to the men
Who carried on in nineteen ten
And shoulder to shoulder we'll win through,
Led by the I.L.G.W.U.

Source: Let's Sing!, Educational Department, International Ladies' Garment Workers' Union, New York City

1. What form of protest is being described in this song?

The Rise of American Power (1890–1920)

Topic Overview

As the United States became a more industrialized and urbanized nation, new economic and social factors contributed to a major shift in America's foreign policy objectives. The nation extended its belief in manifest destiny beyond its borders. By 1917, the United States had acquired an empire. It spread from Puerto Rico in the Caribbean to Panama in Central America to Hawaii in the Pacific Ocean to the Philippines in the South China Sea. In addition, America became involved in diplomatic, economic, and military actions directly related to its new possessions. As presidents Theodore Roosevelt and Woodrow Wilson dominated foreign policy, presidential power also became an issue.

This dramatic change in foreign policy sparked debates between imperialists and anti-imperialists that came to include the pros and cons of our involvement in World War I. President Wilson set war aims in the Fourteen Points. He played a major role at the peace conference at the end of the war. Ultimately, the United States Senate rejected Wilson's efforts. The United States did not ratify the Treaty of Versailles nor did it join the League of Nations. Instead, the nation moved back to its traditional policy of neutrality.

World War I impacted the society, politics, and economy of the United States. Women's role in the war aided their campaign for suffrage. The Great Migration of African Americans also affected American society. The extent of civil liberties in time of war again provoked a serious constitutional debate. In addition, the nation experienced another period of xenophobia, or fear of foreigners.

TOPIC 6

Lesson

1

The United States Becomes a World Power

Key Concept

11.6a In the late 1800s, various strategic and economic factors led to a greater focus on foreign affairs and debates over the United States' role in the world.

Lesson Overview

From 1865 to 1920, a newly industrialized United States moved beyond the borders of North America to become an imperialist power on a global scale. Strategic and economic aims influenced this shift in traditional foreign policy. The nation sought foreign markets, resources, and coaling stations.

As America began to acquire an overseas empire, the nation debated its motivations, policies, and principles and the effects of acquisitions on people at home and abroad. Citizens discussed whether a foreign policy goal of overseas expansion was in the nation's interest. Debate continued over the annexation of Hawaii, causes and effects of the Spanish-American War, the Treaty of Paris of 1898, and annexation of the Philippines.

Controversy persisted as the United States expanded American influence in the Caribbean and Latin America through the creation of the Panama Canal and the implementation of the Roosevelt Corollary. As presidents Theodore Roosevelt and Woodrow Wilson dominated foreign policy, presidential power also became an issue.

Unifying Themes

As you review this lesson take special note of the following themes:

- **Geography, Humans, and the Environment** What geographic factors influenced the acquisition of specific territories by the United States? What geographic factors influenced the selection of nations in which the United States attempted to exercise influence?

- **Development and Transformation of Social Structures** What were the effects of international involvement at the turn of the last century on the United States and other peoples around the world?

- **Power, Authority, and Governance** How did foreign policy actions of presidents William McKinley and Theodore Roosevelt increase both the power of the United States and the power of the presidency? What examples would anti-imperialists and imperialists use in support of their positions while debating America's expansion overseas?

- **Creation, Expansion, and Interaction of Economic Systems** What were the causes of greater international involvement by the United States from 1890 to 1920? How did America's industrialization increase pressures for overseas expansion?

Key People

Theodore Roosevelt

Alfred T. Mahan

Queen Liliuokalani

John Hay

Matthew Perry

William McKinley

George Dewey

Emilio Aguinaldo

William Howard Taft

180 Topic 6: The Rise of American Power (1890–1920)

Key Terms and Events

strategic	joint resolution	Treaty of Paris of 1898
gross national product	sphere of influence	Philippine-American
Manifest Destiny	Open Door Policy	War
Social Darwinism	Gentlemen's Agreement	imperialism
Social Gospel	Spanish-American War	Roosevelt Corollary
tariff	yellow journalism	Big Stick diplomacy
annexation	jingoism	dollar diplomacy

Key Supreme Court Cases

As you review this lesson be sure you understand the significance of this key Supreme Court case:

Insular Cases (1901–1902)

Emerging Global Involvement

Territorial expansion of the United States prior to the 1890s was confined, with two exceptions, to what is now the contiguous 48 states. In 1867, the United States bought Alaska from Russia in order to end Russian trade and exploration in North America. In addition, the Aleutian Islands offered a **strategic** location for a coaling station. That same year the United States annexed uninhabited Midway Island in the Pacific Ocean.

Then, in the 1890s and early 1900s, the United States increasingly focused on foreign affairs. Today, some historians consider this shift to overseas expansion in many ways a resumption of the drive that had been halted by the Civil War. Other historians see its international focus as marking a turning point in the nation's history. A number of factors led the United States into greater global involvement in the late 1800s.

Social Studies Practices
Geographical Context

- Describe the geographic reasoning that led to the acquisition of the following U.S. territories: Ohio River Valley, Florida, Texas, California, Puerto Rico, and the Philippines

- In each case, what were the positive and negative effects on the United States?

Factors that Led to the United States Overseas Expansion

Economic interests influenced the United States to seek foreign markets, resources, and coaling stations in the late 1800s. Other motivations were political, geographic, and cultural.

The Economy Drives Search for New Markets and Raw Materials

In the 1890s, economics linked the domestic and foreign policy goals of the United States. After the Civil War, the Northern economy continued to grow, slowed only by the Panic of 1893, which led to a major depression lasting until 1897.

- Between 1860 and 1897, United States exports tripled.

- By 1898, the United States sold $1.3 billion in overseas exports per year, representing only 10 percent of American production.

- At the same time, from 1865 to 1898, United States imports increased from $238 million to $616 million per year.

- Between 1889 and 1898, American iron and steel exports rose 230 percent.

- By 1890, manufacturing and mining represented 30 percent of the nation's **gross national product (GNP).**

- From 1880 to 1890, farming's percent of the nation's GNP dropped from 28 percent to 19 percent. Technology in agriculture led to fewer farmers producing more goods with an excess available for export.

Stimulus-Based Questions: Bar Graph

Based on the bar graph and the text, answer the following questions.

- What was the value of United States foreign trade in 1870? in 1900? in 1920?
- What are possible explanations of the changes on the chart?
- What evidence supports your explanations?

Value of United States Exports, 1870–1920

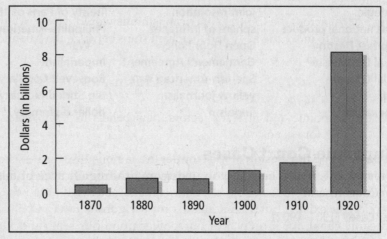

Source: Historical Statistics of the United States, Colonial Times to 1970

Business leaders wanted raw materials from abroad. Business leaders and farmers wanted overseas markets for both their industrial and agricultural products. Overseas markets could provide economic stability, especially when, as in the 1890s, domestic consumption could not absorb the nation's output. Overseas markets could also absorb American exports when the economy at home slowed.

International Rivalry Influences American Expansionism

Most of the country agreed with the business and agricultural interests seeking raw materials and new markets. Other groups also saw the need for the United States to acquire colonies and control valuable sea routes. In the late 19th into the early 20th century, imperialism drove international competition for new markets, naval bases, and colonies. Africa and Asia were major targets of European nations and Japan.

American expansionists were concerned that the United States was already late in entering the competition. They recognized that improvements in transportation and communication technology shortened distances around the world. Communications technology quickly provided information on international markets and on events in other nations that might affect the United States. The nation had to assert itself in an increasingly interdependent and aggressive world. If not seen as a threat by other nations, the United States would become a target even in the Western Hemisphere. This was the position of **Theodore Roosevelt** when he was assistant secretary of the Navy from 1897 to 1898, and later, as vice president and then president.

Expansionists and the Growth of Naval Power

Congress approved the Naval Act of 1890 to build a bigger, modern U.S. Navy. By 1898, 114 triple-steel-hulled warships with steam engines and the latest in weapons were at the core of the 160-ship navy. Behind this growth was the urging of expansionists like navy Captain, later Admiral, **Alfred T. Mahan.** In 1890, Mahan wrote the influential book, *The Influence of Sea Power Upon History, 1660–1783.* Mahan's naval strategy and the building of a bigger and better navy encouraged expansion. Captain Mahan argued that

- throughout history great nations had powerful navies.
- as foreign trade grew, a nation needed a modern steam-powered navy to protect its shipping routes.

- the navy and the merchant fleet needed coaling stations at which to refuel and restock supplies.
- building a canal across the Central American isthmus would cut by two thirds the time needed to move the navy and merchant ships between the Atlantic and the Pacific oceans.

Social, Cultural, and Political Factors Influence American Expansionism

In addition to economic and military factors, new beliefs held by Americans influenced the push for expansion.

Manifest Destiny and the Closing of the Frontier In a famous 1893 essay, historian **Frederick Jackson Turner** argued that the existence of a frontier throughout our history had been vital in shaping the American character. He noted that the frontier no longer existed but "the demands for a vigorous foreign policy, for an interoceanic canal, for a revival of our power upon our seas, and for the extension of American influence to outlying islands and adjoining countries are indications that the forces [of expansion] will continue." Expansionists saw Turner's connection of the frontier to imperialism as further support for extending Manifest Destiny overseas. **Manifest Destiny** is the belief that the United States had a divine mission to expand in order to spread the ideals of freedom and democracy.

Social Darwinism and Imperialism A component of Manifest Destiny is the idea that the American way of life is so superior that the United States is obliged to carry its benefits to other people in other lands. Few wondered whether these other people wanted American "benefits," or recognized that this notion implied that other people and their ways of life were inferior. The belief in Anglo-Saxon superiority was a form of Social Darwinism popular at the time.

You have seen how **Social Darwinism** was used to defend business practices. It was also an ideology that supported imperialism. According to Social Darwinists, the law of nature resulted in the survival of superior people. The same law led to the survival of superior nations that are meant to dominate inferior nations. Believers did not question the lack of scientific evidence to support this theory.

United States Expansion, 1803–1867

Date	Territory	How Acquired
1803	Louisiana Purchase	purchased from France
1819	Florida	occupation, followed by treaty with Spain
1845	Texas	annexation by joint resolution of Congress
1846	Oregon Country	agreement with Great Britain
1848	Mexican Cession	Mexican-American War/treaty with Mexico
1853	Gadsden Purchase	purchased from Mexico
1867	Alaska	purchased from Russia
1867	Midway	annexation

The Missionary Spirit Underlying Manifest Destiny, Social Darwinism, and the missionary movement were feelings of patriotism, nationalism, racism, and a strong sense of cultural superiority. Theodore Roosevelt and Alfred T. Mahan urged expansion for national political and strategic reasons rather than in the interests of commerce alone. Josiah Strong, a minister and Roosevelt's friend, provided American imperialism with a religious, missionary rationale or reason.

Preparing for the Regents

Stimulus-Based Questions: Chart

Using the chart, the text, and the map on page 191, answer the following questions.

- How does the location of Alaska and Midway differ from the other territories on the chart?
- Why would the United States acquire Alaska and Midway?
- How did U.S. foreign policy between 1890 and 1920 change from previous policy directions?
- In what ways was it a continuation of existing foreign policy directions?
- How did U.S. motives for expansion differ between the periods of 1803–1867 and 1890–1914?

Preparing for the Regents

Stimulus-Based Questions: Quote

- After reading the quote, summarize Josiah Strong's point of view on imperialism.
- Then identify the textual evidence that led you to your conclusion.

In *Our Country* (1885), Strong, a minister and social reformer, wrote that to introduce Christianity and "civilization" to others was the mission and that the "Anglo-Saxon, as the great representative of these two ideas, is divinely commissioned to be, in a peculiar sense, his brother's keeper. . . ." Strong's argument continued

The time is coming when . . . the world [will] enter upon . . . the final competition of races. . . . Then this race of unequaled energy, with all the majesty of numbers and the might of wealth behind it—the representative, let us hope, of the largest liberty, the purest Christianity, the highest civilization . . . will spread itself over the earth. . . . And can anyone doubt that the result of this competition of races will be the "survival of the fittest"?

—Josiah Strong, *Our Country: Its Possible Future and Its Present Crisis,* 1885

The **Social Gospel,** a Protestant religious movement of the time, motivated some missionaries to work not only for individual salvation but also for social reform and social justice as well. The number of American Protestant missionaries in China alone grew to about 5,460 by 1914 compared to only 436 in 1874. Missionaries were deeply committed to their work. They helped to spread American cultural, economic, and political views throughout the world. Their voices often added to those who championed the cause of imperialism.

Case Study: The United States Annexes Hawaii

From the beginning of the nineteenth century, Americans—traders, whalers, missionaries—came to Hawaii. Descendants of some of the missionaries developed business interests there.

Queen Liliuokalani

- By 1886, two thirds of Hawaiian sugar was produced on American-owned sugar plantations.
- In 1887, the United States gained the right to establish a naval base at Pearl Harbor.
- By 1890, Americans dominated the islands politically, economically, and militarily, but Hawaii remained an independent country ruled by a monarch.

Then in 1890, Congress, in a new **tariff** law, eliminated the favored status given in 1875 to Hawaiian sugar imports. The new law allowed all sugar to enter the United States duty free but gave sugar cane producers in the United States an incentive to encourage the industry at home. This meant that Americans would be more likely to buy domestic sugar rather than Hawaiian sugar, and American planters in Hawaii would lose money.

At the same time, American planters in Hawaii feared a movement of Hawaiian nationalism led since 1891 by **Queen Liliuokalani.** Challenged both economically and politically, in 1893 American planters and businessmen carried out a successful revolution against the Hawaiian ruler. They were aided by U.S. ambassador to Hawaii John L. Stevens who, without authorization, called in American marines and recognized the government set up after the coup.

The new government quickly asked that the United States annex Hawaii so that their sugar would be considered a domestic import. But President **Grover Cleveland,** just weeks in office, opposed expansion by force against the wishes of the native people. Hawaii remained in the hands of the American sugar interests as the independent Republic of Hawaii with **Sanford B. Dole** as president.

Hawaii did not become a U. S. possession until 1898 during the Spanish-American War. It then became important as a strategic military and commercial link to the Philippines, China, and the rest of East Asia. As in the case of Texas, **annexation** was accomplished by a **joint resolution** rather than a treaty. Hawaii was made a territory in 1900, its first step to statehood. In 1959, it became the 50th state.

The United States Expands its Interests in Asia and the Pacific

In the late 1890s and early 1900s, expanded economic ties with China and Japan led to increasing involvement of the United States in Asia. The acquisition of Hawaii, island bases in the Pacific, and the Philippines added a strategic motive to American interest in the region.

China

American trade with China began in the 1780s through the port of Canton. By the late 1800s, however, Americans were afraid that their economic opportunities in China might be limited. Throughout the nineteenth century, China had been subjected to imperialistic demands by Japan, Germany, Russia, Great Britain, and France. Each nation, except the United States, had gained a **sphere of influence**, a region in which it had exclusive trade, mining, or other economic rights.

Open Door Policy In 1899, Secretary of State **John Hay** tried to secure an economic opportunity in China for the United States. He asked the European powers to keep an "open door" to China. He wanted to ensure through his **Open Door Policy (1899)** that the United States would have equal access to the Chinese market. The European powers, however, met his request with a cool response.

The Boxer Rebellion In 1900, a secret patriotic Chinese society called the Boxers attacked missionaries, diplomats, and other foreigners in China in what is known as the **Boxer Rebellion.** The Boxers were revolting against the Manchu Dynasty and against the intervention of Western powers in China. The Western nations, including the United States, sent troops to restore order. Fearing that rival nations would take even more Chinese land, Hay expanded the **Open Door Policy (1900)** to mean that the current boundaries of China should be preserved.

Secretary of State John Hay

Japan

Japan had developed into a major economic power after 1854, the year in which Commodore **Matthew Perry** ended Japan's isolation by negotiating a treaty opening two Japanese ports to ships from the United States. Unlike China, Japan carried out a far-reaching modernization program making it a major economic power by 1900. From 1900 to 1941, a key aim of American policy in Asia became protecting American economic, political, and territorial interests by providing the **balance of power** to restrict Japanese expansion.

- Japan displayed its growing strength by defeating Russia in the Russo-Japanese War of 1904–1905. President Theodore Roosevelt mediated the Treaty of Portsmouth in an effort to protect American possessions and interests in Asia. It was understood that Japan could remain in Manchuria and annex Korea.

- The United States agreement to the Japanese takeover of Korea was formalized in the 1905 Taft-Katsura Agreement. In return, Japan would not threaten the Philippines.

- In 1906, when the San Francisco schools placed Asian children in separate classes, the Japanese government protested. In 1907, President Theodore Roosevelt's negotiations with Japanese officials resulted in the **Gentlemen's Agreement.** It ended school segregation in San Francisco but also restricted Japanese immigration to the families of those who were already in the United States.

- In 1908, the two nations entered into the Root-Takahira Agreement in which the United States recognized Japan's interest in Manchuria, while the Japanese agreed to uphold the Open Door Policy and support China's independence and integrity. Each nation agreed to maintain the status quo or existing conditions, meaning no attempt would be made to seize the other's territorial possessions.

Preparing for the Regents

Stimulus-Based Questions: Timeline

Examine the timeline to the right, then answer the following questions.

- Which event occurred first—Roosevelt's use of "Big Stick diplomacy" or the Spanish-American War?

- Which events are examples of use of force?

- What other methods of carrying out foreign policy are suggested?

Analyzing Documents

In 1894, the United States Secretary of State said that the Samoan protectorate was

. . . the first departure from our traditional and well-established policy of avoiding entangling alliances with foreign powers in relation to objects remote from this hemisphere.

- What traditional policy does the secretary of state mean?

- What is the secretary's position on U.S. expansionism?

- What specific textual evidence supports your answer?

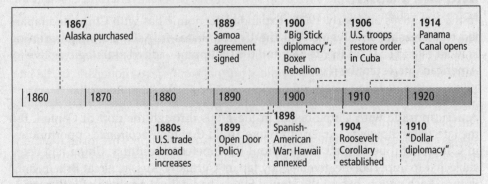

American Imperialism, 1867–1914

| 1867 Alaska purchased | | 1889 Samoa agreement signed | 1900 "Big Stick diplomacy"; Boxer Rebellion | 1906 U.S. troops restore order in Cuba | 1914 Panama Canal opens |

| 1860 | 1870 | 1880 | 1890 | 1900 | 1910 | 1920 |

| | | 1880s U.S. trade abroad increases | 1899 Open Door Policy | 1898 Spanish-American War; Hawaii annexed | 1904 Roosevelt Corollary established | 1910 "Dollar diplomacy" |

Samoa

In 1878, the United States gained the rights to a naval station at Pago Pago in the Samoan Islands. The port was also used by Germany and Great Britain. Samoa is situated in the Pacific on the trade route to Australia. Conflicts arose among the three nations. In 1899, Germany and the United States divided Samoa.

The Causes and Effects of the Spanish-American War

In 1898, the United States began to acquire new territories, making it an imperial power. Most of these territorial gains resulted from the **Spanish-American War**.

The Interests and Actions of the United States, Spain, and Cuba

In the 1890s, Spain, once a great world power, was deeply in debt, its empire reduced. Cuba and Puerto Rico in the Caribbean and Guam and the Philippines in the Pacific Ocean were its only major remaining possessions. Spain's foreign policy objective was to keep control of what it held. In 1895, Cubans rebelled, as did Filipinos in 1896.

Economic By 1898, United States business interests had invested $50 million in Cuba, and Cuban-American trade ran to about $100 million per year with almost all of Cuba's sugar exported to the United States. As in Hawaii, U.S. tariffs played a role in the revolution in Cuba. In 1894, the United States had placed a high protective tariff on Cuban sugar, which had previously entered our nation duty free. Growers in Cuba lost millions because their sugar was no longer competitively priced. Cuba fell into economic chaos. The disruption, combined with resentment of oppressive and incompetent Spanish rule, in 1895 set off another Cuban revolt for independence from Spain. The revolution further endangered American investments. The Cubans fought a guerrilla war. They burned the sugar cane fields and buildings engaged in sugar production to force the Spanish to give up Cuba.

Expansionist From the point of view of American imperialists—including Theodore Roosevelt, Senator Henry Cabot Lodge, and Secretary of State John Hay—the Cuban revolution offered an opportunity to seize territory from a weak Spain. The imperialist cause was aided by widespread condemnation of the tactics of the Spanish military commander, General Valeriano Weyler, who was sent to put down the insurgency. Weyler placed hundreds of thousands of Cuban civilians in reconcentration camps to keep them from aiding the insurgents. By the time that the Spanish-American War began in 1898, about 30 percent of those in camps had died from disease and starvation.

Moving Toward War

Americans' emotions were stirred up as a result of several events and demand for aggressive action against Spain began to grow.

The Yellow Press Americans sympathized with the Cuban revolution and were appalled by the effects of General "Butcher" Weyler's policy. Humanitarian and patriotic feelings were stirred by **yellow journalism,** or sensationalism. In the late 1890s, two of the most famous American publishers, **William Randolph Hearst** of the *New York Morning Journal* and **Joseph Pulitzer** of the *New York World*, were battling for readers in a circulation war. Both newspapers printed sensational stories and pictures about the horrors of the Cuban revolution. The stories routinely exaggerated and distorted events for emotional effect. Hearst and Pulitzer also ran articles that fed a growing **jingoism**, an extreme patriotism and demand for aggressive actions in foreign affairs, that created a warlike climate.

The de Lôme Letter A personal letter written by the Spanish minister to the United States, Enrique Dupuy de Lôme, was printed in the *New York Journal* in February 1898. De Lôme's unfavorable comments—he called President **William McKinley** "weak and catering to the rabble"—made it hard for the president and other political leaders to withstand demands for war.

Sinking of the *Maine* Less than a week after publication of the de Lôme letter, the **USS *Maine*,** an American battleship, exploded and sank in the harbor of Havana, Cuba, killing 266 Americans. Encouraged by the "yellow press," a shocked public blamed Spain, although a later investigation was never able to determine the cause of the explosion nor assign responsibility.

Fighting the Spanish-American War in the Caribbean Sea

In April 1898, despite Spain's agreement to an armistice with Cuba, McKinley asked Congress to declare war. Congress complied. It also approved the **Teller Amendment,** which promised that the United States had no "intention to exercise sovereignty, jurisdiction, or control" over Cuba. Theodore Roosevelt resigned as assistant secretary of the Navy to organize a volunteer cavalry (fought on horseback) unit, the Rough Riders, made up of western cowboys, eastern Ivy League athletes, immigrants, and Native Americans. The publicity led to Roosevelt's election as New York governor, putting him on the road to the presidency.

Fighting the Spanish-American War in the Pacific Ocean

On May 1, 1898, Commodore, later Admiral, **George Dewey,** sailed into Manila Bay in the Philippines with six warships. In the morning, the U.S. Navy destroyed the entire outdated Spanish fleet. In August, American soldiers took the city of Manila. **Emilio Aguinaldo** who, since 1896, had led the fight against the Spanish for Philippine independence set up a provisional Filipino government under a constitution based on that of the United States. Earlier in the war, the U.S. Navy had taken control of Guam.

Roosevelt (center) and the Rough Riders

Preparing for the Regents

Stimulus-Based Questions: Graphic Organizer

Examine the graphic organizer, then answer the following questions.

- Which are the *basic* causes of the war?

- Which are the *immediate* causes of the war?

- What might you add to the causes and/or effects listed?

- Which effects were long-term?

- Was the war a turning point in United States history? If so, why?

Social Studies Practices

Interpreting Evidence

The Pacific is our ocean. . . . And the Pacific is the ocean of the commerce of the future. . . . The power that rules the Pacific, therefore, is the power that rules the world. And, with the Philippines, that power is and will forever be the American republic.

— U.S. Senator Albert J. Beveridge, 1900

- What does the speaker believe is the source of world power for the United States?

- What evidence reveals that the statement is an opinion, not a fact?

- How did the Open Door Policy and acquiring the Philippines affect United States foreign policy for the rest of the twentieth century?

The Spanish-American War Ends

The Spanish-American War lasted four months, with fighting in both the Caribbean Sea and in the Pacific Ocean. In December 1898, the terms of the **Treaty of Paris of 1898** negotiated with Spain

- granted Cuba its independence.
- gave the Philippines to the United States in return for $20 million.
- ceded Puerto Rico and Guam to the United States.

For the United States, the Treaty of Paris of 1898

- led to the acquisition of former Spanish territories that formed the basis of an American empire.
- set off a national debate between imperialists and anti-imperialists.
- increased American involvement in Latin America and in Asia as the nation sought to protect and benefit from its new possessions.

Of the 2,446 Americans who lost their lives, fewer than 400 were killed in combat; the rest died from infection and disease. But the worst of the fighting was yet to come.

The Spanish-American War

Causes	The Spanish-American War	Effects
• United States wants to expand in Latin American and the Pacific. • In Cuba and the Philippines, people rebel against Spanish rule. • Demands for involvement from American expansionists and newspapers. • Explosion sinks American battleship U.S.S. *Maine* in Cuban harbor. Cause of the explosion is unknown, but angry Americans blame Spain.	The Spanish-American War	• United States defeats Spain in less than four months. • Spain recognizes Cuba's independence. United States begins to control Cuban politics and economy. • Puerto Rico, the Philippines, and Guam become United States territories. • United States is recognized as a world power.

The Aftermath of the Treaty of Paris

The Spanish-American War ended with the signing of the Treaty of Paris. Its provisions affected the nation and its new possessions for years to come.

The Philippine-American War

In February 1899, President McKinley secured Senate ratification of the Treaty of Paris of 1898 by a one-vote margin. A month earlier, Aguinaldo, objecting to annexation by the United States, had declared the Philippines a republic. The revolutionaries did not recognize U.S. sovereignty over their republic. The United States did not recognize the sovereignty of the Filipino republic. A brutal **Philippine-American War** followed. The fighting lasted from 1899 until 1902 when the Filipinos surrendered.

More than 4,000 Americans soldiers and some 20,000 Filipinos were killed in this war. An additional 200,000 Filipinos died from starvation and disease. Atrocities were committed by both sides. In 1916, the Jones Act promised the Philippines independence. In 1934, the independence date was set for 1944. This promise was delayed because of World War II but was honored in 1946 when the Philippines became an independent nation.

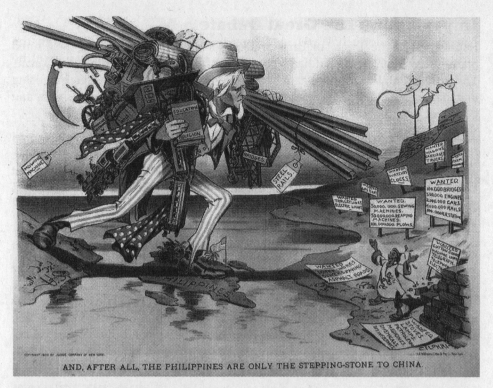

AND, AFTER ALL, THE PHILIPPINES ARE ONLY THE STEPPING-STONE TO CHINA.

Preparing for the Regents

Stimulus-Based Questions: Political Cartoon

- Identify the three land masses in the cartoon.
- Identify items that Uncle Sam is carrying.
- Explain the meaning of the message under the cartoon.
- According to the cartoonist, what motivated the U.S. to annex the Philippines?

Does the Constitution Follow the Flag?

It was left up to the Supreme Court in the **Insular** (island) **Cases** (1901–1902) to determine the status of the residents of the new colonies. The key question was and is does the Constitution follow the flag, meaning do constitutional rights and benefits extend to those living in U.S. territories? The complicated and controversial answer differs by territory and by right or benefit.

Cuba After the Treaty of Paris

U.S. troops remained in Cuba until 1902. They were sent to Cuba twice more between 1902 and 1922. Cuban independence was limited by the **Platt Amendment** (1901), which remained part of the Cuban constitution until 1934. The amendment (1) required that the United States approve treaties between Cuba and other nations, (2) gave the United States the right to lease naval bases in Cuba, and (3) allowed the United States to intervene in Cuba to preserve order or peace.

The Platt Amendment gave the United States the right to lease the **Guantanamo Bay** area "for use as coaling or naval station only." When the treaty was renegotiated in 1934, it stated that the agreement can be broken only by "mutual consent" or U.S. abandonment. Further controversy has surrounded the base. In 2002, President George W. Bush turned part of the base into a detention camp for "enemy combatants." In 2009, President Barack Obama ordered the detention camp closed but faced congressional opposition to its relocation in the United States and problems with transfers of detainees to other nations. In 2018, President Trump ordered that the detention camp be kept open. President Biden's policy is to relocate the 37 who remain.

Puerto Rico After the Treaty of Paris

The **Foraker Act of 1900** provided for a Puerto Rican legislature elected by the people but with a governor and council appointed by the American president. In 1917, Puerto Ricans received United States citizenship. In 1952, the island became a commonwealth. This status gives Puerto Rico many rights of a state excluding sending representatives to Congress. Puerto Ricans participate in primary elections for U.S. president, but they may only vote in a presidential election if they live in the United States, not in Puerto Rico.

Social Studies
Practices
Interpreting Evidence

*It has been a splendid
little war; begun with the
highest motives, carried
out with magnificent
intelligence and spirit.*

—Secretary of State John
Hay, 1898

- How is this description of
a war unusual?

- Why would anti-
imperialists and
pacifists object to this
description?

- Why have some
historians today
suggested that the
war should be called
the Spanish-American-
Cuban-Filipino War or
the War of 1898?

Preparing for
the Regents

**Stimulus-Based
Questions: Chart**

Self-interest is what
determines a nation's
foreign policy. Often that
self-interest is mixed with
or masked by idealism and
nationalism. Examine the
chart and the text to answer
these questions.

- Summarize the
major reasons for the
expansionism of the
United States in the 1890s
and early 1900s.

- Which reasons were
based on self-interest?
idealism? nationalism?

- How did the Hawaiians
and Filipinos show their
nationalism by their
reactions to American
actions and attitudes?

Imperialism: The Great Debate

Ratification of the Treaty of Paris of 1898 set off a great debate in the United States. As with all treaties, it had to be ratified by a two-thirds vote of the Senate. The fundamental question was whether the United States should be practicing **imperialism**—the policy of expanding a nation's power by foreign acquisitions and economic control. Was imperialism compatible with America's identity?

Americans in both political parties, in all regions, and from all social classes could be found on either side of the debate. Emotions were strong. Progressives were also divided. Imperialists included Theodore Roosevelt, Senator Henry Cabot Lodge, and Alfred T. Mahan. Among the anti-imperialists were Andrew Carnegie, Samuel Gompers, Mark Twain, Jane Addams, William Jennings Bryan, Booker T. Washington, and former President Grover Cleveland.

The Arguments of the Anti-Imperialists

The **American Anti-Imperialist League** was organized in 1898 to oppose the annexation of the Philippines and to oppose the Spanish-American War. To the League, imperialism violated the most fundamental beliefs of the nation as expressed in founding documents such as the Declaration of Independence. The anti-imperialists focused on beliefs in liberty, democracy, and the "consent of the governed." The Philippines, Hawaii, and Cuba were all acting on nationalistic motives at the time that Americans intervened.

Nativists among the anti-imperialists argued that the population of the islands we had acquired was of an "inferior race" and could not and should not be absorbed into America. Labor leaders, such as Samuel Gompers, feared that new cheap unskilled labor would take jobs away from Americans and depress wages. Others were proponents of trade across the world without the burden and problems of an empire. Anti-imperialists pointed out the costs of maintaining an empire and the dangers of imperialism dragging the United States into conflicts abroad.

The Arguments of the Imperialists

Imperialists had the support of much of the nation. Their major arguments were political, humanitarian, and economic as well as patriotic. Imperialism was a continuation of the nation's long westward expansion. As with Manifest Destiny, the United States could now carry its beliefs and values overseas to civilize people and convert them to Christianity. The nation needed new markets and resources. The Philippines were in a strategic location to aid trade with China and other nations of East Asia. Imperialists believed that the nation, divided by civil war, depressions, and strikes, could be united around imperialism.

Imperialists' Point of View	Anti-Imperialists' Point of View
The United States needs colonies to compete economically.	Supporting an empire would be a financial burden.
To be a true world power, the United States needs colonies and naval bases.	The United States should concentrate its energies on solving problems at home.
It is the American destiny to expand, and its duty to care for poor, weak peoples.	Nonwhite people cannot be assimilated into American society.
To abandon territories makes the United States appear cowardly before the world.	An empire would involve the United States in more wars.
It is only honorable to keep land that Americans lost their lives to obtain.	It is a violation of democratic principles to annex land and not offer its people the same rights as those of U.S. citizens.

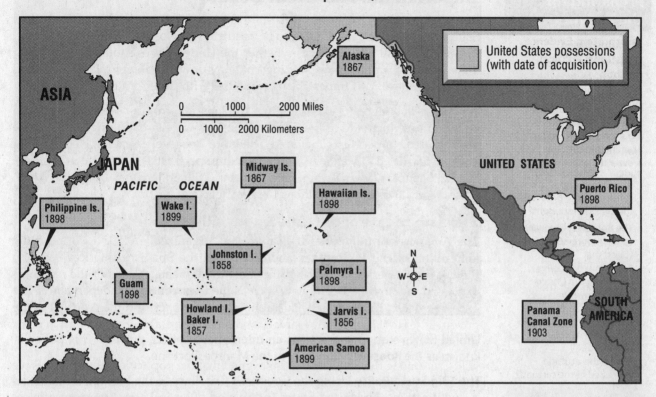

Expanding American Influence in the Caribbean and Latin America

Having acquired an empire, the United States found itself increasingly involved around the globe as it protected its new territories and interests. The Roosevelt Corollary to the Monroe Doctrine and the creation of the Panama Canal are two examples of the expansion of American influence in the Caribbean and Latin America in the first two decades after the Spanish-American War.

The Roosevelt Corollary and the Monroe Doctrine

The **Monroe Doctrine** of 1823 warned foreign powers to stay out of the Western Hemisphere. It was used to support the American annexation of Texas and the Mexican War. It was also used against France at the end of the Civil War, when the French had set up a puppet government in Mexico and withdrew only after the United States massed troops along the Mexican border.

The Venezuelan Border Dispute In 1895, the United States had another opportunity to reaffirm and expand the Monroe Doctrine. Great Britain and Venezuela were involved in a quarrel over the boundary between Venezuela and British Guiana (now Guyana). When Great Britain refused American arbitration, the United States claimed that the British were violating the Monroe Doctrine and forced them to negotiate by threatening war. Secretary of State Richard Olney, in the Olney Interpretation of the Monroe Doctrine, claimed, "Today, the United States is practically sovereign on this continent."

The Roosevelt Corollary In 1904, President Theodore Roosevelt further reinforced, even reinterpreted, the Monroe Doctrine. Economic problems in Venezuela and the Dominican Republic led to threats of European intervention. In both cases, the United States stepped in to restore order. Roosevelt explained American policy in a 1904 message to Congress. If a nation in the Western Hemisphere is guilty of consistently behaving wrongly, he said, the Monroe Doctrine requires that the

Theodore Roosevelt was famous for the statement, *Speak softly and carry a big stick; you will go far.* Examine the cartoon, then answer the questions that follow.

- What does the big stick in the cartoon represent?
- The Roosevelt Corollary to the Monroe Doctrine stated that *Chronic wrongdoing . . . may force the United States, however, reluctantly . . . to the exercise of an international police power.* How is this attitude expressed in the cartoon?

United States step in and act "as an international police power." This policy is known as the **Roosevelt Corollary** to the Monroe Doctrine.

The "Big Stick" Policy Using the Roosevelt Corollary to the Monroe Doctrine as its justification, the United States intervened often in Latin American affairs, usually to maintain economic stability in order to protect American investments and prevent European involvement in the Hemisphere. These actions were conducted using what became known as **Big Stick diplomacy.**

The Panama Canal Since the mid-1850s, the advantages of building a canal across the **isthmus,** or narrow piece of land connecting North and South America, were understood. The growth of United States commerce and the expansion of its navy increased pressure to be able to move naval and merchant ships quickly between the Atlantic and Pacific oceans. The Spanish-American War and the management of the newly acquired empire heightened interest in the project.

Under Theodore Roosevelt, the United States settled on a route across Panama, which, at the time, was part of Colombia. When Colombia seemed reluctant to agree to financial terms, Roosevelt encouraged Panamanians to revolt and declare their independence. A United States naval ship kept the Colombian military from intervening. The United States then quickly negotiated a treaty with the new nation of Panama, which gave the United States a 99-year renewable lease on a ten-mile-wide strip of land, the Panama Canal Zone, across Panama.

Building the canal was a mammoth task. Yellow fever and malaria caused delays. However, workers made the remarkable achievement of completing the canal ahead of schedule and under budget. The canal opened to traffic in 1914.

In 1978, by one vote, the United States Senate approved two treaties with Panama. This meant that in 1979 the United States turned the Canal Zone over to the nation of Panama but continued to run the canal jointly with Panama. On December 31, 1999, the United States returned the Canal to Panama but retained the right to defend it. In 2016, at the cost of about $5.25 billion, the Panama Canal expansion opened. A third set of locks made it possible for today's new container ships and bulk carriers to use the canal.

Dollar Diplomacy The foreign policy of President **William Howard Taft,** elected in 1908, was called **dollar diplomacy** by its critics. Taft described dollar diplomacy as "substituting dollars for bullets." Taft meant that that the United States should use American economic power instead of military force to protect and support any national interests overseas in a way that would help maintain orderly societies in other countries. Ultimately, Taft's dollar diplomacy was unable to moderate the revolutionary forces and economic instability in Latin America.

Intervention in Mexico During the Mexican Revolution, President Woodrow Wilson intervened in Mexico's affairs in order to protect huge American investments there. He also believed in moral diplomacy—conducting foreign affairs in terms of judgments about right and wrong. In 1913, after Victoriano Huerta overthrew the Mexican president and had him murdered, Wilson refused to recognize Huerta's government. The next year, the U.S. Navy seized the port of Vera Cruz to prevent a German ship from landing its cargo of arms for Huerta. Wilson also sent a force into northern Mexico in 1916 in an attempt to capture Pancho Villa, a Mexican rebel whose border raid into New Mexico in 1916 led to American deaths.

The Good Neighbor Policy Under presidents Herbert Hoover (1929–1933) and Franklin D. Roosevelt (1933–1945) the United States attempted to improve its relations with Latin America. Roosevelt backed what came to be called the **Good Neighbor Policy.** This meant less emphasis on intervention and more on cooperation. However, American economic dominance of the region continued.

Latin American Reaction The actions of the United States in Latin America in the 20th century met with protests from the Latin American nations. The attitude and actions of the United States has left a heritage of distrust that persists today.

The United States and World War I

Key Concept

11.6b While the United States attempted to follow its traditional policy of neutrality at the beginning of World War I, the nation eventually became involved in the war. President Woodrow Wilson led the nation into war with the hope of reforming the international order through his Fourteen Points.

Lesson Overview

President Woodrow Wilson entered office in March of 1913, as a Progressive. When World War I began, Wilson at first pursued the nation's traditional policy of neutrality, but in 1917, the United States entered the war. President Wilson expressed his goals in the Fourteen Points. He played a major role at the Versailles Peace Conference but was forced to make compromises in order to gain approval for the League of Nations. Returning to the United States, he forcefully campaigned for Senate approval of the treaty. Ultimately, the United States Senate rejected Wilson's efforts. The United States did not ratify the Treaty of Versailles nor the League of Nations. Instead, the nation moved back to its policy of neutrality. The debates between imperialists and anti-imperialists over the proper course of America's foreign policy included the pros and cons of our involvement in World War I, the Treaty, the League, and the issue of presidential power.

Unifying Themes

As you review this lesson take special note of the following themes:

- **Geography, Humans, and the Environment** How did geographic factors influence the nation's foreign policy decisions before, during, and after World War I?

- **Development and Transformation of Social Structures** In what ways were the Fourteen Points aimed at correcting social and political inequalities and expanding access to human rights in the world? Did the United States conform to the Fourteen Points in its foreign policy?

- **Power, Authority, and Governance** How did the foreign policy actions of President Woodrow Wilson increase both the power of the United States and the power of the presidency? What examples would anti-imperialists and imperialists use in support of their positions regarding Wilson's foreign policy?

- **Creation, Expansion, and Interaction of Economic Systems** How did America's industrial and business interests influence our foreign policy decisions before, during, and after World War I?

Key People

Woodrow Wilson   Henry Cabot Lodge
John J. Pershing

Key Terms and Events

Central Powers	Zimmerman note	reparations
Allied Powers	Fourteen Points	ratify
neutrality	League of Nations	self-determination
freedom of the seas	Treaty of Versailles	
unrestricted submarine warfare		

The Great War

Known as the Great War before the outbreak of World War II, World War I began in Europe in 1914 and lasted until 1918. The United States did not enter the war until 1917. The financial and human costs of this devastating conflict were enormous.

The Causes of World War I

The forces of nationalism, imperialism, and militarism had been developing among the European powers for decades. They were the basic causes of World War I. The alliance system was an immediate cause of the war. The assassination of the heir to the Austro-Hungarian throne in June of 1914 triggered the alliance system, and by August the major European nations were at war.

Nationalism Strong nationalistic competition had developed among France, Great Britain, Russia, Austria-Hungary, and Germany, especially after the unification of Germany in 1871. There was also ethnic unrest within nations. For instance, the Czechs and Slovaks wanted to free themselves from Austro-Hungarian control.

Imperialism Several nations were involved in keen competition for markets and colonies throughout the world.

Militarism The early 1900s witnessed a continual buildup of armies and navies. Germany, for instance, tripled naval construction in order to challenge Great Britain's control of the seas.

The Alliance System As national and imperial goals conflicted, groups of nations organized against each other in an effort to maintain a balance of power and avoid war. If fighting were to break out, members of an alliance were pledged to help each other. The Triple Alliance and the Triple Entente were the two major alliances. When war began, the **Central Powers,** Germany, Austria-Hungary, the Ottoman Empire, and later Bulgaria, fought the **Allied Powers,** Great Britain, France, Russia, and later Italy and the United States.

Europe During World War I, 1914–1918

Preparing for the Regents

Stimulus-Based Questions: Map

Examine the map, then answer the following questions.

- Which nations were the Allied Powers?
- Which were the Central Powers?
- Which nations remained neutral?
- How did geographic location influence a nation's choice of sides?

			1913 Civil war erupts in Mexico		1915 Germans sink *Lusitania*		1917 U.S. enters war; Espionage Act passed		1919 Senate rejects Treaty of Versailles
1910	1911	1912	1913	1914	1915	1916	1917	1918	1919	1920

1914 War begins in Europe

1916 Germany suspends submarine attacks

1918 Fourteen Points announced; Germany surrenders

Social Studies Practices
Cause and Effect

Use the text and these three quotes to answer the questions below, citing supporting evidence. Note the dates on each quote.

. . . impartial in thought as well as in action.
—Woodrow Wilson, 1914

He kept us out of war.
—Wilson campaign slogan, 1916

The world must be made safe for democracy.
—Wilson request for declaration of war, April 2, 1917

- Did United States policy contradict Wilson's earlier statements and therefore involve the U.S. in the war, or Did circumstances beyond the control of the United States lead the nation to break its policy of neutrality?

President Woodrow Wilson

The United States: From Neutrality to War

When the Great War broke out in Europe in the summer of 1914, The United States was officially neutral. By 1917, however, the United States was drawn into the war. There were several reasons for this major shift in our traditional policy of **neutrality**.

Cultural and Ethnic Links Few Americans were truly neutral. Some sympathized with the Central Powers, dominated by Germany and Austria-Hungary. These included German-Americans because of ties to Germany and Irish-Americans because of anti-British sentiments. The majority of Americans favored the Allies. Americans had long-standing cultural ties with Great Britain. Many also felt loyalty to our first ally, France.

Economic Ties American links to the Allies were economic as well as cultural. A British blockade of the North Sea effectively ended U.S. exports to Germany and the other Central Powers, which dropped in value from about $345 million in 1914 to $29 million in 1916. Meanwhile, the value of trade with the Allies quadrupled. American business and agriculture benefited from this trade, much of it financed by U.S. government loans to the Allies, which totaled more than $2 billion by 1917.

President **Woodrow Wilson** interpreted neutrality to the benefit of the Allies. He defended the right of a neutral nation to sell military supplies to nations at war, primarily to Britain and France. Most Americans did not believe that trade with or loans to the Allies violated the nation's neutrality. In fact, President Wilson and his closest advisers favored the Allies. However, even in the 1916 presidential election, Wilson continued to proclaim American neutrality, campaigning on the slogan "He kept us out of war."

Propaganda Aided by their control of the transatlantic cable, the Allies conducted an effective propaganda campaign in the United States. They pictured the war as one of civilized, democratic nations against the barbaric monarchy of Germany.

German Submarine Warfare In 1915, determined to use its new weapon, submarines, or U-boats, to stop trade between the Allies and the United States and to break the British blockade, Germany announced a war zone around Great Britain. The German U-boats would sink enemy ships in the war zone. To avoid attack by error, neutral nations and their citizens should avoid the zone. Because a submarine is very vulnerable when surfaced, Germany ignored international law that required that a warship to stop and identify itself, then board a merchant or passenger ship and remove its crew and passengers before sinking it. In May 1916, Germany announced the Sussex Pledge. Under pressure from the United States, Germany pledged it would not continue submarine warfare against **noncombatants,** meaning civilians and military personnel who do not fight, such as medical and religious personnel.

Freedom of the Seas Germany's attempt to destroy the British blockade by attacking Allied ships was the single most important cause of America's entry into the First World War. Wilson insisted that America as a neutral nation had the right to trade with nations at war and to send its civilians on ships into war zones. Wilson, in defense of the principle of freedom of the seas and in defiance of German demands, would not ban our citizens from traveling on American or British passenger ships. **Freedom of the seas** means the right of all nations to unrestricted travel in international waters in times of peace, except when limits are placed by international agreements, and the right of neutral nations to trade, and their citizens to travel during war as well. The United States defense of this principle was a factor in the undeclared war with France in 1798, the Barbary Wars (1801–1805), the War of 1812, and again in World War I.

Events in 1917 Lead to War A series of events early in 1917 finally led to America's entry into World War I.

- On February 1, Germany announced a policy of **unrestricted submarine warfare**. It warned it would attack without warning all vessels headed for Allied ports. The main reason for Germany's decision was that the war was at a stalemate. Knowing that its move would probably bring the United States into the war, Germany calculated that its U-boats could break the British blockade and defeat the Allies before the United States could get troops to the battlefield.

- Two days later, the United States broke diplomatic relations with Germany. Tension and suspicion increased with the **Zimmermann note** of March 1. This was a secret message from the German foreign secretary, Arthur Zimmermann, to the German minister in Mexico. It urged a German military alliance with the Mexicans, promising them support in regaining their "lost territories" in the southwestern United States. When the message was made public, Americans reacted angrily.

- In March, German U-boats sank five American merchant ships.

- Also in March, the Russian Revolution overthrew the czar. It appeared that more democratic forces would take control in Russia, so that if the United States went to war, it would be joining an alliance of democratic nations.

OCEAN STEAMSHIPS.

CUNARD

EUROPE VIA LIVERPOOL
LUSITANIA

Fastest and Largest Steamer now in Atlantic Service Sails
SATURDAY, MAY 1, 10 A.M.
Transylvania, Fri., May 7, 5 P.M.
Orduna, - - Tues.,May 18, 10 A.M.
Tuscania, - - Fri., May 21, 5 P.M.
LUSITANIA, Sat., May 29, 10 A.M.
Transylvania, Fri., June 4, 5 P.M.
Gibraltar—Genoa—Naples—Piraeus
S.S. Carpathia, Thur., May 13, Noon

NOTICE!
TRAVELLERS intending to embark on the Atlantic voyage are reminded that a state of war exists between Germany and her allies and Great Britain and her allies; that the zone of war includes the waters adjacent to the British Isles; that, in accordance with formal notice given by the Imperial German Government, vessels flying the flag of Great Britain, or of any of her allies, are liable to destruction in those waters and that travellers sailing in the war zone on ships of Great Britain or her allies do so at their own risk.

IMPERIAL GERMAN EMBASSY
WASHINGTON, D. C. APRIL 22, 1915.

Preparing for the Regents

Stimulus-Based Questions: Artifact

America was critical of Germany's use of U-boats. Germany did warn travelers—including passengers of the *Lusitania*—to stay out of the war zone. 1,198 people, including 128 from the United States lost their lives.

- Who issued this notice? When? Where?
- Who is being warned, and what is the warning?
- What type of ship was the *Lusitania*?
- To what port was the *Lusitania* sailing?
- Was the ship British or American?

Unifying Themes
Power and Authority

We shall endeavor . . . to keep the United States of America neutral. In the event of this not succeeding, we make Mexico a proposal . . . make war together, make peace together, . . . and . . . Mexico is to reconquer the lost territory in Texas, New Mexico, and Arizona.

—German foreign secretary Arthur Zimmermann, 1917

- What was Germany's first plan concerning the United States?
- If that plan failed, what did Germany propose to do in alliance with Mexico?
- How did Americans react to this note?
- What specific textual evidence explains why this document was a diplomatic secret?

The United States at War

On April 6, 1917, at the urging of President Wilson, the United States declared war on Germany. Within months American troops were in Europe, fighting on the front.

The Fourteen Points

President Wilson chose to take a stand for the basic principle of freedom of the seas. By banning American overseas travel, he might have avoided war. He also refused to embargo arms to Great Britain in order to obtain a less restrictive blockade for American shipping. Wilson was the first president to end American neutrality and send American troops into a foreign war. These are just a few examples of how President Wilson's foreign policy decisions were often based on his morals and principles.

In January 1918, with the **Fourteen Points,** Wilson rallied the nation and the world to a massive war effort. The Fourteen Points were a statement of his war aims and peace proposals. The purpose of the war was justice for all peoples and nations with a permanent peace based on his Fourteen Points. The Fourteen Points justified America's entry into an overseas war as a selfless, righteous effort on behalf of world peace. With the entry of the United States, the Allies were motivated and the morale of the Central Powers weakened. Wilson became the moral leader of the Allies.

Allies Day, May 1917 by Childe Hassam honors the British, French, and American alliance.

Preparing for the Regents

Stimulus-Based Questions: Speech

- Summarize each of the points.
- Why did Britain oppose Point II?
- Why has Point IV become both imperative and more of a challenge?
- What steps toward self-determination (V) have been taken in the world between WWI and WWII?
- Which points indicate that the speech was anti-imperialist?
- Why was Point XIV most important to Wilson?

Excerpt From The Fourteen Points

. . . for our own part we see very clearly that unless justice be done to others it will not be done to us. The program of the world's peace, therefore, is our program; and that program . . . as we see it, is this:

I. Open covenants of peace, openly arrived at, after which there shall be no private international understandings of any kind but diplomacy shall proceed always frankly and in the public view.

II. Absolute freedom of navigation upon the seas, . . . alike in peace and in war. . . .

III. The removal, so far as possible, of all economic barriers and the establishment of an equality of trade conditions among all the nations consenting to the peace. . . .

IV. Adequate guarantees given and taken that national armaments will be reduced to the lowest point consistent with domestic safety.

V. A free, open-minded, and absolutely impartial adjustment of all colonial claims, based upon a strict observance of the principle that in determining all such questions of sovereignty the interests of the populations concerned must have equal weight with the equitable claims of the government whose title is to be determined. . . .

XIV. A general association of nations must be formed under specific covenants for the purpose of affording mutual guarantees of political independence and territorial integrity to great and small states alike.

In regard to these essential rectifications of wrong and assertions of right we feel ourselves to be intimate partners of all the governments and peoples associated together against the Imperialists. We cannot be separated in interest or divided in purpose. We stand together until the end.

—Woodrow Wilson, speech before a Joint Session of Congress, January 8, 1919

America Fights in the First World War

The United States entered World War I on the side of the Allies in April 1917. American soldiers in meaningful numbers arrived at the front in France in May 1918, just as Germany started a major counter offensive. The United States supplied fresh troops to a war in which both sides were exhausted by years of trench warfare. After four years of war, casualties were in the millions. The Bolshevik Revolution in November of 1917 had resulted in Russia leaving the war. The Germans were shifting their divisions from the Russian front to France.

The entry of the United States tipped the scale in favor of the Allies. The fighting ended on November 11, 1918 with an Allied victory. By the end of the war, 4.8 million Americans had served in the armed forces, 2.8 million of them draftees. Eventually, over 2 million Americans were sent to France organized in a separate command, the **American Expeditionary Force,** led by General **John J. Pershing.** The United States lost about 51,000 men in battle.

Wilson and the Treaty of Versailles

The Fourteen Points became the basis for the peace negotiations held at Versailles, France, beginning in January of 1919. Wilson led the American delegation, the first United States president to leave American soil while in office. Wilson went to Paris as the people's hero. Almost every nation and political group in the world had found something in the Fourteen Points that they liked. This included the Germans who hoped for a peace treaty based on the Fourteen Points. Instead, Germany was not allowed to participate in the peace conference. Russia was also not permitted to attend.

The Paris Peace Conference and the Treaty of Versailles

The Allied leaders, Georges Clemenceau of France, David Lloyd George of Great Britain, and Vittorio Orlando of Italy were cool to Wilson and his Fourteen Points. They knew that Wilson would need to compromise with them in order to preserve his proposal for a league of nations. Wilson wanted a "peace without victory." They did not.

- The Europeans wanted Germany to be punished.
- They expected their nations to be repaid for their losses.
- In some cases, they had already made secret wartime deals involving territorial changes and money settlements that contradicted provisions of the Fourteen Points.

President Wilson opposed many of the provisions of the Versailles Treaty and the treaties with the other Central Powers. He knew that he had to bring home a treaty that the United States Senate would ratify as well as meet the public's high expectations. He made concessions such as allowing France to have the Saar Valley. In 1935, the Saar voted to be returned to Germany. Another compromise was to allow Japan to keep China's Shandong peninsula but promise that at a future date it would again belong to China. Wilson was willing to compromise because the treaties provided for a new world organization, the **League of Nations.** The League, Wilson believed, would correct any problems caused by the peace treaties.

Costs of the War for the Allies

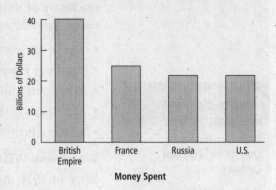

Money Spent

Casualties

Source: V. J. Esposito, *A Concise History of World War I*

Preparing for the Regents

Stimulus-Based Questions: Graph

Examine the graphs, then answer the questions that follow.

- Approximately how many casualties did Russia suffer in the war?
- Approximately how much money did the United States spend on the war?
- What additional information would you need to accurately assess the financial and human cost of World War I?

The most important agreement reached at Versailles was the treaty with Germany, the **Treaty of Versailles.** The League of Nations was part of this treaty. The treaty stated that Germany had to

- accept complete responsibility for causing the war.
- pay huge **reparations** to the Allies.
- give up its military forces.
- cede lands to the new nations of Poland and Czechoslovakia.
- give up its overseas colonies.

Woodrow Wilson and the United States Senate

Early in 1919 most Americans supported the Versailles Treaty. However, the Constitution required the United States Senate to **ratify**, or approve, any treaty and by a two-thirds vote.

Senate Republicans saw Wilson as a braggart and show off because he personally led the 200-member United States delegation to the Paris peace conference. They were angry because Wilson did not name a single Republican to the peace delegation, not even Senator **Henry Cabot Lodge** who was the Senate Majority Leader and chairman of the Senate Foreign Relations Committee. Sixteen Republican senators were **isolationists**. Known as the **Irreconcilables**, they opposed the Treaty. The **Reservationists**, led by Senator Lodge, were a larger group of Republican senators who would, they said, accept the Treaty with changes.

The Struggle to Ratify the Treaty of Versailles

In the summer of 1919, the irreconcilables and the reservationists in the Senate were concerned that joining the League of Nations would involve the United States in future foreign wars. A treaty provision related to the League of Nations said the democratic nations who made up the League had a *moral*, not legal, obligation to aid a member who was under attack. Lodge and others saw this as unconstitutional because it contradicted the right of Congress to declare war.

By September, President Wilson decided that he must bring his message to the people directly. Over the objections of his doctors, the president began an exhausting, fast-paced trip across the country to rally the citizenry in support of the Treaty and the League. In Colorado, he collapsed and had to return to Washington where he suffered a stroke and remained partially paralyzed. The president's illness prevented him from playing an active role in the treaty debate.

In November 1919, two Senate votes on the Treaty failed because Democrats followed Wilson's instructions to vote against ratification that included amendments. Public pressure forced another vote in March of 1920. Once again, and for the last time, ratification failed, with the Democrats voting against Lodge and the reservationists.

THE CHILD WHO WANTED TO PLAY BY HIMSELF.

PRESIDENT WILSON. "NOW COME ALONG AND ENJOY YOURSELF WITH THE OTHER NICE CHILDREN. I PROMISED THAT YOU'D BE THE LIFE AND SOUL OF THE PARTY."

In 1921, the United States made a separate peace with Germany. It never did join the League of Nations. Fundamentally, the nation had voted to retain its traditional foreign policy of nonintervention and acting alone when it did choose to play a role.

The Failure to Ratify the Treaty of Versailles

The failure of the United States to ratify the Treaty of Versailles remains a topic of debate among historians. The Treaty was a victim of traditional foreign policy practices, such as isolationism versus a step toward internationalism and collective security. Partisanship, personalities, feuds, and disillusionment also combined to sink the Treaty.

Some blame falls on Woodrow Wilson and his refusal to compromise. Wilson was a visionary and an idealist. The son of a southern minister, Wilson saw the world in moral terms, supporting good against bad. The votes of the Democrats and the reservationists would have been enough to ratify the treaty. Wilson was inaccessible after his stroke, unable to assess the situation in the Senate and the mood of the country. He communicated almost exclusively through his wife. Under these circumstances, should his fellow Democrats have remained loyal?

Senator Henry Cabot Lodge

Would ratification have been achieved if Wilson had involved Lodge and the Republicans as advisors to the Peace Conference in spite of the hostility between the two men? To what degree did their personal hatred interfere with or even prevent ratification of the Treaty? How valid were Republican concerns that membership in the League of Nations was an "entangling alliance," requiring the involvement of the United States in other nations' conflicts? Did Lodge accurately identify the League's constitutional threat to congressional war-making powers? Would his amendments have resolved this issue?

Woodrow Wilson: His Foreign Policy Legacy

Some historians date the transformation in America's foreign policy from isolationism to internationalism to Woodrow Wilson. They consider the neutrality of the 1920s and 1930s a pause before the United States resumed the role of international leadership introduced by Wilson. They also credit Wilson for being the first major world leader to publicly oppose imperialism and champion **self-determination.** Finally, historians applaud Wilson for recognizing that the modern technology used in the Great War could lead to even worse suffering. Greater effort was required to ensure the creation of an international organization acting collectively for peace.

The primary criticisms of President Wilson's foreign policy come from realists who see Wilson as an idealist and a moralist, unable and unwilling to accept the need to meet force with force in diplomatic affairs. They accuse Wilson of forgetting that the goal of foreign policy is to act in the best interests of the nation.

Unifying Themes
Power, Authority, and Governance

- Was Wilson's Fourteen Points a realistic basis for the peace treaty written at Versailles?
- Why did the Senate fail to ratify the Treaty of Versailles?
- Was the failure to approve the Treaty of Versailles a turning back or a temporary halt in United States foreign policy?

Preparing for the Regents

The history of United States foreign policy can be viewed as a sequence of stages listed below.

1776–1823
Protecting national independence

1824–1897
Fulfilling Manifest Destiny

1898–1918
Emerging global involvement

1919–1940
Limiting international involvement

1941–2017
Accepting world leadership

2017–Present
Debating collective versus unilateral action

- What is always the objective of a nation's versus foreign policy?
- What are the patterns of continuity and of change in U.S. foreign policy?

World War I Affects American Society

Key Concept

11.6c World War I had important social, political, and economic effects on American society.

Lesson Overview

The First World War had profound economic, social, and political effects on American society. Every citizen was called on to participate in the mobilization for the war. The United States economy boomed. Almost five million served in the armed forces. Others stepped in to take their places on the home front, especially women and African Americans. The Great Migration had lasting effects, not only on African Americans, but on all aspects of American society. As in the case of other wars, civil liberties were challenged. One example is the Supreme Court decision in *Schenck* v. *United States* (1919). Unrest continued in the years after the war. A postwar recession and the impact of the Bolshevik Revolution heightened fear of radicals and xenophobia, resulting in the Red Scare.

Unifying Themes

As you review this lesson take special note of the following themes:

- **Geography, Humans, and the Environment** In what ways does the Great Migration illustrate interaction between regions, places, people, and environments?

- **Development and Transformation of Social Structures** How did social and political inequalities affect how the United States conducted World War I? What role did gender, race, ethnicity, and social class play in the United States between 1917 and 1920?

- **Power, Authority, and Governance** How successful was American diplomacy during World War I? Why, how, and by whom were constitutional rights challenged in the United States between 1917 and 1920?

Key People

Woodrow Wilson	Nicola Sacco
Oliver Wendell Holmes, Jr.	Bartolomeo Vanzetti
A. Mitchell Palmer	

Key Terms and Events

Selective Service Act	Espionage Act of 1917
Great Migration	Sedition Act of 1918
nativism	"clear and present danger"
xenophobia	Red Scare
1917 Immigration Act	
literacy test	

Key Supreme Court Cases

As you review this lesson be sure you understand the significance of these key Supreme Court cases:

Schenck v. *United States* (1919)

Abrams v. *United States* (1919)

The United States Mobilizes for War

The United States entered World War I in April 1917. The nation needed, as fast as possible, to recruit, train, and equip an army of close to 5 million, transport it overseas, and continue to support and supply it. At the same time, the United States had to continue sending arms to its allies in Europe. In 1916, even before the United States entered the war, Congress passed the National Defense Act and the Navy Act. Expansion of the armed forces was already underway. That same year Congress also passed the Revenue Act to finance military expansion.

The Draft Issue

In May 1917, Congress passed the **Selective Service Act**, which established a draft. Eventually all males between the ages of 18 and 45 had to register. The constitutionality of the draft was challenged but upheld by the Supreme Court. Those favoring the draft saw it as being fair and democratic. Those opposed to the draft favored voluntary military service. They viewed the draft as an example of the rich and educated exercising power over the poor, the working class, and immigrants.

Mobilizing the Economy and the Workforce

To get the nation's economy geared up for war, certain economic operations were centralized and concentrated through a series of government agencies. Relying on the broad wartime powers of the president, **Woodrow Wilson** used the Council of National Defense to oversee these agencies. For the first time, the government entered fields such as housing and labor relations. It also supervised various public utilities, including the telephone and telegraph.

The War Industries Board (WIB) was created to organize and standardize all aspects of war production. To operate effectively, the WIB worked with newly created agencies such as the War Shipping Board, the Food Administration, the Fuel Administration, and the Railroad Administration. In future times of crisis, such as the Great Depression, this model of cooperation between business and government, refined by experience, was followed.

About 16 percent of male workers went into the military, and their jobs were filled largely by women and African Americans. Immigrants also experienced an increase in employment opportunities.

Women's Role in the War Effort

As men went off to fight in Europe, the roles and contributions of women changed, at least temporarily.

Volunteers Some women contributed to the war effort as volunteers. They used their experience in domestic reform efforts to organize and run volunteer organizations needed to handle new and unexpected problems of war. Some served overseas with groups such as the Red Cross and the Salvation Army.

In the Military More than 21,000 nurses served in the Army Nurse Corps at hospitals in the United States and on active duty in Europe. They were not given a military rank and were denied equal pay. Over 6,000 other women filled clerical jobs in the Army, but as contract civilian employees. The Navy accepted 13,000 women for mostly clerical jobs. These women received military ranks and pay, and, when discharged, veteran's benefits, comparable to those of the Navy men that they replaced.

In the Workplace Opportunities opened for women to move into jobs previously reserved for men, such as in weapons factories. Other examples of jobs new to women and with higher pay were in banks and with the postal service. Most women, however, continued to work in traditionally female jobs, for which there was an increased demand. Only about five percent of the women entering the wartime workforce were new to work outside the home. Between 1910 and 1920, only 500,000 more women were added to the workforce.

Effects Women's contributions to the war efforts were influential in winning ratification of the 19th Amendment. However, for working women World War I did not result in any fundamental and lasting change. At war's end, with the return of male workers, women were expected to quit their jobs or return to more traditional female work. Labor unions lobbied for laws that would limit women holding "men's jobs." In the name of protecting women, laws prohibited overtime and night work for women. Some progress had been made, but most working women remained employed in domestic and personal service or in factory work. American business did continue to grow after the war so that in 1920

- women made up 21 percent of the workforce.
- 25 percent of working women held clerical jobs or worked as telephone operators.
- 13 percent were employed as nurses, teachers, and social workers.

African Americans' Role in the War Effort

Many African Americans felt it was their patriotic duty to serve their country and joined the military. Although subjected to prejudice and discrimination, they served with distinction and honor.

Military Some 2.3 million African Americans registered for the draft and 375,000 served in the military. At the time, open discrimination was common in the segregated American military. Most served in the U.S. Army while only a few served in the Navy and none were accepted by the Marines. Most African American soldiers worked as laborers in noncombat units.

Of the 200,000 African American soldiers sent overseas, only about 42,000 saw combat. They were segregated into two combat divisions and put under command of the French army. The 369th Infantry Regiment, called the *Harlem Hellfighters* by the Germans, fought with distinction in the front lines. Honored by France with its medal for bravery in action, the courageous regiment returned home to New York as heroes. The 369th regimental band brought jazz to France.

Members of the United States Army 369th Infantry Regiment wear their French medals for valor in action.

Political Most African American civil rights leaders supported World War I. To them, "Make the world safe for democracy" meant working for civil rights at home by winning the fight in Europe. Returning African American soldiers sometimes questioned why the liberties and freedoms they had fought to preserve in Europe were denied to them in their own country. Many returned to segregation and Jim Crow laws ready to fight for their own rights as Americans.

Immigrants' Role in the War Effort

The new immigrant population in the United States also chose to support their new country by helping the nation's war effort. They too, however, faced prejudice and discrimination.

In the Military About 500,000 American troops were foreign-born. Although immigrants were 15 percent of the nation's population at the time, about 18 percent of regular soldiers were foreign-born immigrants. African Americans were also overdrafted. 300,000 foreign-born soldiers benefited from laws that allowed them to become citizens because of their military service.

In the Workplace The war had harsh consequences for many immigrant families. Further immigration to the United States came to a halt. Immigrant families already in the country faced fierce social and job discrimination in the antiforeign climate whipped up by the war. All workers were needed in the mobilization for war. Immigrants found jobs in industries such as steel, coal, oil, and lumber. In 1917, immigrants made up one third of the employees at Bethlehem Steel in Pennsylvania.

Unions saw an opportunity to increase membership and recruited immigrants. President Wilson and others advanced labor reforms as part of government efforts to keep factories producing. Contributions of immigrants were highlighted to keep the nation unified.

Underlying tensions remained. Nativism fanned distrust of "hyphenated Americans." When the war ended, businessmen quickly rescinded wartime reforms. Native-born Americans were offered the higher paying jobs, in fact any job, before it went to immigrants returning home. Strikes swept the country.

The Great Migration

The **Great Migration** was a movement between 1915 and 1970 of millions of African Americans from rural Southern areas to urban cities in the North and West. It resulted from **push-pull factors,** such as the combination of the availability of jobs at higher wages elsewhere in the United States and the difficult and often dangerous life in the South from which many African Americans wanted to escape. World War I accelerated the first wave of the Great Migration.

The flow of immigrant labor had ended in 1914 due to the Great War. This created a need for workers to replace those in uniform. Additional workers were needed to meet war production goals. Industries sent agents to the South to recruit African Americans for work in industrial centers such as New York, Boston, Chicago, Cleveland, Detroit, Los Angeles, and Oakland. Southerners objected to this loss of a cheap labor force. At about the same time, floods and destruction of the cotton crop by a beetle, the boll weevil, were devastating Southern agriculture, causing major job losses.

Quality of life issues affected African Americans decisions to leave the South. Northern jobs, even the lowest level ones, paid as much as 70 percent more than wages in the South. Most importantly, Southern Jim Crow laws prevented the exercise of full American citizenship, starting with the fundamental right to vote. The laws limited rights to an education and controlled everyday activities. Parents wanted better economic, educational, and political opportunities, not only for themselves, but for their children. Jim Crow laws were strictly enforced and reinforced with the threat of physical abuse and death. In 1919 alone, 76 African Americans were lynched. In short, the Great Migration was a migration for freedom, a political statement, as well as a search for better economic conditions.

Social Studies Practices
Cause and Effect

- Who participated in the Great Migration from 1915 to 1970?

- What were the causes of it?

- What were the effects of it?

- Was the Great Migration a movement to other parts of the United States or a movement out of the South?

African Americans and the Great Migration

Between 1916 and 1918, close to 500,000 African Americans moved from the South to where there were jobs in the industrial North, Midwest, and West. During the 1920s they were followed by another 700,000. Between 1915 and 1970, slowed only by the Great Depression, some 6 million Southern African Americans emigrated. Today, we see a growing pattern of African Americans returning to the South.

Effects of the Great Migration

African Americans who migrated enjoyed a higher standard of living than in the South. However, they still earned less than white workers and experienced a higher rate of unemployment. Although the newcomers improved their economic situation, they encountered higher prices for rent, food, and other basics. They were not permitted to join labor unions. African Americans still faced segregation, discrimination, and racism. The demography or population pattern of large American cities was altered. The newcomers were concentrated in defined areas in the cities called ghettos. Their reaction was to create in their new urban communities organizations such as the NAACP and the Urban League, movements in civil rights, labor unions, and politics, and the Harlem Renaissance.

Competition for jobs, housing, and political offices increased interracial tensions that, from 1917 through the early 1920s, led to acts of racial violence and riots. In 1917, after experiencing a week of violence that included lynchings and arson, about 6,000 African Americans left East Saint Louis, Illinois. In 1919 there were anti-African American riots in 26 Northern and Southern American cities. And in 1921, 40 city blocks in the prosperous African American Greenwood section of Tulsa, Oklahoma, were looted and burned down. Residents lost their homes, businesses, and, in some cases, their lives.

Patriotism and Propaganda

To President Woodrow Wilson, World War I was a crusade—a war to end all war. His aim was, "The world must be made safe for democracy." These idealistic goals helped mobilize the American people to support the first conflict the United States had ever fought outside the Western Hemisphere.

Propaganda

The United States Committee on Public Information organized a propaganda campaign to encourage patriotism and support for the war. A staff of 150,000 in the United States and overseas used art, music, and words to promote the war effort. Songs, posters, and pamphlets enthusiastically celebrated America, attacked Germany, urged the purchase of Liberty Bonds, and encouraged the conservation of resources needed for war. Planes dropped propaganda leaflets, repeating Wilsonian war aims, over Germany and Austria.

Nativism and Xenophobia

Patriotism was expressed in an outbreak of anti-German **nativism** and **xenophobia** that extended to other immigrant groups. Nativists praise the superiority of America and its way of life and often want to limit

Preparing for the Regents

Throughout United States history there have been movements of people (migrations), voluntary and involuntary, into and within the nation. Some examples are

- Africans' forced migration into enslavement (1619–1808)
- colonial settlement (1600s–1700s)
- forced migration of Native Americans (1800–1880)
- westward expansion (1840–1890)
- rural to urban migration (1870s–1920s)
- European immigration (1840–1860 and 1870–1924)
- Great Migration of African Americans from the South (1915–1930)
- migration west from the Dust Bowl (1930s)
- Second Great Migration of African Americans from the South (1940–1970)
- suburbanization (1945–1960s)
- migration to the Sun Belt (1950–present)
- Documented and Undocumented immigration and asylum seekers (1990–present)

Our Boys in the Trenches

-is there anything they need that you would not give them? Every

LIBERTY BOND

OWNERS WEAR THIS BADGE OF HONOR

YOU buy helps *them* WIN the War. *Buy more Liberty Bonds!*

A liberty bond poster

immigration. American xenophobics, had, in this case, a fear of foreigners and other strangers.

Germans were one of the earliest nationalities to come to America. They arrived in Pennsylvania before the Revolution and again in the 1850s settled in other parts of our nation. However, during World War I, almost nine million German immigrants and those of German ancestry were distrusted as possible spies and traitors. The **Committee on Public Information** raised suspicions with its unrelenting campaign against Germany. Americans shunned German literature and music. Some states banned the teaching of German in schools. Some German language newspapers were driven out of business.

World War I Raises Constitutional Issues

Many well-known Americans were against the nation entering the war. Once the United States committed to the war effort, the social and political climate was one of patriotism and nativism. In addition to those of German background and immigrants in general, socialists, pacifists, anarchists, and anyone opposing or even questioning the war became suspect as possible traitors. Emotions, at times, led to actions that restricted people's civil rights, often in the name of national security.

Opposition to Immigration

Nativism was expressed in the **1917 Immigration Act,** a law passed, over Wilson's veto, even before the United States entered the war. The law extended racial bias against the Chinese and Japanese, creating an Asiatic Barred Zone in East Asia from which immigration to America was prohibited. The law also required a **literacy test.** Its objective was to restrict immigration from Southern and Eastern Europe. It turned out that most could read and write, if not in English, then in the language of their homeland. Of the 800,000 who took the test between 1920 and 1921, only 1,450 were denied entry on the basis of literacy.

The Espionage and Sedition Acts

Two broadly worded acts served to control and punish those who opposed the war effort. The **Espionage Act of 1917** made it a crime to interfere with or to undermine the war effort including by obstructing military operations and recruitment. Inciting insubordination, disloyalty, or mutiny in the military was unlawful. Aiding enemies of the United States during wartime was prohibited. The law allowed the postmaster general to bar "treasonous" materials from the mail.

The **Sedition Act of 1918** amended the Espionage Act to make it a crime "when the United States is at war . . . [to] willfully utter, print, write or publish any disloyal, profane, scurrilous, or abusive language about the form of government of the United States or the Constitution of the United States, or the military or naval forces of the United States, or the flag of the United States, or the uniform of the Army or Navy of the United States."

Under these two acts, the government prosecuted more than 2,100 people and sent 1,500 of them to jail. Pacifists, socialists, and others seen as extremists suffered the most. A special target was the Industrial Workers of the World (IWW), a revolutionary industrial union active in the West. Its leaders were arrested, its strikes broken up, and many of its members interned.

Civil Liberties and *Schenck v. United States*

In 1919, in the landmark case, **Schenck v. United States,** the Supreme Court ruled that free speech could be restricted during wartime. Charles Schenck, the general secretary of the Socialist Party of America, opposed the war. He distributed 15,000

Supreme Court Justice Oliver Wendell Holmes, Jr., known as "the Great Dissenter"

Preparing for the Regents

Stimulus-Based Questions: Supreme Court Opinion

In wartime, civil liberties were restricted. The Red Scare and McCarthyism that followed each of the world wars also led to violations of certain civil liberties.

- According to this Supreme Court ruling, under what circumstances was it constitutional to restrict freedom of speech? Identify the evidence that supports your answer.

- What is the meaning of "to create a clear and present danger" as it is used in the Court decision?

flyers to possible future soldiers urging them to resist the draft. Schenck was prosecuted for violating the Espionage Act. Schenck's argument was that the new law violated his First Amendment right to free speech.

In a unanimous decision, Justice **Oliver Wendell Holmes Jr.,** wrote, "Free speech would not protect a man falsely shouting 'fire' in a theater and causing a panic." Holmes went on to say that in wartime the government has more authority when balanced with constitutional rights. Congress has the right to prevent words that would cause **"a clear and present danger."** Holmes acknowledged that speech cases such as *Schenck* should be assessed on a case-by-case basis. That same year, the Court upheld the Sedition Act, but in that decision the minority expressed concern that freedom of expression was endangered.

. . . the character of every act depends upon the circumstances in which it is done. The most stringent protection of free speech would not protect a man in falsely shouting fire in a theatre and causing a panic. . . . The question in every case is whether the words used are used in such circumstances and are of such a nature as to create a clear and present danger that they will bring about the substantive evils that Congress has a right to prevent. . . . When a nation is at war, many things that might be said in time of peace are such a hindrance to its effort that their utterance will not be endured so long as men fight, and that no Court could regard them as protected by any constitutional right.

— Justice Oliver Wendall Holmes, Jr., *Schenck* v. *United States*, March 3, 1919

In 1920, Congress repealed the Sedition Act. With amendments, the Espionage Act of 1917 remains law. Eugene V. Debs as well as Ethel and Julius Rosenberg were convicted under the Espionage Act. Within months of the *Schenck* decision Justice Holmes dissented in a 7–2 decision in **Abrams v. United States**. He argued that, under the Sedition Act, distributing two leaflets did not constitute a "clear and present danger." Justice Holmes is known as a defender of the First Amendment right of freedom of speech.

Recession, Radicals, Russians, and the Red Scare

In the 1920s, the Red Scare exploited fears about people who were considered un-American, often threatening their civil liberties.

Setting the Red Scare in Motion

Social and economic events within the United States as well as political unrest in Russia set the stage for fear and distrust among Americans.

Dissent Discouraged The imposition in the United States of measures to suppress dissent during World War I took place in what was already a nativist and xenophobic climate. The period before, during, and after the First World War was, as we have seen, one of excitement and patriotic actions but also of individual stress and tensions between Americans. People questioned Who is an American? Minorities experienced discrimination. Protests were often broken up because they were considered unpatriotic and perhaps traitorous. The Espionage and the Sedition Acts suppressed opposition.

Communism In November 1917, the **Bolshevik Revolution,** a second revolution in Russia this time by communists, disrupted the world and threatened the Allied cause in the war. The communist system was openly hostile to American values and beliefs. In America, communists made up less than one percent of the population, but by 1918, an intense fear of communism swept the nation. Also targeted were other groups who were viewed as un-American. Among them were socialists, anarchists, labor leaders, and foreigners. Many xenophobic Americans feared and distrusted foreigners and began to call for the imprisonment or exile of those seen as dissidents, meaning those who disagree or object.

Recession As in the case of most wars, a short recession followed the Great War. The government cancelled $2.5 billion in war contracts within the first month after the armistice. The unemployment rate jumped up. Workers went on strike for better wages in order to keep up with inflation. By March of 1919, inflation was under control and production was starting to increase.

The Red Scare

The **Red Scare,** a crusade against internal enemies was led by Attorney General **A. Mitchell Palmer.** The Red Scare, lasting from late 1918 to 1921, brought together

- the super patriotic sentiment of World War I.
- existing feelings of nativism and xenophobia.
- tensions between Americans.
- fear of radicals in general.
- hysteria over the Bolshevik Revolution and the turmoil it was causing in Europe.
- turmoil caused by job losses, strikes, race riots, and unrest as the war ended.
- concerns due to a postwar recession lasting from late 1918 to 1919.
- vows to avoid future wars as Americans confronted the war deaths and casualties.

The Red Scare was sparked by several events that took place after the war ended. Race riots erupted in more than 25 cities. In Boston, a series of labor strikes climaxed with a walkout by the police. Across the country 365,000 steel workers, mostly immigrants, went on strike to keep the rights that they had won during the war. The companies broke the strike by mobilizing native-born workers in an anti-immigrant campaign that a New York newspaper called "Americanism versus Alienism." Several unexplained bombings, probably by anarchists, added to the hysteria. Many believed that all these events were part of a communist conspiracy.

The Palmer Raids The attorney general ordered the first of the so-called **Palmer Raids** late in 1919. In 33 cities, police without warrants raided the headquarters of communists and other organizations. Eventually they arrested more than 4,000 people, holding them without charges and denying them legal counsel. Some 560 aliens were deported. Palmer's actions and statements soon turned the public against him. However, the Red Scare had lingering effects, discouraging many Americans from speaking their minds freely in open debate, thus squelching their constitutional right to freedom of speech.

Sacco and Vanzetti Closely linked to the Red Scare was the case of **Nicola Sacco** and **Bartolomeo Vanzetti.** These two Italian immigrants—admitted anarchists— were convicted of murder in 1921 in connection with a Massachusetts robbery. Many people questioned the evidence against them, concluding that they were convicted more for their beliefs and their Italian origin than for a crime. In spite of mass demonstrations and appeals, they were executed in 1927. The governor of Massachusetts eventually cleared the two men in 1977.

Base your answers to questions 1 and 2 on the cartoon below and on your knowledge of social studies.

Source: William A. Rogers, "The First Spadeful," 1903

1   What was the goal of President Theodore Roosevelt's action illustrated in this cartoon?

(1) to overthrow the Colombian government and help Panama gain independence

(2) to provide faster access between oceans for commercial and military shipping

(3) to gain access to valuable natural resources in Latin America

(4) to create a strategic advantage in the Spanish-American War

2   Which statement best reflects the outcome of the actions depicted?

(1) Latin American countries became dependent on the U.S. military to defend them against European colonization.

(2) Colombia resented American interference in Latin America and declared war on the United States.

(3) The United States continued to play an active role in the affairs of Panama for much of the 20th century.

(4) Growing anti-imperialism sentiment in the United States eventually led to restoring control of the waterway to Panama.

Base your answers to questions 3 and 4 on the passage below and on your knowledge of social studies.

XIV. A general association of nations must be formed under specific covenants for the purpose of affording mutual guarantees of political independence and territorial integrity to great and small states alike.

Source: President Woodrow Wilson, Fourteen Points, 1918

3   Which statement most accurately describes the reason that Point XIV led to the Senate's rejection of the Treaty of Versailles?

(1) The Senate believed the League of Nations would draw the United States into future international conflicts.

(2) The Senate was unwilling to terminate existing alliances because they were needed to ensure national security.

(3) The Senate felt that Point XIV placed unacceptable restrictions on the nation's imperialist policies.

(4) The Senate feared that European nations would interfere with U.S. policies in the Western Hemisphere.

4   The idea expressed in Point XIV was eventually realized with the formation of the

(1) North Atlantic Treaty Organization

(2) United Nations

(3) National Association for the Advancement of Colored People

(4) European Union

Base your answers to questions 5 and 6 on the passage below and on your knowledge of social studies.

> As to the reasons . . . , undoubtedly, the immediate cause was economic, and the movement began because of floods in middle Alabama and Mississippi and because the latest devastation of the boll weevil came in these same districts. . . . A second economic cause was the cutting off of immigration from Europe to the North and the consequently wide-spread demand for common labor. . . . The third reason has been outbreaks of mob violence in northern and southwestern Georgia and in western South Carolina. These have been the three immediate causes, but back of them is, undoubtedly, the general dissatisfaction with the conditions in the South.

Source: W. E. B. Du Bois, "The Migration of Negroes", *The Crisis*, June 1917

5 What event suggested by Du Bois played a role in the Great Migration?

(1) the First World War

(2) the Immigration Act of 1917

(3) the postwar recession

(4) the Spanish-American War

6 Which effect resulting from the Great Migration was similar to the conditions African Americans were trying to escape?

(1) Competition for jobs led to the same low wages earned in the South.

(2) Farms in the North were soon seriously affected by destructive beetles.

(3) Local governments in northern cities began to pass Jim Crow laws.

(4) Racial tensions led to violence and riots in the North.

Base your answers to questions 7 and 8 on the passage below and on your knowledge of social studies.

> We were tried during a time that has now passed into history. I mean by that, a time when there was hysteria of resentment and hate against the people of our principles, against the foreigner, against slackers, and it seems to me . . . that both you and Mr. Katzmann has done all what it were in your power . . . to agitate still more the passion of the juror, the prejudice of the juror, against us. . . .
>
> But my conviction is that I have suffered for things that I am guilty of. I am suffering because I am a radical and indeed I am a radical; I have suffered because I was an Italian, and indeed I am an Italian; I have suffered more for my family and for my beloved than for myself.

Source: Bartolomeo Vanzetti, statement to the court, April 9, 1927

7 What American attitudes that gained strength during and after the First World War are communicated in Vanzetti's statement?

(1) pacifism and temperance

(2) discrimination and segregation

(3) militarism and nationalism

(4) xenophobia and nativism

8 How did the literacy test of the 1917 Immigration Act reflect Vanzetti's statement?

(1) By its aim to restrict immigrants from southern and eastern Europe, the test demonstrated American prejudice against Italian immigrants.

(2) By its aim to prevent pacifists from entering the United States, the test demonstrated the growing Red Scare in the United States.

(3) By its aim to prevent newcomers from voting in state and national elections, the test demonstrated resentment toward immigrants.

(4) By its aim to control sedition in the United States, the test demonstrated the limiting of free speech.

Base your answers to questions 9 and 10 on the map below and on your knowledge of social studies.

Source: Thomas G. Paterson et al., *American Foreign Policy: A History 1900 to Present*, 1991

9 This map would be most useful for a historian studying

(1) independence movements in Latin America

(2) the North American Free Trade Agreement

(3) humanitarian aid in the Western Hemisphere

(4) United States imperialism in Latin America

10 How did the United States justify most of the actions shown on the map?

(1) by citing the Roosevelt Corollary to the Monroe Doctrine

(2) by deciding it was necessary to respond to German aggression prior to World War I

(3) by designating the actions as part of the United States' Good Neighbor policy

(4) by extending its national policy of containment to Latin America

Base your answers to questions 11 and 12 on the table and image below and on your knowledge of social studies.

Red Cross World War I Statistics

	1914	1918
Number of Chapters	107	3,864
Number of Adult Members	16,708	20,390,173
Number of Junior Red Cross members	n/a	11,418,385
Number of Volunteer Workers	n/a	8,100,000
Number of Paid Staff	25	12,300
Total Contributions Received		$400,000,000
Number of Red Cross nurses enrolled for service with military		23,822
Number of foreign countries in which Red Cross operated		25
American Red Cross war casualties - Female		330

Source: American Red Cross, 2019

Source: Women welders working in the Lincoln Motor Company, circa 1915

11 What statement most accurately reflects the significance of the circumstances shown in the photograph?

(1) Advancements in technology were made as a result of the scientific research conducted by women on the home front.

(2) Wartime labor shortages led to women doing jobs previously reserved for men.

(3) Prejudice against African Americans and immigrants led to only hiring women for work directly related to the war effort.

(4) Factories located near highly populated urban centers benefited most from the funds acquired through liberty bonds.

12 What similar perspective is expressed in both of these documents?

(1) Americans were willing to do whatever was necessary to help the war effort.

(2) Women did most of the work on the home front during World War I.

(3) World War I resulted in a booming economy for the United States.

(4) The war effort in the United States was primarily sustained through volunteerism.

Short Essay Questions

Task: Read and analyze the following documents, applying your social studies knowledge and skills to write a short essay of two or three paragraphs in which you:

- Describe the historical context surrounding documents 1 and 2
- Analyze **Document 2** and explain how *audience*, **or** *purpose*, **or** *bias*, **or** *point of view* affects this document's use as a reliable source of evidence

In developing your short essay answer of two or three paragraphs, be sure to keep these explanations in mind:

Describe means "to illustrate something in words or tell about"

Historical Context refers to "the relevant historical circumstances surrounding or connecting the events, ideas, or developments in these documents"

Analyze means "to examine a document and determine its elements and its relationships"

Explain means "to make plain or understandable; to give reasons for or causes of; to show the logical development or relationship of"

Reliability is determined by how accurate and useful the information found in a source is for a specific purpose

Document 1

But, today, we are raising more than we can consume. Today, we are making more than we can use. Today, our industrial society is congested; there are more workers than there is work; there is more capital than there is investment. We do not need more money—we need more circulation, more employment. Therefore we must find new markets for our produce, new occupation for our capital, new work for our labor. And so, while we did not need the territory taken during the past century at the time it was required, we do need what we have taken in 1898, and we need it now. . . .

Fellow Americans, we are God's chosen people. . . . His great purposes are revealed in the progress of the flag, which surpasses the intentions of Congresses and Cabinets, and leads us like a holier pillar of cloud by day and pillar of fire by night into situations unforeseen by finite wisdom, and duties unexpected by the unprophetic [short-sighted] heart of selfishness.

Source: Senator Albert J. Beveridge, "The March of the Flag" campaign speech, 1898

Document 2

I have read carefully the treaty of Paris [of 1898], and I have seen that we do not intend to free, but to subjugate [control] the people of the Philippines. We have gone there to conquer, not to redeem. . . .

It should, it seems to me, be our pleasure and duty to make those people free, and let them deal with their own domestic questions in their own way. And so I am an anti-imperialist. I am opposed to having the eagle put its talons on any other land.

Source: Mark Twain, *New York Herald*, 1900

Document Analysis for Civic Literacy Essay

Historical Context: Limiting Freedom of Speech

Throughout U.S. history, many constitutional and civic issues have been debated by Americans. One of these constitutional and civic issues is when limits should be placed on free speech.

Task: Read and analyze the documents. Using information from the documents and your knowledge of United States history, write an essay in which you

- Describe the historical circumstances surrounding this constitutional or civic issue
- Explain efforts to address this issue by individuals, groups, and/or governments
- Discuss the extent to which these efforts were successful

Document 1

In its decision in *Schenck* v. *United States* (1919), the Supreme Court found the defendants to be in violation of the Espionage Act of 1917. The Court's unanimous decision supported their conviction as being constitutional and not a denial of their First Amendment rights.

We admit that, in many places and in ordinary times, the defendants, in saying all that was said in the circular, would have been within their constitutional rights. But the character of every act depends upon the circumstances in which it is done. The most stringent protection of free speech would not protect a man in falsely shouting fire in a theatre and causing a panic. . . . The question in every case is whether the words used are used in such circumstances and are of such a nature as to create a clear and present danger that they will bring about the substantive evils that Congress has a right to prevent. It is a question of proximity and degree. When a nation is at war, many things that might be said in time of peace are such a hindrance to its effort that their utterance will not be endured so long as men fight, and that no Court could regard them as protected by any constitutional right. . . . The statute of 1917 . . . punishes conspiracies to obstruct, as well as actual obstruction. If the act (speaking, or circulating a paper), its tendency, and the intent with which it is done are the same, we perceive no ground for saying that success alone warrants making the act a crime.

Source: Justice Oliver Wendell Holmes, Jr., majority opinion in *Schenck* v. *United States* (1919)

1. According to Holmes, when is Congress justified in limiting free speech?

Document 2

In its decision in *Abrams* v. *United States* (1919), the Court found the defendants to be guilty of violating the Espionage Act of 1917. In this case, Justice Oliver Wendell Holmes dissented with the Court's decision.

But, as against dangers peculiar to war, as against others, the principle of the right to free speech is always the same. It is only the present danger of immediate evil or an intent to bring it about that warrants Congress in setting a limit to the expression of opinion where private rights are not concerned. Congress certainly cannot forbid all effort to change the mind of the country. . . .

I think that we should be eternally vigilant against attempts to check the expression of opinions that we loathe and believe to be fraught with death, unless they so imminently threaten immediate interference with the lawful and pressing purposes of the law that an immediate check is required to save the country.

Source: Justice Oliver Wendell Holmes, Jr., dissenting opinion in *Abrams* v. *United States* (1919)

2. In *Abrams*, what is Justice Holmes' definition of when speech can be limited?

Prosperity and Depression

(1920–1939)

Topic Overview

The 1920s and 1930s were decades of cultural and economic changes, resulting in sharp contrasts within the nation. In the 1920s, as the nation became increasingly urbanized, modernized, and commercialized, the American people attempted to return to "normalcy" in foreign and domestic affairs. Many were affected by the First World War, disillusioned and disgusted by the so-called "glory" of war. New technologies created a consumer-goods economy based on mass consumption.

American society was unsettled by these rapid economic, social, and cultural changes. Tensions developed between new and traditional lifestyles. Nativism resurfaced. The nation celebrated the Harlem Renaissance even as African Americans continued to struggle for social and economic equality.

During this period, the nation faced significant domestic challenges, including the Great Depression. All Americans did not share in the good times of the 1920s. Beneath the surface was an economy with structural flaws that brought the Roaring Twenties to an abrupt end with the stock market crash in October 1929. President Herbert Hoover's efforts to control the Depression failed. Starting in 1933, the programs of President Franklin D. Roosevelt, known as the New Deal, worked to overcome the effects of the Great Depression on the United States.

The 1920s: The Clash Between Modern and Traditional Values

Key Concepts

11.7a The 1920s was a time of cultural change in the country, characterized by clashes between modern and traditional values.

Lesson Overview

The Twenties is a decade called the Modern Era, the New Era, the Roaring Twenties, the Jazz Age, the Age of Intolerance, the Lawless Decade, the Machine Age, and the Gilded Age. Taken together, these labels accurately reflect the tensions and conflicts of a decade marked by clashes between modern and traditional values. Following World War I, the United States returned to what President Harding called "normalcy." However, the impact of the war, Prohibition, the new age of consumerism, the automobile, and the growth of suburbs contributed to the creation of a different and new national lifestyle.

While transportation and communications technology served to unite the nation, a clash of values between the new urban-centered life and the legacy of the traditional rural and small-town life exposed contradictions and caused uneasiness and conflict. Women's efforts at self-expression and their changing roles in American society became a controversial symbol of the Roaring Twenties and its values. The Scopes trial highlighted widening differences in religious views. Nativism saw expression in the resurgence of the Ku Klux Klan and the restrictive immigration acts of 1921 and 1924.

Unifying Themes

As you review this lesson take special note of the following themes:

- **Individual Development and Cultural Identity** How did culture, time, place, and geography affect women's personal identity during the Twenties?

- **Time, Continuity, and Change** What were the major causes of the competing interpretations of events that divided the nation in the Twenties? What were the consequences of the resulting clash of values?

- **Civic Ideals and Practices** In the 1920s, how were the civil liberties of socialists, anarchists, labor leaders, foreigners, Catholics, Jews, and African Americans threatened?

Key People

Warren G. Harding

Calvin Coolidge

Henry Ford

F. Scott Fitzgerald

Ernest Hemingway

Key Terms and Events

"normalcy"

Teapot Dome Scandal

pandemic

"Lost Generation"

consumer-oriented economy

mass consumption

Jazz Age

flapper

Kellogg-Briand Peace Pact

Washington Naval Treaty

Prohibition

Anti-Saloon League

Eighteenth Amendment

Twenty-first Amendment

Scopes Trial

Ku Klux Klan

Immigration Act of 1924

1919	1921	1924	1926	1928
18th Amendment ratified	Emergency Quota Act passed; Washington Conference began	Teapot Dome Scandal indictments; National Origins Act; Coolidge elected president	U.S. Marines oversee Nicaragua elections	U.S. signs Kellogg-Briand Pact

1919	1920	1921	1922	1923	1924	1925	1926	1927	1928	1929	1930

1920	1923	1925	1927	1929
Warren G. Harding elected president; 19th Amendment ratified	Calvin Coolidge succeeds Harding	Scopes Trial	Sacco and Vanzetti executed	Stock Market crash

Preparing for the Regents

Stimulus-Based Question: Timeline

Based on the timeline:

- What events on the timeline are examples of a clash of values?

The State of the Nation in the 1920s

The 1920 landslide election of Republican President **Warren G. Harding** and Vice President **Calvin Coolidge** represented the desire of many Americans to remove themselves from the pressures of world politics and the idealistic goals of the Progressive Era. Progressive reform would continue but at a slower pace and only at state and local levels. The nation struggled to come to terms with the cultural and economic effects of the First World War.

Presidents Warren G. Harding and Calvin Coolidge

President Harding and later President Coolidge stood for minimal government. Inaction or cutting back were their government policies. The need for more individual freedom was often cited as a reason for a government action or failure to act. During their administrations, Prohibition lacked rigorous enforcement as did Progressive Era laws.

President Harding was an Ohio newspaper publisher with little experience in politics. Historians credit him for pardoning socialist Eugene V. Debs, who had been jailed for opposing the war, for supporting anti-lynching legislation, and for appointing several dedicated people to his cabinet. Harding campaigned on the slogan **"Return to Normalcy,"** meaning that the nation should go back to its usual pre-war conditions.

The Harding administration was one of scandal and political corruption. Most historians consider it a failed presidency due to a leader who lacked both a vision for the nation and a sense of personal morality. The president gave political jobs to members of the so-called Ohio Gang, corrupt associates who took advantage of him. For example, the head of the Veterans Bureau was convicted and imprisoned for selling hospital supplies for his own profit. The **Teapot Dome Scandal** ended in the conviction of Secretary of the Interior Albert Fall for accepting bribes and no-interest loans from two oil executives in exchange for leasing them government-owned petroleum reserves in Teapot Dome, Wyoming, and Elk Hills, California.

When Harding died in office in 1923, Vice President Calvin Coolidge became president. In 1924, Coolidge won election as president. Coolidge is best known for his strong commitment to business interests and his related laissez-faire approach to the economy.

The Great War Leads to Cultural Changes

World War I triggered a number of the cultural changes in the American society of the 1920s. Young women who had patriotically entered the workforce or the military during the war and young men back home from war did not want to return to the old ways and rules. Many of them felt they had seen too much and done too much in a war for the ideas and ideals of their parents' generation.

Election of 1920

Republican Warren G. Harding 76% of electoral vote

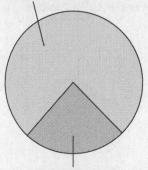

Democrat James M. Cox 24% of electoral vote

Preparing for the Regents

Stimulus-Based Questions: Pie Graph and Speech

Interpreting Evidence

America's present need is not heroics, but healing; not nostrums, [remedies] but normalcy; not revolution, but restoration; not agitation, but adjustment; not surgery, but serenity; not the dramatic, but the dispassionate.

—Warren G. Harding, May 14, 1920

Examine the pie graph and the quotation.

- How does the pie graph support the statement that the 1920 election was a landslide in favor of "normalcy"?

President Calvin Coolidge

Disillusionment The deaths of over 116,000 American military personnel, of whom 45,000 were victims of the 1918–1919 influenza **pandemic,** led to some Americans deciding to live life with abandon, not with an eye to the future. Disillusionment was fed by having witnessed the horrors of a war that wiped out an entire generation of European men. Seeing soldiers who were left disabled, shell shocked (now called PTSD), or injured from poison gas attacks angered and alienated other Americans, as did the 675,000 deaths in the nation from influenza, with high mortality (death) rates, not only for the elderly, but also for children under 5 and for healthy 20 to 40 years old.

Isolationism Feelings of disillusionment also fueled a national movement of postwar **isolationism** different from the traditional American policy of **nonintervention.** Some Americans became members of the "Lost Generation," experiencing isolation on a personal level and expressing their feelings in the literature and art of the 1920s.

Intolerance The intolerance toward **"hyphenated Americans,"** aimed during the war at German-Americans and Austrian-Americans, spread during the 1920s. Nativism, racism, and extreme nationalism saw expression in the Red Scare, the "new" Ku Klux Klan, the Sacco and Vanzetti case, and the Quota Acts. The First Amendment right to dissent, limited during the war, remained in jeopardy. Isolationists labeled as "un-American" the actions and words of those with whom they disagreed. They continued their wartime demand for **one hundred percent Americanism.**

The Cultural Trends of the Roaring Twenties

In the Roaring Twenties, urban, industrial American society welcomed a new lifestyle and adopted new cultural values. Risk-taking, action, freedom, excitement, innovation, experimentation, self-expression, and individualism characterized changes in lifestyle, values, morals, and manners. Wealth, possessions, having fun, and sexual freedom were also some of the new values. They were expressed in fashion, art, music, architecture, and literature.

The State of the Economy Encourages Change

When the war ended, the United States was the most powerful nation in the world. In part, that power rested on the massive growth of the American economy during the war. American prosperity continued into the 1920s. The economy boomed even though government spending decreased. Taxes were lowered. Unemployment was low. Wages were up. The work week was shorter. Many Americans had more leisure time as well as money beyond what they needed for the basics of life. They were spending this "disposable income" to engage in forms of entertainment, such as seeing movies, made possible by technology.

The Role of Technology in Cultural Change

Technology led to the invention of a wider range of products for the home and family. Mass production created a **consumer-oriented economy,** one in which a variety of goods, costing less, were available to more Americans. The technology-driven consumer goods economy was sold to the public by advertising new products as a necessary part of the new culture. Families spent a larger proportion of their income on new **consumer goods,** such as automobiles, appliances, radios, phonographs, and ready-to-wear clothing. American society became one of **mass consumption.** Technological advancements transformed American lifestyle in the 1920s. Technology was, in addition, one of the causes of the social, cultural, and economic upheavals of the decade.

The Effects of New Industries on American Life

The Automobile Industry:

1. stimulated the steel, rubber, paint, glass, and oil industries
2. accelerated a middle-class move to the suburbs that fueled a real estate boom
3. led to an increase in highways and a decline in railroad construction and use
4. produced tractors to replace horses on farms
5. increased social equality as low prices made cars available to Americans at almost all income levels
6. stimulated installment buying
7. contributed to growing sophistication of advertising techniques
8. expanded cities into larger urban areas
9. stimulated development of services such as gas stations, motels, supermarkets, and shopping malls
10. gave greater independence to women and teenagers, changing family life

The Electrical Industry:

1. changed homes, businesses, and cities through electric lights
2. helped double business productivity through electric power
3. transformed life and leisure with electric-powered durable goods such as washing machines, stoves, vacuum cleaners, refrigerators, and irons
4. stimulated installment buying
5. connected people and eased rural isolation through the telephone

Radio and Motion Pictures:

1. helped erase regional differences and homogenize (make very similar) American culture
2. increased people's expectations, often unrealistically
3. helped end rural isolation
4. helped popularize ragtime and jazz
5. provided an outlet for advertising
6. increased interest in politics and spectator sports
7. created nationally known celebrities—stars of radio, sports, and movies

Preparing for the Regents

Stimulus-Based Questions: Chart

In the 1920s, radio, movies, and telephones helped produce a more national culture in which regional differences became less distinct.

- According to the chart, in what ways did the automobile, electrical industry, radio, and motion pictures influence the lifestyle of the 1920s?

- What technology since the 1920s has resulted in further national and even international cultural homogenization?

Marketing and Advertising Influences Cultural Change

The automobile, radio, and movies were all invented well before the First World War, but it was not until the 1920s that they were commercially successful. **Consumerism** flourished in the Roaring Twenties. Technology influenced marketing strategies and made available new means of advertising, such as on the radio. Improvements in print technology made possible more and cheaper ads in magazines and newspapers. Brand names and brand loyalty were promoted. Often goods were purchased over time through installment buying, a type of buying on credit. As a result, between 1919 and 1929 the amount of money Americans spent on household appliances grew by more than 120 percent.

The Automobile Impacts American Culture

Led by **Henry Ford** and the automobile industry, technology developed **standardization** of parts, **mass production,** and the moving **assembly line,** resulting in lower automobile prices. Just over 9 million cars were registered in the United States in 1920 compared to almost 27 million by 1930. The effect of the automobile on the American culture of the 1920s is best expressed in the fact that by 1925 a car was considered a necessity by people at all income levels.

Social Studies Practices

Gathering and Interpreting Evidence

Consider that in the 1920s

- 15 million cars were sold.
- 80 percent were bought on credit.
- a Model T Ford cost $290 in 1920.
- more than 63 percent of U.S. homes had electricity by the end of the decade.
- 10 million families owned radios by 1929.

What additional information do you need in order to have a more complete picture of the effect of new technologies in the 1920s?

Effects of the Automobile The 1920 census made it official that the United States, for the first time in its history, was an urban rather than a rural nation. More than half of the population now lived in an urban center. It was the mass-produced automobile that

- made the nation more mobile with easier access between urban and rural areas.
- disrupted family stability as it was now possible to go off on one's own.
- offered young family members privacy in a place away from parents and chaperones.
- expanded urban areas to include **suburbs** that grew even faster than cities.
- sparked a building boom in real estate and the construction of a national highway system.
- stimulated the growth of industries, such as steel, plate glass, rubber, and oil.
- created new service businesses, such as motels, shopping malls, and gas stations.
- served as an equalizer, with an automobile available to middle-income Americans because of its low price.

A National Culture Develops

Radio and the movies, as well as magazines and newspapers with nationwide circulation, helped to spread the trends and ideas of the changing national culture. The techniques used were very similar to those used by the Committee of Public Information during the Great War. Aspects of the new national culture, such as jazz, were also transmitted via the phonograph and the radio. Young people shared the current trends as they gathered for entertainment at sporting events, dance halls, and speakeasies.

Cultural Conformity Grows The new technology also helped to make American culture more uniform. Americans from one coast to the other tended to use the same products, wear the same styles, see the same movies, and listen and dance to the same music. Regional and class differences were blurred. On the other hand, the easy availability of the latest sounds, scenes, styles, and products made it easier for the traditionalist questioning the modernist to keep up with the changes in American culture. And, young modernists could choose to face or avoid the basic contradiction that while they wanted more individualism and self-expression, they were conforming to a peer culture's code of how to dress, what to buy, and how to behave.

The Cultural Values in the 1920s

TRADITIONAL CULTURE	MODERN VALUES
Honored the Old Ways	Rejected the Old Ways
Community Values	Individual Values
Looked Back	Looked Ahead
Rural	Urban
Older Generation	Younger Generation
Fundamentalist Religion	Modern Religion
Literal Interpretation of the Bible	Science and Technology
Thrift and Self-Denial	Materialism
Old-fashioned Good Manners	Often Deliberately Unmannerly
Conformity	Experimentation
Regression	Revolution
Moderation	Excess
Fidelity and Modesty	Promiscuity
Simple Life	Exciting Life
Pro-Prohibition	Anti-Prohibition

The Clash of Cultural Values in the 1920s

The 1920s was a time of revolution, experimentation, and individualism. Science and technology challenged the old beliefs and way of life. Many felt disillusionment, isolation, and unhappiness. Prohibition had finally succeeded. Red Scare hysteria, the Ku Klux Klan, racism, creationist fundamentalist churches, nativism, and one hundred percent Americanism flourished. In this climate, values clashed.

Cultural Trends Reflected in Arts and Literature

The emerging American cultural changes were reflected in both the media, such as movies, and the literature and arts of the decade. Division emerged as the cultural changes were accepted by some and condemned by other Americans.

The Radio and the Phonograph With a shorter work week and with additional paid vacation, Americans had more leisure time. Between 1923 and 1930, 60 percent of American families purchased radios. Listening to the radio and to records together became the center of family entertainment.

The Movies During the 1920s, movies such as *The Ten Commandments* and the first movie with sound, *The Jazz Singer,* drew as many as 40 million people a week to theaters. The major themes were crime, sex, and love. Movies spread modern ideas. From movies, flappers learned about fashion, style, and modern dating rather than old-fashioned "courting." Americans idolized Charlie Chaplin and heroines such as Mary Pickford and Clara Bow. Protests came from church leaders who condemned scandals involving movie stars and demanded censorship of what they considered scandalous films. The film industry agreed to self-censorship of sexually overt scenes and changed movie endings so that the badly behaved were punished, or at least not rewarded.

Individualism and Heroes The focus on freedom and individualism in the 1920s is seen in the American public's admiration of movie celebrities and sports figures. Babe Ruth was known and applauded across the nation. After his 1927 solo transatlantic flight, **Charles Lindbergh** became a national hero.

Literature The conflict and concern created by changing American values also saw expression in literature. American writers of the 1920s reacted to the Great War by rejecting the values of that generation. They protested the effects of technology and mass consumption on the postwar generation. They criticized the business mentality, the conformity of the times, and the preoccupation with material things. **F. Scott Fitzgerald** named the Twenties the **Jazz Age** and wrote about it in his novels, such as *The Great Gatsby*.

Some writers of the 1920s, such as **Ernest Hemingway,** became **expatriates,** leaving the United States to live in Europe. These expatriates are referred to as the Lost Generation, which is also a name given to Americans and Europeans who came of age during and right after the First World War. Some of the most enduring works of American literature were written in the 1920s.

Some Leading American Writers of the 1920s

Willa Cather	novelist	*My Antonía*
F. Scott Fitzgerald	novelist	*The Great Gatsby*
Ernest Hemingway	novelist	*A Farewell to Arms*
Langston Hughes	poet, novelist	*The Weary Blues*
Zora Neale Hurston	novelist, folklorist	*Their Eyes Were Watching God*
Sinclair Lewis	novelist	*Main Street, Babbitt*
Eugene O'Neill	playwright	*Desire Under the Elms*
Edith Wharton	novelist	*The Age of Innocence*

Art and Architecture The experimentation, alienation, protest, and yearning for individualism of the Twenties was expressed in art movements, such as cubism, surrealism, realism, and Art Deco. Artist Edward Hopper, known for his scenes of isolation and loneliness, and the architect Frank Lloyd Wright are two famous figures of the 1920s.

Women and Their Changing Roles in the 1920s

The conflict between modern and traditional values in the 1920s found expression in the contradictory roles of women. A sign of the changes taking place in the United States of the Twenties was the dramatic shift in women's dress, appearance, behavior, and attitude.

Flappers Influence and Represent the Roaring Twenties

The popular image of young women in the 1920s was the **flapper,** a young, pretty woman with bobbed hair, loose-fitting lightweight clothes, silk stockings rolled up and held with garters, and raised hemlines. She dressed for comfort. She cut off her long hair. She sometimes revealed her knees. She drank alcohol, she smoked, she wore makeup, she drove a car, she danced the Charleston and the fox trot to jazz with her dance partner up close, and she thought for herself.

Although flappers were only a minority of their generation, they both influenced and represented the times. Some women engaged in practices such as drinking and smoking prior to the 1920s. What was different in the Twenties was that the flappers were middle-class, upper middle-class, and upper-class women. They smoked, and in public, at a time when only men smoked. They drank with men as well, and in dance halls and speakeasies. And, before the end of the decade, their mother's generation had adopted some variation of the new ways as did many young working-class women.

The flapper was declaring her new sense of independence and self-expression. She was making a statement of freedom, even rebellion. The flapper became the symbol for the Roaring Twenties, seen as marking the beginning of a modern age. As such, the flapper represented another example in the debate over traditional versus modern values that was dividing the nation.

The 1920s Bring Lifestyle Changes for Women

In the 1920s, women had more choices in life, and there were some attempts to redefine gender roles.

Women in the Workforce In the 1920s, many women migrated to urban centers, where there were jobs and a fast-paced lifestyle. Some earned enough to live on their own in an apartment or a boarding house. By 1930, 10.7 million women were working outside the home, making up almost 25 percent of the workforce. Most working women were single, widowed, or divorced. By 1930, women earned 40 percent of college undergraduate degrees. Many of these college-educated women became teachers, nurses, and social workers, traditional female professional occupations.

Working-class women found jobs in factories, but fewer than 20 percent held the better-paying skilled worker positions. Changes in technology and management created opportunities for middle-class women in white-collar and service industry jobs. They included work as secretaries, salespeople, telephone operators, and beauticians. Because these jobs were labeled "female only," even in hard times women were able to be hired for these and other new occupations.

The Chrysler Building in New York City is a classic example of the Art Deco style.

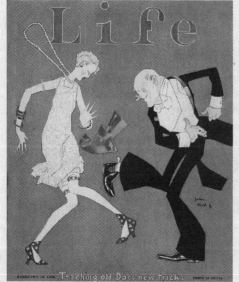

Teaching Old Dogs New Tricks

Women as Wives In the 1920s, a woman's role as a wife was given increased importance with more emphasis placed on companionship in marriage. Families changed during this period as divorce and family planning became more acceptable. Family size decreased; only 20 percent of women who married during the 1920s had five or more children. However, divorce laws continued to favor men. While, by 1930, about one in six married women worked, middle-class wives were expected to stay at home rather than enter the workforce.

Women as Homemakers In earlier times, the family was a producing unit, working together to grow and process much of its needs. Now it was a consuming unit. Marketing and advertising appeals flooded the media, encouraging consumers to buy more goods. With electric washing machines, vacuum cleaners, stoves, and refrigerators, household chores did not require so much time, and there was less need for servants. On the other hand, the typical homemaker now was expected to handle almost all the household tasks herself and to meet higher standards of cleanliness.

Women and Politics In 1920, with the passage of the **Nineteenth Amendment,** women voted in a national election for the first time. Women did not vote in large numbers, nor did they vote as a bloc. They did play a larger public role as reformers, lobbyists, politicians, and political workers. Women ran for and won elective office, primarily at the local level but also for state positions. But, in 1928, there were only seven women in the House of Representatives. Some women became active in political parties. In the 1920s, women reformers developed interest groups to lobby in Washington, D.C. They were attempting reform in a time of deep divisions across the nation.

- From 1920 to 1930, the **Women's Joint Congressional Committee** was one of the most powerful lobbies in Washington, D.C. The Committee secured passage, for only ten years, of a law aimed at reducing infant mortality. It failed in its efforts to pass a child labor law amendment and to create a department of education. As the legacy of the Red Scare continued, the Women's Joint Congressional Committee was accused of being a force for Bolshevism in the United States.

- In 1920, the National American Woman Suffrage Association turned to civic participation in government rather than backing parties and candidates, reorganizing itself as the nonpartisan **League of Women Voters**.

- In 1923, Alice Paul's **National Woman's Party** (NWP) became a single-issue party supporting an **equal rights amendment** to the Constitution. It failed to become law and led to bitter disagreement. Many feminists supported it, but other feminists opposed it because they believed it would do away with special laws protecting female workers.

- In 1928, the pacifist **Women's International League for Peace and Freedom** (WILPF) supported the **Kellogg-Briand Peace Pact** of 1928 that outlawed war except in self-defense. In 1922, the WILPF had supported the 1922 **Washington Naval Treaty,** or the Five Power Treaty, limiting construction of navy ships. The organization and its leader, Jane Addams, were also accused of lack of patriotism and of Bolshevism.

- African American women in the **National Association of Colored Women** (NACW) worked, with little success and help from white women's organizations, against Jim Crow disenfranchisement laws.

Change Raises Constitutional, Civic, and Legal Questions

During the Twenties, serious constitutional, civic, and legal questions were generated, debated, and sometimes resolved. Whether the issue was prohibition, creationism versus evolution, the Red Scare, the Ku Klux Klan, or restricting immigration, tensions, contradictions, distrust, and bitterness often remained.

Using the Law to Confront Problems

Questions that were raised during the Great War and the Red Scare, such as "Who is an American?" and "What is one hundred percent Americanism?," remained. The Bolshevik Revolution, communism, anarchism, and what was considered radicalism continued to raise fears of the unknown. The changing modern values, the technology-driven economy, the Great Migration, and the influx of Southern and Eastern European immigrants caused unease about what was new and different. For some Americans, these tensions took the form of nativism, racism, and intolerance of differences in religion, morals, cultures, and politics. For all Americans, legal questions needed to be confronted.

Prohibition: A Public Health or a Moral Issue?

Prohibition was aimed at African Americans, immigrants, working-class men, and city dwellers. If the lifestyle of the flapper society celebrated the modern, urban, consumption-based culture of the 1920s, national prohibition was a victory for traditional rural culture over urban life, for native-born Americans over immigrants, for fundamentalists over modern religion, for Southerners and Westerners over the Northerners, Easterners, and Midwesterners.

Legislating Prohibition The temperance movement began as a religious movement based in Protestant evangelical churches and rooted in the American reform tradition of the early 1800s. In the late 1890s and early 1900s, with the support of the Populist and Progressive social reform movements, the temperance cause gained strength. Success became a realistic possibility in 1895 when the **Anti-Saloon League,** a national, single-issue, pressure group, began lobbying for prohibition on the state and national levels (see Topic 5). In 1919, aided by the passage of the income tax amendment, the suffrage amendment, nativism, and the super patriotism of World War I, the **Eighteenth Amendment** to the Constitution was ratified.

The Eighteenth Amendment went into effect in January 1920. It imposed a nationwide prohibition of "the manufacture, sale, or transportation of intoxicating liquors within, the importation . . . into, or . . . the exportation . . . from the United States." To implement Prohibition, Congress passed the **National Prohibition Act,** known as the **Volstead Act,** over President Wilson's veto.

The Successes of Prohibition For thirteen years, nationwide prohibition did change drinking habits. Statistics show that Prohibition was a public health success. It slowed the manufacture and sale of alcoholic beverages so that alcohol consumption, especially among working-class Americans, dropped by between 30 and 50 percent nationally. Except for a brief time in the 1970s, alcoholic consumption has not returned to pre-Prohibition levels. The number of deaths from alcoholism and drinking-related diseases also fell sharply. Tainted illegal liquor did, however, cause blindness, paralysis, and death.

Social Studies Practices
Cause and Effect

- How did the income tax amendment, the suffrage amendment, nativism, and the super patriotism of World War I each influence the passage of the Eighteenth Amendment?

- Why is the reaction to the Eighteenth Amendment often compared to the reaction to the 1859 Fugitive Slave Law?

Economic Effects of Prohibition The Eighteenth Amendment forced an entire industry, the fifth largest in the country, out of business. Most of the nation's distilleries, wineries, and breweries closed. The number of alcohol wholesalers dropped by 96 percent and local retailers by 90 percent. It is estimated that the federal government lost $11 billion in tax revenue due to Prohibition while spending over $300 million to enforce it.

Social Effects of Prohibition The male-only rural and urban saloon was a victim of Prohibition. Some 300,000 saloons, often financed by breweries, were owned by first-generation Americans. Saloons were a social institution: a hangout for working men, but also an organizing center for unions and political parties. With Prohibition, liquor was instead sold illegally in dance halls and speakeasies. These became places frequented by college students and other young people, including women. This more positive attitude toward drinking was promoted by the new mass culture through the literature, movies, newspapers, and magazines of the Twenties. Eventually, changes in attitudes toward drinking led to support for repeal.

Enforcement of Prohibition Even though Prohibition was never supported by a majority of the population, most Americans obeyed the new law. However, others created a national organized crime syndicate to make possible the production, transportation, and sale of illegal alcoholic beverages. The public began to worry that Prohibition promoted crime. "Bootleggers" and owners of the speakeasies made huge amounts of money from crime. Law enforcement by 2,500 federal agents and state officials was criticized as ineffective. Enforcement was effective where evenly enforced but was often applied against the poor, immigrants, and African Americans, not the wealthy. Enforcement was to be carried out by both federal and state officials, but neither received enough funding. There were documented incidences of bribery and corruption of both state and federal agents and government officials. While some agents were honored for their work, the methods and behavior of other agents raised concerns of violation of individual rights.

Prohibition Ends The **Eighteenth Amendment** was repealed in December 1933 when the ratification of the **Twenty-first Amendment** ended Prohibition. Americans had raised fundamental questions about the maintenance of law and order in the face of crime and open, public disobedience of the law. They had questioned the limits Prohibition placed on individual freedom and asked if it was the role of government to legislate moral and religious values. These factors led to the repeal of the Eighteenth Amendment. But the immediate cause was the **Great Depression.** In the 1920s, the income tax amendment supplied enough money to the federal government to allow for the loss of tax revenue from alcoholic beverages. But the Great Depression reduced by as much as 33 percent the amount collected in federal income taxes, and no money was paid into the U.S. Treasury from capital gains on stocks. The repeal of Prohibition would also mean jobs in a rebuilt alcoholic beverage industry. Some farmers would benefit with the need for additional grain, particularly barley and corn.

The Scopes Trial

In 1925, the Tennessee legislature passed the Butler Law, which forbade the teaching of Darwin's theory of evolution in any public school or university in the state. The law raised a First Amendment freedom of religion issue.

Creationism Versus Evolution The 1925 **Scopes Trial** was a nationwide media event pitting modern against traditional views, the scientific ideas of Darwinian evolution against the Protestant fundamentalist view of biblical creationism.

Scopes trial lawyers Clarence Darrow (left) and William Jennings Bryan

The American Civil Liberties Union (ACLU) offered to pay all of the expenses of a teacher who would challenge the 1925 Tennessee state law. Dayton, Tennessee, volunteered to be the scene of the trial in order to bring people and publicity to the town. Town leaders asked John Scopes, a new, young biology teacher and football coach to deliberately violate the law. He agreed. At that point, two nationally known lawyers offered to participate in the trial. Scopes was represented by the famous criminal and labor trial lawyer **Clarence Darrow.** The prosecution accepted the assistance of **William Jennings Bryan,** a three-time presidential candidate and firm believer in fundamentalist Christianity.

The trial drew over 100 newspapers and 1,000 people to Dayton. It was the first trial broadcast live on the radio. The judge refused to allow testimony from Darrow's twelve scientific experts. He ruled that the only question was whether or not Scopes had violated the state law. Darrow called Bryan as a witness and examined him about the Bible and creationism. In the process, Darrow's evolutionist views were spread by radio across the nation, while Bryan's confused testimony weakened his fundamentalist arguments. Scopes was convicted and fined $100. On appeal, the Tennessee Supreme Court upheld the Butler Law but acquitted Scopes on a technicality.

Finding that it violated the Constitution's First Amendment establishment clause, in 1968 the United States Supreme Court voided an Arkansas law banning teaching evolution. In its decision in *Epperson* v. *Arkansas* (1968), the Court stated that "Arkansas' law cannot be defended as an act of religious neutrality. . . The law's effort was confined to an attempt to blot out a particular theory because of its supposed conflict with the Biblical account, literally read."

The Revival of the Ku Klux Klan Threatens Civil Liberties

In the 1920s, white supremacist and nativist attitudes encouraged a powerful but short-lived revival of the **Ku Klux Klan.** The first Ku Klux Klan, the vigilante organization active during Reconstruction, had died out in the late 1800s. A reorganized Klan, a secret organization, was formed in 1915 and by 1925 had grown to two to possibly five million members, mostly middle-class men. Like the earlier Klan and the Red Scare, the Ku Klux Klan exploited fears about people who they considered to be un-American, often threatening their civil liberties. While it conducted community activities and involved itself in politics at all levels of

Social Studies Practices
Interpreting Evidence

The Knights of the Ku Klux Klan is a movement devoting itself to the needed task of developing a genuine spirit of American patriotism. . . . They are to organize the patriotic sentiment of native-born white, Protestant Americans for the defense of distinctively American institutions.

—*The Klansman's Manual,* 1925

- What does the Klan mean by "patriotism"?
- Identify the evidence that supports your answer.

government, the Klan also engaged in lynching, whipping, beating, cross burning, and other forms of mob violence against those who, in the Klan's view, were not one hundred percent American.

Lynching is a form of intimidation and terrorism—murder by a mob by torturing and/or hanging a person without due process and in violation of the rule of law. Between 1882 and 1968 at least 4,742 people, of whom 73% were African Americans, were lynched in 46 of the 50 states but concentrated in former Confederate states. Because less than ten percent of those identified as leaders of a lynch mob have been convicted on a local or state level, since 1900 more than 200 anti-lynching bills have been introduced in the Congress. None were passed. Finally, in March 2022 the most recent bill, the Emmett Till Antilynching Act, passed both the House and the Senate and was signed by President Biden. The Act makes lynching a federal civil rights hate crime.

Whom the Ku Klux Klan Opposed To the Klan, the only true Americans were white, Protestant, and American born. Fundamentalist and extremist, the Klan of the 1920s targeted not only African Americans but also Catholics, Jews, and immigrants, especially those from Southern and Eastern Europe. To the Klan, true Americans were also in danger from the "new woman," evolutionists, unions, bootleggers, gamblers, corrupt politicians, lawbreakers, movies, "immorality," foreigners, pacifists, communists, internationalists, and anarchists.

Political Successes of the Second Klan The second Ku Klux Klan expanded beyond the South. In the Southwest and Midwest, it controlled, for a while, politics in the states of Indiana, Texas, Oklahoma, and Colorado. It joined with other organizations to achieve passage of Prohibition and of the Immigration Act of 1924. The Klan played a major role in both the 1924 and 1928 Democratic Conventions. In 1924, it kept the presidential nomination from Al Smith, the Catholic, anti-Prohibition governor of New York, and in 1928, worked to defeat Smith after he was nominated. The Klan led the temporarily successful 1922 effort requiring that all Oregon students attend public school. The aim of the law was to eliminate religious schools. In 1925, a unanimous U.S. Supreme Court declared the Oregon law unconstitutional, a violation of the First Amendment.

The End of the Second Ku Klux Klan By 1930, the second Ku Klux Klan had faded, its membership under 50,000. Financial scandal, embezzlement, kickbacks, and the murder conviction of a nationally known Klan leader all contributed to its fall. A third Klan formed in the 1950s and 1960s to oppose the civil rights movement.

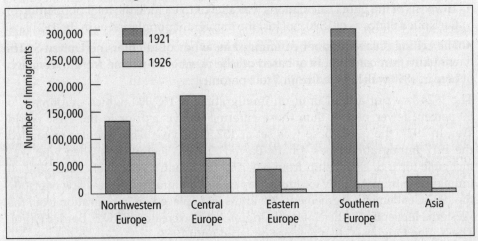

Immigration to the United States, 1921 and 1926

Unifying Themes
Social Structures

- What are the similarities and differences in concern about foreigners and foreign ideas during these events in U.S. history? Consider the historical context and the identity of the foreigners.
- Does historical evidence support adding or eliminating any event?
- 1790s: Alien and Sedition Acts
- 1840s: nativism and the Know-Nothings
- 1882 and 1907: Chinese Exclusion Act and Gentlemen's Agreement
- 1917–1918: suppression of dissent during World War I
- 1920s: Ku Klux Klan, Sacco and Vanzetti case, National Origins Acts
- 1940s: internment of Japanese Americans during World War II
- 1950s: McCarthyism

Unifying Themes
Movement

During the 1920s, immigration from the Western Hemisphere was not limited. Large numbers of Mexicans moved into southwestern cities and Puerto Ricans moved into New York City, most in search of economic opportunities.

- What are the most dramatic changes pictured on the chart?
- What changes were made to immigration laws in the 1920s? Why?

The First Restrictions on European Immigration

The nativism and xenophobia seen in the Red Scare, the Sacco-Vanzetti case, the one hundred percent Americanism movement, and the second Ku Klux Klan were firmly and finally expressed in 1920s immigration legislation. In 1921 and 1924, the first limits on immigration from specific parts of Europe closed the United States to many immigrants.

National Quotas on Immigration After World War I, European immigration resumed, but there was less of a need for workers. In a turbulent time, it was easy to blame real and perceived social and economic problems on immigrant "outsiders." In the postwar recession, immigrants were accused of taking jobs from returning soldiers. Fear of radicals, intolerance, and a desire for conformity fanned the demand to control immigration from Southern and Eastern Europe. These immigrants were seen as a threat to American values. Some immigration opponents used beliefs of the **eugenics movement** to claim that these immigrants were "inferior" people and must be kept out of the nation. Public opinion grew in support of immigration limits. New laws went beyond the 1917 literacy test. For the first time in America's history, laws were passed to radically and selectively cut European immigration.

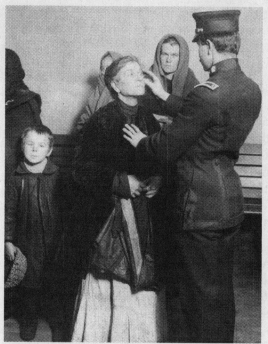

An immigrant going through a physical examination at Ellis Island

Immigration Act of 1921 One of these laws, the **Immigration Act of 1921**—also known as the **Emergency Quota Act** of 1921—established a system that set limits on the numbers of immigrants entering the nation per year and used a **quota system,** the National Origins Formula, to determine those limits. The law capped the number of immigrants to enter the United States annually at 3 percent of the number of immigrants of each European country that were living in the United States in 1910. This temporary act was succeeded by the Immigration Act of 1924.

Immigration Act of 1924 (Johnson-Reed Act) Opponents of immigration who wanted a system based on **ethnicity** believed that the Emergency Quota Act of 1921 still allowed too many "undesirable" immigrants to come to America. The **National Origins Act,** a component of the **Immigration Act of 1924,** established a more restrictive national quota system.

- Quotas in the 1924 law were deliberately based on the 1890 census, not that of 1910, in order to further limit Eastern and Southern European immigration. Immigration from nations in those areas began to increase after 1890.

- The basis of the quota calculations was altered to include the total population of the United States as of 1890, not just the immigrant population as in the 1921 law.

- The ceiling on the number of immigrants who could enter the United States annually from each country based on the number of people from that nation here in 1890 was lowered from 3 to 2 percent.

The 1924 law put a total limit on immigration at 165,000, which amounted to 80 percent fewer people than those entering per year prior to the First World War. In 1929, the quota base was set at 152,574 a year. The law also expanded the 1917 Immigration Act's Asiatic Barred Zone to include any alien who was ineligible for U.S. citizenship from entering the country, effectively excluding all immigration from Asia. By excluding Japanese immigrants, the new law overrode the 1907 Gentlemen's Agreement. No limits were placed on immigration from the Western Hemisphere. The National Origins Act also created the U.S. Border Patrol. The Nation Origins system was not replaced until 1965.

The Harlem Renaissance and Black Nationalism

Lesson Overview

The Jazz Age and the Age of Intolerance, two names for the Twenties, characterize the contradictions of the decade from the point of view of African Americans. Their literary and artistic achievements, particularly those during the Harlem Renaissance, were increasingly integrated into the national culture even as African Americans continued their struggle for social and economic equality. The Harlem Renaissance, through art, music, poetry, essays, and novels, expressed African American racial pride and self-acceptance. The writers and artists also protested racism. The decade saw the rise of Black Nationalism with Marcus Garvey having an influential role. The African American experience in the 1920s reflects the tensions and conflicts of a decade marked by clashes between modern and traditional values.

Key Concept

11.7b African Americans continued to struggle for social and economic equality while expanding their own thriving and unique culture. African American cultural achievements were increasingly integrated into national culture.

Unifying Themes

As you review this lesson take special note of the following themes:

- **Individual Development and Cultural Identity** In what ways did the Harlem Renaissance express the cultural identity of African Americans?

- **Time, Continuity, and Change** Is the Black Nationalism movement an example of continuity or of change in African Americans' drive for freedom and equal rights?

- **Development and Transformation of Social Structures** How did race, education, and class define the participants in the Harlem Renaissance and their work?

- **Civic Ideals and Practices** In what ways did the Harlem Renaissance express a demand for basic rights and freedoms? How was the Harlem Renaissance an expression of diversity in its messages and its mediums?

Key People

W.E.B. Du Bois
Langston Hughes
Alain Locke
Zora Neale Hurston

Louis Armstrong
Edward K. "Duke" Ellington
Marcus Garvey

Key Terms and Events

Harlem Renaissance
Great Migration
National Association for the
   Advancement of Colored People
   (NAACP)
Jazz Age

Black Nationalism
Back to Africa
Universal Negro Improvement
   Association (UNIA)
lynching
Pan-Africanism

The Harlem Renaissance

In the 1920s, African Americans faced Jim Crow segregation in the South and discrimination and racism in much of the rest of the United States. As the decade began, a series of anti-black riots broke out in dozens of cities across the nation. African American soldiers returning home after World War I were seen by some Americans as newly empowered by their military training and war experience, and therefore a threat to the traditional "white order." African American veterans became a special target for violence, discrimination, anti-black race riots, and lynching.

As a result of their experiences overseas and at home, the "New Negro" movement developed. African Americans in the North and Midwest increased their demands for freedom, stood up to discrimination, and expressed racial pride. **W.E.B. Du Bois** summed up their attitude in *The Crisis* when he wrote, "We return. We return from fighting. We return fighting."

The New Negro Movement, or the **Harlem Renaissance,** became one of the most influential cultural and intellectual movements of the 1920s. It was led by a group of African Americans in the New York City neighborhood of Harlem.

Settling in Harlem

From the start of the twentieth century, middle-class African Americans had been moving up from lower Manhattan into Harlem, located in Northern Manhattan between the Hudson River on the West and the Harlem and East rivers on the East. They were joined by Southern sharecroppers and field hands, some of the one million African Americans who left the South in the 1920s. The Harlem Renaissance grew out of the continuation of the **Great Migration** after World War I. Most settled in cities across the North and Midwest, such as New York, Chicago, Detroit, and Cleveland (see Topic 6). Some of these American migrants were the children or grandchildren of slaves. Some had lived through Reconstruction. Many had experienced Jim Crow America.

The Southern migrants who settled in Harlem were joined by immigrants from the Caribbean. The Caribbean immigrants were mostly well-educated, white-collar workers, or middle-class professionals. In 1930, 17 percent of the New York City population was foreign-born African Americans. **Claude McKay,** a Jamaican novelist and poet, was an influential figure in the Harlem Renaissance. He is best known for his novel *Home to Harlem* and his poem "If We Must Die." It called for African Americans to fight back against the anti-black riots of 1919.

The Renaissance also drew African American writers and artists from parts of the nation outside of the South. For example, the poet and writer **Langston Hughes,** born in Missouri and raised in Lawrence, Kansas, came to New York in 1921 to study at Columbia University. He dropped out of college in 1922 to live and write in Harlem. **Aaron Douglas,** painter, illustrator, and arts educator, was raised in Topeka, Kansas, and educated at the University of Nebraska. In 1925, Douglas was on his way to study art in Paris when he stopped in Harlem and stayed.

Defining the Harlem Renaissance

The Harlem Renaissance produced an outburst of different aspects of African American culture. It began with literature, especially novels, poems, and essays. Music, musical theater, theater, and dance were included from the start. A little later, a visual arts movement developed, focused on painting, prints, and sculpture.

The writers and artists of the Harlem Renaissance produced a body of work that expressed their culture and racial pride and impacted the national culture as well. Yet, they never expressed one single political ideology, focus, theme, or style that usually defines a movement. Instead, a strength of the Renaissance was a cultural outpouring of diversity of opinion and in methods or mediums of expression.

The Place In the 1920s and 1930s, Harlem was an urban enclave of 200,000 African Americans. Many lived in poverty or close to it, coping with low-paying jobs and high rents. But Harlem was also the nation's center of African American creativity, excitement, and artistic energy. Galleries, cafés, as well as nightclubs existed among apartments and community centers.

African American History and Culture Explored During this period, African Americans examined aspects of their lives and struggles and expressed their findings in a variety of ways.

- The Harlem Renaissance was a renewal of interest in the history and heritage of the African American. African ancient history, their own Southern rural roots and life in cities were subjects to study, reflect on, and express in a literary or artistic form.

- Another focus was examination of life in Harlem and other African American ghettos in the United States.

- Race and racism and their impact on African Americans received a great deal of attention.

- The participants in the Renaissance studied elements of African and African American cultures, such as spirituals, folklore, and religion, and incorporated them into their art, music, and literature. For example, Langston Hughes and others used the rhythms of jazz and the blues in their poetry.

The Message The artists and writers of the Harlem Renaissance created a distinctive African American culture based on their history and experience.

- Pride in African American culture and identity was defined and expressed in different ways and forms. Their racial pride came with self-acceptance, self-realization, self-expression, and self-confidence.

- The Harlem artists and writers told fellow African Americans that each person has the ability and responsibility to define or identify himself/herself. No one can or should do it for you.

- Their art and writing reflected an assertiveness and militancy in addition to pride. They protested racial injustice and raised questions about their place in a democratic nation.

This message was famously expressed by **Langston Hughes** in a 1926 essay, "The Negro Artist and the Racial Mountain," published in *The Nation*. Hughes wrote

We younger Negro artists who create now intend to express our individual, dark-skinned selves without fear or shame. If white people are pleased we are glad. If they are not, it doesn't matter. We know we are beautiful. And ugly too. . . . If colored people are pleased we are glad. If they are not, their displeasure doesn't matter either. We build our temples for tomorrow, strong as we know how, and we stand on the top of the mountain, free within ourselves.

The Participants Harlem of the 1920s and early 1930s attracted committed intellectuals, writers, artists, musicians, and actors—mainly well-educated members of the African American middle class. They produced a body of work that expressed their culture and racial pride and impacted the national culture as well. Many were reacting to the First World War and the unrealized promises it offered them. Some felt alienated from the society of the 1920s. These feelings were expressed in poetry, novels, essays, and art.

Intellectual Leaders W.E.B. Du Bois, Alain Locke, and Jessie Redmon Fauset were among those who created and sustained the Harlem Renaissance. W.E.B. Du Bois, a founder of the **National Association for the Advancement of Colored People (NAACP),** was the editor of the NAACP's magazine, *The Crisis*. A civil rights activist, sociologist, and historian, he fought against racism, particularly lynching and Jim Crow laws. As the literary editor of *The Crisis,* **Jessie Redmon Fauset** published writings of the Renaissance writers, promoted the realism and truth seeking in their work, and mentored young poets and novelists. **Alain Locke** is called the Father of the Harlem Renaissance because of his 1925 book, *The New Negro: An Interpretation.* An anthology of plays, poems, music, and art, it publicized the work of African Americans and gave a name to the movement.

Literary figures Outstanding writers of the Harlem Renaissance include Langston Hughes, Claude McKay, and **Zora Neale Hurston,** folklorist and author of the novel *Their Eyes Were Watching God.*

Artists In addition to Aaron Douglas, **Jacob Lawrence** was another of the outstanding artists of the Renaissance. He produced a series of 60 paintings tracing the Great Migration.

Harlem nightclubs, such as the Cotton Club, were instrumental in exposing Americans to jazz.

Music and Musicians Jazz was the music of the Harlem Renaissance. It was also the music of the **Jazz Age,** the 1920s. It is now hailed as truly American music. Jazz originated in New Orleans in the late nineteenth and early twentieth centuries. African American musicians blended elements of African, European, and American music to create the distinctive sounds of jazz and the blues. Jazz spread to Kansas City, St. Louis, Chicago, and New York. The development of jazz was aided by and reflected the changes in America in the 1920s. Urbanization with its demographic mobility and the technological innovations of the phonograph and radio carried the new sounds all over the country and abroad.

Louis Armstrong

In Harlem, it was played in the speakeasies and dance halls and clubs as well as the theaters. In New York, it spread to Broadway and to Carnegie Hall. The Cotton Club located in Harlem was a famous jazz club. Staffed by African American musicians, dancers, and waiters, the audience was limited to whites only. On the other hand, the Savoy Ballroom, a jazz nightclub nearby, was racially integrated.

Among the dozens of musicians of the era were Louis Armstrong, Duke Ellington, Count Basie, and singers Billie Holiday and Bessie Smith. **Louis Armstrong** influenced the Jazz Age through his innovative work as a trumpet and cornet player, singer, soloist bandleader, and movie star. **Edward K. "Duke" Ellington** recorded and composed music, performed on the piano, and conducted his own orchestra until his death in 1974. **Bessie Smith,** known as the "Empress of the Blues," was one of the most popular singers of the 1920s.

The Impact of the Harlem Renaissance on the National Culture

The Harlem Renaissance

- further identified, defined, and expanded a rich African American culture.

Bessie Smith

- by rejecting European influences in African American literature and art, encouraged the development of uniquely American art, literature, and music.

- was recognized and sponsorship by mainstream publishers, art galleries, magazines, theaters, and recording companies was offered to African Americans for the first time.

- attracted, for the first time, the interest, attention, and participation of the whole nation by popularizing African American achievements in literature, dance, art, music, and theater. Books, magazines, and other periodicals spread the ideas and experiences of the Renaissance writers.

- influenced the next generation of African American artists and writers, such as Gwendolyn Brooks, James Baldwin, Ralph Ellison, Nobel prize winner Toni Morrison, Alice Walker, and Richard Wright.

- connected the achievements of African Americans to the cultural trends, political debates, controversies, and contradictions of the nation in the Twenties.

- increased communication and exchanges about cultural developments among African American urban centers in the United States as well as internationally.

- attracted renewed interest and influence during the civil rights movement of the 1960s.

The Harlem Renaissance Ends

Although the Harlem Renaissance continued into the mid-1930s, the Great Depression effectively ended it. The sales of books and literary magazines plummeted. Sponsorships, awards, and grants also disappeared. African American-owned businesses struggled to survive. With the end of Prohibition, bars reopened in downtown Manhattan.

African American Racial Pride and Black Nationalism

The emphasis on racial pride was a defining feature of the Harlem Renaissance. The **Black Nationalism** movement of Marcus Garvey was one expression of racial pride.

Origins of Black Nationalism

Black Nationalism first developed in nineteenth-century America. It is a part of the larger history of African American movements demanding economic and social equality from a position of strength, self-confidence, and racial pride. But, rather than an integrated society, supporters of Black Nationalism advocate separation of the races.

Marcus Garvey and Black Nationalism

Marcus Garvey

Marcus Garvey was an intellectual leader of the Harlem Renaissance and of a separatist **Back to Africa** campaign. He founded the **Universal Negro Improvement Association (UNIA)** in Jamaica in 1914, and in 1917 settled in Harlem. Garvey established 700 chapters of the UNIA in thirty-eight states, plus branches in Jamaica, Canada, and Africa. With 4 to 6 million members, the UNIA is said to have been the largest civil rights movement in African American history. Garveyism attracted working-class and lower middle-class African Americans. In Harlem, Garvey published a newspaper, *Negro World*, that reached a circulation of 500,000. Garvey constructed Liberty Hall of Harlem, where he gave political lectures organized much like church services.

Garvey was a powerful speaker and a polarizing personality. His ideas clashed with the philosophies and strategies of other African American intellectuals, such as **A. Philip Randolph** and **W.E.B. Du Bois.** While he and Du Bois encouraged Pan-Africanism, they disagreed on the topic of integration rather than separation. Rivalry for the voice of African Americans was a factor in their relationship: *Negro World* competed with the NAACP's *The Crisis*.

The Philosophy of Marcus Garvey Marcus Garvey was influenced by Booker T. Washington's philosophy. Garvey's philosophy was also affected by his observations of the world after World War I. Garvey thought that African Americans would not be able to overcome the legal barriers of discrimination, such as the Jim Crow Laws, to secure economic and social equality. Therefore, he advocated autonomy, meaning self-determination and self-rule, and separatism. Marcus Garvey

- believed that black people throughout the world had the right to self-determination and encouraged **Pan-Africanism** in particular. Pan-Africanism is a broad principle, with many meanings: the indigenous people from Africa and their descendants throughout the world should be united or they should live in solidarity or they should create a political union. Garvey's position was that he believed "in the principle of Europe for the Europeans, and Asia for the Asians" and "Africa for the Africans at home and abroad."

- promoted a Back to Africa movement, urging all black people in the world to return to Africa, which should be free of white colonial rule.

- advocated Black Nationalism in the form of creating a separate economy and society run for and by African Americans. He promoted separatism, racial pride, and economic independence through the UNIA, his speeches, and *Negro World*.

- adapted the views of Booker T. Washington, whom he admired, on self-improvement, racial pride, education, and black-owned businesses to underpin his separatist model.

- opposed Jim Crow Laws, lynching, and efforts to disenfranchise African Americans.

- rejected striving for a place in American society and government, and instead wanted to create a separatist nation or a separate community for African Americans in the United States.

- created, sponsored, and encouraged development of worldwide black-owned industries and shipping lines consistent with his views on building a separate, autonomous, economic community.

Garveyism Ends Marcus Garvey's UNIA gave financial help to African American businesses to get them started. The organization ran ventures that Garvey developed, including the Black Star Line, a steamship company. Its three ships carried people and cargo between the United States and Africa. In 1921, the Black Star Line shut down. The cause was mismanagement. In 1925, the United States government found Garvey guilty of using the mail to defraud the shareholders of the Black Star Line. In 1927, President Coolidge commuted his sentence and he was deported to Jamaica. Without Garvey, the UNIA fell apart. He died in London in 1940.

Marcus Garvey's Legacy Garvey motivated African nationalist leaders such as Jomo Kenyatta of Kenya and Kwame Nkrumah of Ghana. Garveyism influenced the Rastafari and the Nation of Islam. Garveyism affected Malcolm X, who sought to redevelop a Black Nationalism movement in the United States. With this goal in mind, Malcolm influenced other activists, such as Stokely Carmichael.

The 1930s: The Great Depression and the Government's Response

Key Concept

11.7c For many Americans, the 1920s was a time of prosperity. However, underlying economic problems, reflected in the stock market crash of 1929, led to the Great Depression. President Franklin D. Roosevelt's responses to the Great Depression increased the role of the federal government.

Lesson Overview

The economic prosperity of the 1920s was followed by the Great Depression of the 1930s. Fundamental weaknesses in the national and world economies caused the Great Depression. Worldwide in scope, the Depression affected virtually every aspect of American life. With roots in sharp differences in income levels, unregulated stock market speculation, a flawed banking system, and the overproduction of goods, the Great Depression was triggered by the stock market crash in 1929. Banks failed and businesses shut down, producing widespread unemployment, homelessness, and hunger.

President Herbert Hoover's response to the Great Depression proved ineffective. In 1933, President Franklin D. Roosevelt's New Deal launched ambitious programs of relief, recovery, and reform. The New Deal was based on the belief that government had a responsibility for the social and economic well-being of its citizens. The New Deal dramatically increased the role of government in American life and strengthened the power of the presidency. The entry of the United States into World War II in 1941 put an end to the nation's worst economic collapse. Today, the Great Depression remains the benchmark against which an economic crisis is measured.

Unifying Themes

As you review this lesson take special note of the following themes:

- **Time, Continuity, and Change** What were the causes and consequences of the Great Depression? What is the 21st-century interpretation of President Franklin D. Roosevelt's leadership during the Great Depression?

- **Development and Transformation of Social Structures** How did the New Deal affect the social and economic inequalities of farmers, organized labor, minorities, and women?

- **Civic Ideals and Practices** How was the New Deal belief that government had a responsibility for the social and economic well-being of its citizens put into practice during the Great Depression?

Key People

Andrew Mellon	Eleanor Roosevelt
Herbert Hoover	John Maynard Keynes
Franklin D. Roosevelt	Mary McLeod Bethune
Frances Perkins	Huey Long
Harry Hopkins	

Key Terms and Events

injunction	Great Depression	New Deal
overproduction	underconsumption	deficit spending
speculation	distribution of wealth	collective bargaining
on margin	Hoovervilles	Judicial Reorganization
Great Stock Market	Dust Bowl	Bill
Crash	Bonus Army	

Key Supreme Court Cases

As you review this lesson be sure you understand the significance of this key Supreme Court case:

Schechter Poultry Corporation v. United States (1935)

The Great Depression

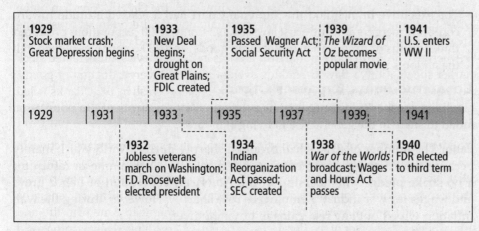

1929	1933	1935	1939	1941
Stock market crash; Great Depression begins	New Deal begins; drought on Great Plains; FDIC created	Passed Wagner Act; Social Security Act	*The Wizard of Oz* becomes popular movie	U.S. enters WW II

1929 1931 1933 1935 1937 1939 1941

1932	1934	1938	1940
Jobless veterans march on Washington; F.D. Roosevelt elected president	Indian Reorganization Act passed; SEC created	*War of the Worlds* broadcast; Wages and Hours Act passes	FDR elected to third term

Preparing for the Regents

Stimulus-Based Questions: Timeline

According to the timeline:

- Which event on the timeline resulted in a migration of farmers?
- Which was a law passed to benefit workers?
- Which act was passed to provide a "safety net"?
- Which acts were passed to provide banking and investment reform?

The 1920s: Business Boom or False Prosperity?

For many Americans, postwar life under Presidents Warren G. Harding and Calvin Coolidge did return to normalcy. Yet beneath the surface, troubling political and economic problems had begun to develop.

Economic Prosperity During the 1920s

The 1920s was a decade of mass production and mass consumption. Americans had more disposable income and they spent it. The standard of living rose for many Americans. Some Americans experienced prosperity, even wealth. Businesses profited from the administration's policies of low taxes, laissez-faire attitude, and high tariffs.

Recession and Recovery The end of World War I was followed by a temporary recession caused by the shift from a wartime to a peacetime economy. For farmers, hardship continued throughout the decade. In other sectors of the economy, a period of economic recovery had begun by 1923, when Calvin Coolidge became president. The Gross National Product (GNP) rose 40 percent. Per capita income went up 30 percent. With little inflation, actual purchasing power—and therefore the standard of living—increased. At the time, few people questioned this Coolidge prosperity.

Pro-Business Policies Big corporations and the wealthy benefited greatly from Coolidge prosperity. For example,

- President Coolidge kept financier **Andrew Mellon** as secretary of the treasury. Mellon acted on the philosophy that government's role was to serve business.

- Businesses and the wealthiest citizens were helped by tax laws that reduced personal income tax rates, particularly for upper income groups, removed most excise taxes, and lowered corporate income taxes.

- The government reduced the national debt and balanced the budget by raising tariffs and demanding repayment of war debts.

Unifying Themes
Economic Systems

Use economic indicators to analyze the state of the economy in the 1920s.

The Gross National Product (GNP) is the total value of all goods and services produced in one year.

Per Capita Income (PCI) means income per individual; it is based on the national income divided by the population.

- Analyze how the government economic policies of the 1920s affected the GNP and PCI.

- In a return to protectionism, the Fordney-McCumber Tariff of 1922 raised tariff rates. Republicans argued that higher tariffs would limit foreign imports, thus protecting United States industry and agriculture from foreign competition. But in actuality, the tariff failed to help farmers and weakened the world economy.

- Regulatory agencies such as the Federal Reserve Board, the Federal Trade Commission, and the Interstate Commerce Commission were headed by people who saw their role as assisting business rather than regulating it.

- The executive branch and the Supreme Court had a relaxed attitude toward corporate mergers and anti-trust laws. By 1929, only 1,300 corporations produced three fourths of American manufactured goods, and 200 companies owned half the nation's wealth.

Economic Boom Bypasses Others

Coolidge prosperity did not benefit everyone. Key segments of the population failed to share in the general rise in living standards.

Labor The number of strikes had dropped sharply during World War I, mainly because the Wilson government supported collective bargaining in return for a no-strike pledge. Membership in the American Federation of Labor grew, and wages for war industry employees rose sharply. However, during the war, inflation wiped out any real gains in buying power.

The 1920s saw a reversal of any union gains. Strikes in the steel, mining, and railroad industries failed, in part, because the government used not only troops to end the strikes but also **injunctions,** which are court orders that prohibit specified actions.

The Supreme Court also ruled against child labor laws and against minimum wages for women and children. In addition, some companies began to offer health and life insurance in hopes of lessening workers' interest in unions. The strategy often worked. Membership in labor unions fell from a high of about 5 million in 1921 to under 3.5 million in 1929.

Real wages for workers increased only slightly during this period, boosted primarily by wages of workers in the new industries, such as communications and automobile manufacturing. This situation meant that only some workers improved their standard of living and could afford to buy the new consumer goods.

Farmers In the 1920s, demographically, almost one half of the population lived in rural areas. The only farmers to benefit from Coolidge prosperity were those involved in large commercial farm operations. For the rest, rural poverty was widespread. The farm depression lasted almost twenty years, until World War II.

Farmers expanded production during World War I in response to rising prices and the worldwide demand for food. Mechanized farm equipment, technology, such as irrigation, and modern farm techniques increased farmers' crop yield per acre. But many farms were too small for mechanization. They could not compete with the corporate farms where the work was done by low-paid migrant labor.

After the Great War, when European farms began producing again, American farmers grew too much compared to what they were able to sell. This **overproduction** caused prices of both farm products and farmland to decrease dramatically. During the 1920s, net farm income fell 50 percent. As farm income fell, many farmers lost their land when they could not make their mortgage payments. By 1930, only about 20 percent of the labor force made a living farming. Between 1920 and 1932, 25 percent of the nation's farms were sold.

Native Americans During the 1920s, Native Americans had the highest unemployment rate of any group and the shortest average life span. Most lived on reservations, without the basics, such as heat and running water.

African Americans African Americans who migrated to the North enjoyed a higher standard of living than in the South. However, they still earned less than white workers and experienced a higher rate of unemployment. A very large majority of African Americans remained in the South, the poorest section of the United States, where they continued to face racism and poverty.

Immigrants The Immigration Act of 1924 halted almost all immigration to the United States. The most recently arrived immigrants were clustered in ethnically separated city ghettoes, struggling economically, and facing demands for assimilation and Americanization.

The Stock Market: Speculation Ends in a Crash

The economic recovery in 1923 helped produce a surge of investment in the stock market. Optimistic business and government leaders saw no end to the boom. They encouraged everyone to play the bull market—that is, the rising stock market. Some families invested their life savings. The profits rolled in until the stock market crashed in October 1929.

Stock Market Speculation The new wealth flowed from a stock market with a deeply flawed structure. Throughout the 1920s, the stock market had grown on **speculation** by people who bought **on margin,** and, in fact, owned only a small portion of their stocks. This meant that buyers could purchase stocks by making only small down payments in cash—sometimes as low as 5 percent of the value of the stocks. They borrowed the rest from brokers, counting on their profits to repay the loans. The system worked as long as stock profits continued.

The Great Stock Market Crash of 1929 The end of the prosperity of the 1920s was marked by a series of plunges in the United States stock market in the fall of 1929 known as the **Great Stock Market Crash.** As the market dropped, many could not meet margin calls, demands to put up the money to cover their loans. The result was panic selling. On October 29 (Black Tuesday) alone, stock values fell $14 billion. Stock values dropped lower and lower in the weeks, months, and years that followed, reaching bottom in July 1932. By then, the market had fallen 89 percent from its September 1929 high point.

The Stock Market Crash

*Based on Standard & Poor's index of common stocks
Source: *Historical Statistics of the United States, Colonial Times to 1970*

Preparing for the Regents

Stimulus-Based Questions: Graph

Based on the graph and your knowledge of social studies, answer the following questions.

- When did the stock market crash occur?
- In what year did stock prices reach their lowest point?
- What role did speculation play in the crash?
- What is the relationship of the stock market crash to the Great Depression?

The Great Depression

The stock market crash triggered the start of the **Great Depression.** It shattered the national sense of optimism and confidence of the 1920s. The crash dramatically exposed the fact that the national economy had serious weaknesses.

Causes of the Great Depression

The Great Depression was caused by an unsound economy—overproduction and underconsumption, overexpansion of credit, and fragile corporate structures—combined with ineffective government action. The growing interdependence of international trade and banking made the effects even more damaging.

Weaknesses in the Overall Economy in the 1920s Weaknesses in the economy expanded before the 1929 stock market crash. The crash dramatically exposed these serious problems with the national economy.

- The **agricultural sector** remained depressed throughout the 1920s, with a worldwide drop in prices.
- **Unemployment** plagued the railroad, coal, and textile industries well before 1929. The railroads were feeling the competition of trucks, and the coal industry of oil.
- **Speculation** in real estate and the resulting building boom had declined.
- The number of **bank failures** was rising as farmers, people speculating in stocks, and consumers buying on credit could not repay their loans.
- As early as the summer of 1929, the economy showed signs of underconsumption. Inventories of unsold goods began to accumulate in warehouses as consumer demand slowed. **Underconsumption,** or overproduction, means that people buy fewer goods than are produced. In other words, supply is greater than demand.

Unequal Distribution of Income Contributing to underconsumption and to the weakness of the economy was an unequal **distribution of wealth.** In the 1920s, a family needed an annual income of $2,500 to have a modest standard of living, but over 60 percent of American families lived on only $2,000 per year, covering just basic needs. Some 40 percent of all families had an income of less than $1,500, which was below the poverty line. At the same time, the nation's 24,000 richest families had a total income *three times as large* as the total income of the 6 million poorest families. In short, while 1 percent of the population owned 59 percent of the nation's wealth, 87 percent of the population owned only 10 percent of the wealth.

As a result, the economy was dependent on the spending of a very small portion of the population. The wealthy people spent their money on luxury goods and on investments. This type of spending was greatly affected by the stock market crash. As output per worker rose, production costs dropped, and corporate profits rose. This benefited the wealthy, not the great mass of the population. Overall, wages were stagnant or had increased only slightly. Often workers could not buy what they produced. As a result, demand dropped. As the economy weakened, this non-purchasing group increased in number and became less and less able to buy even the necessities of life.

Excessive Buying on Credit Excessive buying on credit was one result of the low and unequally distributed wages. The abundance of new products, the sense that these good times would never end, and the availability of easy credit encouraged people to spend money beyond their means.

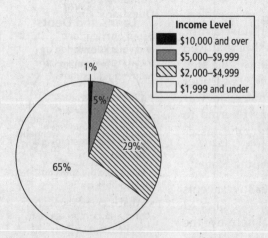

Income Distribution in the United States, 1929

Income Level	
■	$10,000 and over
▨	$5,000–$9,999
▨	$2,000–$4,999
□	$1,999 and under

1%
5%
29%
65%

As the economy slowed, people bought fewer goods in order to be able to pay their installment loans and home mortgages. This underconsumption decreased production and increased unemployment.

Weak Corporate Structure The stock market crash set off the collapse of the nation's business structure. Business consolidations of the 1920s resulted in just a few large companies in each industry. Holding companies controlled the stock of many different corporations and depended on the earnings of the various companies they held. This was a very fragile system, because when one company collapsed, it affected—in a domino fashion—the rest of the holding company.

Weak Banking Structure Some 7,000 banks failed in the 1920s, and thousands more in the early years of the Depression. Many were rural banks that failed when farmers were unable to repay loans. Many banks had inadequate reserves, which made them vulnerable. They had invested too much money in the stock market and made risky loans.

Inadequate Government Policies Actions by the federal government contributed to the Depression.

- Stock market speculation was unregulated by the government.
- Regulation of the nation's 25,000 private banks was limited.
- Tax policies that favored the wealthy resulted in further uneven distribution of income.
- The consolidation of corporations was not challenged under antitrust laws.
- The Federal Reserve Board allowed a low discount rate—the interest charged to member banks. This policy led to stock speculation. The board then raised interest rates in 1931, discouraging spending at just the time when spending would have helped the economy.

Weak International Economy The Great Depression was worldwide. The world's economies were affected by the collapse that was triggered by the crash of the United States stock market. Many European economies had never fully recovered from World War I, and the international economy depended heavily on the economy of the United States. After World War I, the United States became the world's leading **creditor nation,** meaning that other countries owed more to the United States than we owed to them. The United States was also the world's leading industrial producer, exporter, and financier. These changes were due in large part to the payment of war debts by former Allies, who had borrowed from the United States in order to buy war supplies from us.

After the war, European nations argued that their debts should be canceled, but the United States insisted on repayment. American protectionist tariffs, however, limited European trade with the United States and thus reduced European earnings that might have been used to pay off war debts. One step aimed at making repayment easier was the **Dawes Plan,** adopted in 1924. Under this plan, the United States lent funds to Germany so that it could make war reparations as required by the Treaty of Versailles. **Reparations** referred to money Germany owed to the European Allies as payment for economic losses during the war. The Allies would receive their reparations, and, in turn, use the funds to make payments on the war debt they owed to the United States.

When the economy slowed, the United States made even fewer foreign investments and had less money to lend. This meant that foreign nations had less money to buy American goods and often defaulted on loans. The international nature of the banking system can be seen by the fact that banks in both Europe and the United States failed as a result of defaults on loans.

Social Studies Practices
Gathering and Interpreting Evidence

- What were the strengths and weakness of the Dawes Plan?
- Why did it fail to solve U.S.–Europe financial problems?

Postwar Loans and Debts

U.S. loans $ to Germany

Germany pays reparations to Allies

Allies pay war debts to U.S.

Preparing for
the Regents

Stimulus-Based
Questions: Chart

Examine the chart and
then answer the following
questions.

- What is the significance of
the time period covered
in this chart?

- How much did spending
for new housing change
between 1928 and 1932?

- What does the drop in
U.S. exports indicate
about the nature of the
depression?

- How much did
unemployment increase
between 1928 and 1932?

- Based on this chart,
in which year was the
economy in its most
serious state?

Some Economic Changes Between 1928 and 1932
(Figures in millions unless otherwise noted)

	1928	1929	1930	1931	1932
A. United States exports (merchandise)	$5,030	$5,157	$3,781	$2,378	$1,576
B. Spending for new housing	$4,195	$3,040	$1,570	$1,320	$485
C. Farm spending for lime and fertilizer	$318	$300	$297	$202	$118
D. Federal spending	$2,933	$3,127	$3,320	$3,578	$4,659
E. Cash receipts from farming	$10,991	$11,312	$9,055	$6,331	$4,748
F. Lumber production (billions of board ft.)	36.8	38.7	29.4	20	13.5
G. Unemployment (in thousands)	2,080	1,550	4,340	8,020	12,060
H. Average weekly earnings of production workers in manufacturing (actual dollars)	$24.97	$25.03	$23.25	$20.87	$17.05

The Impact of the Great Depression

The Great Depression was a worldwide event with devastating effects. At home, it had a profound personal impact on all Americans, as well as on the economic, political, and social structure of the nation.

Unemployment and Its Effects By 1932, some 12 million people—25 percent of the American labor force—were unemployed. African Americans and unskilled workers were the first to experience unemployment. In 1931, unemployment for African American men was estimated at 66 percent. The human toll was seen in long "bread lines" at soup kitchens. Relief efforts by organizations such as the Red Cross were limited because voluntary contributions slowed down.

As banks failed, people lost their savings; as companies failed, people lost their jobs as well. If you kept your job, your salary might be cut by as much as a third. Men left home to find work elsewhere. Some men just left. Parents looked for ways to stretch what money the family had. Families moved in with relatives. The marriage rate fell by 22 percent. The birth rate dropped, as did college enrollment. Disease increased, as did deaths from starvation and suicide. Parents often went hungry to give what food they had to their children.

Women were criticized and even, in some places, legally banned from working, when men could not find jobs. By 1940, only 15 percent of married women were working, while 50 percent of single women held jobs. However, women's employment data shows an increase in the number working during the Great Depression. "Female-only" occupations in service sectors, such as nursing and clerical work, were less affected than positions in manufacturing that were usually held by men. World War II finally broke this gender barrier.

Preparing for
the Regents

Stimulus-Based
Question: Graph

- Based on the graph,
what was the
relationship between the
unemployment rate and
Hoover's defeat in the
election of 1932?

Unemployment, 1929–1940 (in millions)

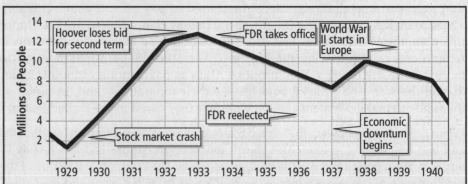

Urban Life In many cities, people were forced out of their homes and apartments for failure to pay their rent. Across the nation, some families who had lost their homes lived in unheated shacks they had built of cardboard, tin, or crates or—if they were lucky—with wood. These communities became known as **Hoovervilles.** Some people slept under old newspapers that they called "Hoover blankets." People selling apples and shoelaces on the street became a common sight.

Rural Life During the Dust Bowl

In the 1930s, the agricultural depression of the 1920s worsened. With more people lacking money, even for food, the already depressed income of farmers dropped by one half. Farm foreclosure sales grew in number. Years of drought in the southern Great Plains combined with unsustainable farming techniques resulted in the **Dust Bowl.**

Causes of the Dust Bowl Starting in the late 1800s, farmers using steel plows cut through the thick grasses that covered the Great Plains. They grew wheat in areas too dry to grow corn. After World War I, when farm prices dropped, farmers responded by overfarming—clearing more land and growing more wheat. The 1930s was a decade of drought. The drought, combined with poor farming methods, resulted in the loss of the topsoil. Modern mechanized plows had crushed the soil and cut into the roots of the native ground cover. The topsoil was no longer protected. For seven years of drought, winds whipped the topsoil into giant dust storms. These Black Blizzards swept across the Great Plains east from New Mexico, Texas, Oklahoma, Colorado, and Kansas to the Atlantic and beyond. With the topsoil went crops, cattle, farms, and livelihoods.

The dust storms began in 1931, covering everything inside as well as outside in a black dust. Day looked like night. Headlights were needed in order to drive through a dust storm. Masks were worn to keep the dust from choking people. There were 14 storms in 1931 and 38 in 1932. They would last for days. By 1934, the drought had spread to 27 states. The worst dust storm happened on Black Sunday, April 14, 1935.

Effects of the Dust Bowl Sixty percent of those living in the Dust Bowl lost their farms. Two and one half million people were displaced. The devastation in the Dust Bowl resulted in a group of migrant farmers called "Okies" moving to California in search of work. While they were only a small percent of those forced to relocate by the storms, the suffering of these Anglo-Americans was made famous in John Steinbeck's novel *The Grapes of Wrath*. In 1936, Los Angeles authorities set up patrols on the Arizona border in order to prevent Dust Bowl migrants from entering California. Once in California, the Okies were subject to discrimination.

In 1933, the Emergency Farm Mortgage Act set aside $200 million to help refinance farm mortgages. In 1935, the New Deal created the **Soil Conservation Service** to help the Dust Bowl region. It established conservation programs, such as crop rotation and contour plowing, paying farmers who used them. The drought finally ended in 1939.

The drought and dust storms of the 1930s made farming in much of the Great Plains nearly impossible.

The Culture of the Great Depression

The sufferings of people during the Great Depression changed the popular culture of the 1930s, as people sought inexpensive and escapist leisure activities.

Sports and Games Spectator sports, especially baseball, remained popular, but fewer people could afford to attend. Instead, they played miniature golf, softball, pinball machines, or the new board game Monopoly®, or they read comic books. *Dick Tracy* was one of the most popular comic strips of the decade.

Movies About one third of the nation's movie theaters closed during the Depression, but each week as many as 90 million people turned out to see Hollywood films. Movies of the 1930s often dealt with issues other than the grim realities of Depression life. Depression-era movies included *King Kong*, *Gone with the Wind*, and *The Wizard of Oz*, as well as cowboy adventures, serials, musicals, comedies, and Walt Disney cartoons starring characters such as Mickey Mouse.

Radio Radio was to the 1930s what television is today—an influential, unifying means of communication. If one owned a radio, it was also a source of free information and entertainment. Radio offered the comedy of George Burns and Gracie Allen or Jack Benny, as well as soap operas, news, sports, serials, and music. Through his fireside chats, President Franklin Roosevelt built and sustained his relationship with the American people.

Literature and the Arts Some popular books, such as detective stories, helped to distract readers from the burdens of Depression life. However, most literature, photography, and paintings of the 1930s reflected the poverty and despair of the times. The photographs of Walker Evans and Margaret Bourke-White revealed the suffering of the people. Government programs provided work for artists, writers, and actors through theater and art projects. Artists painted murals on public buildings. Writers wrote histories and guidebooks about various regions. Actors appeared in plays funded by the Federal Theater Project. Dancers performed, and orchestras played.

Comparing Responses to the Great Depression

The two presidents whose administrations had to contend with the Great Depression had different ideas on how the government should help the nation recover from these difficult times.

President Hoover's Response to the Great Depression, 1929–1933

The first president who had to deal with the deepening depression was **Herbert Hoover.** Hoover took office in 1929, after serving as Coolidge's secretary of commerce. Like Harding and Coolidge, President Hoover believed that the federal government should assist business and limit regulation of it. An engineer by training, Hoover was a good businessman, a self-made millionaire, and a humanitarian. During and after World War I, he had earned an international reputation as a leader of a successful relief effort to aid starving Europeans and to help Europe recover economically.

Hoover's Economic Plan To improve economic conditions, President Hoover

- tried to restore confidence in the American economy with such statements as "Prosperity is just around the corner."

Social Studies Practices
Using Evidence

Reread the section about the culture of the Great Depression, then answer the following questions.

- What forms of entertainment were most popular during the Great Depression?
- What made these forms of entertainment so popular?
- How did the tone of popular entertainment (such as movies and radio) differ from that of art and literature?

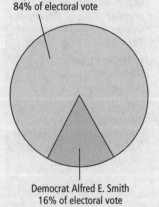

Election of 1928

Republican Herbert C. Hoover 84% of electoral vote

Democrat Alfred E. Smith 16% of electoral vote

- altered his view that government should not become directly involved in the economy. He promoted programs that aided businesses, on the theory that as businesses recovered, economic benefits would trickle down to the workers and consumers.

- allowed the organization of the **Reconstruction Finance Corporation** (1932) to lend money to railroads, mortgage and insurance companies, and banks on the verge of bankruptcy.

- set a precedent for Franklin Roosevelt's New Deal when, in 1932, the Emergency Relief Construction Act provided for federal works projects to create jobs and stimulate the economy.

- obtained voluntary agreements from businesses not to lower wages or prices. However, as companies increasingly faced collapse, they often could not honor these promises.

- halted the payment of war debts to the United States by European nations.

President Herbert Hoover

Hoover's Leadership and Political Skills Despite his efforts in response to the Depression, Hoover's refusal to provide direct relief damaged his image as the nation's leader. Also damaging was his insistence, in the face of worsening conditions, that the economy was improving. President Hoover lacked political and leadership skills when dealing with Congress and the public. He and his administration took two actions in 1932 that doomed the possibility of reelection that November. First, he agreed to support a tax increase that included a sales tax that would fall heavily on poorer citizens. The outcry was so great that the idea did not become law. But Hoover's reputation was hurt.

The Attack on the Bonus Army Hoover's second error of 1932 occurred when thousands of unemployed World War I veterans and their families set up camps in Washington, D.C., demanding early payment of the bonus for their war service due to them in 1945. When the bill for early payment was defeated by Congress, some of the **Bonus Army,** as they were called, refused to leave town. Hoover called out the army to escort the ex-soldiers from the grounds of the Capitol back to their camps. Instead, General Douglas MacArthur used tanks, tear gas, bayonets, and guns against the Bonus Army. The public was outraged by this treatment of veterans, and Hoover's remaining popularity and reelection hopes were destroyed.

Failure of Hoover's Program Herbert Hoover took many steps to use the power of the federal government to stop the growing depression. It was not until 1932 that he changed some of his views, agreeing to increase federal spending to fight the depression. In the end, his efforts were too little. Historians still debate whether Hoover should be praised for the efforts he did make or condemned for not going far enough. For example, President Hoover

- was limited in his ability to act by his failure to grasp the gravity of the economic crisis and its dangers for the United States, its people, and its institutions.

- continued to have great faith in the American economic system, insisting that the forces of the market would eventually set the economy right again.

- believed in cooperation, collaboration, self-help, volunteerism, and private relief efforts rather than governmental action to end the Great Depression.

- opposed direct relief for the homeless and unemployed on the grounds that it would destroy people's self-reliance and **"rugged individualism."** At the same time, he supported raising taxes to balance the federal budget.

**Unifying Themes
Change**

In the large sense the primary cause of the Great Depression was the war of 1914–1918.

—Herbert Hoover, *The Memoirs of Herbert Hoover, Volume 3,* 1952

- Find evidence in the text to support and/or refute Herbert Hoover's opinion about the cause of the Great Depression.

President Franklin D. Roosevelt and Eleanor Roosevelt following his third presidential inauguration

Election of 1932

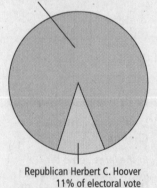

Democrat Franklin D. Roosevelt 89% of electoral vote

Republican Herbert C. Hoover 11% of electoral vote

President Roosevelt's Response to the Great Depression, 1933–1938

In 1932, **Franklin Delano Roosevelt** was elected the thirty-second president. He grew up in a New York family of privilege, one dedicated to public service. He was educated at Harvard University and the School of Law at Columbia University. He held positions as a Democrat in the New York State legislature, as assistant secretary of the navy under Woodrow Wilson, and as governor of New York before being elected president.

Restoring Public Confidence: Master Politician and Communicator Roosevelt inspired support and confidence in people. He was a master politician, an effective communicator, and a natural leader. He used the radio for "fireside chats" with the American public, involving them emotionally in his explanations of what he was doing to solve the nation's economic problems. He had been tested by polio, which left him in a wheelchair, unable to even stand without support. Polio made him tougher, more patient, and more compassionate.

FDR Prepares to Lead the Nation Roosevelt did not come to office committed to a single theory, ideology, or set of beliefs, but rather was a man of action, interested in whatever worked to solve a problem. In order to solve problems, FDR was willing to make choices, often contradictory ones, based on trial and error. He surrounded himself with a group of formal and informal advisers. His cabinet members included the first woman to hold a Cabinet post, **Frances Perkins,** as secretary of labor. Roosevelt's informal advisers, known as the **"brain trust,"** were a group of intellectuals and lawyers, including social worker **Harry Hopkins.** They favored reform and strongly influenced Roosevelt's administration.

FDR's Eyes and Ears: Eleanor Roosevelt Another major influence on Franklin Roosevelt was his wife, **Eleanor Roosevelt.** She was a humanitarian, active on behalf of women and minorities, especially African Americans. As First Lady, she became an important political figure in the nation. She served as the president's eyes and ears, but what he heard and saw was filtered through her progressive views and sensitivity to the plight of others.

FDR's Economic Plan: The New Deal—Relief, Recovery, Reform Roosevelt's program to combat the problems caused by the Depression was called the **New Deal.** The programs of the New Deal had the following goals: relief for those people who were suffering, recovery for the economy, so it could grow again, and reform measures to avoid future depressions. The strategies used by the New Deal included

- passing relief measures that involved the federal government in the nation's economy to a greater degree than ever before. This direct governmental action was justified by using the commerce and elastic clauses of the Constitution.

- taking fiscal action to stimulate the economy and reduce unemployment by lowering taxes and increasing government spending.

- assuming responsibility for the general welfare by protecting people against risks that they could not handle on their own.

- increasing the regulatory role of the federal government over banks, businesses, and the stock exchange.
- adopting **deficit spending,** particularly after the 1937–1938 recession, as a means of reviving the economy. This policy was based on the theories of economist **John Maynard Keynes,** who argued that the government must spend huge amounts of money to encourage the increase in production levels and purchasing power, resulting in economic recovery.

Comparing Presidential Responses to the Great Depression	
Our Republican leaders tell us economic laws . . . cause panics which no one could prevent. But while they prate of [chatter about] economic laws, men and women are starving . . . I pledge you, I pledge myself, to a new deal for the American people. —Franklin D. Roosevelt, acceptance speech, Democratic National Convention, July 2, 1932	*The urgent question today is the prompt balancing of the budget. When that is accomplished, I propose to support adequate measures for relief of distress and unemployment.* —President Herbert Hoover, press conference statement, 1932

Preparing for the Regents

Stimulus-Based Questions: Speeches

Both of these quotes are from speeches made during the 1932 presidential campaign.

- Which speech has a greater sense of urgency?
- Which man is more optimistic? Why?
- What is the clearest difference in their approach to the Great Depression?

Roosevelt's New Deal Program

In the first 100 days after Roosevelt took office, he worked with Congress to set up programs and projects aimed at getting the nation out of the Great Depression.

Relief Legislation of the New Deal

Congress passed a wide range of relief legislation as part of the New Deal.

Emergency Banking Act, 1933 Roosevelt's first act as president was to stop the collapse of the national banking system by declaring a **bank holiday** and closing the nation's banks. The time was used to assure the public that it could have confidence in the banks once they reopened. The law required the examination of banks to ensure that only financially sound banks were operating. In the same month, Roosevelt began to take the United States off the gold standard.

Federal Emergency Relief Act (FERA), 1933 Between 1933 and 1935, some $500 million was provided for distribution by states and cities for direct relief and work projects for hungry, homeless, and unemployed people.

Public Works Administration (PWA), 1933 Operating from 1933 until 1939, the PWA provided jobs through construction projects, such as bridges, housing, hospitals, schools, and aircraft carriers. The PWA also moved government money into the economy. It was hoped that this "pump priming" would create jobs, revive production, and lead to more consumer spending.

Civilian Conservation Corps (CCC), 1933 Between 1933 and 1942, the CCC provided work for 2.5 million young men ages 18 to 25 conserving natural resources. Only 8,000 young women joined the CCC.

Works Progress Administration (WPA), 1935 From 1935 until 1943, the Works Progress Administration provided jobs for 25 percent of adult Americans. The agency was created to replace direct relief with public works projects. The WPA spent more government money than any other program.

San Francisco's Golden Gate Bridge, built between 1933 and 1937, was a WPA project.

While WPA workers built roads, bridges, and other public works, the program also offered work to writers, and artists. Critics attacked the cultural work projects in particular. Others criticized the WPA for being inequitable. However, the WPA provided jobs for over 8.5 million people who left a legacy in books, artwork, and public buildings, dams, tunnels, and stadiums still in use.

Recovery Legislation of the New Deal

Congress also passed a wide range of recovery legislation as part of the New Deal.

National Industrial Recovery Act (NIRA), 1933 Created to administer the NIRA, the National Recovery Administration (NRA) worked with businesses to help them recover. The NRA set "codes of fair competition" within industries to maintain prices, minimum wages, and maximum hours. The public was encouraged to buy from companies that followed the NRA codes. The NIRA was not popular, however. Some consumers complained that the NRA plan raised prices. Companies opposed the provisions giving unions the right to organize. Small companies felt at a disadvantage compared to larger companies. The NIRA was declared unconstitutional in 1935.

Home Owners Loan Corporation (HOLC), 1933 This agency was created to help homeowners save their houses from foreclosure. It provided funds to pay off mortgages and financed over one million new long-term mortgages at lower, fixed-interest rates.

First Agricultural Adjustment Act (AAA), 1933 The aim of the AAA was to raise farmers' income by cutting the amount of surplus crops and livestock. In that way, farmers would be able to sell their crops at the same prices of the years 1909 to 1914, a time when farm prices were high. The government paid farmers for reducing the number of acres they planted. Large farmers, rather than small farmers and tenant farmers, benefited from the AAA. The public was outraged at the destruction of crops and animals in order to keep production down. However, farm prices did increase. Although the AAA was declared unconstitutional in 1936, the principle of farm price supports had been established.

Federal Housing Administration (FHA), 1934 The FHA was created by the National Housing Act to insure bank mortgages. These mortgages were often for 20 to 30 years and at down payments of only 10 percent.

Second Agricultural Adjustment Act (AAA), 1938 The second AAA was passed when farm prices fell in 1938. The government paid farmers to store portions of overproduced crops until the price reached the level of prices from 1909 to 1914. America's farmers did not regain prosperity until the 1940s, when World War II brought increased demand for food.

Reform Legislation of the New Deal

Congress also passed a wide range of reform legislation as part of the New Deal.

Glass-Steagall Banking Act, 1933 This banking act aimed at restoring and maintaining stability in the national economy. It created the Federal Deposit Insurance Corporation (FDIC), which guaranteed individual bank deposits up to $5,000. The Glass-Steagall Act separated investment banks from commercial ones, prohibiting commercial banks from involvement in securities markets.

Securities Exchange Act, 1934 Created to promote economic stability, the Securities and Exchange Commission (SEC) has the authority to regulate stock exchanges and investment advisers. SEC powers included the right to bring action against those found practicing fraud. The SEC could require financial information about stocks and bonds before they were sold.

Social Security Act, 1935 The 1935 Social Security Act was a combination of public assistance and insurance. The law had three main parts: (1) It provided old-age insurance, paid by a tax on both the employer and employee while the employee was working. The worker and employer, not the government, funded this part of social security. (2) It provided unemployment insurance for workers, paid by employers. (3) It gave assistance to dependent children and to the elderly, ill, and handicapped.

National Labor Relations Act (Wagner Act), 1935 The Wagner Act, named for its author, New York Senator Robert Wagner, guaranteed labor the right to form unions, to practice **collective bargaining,** and to take collective action, such as strike, to support these actions. It created the National Labor Relations Board (NLRB) to ensure that elections to select unions were conducted fairly. The NLRB could also halt practices such as blacklisting, made illegal by this law.

Fair Labor Standards Act, 1938 This law, also called the Wages and Hours Act, set a minimum wage (originally 25 cents per hour) and a maximum work week (originally 44 hours) for workers in industries involved in interstate commerce. The law also banned child labor in interstate commerce. It is one of many examples of New Deal legislation passed using the power given to Congress to regulate interstate commerce.

The New Deal and Organized Labor

Roosevelt was interested in helping workers primarily through social legislation, such as social security. He also wanted to work cooperatively with business, as seen in the NIRA legislation. By 1935, when the NIRA was ruled unconstitutional, and with it the section that ensured labor the right to form unions, Roosevelt supported the Wagner Act as a means of aiding labor. He had turned away from business and saw organized labor unions as a force in society that would balance the power of big business. This pro-labor attitude of the New Deal resulted in an increase in union membership, which by 1938 had reached 7 million. In a 1937 case, the Supreme Court upheld the constitutionality of the NLRA.

The New Deal's Impact on Minorities and Women

The New Deal legislation affected Native Americans, African Americans, Latinos, and women in a variety of ways.

Native Americans and the New Deal In 1924, Native Americans were finally granted citizenship by Congress. However, Native Americans continued to suffer under the government policy of forced assimilation enacted in 1887 by the Dawes Act. Under Roosevelt and the New Deal, government policy changed to one of tribal restoration. The 1934 **Indian Reorganization Act,** also called the **Wheeler-Howard Act,** was passed. The bill's aim was to restore tribal self-government as well as Native American languages, customs, and religious freedom. Another New Deal program provided for the education of Native American children under the Bureau of Indian Affairs.

African Americans and the New Deal African Americans were not a well-organized interest group in the 1930s. They benefited less from the New Deal than did other groups. Roosevelt was not a strong advocate of civil rights, in part because he did not want to alienate Southern Democrats in Congress, whose votes he needed to pass New Deal legislation. He did not support African American efforts to abolish the poll tax or to pass an anti-lynching law. However, within the New Deal programs, Eleanor Roosevelt and Harry Hopkins gave strong support to African Americans. As many as 50 African Americans were appointed to posts in various New Deal agencies. The most influential among them was **Mary McLeod Bethune,** who served in the National Youth Administration. While African Americans protested discrimination within New Deal programs, some 40 percent of the nation's African Americans received help through a New Deal program.

Latinos and the New Deal Many Latinos worked in agriculture and were hit particularly hard by the Depression. "Okies" fleeing the Dust Bowl competed with Mexicans and Mexican Americans for migrant farm work in California. While the New Deal provided relief for these workers, the government's policy was to stop immigration and return to Mexico any unemployed noncitizens.

Women and the New Deal Like African Americans, women were not an organized group during the 1930s. As you have read, women experienced fewer layoffs during this period, because they worked in low-paying female-only jobs less affected by the Depression. Women earned about 50 cents for every dollar a man was paid, and they were often expected to give up jobs to male heads of families. The belief that the proper work for women was that of a wife and mother remained strong. Many New Deal programs simply would not hire women. While women made little progress in the workplace, the New Deal did help women in government. More women ran for and won political office, although they were still far outnumbered by men.

Evaluating FDR's Leadership: 1936 Election Mandate

In his first term, Roosevelt won the support of large numbers of Americans. Popular belief in him and in his New Deal program translated into votes. Roosevelt carefully built what is known as the **New Deal coalition,** a voting bloc that embraced the solid Democratic South, new immigrant workers, the big cities, African Americans who had previously voted Republican, organized labor, the elderly, and farmers who usually voted Republican. This coalition emerged in the 1936 election, when Roosevelt was reelected to a second term. Roosevelt received a mandate, or a clear endorsement, from the electorate, carrying all but two states. This shift in the two-party system was to dominate American politics over the next generation.

Social Studies Practices
Compare and Contrast

- How did the Indian Reorganization Act of 1934 compare to the Dawes Act of 1887 in terms of government goals and Native Americans' reactions to it?

Social Studies Practices
Organizing Evidence

The New Deal affected various groups in different ways. To help you understand how different people were affected by the New Deal, create a chart showing the impact of the New Deal on

- African Americans
- Latinos
- women

Evaluating FDR's Leadership: Relief and Recovery Efforts

Descriptions of Franklin Roosevelt, whether by those around him or historians today, focus on his optimism and sense of hope, his willingness to experiment, to acknowledge success, to admit failure and move on. Roosevelt agreed with those who believed that the Great Depression was a national crisis that could destroy capitalism and democracy. The New Deal provided relief by providing farm subsidies and offering employment through the CCC and WPA.

Evaluating FDR's Leadership: Reform Efforts

An overriding New Deal objective was to bring security to the American people. Roosevelt sought to make the national economy more stable and to preserve capitalism by moving away from laissez-faire capitalism to create a more stable capitalist economy. To that end, the New Deal created the FDIC, the SEC, and the NLRB. Other laws to make life more secure included the Social Security Act, the Federal Housing Authority Act, and the Fair Labor Standards Act.

FDR and the New Deal: Constitutional Issues

Franklin Roosevelt and his program for relief, recovery, and reform provoked controversy. Criticisms came from those who felt that it was too radical or went too far as well as from those who felt its programs were too conservative or did not go far enough.

Supreme Court Reactions to New Deal Legislation

Throughout the New Deal, the Supreme Court majority practiced judicial restraint, narrowly interpreting the interstate commerce clause and striking down many of FDR's programs, which were based on a broad interpretation of that part of the Constitution. In a series of decisions, the Court ruled that several key New Deal laws were unconstitutional.

Supreme Court and the NIRA The National Industrial Recovery Act (NIRA) was declared unconstitutional in **Schechter Poultry Corporation v. United States (1935).** The Court ruled that the law illegally gave Congress power to regulate intrastate commerce, or commerce within a single state, and violated the separation of powers by giving the legislative powers to the executive branch.

Supreme Court and the AAA The Supreme Court struck down the Agricultural Adjustment Act (AAA) in **United States v. Butler (1936)** on the grounds that agriculture was a local, not an interstate, matter under the provisions of the Tenth Amendment.

Tennessee Valley Authority (TVA), 1933: Model Yardstick or Creeping Socialism?

The federally funded TVA provided jobs, cheap electricity, and flood control to poor rural areas of seven states through dam construction on the Tennessee River and its tributaries. The TVA was made possible through the efforts of Republican Senator George Norris of Nebraska. The TVA was praised as a bold experiment in government intervention to meet regional needs. The TVA was also attacked as "creeping socialism."

Unifying Themes
Transformation of Social Structures

The Supreme Court's ruling in *Schechter Poultry* v. *United States* (1935) was based in part on a narrow definition of the interstate commerce clause. It also considered the NIRA law a violation of separation of powers.

- Review *Gibbons* v. *Ogden* (1824) regarding the interstate commerce clause.

- Review *Marbury* v. *Madison* (1803) regarding separation of powers.

- What is meant by separation of powers?

- Explain the Court's ruling in *Schechter* and the dissent.

Do We Want A Ventriloquist Act In The Supreme Court?

FDR's "Court-Packing" Proposal: Constitutional Challenge

Supreme Court opposition to FDR's programs continued with the Court consistently vetoing New Deal legislation. Roosevelt asked Congress to approve a law that would permit the president to increase the number of judges from nine to fifteen if the judges refused to retire at the age of 70. The request was seen as a constitutional challenge. It set off one of the biggest controversies of the New Deal.

The **Judicial Reorganization Bill**—or the **"court-packing"** plan, as its opponents called it—was intended to make the Supreme Court approve the New Deal laws. It never became law because it would have threatened the separation of powers and the system of checks and balances. Perhaps Roosevelt did succeed with his goal, however. The Supreme Court did not void another New Deal law. Roosevelt eventually appointed seven Supreme Court justices.

New Deal Controversy, Criticism, and Opposition

Although Americans seemed to support many of the New Deal programs, there were voices of opposition against Roosevelt and his ideas.

The Third-Term Controversy

Several constitutional questions were raised during the New Deal years, among them the third-term controversy when, in 1940, President Roosevelt challenged the unwritten constitution, winning both a third and a fourth term (1944). In 1951, the **Twenty-second Amendment,** setting a two-term limit for president, was ratified.

Preparing for the Regents

Compare the New Deal to other reform movements, such as Progressivism and the Great Society.

- Do they too appear to have stages?

Political Opposition

In his first two terms, Roosevelt's strongest opposition was from big business. In 1934, the **American Liberty League** was formed. It claimed that Roosevelt was exercising too much power as president. It attacked the New Deal for being financed through deficit spending. The group expressed fear that the American free-enterprise system was being destroyed.

Radical groups such as the Communist Party also offered alternatives to the New Deal but failed to gain any major public support. Meanwhile, the pro-Nazi German-American Bund became active, as did the Black Shirts, fascists who supported the views of Italian dictator Benito Mussolini. The New Deal was battling both the Great Depression and the threat of war from Europe and Japan.

The Socialist Party in America drew some increased support, although some members began to vote for Roosevelt. Unlike the Communist Party, the Socialists believed in the use of democratic means to make changes in the American economic structure.

As frustration grew in the face of the prolonged depression, various individuals entered the political scene, each criticizing the New Deal and often offering simplistic solutions to the economic crisis. These men included:

- Francis E. Townsend, who created a financially impossible plan to provide government pensions for the elderly.
- Father Charles E. Coughlin, a Catholic priest who blamed business owners, especially Jewish ones, for the economic crisis.
- **Huey Long,** a powerful United States senator and governor from Louisiana, who proposed that income and inheritance taxes on the wealthy be used to give each American a $2,500 income, a car, and a college education.

Evaluating the New Deal

Most historians agree on the following assessment of the New Deal:

- World War II was largely responsible for ending the Great Depression. The New Deal provided relief and improved but did not solve unemployment, the farm crisis, and underconsumption.
- Nevertheless, the New Deal did help people cope with the effects of the Great Depression while preventing economic, political, and social disaster.
- The New Deal restored confidence in government while it increased the power of the presidency and the federal government.
- The government assumed a role and a responsibility in more aspects of the economic and social life of its citizens.
- The New Deal preserved the free-enterprise system, instituting reforms to provide stability and encourage growth.
- The deficit spending of the New Deal raised the national debt.

Multiple-Choice Questions for Regents Practice

Base your answers to questions 1 and 2 on the graph and table below and on your knowledge of social studies.

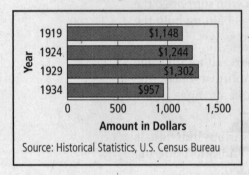

Average Annual Earnings of Factory Workers

Year	Amount in Dollars
1919	$1,148
1924	$1,244
1929	$1,302
1934	$957

Source: Historical Statistics, U.S. Census Bureau

Consumer Spending (in millions) on Select Items and Value of Stock

Category	1929	1933
Food	$19.5	$11.5
Housing	$11.5	$7.9
Clothing	$11.2	$5.4
Automobiles	$2.5	$0.8
Medical care	$2.9	$2.0
Philanthropy	$1.2	$0.9
Value of shares on New York Stock Exchange	$89.7	$22.2

Source: Historical Statistics of the United States, U.S. Census Bureau

1 Which claim is best supported by the data shown in both the graph and chart?

(1) The U.S. economy was at its weakest point just before the 1929 stock market crash.

(2) The military buildup during World War I sustained the U.S. economy through the 1920s.

(3) The economic prosperity of the 1920s in the United States greatly declined in the 1930s.

(4) The unstable U.S. economy of the 1930s caused the reduction of the costs of everyday goods.

2 Based on the graph and chart, what problem arose during the 1930s?

(1) Unemployment grew to 48 percent as key industries failed throughout the nation.

(2) Wealthy Americans had to provide more money to help the poor.

(3) People risked their money on stocks that were now more affordable.

(4) Americans had less income to spend on important basic needs.

Base your answer to question 3 on the passage below and on your knowledge of social studies.

> When Roosevelt sent the New Deal to the South he gave us a whole new political orientation, and we in the Southern black community began to identify him as a friend. . . . And, one of the major things that he did at that time was to send his wife as a kind of ambassador above and beyond politics to express the spiritual intent of the New Deal. And though she never came to Waycross, our picture of her was of a woman who cared. And she had a friend named Mary McLeod Bethune, who was a member of tremendous importance in the black community, and those two women began to symbolize for us what the New Deal was, who Roosevelt was, and what the response to the Depression was, how it was being led and orchestrated by kindly forces.

Source: Ossie Davis, interview for *The Great Depression*, PBS, August 29, 1992

3 What claim about Roosevelt can best be supported by this document?

(1) By delegating some of his presidential responsibilities to his wife and others, FDR was able to focus his efforts on getting his New Deal programs through Congress.

(2) By creating New Deal programs that focused on the needs of Americans in the South, FDR significantly reduced the number of unemployed African Americans.

(3) By including women in his group of advisors, FDR obtained public support for reducing government's role in the nation's social and economic affairs.

(4) By sending representatives who conveyed concern for Americans and confidence in his leadership, FDR gained support for his plans for recovery.

Base your answers to questions 4 and 5 on the image below and on your knowledge of social studies.

Source: Magazine advertisement for Hupp Motor Car Corporation, Detroit, Michigan, 1927

4 What aspect of American culture that developed during the 1920s is best reflected in this advertisement?

(1) Car ownership was considered the greatest expression of a flapper's wealth.

(2) Advertising focused on the wealthy as only they could afford the expensive new technology.

(3) Excess income allowed Americans to buy more consumer goods than ever before.

(4) Leisure time increased, and getting out of the city became a regular activity for many.

5 What problem arose for consumers who chose to make purchases such as this during the 1920s?

(1) People bought many items on credit and could not afford to pay their debts when the economy weakened.

(2) Industries that were detrimental to the environment developed as a result of new products such as the automobile.

(3) Americans spent more on consumer goods than on stocks, and the stock market became dangerously unstable.

(4) The federal government saw the excess spending and decided to benefit from it by levying an income tax.

Base your answers to questions 6 and 7 on the cartoon below and on your knowledge of social studies.

Source: O. Seibel, "The Supreme Court Under Pressure," 1937

6 What is the cartoonist's point of view on the actions of President Roosevelt?

(1) President Roosevelt is attempting to exert influence over the Supreme Court.

(2) President Roosevelt wants to strengthen the judiciary by reducing the number of courts.

(3) President Roosevelt is a strong believer in the system of checks and balances.

(4) President Roosevelt needs the Judiciary to balance power against a hostile Congress.

7 This cartoon was most likely created in response to President Roosevelt's

(1) decision to break tradition and run for a third term

(2) effort to increase the size of the Supreme Court

(3) desire to increase the power of the executive branch

(4) growing support for America's entry into World War II

Base your answers to questions 8 and 9 on the table below and on your knowledge of social studies.

U.S. Immigration Quotas of Select Countries

Country	Quotas	
	Under Immigration Act of 1921	Under Immigration Act of 1924
Great Britain	77,342	34,007
Germany	67,607	51,227
Italy	42,057	3,845
Poland	31,146	5,982
Russia	24,405	2,248
Sweden	20,042	8,961
Czechoslovakia	14,357	3,073
Norway	12,202	6,453

Source: 1929 Statistical Abstract, U.S. Census Bureau

8 The policy changes shown on the chart were a direct result of the growing

(1) influence of the Ku Klux Klan in local, state, and national government

(2) demand to allow only English speakers to come to the United States

(3) nativism that saw immigrants as a threat to American values and beliefs

(4) need to employ American women when soldiers returned after World War I

9 The Immigration Act of 1917 differed from these two later policies in that it

(1) focused on limiting the number of communists from entering the United States

(2) included the first immigration ban on a region by creating an Asiatic Barred Zone

(3) promoted the removal of radical Americans to select countries in Europe

(4) greatly restricted the number of immigrants allowed from Eastern and Southern Europe

Base your answers to questions 10 and 11 on the map below and on your knowledge of social studies.

Extent of the Dust Bowl

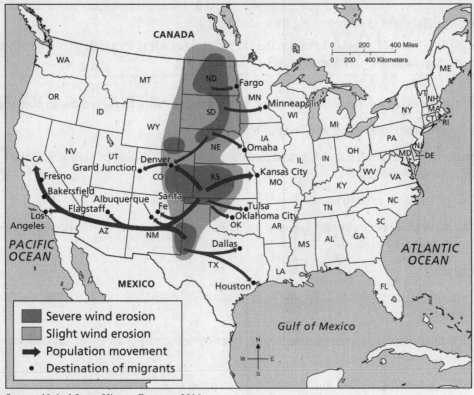

Source: *United States History,* Pearson, 2016

10 What was the primary cause of the events shown on the map?

(1) sharp decline in temperatures combined with destructive thunderstorms

(2) poor farming methods combined with a severe drought

(3) deforestation as a result of an increase in population in the Great Plains

(4) abandoned land eroded when tenant farmers joined the Great Migration

11 Which statement most accurately describes the consequence of the migration patterns shown on the map?

(1) The millions of farm workers who were displaced by the Dust Bowl added to the competition for jobs during the Depression.

(2) The movement of farmers out of the Great Plains allowed the small farms that remained to increase in size and control prices.

(3) The trend in migration out of the Dust Bowl region lasted through World War II, when farm workers returned to help supply recovering nations.

(4) The economic struggles of farms in the East were magnified when the farms in the West and Southwest gained more workers and could reduce their prices.

Task: Read and analyze the following documents, applying your social studies knowledge and skills to write a short essay of two or three paragraphs in which you:

- Describe the historical context surrounding these documents
- Identify and explain the *relationship* between the events and/or ideas found in these documents (Cause and Effect, *or* Similarity/Difference, *or* Turning Point)

In developing your short essay answer of two or three paragraphs, be sure to keep these explanations in mind:

Describe means "to illustrate something in words or tell about it"

Historical Context refers to "the relevant historical circumstances surrounding or connecting the events, ideas, or developments in these documents"

Identify means "to put a name to or to name"

Explain means "to make plain or understandable; to give reasons for or causes of; to show the logical development or relationship of"

<u>Types of Relationships:</u>

Cause refers to "something that contributes to the occurrence of an event, the rise of an idea, or the bringing about of a development"

Effect refers to "what happens as a consequence (result, impact, outcome) of an event, an idea, or a development"

Similarity tells how "something is alike or the same as something else"

Difference tells how "something is not alike or not the same as something else"

Turning Point is "a major event, idea, or historical development that brings about significant change. It can be local, regional, national, or global"

Document 1

"Yes, You Remembered Me"

Source: Clarence D. Batchelor, "The Forgotten Man," 1936

Document 2

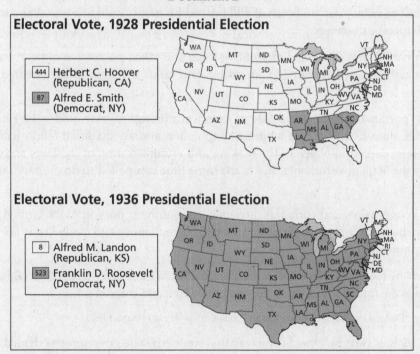

Electoral Vote, 1928 Presidential Election

444 Herbert C. Hoover (Republican, CA)
87 Alfred E. Smith (Democrat, NY)

Electoral Vote, 1936 Presidential Election

8 Alfred M. Landon (Republican, KS)
523 Franklin D. Roosevelt (Democrat, NY)

Source: *Encyclopaedia Britannica*

Document Analysis for Civic Literacy Essay

Historical Context: Equality

Throughout United States history, many constitutional and civic issues have been debated by Americans. These debates have resulted in efforts by individuals, groups, and governments to address these issues. These efforts have achieved varying degrees of success. One of these constitutional and civic issues is the meaning of equality.

Task: Read and analyze the document. Using information from the document and your knowledge of United States history, write an essay in which you

- Describe the historical circumstances surrounding this constitutional or civic issue
- Explain efforts to address this constitutional or civic issue by individuals, groups, and/or governments
- Discuss the extent to which these efforts were successful

Describe means "to illustrate something in words or tell about it"

Explain means "to make plain or understandable; to give reasons for or causes of; to show the logical development or relationship of"

Discuss means "to make observations about something using facts, reasoning, and argument; to present in some detail"

We complain:

1. That nowhere in the world, with few exceptions, are black men accorded equal treatment with white men, although in the same situation and circumstances, but, on the contrary, are discriminated against and denied the common rights due to human beings for no other reason than their race and color. . . .

2. In certain parts of the United States of America our race is denied the right of public trial accorded to other races when accused of crime, but are lynched and burned by mobs, and such brutal and inhuman treatment is even practiced upon our women.

3. That European nations have parceled out among them and taken possession of nearly all of the continent of Africa, and the natives are compelled to surrender their lands to aliens and are treated in most instances like slaves.

4. In the southern portion of the United States of America, although citizens under the Federal Constitution, and in some States almost equal to the whites in population and are qualified land owners and taxpayers, we are, nevertheless, denied all voice in the making and administration of the laws and are taxed without representation by the State governments, and at the same time compelled to do military service in defense of the country.

5. On the public conveyances and common carriers in the southern portion of the United States we are jim-crowed and compelled to accept separate and inferior accommodations and made to pay the same fare charged for first-class accommodations. . . .

6. . . . Our children are forced to attend inferior separate schools for shorter terms than white children, and the public school funds are unequally divided between the white and colored schools.

Source: Marcus Garvey, "Declaration of Rights of the Negro Peoples of the World," August 1920

1. According to Marcus Garvey, what is one way that southern state governments denied the rights of African Americans?

World War II (1935–1945)

Topic Overview

After the experiences of World War I, the United States attempted to follow a policy of neutrality. The nation suffered both with the loss of lives and financial expense as a result of helping to end World War I in Europe. During the 1930s the rise of totalitarian governments in Germany, the Soviet Union, and Japan caused President Franklin D. Roosevelt to balance neutrality with gradual limited assistance to Great Britain and other countries known as the Allies.

When the United States entered World War II in 1941, it could not have predicted how much the events of the next four years would impact the nation. These events were a time of transformation for the United States domestically and internationally as it took on the role of a global leader. On the home front, life changed for women, African Americans, Japanese Americans, and others. In foreign affairs, President Roosevelt took on a new world leadership position as he worked with other Allied leaders.

In the 1930s, Nazi Germany began the planned genocide of millions of Jews and other people they considered "undesirable." This horrific event is known as the Holocaust. After World War II, the United States and other countries took part in efforts to prevent such atrocities from ever occurring again.

United States Neutrality and Entry into World War II

Key Concept

11.8a As situations overseas deteriorated, President Roosevelt's leadership helped to move the nation from a policy of neutrality to a pro-Allied position and, ultimately, direct involvement in the war.

Lesson Overview

Following World War I, the United States had returned to its policy of isolationism. However, the nation remained active internationally both diplomatically and economically. The Neutrality Acts gave way to pro-Allied positions, including "cash and carry" and Lend-Lease. The United States negotiated with Japan in an effort to stop Japanese aggression in the Pacific prior to the start of the war. American isolationism ended with the Japanese attack on Pearl Harbor, which caused the American entry into World War II.

As president, Franklin D. Roosevelt served as commander in chief and chief diplomat working with the Allied nations during wartime. Technological advances altered the nature of war and the extent of its devastation. As a result of air power, civilians now became targets. Ultimately, President Truman decided to use the atomic bomb against the Japanese to bring an end to the war.

Unifying Themes

As you review this lesson take special note of the following themes:

- **Power, Authority, and Governance** What caused President Roosevelt to move the nation from a policy of neutrality to a pro-Allied position? What ultimately caused his decision to directly involve the United States in World War II?

- **Civic Ideals and Practices** After World War I, why did many Americans urge the United States government to follow a policy of neutrality? Why did other citizens push for a policy of isolationism?

- **Science, Technology, and Innovation** In what ways did the technological innovations of World War II alter military tactics and civilian life? What were some negative consequences of the use of scientific advances during this time period?

Key People

Franklin D. Roosevelt

Adolf Hitler

Benito Mussolini

Francisco Franco

Winston Churchill

Emperor Hirohito

Key Terms and Events

isolationism

neutrality

Neutrality Acts

"cash and carry"

Twenty-second Amendment

totalitarian

fascism

appeasement

Grand Alliance

Lend-Lease Act

attack on Pearl Harbor

Allies

Axis Powers

Manhattan Project

atomic bomb

Hiroshima

Nagasaki

In the 1920s and 1930s, the United States pursued the policies of neutrality and isolationism. In order to understand the reasons for these policies, we must examine the lingering impact of World War I.

Isolationist Sentiment After World War I

The United States had been reluctant to enter World War I. Fighting had begun in Europe in 1914, and the United States stayed out of the war until 1917. Between April 1917, when the United States formally declared war, and Germany's surrender in November 1918, some 48,000 American soldiers were killed in battle while 2,900 were declared missing in action and 56,000 soldiers died of disease. These losses were far less than those of the European nations, some of which had lost millions of soldiers and civilians. Nevertheless, the American losses were great enough to cause Americans to take a close look at the reasons for the entry of the United States into the war and at the nation's foreign policy.

Isolation and Neutrality

Isolationism and neutrality are similar foreign policies, but an important difference exists between them. **Isolationism** is a national foreign policy of remaining apart from political or economic entanglements with other countries. Strict isolationists do not support any type of contact with other countries, including economic ties or trade activities.

When a country chooses a policy of **neutrality,** it deliberately takes no side in a dispute or controversy. Countries following this path are often referred to as being nonaligned or noninvolved. Neutral nations do not limit their trading activities with other nations, unless a trading partnership would limit that country's ability to stay politically noninvolved.

Social Studies Practices
Geographic Reasoning

- How did the United States' location relative to Europe and Asia contribute to its isolationist sentiment before and after World War I?

Preparing for the Regents

Many questions on the exam will require you to distinguish between similar concepts and terms.

- What is the difference between isolationism and neutrality?

Events Preceding American Involvement in World War II

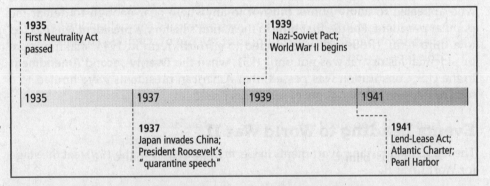

1935	1937	1939	1941
1935 First Neutrality Act passed		**1939** Nazi-Soviet Pact; World War II begins	
	1937 Japan invades China; President Roosevelt's "quarantine speech"		**1941** Lend-Lease Act; Atlantic Charter; Pearl Harbor

Historical Roots of Isolationism and Neutrality

The roots of isolationist and neutralistic sentiments in the United States can be traced to the late eighteenth and early nineteenth centuries.

Precedent Set by George Washington As President, George Washington set the precedent of American neutrality—but not isolationism. He knew that trade was necessary for the new nation, but that alliances might force it into war. In 1793, Washington issued his Proclamation of Neutrality. In his farewell address of 1796, he warned the nation to "avoid entangling alliances."

• How did the Monroe
Doctrine contribute
to isolationist and
neutralistic sentiments in
the United States prior
to World War II?

Unifying Themes
Time, Continuity, and
Change

The Neutrality Acts of the
1930s reflect the efforts
of Congress to avoid the
foreign policy mistakes
that led the country
into World War I. The
Neutrality Acts passed
in 1935, 1936, and 1937
declared that the United
States would withhold
weapons and loans of
money from all nations at
war and that U.S. citizens
who traveled on ships
belonging to nations
at war did so at their
own risk. The acts also
required that nonmilitary
goods sold to nations at
war be paid for in cash
and transported by the
purchaser.

• What events in the
nation's history caused
the government to be
wary of Americans'
involvement in ocean
trade and travel?

Monroe Doctrine The Monroe Doctrine reinforced the neutrality of the United States toward Europe. In 1823, President Monroe stated that the United States would not interfere in European affairs. He also warned European powers to remain out of the affairs of nations in the Western Hemisphere.

Pre–World War II Isolationism

In 1934, when the United States was trying to recover from the worst economic depression in its history, Senator Gerald Nye led an investigation into the reasons the United States entered World War I. The committee concluded that the United States had gone to war at the encouragement of financiers and armament makers, eager for profits. As a result of this investigation, many Americans supported a return to isolationism.

In 1935, the Senate refused to allow the United States to join the World Court. That same year, Congress passed the first of a series of **Neutrality Acts,** which prevented Americans from making loans to nations at war. Any sales of goods to such nations were strictly on a **"cash and carry"** basis. In 1937, President Franklin D. Roosevelt made his famous quarantine speech, in which he stated that the United States would attempt to quarantine the warring nation "patients" in order to protect the rest of the world. In 1941, the famous aviator Charles Lindbergh made a speech encouraging isolationism.

Presidential Election of 1940

In 1940, President **Franklin D. Roosevelt** faced a challenge no other president had faced. He had helped the nation to survive the worst depression in its history while watching the rise of dictators in Europe and Asia. Roosevelt was at the end of his second term as president of the United States. Since the precedent set by President George Washington, no president had served more than two terms. This practice was not set by law at that time but was considered a respected tradition.

Roosevelt surprised the nation by campaigning for and accepting the Democratic Party's nomination for a third term. He ran against Republican Wendell L. Willkie, who appealed to many voters but not to anywhere near enough to defeat the popular president. For the first time in the nation's history, a president was elected to a third term. (Roosevelt was elected to a fourth term in 1944, making more presidential history.) It was not until 1951, when the **Twenty-second Amendment** to the U.S. Constitution was passed, that American presidents were limited to a total of two terms or ten years of service as president.

Events Leading to World War II

The rise of totalitarian governments in Germany and Italy in the 1930s set the stage for World War II.

The Rise of Totalitarian Governments

In **totalitarian** governments, one political party has complete control over the government and bans all other parties. Totalitarian governments rely on terror to suppress individual rights and silence opposition.

In Germany and Italy, totalitarian governments were established based on the philosophy of fascism. **Fascism** places the importance of the nation above all else, and individual rights and freedoms are lost. Nazi Germany (led by **Adolf Hitler**) and fascist Italy (led by **Benito Mussolini**) were two fascist governments characterized by extreme nationalism, racism, and militarism (desire to go to war).

Hitler and Mussolini provided military assistance to **Francisco Franco**, a fascist leader in Spain who was attempting to overthrow the republican government. The devastating Spanish Civil War that erupted in 1936 became a "dress rehearsal" for World War II. The war in Spain was a testing ground for new weapons and military strategies that were later used in World War II.

In the United States, opinions about support for the Spanish Civil War were divided. Some Americans traveled to Spain to fight for the republican cause. The United States government, however, continued to pursue a policy of neutrality. Congress passed a resolution forbidding the export of arms to either side in 1937. Franco won the Spanish Civil War in 1939, established a fascist government, and remained leader of Spain until his death in 1975.

Major World Events, 1918–1941

1918 Germany surrenders. World War I is concluded.	**1935** Italy invades Ethiopia. The United States passes the first Neutrality Act.
1919 Germany signs the Treaty of Versailles. The United States refuses to approve the Treaty of Versailles.	**1936** Hitler reoccupies the Rhineland. The German/Italian Axis is formed. The Spanish Civil War begins (ending in 1939). The United States passes the second Neutrality Act. The United States votes for nonintervention at the Pan-American Conference.
1921 Great Britain, France, and Japan attend the Washington Naval Conference on limiting arms. The conference produces the Four Power and Nine Power treaties.	
	1937 Japan invades China. Japan sinks an American gunboat in Chinese waters. The United States passes the third Neutrality Act, including a "cash and carry" plan.
1922 Benito Mussolini becomes Italy's fascist dictator. The USSR is officially formed, following the communist victory in the Russian Revolution.	
	1938 Germany annexes Austria (the *Anschluss*). Hitler demands the Sudetenland of Czechoslovakia. Great Britain, France, and Germany sign the Munich Pact, giving in to Hitler's demands.
1923 Adolf Hitler writes *Mein Kampf* in prison.	
1924 In the USSR, Lenin dies. Stalin continues his rise to power.	
	1939 A German/Soviet nonaggression pact is signed. Japanese and American relations are deadlocked. The United States Senate refuses to grant aid to Great Britain or France. Hitler invades Poland, marking the beginning of World War II.
1928 The Kellogg-Briand Pact outlawing war is signed by 62 nations. The pact contains no method of enforcement.	
1929 The most serious economic depression in history begins, continuing through the 1930s.	
	1940 Germany occupies Norway, Denmark, the Netherlands, Belgium, Luxembourg, and France. Germany attacks Great Britain. Japan joins the Axis Powers. President Roosevelt arranges to supply destroyers to Great Britain. Congress passes the Selective Training and Service Act, the first peacetime draft in United States history.
1930 Japan occupies Manchuria.	
1932 Japan seizes Shanghai. The United States issues the Stimson Doctrine, condemning Japanese aggression against Manchuria.	
1933 Hitler assumes power in Germany. Japan announces its withdrawal from the League of Nations. President Roosevelt announces the Good Neighbor Policy in Latin America. The USSR is formally recognized by the United States. Nazi Germany begins operation of the first concentration camp at Dachau, near Munich.	**1941** Germany invades the USSR. The United States passes the Lend-Lease Act, granting aid to countries whose defense was seen as critical to the defense of the United States. President Roosevelt and Prime Minister Churchill agree to the Atlantic Charter. Japan attacks the United States at Pearl Harbor. The United States enters World War II.

Major World Events, 1918–1941

The "Major World Events, 1918–1941" chart above summarizes the major events between the end of World War I and the entry of the United States into World War II. As you review the chart, look for relationships between events in order to understand how certain events caused others that occurred later. Some events in the chart are so significant that they require further discussion.

Social Studies Practices
Compare and Contrast

One way to remember the meaning of the term *totalitarianism* is from the word *total*: totalitarian governments have total control over every aspect of life. They suppress all individual rights and silence all opposition with threats. Fascism places the importance of the nation above individual rights.

- What is the relationship between totalitarianism and fascism?

Preparing for the Regents

Stimulus-Based Questions: Chart

Examine the chart then answer these questions.

- How might dissatisfaction with the outcome of World War I and economic depression have contributed to the rise of dictators in Italy and Germany?
- Which events described in the chart represent actions of appeasement on the part of France and Great Britain?

Munich Agreement With the signing of the Munich Agreement in 1938, Great Britain and France allowed Germany to annex the Sudetenland, a region of Czechoslovakia with a large German-speaking population. Hitler convinced the British prime minister, Neville Chamberlain, and the French premier, Édouard Daladier, that Germany would make no further territorial demands in Czechoslovakia after annexing the Sudetenland.

When Chamberlain returned to Great Britain with this agreement, he told the world that he had achieved "peace for our time." Six months later, however, Hitler seized the rest of Czechoslovakia. Great Britain and France had resorted to the policy of **appeasement,** which means to agree to the demands of a potential enemy in order to keep the peace. Hitler demonstrated by his action that he could not be permanently appeased, and the world learned a costly lesson.

American Actions and Alliances In 1940, legislation to create a U.S. military draft was controversial as it raised fears that the United States would be drawn into war. Congress took this action although it was clearly still attempting to keep the United States out of another war. Also, in 1940, President Franklin D. Roosevelt agreed that the United States and Great Britain, whose Prime Minister was **Winston Churchill,** would become formal allies to defeat the aggressors. This became known as the **Grand Alliance.** The two men didn't always share common political aims, but they shared a common enemy.

Lend-Lease Act Although the United States was officially committed to a policy of neutrality, President Roosevelt soon found a way around the Neutrality Acts to provide aid, including warships, to Great Britain. In 1941, Roosevelt convinced Congress to pass the **Lend-Lease Act,** which allowed the United States to sell or lend war materials to "any country whose defense the President deems vital to the defense of the United States." Roosevelt said that the nation would become the "arsenal of democracy," supplying arms to those who were fighting for freedom.

Japanese Aggression in Asia Since the 19th century, the United States had a long history of trading with both China and Japan. Its Open Door trade policy with China allowed the United States to maintain access to China's natural resources and its markets. Japan industrialized much sooner and faster than China and also desired resources from China as well as from Southeast Asia. In 1931, Japan invaded Manchuria, a part of mainland China. In 1937, to the alarm of the United States, Japan invaded and took control of large areas of coastal China. Since 1911, the United States had an agreement to sell war materials to Japan, but by 1939 as a result of Japan's aggression that sales agreement with Japan had ended.

At the same time, Germany and the Soviet Union had signed a nonaggression pact, which caused Japan to increase its militarism in Asia. Japan then allied itself with Germany to attack the British colony of Burma and French colonies in Southeast Asia. Tensions between the United States and Japan grew as the United States was importing oil, tin, and rubber from European colonies in this region. Also, the United States was strongly supporting China with Lend-Lease aid overland via the Burma Road. This important supply route was closed as a result of the Japanese invasion. By early 1941, diplomatic and economic negotiations between the United States and Japan had ceased being productive. The United States was unable to stop Japanese aggression in Asia without declaring war, which it was unwilling to do.

Japan Attacks Pearl Harbor President Roosevelt had promised that the United States would not fight in a war in which the country was not directly involved. However, on December 7, 1941, Japanese war planes attacked the U.S. Navy

Unifying Themes
Power and Authority

President Roosevelt explained the Lend-Lease Act to the American people through the use of a simple comparison:

"If your neighbor's house is on fire, you don't sell him a hose. You lend it to him and take it back after the fire is out."

- How did the Lend-Lease Act lead to greater U.S. involvement in the war?

fleet at Pearl Harbor, Hawaii. Roosevelt called the attack a day that would "live in infamy," a day that Americans would never forget. This surprise attack shattered the American belief that the Atlantic and Pacific oceans would safely isolate the United States from fighting in Europe and Asia. The **attack on Pearl Harbor** fueled American nationalism and patriotism.

The day after the attack, Congress agreed to President Roosevelt's request to declare war on Japan, thus entering World War II. As a nation recently recovering from its worst economic depression in its history, the United States financed a great part of its involvement in World War II with the sale of government war bonds.

World War II in Review

World War II began in 1939, when German forces invaded Poland. The United States entered the war two years later, after the Japanese attacked Pearl Harbor. By 1942 the United States and Great Britain entered into a formal agreement with the Soviet Union to allow that country to join their existing Grand Alliance. War in Europe ended in May 1945, and fighting in the Pacific ended on August 14, 1945, when the Japanese surrender brought World War II to a conclusion.

Major Powers

The war pitted 26 nations united together as the **Allies** against eight **Axis Powers.** The major powers among the Allies were Great Britain, the Soviet Union, and the United States. Germany, Italy, and Japan were the major Axis nations. Leaders of the major powers are listed below.

Unifying Themes
Science and Technology

• How did advances in aviation technology contribute to changes in American isolationist sentiments?

Social Studies Practices
Gathering Evidence

• Who were the three major Allied Powers?
1.
2.
3.
• Who were the three major Axis Powers?
1.
2.
3.

Leaders During World War II

Allies	
• Great Britain	Winston Churchill, Prime Minister
• USSR	Joseph Stalin, Communist dictator
• United States	Franklin D. Roosevelt, President until his death in April 1945
	Harry S. Truman, President following Roosevelt's death
	Dwight D. Eisenhower, Supreme Commander of Allied troops in Europe
	Douglas MacArthur, Commander of the Allied troops in the Pacific
• France	Charles de Gaulle, leader of the Free French during the Nazi occupation

Axis Powers	
• Germany	Adolf Hitler, leader of the National Socialist German Workers' Party (Nazis), known as "Der Führer" ("The Leader")
• Italy	Benito Mussolini, Fascist dictator known as "Il Duce" ("The Leader")
• Japan	Emperor Hirohito
	Hideki Tojo, General and Prime Minister

Major Events

World War II was fought primarily in two major regions: Europe and North Africa and in the Pacific. Major military engagements and turning points in World War II are presented on the next two pages.

Europe During World War II

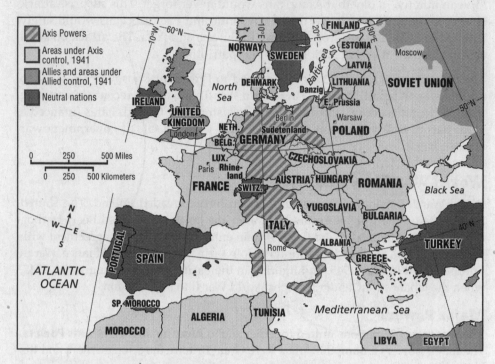

Legend:
- Axis Powers
- Areas under Axis control, 1941
- Allies and areas under Allied control, 1941
- Neutral nations

Major Events of World War II

- **1939** Germany invades Poland with a rapid attack by armored vehicles supported by airplanes. This is known as a blitzkrieg, or "lightning war."

- **1940** Denmark, Norway, Belgium, the Netherlands, and much of northern France fall to Nazi invasion. Battle of Britain—months of terrifying air raids by Germany against Great Britain known as the blitz.

- **1941** Germany invades the Soviet Union. The siege of Leningrad begins and lasts 17 months. Japan attacks Pearl Harbor, Hawaii. The United States enters the war.

- **1941–1942** Japan seizes the Philippines, Burma, Singapore, the Dutch East Indies, and French Indochina. Japan continues to press southward toward Australia.

- **1942** Battle of Midway in the Pacific. The United States regains naval superiority in the Pacific.

- **1942–1943** Battle of Stalingrad. German troops are forced to surrender after thousands have been killed. This battle marks a turning point in the East and allows Russian soldiers to begin to move west.

- **1943** In North Africa, Allied troops defeat Axis armies for control of the Mediterranean Sea and the Suez Canal.

- **June 6, 1944** Allied invasions of Normandy, France, across the English Channel. This was the largest such invasion in history, involving over 150,000 soldiers. This invasion was known by the code name Operation Overlord and the D-Day Invasion.

- **1944–1945** Bitter fighting in the Pacific (for example at Leyte, Iwo Jima, and Okinawa) costs thousands of American lives.

- **December 1944** Battle of the Bulge. A surprisingly strong response by German troops slows the movement of Allied forces eastward to Germany.

- **April 12, 1945** Franklin Roosevelt dies unexpectedly from a cerebral hemorrhage.

- **April 1945** Allied troops from the East and West meet at the Elbe River in Germany. Hitler commits suicide.

- **May 8, 1945** The end of war in Europe, celebrated as V-E Day (Victory in Europe).

- **August 6, 1945** The United States drops an atomic bomb on the Japanese city of Hiroshima.

- **August 9, 1945** The United States drops an atomic bomb on the Japanese city of Nagasaki.

- **August 14, 1945** Hirohito announces Japan's defeat to the Japanese people.

- **September 2, 1945** Japan formally surrenders.

Preparing for the Regents

Stimulus-Based Questions: Timeline

Examine the timeline. Then answer the following questions.

- What was the significance of the Battle of Midway?
- Which ended first, the war in Europe or the war in the Pacific?
- What event would be considered a turning point in favor of the Allies? Why?

World War II in the Pacific

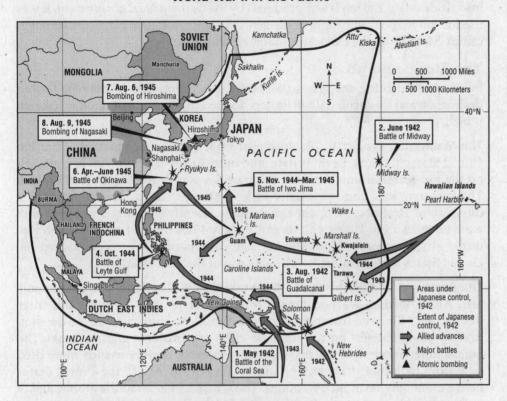

Technology and World War II

The technological advancements made before and during World War II forever changed warfare. Some of these innovations led to beneficial technologies that we use today while others caused utter devastation.

New Innovations

The years immediately prior to the United States entry into World War II and then the actual war years (1941–45) were years of great technological advancement. New and larger naval vessels were developed to become aircraft carriers. This allowed for increased naval and air force mobility. New, bigger, and faster aircraft were developed by both sides, which could carry larger and larger bombs. These planes became the forerunners of today's cruise missiles. The early use of rockets during this time period led to the Space Age and the Space Race of the 1950s and beyond.

Radar and sonar techniques were developed, which proved crucial to the Allied forces. Radar was vital especially during the German bombing of London and southeast England. Even with the radar of the day, thousands of English civilians were killed by German bombs. Near the end of the war, Allied bombs were used against military and civilian targets in Germany, causing major destruction and loss of life. With the widespread use of submarines, sonar technology enabled detection of underwater enemies. An assortment of new materials for aircraft were developed, including nylon and bakelite. That development eventually led to a variety of modern plastics. Very early electronic computers were just beginning to be developed and were used on a limited basis.

Although penicillin was discovered in 1928, it was not mass-produced until 1942. Given wartime injuries and diseases the demand for it was high. Plasma was discovered and used as a short-term blood substitute for injured military personnel.

All medical discoveries were not used in positive ways, however. A cyanide-based insecticide called Zyklon B was produced by the German Nazi government. It was used to kill millions of people in the genocide taking place in Nazi concentration camps. More about the Holocaust follows in this topic.

The Atomic Bomb

In an effort to bring the war to a speedy conclusion and to prevent further destruction and loss of life, Allied leaders decided to embark on an atomic research project.

The Manhattan Project In the spring of 1943, a group of scientists from the United States, Canada, Great Britain, and other European countries began work on the top-secret atomic research program known as the **Manhattan Project.** The research was done primarily at Los Alamos, New Mexico, under the direction of Dr. Robert Oppenheimer. Many scientists involved in the project were refugees from Hitler's Germany. By July 1945, the first **atomic bomb** was tested at Alamagordo, New Mexico. The success of this project enabled the United States to determine the ultimate use of the new weapon.

The Bombings of Hiroshima and Nagasaki Within days after the first atomic test, Allied leaders warned Japan to surrender or face "prompt and utter destruction." Since no surrender occurred, President Truman made the decision to drop atomic bombs on the Japanese cities of **Hiroshima** and **Nagasaki.** The bombs killed more than 100,000 Japanese instantly, and thousands more died later from radiation sickness. For a time after World War II, the United States held a monopoly on atomic weapons. The world had entered the atomic age. A controversial issue that resulted from World War II was the morality of nuclear warfare. The topic continues to be debated in the twenty-first century.

Japan Surrenders Within days of the devastating bombings of Hiroshima and Nagasaki, Japan formally surrendered, and World War II came to an end. Following Japan's surrender, the United States occupied Japan under the leadership of General Douglas MacArthur. A new constitutional monarchy introduced democratic reforms that included a democratic constitution dictated by MacArthur. **Emperor Hirohito** retained his throne but only as a figurehead.

Preparing for the Regents

Turning Point

Several alternatives were considered before dropping the atomic bombs on Hiroshima and Nagasaki, Japan. The final decision rested with President Truman who decided to use the bombs to end the war as quickly as possible and thereby save American lives.

- Why might the dropping of the atomic bombs be considered a turning point in American history?

Preparing for the Regents

Stimulus-Based Questions: Chart

Study the chart at right, then answer the following questions.

- Which country had the greatest number of military casualties during World War II?
- How did technology have an effect on the casualty numbers?

Casualties in World War II

Country	Military Dead	Military Wounded	Civilian Dead
Great Britain	373,000	475,000	93,000
France	213,000	400,000	108,000
Soviet Union	11,000,000	14,102,000	7,000,000
United States	292,000	671,000	*
Germany	3,500,000	5,000,000	780,000
Italy	242,000	66,000	153,000
Japan	1,300,000	4,000,000	672,000

All figures are estimates   * Very small number of civilian dead

Wartime Life in the United States

Lesson Overview

An American didn't have to be a member of the military during World War II to experience the impact of the war. American business was drawn out of the Great Depression to convert production facilities for wartime use. American women and members of minority groups suddenly became valuable and necessary members of the workforce. Others suffered new and unexpected forms of discrimination as they were wrongfully associated with America's enemies.

Key Concept

11.8b United States entry into World War II had a significant impact on American society.

Unifying Themes

As you review this lesson take special note of the following themes:

- **Time, Continuity, and Change** How did the Japanese attack on Pearl Harbor influence life within the United States for Japanese Americans, especially on the West Coast?

- **Development and Transformation of Social Structures** In what ways did World War II change the role of women in American society?

- **Power, Authority, and Governance** Describe an event during World War II in the United States that could be considered an abuse of power.

Key People

Tuskegee Airmen

Harry S. Truman

Key Terms and Events

mobilization
Rosie the Riveter
Executive Order 9981
Nisei
Executive Order 9066
Wartime Relocation Authority (WRA)
"Government Issue" (G.I.)

Code Talkers
demobilization
Fair Deal
G.I. Bill of Rights
Taft Hartley Act (1947)
National Security Act (1947)
"Baby Boom"

Key Supreme Court Cases

Korematsu v. *United States (1944)*

American Patriotism

After the United States entered the war, the nation moved to full-scale wartime production and **mobilization** of the armed forces. Americans rallied behind the war effort.

With the exception of the attack on Pearl Harbor, Hawaii, and battles on several Pacific islands, World War II was not fought on American soil. Nonetheless, America's coastal areas and large cities held blackout drills in case of attack. Americans supported the war effort by rationing food, gasoline, and other necessities and luxuries.

Unifying Themes
Economic Systems

Between 1939 and 1945, federal spending increased from $9.4 billion to $95.2 billion. The government financed about 41 percent of the war costs by increasing taxes. The rest of the money needed was borrowed from banks, private investors, and the public. Such deficit spending—government spending of borrowed money—turned the depressed economy of the 1930s around almost overnight. It also created a huge national debt. During this period, federal economic controls increased.

- Why did the American public support the increased taxes and the development of deficit spending?

During the war, the federal government used rationing to provide more resources for the military. Rationing meant that the availability of many consumer goods was very limited. Government campaigns encouraged Americans to have "meatless Tuesdays," and many Americans planted "victory gardens" to increase the food supply. Hollywood entertainers made special presentations to persuade citizens to buy war bonds to help the government finance the war.

The Role of American Women

World War II brought dramatic changes to the lives of American women in the military and in the civilian workforce.

In the Military During the war, more than 200,000 women joined the military services. Women served in separate units from men, such as in the Women's Army Corps (WAC), and performed vital military duties. They operated radios and repaired planes and vehicles. They were also assigned, along with men, to clerical duties.

In the Civilian Workforce When millions of men joined the military, employment opportunities opened up to women. Many women took jobs that had once been open to men only. More than five million women eventually worked in factories devoted to wartime production, although their pay never came close to equaling men's pay. One song about a woman named Rosie the Riveter became popular during the war years because it captured the sense of duty and patriotism felt by millions of women. The term **"Rosie the Riveter"** became a slang term for all women who worked in wartime factories.

Resulting Changes Women's wartime work resulted in important changes in employment and lifestyle, even after the war. Before the war, most employed American women were young and unmarried. During the war, large numbers of married women and mothers who had never worked outside the home took

Women factory workers

jobs. This trend continued after the war. Although many women willingly returned to the roles of wife and mother at the end of the war, thousands more remained in the workforce, which improved their standard of living.

The entry of women into the paid workforce during World War II marked the beginning of a long-term trend. Women continued to enter the workforce throughout the rest of the century. New issues became important. For example, child care became important during the war years, and it remains an important issue today.

African Americans

The experiences of African Americans during the war years provided the foundation of the civil rights movement of the 1950s and 1960s.

African Americans in the Military Nearly one million African American men and women served in the military during World War II. Military units were segregated, and initially, African American soldiers were limited to support roles. Once the war went on, these soldiers soon saw combat, and many became distinguished themselves.

One example of such heroism was the **Tuskegee Airmen,** the first black military pilots. These 994 fighter pilots were some of the most decorated fliers of the war effort, but they fought two wars, one overseas against a foreign enemy and the other against racism at home. In 1948, President **Harry S. Truman** showed his support for civil rights by issuing **Executive Order 9981,** which led to the end of racial segregation in the military.

At Home In the 1940s, many southern African Americans began moving to northern cities in search of economic opportunity and freedom from discrimination. However, they met discrimination in the North. Race riots broke out in Detroit and New York City in the summer of 1943. Membership in civil rights organizations grew as African Americans struggled against discrimination.

African Americans did experience some gains during the war years. Politically, their migration north had made them a significant voting bloc in urban areas. Economically, new jobs in war industries brought many African Americans the chance to earn more than they ever had before. Despite these gains, African Americans experienced discrimination and inequality in salaries in the workplace. The black press urged that the struggle for freedom be fought on two fronts— overseas and at home as well.

Japanese Americans

Thousands of Japanese Americans faced hardship and economic losses after the attack on Pearl Harbor, Hawaii.

Japanese Immigration to America Immigrants from Japan began arriving in the United States in the early 1900s. These immigrants settled mainly on the west coast of the United States. By 1941, thousands of Americans of Japanese descent, called **Nisei,** had been born in the United States and were American citizens. Many had never been to Japan, and many had no desire to go there.

Wartime Relocation Authority (WRA) After the Japanese attack on Pearl Harbor, many Americans feared that Japanese Americans presented a threat to national security. Anti-Japanese sentiment grew, and in 1942, President Roosevelt issued **Executive Order 9066,** establishing military zones for the imprisonment of Japanese Americans. The agency responsible for handling this internment process was the **Wartime Relocation Authority (WRA).** More than 100,000 people of Japanese descent were forced to leave their homes and move to WRA camps, hastily constructed military-style barracks ringed with barbed wire and guarded by troops.

Social Studies Practices
Cause and Effect

• What trend emerged following World War II in regard to women's participation in the labor force?

Social Studies Practices
Chronological Reasoning

• How might the experiences of African Americans during World War II have contributed to the rise of the civil rights movement during the 1950s and 1960s?

Unifying Themes
Civic Ideals and Practices

Since the United States was fighting on the same side as China, the Magnuson Act of 1943 repealed the Chinese Exclusion Act and gave Chinese Americans the right to vote. American citizens from India gained the right to vote in 1946, while Japanese Americans were granted suffrage in 1952.

"It is a fact that the Japanese navy has been reconnoitering [investigating] the Pacific Coast. . . . It is [a] fact that communication takes place between the enemy at sea and enemy agents on land."

- Would the writer of this excerpt have supported the Supreme Court's decision in *Korematsu* v. *United States?*

- Explain your answer.

The concept of majority rule may threaten individual rights. The *Korematsu* case shared a similarity with *Plessy* v. *Ferguson* (1896) in that specific groups were being targeted by the government based on race or ethnicity. Which groups were targeted by each case and why?

- *Korematsu* v. *United States*

- *Plessy* v. *Ferguson*

On the exam you will need to know some specialized vocabulary: *Latino* means a person from Latin America (Central or South America), *Hispanic* means someone who is Spanish-speaking and of Spanish origin, *Chicano* means a male of Mexican origin.

High-school recess period, Manzanar Relocation Center, California

Korematsu* v. *United States In the 1944 landmark case ***Korematsu* v. *United States*,** the Supreme Court upheld the forced evacuation as a reasonable wartime emergency measure. However, no acts of Japanese American sabotage or treason were ever identified, and thousands of Nisei fought honorably in the war. Almost 50 years after World War II, the United States government admitted that the wartime relocation program had been unjust. In 1988, Congress voted to pay $20,000 to each of the approximately 60,000 surviving Americans who had been interned. The first payments were made in 1990. The government also issued a formal apology.

Nisei Soldiers Despite the injustices endured by Japanese Americans, thousands proved their loyalty by serving in the U.S. armed forces, primarily in Europe. The 442nd Regimental Combat Team, made up entirely of Japanese Americans, won more medals for bravery than any other unit of its size in the war. Daniel Inouye, a soldier in World War II who lost his right arm in the war, became a United States Senator from Hawaii. He served from 1963 until his death in 2012. He was known for telling of when he returned from the war in uniform and tried to get a haircut in the United States. A barber refused him using an ethnic slur directed at Inouye, a returning American soldier in uniform without his right arm.

Mexican Americans and Latino Americans

Mexican Americans were another large minority group who served the United States during World War II both in combat and on the home front. Over 500,000 Latinos (persons of Latin American origin) served in the military in both the Pacific theater and in Europe. This number includes about 350,000 Mexican Americans and over 50,000 Puerto Ricans. Latino soldiers were especially valuable in the defense of the Philippines as most spoke Spanish as well as English. A Mexican American from East Los Angeles, Marine Guy Gabaldon, also knew Japanese as a result of growing up in an ethnically diverse neighborhood. This asset was extremely beneficial when he was serving in Saipan in the South Pacific. Gabaldon captured 1,500 Japanese soldiers using his skill with language and was given the nickname the "Pied Piper of Saipan."

Latino women were also talented and bilingual and served in the military as linguists, nurses, and Red Cross aids. These women were able to break through both gender and cultural barriers. Thousands of Latino men and women worked in vital jobs on the home front, such as in mines, shipyards, and airplane factories. Thousands of Mexicans were also needed for agricultural jobs and as railroad workers. Many came to the United States under a special program to permit guest workers.

After the war, these Latinos thought that their wartime sacrifices had earned them equal rights just as other minority groups believed. Instead they, too, often faced discrimination. Many wartime Latino leaders came home to become civil rights leaders. Dr. Hector Garcia founded the American G. I. Forum, a group still active in working for Latino rights in health care, education, labor agreements, and the court system. G.I. is short for **"Government Issue"** and was a slang term used for American soldiers.

Native Americans

Native Americans, who represent dozens of Indian tribes, also served in the American military during World War II. Although they served in the military in many capacities, one of their most valuable and unique contributions was to serve as **Code Talkers.**

During World War I, members of the Choctaw tribe began the practice by using their native language to pass secure messages. Adolf Hitler knew that this had occurred and tried to have a team of his own learn Native American languages before the actual outbreak of World War II. They were unsuccessful largely due to the number of dialects that exist.

The Navajo Code Talkers were very important to the campaign in the Pacific and Comanche Code Talkers transmitted messages at the invasion of Normandy, June 6, 1944, also known as D-Day. In the Pacific, the Japanese were known to be good at breaking the security codes of their enemies but they were puzzled by the Navajo Codes. They were never able to break the Navajo Codes, which were crucial to the American communication during fighting in the huge Pacific Theater.

Many Americans have seen the familiar photograph and statue called "Raising the Flag on Iwo Jima." It is considered one of the most iconic and recognizable images of World War II. What many Americans don't know is that one

Raising the Flag on Iwo Jima

of soldiers holding the flag was Native American. Ira Hayes was a full blood Pima Native America from Arizona. He grew up on a Pima reservation and enlisted in the Marines when World War II began. In 1944, he was part of the American invasion force at Iwo Jima. To signal the end of Japanese control of the island, Hayes and five other soldiers raised the flag on the top of Mt. Suribachi. When Hayes died at 32, he was buried at Arlington National Cemetery. He suffered for years from his memories of battles and lost friends. Today, his death would be considered a result of Post-Traumatic Stress Disorder (PTSD), which is diagnosed among soldiers returning from the wars in Iraq and Afghanistan.

Like African Americans and Mexican Americans, Native Americans as a whole continued to suffer various forms of discrimination during and after World War II. Several states would not allow Native Americans to vote. They were paid less for the same work that white Americans performed in wartime industries.

During the war, the government seized some reservation lands that had oil, gas, lead, zinc, copper, and other resources. The Manhattan Project used Navajo helium to make the atomic bomb. Two internment camps for Japanese Americans were built on reservations in Arizona. In the end, about 876,000 acres of Native American land was used for the war effort without thought to what was to happen to many of the tribal inhabitants.

Demobilization

During the war, American factories, geared up for wartime production, had helped the nation recover from the Great Depression. After the war ended, the challenge was to convert from a wartime to a peacetime society. The United States underwent a period of **demobilization,** or the movement from a military to a civilian status. The United States armed forces reduced from 12 million members to 1.5 million. Factories that had made planes and tanks now began producing consumer goods. This met a pent-up consumer demand for everything from cars to washing machines. It also meant ensuring that the nation would not slip back into depression.

Truman's Legislative Program During President Truman's administration, legislation was passed to deal with different issues raised by demobilization. Truman's legislative program, aimed at promoting full employment, a higher minimum wage, greater unemployment compensation for workers without jobs, housing assistance, and other items, was known as the **Fair Deal,** a play on words from Franklin D. Roosevelt's New Deal.

Servicemen's Readjustment Act of 1944 This act authorized billions of dollars to pay for veterans' benefits, such as college education, medical treatment, unemployment insurance, and home and business loans. This **GI Bill of Rights,** or the GI Bill, made it possible for more people to attend college and buy homes than ever before.

Employment Act of 1946 This act made full employment a national goal. It also set up a Council of Economic Advisors to guide the president on economic matters.

An End to Price Controls Wartime legislation had put controls on the prices of most goods. In 1946, the government moved to end most such controls. However, the end of controls coupled with a tax cut caused a rapid increase in inflation. For example, food prices soared 25 percent in just two years.

Unifying Themes
Continuity and Change

• What kinds of programs did the government develop to assist Americans in post–World War II society?

The Taft-Hartley Act Workers' wages could not keep up with inflation after the war. Major strikes were held as unions pushed for higher wages. In 1947, antiunion feelings grew and led Congress to pass the **Taft-Hartley Act** over Truman's veto. The act

- provided an 80-day "cooling-off" period through which the president could delay a strike that threatened national welfare.
- barred the closed shop, under which workers had to belong to a union before being hired.
- allowed states to pass "right-to-work laws," which said workers could take jobs and not have to join a union.
- banned union contributions to political campaigns.
- required union leaders to swear they were not communists.

National Security Concerns

During Truman's administration, the **National Security Act of 1947** was passed. This created the National Military Establishment, which later became the Department of Defense. The act also created the Central Intelligence Agency to oversee intelligence-gathering activities. Truman also issued Executive Order 9981, banning discrimination in the armed forces.

The Baby Boom

In addition to problems caused by converting to a peacetime economy, the nation also experienced the largest population explosion in its history. The economic hardships of the Great Depression that had encouraged smaller families were gone. Families grew larger. This **"baby boom"** led to the expansion of many public services, especially schools. The rapid growth in personal income in the decade after World War II also contributed to an expansion of the middle class.

More than 70 million babies were born during the "baby boom" era.

Preparing for the Regents

The Taft-Hartley Act of 1947 was a setback for organized labor. It gave the President the power to delay (through court injunction) any strike that took place within an industry that the President deemed important to the nation's health or safety.

- Identify one or two industries that would be considered important to the nation's health or safety.

Unifying Themes
Expansion of an Economic System

- How did the prosperity of the 1940s and 1950s influence the nation's population growth rate?

The Holocaust and Postwar Efforts for Justice and Peace

Lesson Overview

When Adolf Hitler rose to power in Germany, he did so by finding a scapegoat, someone to blame for Germany's problems after World War I. By appealing to anti-Semitism, feelings of hatred against Jewish people, Hitler encouraged the Germans to turn viciously on all Jewish people. His policies turned into genocide, which is the deliberate murder of an entire people. Over time the American public became aware of the horrific events that were happening as Nazi Germany seized control of more and more territory.

After the war ended, the Nuremberg War Crimes trials occurred with American leadership. The United Nations (UN), a new international organization, was created to ensure peace among nations. First Lady Eleanor Roosevelt played a key role in the UN's creation of the Universal Declaration of Human Rights.

Unifying Themes

As you review this lesson take special note of the following themes:

- **Power, Authority, and Governance** How did those in power abuse that power during the Holocaust?
- **Civic Ideals and Practices** How is the Holocaust an example of the lack of respect for diversity in a nation?
- **Global Connections and Exchange** What challenges might the United Nations face in its efforts to achieve its goals?

Key People

Adolf Hitler
Robert Jackson

Eleanor Roosevelt

Key Terms and Events

extermination
genocide
The Final Solution
concentration camps

Holocaust
St. Louis
United Nations

The "Final Solution"

Early in his rise to power, Germany's chancellor, **Adolf Hitler,** seized Jewish property, homes, and businesses and barred Jews from many jobs. At the Wannsee Conference of 1942, the Nazis set as a primary goal the total **extermination,** or **genocide,** of all Jews under their domination. This effort was to be kept secret from the German people and from the rest of the world. Hitler's plan to eliminate the Jews was known to the Nazis as the **Final Solution.**

The Horror of Concentration Camps

In the 1930s, the Nazis began to build **concentration camps** to isolate Jews and other groups from society and provide slave labor for industry. As Hitler's conquest of Europe continued, the camps became factories of death. More than six million Jews were killed in the camps as were another four million people—dissenters, Gypsies, homosexuals, the mentally and physically handicapped, Protestant ministers, and Catholic priests. Today, concentration camps and death camps with names such as Auschwitz, Treblinka, and Dachau stand as memorials to the incredible human suffering and death of this time, a period in history now called the **Holocaust.**

The United States and other nations failed to take strong action to rescue Jews from Nazi Germany before World War II. In 1939, the *St. Louis,* a passenger ship carrying more than 900 Jewish refugees, left Europe for Cuba, but when they arrived, most of the refugees were denied permission to land there. During part of their voyage, Jewish refugees on board could see the Florida coastline. The refugees were also denied permission to enter the United States, and the ship was forced to return to Europe. Most of the ship's passengers eventually were killed in the Holocaust.

After the war broke out, the Allies still failed to speak out forcefully against the treatment of Jews or to make direct attempts to stop the genocide. Near the very end of the war, Jewish leaders in the United States begged the army to bomb known sites of specific concentration camps. The United States refused to do so based on the grounds that bombing those areas would cause certain death to those at the sites. It was argued that individuals were doomed to death and that this could save future detainees. Only toward the end of the war did the United States create the War Refugee Board to provide aid for Holocaust survivors.

The United States Army did liberate camps in existence in May 1945 at the end of World War II. Some of the freed prisoners did not survive long after the liberation but many did. Some of those who were young at that time are still alive today and some live in the United States. Hundreds of survivors have lived to give testimony to their horrific experiences.

War Crimes Trials

As a result of the Potsdam Conference, a final chapter to the Holocaust occurred in Nuremberg, Germany, in 1945 and 1946. At that time an international military court tried 24 high-level Nazis for atrocities committed during World War II. United States Supreme Court Justice **Robert Jackson** served as Chief Prosecutor for the United States. In that position he made arguments against the Nazi war criminals. When this court found former Nazis guilty of "crimes against humanity," a precedent was established that soldiers, officers, and national leaders could be held responsible for such brutal actions. Escaped Nazis who were found after the end of the war—even decades later—were also brought to trial for war-related crimes

Among the most infamous Nazis who were tried and convicted was Adolf Eichmann. He was captured in Argentina in 1960 and tried in Israel for the torture and deaths of millions of Jews. Eichmann was convicted of crimes against humanity and was hanged in 1962. Klaus Barbie, known as the "Butcher of Lyon" (France), was also apprehended and tried in 1987 for his wartime brutality against Jews.

War crime trials in Japan led to the execution of former Premier Tojo and six other war leaders. About 4,000 other Japanese war criminals were also convicted and received prison sentences.

Social Studies Practices

Interpreting and Using Evidence

- What important legal precedent was set at the Nuremberg trials?

The United Nations

American foreign policy changed dramatically as a result of World War II. Even before the conclusion of the war, the United States began planning for an international peacekeeping organization. Plans were made at the Yalta Conference for a United Nations Conference to be held in San Francisco in April 1945. The Soviet Union, under the leadership of Joseph Stalin, agreed to participate in planning the new organization, which would be known as the United Nations. The United States Senate approved the United Nations Charter by a vote of 82 to 2.

Organization of the United Nations

The structure of the **United Nations** (UN) includes a General Assembly of all its members and a Security Council of 15 members. The Security Council consists of ten rotating member nations and five permanent members. (The original permanent members were the United States, Great Britain, the Soviet Union, China, and France. After the breakup of the Soviet Union, the Russian Federation became a permanent member.) The General Assembly serves as a forum for world leaders to speak on a variety of concerns.

Although the UN has become militarily involved in a number of world crises, most of its members would agree that its greatest accomplishments have been in fighting hunger and disease and in promoting education. The headquarters of the United Nations is in New York City.

Universal Declaration of Human Rights

In 1946, President Truman appointed former First Lady **Eleanor Roosevelt** as a United Nations delegate, the only woman in the American delegation. The committee that Eleanor Roosevelt led authored the Universal Declaration of Human Rights, a proclamation that is still part of the guiding philosophy of the UN today. In the postwar years, people all over the world were especially eager to have an international organization succeed at defining human rights for all people.

Preparing for the Regents

Stimulus-Based Questions: Chart

- Which branch of the United Nations would help two countries resolve a legal dispute?
- Which branch sets UN policies?
- Why might it be difficult for the Economic and Social Council to achieve its goals?

The United Nations

Security Council
- Investigates situations that threaten peace
- Sets UN policies
- Works for peaceful settlement of disputes

General Assembly
- Discusses world problems
- Votes on actions
- Controls UN budget

Secretariat
- Coordinates work of all UN agencies
- Is headed by Secretary General

Economic and Social Council
- Works for improved economic and social conditions
- Cooperates with member nations to improve standards of living
- Promotes human rights

Trusteeship Council
- Administers territories that are not self-governing
- Helps such territories work toward independence

International Court of Justice
- Helps settle legal disputes between nations
- Gives legal opinions to General Assembly

Multiple-Choice Questions for Regents Practice

Base your answers to questions 1 and 2 on the speech below and on your knowledge of social studies.

> If Great Britain goes down, the Axis powers will control the continents of Europe, Asia, Africa, Australia, and the high seas—and they will be in a position to bring enormous military and naval resources against this hemisphere. It is no exaggeration to say that all of us, in all the Americas, would be living at the point of a gun—a gun loaded with explosive bullets, economic as well as military. . . .
>
> The people of Europe who are defending themselves do not ask us to do their fighting. They ask us for the implements of war, the planes, the tanks, the guns, the freighters which will enable them to fight for their liberty and for our security. Emphatically we must get these weapons to them, get them to them in sufficient volume and quickly enough, so that we and our children will be saved the agony and suffering of war which others have had to endure. . . .
>
> We must be the great arsenal of democracy. For us this is an emergency as serious as war itself. We must apply ourselves to our task with the same resolution, the same sense of urgency, the same spirit of patriotism and sacrifice as we would show were we at war.

Source: President Franklin D. Roosevelt, "Arsenal of Democracy" fireside chat, December 29, 1940

1 What program is President Roosevelt defending in this speech?

(1) New Deal legislation

(2) Lend-Lease Act

(3) the military draft

(4) GI Bill of Rights

2 What best explains the reluctance of the United States to join Great Britain in war?

(1) the superiority of British warships and ammunition

(2) the possibility that the Axis powers might defeat the Allies

(3) the human and financial costs of American involvement in World War II

(4) the fear that Great Britain might try to regain control of the United States

Base your answers to questions 3 and 4 on the speech below and on your knowledge of social studies.

> The thoughts and hopes of all America—indeed of all the civilized world—are centered tonight on the battleship *Missouri*. There on that small piece of American soil anchored in Tokyo Harbor the Japanese have just officially laid down their arms. They have signed terms of unconditional surrender.
>
> Four years ago, the thoughts and fears of the whole civilized world were centered on another piece of American soil—Pearl Harbor. The mighty threat to civilization which began there is now laid at rest. It was a long road to Tokyo—and a bloody one.
>
> We shall not forget Pearl Harbor.
>
> The Japanese militarists will not forget the U.S.S. *Missouri*.
>
> The evil done by the Japanese war lords can never be repaired or forgotten. But their power to destroy and kill has been taken from them.

Source: President Harry S. Truman, radio address, September 1, 1945

3 Which significant development in history is President Truman addressing?

(1) Truman is outlining his plan to end World War II.

(2) Truman is announcing the Japanese surrender in World War II.

(3) Truman is praising the military for success in the South Pacific.

(4) Truman is recognizing the United Nations as a new organization for world peace.

4 What event directly preceded the event described in Truman's speech?

(1) the surrender of Nazi Germany

(2) the Japanese attack on Pearl Harbor

(3) the use of atomic bombs at Hiroshima and Nagasaki

(4) the death of President Franklin D. Roosevelt

Base your answers to questions 5 and 6 on the images below and on your knowledge of social studies.

Source: U.S. propaganda posters, 1940s

5   What claim about the actions of Americans on the home front is supported by both of these posters?

   (1) Buying war bonds helps the war effort as well as the economy.

   (2) Complying with food and materials rationing is required by law.

   (3) Working in wartime industries improves military morale and technology.

   (4) Using limited resources wisely will win the war.

6   Who had the most to lose if Americans did not follow the suggestions made by these posters?

   (1) big business in the United States

   (2) Americans on the home front

   (3) the American military

   (4) foreign allies of the United States

Base your answers to questions 7 and 8 on the speech below and on your knowledge of social studies.

> Yesterday, December 7, 1941—a date which will live in infamy—the United States of America was suddenly and deliberately attacked by naval and air forces of the Empire of Japan. . . .
>
> The attack yesterday on the Hawaiian Islands has caused severe damage to American naval and military forces. I regret to tell you that very many American lives have been lost. In addition, American ships have been reported torpedoed on the high seas between San Francisco and Honolulu. . . .
>
> As Commander in Chief of the Army and Navy I have directed that all measures be taken for our defense. . . .
>
> I believe I interpret the will of the Congress and of the people when I assert that we will not only defend ourselves to the uttermost but will make very certain that this form of treachery shall never again endanger us. . . .
>
> I ask that the Congress declare that since the unprovoked and dastardly attack by Japan on Sunday, December 7, 1941, a state of war has existed between the United States and the Japanese Empire.

Source: President Franklin D. Roosevelt, Address to Congress, December 8, 1941

7 The event described in the passage was such a surprise to Americans because, prior to the event, the

   (1) U.S. military had just surrendered territory it held in China to the Japanese
   (2) American government had started supplying Japan through the Lend-Lease Act
   (3) U.S. military and the Japanese had just agreed to the Grand Alliance
   (4) American government had been using diplomacy in order to appease the Japanese

8 Why might President Roosevelt's speech be considered a turning point in U.S. history?

   (1) The United States had been increasing its supply of arms and warships since the end of World War I.
   (2) The United States had been trying to help the Allies without actually getting into the war.
   (3) The president was assuming a new executive power by declaring war against Japan.
   (4) The president blamed Japan for attacking another country.

Short Essay Questions

Task: Read and analyze the following documents, applying your social studies knowledge and skills to write a short essay of two or three paragraphs in which you:

- Describe the historical context surrounding these documents
- Identify and explain the *relationship* between the events and/or ideas found in these documents (Cause and Effect, *or* Similarity/Difference, *or* Turning Point)

In developing your short essay answer of two or three paragraphs, be sure to keep these explanations in mind:

Describe means "to illustrate something in words or tell about it"

Historical Context refers to "the relevant historical circumstances surrounding or connecting the events, ideas, or developments in these documents"

Identify means "to put a name to or to name"

Explain means "to make plain or understandable; to give reasons for or causes of; to show the logical development or relationship of"

Types of Relationships:

Cause refers to "something that contributes to the occurrence of an event, the rise of an idea, or the bringing about of a development"

Effect refers to "what happens as a consequence (result, impact, outcome) of an event, an idea, or a development"

Similarity tells how "something is alike or the same as something else"

Difference tells how "something is not alike or not the same as something else"

Turning Point is "a major event, idea, or historical development that brings about significant change. It can be local, regional, national, or global"

Document 1

Posters with instructions to Japanese Americans were hung in various regions in California. They detailed Civilian Exclusion Order #41, which required the removal of people of Japanese ancestry from these regions by May 11, 1942.

WESTERN DEFENSE COMMAND AND FOURTH ARMY
WARTIME CIVIL CONTROL ADMINISTRATION
Presidio of San Francisco, California
May 5, 1942

INSTRUCTIONS
TO ALL PERSONS OF
JAPANESE
ANCESTRY

Source: Civil Exclusion Order #41, 1942

Document 2

A monetary sum and words alone cannot restore lost years or erase painful memories; neither can they fully convey our Nation's resolve to rectify injustice and to uphold the rights of individuals. We can never fully right the wrongs of the past. But we can take a clear stand for justice and recognize that serious injustices were done to Japanese Americans during World War II.

In enacting a law calling for the restitution and offering a sincere apology, your fellow Americans have, in a very real sense, renewed their traditional commitment to the ideals of freedom, equality, and justice. You and your family have our best wishes for the future.

Source: President George H. W. Bush, letter of apology to Japanese Americans affected by the U.S. internment policy, October 1990

Document Analysis for Civic Literacy Essay

Historical Context: Human Rights

Throughout United States history, many constitutional and civic issues have been debated by Americans. These debates have resulted in efforts by individuals, groups, and governments to address these issues. These efforts have achieved varying degrees of success. One of these constitutional and civic issues is human rights.

Task: Read and analyze the document. Using information from the document and your knowledge of United States history, write an essay in which you

- Describe the historical circumstances surrounding this constitutional or civic issue
- Explain efforts to address this constitutional or civic issue by individuals, groups, and/or governments
- Discuss the extent to which these efforts were successful

Describe means "to illustrate something in words or tell about it"

Explain means "to make plain or understandable; to give reasons for or causes of; to show the logical development or relationship of"

Discuss means "to make observations about something using facts, reasoning, and argument; to present in some detail"

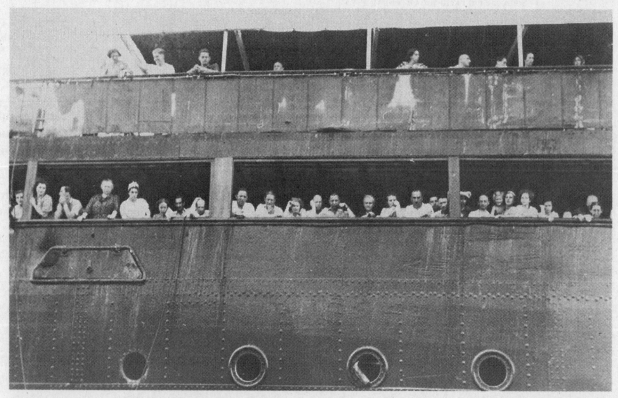

This a partial photograph of the ship St. Louis, with Jewish passengers near the Havana, Cuba harbor in 1939. The United States Holocaust Museum exhibits such documents to illustrate Jewish refugees searching for safety.

1. What was happening in Germany that would have motivated these refugees to flee to Cuba?

The Cold War Era (1945–1990)

Topic Overview

The end of World War II brought the desire to prevent such devastation from ever happening again. The uneasy wartime alliance between the United States and the Soviet Union dissolved as the Cold War took hold. Communism spread through the efforts of the Soviet Union and later China. The United States worked to strengthen its influence in Western Europe and Asia by providing economic aid and building strategic alliances. A growing anxiety about the spread of communism led the United States to become more deeply involved in global affairs, while also fearing communist influence at home.

The United States became involved in such distant and wide-ranging locations as the newly formed divided Germanys, Cuba, Vietnam, and the Middle East. A nuclear arms race began as well as a race for superiority in space exploration. These races occurred primarily between the United States and the Soviet Union (the Union of the Soviet Socialist Republics, or USSR.) There were tense times in foreign policy for the United States that sometimes led to war. Diplomatic relations during this period were also crucial to the effort of peaceful coexistence.

The Cold War Begins

Key Concept

11.9a After World War II, ideological differences led to political tensions between the United States and the Soviet Union. In an attempt to halt the spread of Soviet influence, the United States pursued a policy of containment.

Lesson Overview

Decisions made at wartime conferences applied to Poland and other areas of Eastern Europe and postwar Germany. Continuing disagreements over these decisions helped bring about the start of the Cold War. The United States began a policy of containment. Examples of this policy are the Truman Doctrine, the Marshall Plan, the North Atlantic Treaty Organization, and United States actions during the Berlin Blockade. These actions represented a shift in American foreign policy. Domestically, the United States experienced concerns about the spread of communism. The rise of McCarthyism brought the Cold War home and divided the nation.

Unifying Themes

As you review this lesson take special note of the following themes:

- **Time, Continuity, and Change** How did the results of World War II impact the United States and its relationship with other nations? Why did the American use of the atomic bomb cause a variety of reactions around the world? Why did the United States change from being allies with the Soviet Union to becoming enemies?

- **Power, Authority, and Governance** Why did the Western democracies clash with the Soviet Union, their former ally? How did diplomacy play a role in competing ideologies following World War II? How did the fear of communism lead to the violations of some people's civil rights in the United States?

- **Creation, Expansion, and Interaction of Economic Systems** Explain the economics of the Berlin Blockade. What countries were involved? How did the United States use economics to develop its alliances after World War II?

Key People

Franklin D. Roosevelt	George C. Marshall
Winston Churchill	Alger Hiss
Chiang Kai-shek	Joseph McCarthy
Joseph Stalin	Ethel and Julius Rosenberg
Harry S. Truman	

Key Terms and Events

Atlantic Charter	Truman Doctrine	Warsaw Pact
Yalta Conference	Marshall Plan	38th parallel
communism	Cold War	HUAC
containment	Berlin Blockade	McCarthyism
"iron curtain"	NATO	Red Scare

Wartime Diplomacy

During World War II, leaders of the Allied nations met in a series of conferences to discuss wartime strategies and plans for the postwar world. Key meetings are described below.

Atlantic Charter Meeting, 1941 President **Franklin D. Roosevelt** and British Prime Minister **Winston Churchill** met on battleships in the North Atlantic to agree on certain principles for building a lasting peace and establishing free governments in the world. The document containing these agreements was called the **Atlantic Charter.**

Casablanca, 1943 Roosevelt met with Churchill to plan "victory on all fronts." They used the term "unconditional surrender" to describe the anticipated Allied victory.

Cairo, 1943 Roosevelt, Churchill, and **Chiang Kai-shek** of China discussed the Normandy invasion.

Tehran Conference, 1943 Roosevelt and Churchill met with the Soviet Union's leader, **Joseph Stalin,** to discuss war strategy and plans for the postwar world.

Yalta, 1945 Roosevelt, Churchill, and Stalin outlined the division of postwar Germany into spheres of influence and planned for the trials of war criminals. The Soviet Union promised to enter the war against Japan. At the **Yalta Conference,** the three leaders agreed to split Germany into four zones, each under the control of one of the major Allies. Stalin promised to allow elections in the nations his army liberated from the Germans in Eastern Europe. However, Stalin did not fulfill this promise.

Potsdam Conference, 1945 Allied leaders warned Japan to surrender to prevent utter destruction. President Roosevelt died suddenly in April 1945, and Vice President **Harry S. Truman** became President. Truman represented the United States at this conference.

The United States emerged from World War II as the world's greatest military power. Compared to other nations, it had suffered relatively little physical destruction. For a short time, the United States held a monopoly on the ability to use nuclear power. After World War II, the United States was aware of its strength as a nation and its responsibility to preserve world peace.

Social Studies Practices
Using Evidence

• How did the agreements at Yalta set the stage for the problems that later arose during the Cold War?

The United States and the World, 1945–1954

1945 World War II ends		1949 NATO formed		1953 Cease-fire in Korea	
1945	1947	1949	1951	1953	1955
	1947 Marshall Plan; Truman Doctrine		1950 Korean War begins; Rosenbergs arrested		1954 McCarthy censured by Senate

Preparing for the Regents

Stimulus-Based Question: Timeline

Review the timeline, then answer the following questions.

• In what year was NATO formed?
• Why would the Marshall Plan and the Truman Doctrine have occurred at the same time?

Containment as a Foreign Policy

American foreign policy after World War II was influenced by two factors: the willingness of the United States to become involved in international peacekeeping efforts and its determination to prevent the spread of **communism.** Containment of communism to the areas where it already existed was a central part of American foreign policy during the Cold War.

Social Studies Practices
Gathering and Using Evidence

- How did communism spread to Eastern Europe?

- What had Stalin promised at Yalta in regard to Eastern Europe?

Growing Distrust of the Soviet Union

In 1939, Germany and the Soviet Union had signed a nonaggression treaty, but after Germany violated the pact, the Soviet Union sought a new alliance to protect itself from Germany. The United States then allied with the Soviet Union throughout World War II. Although they were allies, American and Soviet leaders did not fully trust one another. After the war, it became apparent that the only common goal shared by the United States and the Soviet Union was the defeat of the Axis powers.

After World War II, the Soviet Union was viewed as a grave threat to the security of the noncommunist world. In defeating Nazi Germany, the Soviets had moved troops into the nations of Eastern Europe. After the war, the Soviet Union actively supported communist governments in those nations.

The United States, which had emerged as a superpower nation, took on the task of limiting communist expansion—a policy known as **containment.** The goal of containment was to confine communism to the area in which it already existed—the Soviet Union and the Eastern European nations. American presidential power increased during this time period as the United States sought to carry out this new policy.

Following are key foreign policy developments related to the containment of communism immediately after World War II.

Churchill's "Iron Curtain" Speech

In his 1946 speech at Westminster College in Fulton, Missouri, Prime Minister Winston Churchill of Great Britain cautioned the world about the threat of communist expansion. He warned that "from Stettin in the Baltic to Trieste in the Adriatic, an 'iron curtain' has descended across the Continent." Churchill's phrase **"iron curtain"** drew a clear picture of the postwar world. There had come to be recognizable division between the free Western Europe and the communist Eastern Europe.

Preparing for the Regents

Stimulus-Based Question: Political Cartoon

Examine the cartoon at right, then answer the following questions.

- What major world event has recently ended?

- Describe the buildings below the climber.

- Why is the climber named "Europe"?

- What is the importance of the climber's rope?

- What does the caption mean?

In one or two sentences, write a summary of the idea this cartoon is conveying.

The Way Back

The Truman Doctrine

Before World War II, Great Britain had been a powerful force in the Mediterranean. The tremendous losses and expense of World War II, however, weakened Great Britain's influence there. The Soviet Union, which had long been striving for access to the Mediterranean Sea by way of the Turkish straits, sought to extend its influence in the area.

The Soviets supported communist rebels in their attempt to topple the government of Greece. This led the United States to try to contain the spread of communism in the Mediterranean region. On March 12, 1947, President Truman asked Congress for $400 million in aid to Turkey and Greece. He called on the United States to support free people in resisting control by armed minorities or outside pressures. Truman believed that the failure of the United States to act at this time would endanger both the nation and the free world.

Congress approved Truman's request. By 1950, more than $660 million had been spent in aid to Turkey and Greece. This policy of economic and military aid became known as the **Truman Doctrine.** It represents a major step in the evolution of American foreign policy further away from isolationism and neutrality.

The Marshall Plan

World War II left much of Europe in ruins. Major cities and industrial centers were destroyed. Survivors of the war struggled to find food, shelter, and clothing. Dissatisfaction with such conditions grew rapidly. In many war-torn countries, the Communist Party seemed to offer solutions to such problems.

To prevent the spread of communist influence in Europe, General **George C. Marshall,** secretary of state under President Truman, announced a new economic aid program called the **Marshall Plan.** In a speech delivered on June 5, 1947, Marshall announced that the United States was against "hunger, poverty, desperation, and chaos." Between 1948 and 1952, about $13 billion in economic aid was allocated by the Republican-dominated Congress for the rebuilding of Europe under the Marshall Plan. The largest amount went to Great Britain, France, Italy, and West Germany.

This aid enabled Western Europe to begin consumer production once more and to build prosperous economies. Both Western Europe and the United States felt that, with stabilized and improving economies, communist expansion would be halted.

The Beginning of the Cold War: Germany 1948–1949

At the end of World War II, Germany was divided into four zones of occupation controlled by Great Britain, France, the Soviet Union, and the United States. Berlin, the capital of Germany, was located in the Russian sector. However, the city was divided into four sections, each controlled by one of the four Allies. Disagreements during this period of occupation marked the beginning of the **Cold War,** a period of tension between the United States and the Soviet Union from the end of World War II to 1991.

The Berlin Blockade The United States, France, and Great Britain cooperated in governing the western sectors of Germany. Unable to reach agreement with the Soviet Union over the eventual unification of Germany, the three Western powers decided to unify their zones without the Soviet zone. In 1949, the Federal Republic of Germany, commonly known as West Germany, was established. The Soviets opposed the establishment of this separate government. Prior to that, on June 24, 1948, the Soviets had cut off all access to West Berlin by blockading the roads leading to the city, all of which had to go through the Soviet-controlled sector of Germany. The Soviets hoped that the **Berlin Blockade** would force the Western powers out of Berlin.

The Berlin Airlift The United States, Great Britain, and France would not back down. Recognizing that West Berlin could not get supplies by road anymore, the Western powers began an airlift of food, clothing, coal, medicine, and other necessities to the city. Almost a year later, on May 12, 1949, the Soviets recognized their defeat in the area and ended the blockade. Shortly afterward, the Soviets announced the formation of the German Democratic Republic, commonly known as East Germany. In 1955, West Germany was given full sovereignty. The West had learned once again that although World War II was over, its struggle against aggressor nations was not.

Point Four Program

The United States recognized that the Soviet Union's expansionist aims were targeted not only at Europe but at developing nations of the world as well. In 1950, Congress approved President Truman's Point Four Program, which provided nearly $400 million for technical development programs in Latin America, Asia, and Africa. The Point Four Program was designed to modernize and strengthen the economies of developing nations and thereby discourage the growth of communism.

The North Atlantic Treaty Organization

The United States and other Western European nations also fought the spread of communism by forming alliances. In April 1949, the United States and 11 other Western nations signed a collective security agreement called the North Atlantic Treaty. This agreement bound the participating nations to act together for their common defense. Members pledged that an attack on any one of them would be considered an attack on all of them. This is known as a system of mutual defense. Defense arrangements were coordinated through the North Atlantic Treaty Organization **(NATO).** The Soviets later formed an opposing alliance with seven Eastern European nations under the **Warsaw Pact.**

In 1949, President Truman announced that the Soviet Union had successfully exploded an atomic bomb. Fearing the power that this gave the Soviets, the United States worked to strengthen its influence in the world by committing several billion dollars in assistance to countries in Western Europe and elsewhere.

Unifying Themes
Time, Continuity, and Change

NATO represented the principle of mutual military assistance, or collective security. By joining NATO, the United States dropped its opposition to military treaties with Europe for the first time since the Monroe Doctrine. As a member of NATO, the United States became actively involved in European affairs.

- How is this an example of the United States using its policy of containment?

Preparing for the Regents

Stimulus-Based Question: Map

After losing more than 20 million people during the war and suffering widespread destruction, the Soviet Union was determined to rebuild in ways that would protect its own interests. One way was to establish satellite nations, countries subject to Soviet domination, on the western borders of the Soviet Union.

- How does this map illustrate the Soviet Union's desire to protect itself from noncommunist rivals?

The Cold War in Europe

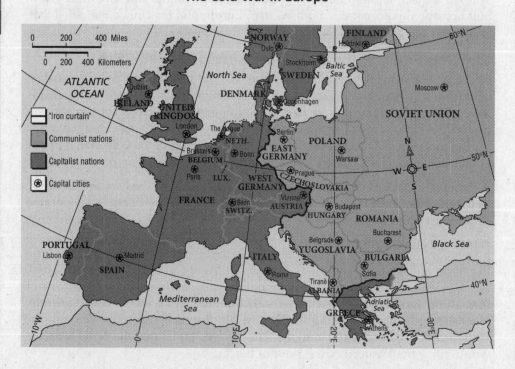

European Cooperation

In order to rebuild and strengthen their economies after the war, Western European nations made ever-increasing efforts at economic cooperation. In 1951, the European Coal and Steel Community formed to enable six European nations to set prices and regulate the coal and steel industries. By 1957, the scope of economic cooperation had broadened to include efforts to improve transportation and eliminate tariff barriers within Europe. Those same six nations signed a treaty in 1957 to form the European Economic Community (EEC), also known as the Common Market. As economic cooperation continued to broaden, this organization later transformed into the European Union (EU) that exists today.

The European Union has experienced many changes in recent years. The European Parliament, the legislative branch of the EU, now has the power to approve or reject the EU's budget. In 1999, eleven member states began using a common currency called the euro. The EU continues to grapple with such key issues as increasing employment opportunities for citizens in all member nations. The EU today has 27 member states. The United Kingdom left the EU in January 2020.

Containment in Asia

During World War II, the United States had been an ally of China and an enemy of Japan. After the war, the United States reversed its political alliances in Asia. With its new constitutional democracy, Japan became an American ally. Meanwhile, a communist takeover in China made the United States increasingly suspicious of and hostile to that nation.

Communist Victory in China

In the 1930s, China had plunged into civil war. Mao Zedong, leader of the communist forces in China, sought to defeat the nationalist regime of Chiang Kai-shek. In 1949, the communist forces defeated the nationalists and renamed the now communist-led country the People's Republic of China. Chiang Kai-shek and the nationalists fled to the island of Taiwan.

The United States was alarmed by this development because it feared that communism would spread beyond China. Because the United States had overseen the initial rebuilding of postwar Japan and had helped put a new constitutional democracy in place, it did not want to see communism spread to Japan. Support for Japan was now seen as a way of offsetting communist China's influence in Asia.

The Korean War

During World War II, Korea had been occupied by Japan. At the end of the war, Korea was divided along the **38th parallel,** or line of latitude. The northern zone was under the influence of the Soviet Union, and the southern zone was controlled by the United States. By 1948, the southern zone had elected an anticommunist government headed by Syngman Rhee and was now called the Republic of Korea. In the northern zone, now named the Democratic People's Republic of Korea, a communist government ruled.

Fighting Begins North Korea invaded South Korea in 1950 in an attempt to unify the country. President Truman responded to this invasion by committing American troops to major involvement in the Korean conflict.

MacArthur in Command General Douglas MacArthur, a World War II hero, was sent to command the United States military in Korea. Troops from the United States, along with small numbers of soldiers from other UN member

Unifying Themes
Continuity and Change

It was a major decision for Great Britain to leave the EU and only happened after long debates and disagreements. The decision was called Brexit by the media.

Social Studies Practices
Cause and Effect

• How might the victory of the communists in the Chinese civil war in 1949 have contributed to United States involvement in the Korean War in 1950?

Social Studies Practices
Gathering and Interpreting Evidence

• Who fought on the side of communist North Korea during the Korean War?

• Who fought on the side of anticommunist South Korea during the Korean War?

• How did the sides in the conflict illustrate the growing Cold War tensions?

nations, were soon involved in battles as fierce as those of World War II. A particularly devastating loss came at the Yalu River, when Chinese forces entered the conflict and pushed UN troops south. By the middle of 1951, the war had reached a stalemate. Fighting continued, but neither side was able to advance successfully.

Disagreement over the objectives and military strategies of the Korean War caused a major conflict between President Truman and General MacArthur. Although Truman was a civilian, the Constitution makes the president the commander in chief of the armed forces. When General MacArthur disagreed with Truman publicly about the conduct of the war, the President recalled him to the United States and dismissed him from command.

President Harry Truman (left) and General Douglas MacArthur

Hostilities End Although truce talks began in June 1951, no resolution was reached before the American presidential election of 1952. During that campaign, the Republican candidate, World War II hero Dwight D. Eisenhower, promised that if he were elected president, he would go to Korea to aid in the peace negotiations. Eisenhower won the election and did keep his campaign promise, but a truce, or cease-fire, was not officially signed until July 27, 1953.

The war in Korea lasted for more than three years and cost more than $15 billion. Approximately 34,000 Americans and one million Koreans and Chinese died in the conflict. At the end of the Korean War, Korea remained a divided nation and has continued in that political situation into the twenty-first century.

New Directions The policy of containment took a different course with American involvement in the Korean conflict. Early containment efforts focused primarily on economic aid programs. With the Korean War, the United States now showed its willingness to undertake military action to contain communism if it was necessary. American experiences in Korea were a warning of future global confrontations between democratic and communist opponents.

The Cold War at Home

Even as the United States defended democratic freedoms worldwide, sometimes those same freedoms were in danger at home. The spreading of communism to China and the apparent growing strength of the Soviet Union led some Americans to fear that communism could spread to the United States. This fear led some Americans to take actions that violated the civil rights of others. Many Americans charged that communist agents were trying to subvert, or destroy, the American political system. Other Americans responded that the actions of anticommunists were more subversive of American values and more dangerous to the nation.

Looking for Communists

The fear of communism in the United States had its roots in the period before World War II. Anticommunist activity began in the 1930s.

HUAC In 1938, the House Un-American Activities Committee **(HUAC)** was formed as a temporary investigative unit to look into communist activity in the United States. HUAC operated for more than 30 years. Its well-publicized probe of the movie industry in the 1940s and 1950s led to the blacklisting, or cutting off from employment, of many actors, writers, and directors.

J. Edgar Hoover, director of the Federal Bureau of Investigation, often aided HUAC investigations. Critics argued that Hoover conducted anticommunist activities that often violated the civil rights of Americans.

The Smith Act In 1940, Congress passed the Smith Act, which made it illegal for anyone to advocate "overthrowing . . . any government in the United States by force" or to "affiliate" with groups that called for such action.

In the 1951 landmark case of *Dennis* v. *United States*, the Supreme Court upheld the Smith Act. Eugene Dennis, general secretary of the Communist Party in the United States, and ten others were convicted of advocating the violent overthrow of the government.

Two Supreme Court decisions in 1957 weakened the intent of the Smith Act. In *Watkins* v. *United States*, the Court ruled the HUAC could not punish witnesses who refused to cooperate with its investigations. In *Yates* v. *United States*, the Court ruled that the Smith Act applied only to those who teach or advocate direct "action" to overthrow government, not to those who merely advocate it in principle.

The Loyalty Program In 1947, President Truman fueled anticommunist feelings by ordering a Loyalty Review Board to conduct security checks on thousands of government employees. Those whose loyalty was considered doubtful were dismissed.

In the early 1950s, Robert Oppenheimer, who had led the research to develop the atomic bomb, voiced his opposition to building the new, more destructive hydrogen bomb. This action and his past association with others whose loyalty was being questioned led to a government hearing about his own loyalty. He was determined to be a "loyal citizen," but his security clearance was removed, and he was barred from future government research.

The Hiss Case The Alger Hiss case led many Americans to believe that there was a reason to fear that there were communists in the government. In 1948, **Alger Hiss,** a former adviser to President Roosevelt, was charged with having been a communist spy during the 1930s. Whittaker Chambers, a former Communist Party member, made these charges, which Hiss denied. A congressional committee investigated them.

A young Republican committee member from California, Richard Nixon, believed that Hiss was guilty. Nixon's pursuit of the case and Hiss's eventual conviction on perjury charges made Nixon a national figure. The conviction also added weight to Republican charges that Roosevelt and Truman had not been alert enough to the dangers of communism.

McCarthyism

Against this political background, Senator **Joseph McCarthy** of Wisconsin began his own hunt for communists. In 1950, McCarthy charged he had a list of State Department employees known to be communists. Over the next four years, McCarthy went on to charge that many other people and government agencies had been corrupted by communism. He used the term "infiltrated" to describe how the people he accused had secretly obtained government positions.

McCarthy made bold accusations without any evidence. This tactic became known as **McCarthyism.** He ruined the reputations of many people he carelessly accused of being communists. Meanwhile, the Rosenberg case and congressional legislation helped win public support for McCarthy's actions.

The Rosenberg Case In 1950, **Ethel and Julius Rosenberg** and Morton Sobell were charged with giving atomic secrets to the Soviet Union during World War II. After a highly controversial trial, they were convicted of espionage. The Rosenbergs were sentenced to death and Sobell to prison. The Rosenbergs were executed in 1953.

Congressional Legislation In the same year the Rosenbergs were arrested, Congress passed the McCarran Internal Security Act. The law aimed at limiting the actions of anyone the government considered a threat to United States security. The McCarran-Walter Act of 1952 restricted the immigration of persons from communist-dominated nations in Asia and southern and central Europe. President Truman vetoed the bill, but Congress passed it over his veto.

McCarthy's Fall In 1954, McCarthy charged that even the army was full of communists. He held televised investigations into these charges. For the first time, millions of Americans saw McCarthy's bullying tactics for themselves. His public support quickly faded, and in December 1954, the Senate censured, or denounced, him for "conduct unbecoming a member."

The fall of McCarthy ended the **Red Scare** of the 1950s, although anticommunist attitudes lingered as the Cold War continued to drag on. During this time, the tactics of Senator McCarthy were criticized because he violated important constitutional liberties. The term *McCarthyism* has come to mean the use of methods of investigation and accusation that are regarded as unfair, in order to suppress opposition.

The Vietnam War in the Cold War Era

Lesson Overview

The fear of communist expansion led the United States to become increasingly involved in Southeast Asia. This involvement led to the Vietnam War. As the war dragged on, American support began to erode. The combination of negative public opinion and the inability of the military to achieve clear-cut victory led to a gradual withdrawal from the war. Meanwhile, great social and cultural changes were taking place in many parts of American society.

Key Concept

11.9a After World War II, ideological differences led to political tensions between the United States and the Soviet Union. In an attempt to halt the spread of Soviet influence, the United States pursued a policy of containment.

Unifying Themes

As you review this lesson take special note of the following themes:

- **Time, Continuity, and Change** Why did the United States become involved in Vietnam? How did the decisions made by Presidents Johnson and Nixon affect how the Vietnam War was conducted? What social and cultural changes developed in the 1960s? Why do you think these changes occurred at this particular time period?

- **Power, Authority, and Governance** How did Congress limit the power of the president in wartime? Why did Congress decide this was necessary?

Key People

Dwight D. Eisenhower

John F. Kennedy

Lyndon B. Johnson

Richard Nixon

Henry Kissinger

Key Terms

brinkmanship

domino theory

SEATO

Gulf of Tonkin Resolution

guerrilla war

hawks

doves

Vietnamization

War Powers Act

The Cold War Continues

The United States emerged from World War II as the strongest nation in the world. It controlled the atomic bomb, and its economy was undamaged by the destruction of the war. The Soviet Union, however, quickly became America's chief rival. By 1949, it too had the atomic bomb. It had also taken control of most of the nations of Eastern Europe and was seeking to extend its influence elsewhere.

As you read in the previous lesson President Harry S. Truman began the policy of containment after the war in an attempt to limit the spread of communism. As the United States and the Soviet Union—the two world superpowers—attempted to maintain a balance of power, a Cold War developed.

The Cold War, 1950–1960

1950	1953	1956	1960
Korean War begins	Korean War ends	Suez crisis begins; Hungarian revolt	U-2 shot down over USSR

| 1950 | 1952 | 1954 | 1956 | 1958 | 1960 |

| | 1952 | | 1955 | 1959 | |
| | Dwight D. Eisenhower elected president | | Summit conference in Geneva | Castro wins power in Cuba | |

Eisenhower's Foreign Policy

As President, **Dwight D. Eisenhower** continued Truman's basic policy of containment. However, he and his secretary of state, John Foster Dulles, introduced some new ideas. Eisenhower worried that defense spending would bankrupt the nation. Yet he feared that the Soviets might see cutbacks in military spending as a sign of weakness.

Eisenhower and Dulles instead devised a "new look" for the nation's defense. The United States would rely more heavily on air power and nuclear weapons than on ground troops. Dulles announced a policy of massive retaliation. This meant that the United States would consider the use of nuclear weapons to halt aggression if it believed the nation's interests were threatened. Dulles further stated that the nation must be ready to go "to the brink of war" in order to preserve world peace. This policy of **brinkmanship** greatly increased world tensions during the 1950s.

Foreign Policy in Asia

Asia became a major area of concern for United States foreign policy. The communist victory in China in 1949 raised fears of further communist expansion. The war in Korea, even though it ended in what was basically a draw in 1953, added to these fears.

The Domino Theory As communists took control of the governments of China and, later, some nations of Southeast Asia, American worries about communist expansion increased. Eisenhower stated that the United States must resist further aggression in the region and explained what came to be known as the **domino theory.** The nations of Asia, he said, were like a row of dominoes standing on end. If one fell to communism, the rest were sure to follow.

SEATO One way to resist aggression, Dulles claimed, was through alliances. To mirror the formation of NATO in Europe, Dulles in 1954 pushed for the creation of the Southeast Asia Treaty Organization **(SEATO).** Its original members— Pakistan, Thailand, the Philippines, Australia, New Zealand, Great Britain, and the United States—pledged to meet any "common danger" from communist aggression.

Fear of communist expansion led the United States to become deeply involved in Southeast Asia. Review the chart on the next page to learn about the growing involvement of the United States in this region.

Unrest in Asia, 1945–1960

Date	Event
September 1945	World War II ended in Asia; Ho Chi Minh, a member of the Communist party since 1920, proclaimed the Democratic Republic of Vietnam.
1946–1949	France, which had controlled Vietnam since the nineteeth century, appointed a "puppet leader" named Bao Dai, who was ineffective against the power of Ho Chi Minh.
1949	Mao Zedong declared the (Communist) People's Republic of China; recognized the Vietnamese government of Ho Chi Minh in 1950.
1950–1953	United States fought in the Korean War and provided the French with financial aid in their struggle to hang onto Vietnam.
1953–1954	President Eisenhower debated how far the United States should go in backing the French.
1954	The forces of Ho Chi Minh defeated the French at Dienbienphu; Geneva Accords divided Vietnam at the 17th parallel; North and South Vietnam agreed to hold elections in 1956 to reunite the country; the United States joined with seven Asian and European nations in the Southeast Asia Treaty Organization (SEATO), an anticommunist pact which extended protection to Vietnam.
1955	United States under President Eisenhower increased aid to South Vietnam.
1956	South Vietnamese President Ngo Dinh Diem, fearing the popularity of Ho Chi Minh, refused to hold elections scheduled under the Geneva Accords.
1960	Ho Chi Minh recognized the Vietcong, Communist guerrillas in South Vietnam, as the National Liberation Front (NLF) of Vietnam; President Kennedy sent Vice President Johnson to study the crisis in Vietnam.

Kennedy and Growing Involvement in Vietnam

President **John F. Kennedy** shared Eisenhower's belief in the domino theory. He therefore continued to support the Diem regime. By 1963, the number of United States "advisers" in South Vietnam totaled about 17,000. That year, 489 Americans died in the fighting in Vietnam.

American advisers urged Diem to adopt reforms to broaden his support. Diem, however, brutally suppressed all opponents and ruled as a dictator. On November 2, 1963, the South Vietnamese military overthrew Diem, with the knowledge and approval of the United States. Around the same time, the White House announced that it intended to withdraw all United States military personnel from Vietnam by 1965. Kennedy was unable to keep this promise because he was assassinated on November 22, 1963.

Johnson and the Escalation of War in Vietnam

Under the Constitution, only Congress can declare war. However, by 1964, three presidents—Eisenhower, Kennedy, and **Lyndon B. Johnson**—had sent United States aid and troops into Vietnam. Each did so by acting as the commander in chief of the nation's military forces.

Unifying Themes
Time, Continuity, and Change

In 1964, Congress passed the Gulf of Tonkin Resolution. The resolution, which empowered the President to "repel an armed attack against the forces of the United States," was used to escalate U.S. bombings in North Vietnam.

- What obstacles did U.S. troops fighting in Vietnam face?

Social Studies Practices
Geographic Reasoning

Laos shares a long border with North Vietnam. During the Vietnam War, the dense jungle terrain made it difficult for U.S. and South Vietnamese forces to cut off the supply lines that ran between Laos and North Vietnam.

- How might this role as supplier have had an impact on Laos later in the war?

The Gulf of Tonkin Resolution

On August 4, 1964, President Johnson escalated the war dramatically. He announced on television that American destroyers had been the victim of an unprovoked attack by North Vietnamese gun boats. (It later appeared that the ships might have been protecting South Vietnamese boats headed into North Vietnamese waters.) The next day, Johnson asked Congress for the authority to order air strikes against North Vietnam. With only two dissenting votes, Congress passed the **Gulf of Tonkin Resolution.** The resolution empowered "the President, as commander in chief, to take all necessary measures to repel any armed attack against the forces of the United States and to prevent further aggression." Johnson used the resolution to justify expansion of the war. By April 1965, U.S. planes regularly bombed North Vietnam.

A Guerrilla War

At first, United States military leaders expected that the nation's superior technology would guarantee victory. However, they soon found themselves bogged down in a **guerrilla war** fought in the jungles of Southeast Asia. The enemy did not wear uniforms, and no clear battlefront emerged. Thousands of Vietnamese casualties occurred each month as the United States dropped more bombs on Vietnam, an area about twice the size of New York State, than it had used on Nazi Germany during the heaviest months of fighting during World War II.

Vietnam, 1968

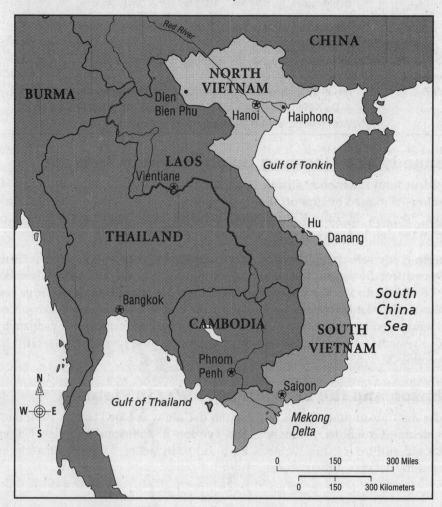

Reasons for War

The massive commitment in Vietnam raised questions in the minds of many Americans about why the United States got involved in Vietnam and why it stayed there. The administration argued that the United States was involved in Vietnam to prevent the fall of Vietnam to communism, to stop the rise of aggressor governments, and to protect the nation's position as a superpower and defender of democracy. However, as the war dragged on, many Americans began to question these motives.

Resistance to the War

By late 1965, an antiwar movement had begun to take shape in the United States.

Hawks and Doves In Congress, there were differences of opinion concerning the war. Some stood solidly behind the president and argued in favor of victory at any cost. These members were known as **hawks.** Those who favored immediate withdrawal and an end to the war were known as **doves.**

Student Protests College campuses became centers of political protest against the war. The University of California, Berkeley campus, became a leader in anti-Vietnam War protests. The name *Berkeley* became synonymous with the activities of the protest movement. Students organized a new form of protest called teach-ins, or meetings in which speakers, usually promoting unconditional American withdrawal from Vietnam, held study sessions and rallies.

The strongest antiwar group in the 1960s was Students for a Democratic Society (SDS), founded in 1960. SDS was antiestablishment, or against big business and government. It led demonstrations, sit-ins, draft-card burnings, and protests against universities with "pro-establishment" regulations. By 1969, the organization had collapsed into a number of splinter groups. However, SDS's legacy of protest against authority remained a strong force into the 1970s.

Protest Marches People of all ages joined in protest marches against the war. The first huge march took place in Washington, D.C., in 1965. In 1967, some 300,000 Americans marched in New York City. That same year, another 50,000 tried to shut down the Pentagon.

Draft Resisters In 1967, former Olympic boxing light heavy-weight gold medal winner Muhammad Ali (Cassius Clay) refused to take the oath of induction into the army after being drafted. He was found guilty of draft evasion but remained free on appeal until 1971, when the Supreme Court overturned his case. By 1968, about 10,000 draft resisters, people unwilling to serve in the military after being drafted, had fled the country for Canada.

The nation's youth became increasingly divided as some chose to fight for the United States in Vietnam, while others sought deferments to go to college. A large number of minorities, who could not afford the cost of college, responded to the draft and went to Vietnam. The attitude of American youth became increasingly hostile toward the Johnson administration and all war-related issues. In 1968, Lyndon Johnson announced his decision not to run for a second term as president. This was largely due to his low popularity ratings as a result of his Vietnam War policies.

Preparing for the Regents

On the examination, you will need to have a thorough understanding of U.S. foreign policy.

List three reasons President Johnson's administration used to justify U.S. involvement in Vietnam.

1.

2.

3.

Unifying Themes
Civic Ideals and Practices

College campuses became centers of the antiwar movement in the United States. Students organized teach-ins and other protests aimed at getting the Johnson administration to end U.S. involvement in Vietnam. Protest marches featuring people of all ages took place in major cities.

- How do the actions of the antiwar movement reflect the principles of American democracy?

The 1960s—Political and Social Upheaval

Some political analysts who studied the events of 1968 believed the nation had survived one of the biggest tests to its political institutions since the Civil War. The 1960s had been shaped by two movements: the Civil Rights Movement and the antiwar movement. The political turmoil of the decade helped produce great social upheaval, especially among the nation's youth.

Some young people became disillusioned with traditional American values. For the first time in United States history, thousands of Americans flaunted the use of illegal drugs, often popularized in rock music. Many young Americans referred to themselves as hippies or flower children. They claimed to be searching for a freer, simpler way of life. Communal living attracted thousands of youths who adopted lifestyles foreign to older Americans. Some spoke of a generation gap between youth and people over 30.

The Civil Rights Movement and the Vietnam War also divided Americans. The assassinations of Dr. Martin Luther King, Jr., in April 1968 and of Robert F. Kennedy in June 1968, heightened emotions, resulting in demonstrations and riots.

Social Studies Practices
Gathering and Using Evidence

- Identify three events that occurred during 1968 that caused that year to be associated with political and social upheaval.
- Explain your reasoning behind your choice of each event.

Key Events of 1968

Month	Event
January	• North Vietnam launched the Tet (New Year's) offensive, using Soviet-made jets and weapons for the first time.
March	• Eugene McCarthy, a peace candidate and leading "dove," won the Democratic presidential primary in New Hampshire. • Robert Kennedy announced his candidacy for the presidency. • President Johnson announced that he would not seek reelection and that he would devote the remainder of his term to trying to end the war. The war had hurt his popularity with voters.
April	• American forces in Vietnam reached 549,000; combat deaths climbed to 22,951. • North Vietnam announced its willingness to enter into peace talks. • An assassin claimed the life of Dr. Martin Luther King, Jr.
May	• Preliminary peace talks with the North Vietnamese began, but serious negotiations would not take place for several years.
June	• An assassin claimed the life of Robert Kennedy shortly after his victory in the California Democratic presidential primary.
August	• The Democratic National Convention nominated Hubert Humphrey amid the worst political rioting and demonstrations any convention had ever experienced; Humphrey (Johnson's Vice President) inherited a divided party and sought election in a divided nation. • The Republican National Convention nominated Richard Nixon, whose only serious challenger was Ronald Reagan. • The American Independent party nominated Governor George Wallace of Alabama, showing that a third party could attract white-backlash voters who opposed the Civil Rights Movement.
November	• Nixon won the 1968 election with 43.4% of the popular vote; Humphrey claimed 42.7%; Wallace took 13.5%.

Nixon and the End of the Vietnam War

By 1969, President **Richard Nixon** faced a national crisis. The Vietnam War had turned into the nation's most costly war. American support for the war was at an all-time low.

Winding Down the War

Nixon did not bring an end to the war right away. In fact, for a time, he widened American military activities, attacking North Vietnamese supply routes out of Laos and Cambodia. This expansion of the war in Indochina caused increased human and financial losses for the United States.

Vietnamization Nixon called for **Vietnamization** of the war, or a takeover of the ground fighting by Vietnamese soldiers. Both Kennedy and Johnson had favored this approach, but neither had been able to make it work. While Nixon promoted Vietnamization, he also bombed neighboring Cambodia, which he claimed served as a base for North Vietnamese guerrillas.

The bombings triggered a large student protest at Kent State University in Ohio. By the time the National Guard broke up the demonstration, four students lay dead and nine others wounded. More and more Americans were questioning the role of the United States in Vietnam, yet President Nixon increased bombing raids on North Vietnam throughout 1970.

Peace With Honor Nixon's chief foreign policy adviser, **Henry Kissinger,** met in Paris with North Vietnamese officials seeking an end to the war. For several years, negotiations remained deadlocked. Finally, on January 15, 1973, Nixon announced that "peace with honor" had been reached and that a cease-fire would soon take effect.

The War Powers Act

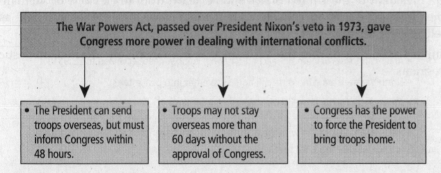

The War Powers Act, passed over President Nixon's veto in 1973, gave Congress more power in dealing with international conflicts.

• The President can send troops overseas, but must inform Congress within 48 hours.

• Troops may not stay overseas more than 60 days without the approval of Congress.

• Congress has the power to force the President to bring troops home.

The War Powers Act

In November 1973, Congress passed the **War Powers Act** over Nixon's veto. This law helped reverse the precedent set by the Gulf of Tonkin Resolution, which gave the President sweeping powers in Vietnam. The War Powers Act included the following provisions

• The President had to notify Congress within 48 hours of sending troops into a foreign country. At that time, the President would have to give Congress a full accounting of the decision.

• The President had to bring the troops home within 60 days unless both houses voted for them to stay.

For the examination,
it will be important
to understand the
significance of historical
events, not just the dates
of and participants in
those events.

- Overall, was the Vietnam
  War a success or a
  failure? Why?

- What enduring lessons
  were learned from the
  war?

- How has the Vietnam
  War continued to
  be remembered in
  American society?

Vietnam and Limits on United States Power

When the United States finally withdrew from Vietnam, the North Vietnamese overran South Vietnam. For two years, the United States poured billions of dollars of aid into South Vietnam. However, on April 30, 1975, the government in Saigon collapsed. Bitterness over the war persisted. When the president asked for funds to evacuate the South Vietnamese who had helped the United States, Congress refused. In the end, some 100,000 people fled the country.

The United States had tried for 20 years to guarantee freedom to the people of South Vietnam. However, the United States ultimately could not count its efforts as a success. In the conflict, some 58,000 Americans died, and another 300,000 were wounded. The United States spent over $150 billion on the war effort. Not only did Vietnam fall to communism, but so did its neighbors Cambodia (Kampuchea) and Laos. Throughout the late 1970s and 1980s, the United States sought to understand the Vietnam experience. It was the subject of films, books, and national monuments such as the Vietnam Veterans Memorial in Washington, D.C.

Conclusions Drawn From U.S. Involvement in Vietnam

The following is a list of conclusions drawn from the Vietnam War era.

- The American political system acted in response to a variety of public pressures.

- Modern war technology was not always powerful enough if an opponent was armed with a determined spirit of nationalism.

- Successful military efforts required a well-prepared and supportive public. (Compare, for example, the differing experiences in Vietnam and World War II.)

- The United States was committed to a foreign policy that supported the global nature of United States involvement in foreign affairs.

- The United States questioned its role as a police officer to the world.

- The President of the United States should learn from the lessons of Vietnam when foreign policies are considered that could cause loss of American lives as well as great financial cost.

- Military spending during the Vietnam War era negatively affected domestic programs.

The Arms Race and Changes in U.S. Foreign Policy

Lesson Overview

During the 1950s through the early 1970s, the Cold War was brought about by competition between the United States and the Soviet Union for power and influence in the world. Specific examples of this can be seen in events related to the arms race and space race. Events ranged from the fear of a world war during the Cuban Missile Crisis to surprising periods of goodwill towards communist China a decade later. President Nixon's desire to maintain personal power in the presidency eventually caused him to be the first and only president to date to resign the office.

Unifying Themes

As you review this lesson take special note of the following themes:

- **Time, Continuity, and Change** Why did President Nixon decide to change American foreign policy with the Soviet Union? How did this policy evolve over time?

- **Power, Authority, and Governance** How did President Kennedy demonstrate American power in the Cuban Missile Crisis? How and why did President Nixon abuse his presidential powers in the Watergate crisis? What was the ultimate result of this abuse of power? How did it occur that Gerald Ford became President of the United States?

Key People

Dwight D. Eisenhower	John F. Kennedy
Nikita Khrushchev	Richard M. Nixon
Fidel Castro	

Key Terms and Events

nuclear arms race	Nuclear Test Ban Treaty
balance of power	détente
Sputnik	SALT
space race	Watergate scandal
Cuban Missile Crisis	

The Arms Race

The United States used the first atomic bombs in history in August 1945 in Japan in a successful effort to bring World War II to a close. As you read in Topic 8, the use of these atomic bombs caused major loss of life and destruction. This also began a dialogue about the morality of nuclear warfare.

By 1949, the Soviet Union showed the world that it too had developed an atomic bomb. The United States and the Soviet Union became rivals and the **nuclear arms race** began. The two nations began by stockpiling nuclear and nonnuclear weapons. The United States exploded a hydrogen bomb in 1952, and the Soviets tested one a year later. Both nations rushed to develop missiles capable of carrying nuclear weapons. The **balance of power** became a balance of terror.

Key Concept

11.9b The United States and the Soviet Union engaged in a nuclear arms race that eventually led to agreements that limited the arms buildup and improved United States–Soviet relations.

Preparing for the Regents

Some questions in the exam will require you to identify a central effect of a specific event.

- Why would the Soviet launch of *Sputnik* cause the federal government to increase spending on the study of math and science in schools?

The inside of an underground fallout shelter on Long Island, New York, in 1955

In 1953, President **Dwight D. Eisenhower** announced the Atoms for Peace Plan at the United Nations. The plan called for United Nations supervision of a world search to find peaceful uses for nuclear technology. The Soviet Union refused to participate. Americans were encouraged to build fallout shelters in homes, schools, and public buildings to enable survival in the case of nuclear attack.

In 1957, the Soviets launched a satellite, *Sputnik,* into orbit around the earth. The arms race then became a **space race** as the United States rushed to launch its own satellites, some for military purposes.

Changing Relations With the Soviet Union

Tensions between the United States and the Soviet Union rose and fell during Eisenhower's time in office. Joseph Stalin, leader of the Soviet Union since the 1920s, died in 1953. In time, **Nikita Khrushchev** took over as the head of the Soviet government. This change marked a temporary easing of Cold War tensions as the Soviets began to focus more on improving conditions within their own nation.

Peaceful Coexistence Relations between the superpowers gradually improved. In 1955, the leaders of the United States, the Soviet Union, Great Britain, and France held the first summit meeting since World War II in Geneva, Switzerland. The superpower leaders began talks on disarmament that, in time, led to a suspension of nuclear testing.

Poland and Hungary In 1956, riots by Polish workers won concessions from the communist Polish government. Inspired by this, students and workers in Hungary began demonstrations that ended with the Soviet Union sending tanks and troops to bring that nation firmly back under communist control. The suppression of the Hungarian revolt cooled relations between the United States and the Soviet Union.

Camp David Relations improved again by 1959. Khrushchev visited the United States. Khrushchev and Eisenhower held lengthy talks at Camp David, the presidential retreat near Washington, D.C. The spirit of goodwill that grew at these talks encouraged the leaders to announce another summit meeting in Paris in 1960.

The U-2 Incident The Paris summit proved a disaster. Shortly before it opened, the Soviet military shot down an American U-2 aircraft deep within Soviet territory. The pilot admitted that he had been spying on Soviet military bases.

Cuba In 1956, **Fidel Castro** began a revolt against the government of Cuban dictator Fulgencio Batista. When the revolt ended with Castro's victory in 1959, the United States quickly recognized the new government. Castro, however, soon adopted policies that angered the Eisenhower administration. He limited civil liberties and imprisoned political opponents. He also nationalized key industries and turned to the Soviet Union for aid. Castro was turning Cuba, just 90 miles from Florida, into a communist nation. Large numbers of Cubans fled Castro's rule, with many settling in southern Florida. Some worked actively to end Castro's rule. Meanwhile, they became an immigrant group that contributed to the richness of the American multicultural experience.

Social Studies Practices
Cause and Effect

• Why did the policies of Fidel Castro anger the Eisenhower administration?

The Kennedy Administration

By 1960, President Eisenhower, a Republican, had completed two terms in office. **John F. Kennedy,** a Democrat, won the presidency in the election of 1960 in a very close race against Eisenhower's vice president, **Richard M. Nixon.**

The Space Program

Following the successful launch of a Soviet cosmonaut, the first man in space, in 1961, President Kennedy committed the nation to a space program with the goal of landing a person on the moon by the end of the 1960s. In 1962, John Glenn became the first person to orbit the earth. In July 1969, six years after Kennedy's death, astronaut Neil Armstrong stepped onto the moon's surface. That effort cost some $25.4 billion.

Kennedy and Latin America

The United States has been deeply involved in the affairs of Latin America since early in its history. Latin American nations often resented such intervention, and United States policies sometimes left a legacy of anger and hostility. In the 1960s, the United States had an uneasy relationship with many Latin American nations. While President Kennedy supported the Cold War policies begun under President Truman, Kennedy hoped to warm ties with Latin America through the Alliance for Progress. Some of President Kennedy's most significant foreign policy decisions involved Latin America.

The Alliance for Progress Kennedy hoped to improve relations with Latin America and stop the spread of communism there through the Alliance for Progress, which pledged $20 billion to help economic development in the region. However, funds often went to aid repressive governments simply because they were anticommunist.

The Bay of Pigs After President Kennedy took office, he approved a CIA (Central Intelligence Agency) plan to overthrow Fidel Castro, the communist leader of Cuba. The plan called for Cuban exiles—supplied with U.S. arms, material, and training—to invade Cuba and set off a popular uprising against Castro. The invasion took place on April 17, 1961, at a location called the Bay of Pigs, about 90 miles from Havana. No uprising followed, and Castro's troops quickly crushed the invading forces, to the embarrassment of Kennedy and the United States government.

The Cuban Missile Crisis Fearing another U.S. invasion attempt, Castro agreed to a Soviet plan to base nuclear missiles aimed at the United States in Cuba. Kennedy learned of the plan while the bases were under construction. On October 22, 1962, he announced a naval blockade, or quarantine, of Cuba and demanded that the Soviets withdraw the missiles. The **Cuban Missile Crisis** brought the United States and the Soviet Union to the brink of war, but the Soviets backed down and withdrew their missiles.

Kennedy had clearly demonstrated that the United States would not tolerate a Soviet presence in the Western Hemisphere just 90 miles from its shores. By doing so, Kennedy also helped the nation recover some of the prestige it had lost in the failed Bay of Pigs invasion.

Nuclear Test Ban Treaty

In 1963, the United States, Soviet Union, and Great Britain signed a **Nuclear Test Ban Treaty** in which they agreed not to test nuclear weapons in the air, in outer space, or under the sea. Underground testing was permitted.

Preparing for the Regents

Turning Point

• Why is the Cuban Missile Crisis of 1962 considered a turning point in U.S.–Soviet relations?

From Cold War to Détente

When John F. Kennedy was assassinated in 1963, his vice president, Lyndon Johnson became president. Johnson won reelection in 1964 but in 1968 he chose not to run for reelection. In the election of 1968, Richard M. Nixon, a Republican, won the presidency. Although President Nixon's main foreign policy objective was ending the Vietnam War, he had other foreign policy interests as well.

Nixon Doctrine

In 1969, Nixon announced what became known as the Nixon Doctrine. This doctrine stated that the United States would no longer provide direct military protection in Asia. Even though the Vietnam War was not yet concluded, the president promised Americans that there would be no more Vietnams for the United States.

A New Policy Toward China

The United States had not had diplomatic relations with the People's Republic since the 1949 communist revolution. Under President Nixon the United States adopted a new foreign policy toward China.

Presidential Visit In 1971, Nixon stunned Americans by announcing that he had accepted an invitation to visit China. On February 21, 1972, Nixon arrived in China. National Security Adviser Henry Kissinger accompanied the president on his peace mission.

Opening the Door After more than 20 years of hostility, President Nixon and Chinese leaders Mao Zedong and Premier Zhou Enlai agreed to open the door to normal diplomatic relations. Nixon's visit cleared the way for economic and cultural exchanges. American manufacturers, for example, now had a new market for their products. By following a policy toward China that was separate from the Soviet Union, Nixon underscored the splits that had occurred within communism. This visit ultimately reduced tensions between the United States and China.

President Richard Nixon (right) shakes hands with Mao Zedong during the president's visit to China in 1972.

A New Policy Toward the Soviet Union

Nixon balanced his openness with China by looking for ways to ease tensions with the Soviet Union, China's communist rival.

Détente Nixon and Kissinger shaped a policy called **détente.** The goal of détente was to bring about a warming in the cold war. It was called an effort to thaw the icy relationship of the Cold War era. In contrast to President Truman's policy of containment, President Nixon's policy of détente was designed to prevent open conflict. During the Nixon administration, the foreign policy of the United States was shaped by *Realpolitik,* a political philosophy favored by Kissinger. The meaning of *Realpolitik* is power politics. Therefore, in its dealings with China and the Soviet Union, the United States made its decisions based on what it needed to maintain its own strength—regardless of world opinion. President Nixon underscored his willingness to pursue détente by visiting the Soviet Union in May 1972. He was the first president since World War II to make such a journey.

SALT While in Moscow, Nixon opened what became known as the Strategic Arms Limitations Talks **(SALT).** These talks led to a 1972 agreement called the SALT Agreement. The agreement set limits on the number of defensive missile sites and strategic offensive missiles each nation would keep.

Nixon's Space Program

Advances in the space program occurred during the Nixon administration. In 1969, American astronaut Neil Armstrong became the first person to walk on the moon. The triumph of seeing Armstrong plant a United States flag on the moon's surface marked a bright spot in an otherwise troubled decade.

The Watergate Affair

In 1972, the Republicans nominated Nixon for reelection. The Democrats selected George McGovern. President Nixon claimed credit for bringing down inflation and scoring foreign policy triumphs abroad. He swept to victory, carrying the largest popular majority in United States history. Yet less than two years later, Nixon resigned from office.

- **What happened** an illegal break-in to wiretap phones in the Democratic Party headquarters with electronic surveillance equipment
- **Where** Watergate Towers, an apartment complex in Washington, D.C.
- **When** June 17, 1972
- **Who** the Committee to Reelect the President, acting with the knowledge of several high-level Nixon advisers
- **Why** to secure information to undermine the Democratic campaign against Nixon

The Cover-Up

Police captured the "burglars," who carried evidence linking them to the White House. Nixon did not know about the plan until after it happened. However, he then ordered a cover-up, which was a crime under federal law.

The Investigation Reporters from the *Washington Post* probed into the case, now known as the **Watergate scandal,** but their reports did not hinder Nixon's reelection. Then, in 1973, the Senate set up a committee to look into "illegal, improper, or unethical activities" in the 1972 election. For more than a year, the Senate committee came closer and closer to implicating President Nixon.

Unifying Themes
Science and Technology

- Why was it significant that an American was the first person to set foot on the moon?

Social Studies Practices
Chronological Reasoning and Cause and Effect

The Watergate affair was a serious scandal that brought down a president.

- What was the reason behind the Watergate break-in?
- What was Nixon's role?
- How did Nixon's involvement in the Watergate affair lead to his resignation?
- How did the Watergate affair prove that the system of checks and balances works?

Resignation of Agnew While the Watergate hearings were under way, the Justice Department charged Vice President Spiro Agnew with income tax evasion. Agnew resigned, and Nixon appointed Gerald R. Ford, the minority leader in the House of Representatives, as vice president.

The Tapes In mid-1973, the Senate committee learned that the White House had kept tape recordings of key conversations between Nixon and his top aides. Nixon refused to turn over the tapes. During the summer, the committee opened the hearings to television. The televised proceedings had the appeal of a soap opera as millions of Americans watched.

Nixon Resignation The situation ended when the Supreme Court ordered Nixon to surrender the tapes in its ruling in *United States* v. *Richard Nixon*. Based on evidence in the tapes, the House Judiciary Committee began voting on articles of impeachment against the president. To avoid impeachment, Nixon resigned on August 9, 1974, becoming the first president to do so. On noon of that day, Gerald Ford took the oath of office. Ford became the first nonelected president. To fill the office of vice president, Ford named Nelson Rockefeller, the former governor of New York.

The Significance of Watergate

Although Nixon was never charged with any specific crimes, President Ford pardoned him. Ford hoped to end what he called "our long national nightmare." Many of Nixon's advisers, however, were found guilty of crimes and sentenced to prison. The incident showed, as Ford put it, that "the Constitution works." The system of checks and balances had stopped Nixon from placing the presidency above the law. One impact of the Watergate scandal was a decline in the public's trust in government. New regulations limited campaign donations and the actions of some lobbyists.

Unifying Themes
Change

The 25th Amendment passed in 1967 established the procedure for Gerald Ford to become president.

• Why was this amendment necessary?

Gerald Ford takes the presidential oath of office following Nixon's resignation.

The Growth of Tensions and Conflict in the Middle East

Lesson Overview

When World War II ended in 1945, over six million Jews had died in the Holocaust. Across Europe, many Jews who survived were living in refugee camps and displaced person camps. Thousands of Jews were trying to return to what they considered their ancient and native homeland, Palestine. By 1948, the state of Israel had been created. However, it led to discord and conflict between Arabs and Jews. The United States took an active role in trying to achieve peace between Arab nations and Israel with some success. The United States also tries to maintain peace in the Middle East to ensure American interests are protected.

Unifying Themes

As you review this lesson take special note of the following themes:

- **Time, Continuity and Change** Why have efforts at peace been so difficult to achieve between the Arabs and the Israelis?

- **Geography, Humans, and the Environment** Why does the Middle East play such an important role in American foreign policy?

- **Power, Authority, and Governance** How has power been maintained in this area of the world?

Key People

Yasser Arafat   Menachem Begin
Anwar el-Sadat   Jimmy Carter

Key Terms and Events

partition   Camp David Accords
Palestine Liberation Organization   terrorism
Intifada

The Creation of the State of Israel

When the horrific events of the Holocaust became known around the world after World War II, support for the creation of a Jewish nation in Palestine grew. However, the region in Palestine that was in question was the homeland of Palestinian Arabs, who had been living in the region for thousands of years. To resolve the issue, the UN **partitioned,** or divided, the region into an Arab state and a Jewish state.

Although the state of Israel was quickly recognized by the United States as well as the Soviet Union, the battle for Israel's existence was far from over. Tensions between Jews and Arabs would often lead to conflict and outright war. Review the chart on the next page to learn about the struggle in establishing and maintaining the nation of Israel.

Key Concept

11.9c American strategic interests in the Middle East grew with the Cold War, the creation of the State of Israel, and the increased United States dependence on Middle Eastern oil. The continuing nature of the Arab-Israeli dispute has helped to define American policy in the Middle East.

Social Studies Practices
Chronological Reasoning

- Using the information in the chart, draw some conclusions about what was happening to Israeli citizens between 1948 and 1973.

Date	Event
1945	World War II ends, and the events of the Holocaust are made public worldwide.
1947	The United Nations partitions (divides) Palestine between Jews and Arabs.
May 1948	Great Britain's withdrawal from the area takes effect. Israel declares itself an independent nation.
May 1948	The United States and the Soviet Union formally recognize the nation of Israel.
May 1948	Six neighboring Arab nations invade Israel. Israel defeats its invaders, gaining large tracts of Arab land and causing over 700,000 Arabs to become refugees.
1956	The Suez Canal in Egypt is nationalized, or taken over by the Egyptian government. Egypt closes the canal to Israeli shipping. Supported by the British and the French, Israel invades Egypt. The UN stations a UN Emergency Force on the Egyptian side of the Egypt-Israel border leads Israel to withdraw and Egypt to reopen the canal.
1967	Israel wins the Six Day War against Egypt, Jordan, and Syria. Israel gains significant additional land.
1967	Eight Arab nations meet and agree on the Khartoum Resolution that expresses their stance against the state of Israel: "No peace with Israel, no recognition of Israel, no negotiations with it."
1973	Yom Kippur War (a Jewish high holy day) is started by Egypt and Syria. Israel defeats its attackers, and the United States helps negotiate a cease-fire agreement.

Organizations Working Against Israel

The **Palestine Liberation Organization** (PLO) was established in 1964. Its goal was to win self-rule for the Arab Palestinians and to end the presence of Israel in the area. The organization used terrorist activities and secret attacks on Israelis to gain their objectives. One of the group's leaders was **Yasser Arafat,** who helped coordinate and direct guerrilla attacks on Israel.

In the early 1990s, Arafat made a speech to the UN declaring the need to establish peace among the states of Palestine, Israel, and their neighbors. This led to a peace process that resulted in the Oslo Accords of 1993. However, peace did not last, and conflict remains among the nations. The PLO still exists today and pushes for a two-state solution to the Palestine-Israel conflict.

In the 1980s and 1990s, young Palestinians formed the **Intifada,** which means "uprising." The group fought in the streets and in surprise demonstrations against the Israelis. Many civilians on both sides died during this time period.

The Camp David Accords

In 1977, Egyptian President **Anwar el-Sadat** surprised the world by visiting Israeli Prime Minister **Menachem Begin.** In 1978, President **Jimmy Carter** seized the opportunity for bringing peace to the Middle East by inviting the two leaders to Camp David, the president's retreat in Maryland. There, Sadat and Begin hammered out the terms for a peace treaty known as the **Camp David Accords.**

Unifying Themes
Power and Authority

- Why would an American president like President Carter try to use his authority to bring about peace between the Israelis and their neighbors?

President Carter (center), Egyptian President Sadat (left), and Israeli Prime Minister Begin clasp hands after signing the Camp David Accords

The two leaders signed the treaty in 1979. Other Arab nations, however, still refused to recognize Israel. Sadat was later assassinated by Muslims opposed to Sadat's goals for peace.

Other American Efforts to Broker Peace

The United States places a great deal of importance in achieving peace in the Middle East. Like President Carter, several presidents have tried to broker peace through diplomatic methods.

- President Clinton continued to try to achieve peace in the Middle East by hosting the Camp David Summit for Israeli and Palestinian leaders. It did not produce lasting peaceful results. Problems between the Israelis and the Palestinians continued, with repeated incidents of suicide bombers and cross-border attacks by both sides. Attempts were made by the United States to develop compromise solutions, but episodes of violence delayed peacekeeping efforts.

- In November 2007, President George W. Bush hosted a Middle East Peace Conference in Annapolis, Maryland, which brought together Israeli Prime Minister Ehud Olmert and Palestinian President Mahmoud Abbas, as well as representatives from 49 other countries. The leaders agreed to work on details of a peace treaty. The effort did not have long-term success. The area continues to be troubled with violence and disagreeing factions.

- During President Barack Obama's administration, Secretary of State Hillary Clinton returned frequently to the Middle East, indicating that the administration took the issues in the area seriously. Obama and Clinton were both clear in the American support of Israel.

- Since 2016, President Trump and his administration have indicated continuing support for Israel. The president's son-in-law, Jared Kushner, acting for the president, has made multiple trips to Israel.

The United States is an important ally to Israel. Israel benefits from the support of its much larger and more powerful friend. Israel's safety and security are also important to the United States. The United States seeks, with many world nations, to see peace and an end to wars in the Middle East. There are ongoing problems in the negotiations for peace between the Arabs and the Israelis. Currently, Israel has lost some support from its few Arab friends as the Palestinian issues remain unresolved.

**Unifying Themes
Continuity**

- What examples can you find that demonstrate continuity in American foreign policy toward Israel?

Oil: A Source of Tension in the Middle East

Achieving peace in the Middle East is not just dependent on Arab-Israeli relations but also on a key resource—oil. Over 65 percent of the world's oil reserves are located in the Middle East. This valuable commodity has been a source of conflict in the region as nations vie for control over this prized resource. The United States is dependent on oil from the Middle East. During the Cold War, American foreign policy in the Middle East centered on protecting its interests in the region, which remains the focus of American foreign policy in the region to this day.

Iran In 1954, the prime minister of Iran tried to nationalize that country's foreign-owned oil industry. The United States, through the Central Intelligence Agency, secretly arranged the overthrow of the prime minister's government and the restoration of the shah to the throne of Iran. This action helped secure America's supply of oil at the time but caused problems for the nation in years to come.

Iran-Iraq War In 1980, Iraqi troops invaded Iran. Iraqi President Saddam Hussein wanted to seize control of an oil-rich region on Iran's western border that was under dispute by the two nations. When both sides began to attack oil tankers in the Persian Gulf, the United States and other Western nations sent warships to secure the shipping lanes and ensure the movement of oil. A ceasefire was eventually brokered in 1988 by the United Nations. As you will read in Topic 11, the outcome of this war eventually led to the Persian Gulf War fought between Iraq and the United States in 1990.

Turmoil in the Middle East

During the Cold War, religious and political turmoil in the Middle East helped increase tensions in this already unstable region.

Hostage Crisis In 1979, a revolution led by Islamic fundamentalists toppled the pro-American shah, Reza Pahlavi. The shah, suffering from terminal cancer, requested treatment in the United States, and President Carter agreed. Islamic rebels struck back by seizing the United States embassy in Tehran and holding more than 50 Americans hostage. The United States worked with the government of Iran to negotiate their release. Finally, after 444 days, the negotiations were settled and the Iran hostage crisis had come to an end.

Lebanon An international peacekeeping force went into Lebanon to try to end bloody fighting between Christians and Muslims. In October 1983, U.S. marines became the target of terrorists when a bomb-laden truck drove into their barracks, killing more than 300 people. In 1984, President Ronald Reagan admitted the peacekeeping effort had failed and withdrew American troops.

Terrorism Global concern was raised by an increase in **terrorism,** or random acts of violence to promote a political cause, in the Middle East. In some countries, Islamic fundamentalists engaged in terrorism against those believed to be enemies of Islam. Political terrorist groups such as Al Qaeda and ISIS grew out of the unrest in the Middle East during the Cold War. In Topic 11, you will learn about the effects terrorism has had on the United States and the world as a whole.

Unifying Themes
Continuity and Change

- Using events on this page, trace how U.S. interests and actions have both stayed the same and have changed toward Iran.

The End of the Cold War

Lesson Overview

The Berlin Wall, separating the democratic city of West Berlin from the communist city of East Berlin, served as a powerful and visible symbol of the Cold War from 1961 until 1989. During those 28 years, many people died trying to illegally cross through or get over the Wall. The differences in standards of living on either side were clearly visible. West Berlin was a vibrant, bustling city like other cities of its type in Western Europe and the United States. East Berlin changed little from postwar days of damaged or gloomy architecture and limited consumer goods.

Berlin as a divided city was an example to the world of a comparison between democracy and capitalism and communist politics and economics. When the Wall was pulled down unexpectedly in 1989, it not only opened the door to East Berlin but to all of Eastern Europe and the changes that were to follow.

Key Concept

11.9d A combination of factors contributed to the end of the Cold War, including American policies and Soviet economic and political problems that led to the loss of Soviet control over Eastern Europe.

Unifying Themes

As you review this lesson take special note of the following themes:

- **Time, Continuity, and Change** Why did economic changes in Western Europe and the United States in the post–World War II era encourage the end of the Cold War?

- **Power, Authority, and Governance** How did the use of power by Soviet President Gorbachev encourage governmental changes in his own country and others? What role did the power of the United States play in these changes?

Key People

John F. Kennedy

Nikita Khrushchev

Mikhail Gorbachev

Ronald Reagan

Key Terms and Events

Berlin Wall

glasnost

command economy

perestroika

market economy

Post–World War II

Since World War II, the division of Germany into a communist East Germany and a democratic West Germany had added to Cold War tensions. President **John F. Kennedy** and Soviet Premier **Nikita Khrushchev** met in Austria in June 1961 to discuss relations between the United States and the Soviet Union. Khrushchev thought that the Bay of Pigs disaster revealed American weakness, and he tried to threaten Kennedy into removing NATO troops from Europe. Instead, Kennedy increased U.S. military and financial commitment to West Germany.

The Building of the Berlin Wall

Response to the American moves came in August 1961 when the East German government built a wall between East and West Berlin. The **Berlin Wall** was meant to stop the flood of East Germans escaping to freedom in the West and quickly became a symbol of tyranny. In June 1963, Kennedy visited West Berlin, renewing the American commitment to defend that city and Western Europe. In a famous speech, he said that he and all people who wanted freedom were citizens of Berlin.

Renewal of Détente

In 1985, **Mikhail Gorbachev** became the new charismatic leader of the Soviet Union. Gorbachev criticized some of Reagan's defense policies and called for a renewal of détente. Gorbachev helped further relations by announcing his new policies of *glasnost* and *perestroika*.

Glasnost Gorbachev's policy of ***glasnost*** called for greater openness, including increased political freedom in the Soviet Union and Eastern Europe. This new attitude of the Soviet government was welcomed by both citizens of the Soviet Union and the western world as well. The individual republics that had been united into the Soviet Union decades before began to think about the possibility of regaining their political and economic independence.

Perestroika The Soviet Union had been following a communist economic system since the Russian Revolution in 1917. This meant that they had a **command economy.** The government owned and controlled all economic enterprise. The Soviet Union suffered such huge losses of life and damage to businesses and infrastructure during World War II that it was unable to compete economically during the postwar years with the United States or even recovering Western Europe. Remember Western Europe was receiving aid as a result of the Marshall Plan and the Truman Doctrine in the immediate postwar years.

The policy of ***perestroika*** allowed a measure of free enterprise to improve economic conditions within the Soviet Union. The very gradual transformation to a **market economy** was another welcome beginning to Soviet citizens. The standard of living in the Soviet Union and in other countries in Eastern Europe under Soviet domination lagged far behind the modernizing and industrializing United States and Western Europe. Gorbachev and his wife travelled to the United States and Western Europe and could compare for themselves the differences and the availability of consumer goods.

In 1987, on the diplomatic front, the United States and the Soviet Union reached an agreement to eliminate short-range and medium-range land-based missiles.

Preparing for the Regents

Some questions in the exam will require you to identify the significance of an event, action, idea, or development.

- How did Soviet leader Mikhail Gorbachev work to improve relations with the United States?

The End of the Cold War

Causes		Results
• Anticommunist movements gained force in Eastern Europe. • Soviet leader Mikhail Gorbachev encouraged Eastern European leaders to adopt more open policies.		• Reform leaders came to power after free elections in Poland and Czechoslovakia. • New governments took charge in Bulgaria, Hungary, Romania, and Albania. • Berlin Wall fell, East and West Germany were reunified. • Soviet Union broke apart.

On October 10, 1989, the day after the East German government opened the Berlin Wall, West Germans and East Germans unite to celebrate the fall of the symbolic structure.

The Fall of the Wall

In 1987, President **Ronald Reagan** visited the city of Berlin and stood at the famous Wall. He challenged the Soviets to "Tear down this Wall." The Berlin Wall stood as a strong Cold War symbol until 1989. In that year, political change sweeping through Eastern Europe led East Germany to tear down the wall. By October 1990, the rapid political changes in the region had led to the reunification of the two Germanys as a single nation for the first time since the end of World War II.

New Nations Are Established and Former Nations Re-Emerge

The impact of Gorbachev's policies encouraged independence movements in the Baltic republics of Lithuania, Latvia, and Estonia. In Poland in 1989, the first free elections in 50 years occurred. By 1991, the Soviet Union as a "union" was no more. The former republics declared themselves independent states such as Russia, Ukraine, Georgia, Uzbekistan, and others. This was not an easy process as many of the newly independent areas had to deal with ethnic minorities within their borders. In Eastern Europe, Czechoslovakia split into the Czech Republic and Slovakia. In December 1991, Gorbachev resigned as the changes he had encouraged occurred and as hardline communist leaders worked against these changes.

Base your answers to questions 1 and 2 on the letter below and on your knowledge of social studies.

> Dear Mr. President,
>
> We write to you because the Senate will play a major part in decisions affecting the Middle East in the time ahead, and, like any President, you will need strong support in your efforts to contribute to the cause of peace in the Middle East.
>
> With this in mind we join in assuring you that you do have strong support in the Senate for your efforts to help Israel and the Arab nations secure a genuine and lasting peace.

Source: Letter from a group of nine U.S. senators to President Jimmy Carter, June 28, 1977

1   This letter supported President Carter in his efforts to

(1) negotiate the Camp David Accords

(2) end the Arab nations' oil embargo against the United States

(3) negotiate the freeing of the American hostages in Iran

(4) get the U.S. economy out of a period of stagflation

2   According to the U.S. Constitution, why will President Carter "need strong support" from the Senate to negotiate peace in the Middle East?

(1) Only the Senate has the power to try cases of impeachment.

(2) The Senate must ratify all treaties.

(3) U.S. ambassadors must report to the Senate.

(4) Senators are up for reelection every six years.

Base your answers to questions 3 through 5 on the passage below and on your knowledge of social studies.

> **Section 2.(c)**
> The constitutional powers of the President as Commander-in-Chief to introduce United States Armed Forces into hostilities, or into situations where imminent involvement in hostilities is clearly indicated by the circumstances, are exercised only pursuant to (1) a declaration of war, (2) specific statutory authorization, or (3) a national emergency created by attack upon the United States, its territories or possessions, or its armed forces.

Source: The War Powers Act, 1973

3   The purpose of this legislation is to describe the

(1) transfer of the power of commander in chief from the executive to the legislative branch

(2) limits placed on the ability of the president to send American troops into war

(3) transfer of the power to declare war from the legislative to the executive branch

(4) limits placed on the powers of Congress to override a presidential executive order

4   President George W. Bush complied with this legislation when he

(1) established that there is an "Axis of Evil" made up of Iraq, Iran, and North Korea

(2) spoke to first responders and vowed revenge for the September 11th attacks

(3) asked Congress for authorization for the use of military force in Iraq

(4) signed into law the Patriot Act as a way to prevent future terrorist attacks

5   Which historical event was the reason for the creation of this legislation?

(1) the Civil Rights Movement

(2) World War II

(3) the Vietnam War

(4) the September 11th attacks

Base your answers to questions 6 through 8 on the cartoon below and on your knowledge of social studies.

National-Security Blanket

Source: Herb Block, *Washington Post*, 1973

6   The cartoonist would support the claim that

   (1) Richard Nixon led the break-in at the Watergate hotel

   (2) Richard Nixon opened the nation to trade with Communist China

   (3) Richard Nixon attempted to obstruct justice by concealing evidence

   (4) Richard Nixon supported the policy of Vietnamization

7   What was the outcome of the events depicted in this cartoon?

   (1) the escalation of the Vietnam War

   (2) the resignation of the president

   (3) the passage of the War Powers Act

   (4) the visit of the president to Communist China

8   At the same time this cartoon was published, what foreign policy development contributed to the growing distrust in government?

   (1) the Vietnam War

   (2) the Soviet invasion of Afghanistan

   (3) the Nuclear Test Ban Treaty

   (4) the Camp David Accords

Multiple-Choice Questions for Regents Practice

Base your answers to questions 9 and 10 on the image below and on your knowledge of social studies.

Source: Lionel Cironneau, *Associated Press*, 1989

Base your answers to questions 11 and 12 on the cartoon below and on your knowledge of social studies.

Source: Leslie Gilbert Illingworth, *Daily Mail*, 1962

9   This image is most closely associated with

(1) the end of the Cold War

(2) student protests of the war in Vietnam

(3) the end of World War II in Europe

(4) American air strikes against Yugoslavia in the Kosovo War

10   The United States assisted in the outcome depicted in this image by

(1) encouraging democracy in Eastern Europe

(2) creating the House Un-American Activities Committee

(3) re-instituting a policy of isolationism

(4) placing a blockade around East Berlin

11   Which historical event is most closely associated with this arm-wrestling match between Soviet leader Khrushchev and President Kennedy?

(1) the Berlin Airlift

(2) the Cuban Missile Crisis

(3) the Vietnam War

(4) the Bay of Pigs Invasion

12   What later development would change the political situation illustrated in this cartoon?

(1) the Nuclear Test Ban Treaty

(2) the Camp David Accords

(3) the Paris Agreement

(4) the Iran Nuclear Deal

Base your answers to questions 13 and 14 on the passages below and on your knowledge of social studies.

The truth of the matter is that Europe's requirements for the next three or four years of foreign food and other essential products—principally from America—are so much greater than her present ability to pay that she must have substantial additional help, or face economic, social and political deterioration of a very grave character.

Source: Secretary of State George C. Marshall, speech at Harvard University, June 5, 1947

Article 5
The Parties agree that an armed attack against one or more of them in Europe or North America shall be considered an attack against them all and consequently they agree that, if such an armed attack occurs, each of them, in exercise of the right of individual or collective self-defense . . . will assist the Party or Parties so attacked by taking forthwith, individually and in concert with the other Parties, such action as it deems necessary, including the use of armed force, to restore and maintain the security of the North Atlantic area.

Source: North Atlantic Treaty, April 4, 1949

13 A historian would best use these documents to study contemporary viewpoints on

(1) the division of West Berlin

(2) America's decision to defend South Korea

(3) the spread of McCarthyism

(4) immediate post–World War II Europe

14 What similarities exist between these two methods for containment?

(1) Both of these methods are in accordance with the Truman Doctrine.

(2) Both methods led to the eventual creation of NATO.

(3) Both methods were used to overcome the Berlin Blockade.

(4) Both methods would lead to direct military conflict in Eastern Europe.

Short Essay Questions

Task: Read and analyze the following documents, applying your social studies knowledge and skills to write a short essay of two or three paragraphs in which you:

- Describe the historical context surrounding these documents
- Identify and explain the *relationship* between the events and/or ideas found in these documents (Cause and Effect, *or* Similarity/Difference, *or* Turning Point)

In developing your short essay answer of two or three paragraphs, be sure to keep these explanations in mind:

Describe means "to illustrate something in words or tell about it"

Historical Context refers to "the relevant historical circumstances surrounding or connecting the events, ideas, or developments in these documents"

Identify means "to put a name to or to name"

Explain means "to make plain or understandable; to give reasons for or causes of; to show the logical development or relationship of"

<u>Types of Relationships:</u>

Cause refers to "something that contributes to the occurrence of an event, the rise of an idea, or the bringing about of a development"

Effect refers to "what happens as a consequence (result, impact, outcome) of an event, an idea, or a development"

Similarity tells how "something is alike or the same as something else"

Difference tells how "something is not alike or not the same as something else"

Turning Point is "a major event, idea, or historical development that brings about significant change. It can be local, regional, national, or global"

Document 1

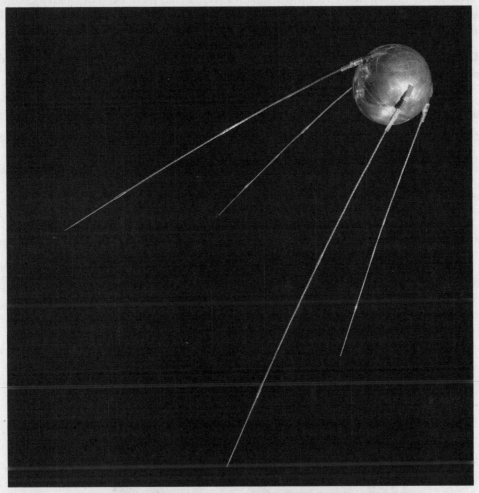

Sputnik was the world's first artificial satellite, launched in 1957 by the Soviet Union.

Document 2

First, I believe that this nation should commit itself to achieving the goal, before this decade is out, of landing a man on the moon and returning him safely to the earth. No single space project in this period will be more impressive to mankind, or more important for the long-range exploration of space; and none will be so difficult or expensive to accomplish. We propose to accelerate the development of the appropriate lunar space craft. We propose to develop alternate liquid and solid fuel boosters, much larger than any now being developed, until certain which is superior. We propose additional funds for other engine development and for unmanned explorations—explorations which are particularly important for one purpose which this nation will never overlook: the survival of the man who first makes this daring flight. But in a very real sense, it will not be one man going to the moon—if we make this judgment affirmatively, it will be an entire nation. For all of us must work to put him there.

Source: President John F. Kennedy, speech before a Joint Session of Congress, May 25, 1961

Document Analysis for Civic Literacy Essay

Historical Context: Political Protest

Throughout United States history, many constitutional and civic issues have been debated by Americans. These debates have resulted in efforts by individuals, groups, and governments to address these issues. These efforts have achieved varying degrees of success. One of these constitutional and civic issues is political protest.

Task: Read and analyze the document. Using information from the document and your knowledge of United States history, write an essay in which you

- Describe the historical circumstances surrounding this constitutional or civic issue
- Explain efforts to address this constitutional or civic issue by individuals, groups, and/or governments
- Discuss the extent to which these efforts were successful

Describe means "to illustrate something in words or tell about it"

Explain means "to make plain or understandable; to give reasons for or causes of; to show the logical development or relationship of"

Discuss means "to make observations about something using facts, reasoning, and argument; to present in some detail"

Source: Charles Dixon, *The Boston Globe*, 1966

1. What actions did students take in attempt to end the war in Vietnam?

Social and Economic Change/Domestic Issues

(1945–Present)

Topic Overview

In the life of a country, 75 years can be a busy period of growth and innovation, or simply the passage of time. The United States has experienced significant economic, political, and social changes during the last 75 years.

During this span of time in the United States, there have been multiple and major efforts for the improvement of civil rights for minority groups. Those groups include African Americans, women, persons with disabilities, and others. Some changes have happened through legislation. In other cases, the Supreme Court through its decision-making powers has changed the lives of Americans to increase individual rights.

Other groups have focused attention on the environment. There are serious challenges facing the nation, such as water and air pollution and global warming. Presidential administrations during this time have chosen either to take on a major role in these issues or to have little concern with them.

During these years, the United States has enjoyed economic growth as well as economic decline. Presidents and political parties have disagreed over the best approach to solve some of these concerns.

The African American Civil Rights Movement

Lesson Overview

During World War II and the years following the war, the lives of African Americans changed in such significant ways that they could no longer tolerate the long years of discrimination and racism that were occurring in the United States. African American soldiers, fighting for democracies overseas and on the home front, found a lack of democracy more unacceptable when they returned home. African American men and women who had jobs in war plants at home were regularly denied the right to vote, especially in southern states. Their children were unable to attend integrated schools in many areas, again especially in the South.

Incidents in the 1950s and 1960s propelled new African American organizations to form and unite to fight for equality. Leaders emerged such as Dr. Martin Luther King, Jr., who motivated thousands to stand up for their basic rights as Americans. Some young leaders and activists such as Congressman John Lewis are still working for African American rights today.

Unifying Themes

As you review this lesson take special note of the following themes:

* **Individual Development and Cultural Identity** How did African Americans work to function effectively in their struggle for equal rights? Who were some of the leaders of the civil rights movement? What difficulties did they have?

* **Time, Continuity, and Change** What were some of the events that were harmful to the struggle of African Americans, and why was this the case? How did African American leaders turn some of these events into unifying activities?

* **Development and Transformation of Social Structures** What kinds of social and political inequalities did African Americans suffer in the United States after the end of World War II? How were some of these inequalities resolved?

* **Power, Authority, and Governance** What specific changes occurred in the United States as a result of governmental actions that attempted to improve the lives of African Americans?

* **Civic Ideals and Practices** Why did African Americans have such a struggle to gain civic equality?

Key People

Earl Warren	Lyndon B. Johnson
Rosa Parks	Fannie Lou Hamer
Martin Luther King, Jr.	Stokely Carmichael
George Wallace	Malcolm X

Key Terms and Events

NAACP

school desegregation

Little Rock Nine

Montgomery Bus Boycott

SCLC

SNCC

civil disobedience

Birmingham protest

March on Washington

Civil Rights Act of 1964

Twenty-fourth Amendment

Fair Housing Act

Voting Rights Act of 1965

Key Supreme Court Cases

As you review this lesson be sure you understand the significance of these key Supreme Court cases:

Brown v. *Board of Education of Topeka, Kansas* (1954)

Heart of Atlanta Motel, Inc. v. *United States* (1964)

A Renewed Struggle for Civil Rights

Since the period of Reconstruction after the Civil War, African Americans faced discrimination, especially in southern states. Jim Crow laws limited their freedoms. For generations, white southerners continued to maintain economic, social, and political control over the South. Until well into the twentieth century, much of the South was segregated, or separated by race. Although such segregation was less apparent in the North, African Americans were generally restricted to poorer neighborhoods and lower-paying jobs.

After World War II, there was a renewed interest in achieving equal rights in all areas of life. Not until 1947 were African Americans permitted to play on major league baseball teams in this country. In that year, Jackie Robinson joined the Brooklyn Dodgers. This was one sign that public attitudes on segregation were beginning to change.

President Truman appointed a presidential commission on civil rights in 1946. Based on its report, Truman called for the establishment of a fair employment practices commission. Congress, however, failed to act on the idea. Using his powers as commander in chief, Truman issued Executive Order 9981, banning segregation in the armed forces. He also strengthened the Justice Department's civil rights division, which aided African Americans who challenged segregation in the courts.

Preparing for the Regents

Turning Point

- Why is it considered a turning point in the struggle for civil rights when Jackie Robinson joined the Brooklyn Dodgers?

Social Studies Practices

Using Evidence

The struggle to secure African American civil rights required the efforts of countless dedicated activists, organizers, and political leaders. What are two changes that President Truman made that had an impact on civil rights?

1.

2.

Civil Rights Milestones, 1947–1957

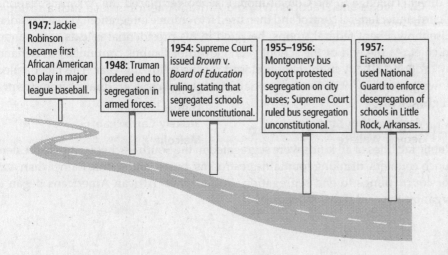

1947: Jackie Robinson became first African American to play in major league baseball.

1948: Truman ordered end to segregation in armed forces.

1954: Supreme Court issued *Brown* v. *Board of Education* ruling, stating that segregated schools were unconstitutional.

1955–1956: Montgomery bus boycott protested segregation on city buses; Supreme Court ruled bus segregation unconstitutional.

1957: Eisenhower used National Guard to enforce desegregation of schools in Little Rock, Arkansas.

Civil Rights and the Courts

In the 1950s, the Supreme Court made several important decisions concerning the civil rights of African Americans.

The Warren Court In 1953, a vacancy occurred on the Supreme Court. President Eisenhower appointed **Earl Warren,** former governor of California, as chief justice. Warren presided over the Supreme Court until 1969. During that period, the Court reached a number of decisions that deeply affected many areas of American life. Among the most far-reaching of the Warren Court's decisions were those dealing with civil rights for African Americans.

Brown* v. *Board of Education Only a year after he became chief justice, Warren presided over the Court as it reached a landmark decision in ***Brown* v. *Board of Education of Topeka, Kansas*** (1954). The Supreme Court actually combined several cases related to overturning state laws that allowed for school segregation in Kansas, Delaware, South Carolina, Virginia, and also in Washington, D.C. There were nearly 200 plaintiffs, including Oliver Brown, for whom the case was named. Linda Brown, his daughter, was a young African American student who requested the right to attend a local all-white school in her Topeka neighborhood, rather than attend an all-black school that was farther away. She was refused this opportunity by the Topeka, Kansas, Board of Education.

The 1896 *Plessy* v. *Ferguson* decision had held that separate but equal public facilities were legal. Schools were such public facilities, and Brown was refused admittance to the all-white school.

The National Association for the Advancement of Colored People **(NAACP)** joined the case and appealed it all the way to the Supreme Court. In a unanimous decision, the Court reversed its ruling in *Plessy* v. *Ferguson* and held that in the field of public education, "the doctrine of separate but equal has no place."

Little Rock Although the *Brown* case opened the door for desegregation, integration did not follow immediately. Many Americans were shocked by the decision. In the South, whites began campaigns of "massive resistance" to public **school desegregation.**

Although the Supreme Court had ordered that school integration go forward "with all deliberate speed," many school systems openly defied the ruling. In 1957, the governor of Arkansas, Orval Faubus, ordered the state's National Guard to prevent nine African American students from attending Central High School in Little Rock. These students became known as the **Little Rock Nine.**

President Eisenhower was reluctant to step in, but the governor's defiance was a direct challenge to the Constitution. Eisenhower placed the Arkansas National Guard under federal control and then used it to enforce integration. When President Eisenhower sent federal troops, he acted in his presidential role as commander in chief. At the end of the school year, Governor Faubus continued his defiance by ordering all city high schools closed for the following year. The tactic failed, however, and in 1959, the first racially integrated class graduated from Central High School.

African American Activism

Public facilities of all kinds were segregated in the South—schools, movie theaters, lunch counters, drinking fountains, restrooms, buses, and trains. Rather than wait for court rulings to end segregation, in the 1950s, African Americans began to organize the civil rights movement.

Unifying Themes
Power and Authority

Brown v. *Board of Education of Topeka, Kansas* (1954) established that facilities separated by race were unequal. The decision reversed *Plessy* v. *Ferguson* (1896) and made integration of schools possible.

- How did the governor of Arkansas respond to *Brown* v. *Board of Education of Topeka, Kansas*?

- Was President Eisenhower's response to Governor Faubus' action justified?

- What may have been the result had Eisenhower not sent in the National Guard?

Unifying Themes
Cultural Identity

African Americans began to take direct action to end segregation following *Brown* v. *Board of Education* (1954). Boycotts of schools, lunch counters, and buses, for example, began.

- How did the actions of Rosa Parks and Martin Luther King, Jr., change attitudes toward segregation?

Major Civil Rights Protests, 1954–1965

Year	Event	Outcome
1954	*Brown v. Board of Education*	Supreme Court ruled that separate educational facilities for whites and African Americans are inherently unequal.
1955–1956	Montgomery Bus Boycott	Alabama bus company was forced to desegregate its buses. Martin Luther King, Jr., emerged as an important civil rights leader.
1961	Freedom Rides	Interstate Commerce Commission banned segregation in interstate transportation.
1963	James Meredith sues University of Mississippi for admission	Supreme Court upheld Meredith's right to enter the all-white institution.
1963	Protest marches in Birmingham, Alabama	Violence against peaceful demonstrators shocked the nation. Under pressure, Birmingham desegregated public facilities.
1963	March on Washington	More than 200,000 people demonstrated in an impressive display of support for civil rights.
1965	Selma March (Alabama)	State troopers attacked marchers. President Johnson used federal force to protect route from Selma to Montgomery and thousands joined march. On the 50th anniversary of the March (2015) President and Mrs. Obama led lawmakers and civil rights activists in a march in the same location. In a speech that day the President said that "our march is not yet finished" and cited the need for the full restoration of the Voting Rights Act which has been weakened in some states.

In Montgomery, Alabama, in 1955, an African American seamstress named **Rosa Parks** refused to give up her seat to a white man and move to the back of the bus, as was required by law. She was arrested for violating the law, and her action inspired a boycott of the city's buses known as the **Montgomery Bus Boycott.**

A young Baptist minister, **Martin Luther King, Jr.,** emerged as a leader of the protest. King had studied the nonviolent methods of Mohandas Gandhi and Henry David Thoreau. His dynamic speaking style drew the attention and support of large numbers of people.

The boycott lasted 381 days. In the end, the Supreme Court ruled that segregation of public buses was illegal. Although Parks had not planned her action that day, her stand against injustice led the way for others.

Civil Rights Legislation

Congress also made some moves to ensure civil rights for African Americans. In August 1957, it passed the first civil rights act since Reconstruction. The bill created a permanent commission for civil rights and increased federal efforts to ensure blacks the right to vote. Another bill in 1960 further strengthened voting rights.

Although these bills had only limited effectiveness, they did mark the beginning of change. Martin Luther King, Jr., once remarked that it was impossible to legislate what was in a person's heart, but that laws can restrain the heartless. During this time, some southern Senators attempted to delay passage of civil rights legislation by using a filibuster. This is an effort by one or more senators to speak continuously on the floor of the Senate until support for their view can be gained or until the Senate leaders decide to delay the proposed bill. Filibusters may last several weeks and can be ended only by a special vote called cloture, which can close debate.

Rosa Parks

During the 1960s, the struggle of African Americans to win equality before the law grew more intense. In their fight, African Americans were seeking to overcome a heritage of racism that had been a part of American thought and tradition for more than 300 years. Many African Americans were working together for the common goal of justice and equality. The successes they gained would deeply affect many parts of American society.

African Americans Organize

African Americans formed a number of different groups that used a variety of approaches in the attempt to achieve justice and equality. In the early 1960s, many groups followed the nonviolent methods introduced by Dr. Martin Luther King, Jr., and the Southern Christian Leadership Conference **(SCLC),** an organization of clergy who shifted the leadership of the civil rights movement to the South. Another organization, the Student Non-Violent Coordinating Committee **(SNCC),** initially used nonviolent methods to promote the movement with its freedom rides and voter registration efforts.

Many civil rights activists used a form of protest called **civil disobedience.** This means the deliberate breaking of a law to show a belief that the law is unjust. For example, they attempted to use segregated facilities at interstate train stations and bus depots. Usually, they were arrested for such acts; often, they were beaten.

James Meredith The push to integrate education continued. In 1962, James Meredith, an African American Air Force veteran, made headlines when he tried to enroll at the all-white University of Mississippi. The governor of the state personally tried to stop Meredith from enrolling. Riots broke out, and federal marshals and the National Guard were called up. Although he had to overcome continued harassment, Meredith did finally enter and eventually graduate from the university.

Greensboro Practicing civil disobedience, demonstrators protested such discrimination as segregated lunch counters and buses. Sit-ins at lunch counters—the 1960s version of fast-food restaurants—began at Greensboro, North Carolina, in 1960. There, a group of African Americans sat at a "whites only" lunch counter and refused to leave until served. As such protests became popular, some sympathetic whites often joined the sit-ins.

Major African American Organizations

Organization	Date of Founding	Background
National Association for the Advancement of Colored People (NAACP)	1909	Organized by black and white progressives; W. E. B. Du Bois an early leader; favored court challenges to segregation; appealed primarily to the professional and college-educated
National Urban League	1910	Began as the Urban League; devoted to empowering African Americans to enter the economic and social mainstream, and to secure economic self-reliance, equality, power, and civil rights
The Nation of Islam	1930	Known as Black Muslims, founded as a black separatist religious group; became the voice of black nationalism in the 1960s; Muhammad Ali converted in 1964; Malcolm X, a leading spokesperson, assassinated in 1965
Congress of Racial Equality (CORE)	1942	Became best known for the "freedom rides" of the 1960s, efforts to desegregate interstate transportation
Southern Christian Leadership Conference (SCLC)	1957	Founded by Martin Luther King, Jr., to encourage nonviolent passive resistance; organized black Christian churches
Student Nonviolent Coordinating Committee (SNCC)	1960	In early days, used nonviolent civil disobedience in sit-ins and boycotts; later supported the idea of "black power" put forward by Stokely Carmichael; he explained this phrase to mean that African Americans should work together to use their economic and political power to gain equality

Birmingham In 1963, Dr. Martin Luther King, Jr., and the SCLC began a campaign to bring integration to Birmingham, Alabama, which many considered to be the most segregated city in the South. At a protest march, police used dogs and fire hoses to break up the marchers and arrested more than 2,000 people. One of those jailed was King, who then wrote his famous "Letter from a Birmingham Jail," in which he defended his methods of nonviolent civil disobedience and restated the need for direct action to end segregation.

Television cameras brought the scenes of violence at the **Birmingham protest** to people across the country. This helped build support for the growing civil rights movement. In Birmingham, the protests eventually resulted in the desegregation of city facilities.

Medgar Evers White reaction to African American protests sometimes turned deadly. Medgar Evers, field secretary of the NAACP, had been working to desegregate Jackson, Mississippi. In June 1963, Evers was murdered by a sniper outside his home.

University of Alabama Also in June 1963, Governor **George Wallace** of Alabama vowed to stop two African American students from registering at the state university. Pressure from President Kennedy and the later arrival of the National Guard forced Wallace to back down. The two students enrolled peacefully.

The March on Washington The growing civil rights movement moved President Kennedy to deliver a televised speech to the nation in June 1963 on the need to guarantee the civil rights of African Americans. This marked the first speech by a president specifically on this issue. Eight days later, he sent the most comprehensive civil rights bill in the nation's history to Congress.

Civil rights groups organized the **March on Washington,** a huge march on Washington, D.C., in August 1963, to show support for the bill. At the march, Dr. Martin Luther King, Jr., delivered his famous "I have a dream" speech to a crowd of more than 200,000 participants. In the speech, he eloquently expressed his hopes for a unified America.

Not all Americans shared King's dream, however. Just a few weeks after the March on Washington, white terrorists bombed an African American church in Birmingham, killing four young girls.

Preparing for the Regents

More than fifty years later, African Americans are still struggling with discriminatory practices by police. Baltimore, Maryland, and Ferguson, Missouri, and other locations have been the site of riots against police.

• Why do you think these events continue to happen?

The March on Washington

President Johnson and Civil Rights Legislation

After the assassination of John F. Kennedy in November 1963, the new president, **Lyndon B. Johnson,** recognized the urgency of pushing forward with civil rights legislation.

Civil Rights Act of 1964

Johnson worked tirelessly for the passage of a civil rights bill, and in July 1964, he signed the **Civil Rights Act of 1964,** the most sweeping civil rights law in American history. The bill called for

- protection of voting rights for all Americans.
- opening of public facilities (restaurants, hotels, stores, restrooms) to people of all races.
- a commission to protect equal job opportunities for all Americans.

Passage of the Civil Rights Act came just months after ratification of the **Twenty-fourth Amendment** to the Constitution, which abolished the poll tax in federal elections. A poll tax was a fee that had to be paid before a person could vote. The poll tax had prevented poorer Americans—including many African Americans—from exercising their legal right to vote.

The Civil Rights Act of 1964 outlawed race discrimination in public accommodations, including motels that refused rooms to African Americans. In the landmark Supreme Court case *Heart of Atlanta Motel* v. *United States* (1964), racial segregation of private facilities engaged in interstate commerce was found unconstitutional. Title VIII of the Civil Rights Act of 1968, also known as the **Fair Housing Act**, prohibits discrimination in the sale, rental, or financing of dwellings based on race, color, national origin, sex, or familial status.

The Voting Rights Act of 1965

Many southern states continued to resist civil rights legislation and Supreme Court rulings. Southern resistance to civil rights laws angered Johnson. He proposed new legislation, which was passed as the **Voting Rights Act of 1965.** This bill

- put an end to literacy tests—tests of a person's ability to read and write that had often been misused to bar African American voters.
- authorized federal examiners to register voters in areas suspected of denying African Americans the right to vote.
- directed the attorney general of the United States to take legal action against states that continued to use poll taxes in state elections.

Changes in the Civil Rights Movement

The summer of 1964 was known as "Freedom Summer" for its many demonstrations, protests, voter registration drives, and the March on Washington. Freedom Summer and the passage of the Voting Rights Act a year later marked high points of the civil rights movement.

New Leaders in the Movement

As the African American civil rights movement gained momentum, new leaders began to emerge.

Fannie Lou Hamer In Mississippi, the African American voter registration was so low that the Mississippi Freedom Democratic Party (MFDP) was formed as an alternative to the existing Democratic Party. The year 1964 was a presidential election year. **Fannie Lou Hamer**, a representative of the MFDP and an active black

Preparing for the Regents

Turning Point

- Why is the Civil Rights Act of 1964 considered a turning point in the struggle for civil rights?

Social Studies Practices

Organizing Information

In the space below, list three provisions of the Voting Rights Act of 1965. Which do you think is the most significant? Why?

1.

2.

3.

civil rights activist in the state, attended the National Democratic Party Convention. She spoke at the convention, describing the difficulties African Americans had in attempting to vote in Mississippi.

The MFDP was offered a compromise of two delegate seats "at large," meaning they were not designated by state. They were also told that there would be an effort to increase minority representation in the future. The MFDP rejected the offer, and the regular Democratic representatives also left the convention in protest that the compromises had even been offered. Fannie Lou Hamer continued a long career in civil rights activism, drawing large crowds when she spoke. She died in 1977.

Stokely Carmichael By the mid-1960s, some civil rights activists became frustrated that the new legislation had not improved conditions enough. Some, like **Stokely Carmichael,** demanded "Black Power," stressing that African Americans should take total control of the political and economic aspects of their lives. Some advocated the use of violence. Meanwhile, more moderate leaders continued to call for nonviolent methods of protest. These splits weakened the effectiveness of the civil rights movement.

Malcolm X A new, more militant leader, **Malcolm X,** began to attract a following from African Americans who were frustrated by the pace of the civil rights movement. Malcolm X spoke against integration, instead promoting black nationalism, a belief in the separate identity and racial unity of the African American community. A member of the separatist group Nation of Islam until 1964, Malcolm X broke with that group to form his own religious organization, called Muslim Mosque, Inc. After a pilgrimage to the Muslim holy city of Mecca in Saudi Arabia, during which he saw millions of Muslims of all races worshipping peacefully together, he changed his views about integration and began to work toward a more unified civil rights movement. He had made enemies, though, and in February 1965, he was assassinated at a New York City rally.

Violence as a Result of the Movement

Although many Americans supported the African American civil rights movement, there were many who did not support the movement, and tensions between whites and blacks increased. Eventually, these tensions blew up into terrible and deadly violence.

Riots In 1964 and 1965, frustration at the discrimination in housing, education, and employment boiled over into riots in New York City, in Rochester, New York, and in the Watts neighborhood of Los Angeles. In Watts alone, 34 people were killed, and more than a thousand were injured. The federal government set up the Kerner Commission to investigate the cause of the rioting. It concluded that the riots were a result of the anger that had been building in many of America's inner cities.

Assassinations Dr. Martin Luther King, Jr., had been awarded the Nobel Peace Prize in 1964 "for the furtherance of brotherhood among men." He remained a leading speaker for African American rights, even as splits developed in the civil rights movement. As a supporter of the underprivileged and the needy, King went to Memphis, Tennessee, in April 1968 to back a sanitation workers' strike. There he was shot and killed by a white assassin. The death of the leading spokesperson for nonviolence set off new rounds of rioting in American cities.

Just two months after King's death, Senator Robert F. Kennedy, brother of the late president and now a presidential candidate committed to civil rights, was assassinated. The shock of these deaths and the increasing urban violence made the goals of King and the Kennedys seem far off to many Americans.

Unifying Themes
Time and Change

In the 1960s, many African Americans felt that they should take more control over the political and economic conditions in their lives. A new leader named Malcolm X emerged and began to attract attention from more militant individuals.

• How were Malcolm X's beliefs different from those of Martin Luther King, Jr.?

Preparing for the Regents

Turning Point

• Why is the assassination of Martin Luther King, Jr., in 1968 considered a turning point in history?

Other Movements for Change

Key Concept

11.10b Individuals, diverse groups, and organizations have sought to bring about change in American society through a variety of methods.

Lesson Overview

It has been 75 years since the end of World War II. During that time, tremendous changes have occurred in many aspects of American life. This section reviews the civil rights that have been gained by women, Native Americans, Latino Americans, Americans with disabilities, persons formally accused of crimes, students, and the LGBT community. There have also been new efforts to improve the condition of the environment and to plan for the future. The topic of immigration to the United States has been a challenging issue throughout American history, and it continues to be so.

Unifying Themes

As you review this lesson take special note of the following themes:

- **Individual Development and Cultural Identity** In what ways have various ethnic groups worked to achieve equal opportunities while maintaining aspects of their own cultures? What kinds of legal difficulties have specific ethnic groups faced?

- **Time, Continuity, and Change** How have Supreme Court cases had the power of law in settling some civil rights issues? Cite a few specific examples of how individual Americans won a particular civil right.

- **Development and Transformation of Social Structures** Why did the case *Brown* v. *Board of Education of Topeka*, *Kansas* cause such turmoil in so many school districts, especially in the South? How did the Stonewall Inn riots bring to attention a largely ignored segment of the population?

Key People

Betty Friedan	Cesar Chavez
Russell Means	Rachel Carson

Key Terms and Events

The Feminine Mystique	LGBT movement
Equal Rights Amendment	*Silent Spring*
Equal Pay Act	Environmental Protection Agency
Title IX	Clean Air Act of 1970
American Indian Movement	Clean Water Act of 1972
Chicano movement	Endangered Species Act of 1973
Individuals with Disabilities Education Act	Immigration and Nationality Act of 1965
Americans with Disabilities Act	Immigration Act of 1990
Gay Rights movement	Immigration Reform and Control Act of 1986
Stonewall Inn riots	

Key Supreme Court Cases

As you review this lesson be sure you understand the significance of these key Supreme Court cases:

Roe v. *Wade* (1973)
Mapp v. *Ohio* (1961)
Gideon v. *Wainwright* (1963)
Miranda v. *Arizona* (1966)
Engel v. *Vitale* (1962)
Tinker v. *Des Moines School District* (1969)
New Jersey v. *TLO* (1985)

The Women's Rights Movement

Like African Americans, women had long been denied equal rights in the United States. The successes of the African American civil rights movement in the 1960s highlighted the need for organized action by women to achieve similar goals.

Past Successes, New Goals

The women's rights movement was not just a product of the 1960s. The struggle for equality had been a long one. Some of the key events in the struggle are listed below.

1848 The Seneca Falls Convention marked the beginning of the organized women's rights movement in this nation.

1870 Passage of the Fifteenth Amendment granted the vote to African American men but not to any women. Susan B. Anthony arranged to have a women's suffrage amendment introduced in Congress. It was defeated there, but Anthony and others continued the fight for the right to vote.

1920 Ratification of the Nineteenth Amendment gave women the right to vote.

1940s Thousands of women took jobs in war-related industries during World War II.

By the 1960s, women had exercised the right to vote for 40 years, yet women still had not achieved equal status with men economically and socially. Women's groups renewed demands for a variety of goals, including more job opportunities, equality of pay with men, and an end to discrimination based on sex.

Presidents Kennedy and Johnson appointed no women to major posts in their administrations. Yet, in those years, fundamental changes occurred.

- More and more women entered fields that men had traditionally dominated, such as law, medicine, engineering, and the sciences.

- In 1963, **Betty Friedan** wrote *The Feminine Mystique*, a book arguing that society had forced American women out of the job market and back into the home after World War II. The book was influential because it energized a new women's rights movement. Friedan said that not all women were content with the role of homemaker and that more job opportunities should be open to women.

- Title VII of the Civil Rights Act of 1964 barred job discrimination on the basis of sex as well as race.

- The National Organization for Women (NOW) formed in 1966 to push for legislation guaranteeing equality for women.

- Congress approved the **Equal Rights Amendment** (ERA) in 1972 and sent it to the states for ratification. This proposed amendment has never been ratified,

Social Studies Practices

Gathering and Using Evidence

- List five important events of the women's rights movement of the 1960s and early 1970s.

- Which event do you consider to be the most significant? Why?

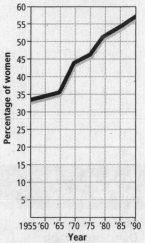

Women Working Outside the Home, 1955–1990

Source: *Statistical Abstract of the United States*

Preparing for the Regents

Stimulus-Based Questions: Graph

- According to the line graph, between which years did the number of women working outside the home first exceed 50 percent?

- What factors may have caused that change?

although there has been renewed interest lately. The amendment stated "equality of rights under the law shall not be denied or abridged by the United States or any state on account of sex."

- The Equal Opportunity Act of 1972 **(Equal Pay Act)** required employers to pay equal wages for equal work.
- **Title IX** of the Educational Amendments Act of 1972 gave female college athletes the right to the same financial support as male athletes.

In the landmark case of **Roe v. Wade** (1973), the Supreme Court ruled that a woman's right to terminate a pregnancy is constitutionally protected. Laws making abortion a crime were overturned because they violated a woman's right to privacy. The Supreme Court held that the states could limit abortion only after the first six months of pregnancy. Challenges to the decision in *Roe* v. *Wade* have continued for decades afterward. In recent years, some states have approved legislation that places additional limits on abortions.

Affirmative Action Some of the laws guaranteeing equal opportunities for women, African Americans, and other minority groups called for affirmative action. This meant taking positive steps to eliminate the effects of past discrimination in hiring. In practice, it often meant giving preference to members of such groups when hiring workers or accepting applicants to schools. These affirmative action programs were begun during the Johnson administration of the 1960s.

Women's Rights Vocabulary The term *feminism* refers to the belief that women should have the same economic, social, and political rights as men. The women's rights movement is sometimes called the feminist movement.

The term *sexism* refers to beliefs or practices that discriminate against a person on the basis of sex. The women's movement directed its efforts at removing sexist terminology, practices, and literature from American business and education.

Median Income of Men and Women, 1965–2015

Source: U.S. Bureau of Labor Statistics; Institute for Women's Policy Research

"Founding Fathers! How come no Founding Mothers?"

Preparing for the Regents

Stimulus-Based Question: Political Cartoon

Examine the cartoon, which features a painting by John Trumbull that shows the signing of the Declaration of Independence.

• What criticism about this painting are the two characters giving?

The term *glass ceiling* is used to describe a mid-level position to which women might be promoted in many jobs but which allowed women to see upper-level, better-paying positions that were held by men and were not open to women. This type of unspoken discrimination occurred in all types of employment and can still be found today.

Setbacks for the Women's Rights Movement

Not all Americans supported the women's rights movement. Some argued that women already had equal rights. Others claimed that those goals undermined "traditional" values. In 1971, President Nixon vetoed a bill that would have provided for a national system of day care for the children of working mothers. His reason for vetoing the bill was that he believed that the family rather than the government should be responsible for the care of children.

Social Studies Practices
Interpreting Evidence

• Why might some women support the women's rights movement of the 1960s, while others might oppose it?

Critics also charged that affirmative action programs were a kind of reverse discrimination, in which white males lost chances at jobs to less-qualified women and members of minority groups. In 1979, the Supreme Court ruled in *Regents of the University of California* v. *Bakke* that the school used racial quotas when deciding on applicants to medical school. This meant that Allan Bakke was rejected admission to the medical school in favor of less-qualified applicants. The Court ruled that Bakke had been denied equal protection under the Fourteenth Amendment. It nevertheless found that other affirmative action programs may be constitutional.

The proposed ERA generated tremendous controversy. Opponents claimed that the women's rights movement had led to rising divorce rates, increasing numbers of abortions, and the growing acceptance and recognition of homosexuality—all threats to traditional values, said critics. Ratification of the ERA, they argued, would cause still more problems for American society. By the 1982 deadline, the ERA was three states short of ratification and thus was defeated. There have been recent endeavors to renew efforts to pass an Equal Rights Amendment.

Preparing for the Regents

Some questions in the exam will require you to identify a central effect of a specific event.

• Why did the proposed Equal Rights Amendment cause controversy?

In the late 1980s and 1990s, women's groups began to demand legal protection against physical and mental abuse directed toward both women and children. Lawsuits began to occur to protest sexual harassment, especially in the workplace.

Other Groups Struggle for Their Rights

In addition to the African American and women's civil rights movements, Native Americans, Latinos, and disabled Americans fought for equality and justice.

Native Americans

Unifying Themes
Authority and Governance

- How did the federal government change its policies toward Native Americans in the early 1900s? What were the effects of these changes?

In the twentieth century, some conditions for Native Americans had improved. They were granted full citizenship in 1924 by the Indian Citizenship Act. With citizenship came the right to vote but some states imposed restrictions that lasted until the 1960's. Franklin Roosevelt's Indian Reorganization Act of 1934 (Wheeler-Howard Act), known as the Indian New Deal, revised earlier government policies to rebuild tribes and promote tribal cultures. As Native Americans' circumstances improved, their population began to increase. Nevertheless, conditions for many remained poor. The per capita income of Native Americans was well below the poverty level. Rates of alcoholism and suicide were the highest of any ethnic group in the United States. Unemployment rates were far higher than the national average, and the high school dropout rate was near 50 percent.

Native Americans Organize In the early 1950s, Congress had enacted legislation to lessen government control over reservations, but this led to the loss of property by many Native Americans and forced some onto welfare. During the Johnson administration, the government tried to improve conditions by starting new programs to raise the standard of housing and to provide medical facilities, educational institutions, and vocational training.

Preparing for the Regents

Some questions in the exam will require you to explain how people made an effort to address an issue.

- What problems did Native Americans face in the 1960s and 1970s?
- How did they draw attention to their plight?

Native Americans began demanding greater responsibility in making decisions that affected their lives. Native Americans took inspiration from the African American civil rights movement. They began to call for "Red Power" and formed the **American Indian Movement** (AIM) to further their goals. **Russell Means,** a member of the Oglala Lakota tribe, was a founder of this movement. Means became the first national director of AIM.

In 1969, a group of militant Native Americans seized Alcatraz Island in San Francisco Bay with the demand that it be turned into an Indian cultural center. In 1972, members of AIM occupied the Bureau of Indian Affairs in Washington, D.C., demanding rights and property they said were guaranteed to them under earlier treaties. In 1973, AIM members occupied the reservation village of Wounded Knee, South Dakota, site of the last battle in the Indian wars of the 1800s. The takeover lasted two months, with the militants demanding changes in policies toward Native Americans.

Means was a leader and participant in the activities at Alcatraz and Wounded Knee. He said that there was a "Buckskin Curtain" separating American Indians from the American government and the white population. In his struggle for rights for American Indians, Means said that anyone who was born in the Western Hemisphere was a "Native American" and that he and all the tribes were "American Indians." Means also stressed that justice can be measured in the United States by how native people are treated. With this statement, he would then note the many injustices to American Indians.

Although these actions did not always achieve Native Americans' goals, the agitation did draw attention to their problems. Throughout the 1970s, court decisions tried to remedy earlier treaty violations. By 1989, Native Americans had been awarded more than $80 million as compensation for lost land. In addition, government policies changed again. The Indian Self-Determination and Education Assistance Act of 1975 gave Native Americans more control over reservations.

Also, the post of Assistant Secretary of the Interior for Indian Affairs was created in 1975 to protect Native American interests.

New York State and Native Americans Some major court cases involving Native American rights have taken place in New York State. For example, in *County of Oneida* v. *Oneida Indian Nation of New York State* (1985), the Supreme Court ruled that Native Americans had a right to sue to enforce their original land rights. The Court further stated that New York's purchase of 872 acres from the Oneida Indians in 1795 was illegal, because it was neither witnessed by federal agents nor approved by Congress. Both these steps were required under the federal Indian Trade and Non-Intercourse Act of 1793. Such court decisions have encouraged other Native American groups in New York State and across the nation to sue for return of lost lands.

Controversies occurred in northern New York regarding the St. Regis Indian Reservation, or Akwesasne Mohawk Reservation as it is also known. Violence erupted on the 14,000-acre reservation, which stretches into southern Canada, in the spring of 1990. At issue was gambling on the reservation. The incident involved questions of which Native American group controlled reservation policy as well as the role New York State has in dealing with the reservation. By 2019, there were a number of Native American owned and operated gambling casinos, gas stations, and other related services across New York State.

A very recent example of political progress for Native Americans as well as women occurred in the congressional elections of 2018. Deb Haaland, a Native American lawyer from New Mexico, and Sharice Davids, a Native American lawyer from Kansas, were the first two Native American women elected to the House of Representatives.

Latinos

People from the nations south of the United States may be identified in a number of proper terms. The word *Latino* refers to people whose family origins are from any of the nations known as Latin America. *Latina*/s refers to a female or group of only females. The largest number of Latinos is Mexican Americans. Although sometimes known as Chicanos, this term is less accurate as it really only refers to Mexican American males. The term *Hispanic* is used for people whose family origins are in the Spanish-speaking nations of Latin America. For example, a native Mexican man would qualify as a Chicano, a Latino, and a Hispanic. A native Brazilian male would be Latino but not Hispanic as Brazil was colonized by Portugal and still speaks Portuguese.

It is important to understand the proper terminology, but regardless of the term, Latino immigrants to the United States have often been denied equal opportunities in employment, education, and housing. Addressing these issues was the focus of the **Chicano movement** of the 1960s.

By the early 1960s, large numbers of Latinos were employed as farm workers, often as migrants. They faced problems of discrimination, poor pay, and hazardous working conditions. In 1962, a Chicano named **Cesar Chavez** emerged as a labor leader in California, starting a union for migrant farm workers. This union became the United Farm Workers. Since these efforts were occurring at the same time as the civil rights movement for African Americans was gaining momentum, and some were using the term *Black Power*, the Latino leaders used the term *Brown Power*.

Unifying Themes
Power and Authority

The Supreme Court case *County of Oneida* v. *Oneida Indian Nation of New York State* (1985) established that Native American tribes had the right to sue state governments to reclaim their tribal lands.

• Why is *County of Oneida v. Oneida Indian Nation of New York State* important in the struggle for Native American equality?

Social Studies Practices
Interpreting and Using Evidence

Identify the correct term for each of the following in addition to each country of origin:

1. a woman from Cuba

2. a man from Honduras

3. a woman from Argentina

Cesar Chavez

Chavez's work in California was especially helpful to grape and lettuce pickers in their struggle for higher wages and better working conditions. Chavez's efforts at boycotts of grapes and lettuce increased public support for the goals of farm workers. Some rural areas of New York State have seasonal Latino migrant populations who work on fruit and vegetable farms. Other areas, like major urban metropolitan areas such as New York City and Rochester, for example, have large Latino American resident populations.

Chavez, like Dr. Martin Luther King, Jr., believed in nonviolent methods. Chavez continued to serve as spokesperson for farm workers until his death in 1993. He helped raise the self-esteem of the nation's growing Latino population by making their contributions to the American economy and culture more visible. Latinos began to organize against discrimination in the 1960s and succeed in making strides toward their goals, as shown in the graphic organizer below.

Latino Victories in the 1960s

Latino Victories		
Labor	**Politics**	**Civil Rights**
• Under the leadership of Cesar Chavez, United Farm Workers union made important financial, health, and safety gains for farm workers.	• Voters elected Texans Henry Gonzalez and Eligio de la Garza to the House of Representatives. Joseph Montoya of New Mexico was elected to the Senate.	• Mexican American Legal Defense and Education Fund helped Mexican Americans gain civil rights and encouraged Mexican American students to become lawyers.

People With Disabilities

Americans with disabilities have endured a long struggle to gain their full rights in American society. In the nation's early years, care of the handicapped was usually left to their families, often resulting in neglect or abuse. Reformers began to work for change in the early 1800s. For example, in Massachusetts, Dorothea Dix led a campaign to improve conditions for mentally ill people, resulting in the founding of more than 30 state institutions to care for them.

Education Educational opportunities for hearing-impaired students were gradually widened. Gallaudet College in Washington, D.C., was founded in 1857, and today that institution is internationally recognized for its educational programs for hearing-impaired students. In the late 1980s, its students successfully demonstrated to win the appointment of a hearing-impaired person as president of the college. In New York State, the National Technical Institute for the Deaf at the Rochester Institute of Technology is another school for the hearing impaired whose programs have won wide recognition. The school provides deaf students with college training in technical and scientific fields.

Educational opportunities were also widened for visually impaired students. In 1829, the Perkins School for the Blind opened in Boston and quickly became a model for schools elsewhere. Although such schools still exist and serve important functions, many visually impaired students today attend regular schools under a practice called mainstreaming. The idea behind mainstreaming is to bring handicapped students out of the isolation of special schools and into the "mainstream" of student life.

Programs and Legislation for People With Disabilities The federal government has been especially active in setting out new programs and policies for people with disabilities.

- President Kennedy established the Presidential Commission on Mental Retardation to study and highlight the problems of the mentally handicapped individuals in American society.

- President Kennedy also backed the establishment of the Special Olympics to provide both a showcase and encouragement for athletes with handicapping conditions.

- The Rehabilitation Act of 1973, Section 504, barred discrimination against people with disabilities in any programs, activities, and facilities that were supported by federal funds.

- The Education for All Handicapped Children Act of 1975, now called the **Individuals with Disabilities Education Act** (IDEA), ensured a free, appropriate education for children with disabilities, including special education and related services.

- The **Americans with Disabilities Act of 1990** (ADA) prohibited discrimination in employment, public accommodation, transportation, state and local government services, and telecommunications. Benefits of the act included greater accessibility to public buildings and transportation for people who use wheelchairs and the availability of electronic devices to allow hearing-impaired people to use telephones and enjoy movies.

- In October 2010, new federal legislation known as Rosa's Law replaced the phrase "mentally retarded" with "intellectual disabilities" in health, education, and labor policy.

Activism by disabled veterans, especially from the Vietnam War, drew increased attention to the needs of people with disabilities. Celebrities have also taken up the cause of working for increased congressional funding of medical research. Some examples include actors such as the late Elizabeth Taylor for AIDS research, the late Christopher Reeve for spinal cord injuries research, and Michael J. Fox for Parkinson's disease research.

Schools began to mainstream students with disabilities into regular classrooms. Students who previously might have attended special schools with other students with similar disabilities have begun to attend regular public schools in a major attempt at deinstitutionalization. These efforts are known as programs of inclusion.

The Supreme Court and Rights of the Accused

During the 1960s, several cases came before the Supreme Court of the United States in Washington that had to do with the rights of a person accused of a crime. In this section, a few of the most important cases are described. They are considered landmark cases of the Supreme Court because their results impacted many Americans and would last over a long period of time.

Mapp v. *Ohio* (1961) In 1957, in Cleveland, Ohio, police searched the home of Dollree Mapp, looking for a suspect in a bombing case. Mapp never saw a warrant for the search and protested the search, but a search was conducted anyway. During the search, police found a trunk with some materials that they called obscene. Mapp was arrested for being in possession of the materials. She was found guilty but, working with an attorney, protested that police did not have a warrant to look through her whole house in search of the suspect.

Social Studies Practices
Cause and Effect

- How did the Americans with Disabilities Act (1990) change the lives of people with handicaps?

Social Studies Practices
Gathering and Using Evidence

- What are the "rights of the accused"?

- How do these cases support the role of the Supreme Court as the interpreter of the U.S. Constitution?

Dollree Mapp

In 1961, the case eventually went before the Supreme Court. The Court ruled that Mapp's rights had been violated. The Court ruled that the 4th and 14th amendments protect a citizen from illegal searches. The exclusionary rule was applied to state courts. This meant that evidence obtained unconstitutionally, in this case without a search warrant, could not be used in federal or state courts. In other words, it had to be excluded from the trial proceedings.

***Gideon* v. *Wainwright* (1963)** Clarence Earl Gideon was accused of breaking into a Florida pool hall and stealing money from the vending machines. Gideon had no financial resources and requested that an attorney represent him in court. He was refused an attorney since it was not a case involving the possibility of the death penalty. Gideon attempted to represent himself but did not have the knowledge to be successful. Gideon was found guilty and was sentenced to five years in prison. While in prison, Gideon spent as much time as he could studying the law. He eventually wrote to the Supreme Court, requesting that his case be reviewed as he was sure he was entitled to a lawyer from everything he read.

Clarence Gideon

The Supreme Court agreed to hear the case and ruled unanimously that the 6th Amendment's right to an attorney, which was applied to the states by the 14th Amendment, required that a state provide lawyers for poor people accused of felony crimes, not just capital crimes.

***Miranda* v. *Arizona* (1966)** Ernesto Miranda was arrested in Arizona and charged with kidnapping and rape. After hours of questioning by police, Miranda confessed to the crimes. After his case was tried and he received a long prison sentence, Miranda said that the police had not informed him of any of his rights. These rights included his right to not incriminating himself when he was charged as well as his right to an attorney. His case was joined with three other similar types of cases that were brought before the Supreme Court in 1966.

The decision of the Supreme Court in the *Miranda* case established the requirement that, prior to questioning, those accused of a crime must be told that they have the right to remain silent, the right to a lawyer, and that what they say can be used against them in a court of law. Police officers now are very careful to inform accused persons of these rights. If you have ever seen a "police show," you have probably seen this take place. This is now referred to as Mirandizing the accused person. Evidence obtained without this warning may not be used in court under the exclusionary rule, which was similarly used in *Mapp*.

Ernesto Miranda

The Supreme Court and the Rights of Students

Just as accused persons in the United States have gained rights as a result of Supreme Court decisions, so too have students. Following are a few examples of cases in which American students have seen their rights affirmed by the Court. Again, these cases are known as landmark cases because their decisions have had such a wide-reaching impact.

***Engle* v. *Vitale* (1962)** During the 1958–59 school year in Hyde Park, New York, a small group of parents led by William Engel approached the school board (Vitale was the president of the board), requesting that a prayer not be recited every morning in schools in the district. The prayer had been written and approved by the New York State Board of Regents, the state's governing board for all schools within the state. The local school board refused and said that any students who did not want to participate could remove themselves from the classroom while the prayer was being said. The parents felt that this was discriminatory for their children and caused them to be isolated from their classmates.

The case went to the state's highest court, which upheld the decision of the school board. The parents then appealed their case to the Supreme Court. The Court ruled that no public school could require students to say a prayer or to absent themselves from the classroom for that prayer. The decision stated that reciting an official prayer in the schools violated the 1st Amendment's establishment of religion clause, which was applied to the states by the 14th Amendment. It also stated that although students were not required to say the non-denominational prayer, its recitation in class put the students under pressure. Since this decision impacted all schools in the United States, it is considered a landmark decision.

***Tinker* v. *Des Moines School District* (1969)** In 1966, Mary Beth Tinker and her brother John and a few other students decided to wear a black armband to school to protest the war in Vietnam. School officials demanded that the students remove the arm bands while in school. When the students refused to remove the arm bands, the students were suspended. The Des Moines, Iowa, school board maintained that the students had no right to wear the arm bands to school as the board claimed that the arm bands were disruptive.

When the students returned to school, they decided to wear black for the rest of the school year. Eventually, their case went all the way to the Supreme Court. The decision of the Supreme Court was that the black arm bands alone were not disruptive of the school day and that students had the right to express their opinions as long as they did nothing to disrupt the normal school day and events. The Court's decision held that the 1st Amendment covers student rights and a safe school environment.

***New Jersey* v. *TLO* (1985)** This case occurred when the accused was a 14-year-old juvenile, and to protect her privacy only the initials of her name, TLO, were used during the case. TLO and another girl were found by a teacher smoking in a girls' restroom at school. They were taken to the principal's office, where the other student admitted smoking but TLO denied the activity. As a result, the principal decided to search TLO's purse and he found cigarettes, drug paraphernalia, marijuana, and documentation of drug sales. TLO and her family claimed that her rights had been violated by an unreasonable search. The case went through the New Jersey courts. TLO was found guilty of drug possession and was sentenced to one year in a juvenile facility. TLO and her family challenged the ruling, and the case eventually went to the Supreme Court.

The Court affirmed that the 4th Amendment prohibition on unreasonable searches and seizures applied to school officials, but in this case the Court determined that school rules had been broken. The Court then ruled that the necessity of maintaining discipline allowed for searches when there are *reasonable grounds* that the law or school rules have been broken. It was determined that within the school setting students do not have the same rights as they would in other places, given the need of the school to maintain order.

There are many other cases that illustrate how students have had their rights guaranteed and protected by the Supreme Court. The cases described here are excellent places to start to appreciate this topic.

Gay Rights and the LGBT Movement

June 2019 marks the 50th anniversary of an event that is considered the beginning of public recognition of a **Gay Rights movement** in the United States. In the Greenwich Village area of New York City, there were a number of gay bars. Regularly, the New York State Liquor Authority would refuse licenses to bars with gay customers. The Stonewall Inn was such an establishment.

Social Studies Practices
Gathering and Interpreting Evidence

- What other issues might students have in school that could end up in the courts?
- Investigate one of those topics to try to find other cases dealing with student rights.

In late June 1969, a routine police raid on the Stonewall Inn turned violent, and eventually hundreds and then thousands of people participated in six days of demonstrations. During the **Stonewall Inn riots,** there were injuries and multiple arrests.

These events all served to motivate gay and lesbian Americans to organize and to work for equal rights and recognition in the United States. In 2016, the Stonewall Inn became a National Historic Landmark representing the struggle for civil rights, and is operated by the National Park Service. On the last Sunday in June in New York City, a Gay Pride Parade occurs annually. Rainbow colors have been adopted as a symbol of the movement, and rainbow-colored flags fly at the parade.

In the fifty years of this movement, it has been enlarged gradually over the years and is identified with the letters *LGBT*. These letters stand for *lesbian, gay, bi-sexual,* and *transgender.* In very recent times, the letter *Q* is sometimes added to the other four letters to represent the overall historic term *queer.* The addition of the *Q* is acceptable to many in the **LGBT movement** and seen as an offensive slur by others.

The following are some of the significant events that have occurred during the years since the Stonewall Inn riots:

1978 Harvey Milk, one of the country's first openly gay elected officials, was assassinated in San Francisco.

1981 The AIDS/HIV (Acquired Immune Deficiency Syndrome) crisis was first identified in the United States. In recent years, the number of new cases in the United States has significantly declined, and there are new pharmaceutical advances helping those living with the disease.

1987 Congressman Barney Frank announced publicly that he was gay. "Coming out" became the term associated with making one's sexual preference public.

1994 "Don't Ask, Don't Tell" (DADT) was enacted in an effort to allow gay members of the military to continue to serve without identifying their sexual preference.

1996 The National AIDS Memorial was dedicated in San Francisco's Golden Gate Park.

1998 The Matthew Shepard Memorial was dedicated on the campus of the University of Wyoming at Laramie in memory of a student who was beaten and left to die as a result of being gay.

2009 The 1968 first hate crimes legislation was strengthened with new, more inclusive legislation that aimed at crimes or violence based on gender or sexual orientation.

2011 DADT (see 1994 above) was repealed as being discriminatory.

2015 The Supreme Court ruled on the case of *Obergefell* v. *Hodges* (see below).

By spring 2015, thirty-seven states legalized gay marriage, including New York State. For this reason and related issues, a bill signed into law in 1996 by President Clinton called the Defense of Marriage Act (DOMA) was brought before the Supreme Court. The Court ruled that DOMA is unconstitutional. The ruling stated that if a state provides for legal same-sex marriages, the federal government must recognize these marriages as legal too. This opened the door for equal treatment in economic, medical, legal, and social issues. In June 2015, in *Obergefell* v. *Hodges,* the Supreme Court ruled that same-sex marriages were legal in all fifty states. That evening, the White House, usually lit by white lights at night, was illuminated with a rainbow of colors.

Unifying Themes
Development and Transformation of Social Structures

• Using the terms *cause* and *effect* in your answer, describe how any three of these events are related to each other.

Other Major Domestic Issues Faced by the Nation

In addition to the civil rights movements that developed in the mid- to late 1900s, the nation was challenged by a variety of other domestic issues. These challenges included environmental protection and immigration reform.

Environmental Issues and Changes

In 1961, **Rachel Carson** wrote a book called *Silent Spring,* which identified the hazards of agricultural pesticides. Carson was a writer, scientist, and environmentalist who brought the first widespread public attention to serious concerns related to air and water pollution. Her work inspired the environmental movement and legislation.

The **Environmental Protection Agency** (EPA), established in 1970 during the Nixon administration, coordinates federal programs to combat pollution and protect the environment. Its creation was an indicator of how important the environment was becoming to the nation. The first Earth Day celebration occurred in April 1970 to bring attention to multiple environmental concerns.

Air Pollution The **Clean Air Act of 1970** was a major comprehensive federal law addressing topics related to air pollution. Acid rain, created by toxic air pollution, continued to threaten forests, lakes, and wildlife in the United States. President Jimmy Carter supported environmental programs, but inflation and energy shortages prevented him from undertaking ambitious programs to protect the environment. Coal polluted the air, but the nation needed coal to offset oil shortages. The nation needed to clean up the air, but emission devices for cars and factories pushed up prices. The Clean Air Act was amended in 1977 to set new goals since many parts of the country did not meet the standards set by the 1970 act. It was amended again in 1990 to address problems such as acid rain, ground level ozone, stratospheric ozone depletion, and air toxins.

Water Pollution In an attempt to address water pollution in the United States, Congress passed the **Clean Water Act of 1972** (CWA). It was the first time legislation had been undertaken on this issue since the Federal Water Pollution Control Act of 1948. The 1972 CWA set specific guidelines for individuals and businesses with regard to water pollution and required government standards. With increased publicity, Americans began to appreciate the damage that had been done by industrial pollution in particular. Many groups organized to reduce and clean up pollution on the land, in the water, and in the air.

Protection of Animals and Plants Concern for the environment involved protecting the quality not only of human life but also the lives of other living things. The **Endangered Species Act of 1973** (ESA) included both plants and animals in its detailed identification of American species that could become extinct. The term *endangered* identifies those species which are most in danger of becoming extinct in the near or immediate future. Species that are identified as "threatened" exist in slightly larger numbers or quantities, but they are still considered in danger of becoming extinct in the future. The United States was divided into large zones composed of states with similar vegetation and animals and ESA staff serve each area.

During the Reagan administration of the 1980s, there was little new environmental legislation. Although Reagan was praised for his efforts on issues to protect California's forests, lakes, rivers, and ocean shoreline, he was much less interested in national environmental concerns. Reagan's philosophy was to encourage large private businesses and industries and was in favor of less government intervention. Reagan was known to have difficulty appreciating concerns about the extent of acid rain and pollution.

Environmental Progress and Reversal By the 1990s, recycling efforts were organized to reuse paper, glass, plastic, and aluminum. Community organizers opposed plans to convert vacant lands into dumpsites. Communities have the effects of industrial pollution on the groundwater that people drink. In response to public pressure, the federal government enacted laws requiring automobile manufacturers to put antipollution devices on their cars. Since the first Earth Day celebration in 1970, the American people, along with the rest of the world, have begun to realize their obligation to protect the environment for future generations.

In 2007, former Vice President Al Gore won a Nobel Peace Prize for his efforts to increase public understanding of issues related to global warming. This followed his widely viewed documentary film, *An Inconvenient Truth*.

Unifying Themes
Time and Change

• Find examples of how attitudes about the environment and climate have changed over the last fifteen years.

The phrase "going green" has come to mean the conscious efforts of Americans to conserve energy in all aspects of daily life. Presidents Clinton, Bush (43), and Obama have all directed efforts within the White House itself to increase energy efficiency. Efforts that extend from the First Family to all American families include activities such as recycling, installation of energy-efficient light bulbs, the use of solar power where possible, appropriate conservation of heating and cooling sources, and other individual initiatives.

President Donald Trump has made no secret of his disbelief in global warming. Trump supports eliminating or loosening controls on industries that were enacted to protect the environment. The EPA has been reduced in size during the Trump administration, and issues about climate control are not seen as serious concerns.

In November 2016, about 150 countries agreed to the Paris Agreement of the United Nations Convention on Climate Change. These nations recognized the need to strengthen the global response to the threat of climate change by making efforts to limit global temperature rise. The goal is to limit and decrease greenhouse gas emissions. In his first few months as president, Trump announced that he was withdrawing the United States from the International Paris Agreement of 2016.

Following the congressional elections of 2018, some new representatives and some returning representatives advocated a Green Revolution to promote environmental issues. Their aim is to revive the government's commitment to protecting the environment.

Immigration Legislation

Although the United States is considered a nation of immigrants, immigration to the United States has experienced many waves. There have been periods of no legislation at all and periods of very strict legislation. During the Depression years of the 1930s and the war years of the 1940s, there was very limited interest in immigration to the United States.

Immigration and National Security In 1950, Congress passed the McCarran Internal Security Act. The law aimed at limiting the actions of anyone the government considered a threat to the security of the United States. The McCarran-Walter Act of 1952 restricted the immigration of persons from communist-dominated nations in Asia and southern and central Europe. President Truman vetoed the bill, but Congress passed it over his veto.

Reducing Restrictions In 1965, Congress passed the **Immigration and Nationality Act of 1965** (the Hart-Celler Act). This legislation was signed by President Johnson at the Statue of Liberty. It formally ended an admissions policy based solely on race and ethnicity. This legislation focused more on family reunification and on persons who could prove they had skills needed by the United States.

Since this Act was passed, over 18 million new immigrants have come to the United States, many from Asia and Latin America. The Act has been seen as an extension of the civil rights movements of the 1960s. The **Immigration Act of 1990** reduced immigration restrictions even more by increasing the total number of immigrants who could enter the United States every year.

Undocumented Workers In an effort to cut down on the number of undocumented workers living in the United States, Congress passed the **Immigration Reform and Control Act of 1986,** which forbade employers from hiring illegal immigrants. This new legislation did not solve the problem of the thousands of people who enter the United States illegally every year. These immigrants often work in sweatshop-type factories, live in substandard housing, and are paid very low wages.

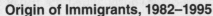

Origin of Immigrants, 1982–1995

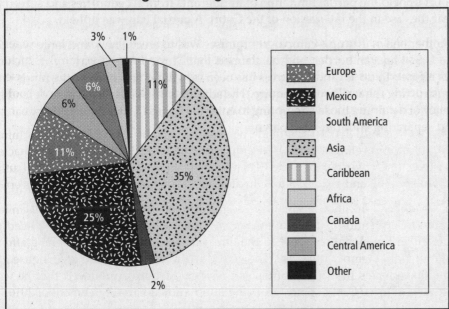

Preparing for the Regents

Stimulus-Based Question: Circle Graph

- Which area of the world sent the largest percentage of immigrants during the time period shown?

- What event or events may have impacted those immigrants?

Border Protection The George W. Bush (43) administration had to deal with several issues relating to immigration, some of which became more serious after the attacks of September 11, 2001. The Real ID Act of 2005 strengthened security requirements at U.S. borders and gave the Director of Homeland Security additional powers. Several proposals were introduced in both houses of Congress to increase border patrols and protection, restrict illegal immigration, and strengthen anti-terrorism laws. There was also extensive discussion over funding bills to construct a wall along the U.S. border between Mexico and the United States. This produced mixed reactions on both sides of the border.

Immigration Reform

A major goal of the Obama administration was immigration reform. Some efforts were not successful. However, there has been acknowledgment by both political parties that there must be new attempts at solutions to deal with the number of people trying to immigrate to the United States, both legally and illegally, and also the large number of undocumented immigrants already living in this country.

The children born in the United States to undocumented immigrants have attracted particular attention due to their large numbers and the fact that many are graduating from colleges and universities and trying to enter the job market. A bipartisan group of senators made some progress on this national goal, but no new legislation has been passed. These young people are known as "Dreamers" and they await action on the Deferred Action for Childhood Arrivals law (DACA).

In 2014, the United States experienced a swelling of numbers of unaccompanied minors (children) from Guatemala, Honduras, El Salvador, and Mexico. This put an increased strain on relations with Mexico and the other countries and on social services and educational facilities in the southern border states in the United States. By some estimates, the number was four times the number of illegal immigrants from 2012.

Since President Donald Trump came into office in 2017, there has been an increased emphasis on problems related to immigration. The Trump administration has taken a very hard-line approach to illegal immigrants. While a presidential candidate, Trump promised to enact a ban against Muslims entering the United States. Early in his presidency, he signed an Executive Order blocking immigration from six Muslim-majority nations. Lower courts halted the travel ban, but the Supreme Court upheld the partial limitation of immigrants from six countries and agreed to hear the case in the fall session of the Court. A partial ban was upheld.

Another one of Trump's campaign promises was to erect a new and large wall on the U.S.–Mexican border, and he claimed that Mexico would pay for it. Mexico has refused to do so, and Congress has been unwilling to authorize the funds that constructing the wall would require. The administration has also had to defend its policy of detaining those attempting to enter the United States in temporary camps and separating children from parents.

The Economic and Social Role of Government

Lesson Overview

From the 1960s through the present, different political philosophies, promoted by different presidential administrations, have impacted the American people. American presidents can be the primary force in effecting change for better or worse, depending on personal situation and circumstances. Americans have come to expect a certain level of governmental economic involvement in daily life. Events from the Great Depression of the 1930s through the Great Recession of the early 21st century have impacted economic policies. Both major political parties, Republicans and Democrats, have struggled to meet the needs of their constituents.

Key Concept

11.10c Varying political philosophies prompted debates over the role of the federal government in regulating the economy and providing a social safety net.

Unifying Themes

As you review this lesson take special note of the following themes:

- **Individual Development and Cultural Identity** Why did government benefits for Americans change between the 1960s and the 1990s? How have changes continued to occur with regard to the government and health care?

- **Power, Authority, and Governance** In what ways does the government need to protect its citizens to continue existing social and economic programs? What potential problems exist in this effort?

- **Creation, Expansion, and Interaction of Economic Systems** How did the goals of President Johnson differ from those of President Reagan in the development of economic and social policies?

Key People

Franklin D. Roosevelt

Lyndon B. Johnson

Ronald Reagan

Key Terms and Events

social safety net

Great Society

Medicare

Medicaid

supply-side economics

Reaganomics

Great Recession

Affordable Care Act

The Growth of Big Government

At various times in American history, the government has wrestled with problems related to the social well-being of the country. Many felt that the government should stay out of economic affairs. You may remember the term *laissez-faire*.

Roosevelt's New Deal

During the Great Depression of the 1930s, when millions were suffering and unemployed, President **Franklin D. Roosevelt** began the New Deal programs. Many of those programs were intended to solve immediate problems and were not intended to be long lasting.

Some of these programs created what is known as a **social safety net,** that is, a program intended to prevent the economic and social disaster that occurred during the Great Depression. One major program still in existence is the Social Security Act.

The 1935 Social Security Act was a combination of public assistance and insurance. The law had three main parts: (1) It provided old-age insurance, paid by a tax on both the employer and the employee while the employee was working. The worker and the employer, not the government, funded this part of Social Security. (2) It provided unemployment insurance for workers, paid by employers. (3) It gave assistance to dependent children and to the elderly, ill, and handicapped.

The Great Society of the 1960s

President **Lyndon Johnson's** domestic policy goals for the United States, known as the **Great Society,** continued and expanded upon traditions begun during Franklin Roosevelt's New Deal of the 1930s.

Medicare The **Amendments to the Social Security Act** (1965) provide health insurance and some types of health care to those over the age of 65. All workers pay a Medicare tax directly from their paychecks. Citizens receiving Medicare must pay part of their Medicare cost. Generally, recipients pay by having what they owe taken directly from their monthly paycheck as Social Security benefits. Medicare is not a "totally free" government program. This program has become increasingly expensive as health costs have risen, health care has improved and people are living longer. Also, the percentage of recipients has increased as compared to the number of workers contributing.

Medicaid (1965) is a program that provides states with funds to help the needy who are not covered by Medicare. In recent years, states have been expected to pay for part of the cost of Medicaid.

Reagan and the Economic Challenges of the 1980s

A former actor, **Ronald Reagan** appealed to many Americans with his references to the "good old days" and his patriotic speeches. He used his prepared speeches to promote a conservative approach to government and the economy. He targeted inflation as his top priority and argued that big government was the cause of inflation. "In the present crisis," said Reagan, "government is not the solution to our problem; government is the problem."

During his first term in office, President Reagan supported a domestic program backed by both presidents Eisenhower and Nixon. Like his Republican predecessors, he supported New Federalism, a policy that turned over federal control of some social welfare programs to the states.

Supply-Side Economics Reagan called for cuts in taxes on businesses and individuals, especially those with large incomes. The president believed that they would reinvest in more businesses. These businesses would hire more workers and increase the supply of goods and services. Reagan argued that **supply-side economics,** or the trickle-down theory, would end inflation without increasing the national debt. His ideas later became known as **Reaganomics.** His critics at the time were highly skeptical of his plans and called his economic theories "voodoo" economics or "magic tricks." Ultimately, the wealthy benefited more than others.

Balancing the Budget Reagan tried to balance the budget by reducing many social welfare programs. He also made sharp cuts in the Environmental Protection Agency. Despite such efforts, however, the national debt climbed throughout Reagan's presidency. Reagan, nicknamed the Great Communicator by some journalists, used his charm and persuasive talents to convince many Americans to support a plan aimed at creating a balanced budget by the early 1990s.

Reagan and his supporters promised to make deep cuts in federal programs. Only a few select programs, such as Social Security and defense, were to be spared. Reagan also called for simplification of tax laws and tax cuts for about 60 percent of Americans. It was believed that tax cuts would encourage economic growth. Some people charged that the cuts favored the rich. In fact, by the late 1980s, wealth was more unevenly distributed than at any time since the end of World War II.

Despite drastic actions by the federal government, the national debt climbed. This was due, in part, to a huge trade imbalance, a situation in which a nation imports more goods than it exports. At the start of Reagan's second term, the trade deficit approached $150 billion.

President Reagan uses charts to gain support from the American public to pressure Congress to approve his budget.

The George H. W. Bush (41) Administration and Economics

During his presidential election campaign of 1988, President George H. W. Bush had promised voters no new taxes. However, as the budget deficit mounted, Bush was forced to break this promise in 1990. By 1992, an economic recession caused increased layoffs and rising unemployment. Also, in 1990, the misuse of funds by savings and loan institutions surfaced. American taxpayers paid hundreds of billions of dollars to bail out the savings and loan industry.

The Bill Clinton Administration and Economics

In 1993, President Clinton presented to Congress a health care reform plan that would ensure health insurance for all Americans. Critics of the plan complained that it was too expensive and complex and would limit choices in health care. In 1994, Congress rejected Clinton's plan. Since the 1990s, the primary issue concerning health care in the United States has been the increasing cost of medical insurance. Growing numbers of Americans have become unable to afford health care insurance.

It became clear that the Social Security program, begun during the Great Depression, would run into trouble because of changing demographics. The number of recipients is increasing rapidly due to longer life spans and the aging baby boomer generation. Several plans to fund Social Security were considered, but no plan was agreed upon during the Clinton administration.

The George W. Bush (43) Administration and Economics

President George W. Bush attempted a tax cut and rebates to taxpayers early in his administration, and in 2008 taxpayers received rebate checks of $300 to $1,200. Starting in 2007, the economy showed signs of a possible recession, especially in the housing market as thousands of homeowners struggled to meet mortgage payments and others faced bank foreclosures. In 2007, Congress approved an increase in the minimum wage from $5.15 to $5.85, with an increase to $7.25 by 2009.

The Federal Reserve Board has lowered its interest rate several times, including a drop of 0.75 percent, the largest in the history of the Federal Reserve Board. By early spring 2009, the Federal Reserve interest rate was actually at a record-breaking 0 percent. All of these actions were an effort to reverse the **Great Recession.** By late 2008, the recession was being described as the worst economic downturn since the Great Depression of the 1930s.

President Bush wanted to make Social Security reform a primary agenda item. The president's plan to allow younger workers to choose private accounts for a portion of their Social Security contributions drew praise as well as criticism. The president also tried to reform the Medicare program. A major concern with these programs is that the number of Americans eligible for them is growing. There is an increasing senior citizen population due to the aging of the "baby boom" generation. At the same time, there are fewer workers contributing to the system, due to declining American birth rates of the 1970s and 1980s. One solution that has begun to be phased in would be to raise the age of eligibility.

The Barack Obama Administration and the Great Recession

President Obama took office as the United States faced its most serious economic crisis since the Great Depression.

Bail-Outs The President came into office knowing that an enormous economic stimulus plan would be necessary to solve this crisis. Some major banks had failed and other companies, primarily the massive AIG Insurance Company, needed billions of dollars of American taxpayer money, known as "bail out" money, to prevent them from collapsing. About $700 billion in what is known as TARP money, or the Troubled Asset Relief Program, was used to help banks that were in danger of failing.

The unemployment rate in some parts of the United States was at its highest rate in almost 25 years, between eight and ten percent. Ben Bernanke, the Chairman of the Federal Reserve Board, was called to Capitol Hill several times to explain the policies that the Fed was implementing to remedy the crisis. There was general support for the president's efforts to keep the three major American automotive companies, General Motors, Ford, and Chrysler, economically afloat. The difference with the money being lent to the auto industry is that it is being paid back to the taxpayers through the government. Other major billion-dollar spending plans have received more criticism. A major sticking point with the bailout funds was the discovery by the White House, Congress, and the public that millions of dollars of taxpayer money went to pay bonuses for executives at failing companies.

Mortgage Scandal Another economic problem at this time was that many homeowners could not afford to pay the money they owned on their homes (called a mortgage). When banks didn't receive their payments, they could take back the homes or foreclose on them. Several large banks were found to be guilty of both allowing and encouraging home buyers to obtain mortgages that they would have severe difficulty in paying.

Unifying Themes
Economics

Adding to the economic crisis of the Obama Administration was the fact that the United States had had a trade deficit for the previous two decades. This was a result of the United States importing more than it exports. China had become a major source of American imports to the benefit of the Chinese economy.

During the recession, many people lost their homes when banks foreclosed on them. A foreclosure happens when a buyer or buyers cannot afford to pay the money owed to the lender. Housing prices dropped, causing a ripple effect in the whole economy. Several large banks collapsed.

In 2010, President Obama signed a sweeping reform bill aimed at ending the practices that had allowed bank and investment companies to cause the recession. It created federal oversight over financial institutions which included credit card rates, bank fees, mortgage programs, and car loans.

Affordable Care Act Also, in 2010, President Obama made history by signing the Patient Protection and Affordable Care Act, known as the **Affordable Care Act** for short. Health care reform had been a major goal of the President and the Democratic Party. The bill passed with a narrow margin over fierce Republican opposition. The law is being phased in over several years and has provisions to forbid insurance companies to deny health care coverage to applicants, to extend coverage to young adults until they are 26 if living at home, and to eventually require all Americans to obtain health care insurance.

By 2016, Republicans tried over 60 times to repeal the law, which has become known as Obamacare, especially by those who want it repealed, but so far they have been unsuccessful. A campaign pledge of President Trump was to repeal the Affordable Care Act. As of spring 2019, the President has been unsuccessful in getting a majority of Congress to repeal and replace it.

House and Senate Democrats protest attempts to repeal the Affordable Health Care Act in early 2019.

Base your answers to questions 1 and 2 on the passage below and on your knowledge of social studies.

> We affirm the philosophical or religious ideal of nonviolence as the foundation of our purpose, the presupposition [foundation] of our faith, and the manner of our action. Nonviolence as it grows from Judaic-Christian traditions seeks a social order of justice permeated [filled] by love. Integration of human endeavor represents the crucial first step towards such a society.
>
> Through nonviolence, courage displaces fear; love transforms hate. Acceptance dissipates [melts away] prejudice; hope ends despair. Peace dominates war; faith reconciles doubt. Mutual regard cancels enmity [hatred]. Justice for all overthrows injustice. The redemptive community supersedes systems of gross social immorality.

Source: Student Nonviolent Coordinating Committee, statement of purpose, April 1960

1 The Student Nonviolent Coordinating Committee put these beliefs into action when they

(1) organized freedom rides through the segregated South

(2) provided legal defense for Linda Brown

(3) attempted to desegregate Little Rock Central High School

(4) organized the March on Washington

2 Which organization would disagree with the methods described in this document?

(1) the Freedmen's Bureau

(2) Southern Christian Leadership Conference

(3) the Black Panthers

(4) NAACP

Base your answers to questions 3 and 4 on the poster below and on your knowledge of social studies.

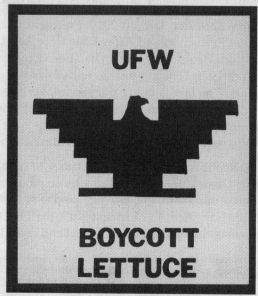

Source: UFW boycott poster, circa 1970, Library of Congress

3 Which individual is most closely associated with the action promoted in this poster?

(1) Fannie Lou Hamer

(2) Betty Friedan

(3) Lyndon Johnson

(4) Cesar Chavez

4 What was the main objective of this event?

(1) payment for lost Native American lands

(2) reduction of manual labor on farms

(3) equal rights for Mexican Americans

(4) better wages for migrant workers

Base your answers to questions 5 through 7 on the images below and on your knowledge of social studies.

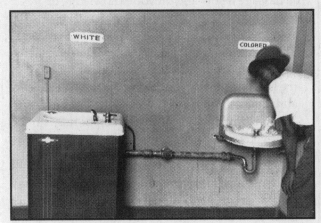

Source: Water fountains in North Carolina, Magnum Photos, 1950

Source: Clay Bennett, *Chattanooga Times Free Press*, November 5, 2008

5   What is a cause of the situation shown in the photograph?

(1) Harlem Renaissance

(2) poll taxes

(3) Jim Crow laws

(4) March on Washington

6   What historical event is referenced in the cartoon?

(1) the election of Barack Obama

(2) the passage of the Civil Rights Act

(3) the decision in *Brown* v. *Board of Education*

(4) the impeachment of Bill Clinton

7   According to these two images, what has changed between the 1950s and the 2000s?

(1) Legal segregation no longer exists in the United States.

(2) An executive order from the president ended the segregation of water fountains.

(3) The Constitution now allows African American candidates to run for political office.

(4) The civil rights movement has shifted tactics over the last 50 years.

Base your answers to questions 8 and 9 on the passage below and on your knowledge of social studies.

> *Question:* Mr. President, many people in Congress believe in . . . the budget cuts, but are very concerned about the tax cuts. They fear it will be inflationary. How do you plan to combat that fear among Congress?
>
> *President Reagan:* Well, I mentioned that last night, this fear that the tax cuts would be inflationary. First of all, a number of fine economists . . . don't think that that's so. But also we've got history on our side. Every major tax cut that has been made in this century in our country has resulted in even the government getting more revenue than it did before, because the base of the economy is so broadened by doing it.

Source: President Ronald Reagan, Question-and-Answer Session on the Program for Economic Recovery, February 19, 1981

8 What course of action is being recommended by President Reagan?

(1) cutting taxes to grow the economy

(2) increasing government spending

(3) reverting to inflationary policies

(4) decreasing spending on the military

9 The ideas expressed by President Reagan promote the theory of

(1) the need for a social safety net

(2) increasing the role of government

(3) laissez-faire economics

(4) taxation without representation

Base your answers to questions 10 and 11 on the passage below and on your knowledge of social studies.

> These considerations lead to the conclusion that the right to marry is a fundamental right inherent in the liberty of the person, and under the Due Process and Equal Protection Clauses of the Fourteenth Amendment couples of the same-sex may not be deprived of that right and that liberty. . . .
>
> As some of the petitioners in these cases demonstrate, marriage embodies a love that may endure even past death. It would misunderstand these men and women to say they disrespect the idea of marriage. Their plea is that they do respect it, respect it so deeply that they seek to find its fulfillment for themselves. Their hope is not to be condemned to live in loneliness, excluded from one of civilization's oldest institutions. They ask for equal dignity in the eyes of the law. The Constitution grants them that right.

Source: Supreme Court Justice Anthony Kennedy, majority opinion in *Obergefell* v. *Hodges,* 2015

10 The decision in *Obergefell* v. *Hodges* was a major victory in the civil rights efforts of the

(1) American Indian movement

(2) people with disabilities movement

(3) women's rights movement

(4) LGBT movement

11 What effect did the decision in *Obergefell* v. *Hodges* have on the states?

(1) States were required to change their laws banning same-sex marriages to ensure due process was followed.

(2) States were required to recognize all same-sex marriages as a result of the equal protection clause.

(3) States were required to repeal any "Don't Ask, Don't Tell" laws as they were now deemed to be discriminatory.

(4) States were required to amend their constitutions to include provisions that redefined who could legally marry.

Base your answers to questions 12 and 13 on the map below and on your knowledge of social studies.

School Desegregation in the South, 1954–1964

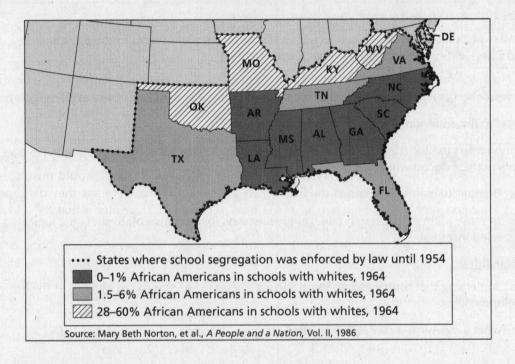

•••• States where school segregation was enforced by law until 1954
■ 0–1% African Americans in schools with whites, 1964
▨ 1.5–6% African Americans in schools with whites, 1964
▨ 28–60% African Americans in schools with whites, 1964

Source: Mary Beth Norton, et al., *A People and a Nation*, Vol. II, 1986

12 A historian could best use this map to study

    (1) the impact of the decision in *Brown* v. *Board of Education*

    (2) the use of affirmative action programs in the South

    (3) the implementation of school busing programs

    (4) the impact of the Civil Rights Act of 1964

13 Which conclusion can be drawn from the map?

    (1) By 1964, a majority of southern states had no integrated schools.

    (2) Northern states had similar issues of segregation as Southern states.

    (3) State governments were slow to follow court orders to desegregate.

    (4) Prior to 1954, most African American students attended integrated schools in the South.

Task: Read and analyze the following documents, applying your social studies knowledge and skills to write a short essay of two or three paragraphs in which you:

- Describe the historical context surrounding these documents
- Identify and explain the *relationship* between the events and/or ideas found in these documents (Cause and Effect, *or* Similarity/Difference, *or* Turning Point)

In developing your short essay answer of two or three paragraphs, be sure to keep these explanations in mind:

Describe means "to illustrate something in words or tell about it"

Historical Context refers to "the relevant historical circumstances surrounding or connecting the events, ideas, or developments in these documents"

Identify means "to put a name to or to name"

Explain means "to make plain or understandable; to give reasons for or causes of; to show the logical development or relationship of"

<u>Types of Relationships:</u>

Cause refers to "something that contributes to the occurrence of an event, the rise of an idea, or the bringing about of a development"

Effect refers to "what happens as a consequence (result, impact, outcome) of an event, an idea, or a development"

Similarity tells how "something is alike or the same as something else"

Difference tells how "something is not alike or not the same as something else"

Turning Point is "a major event, idea, or historical development that brings about significant change. It can be local, regional, national, or global"

Document 1

We are confronted primarily with a moral issue. It is as old as the scriptures and is as clear as the American Constitution.

The heart of the question is whether all Americans are to be afforded equal rights and equal opportunities, whether we are going to treat our fellow Americans as we want to be treated. . . .

The fires of frustration and discord are burning in every city, North and South, where legal remedies are not at hand. Redress is sought in the streets, in demonstrations, parades, and protests which create tensions and threaten violence and threaten lives.

We face, therefore, a moral crisis as a country and as a people. It cannot be met by repressive police action. It cannot be left to increased demonstrations in the streets. It cannot be quieted by token moves or talk. It is a time to act in the Congress, in your State and local legislative body and, above all, in all of our daily lives. . . .

Next week I shall ask the Congress of the United States to act, to make a commitment it has not fully made in this century to the proposition that race has no place in American life or law.

Source: President John F. Kennedy, radio and television address to the American people, June 11, 1963

Document 2

To enforce the constitutional right to vote, to confer jurisdiction upon the district courts of the United States to provide injunctive relief against discrimination in public accommodations, to authorize the Attorney General to institute suits to protect constitutional rights in public facilities and public education, to extend the Commission on Civil Rights, to prevent discrimination in federally assisted programs, to establish a Commission on Equal Employment Opportunity, and for other purposes.

Be it enacted by the Senate and House of Representatives of the United States of America in Congress assembled, That this Act may be cited as the "Civil Rights Act of 1964."

Source: Civil Rights Act of 1964

Document Analysis for Civic Literacy Essay

Historical Context: Conservation and Environmental Protection

Throughout United States history, many constitutional and civic issues have been debated by Americans. These debates have resulted in efforts by individuals, groups, and governments to address these issues. These efforts have achieved varying degrees of success. One of these constitutional and civic issues is conservation and environmental protection.

Task: Read and analyze the document. Using information from the document and your knowledge of United States history, write an essay in which you

- Describe the historical circumstances surrounding this constitutional or civic issue
- Explain efforts to address this constitutional or civic issue by individuals, groups, and/or governments
- Discuss the extent to which these efforts were successful

Describe means "to illustrate something in words or tell about it"

Explain means "to make plain or understandable; to give reasons for or causes of; to show the logical development or relationship of"

Discuss means "to make observations about something using facts, reasoning, and argument; to present in some detail"

There was a strange stillness. The birds, for example—where had they gone? Many people spoke of them, puzzled and disturbed. The feeding stations in the backyards were deserted. The few birds seen anywhere were moribund [declining]; they trembled violently and could not fly. It was a spring without voices. On the mornings that had once throbbed with the dawn chorus of robins, catbirds, doves, jays, wrens, and scores of other bird voices there was no sound; only silence lay over the fields and woods and marsh.

On the farms the hens brooded, but no chicks hatched. The farmers complained that they were unable to raise any pigs—the litters were small and the young survived only a few days. The apple trees were coming into bloom but no bees droned among the blossoms, so there was no pollination and there would be no fruit.

The roadsides, once so attractive, were now lined with browned and withered vegetation as though swept by fire. These, too, were silent, deserted by all living things. Even the streams were now lifeless. Anglers no longer visited them, for all the fish had died.

In the gutters under the eaves and between the shingles of the roofs, a white granular powder still showed a few patches; some weeks before it had fallen like snow upon the roofs and the lawns, the fields and streams.

No witchcraft, no enemy action had silenced the rebirth of new life in this stricken world. The people had done it to themselves.

Source: Rachel Carson, *Silent Spring*, 1962

1. According to Rachel Carson, what changes were taking place to the environment?

The United States in a Changing World (1990–present)

Topic Overview

The United States political and economic status in the world has faced external and internal challenges related to international conflicts, economic competition, and globalization. Throughout this time period, the nation has continued to debate and define its role in the world. Simultaneously, the nation has faced national issues, such as environmental concerns, changing demographics, gun control issues, random violence, immigration, national well-being, and other concerns.

Foreign and Domestic Issues of the 1990s

Lesson Overview

In 1988, George H.W. Bush (41), a conservative Republican from Texas defeated the Democratic candidate, Michael Dukakis, for the presidency. President Bush (41), who had been Reagan's vice president, served during the end of the Cold War. After serving one term, President Bush was defeated by Arkansas Governor Bill Clinton. Both presidents struggled with what has been called the Vietnam Syndrome. That is, both administrations were challenged by the need to keep the United States from involving itself in military crises around the globe. No president can be concerned with only foreign or only domestic policy issues. This section reviews the issues faced by these presidents of the 1990s.

Unifying Themes

As you review this lesson take special note of the following themes:

- **Time, Continuity, and Change** What domestic and international conflicts caused problems for the United States during this time?

- **Power, Authority, and Governance** In what ways did the United States government use its power at home and abroad? In what cases did the United States choose not to intervene in overseas conflicts?

- **Global Connections and Exchange** How did values of other cultures clash with values of the United States?

Key People

George H.W. Bush

Saddam Hussein

Ross Perot

Bill Clinton

Madeleine K. Albright

Key Terms and Events

Vietnam Syndrome

Persian Gulf War

ethnic cleansing

NAFTA

GATT

World Trade Organization

The George H. W. Bush (41) Administration

A member of a family that had a long tradition of public service, President **George H.W. Bush** had decades of military and government experience he could turn to during his presidency. This would prove necessary as he faced a world undergoing significant changes.

Domestic Events

Like Reagan, President Bush faced domestic challenges, especially pertaining to the nation's economy.

Economic Troubles During the election campaign, Bush had promised voters no new taxes. However, as the budget deficit mounted, President Bush was forced to break this promise in 1990.

In 1990, the misuse of funds by savings and loan institutions surfaced. American taxpayers paid hundreds of billions of dollars to bail out the savings and loan industry. By 1992, an economic recession caused increased layoffs and rising unemployment.

Supreme Court Appointments Due to vacancies on the Supreme Court during his administration, President Bush appointed two new justices: David Souter in 1990 and Clarence Thomas in 1991. Thomas was confirmed by the Senate after controversial hearings in which he was charged with sexual harassment by Anita Hill, a former employee.

Foreign Events

President Bush focused greatly on foreign affairs. The breakup of the Soviet Union changed what had been the world order since World War II. American involvement in the Middle East would have long-term effects for the nation.

End of the Cold War In November 1989, the world watched in amazement as Germans tore down the Berlin Wall—a symbolic reminder of the division between the communist and democratic worlds. Throughout the winter of 1990, communist governments in Eastern Europe crumbled. In 1990, Gorbachev received the Nobel Peace Prize for relaxing control over former Soviet satellites. In October of that year, East and West Germany were formally reunited. A failed coup by hardline communist leaders in 1991 led to the dissolution of the Soviet Union and the 1992 formation of a Commonwealth of Independent States.

The Vietnam Syndrome As you read in Topic 9, over 58,000 American lives were lost as a result of American involvement in the Vietnam War. Thousands more came home seriously wounded. Following that experience, the term **Vietnam Syndrome** came to be used to describe American unwillingness to commit the American military anywhere in the world unless it was considered absolutely necessary to protect United States national interests. Ronald Reagan used the term in August 1980 in a campaign speech, and its use has reoccurred as conditions prompted over the years since. President Bush as well as subsequent presidents made foreign policy decisions based at least in part on the Vietnam Syndrome.

Invasion of Panama As president, Bush continued Reagan's war on drugs. In 1989, he ordered United States troops into Panama to capture General Manuel Noriega, the dictator of Panama, and return him to the United States to face drug charges. In 1992, Noriega was sentenced to serve 40 years in federal prison.

Persian Gulf War In August 1990, Iraqi leader **Saddam Hussein** invaded the oil-rich nation of **Kuwait**. President Bush responded by sending United States troops into Saudi Arabia, with the agreement of Saudi leaders. The United Nations condemned Iraq's actions and approved economic sanctions against Iraq. The UN also authorized a joint military buildup in Saudi Arabia, called Operation Desert Shield. The United States involvement reflected its long-term commitment to protecting oil resources.

President George H.W. Bush visits American troops in Saudi Arabia during Operation Desert Shield.

Operation Desert Shield became **Operation Desert Storm** in January 1991 when the United States, with a troop force of over 500,000 (the largest American military commitment since Vietnam), and Allied troops from a number of other nations began a total air assault on Iraq. By the end of February, Bush ordered a cease-fire, and Iraq accepted all UN demands to end the **Persian Gulf War.** More than 300 Allied lives were lost. The Iraqi death toll was estimated at 100,000. President Bush knew his actions were taking a risk for the United States and when this fast military action was completed he commented that he had "kicked the Vietnam Syndrome" by bringing the military home quickly and with limited losses.

Election of 1992

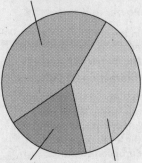

Democrat Bill Clinton 43% of popular vote

Independent Ross Perot 19% of popular vote

Republican George Bush 38% of popular vote

Bosnia and the Balkans The end of the Bush administration was marked by the outbreak of violence in the Balkans. In 1991, Slovenia and Croatia declared their independence from Yugoslavia and fighting broke out throughout the area. Millions became refugees during the fighting. Bosnian Serbs, led by Slobodan Milosevic, carried out **ethnic cleansing,** or genocidal warfare, killing thousands of innocent civilians. It would be the next administration that had to deal with this crisis.

The Election of 1992

In the 1992 presidential election, President George H.W. Bush ran for re-election as the Republican candidate with Dan Quayle as his running mate. The Democrats selected Arkansas governor Bill Clinton as their candidate, with Al Gore as his running mate. Texas billionaire **Ross Perot,** an independent challenger, also entered the race. Perot ran as a candidate from what he called the Independent Party. A major issue of the campaign concerned the state of the American economy. Clinton also made Bosnia an issue and promised to take strong action there.

Clinton carried 32 states with a total of 370 electoral votes. Although Perot did not earn any electoral votes, he received over 19 million popular votes. Women, African Americans, and Latino Americans were elected to Congress in record high numbers in 1992.

The Bill Clinton Administration

President **Bill Clinton** served from 1993 until President Bush's son George W. Bush (43) was inaugurated in 2001 after he defeated President Clinton's vice president Al Gore in the race for the White House. Before he left office, Clinton became the second president in American history to experience an impeachment trial.

Domestic Issues

As president, Bill Clinton tried to address major issues facing Americans. Health care and the viability of Social Security were high priorities but controversial and continue to be so today.

President Bill Clinton

Health Care Reform In 1993, President Clinton presented to Congress a health care reform plan that would ensure health insurance for all Americans. Critics of the plan complained it was too expensive, complex, and limited in choices for health care. In 1994, Congress rejected Clinton's plan. Since the 1990s, the primary issue concerning health care in the United States has been the increasing cost of medical insurance. In the twenty-first century, growing numbers of Americans have been unable to afford health care insurance.

Social Security It became clear that the Social Security program, begun during the Great Depression, would run into trouble because of changing demographics. The number of recipients is increasing rapidly due to longer life spans and the aging baby boomer generation. Several plans to change or improve funding for Social Security have been considered, but no plan has been agreed upon.

Supreme Court Appointees With his nominations of Ruth Bader Ginsburg and Stephen Breyer, President Clinton became the first Democratic president in 26 years to name a Supreme Court justice.

The 1994 Congressional Elections In 1994, Republicans took majority control of Congress for the first time in 40 years.

Foreign Issues

The Clinton administration attempted to help with humanitarian issues overseas, some of its initiatives were more successful than others. International trade agreements greatly improved the nation's economy.

The Former Yugoslavia Tensions between ethnic groups in the former Yugoslavia led to war in Bosnia in the early 1990s. The United States helped win an agreement between the two sides in 1995. In 1998, violence erupted in **Kosovo,** where Serbian forces massacred ethnic Albanian civilians. A brief bombing campaign by NATO forced the Serbs to withdraw. Many Serbian leaders then were arrested for war crimes and tried. The United States participated in this military crisis with the NATO troops.

Rwanda Located in central Africa, the country of **Rwanda** gained its independence from Belgium in 1962. The country is composed of two major tribes the Tutsi and the Hutu. The Rwandan civil war in 1994 began a period of genocide in which it is estimated that over 1,000,000 Rwandans died. The United States did not become involved in this conflict. The Vietnam Syndrome was often cited for the American reluctance to enter the fighting. In 2013, former President Clinton stated that it was one of his biggest regrets that his administration had not tried to help stop the slaughter in Rwanda, one of the poorest countries in the world.

Haiti In 1994, President Clinton ordered U.S. troops to lead a multinational force into Haiti to restore a legitimate government after years of dictatorships and unrest. During the rest of the decade, millions of dollars in aid was pledged to Haiti by many countries but little was sent due to the continuing lack of a stable government in that area.

Global Economy In 1992, President Clinton signed into law the **North American Free Trade Agreement (NAFTA),** which was created in an effort to break down trade barriers among the United States, Canada, and Mexico. During the Trump administration, a replacement was negotiated with better terms for the United States. On July 1, 2020, the United States-Mexico-Canada Agreement (USMCA) replaced NAFTA, creating a more balanced trade and improving conditions for American workers.

During the Clinton administration, American trade in Europe continued to be strong despite the formation of the **European Union,** a trade organization designed to break down trade barriers within Europe. The **General Agreement on Trade and Tariffs (GATT)** was formed in 1947 with 23 nations to encourage international trade. In 1995, the **World Trade Organization** was formed from GATT and included many other nations as well. These organizations are an example of globalization or global interdependence.

Economic Prosperity In the 1990s, the United States enjoyed the longest period of economic growth in its history.

The 1996 and 1998 Elections

At the end of 1995, disagreements between Republicans and President Clinton over the budget led to a shutdown of the federal government. During the 1996 presidential campaign, Clinton focused public attention on the Republicans' role in the shutdown. He also adopted several Republican issues by signing welfare

**Unifying Themes
Power and Authority**

In the early 1990s, war erupted in the Balkans as the former Yugoslavia fell into a bitter civil war.

- How did President Clinton handle tensions between ethnic groups in the former Yugoslavia in the 1990s?
- What gave President Clinton the authority to take this action?

**Unifying Themes
Global Exchange**

By the 1990s, the economies of many nations had become more interdependent.

- Name two organizations or agreements designed to improve trade among member nations.
- To which of these does the United States belong?
- How might interdependence affect the nation and its citizens?

reform into law and supporting a balanced budget. Clinton easily won reelection. Republicans maintained their congressional majority after both elections, but Democrats gained five House seats in 1998.

Scandal and Impeachment

Some of President Clinton's activities were the subject of investigations, including the Whitewater affair, which accused him and his wife, Hillary Rodham Clinton, of involvement with an illegal real estate scheme in Arkansas. The Clintons were never formally charged.

In 1998, a special prosecutor accused President Clinton of several offenses, including lying under oath about his relationship with a White House intern. On December 19, 1998, the House impeached President Clinton on charges of perjury and obstruction of justice. The Senate acquitted President Clinton two months later.

This result was similar to President Andrew Johnson's impeachment trial in 1868. Both presidents went through the impeachment process and both won acquittals in the Senate. However, there was a major difference between the impact of the impeachment on each president. President Andrew Johnson lost power in Washington, whereas President Clinton remained an extremely popular political figure.

Historic Appointment

In late 1996 at the beginning of his second term in office, President Clinton nominated **Madeleine K. Albright** to be secretary of state. After being unanimously confirmed by the U.S. Senate, she was sworn in as the 64th secretary of state in January 1997. Secretary Albright was the first female secretary of state. Since then two other women have held that position, Condoleezza Rice in the Bush (43) administration and Hillary Rodham Clinton in the Obama administration.

The War on Terror and Other Policies of the Early 2000s

Lesson Overview

The surprise terrorist attacks on September 11, 2001, had a major impact on American life. There had never been such an attack on the American homeland. You will recall from Topic 8 the Japanese attack on the Naval Base at Pearl Harbor, Hawaii, on December 7, 1942. That event caused the United States to enter World War II. The horrific events of 2001 caused the United States to declare a War on Terror. New legislation was written and a new federal department was established to provide greater security to the United States. Ultimately, the United States sent troops overseas in what became our longest war. President George W. Bush held the office for two terms and President Barack Obama, the first African American president, succeeded him in 2008.

Key Concept

11.11b in response to the terrorist attacks of September 11, 2001, the United States launched the War on Terror, which involved controversial foreign and domestic policies.

Unifying Themes

As you review this lesson take special note of the following themes:

- **Time, Continuity, and Change** How did the events of September 11, 2001, impact the Bush administration? the United States as a whole?

- **Development and Transformation of Social Structures** What role did diversity play in the years following the September 11th attacks in the United States?

- **Power, Authority, and Governance** How and why did the government begin to limit some personal freedoms after September 11th?

- **Civic Ideals and Practices** How did the events of September 11th impact the average life of American citizens?

Key People

George W. Bush	Dick Cheney
Al Gore	Condoleezza Rice
Osama bin Laden	Hillary Clinton
Saddam Hussein	Barack Obama

Key Terms and Events

swing state	weapons of mass destruction
September 11, 2001 attacks	(WMD)
War on Terror	Operation Iraqi Freedom
USA Patriot Act of 2001	Taliban
Department of Homeland Security	

The Historic 2000 Presidential Election

In the presidential election of 2000, Texas Governor **George W. Bush** ran as the Republican candidate against the Democratic candidate Vice President **Al Gore**. In one of the closest presidential races in history, Florida emerged as the key state because its electoral votes could decide the winner. The popular vote in Florida was so close that a recount of ballots was ordered by law. The election ended when the Supreme Court ruled to discontinue the recounts in the case *Bush* v. *Gore* (2000).

Election of 2000

Republican George W. Bush
50.5% of electoral vote

Democrat Al Gore
49.5% of electoral vote

Although Gore won the popular vote, Bush won the electoral vote. The election marked the first time the Supreme Court intervened in a presidential election.

The presidential election of 2000 was also the first election since the Hayes/Tilden election of 1876 in which the winner of the popular vote—Tilden in 1876 and Gore in 2000—did not win the electoral vote.

This election also popularized the term **swing state,** which is a term used for a state in which the voters are almost evenly divided between the major parties. Candidates and political experts acknowledge that either major party candidate could win the popular vote and therefore that state's electoral votes. Swing states such as Florida, Ohio, and Michigan were also crucial to the elections of 2004 and 2008. In the 2016 election, swing states included Ohio and Wisconsin.

The George W. Bush (43) Administration and the War on Terror

Nine months after President George W. Bush was inaugurated an event occurred that forever changed the nation. From that moment, the policies and actions of the Bush administration were shaped by the events on September 11, 2001.

September 11, 2001 and Resulting Events

On September 11, 2001, the United States suffered the worst attack on American soil in United States history. **Al Qaeda,** a terrorist organization led by **Osama bin Laden,** caused the deaths of almost 3,000 people, primarily American citizens. Two passenger planes were hijacked and flown into the high-rise buildings known as the World Trade Center in New York City. At the same time, another plane flew into the Pentagon in Washington, D.C. A fourth plane was unable to attack its intended target as heroic passengers attempted to overtake the hijackers but crashed into farmland in Shanksville, PA, killing all aboard.

President Bush focused largely on foreign policy after the **September 11, 2001 attacks.** The president called the attacks "acts of war" and committed the country to a **War on Terror**—a campaign against terrorists. American forces attacked military sites and terrorists training camps in **Afghanistan.** A major goal of this campaign was to aid in the overthrow of the Taliban rule and to find and bring to justice the al Qaeda leader, Osama bin Laden. Bush urged Americans not to expect one battle but a lengthy campaign unlike any other they have ever seen.

The passage of the **USA Patriot Act of 2001** and the creation of the Department of Homeland Security reflect the determination of the United States government to prevent future terrorist attacks. The USA Patriot Act of 2001 gave sweeping new powers to government agencies, which in some cases limited the privacy of American citizens. The USA Patriot Act name was based on the phrase, Uniting and Strengthening America by Providing Appropriate Tools Required to Intercept and Obstruct Terrorism. Some of the provisions of the Act included

- increasing use of government surveillance against more crimes.
- using tracking methods by the FBI.
- increasing methods of investigation.
- facilitating information sharing between various government agencies.

President George W. Bush announcing the War on Terror before a Joint Session of Congress

- utilizing new technologies.
- prohibiting harboring of terrorists within the country.
- enhancing penalties for crimes related to terrorism, which included crimes on mass transit and those of bioterrorists.

The reaction of Americans to this Act was mixed. Many were thankful for stricter regulations and any effort to protect American citizens. Others protested what was called an invasion of privacy into American lives. Travel by air in particular changed significantly as numbers of security guards were increased and stricter pre-boarding screenings were imposed. Eventually, the Senate allowed most portions of the Patriot Act to expire in June 2015.

To coordinate federal government efforts, the **Homeland Security Act** created a new Cabinet-level department, the **Department of Homeland Security.** Its job was to coordinate the efforts of more than 40 federal agencies in fighting terror. These agencies include the CIA, FBI, and the National Guard. In 2002, President Bush and Congress created the independent, bipartisan National Commission on Terrorist Attacks upon the United States. After extensive hearings by the Commission, a detailed report was released in the summer of 2004. One of its major recommendations was to unify the United States Intelligence Community under the leadership of a new National Intelligence Director.

War in Iraq In late 2002 and early 2003, the Bush administration warned **Saddam Hussein** to eliminate Iraq's **weapons of mass destruction (WMD).** Hussein claimed not to have any WMD. The United Nations sent an inspection team, which reported little success finding these weapons. The United States worked to gain United Nations support for an invasion of Iraq. Failing to gain this support, a small number of countries led by the United States and Great Britain attacked Iraq in March 2003. This action strained foreign relations with France, Germany, and Russia. This campaign is known as **Operation Iraqi Freedom.** More than 200,000 American troops were sent to the area. For the first time, the United States military allowed reporters to be "embedded" with the troops. By the end of the war, in 2011, over 170 journalists had been killed. Bush prematurely declared an official end to the war on May 1, 2003 using the words "Mission Accomplished."

**Unifying Themes
Power and Authority**

- How did President Bush's actions during the war in Iraq demonstrate his use of presidential power?

In July 2003, both sons of Saddam Hussein were killed in a shootout with U.S. forces in Mosul, Iraq. Hussein escaped capture until December 2003. An Iraqi Governing Council was established in 2003 with the goal of making Iraq an independent, democratic nation. American casualties continued to rise as the military met resistance. President Bush defended the war on the grounds that a brutal dictator who had terrorist links and was hiding WMD should be removed. Given the rising loss of human lives and financial costs to the United States and the failure to find WMD, critics questioned the Bush administration's activities in Iraq and its long-term plan for the country.

During 2004, President Bush and Secretary of Defense Donald Rumsfeld faced serious questions about the treatment of Iraqi prisoners after reports disclosed abuse by American troops. Some soldiers were found guilty and sentenced to prison terms. In January 2005, with American and Coalition Forces' support, the new Iraqi government held its first democratic elections under extremely tight security. Insurgents who opposed the new government and the American presence in Iraq continued violent attacks on both military and civilians in Baghdad and elsewhere.

In 2006, President Bush replaced Secretary of Defense Rumsfeld with Robert Gates, who agreed to continue in that position in President Obama's administration. Early in 2007, the Bush administration was forced to answer questions about the poor treatment of many returning wounded soldiers. At the end of 2007, several Army leaders were dismissed from their jobs as a result of the conditions at Walter Reed Medical Center in Washington.

Although the new Iraqi government made some progress at establishing democracy, the two most powerful Islamic sects, the Shiites and the Sunnis, continued to have difficulties working together. The trial of Saddam Hussein concluded with his being found guilty of multiple murders. He was hanged on December 30, 2006. By 2007, the violent actions of the insurgents moved Iraq into a civil war. Daily violence and loss of life increased as American and coalition troops tried to maintain order. With these events, President Bush's popularity ratings with the American public declined to the lowest levels of his presidency. There was growing antiwar pressure from mainstream Americans as the number of Americans dead and wounded continued to grow. The Vietnam Syndrome, which had not stopped the United States from entering into a war with Iraq, was now returning in the minds of many Americans. Early in 2007, Great Britain, America's strongest ally in the Iraqi war, began to withdraw its troops from Iraq.

Despite the attempts of Congress to limit the increase of troops in Iraq, President Bush announced a new strategy called a "Surge" in which American troop strength increased to over 160,000. This plan was an effort to control the number of suicide bombers, car bombs, and roadside attacks by Iraqi insurgents that had caused thousands of Iraqi deaths. The Surge did meet with some success, but American war deaths in 2007 increased to their highest level since 2003. The estimates of the cost of the war in Iraq vary widely, but the cost is currently believed to be more than $800 billion. Over 5,000 American servicemen and servicewomen have been killed in Iraq and thousands more have been seriously wounded.

Afghanistan Following the Soviet occupation of Afghanistan from 1979 until the end of the 1980s, millions of Afghans fled their country, and Afghan fighters fought a resistance movement to force the Soviets to leave. In the 1990s, a reactionary, extremist Islamic fundamentalist group known as the **Taliban** took over the Afghan government and imposed strict, conservative laws on the population. Women were forced to wear traditional coverings and to remain primarily in their homes.

In 2001, President Bush gave the Taliban government an ultimatum. Unless they turned over Osama bin Laden, who had been coordinating terrorist attacks from Afghanistan, the United States would attack the country. Bin Laden was not turned over. Later that year, NATO forces led by the United States forced the Taliban from power. Many of the surviving Taliban fled across the border into Pakistan where they continued to launch attacks across the border. In 2006, President Bush visited the area under very heavy security to emphasize the desire of the United States to cooperate with that part of Asia. In 2007, Vice President **Dick Cheney** visited Afghanistan, and suicide bombers attempted to attack the secured compound where the vice president was staying.

Osama bin Laden was killed by United States Special Forces on May 1, 2011. Continued American involvement in Afghanistan is considered crucial to American goals and interests in the region. By the spring of 2019, over 2,300 U.S. service members have died as a result of the war in Afghanistan. As in the case of the war in Iraq, estimates of total cost vary widely. By 2019, the cost of the war in Afghanistan is estimated by some sources to be over $690 billion in total spending.

With the death of bin Laden and some other al Qaeda leaders, the terrorist organization lost some of its power. The antidemocratic Taliban exists as an extremist Islamic force in Afghanistan and Pakistan. The United States military in the area continues to try to destroy the influence of both organizations. A stable democratic government without the opportunity for terrorism in both countries is a goal of U.S. foreign policy.

Domestic Policies and Issues

Although greatly focused on events abroad, President Bush also had domestic policies he wished to pursue and domestic issues that required his attention.

Educational Reform On January 8, 2002, President Bush signed into law a major educational reform bill called No Child Left Behind. The plan called for increased student and teacher accountability and targeted funds for improving schools. Critics said that it did not accomplish what it needed to do to improve American education.

Immigration Issues The Bush administration had to deal with several issues relating to immigration, some of which became more serious after the attacks of September 11, 2001. The Real ID Act of 2005 strengthened security requirements at U.S. borders and gave the Director of Homeland Security additional powers. Several proposals were introduced in both houses of Congress to increase border patrols and protection, restrict illegal immigration, and strengthen anti-terrorism laws. There was also extensive discussion over funding bills to construct a wall along the U.S. border between Mexico and the United States. This produced mixed reactions on both sides of the border.

Social Security President Bush wanted to make Social Security reform a primary agenda item. The president's plan to allow younger workers to choose private accounts for a portion of their Social Security contributions drew praise as well as criticism. The president also tried to reform the Medicare program. A major concern with these programs is that the number of Americans eligible for them is growing. There is an increasing senior citizen population due to the aging of the "baby boom" generation. At the same time, there are fewer workers contributing to the system, due to declining American birth rates of the 1970s and 1980s. Some suggest a solution would be to raise the age of eligibility.

Mass Acts of Violence In 2007, following several years of mass acts of violence in schools and on college campuses, the most deadly shooting rampage in United States history at that time took place, with 33 students, including the killer, dead at Virginia Tech in Blacksburg, Virginia. Later in 2007, a sniper in an Omaha, Nebraska, shopping mall killed eight people, while in February 2008, another gunman killed five students as well as himself at Northern Illinois University. Each incident of this type of violence renewed the debate among Americans about gun control.

Taxes and the Economy Bush attempted a tax cut and rebates to taxpayers early in his administration. In 2008, taxpayers received rebate checks of up to $1,200. From 2007, however, the economy showed signs of a recession, especially in the housing market as thousands of homeowners struggled to meet mortgage payments and others faced bank foreclosures. Eventually, banks and mortgage companies were investigated and found to have encouraged borrowers to borrow more than they could afford to pay back. Some of these borrowers struggled to pay their mortgages because they became unemployed due to outsourcing. In 2007, Congress approved a minimum wage increase. The Federal Reserve Board lowered its interest rate several times, including a drop of 0.75 percent, the largest in the Board's history.

Preparing for the Regents

Remember that current topics like Afghanistan and the Taliban, who continue to be a threat to Western ideas in that country, are valid topics for both multiple-choice and essay questions.

• Why do Western nations such as the United States continue to oppose the goals of the Taliban?

Unifying Themes
Global Connections

The term "outsourcing" has been used in the last decade to describe the strategy of American businesses sending work to foreign countries to save money in production costs. This benefits the foreign countries but hurts workers in the United States and causes a rise in American unemployment.

• Can you suggest something that the U.S. government might do to discourage "outsourcing"?

Election of 2004

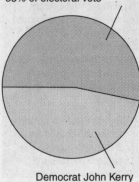

Republican George W. Bush
53% of electoral vote

Democrat John Kerry
47% of electoral vote

By early spring 2009, the Federal Reserve interest rate was at a record-breaking low of 0 percent. All of these actions were in an effort to reverse the threat of a recession. Yet, by late 2008, the recession was described as the worst economic downturn since the Great Depression of the 1930s.

Election of 2004 In November 2004, George W. Bush, the Republican incumbent won a close race against challenger, Massachusetts Senator and Vietnam War veteran, John Kerry. Dr. **Condoleezza Rice**, former National Security Advisor, became the first African American woman to hold the position of secretary of state. Within the first few months of being appointed secretary of state, Rice made trips to Europe, the Middle East, and parts of Asia.

The 2008 Election and Its History-Making Candidates

Early in 2007, several candidates entered the race for the presidency. Some of these candidacies were particularly historic because they represented "firsts" in American history. New York Senator **Hillary Clinton** was both the first former First Lady and the first female from a major political party (Democratic) to run for president. Illinois Senator **Barack Obama**, also a Democrat, was the first African American to be considered a serious presidential candidate from a major party. In the early 2008 democratic primaries, Obama won in Iowa, and Clinton won in New Hampshire, setting the stage for weeks of continuing debates and campaign travel for both.

Arizona Senator John McCain, the Republican front runner, took a strong lead over his opponents. In February 2008, Ralph Nader announced that he would run again for president as a third-party candidate. Previously, in the 2000 election, when Nader ran as a third-party candidate, he was blamed for taking votes from the Democratic candidate.

Preparing for the Regents

Turning Point

• For what reasons could the election of 2008 be considered a turning point in United States political history?

Throughout the spring of 2008, Hillary Clinton and Barack Obama, each won primaries. The candidates attracted different groups of voters, and each continued to build large numbers of delegate votes. As the primary season continued, Senator Clinton gradually fell behind both in convention delegates and in campaign money raised. Senator Clinton refused to quit, stayed on the primary ballot and continued to win states until the very last day of the primaries, June 3, 2008. That evening, Obama clinched the Democratic nomination.

Both candidates congratulated each other on their success at bringing so many new voters into the political process. Their candidacies drew thousands of new voters representing several groups, such as younger voters, African Americans, and Hispanics. The increase in eligible Democratic voters concerned the Republican party leadership as they tried to retain control of the White House despite declining popular support for President George W. Bush.

Election of 2008

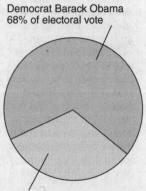

Democrat Barack Obama
68% of electoral vote

Republican John McCain
32% of electoral vote

Barack Obama became the Democratic candidate for president and he selected Senator Joseph Biden of Delaware as his vice-presidential running mate. Senator McCain chose Sarah Palin, governor of Alaska, to be his vice-presidential running mate. The election results were clear by the evening of Election Day on November 4, 2008. John McCain conceded the election to Barack Obama. Ralph Nader took in around 700,000 votes and did not have enough voters to earn one electoral vote. Obama earned 365 electoral votes compared to McCain's 173. The results of the races for the Senate and the House of Representatives also favored the Democrats, and for the first time in a number of years, Democrats controlled both the legislative and executive branches of government.

The Barack Obama Administration

When President Barack Obama, First Lady Michelle Obama, and their two young daughters moved into the White House following his inauguration on January 20, 2009, they made American history. They were the first African American family to serve in this role.

President Barack Obama

Domestic Issues

As a result of the 2008 recession, President Obama's primary focus was the nation's economy. However, his domestic agenda included addressing equal rights and health care.

The Economy President Obama took office as the United States faced its most serious economic crisis since the Great Depression of the 1930s. The president came into office knowing that an enormous economic stimulus plan would be necessary to solve this crisis. Some major banks had failed and other companies needed billions of dollars of American taxpayer money, known as "bailout" money, to prevent them from collapsing. About $700 billion in what is known as TARP money, or the Troubled Asset Relief Program, was used to help banks that were in danger of failing. The unemployment rate in some parts of the United States was at its highest rate in almost 25 years, between eight and ten percent.

The chairman of the Federal Reserve Board was called to Capitol Hill several times to explain the policies that the Fed was implementing to remedy the crisis. There was general support for the president's efforts to keep the three major American automotive companies economically afloat. The difference with the money being lent to the auto industry was that it was being paid back to the taxpayers through the government. Other major billion-dollar spending plans received more criticism. A major sticking point with the bailout funds was the discovery that the businesses used millions of dollars of taxpayer money to pay bonuses for executives at failing companies.

Another economic problem at this time was that many homeowners could not afford to pay the money they owned on their homes (called a mortgage). When banks didn't receive their payments, they could take back the homes or foreclose on them.

Fair Pay The first act that President Obama signed into law was the Lilly Ledbetter Fair Pay Act of 2009. This law was the result of an original suit filed by Lilly Ledbetter over pay discrimination in 1998. In 2007, after years of disputes in the courts, the Supreme Court ruled in a 5 to 4 decision that too much time had passed between the discrimination and the filing of the suit. An attempt at an Act to correct the situation in the future was defeated by a Republican majority in 2007. After President Obama's election in 2008, Congress quickly passed a new 2009 version of the Fair Pay Act named for Ms. Ledbetter and ending the issues of timing for filing a pay discrimination suit.

Health Care In March 2010, President Obama made history by signing the Health Care Reform Bill. Health care reform had been a major goal of the president and the Democratic Party. The bill passed with a narrow margin over fierce Republican opposition. The law was phased in over several years and has provisions to forbid insurance companies to deny health care coverage to applicants, to extend coverage to young adults until they are 26 if living at home, and to eventually require all Americans to obtain health care insurance. Republicans have tried over 60 times to repeal the law, also known as the Affordable Care Act, but so far have been unsuccessful.

Unifying Themes
Global Connections

Adding to the economic crisis of the Obama administration was the fact that the United States had had a trade deficit for the previous two decades. This was a result of the United States importing more than it exported. China had become a major source of American imports to the benefit of the Chinese economy.

Unifying Themes
Power

In June 2015, the Supreme Court ruled in the case of *King* v. *Burwell* that the Affordable Care Act (often called Obamacare) is legal and constitutional. This decision was a major accomplishment for the Obama administration.

• How is this case an example of the use of checks and balances?

Other Domestic Issues

- Millions of dollars of the government stimulus plan were marked for use by the states to improve education.

- Another domestic need that received stimulus dollars was the repair of the American infrastructure.

- During the spring of 2013, a bipartisan Senate committee made significant progress on the possible passage of new immigration legislation. It still has yet to be debated or voted on by the House.

- Efforts toward Social Security reform were made by the Obama administration, but they could not get congressional approval.

- Since 2014, a number of African Americans encountered incidents of deadly violence by police officers. These well-documented and publicized events caused reactions from peaceful protests and requests for equal treatment under the law to street riots in areas as diverse as Missouri, Maryland, and New York.

Election of 2012

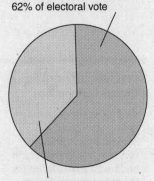

Democrat Barack Obama
62% of electoral vote

Republican Mitt Romney
38% of electoral vote

2010 Congressional Elections President Obama, a Democrat, had the good fortune to be working with a Democratic majority in both the Senate and the House of Representatives during his first two years in office. In November 2010, a Republican majority retook control of the House. The Senate lost some seats to Republicans but retained a Democratic majority. These Republican gains were seen as a protest against various Obama policies, such as conduct of the wars in Iraq and Afghanistan, the failure to significantly reduce the deficit, consistently high unemployment, the passage of the Health Care Reform Bill, and the failure to adopt immigration reform.

The Presidential Election of 2012

As an incumbent, President Barack Obama did not face any opposition for the Democratic presidential nomination. Mitt Romney, a former governor of Massachusetts, earned the Republican nomination. President Obama won the election and took the oath of office for his second term as president in January 2013.

Foreign Issues

As previous presidents before him, Obama had to contend with wars and political unrest in the Middle East. Terrorism and its threat to the nation's security influenced U.S. foreign policy.

Secretary of State John Kerry visits American troops stationed in Kabul, Afghanistan, in 2016

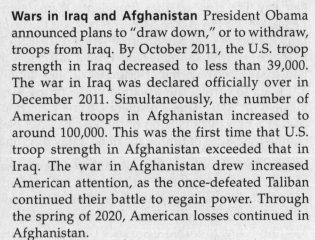

Wars in Iraq and Afghanistan President Obama announced plans to "draw down," or to withdraw, troops from Iraq. By October 2011, the U.S. troop strength in Iraq decreased to less than 39,000. The war in Iraq was declared officially over in December 2011. Simultaneously, the number of American troops in Afghanistan increased to around 100,000. This was the first time that U.S. troop strength in Afghanistan exceeded that in Iraq. The war in Afghanistan drew increased American attention, as the once-defeated Taliban continued their battle to regain power. Through the spring of 2020, American losses continued in Afghanistan.

The United States position was that the Afghan government must be helped in its effort to maintain stability against both the Taliban and terrorist organizations, such as al Qaeda and ISIS.

Arab Spring The spring of 2011 was termed the Arab Spring due to the political uprisings against established and often dictatorial governments in Egypt, Yemen, Bahrain, Libya, Syria, and elsewhere. As part of a NATO mission, the United States participated in attacks on Libya to assist rebels in removing long-time dictator Muammar Gadhafi. In October 2012, a terrorist attack occurred against the United States mission in Benghazi, Libya, which killed the United States ambassador and three other Americans. The surprise attack caused a series of congressional investigations concerning the issue of how well the United States could defend itself in dangerous foreign locations.

Syria The Syrian civil war drew international attention due to the loss of thousands of lives, including thousands of civilians, women, and children. Some sources estimate that there were more than 450,000 deaths in Syria. There were also estimated to be almost 11 million refugees who fled the fighting. These refugees sought safety in nearby Middle Eastern countries, in Turkey, in North Africa, and also in European nations. President Obama pledged the United States to accept some refugees. The admission of Syrian refugees to the United States became a controversial topic due to the concern of many Americans that terrorists might use this opportunity to enter the United States. The Syrian government was accused by some nations of using chemical warfare against its own citizens.

ISIS At the same time as the United States involvement in Iraq was ending and the Syrian civil war was escalating, a new extremely violent terrorist group, ISIS, was becoming active in the Middle East. ISIS is a group claiming to be the Islamic State of Iraq and Syria (also ISIL, Islamic State of Iraq and Levant, the geographic area). This terrorist group is responsible for numerous public violent executions of Westerners as well as thousands of others who disagree with their practices. The goal of ISIS is to create a hardline Islamic state that includes both Syrian and Iraqi territory. In the spring of 2019, heavy fighting occurred in eastern Syria that involved United States troops. ISIS forces have been forced out of their last positions and have lost any territory that they had still claimed. By 2020, President Trump withdrew American troops from Syria.

2014 Congressional Elections

As a result of the 2014 midterm elections, the Republican Party regained control of both houses of Congress. For this term, there were more Republicans serving in Congress than there had been in fifty years. Because President Obama was a Democrat, he had more difficulty in trying to enact his goals for his second term.

Preparing for the Regents

Turning Point

In April 2010, President Obama signed a Nuclear Arms Reduction Treaty with Russia. With Senate approval, it was the first step in many years taken by nations with nuclear weapons to agree to limit their development. In 2015, Secretary of State John Kerry was involved in negotiations with Iran related to limitations on their ability to produce nuclear weapons.

The Economic and Social Effects of Globalization on the Nation

Key Concept

11.11c Globalization and advances in technology have affected the United States economy and society.

Lesson Overview

The United States began as a nation of farmers. Today, it is one of the leading economic and political powers in the world. Because of the advanced technology of the postindustrial age, the world has become what some call a "global village." Because of increased interdependence, major events in one part of the world have an impact upon the rest of the world. Technology and multinational corporations have helped to increase job growth. Population growth, longer life spans, and environmental concerns challenge the United States as well as other countries. The president of the United States is ultimately responsible for dealing with a wide range of issues related to both the United States and the world.

Unifying Themes

As you review this lesson take special note of the following themes:

- **Time, Continuity, and Change** How have forms of business organization changed since World War II? Why has this changed occurred?

- **Geography, Humans, and the Environment** Identify some major environmental concerns of the 21st century. In what ways are individuals, organizations, and government dealing with environmental concerns?

- **Creation, Expansion, and Interaction of Economic Systems** Why are China and the United States tied economically? How do multinational companies impact economic growth in the United States and in the global economy? How has the emergence of a global economy strengthened the interdependence of nations?

- **Science, Technology, and Innovation** How has technology impacted life in the 21st century?

Key People

Hillary Rodham Clinton	Donald J. Trump
Joseph R. Biden	Kamala Harris

Key Terms and Events

globalization	Earth Day
multinational corporations	climate change
alternative energy sources	global warming
Internet	

Congressional Elections of 2016

The 2016 congressional elections resulted in both houses of Congress continuing with Republican majorities. Democrats in the Senate increased by two, with two others identified as Independent but who caucus (meet) with the 46 Democrats. Republicans held 52 seats. In the House of Representatives, Republicans won 241 seats with Democrats at 194.

Presidential Election of 2016

One of the earliest announced Democratic candidates for the 2016 election was **Hillary Rodham Clinton,** former Senator from New York State, former secretary of state, and also former First Lady. Clinton won the nomination and was the first female candidate for president from a major party.

Donald J. Trump, a New York self-proclaimed billionaire, businessman, land developer, and reality TV show figure, surprised the Republican Party by attracting thousands of supporters across the United States. Trump became famous for his outspoken and negative opinions toward Mexicans, immigration, women, the handicapped, some veterans, and Muslims. Many conservative Republicans expressed concerns that Trump should not be allowed to become the voice of the party. Trump clinched the nomination at the Republican Convention. Donald Trump chose Mike Pence to be his vice-presidential running mate.

After a close and hard-fought campaign, Democrat Hillary Rodham Clinton won the popular vote with 65,853,516 votes cast (48.5%). Republican Donald J. Trump had 62,979,879 popular votes. Trump won the presidency by winning the electoral vote with 306 votes (56.9%) over Clinton's 232 votes.

The Donald J. Trump Administration

With his inauguration in January 2017, Donald Trump became 45th president of the United States. During his campaign, he made a number of pledges to voters. Within the first weeks of his administration, he began to act on these promises as he endeavored to change a variety of domestic and foreign policies enacted by previous presidents.

Domestic Issues

- A campaign pledge of President Trump was to repeal the Affordable Care Act (known as Obamacare). The president was unsuccessful in getting a majority of Congress to repeal and replace it.

- President Trump also promised to have Mexico pay for a large, new wall separating the two countries. Mexico has refused to pay for such a wall, and its construction continues to be controversial.

- Early in his presidency, Trump signed an Executive Order blocking immigration from six Muslim majority nations. Lower courts halted the travel ban, but the Supreme Court upheld the partial limitation of immigrants from six countries and agreed to hear the case. The Court upheld the ban in June 2018.

- As a result of widespread concern over possible Russian interference in the 2016 election, former FBI Director Robert Mueller was appointed as Special Counsel to lead an investigation starting in May 2017. Within a year, some close associates of the president were indicted, but the president repeatedly claimed to have no involvement with the Russians. The report was released to Attorney General William Barr in late March 2019. Within 48 hours, Barr released to Congress a four-page letter summarizing the report and claiming that the president was found not to be guilty of collusion with the Russians. When the nearly 400-page Mueller report was released publicly, with large sections redacted (deleted), immediate controversy occurred. The report concluded that Russia interfered in the 2016 presidential election to favor the election of Donald Trump. Thirteen Russians were indicted and found guilty of interference. Previously the Office of Legal Counsel has held that a "sitting president" (in office) cannot be indicted. The report did not conclude that Trump committed a crime but also did not exonerate (excuse) him.

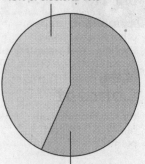

Election of 2016

Democrat Hillary Clinton
43% of electoral vote

Republican Donald J. Trump
57% of electoral vote

President Donald J. Trump

Unifying Themes
Civic Ideals: Respect for Diversity

Try to identify names of other Black victims of the police that protesters demonstrated on behalf of. Why were they seen as symbols of this movement? Why did protesters want the Confederate flag removed from public places?

- On May 25, 2020, while being arrested on suspicion of passing a counterfeit $20.00 bill, George Floyd, a 46-year-old African American man, was murdered by a white police officer in Minneapolis, Minnesota. The officer, as well as others on the scene, were later convicted for their actions. This incident spurred nationwide demonstrations against injustices by white police officers and courts against Black Americans. In 2013, the Black Lives Matter movement had started in response to the acquittal of a citizen who was charged with the murder of a Black teenager in Florida. This movement gained increased momentum and publicity with the Floyd case, especially since a video of the incident, filmed by a teenage spectator, was widely seen. Millions of people participated in protests. These were the largest national protests for civil rights since the civil rights protests of the 1960s. Other deaths of Black people caused by law enforcement were publicized across the country. Changes that have occurred as a result of these protests have included the removal of the Confederate flag and monuments to the Confederacy in public places. Name changes have taken place for streets, public buildings, schools, team mascots, and food and drink brands.

Foreign Issues

Trump supported a policy of placing the interests of the United States before anything else. This sometimes undermined the actions of previous presidents, shifting America's stance on issues and programs.

First International Trip President Trump took his first overseas trip as president in May 2017. He visited Saudi Arabia, Israel, Vatican City, and Brussels, Belgium, for a NATO meeting and Sicily, Italy, for a G7 meeting. (The G7 nations are the most industrialized nations in the world and were formed as a group in 1975.) In early June 2017, Trump announced that the United States would withdraw from the Paris Agreement of 2016, and international agreement addressing climate change.

Syria Early in his administration, President Trump authorized an American air strike on a Syrian air base believed to have been used in chemical warfare against Syrian civilians. A second strike against the use of chemical warfare occurred in 2018.

North Korea From 2013 through 2018, North Korea's communist leader, Kim Jong Un, continued to increase tensions with threats of the use of nuclear power against the United States and South Korea. North Korea claimed early in 2016 to have successfully tested a hydrogen bomb. This action was condemned by the United Nations Security Council with the threat of new sanctions against North Korea. President Trump made a surprise announcement that he would meet Kim Jong Un in 2018. In April 2018, a surprise news event pictured the leaders of North and South Korea agreeing to end hostilities. A second meeting occurred months later in Saigon between President Trump and Kim Jong Un but ended abruptly with little accomplished.

Social Studies Practices
Gathering and Interpreting Evidence

Take a few minutes at home to look at as many items as you can from clothing to kitchen appliances to electronics to toys to find and identify the "Made in . . ." label. You will probably have quite a list of "Made in China" items.

- What does this suggest about China's effect on the American economy?

China As you read in Topic 9, the Nixon administration reopened trade with China in 1972. Since then the Chinese economy has grown steadily and the country is now a major financial force in the global marketplace. In fact, the United States has had a serious trade deficit with China for a number of years. This means that the United States is a major consumer of inexpensive Chinese goods. We buy more from China than we sell to China. To deal with the imbalance of trade, President Trump began placing a series of tariffs on products from a number of countries, including China. In response, China levied tariffs on American products. After Trump reduced some tariffs with China, the Chinese were willing to come to the negotiations table.

In January 2020, Trump announced that the United States and China signed a new trade agreement. Aside from the goal of improving trade for American consumers as soon as possible, a goal of the president was to reduce the nation's trade deficit before the 2020 presidential election. The Chinese would buy more agricultural and manufactured goods from the United States, and the United States would cut back on some tariffs on Chinese goods sold in the United States.

One concern is that any new trade deal must have an agreed upon method of enforcement. This has been a problem in negotiations with previous administrations. In an effort to improve relations with China, the president traveled to China and the Chinese Premier Xi Jinping visited the president at his Florida home. In such situations, the Chinese are concerned about the possible undercutting of the Communist Chinese Party's control of the economy. The first phase of the new agreement provided bilateral negotiations between the two countries as difficulties may arise.

Mexico and Canada Twenty-five years after the Clinton administration negotiated NAFTA (see page 367), the Trump administration agreed to a modernized version of the trade agreement. Known as USMCA, (United States, Mexico, Canada), the agreement offers new protections for "innovators and creators," stronger enforcement provisions, financial services, rights for labor, and environmental protections. The agreement went into effect in the spring of 2020.

Globalization

The negotiations with China are a good example of the globalization of the world economy. **Globalization** is the process of interaction and integration among peoples, companies, and governments on a worldwide basis. Businesses or other organizations develop international influence or start operating on an international scale. It involves the diffusion of products, technological information, and jobs across national borders and cultures. In economic terms, globalization describes an interdependence of nations around the globe fostered through free trade.

Since the 1800s, the organization of American businesses has changed from single ownership and partnerships to corporations. In the post–World War II period, many corporations have become **multinational corporations,** or businesses with bases of operation in many nations. Multinational banks and lending institutions make it easier to transfer capital across the globe. This trend can help spread American influence internationally but may not always bring good results for the American worker who needs and expects higher wages than workers do in less affluent countries.

In the United States during the twentieth century and since the beginning of the twenty-first century, federal prosecutions of corporations such as Standard Oil, AT&T, and Microsoft were based on alleged violations of antitrust laws. There has also been reduced competition in the airline industry, which has ultimately hurt the consumer.

Challenges Facing the Nation in the 21st Century

The United States is trying to address a variety of issues that affect the nation.

Continued Acts of Mass Violence

The issue of gun control continues to be hotly debated. Random urban violence, as well as highly publicized shootings, have caused millions of Americans to reconsider their attitudes toward the availability of guns in this nation.

Unifying Themes
Global Connections and Exchange

Try to make connections between globalization as described and the new problems of the Global Pandemic. Hundreds of cargo ships were stalled in worldwide ports causing major problems and delays in what is called the "supply chain." Make a list of how you or your family are or were impacted by this situation.

Unifying Themes
Time, Continuity, and Change

- What kinds of settings were touched by gun violence in the events listed?
- How many states were impacted by these events?
- Identify some similarities and some differences in this series of events.
- After reviewing these events, what conclusion(s) might you draw?

- As they target children and other young people, school shootings have served as symbols of out-of-control gun violence for many. In December 2012, a lone gunman attacked an elementary school in Newtown, Connecticut, causing the deaths of 20 young children and six educators. Since then, efforts to limit the sale of guns, especially assault rifles, have increased. In February 2018, 17 deaths of students and teachers occurred in Parkland, Florida, following an attack by a teenage former student. The Parkland, Florida, shooting inspired a national youth movement aimed at ending school violence. In 2019, a bill limiting the power of certain rifles was passed by Congress. Still, shootings at schools occur with disturbing frequency.

- Some mass shootings have occurred in houses of worship as people gathered for religious services, such as a November 2017 attack at a church in Texas in which 26 people were killed. When 11 worshippers were killed in an October 2018 attack on a Pittsburgh synagogue and 6 were killed in a December 2019 attack on a kosher market in New Jersey, people brought up concerns about heightened antisemitic sentiment leading to violence against the Jewish community.

- An extremist targeted a different community in 2016 when he shot over 100 people, resulting in 49 deaths, at a gay bar in Orlando, Florida. The gunman was a native-born American with self-proclaimed ties to ISIS. Other people caught by violence while enjoying themselves included the 12 people killed by a gunman in November 2018 at a Thousand Oaks, California, bar. People doing everyday tasks such as grocery shopping have also been shot, such as the 22 dead and 24 injured at an El Paso, Texas, Walmart in August 2019.

- On May 14, 2022, a racially motivated shooting killed 10 people and injured three at a grocery store in Buffalo, New York. Eleven of the victims were Black.

The National Rifle Association continues to be one of the strongest lobbying groups in the United States and remains committed to the rights of gun owners. This topic will continue to be a controversial one for years to come. Random gun violence in workplaces, shopping malls, universities, and even health care facilities continues to be a serious problem.

2018 Congressional Elections

The 2018 congressional elections resulted in the Democratic Party regaining control of the House of Representatives with 235 seats, a gain of 42 seats. Republicans held 200 seats. At the time of the election, there were 7 vacant seats. Significantly, 36 new women won seats in the House. Of these women, two were 29 years old, two were the first Native American women to ever be elected and two were the first Muslim women to be elected. The number of Latino and Asian Americans increased as well. At least 10 members identify as LGBTQ. Nancy Pelosi, a member from California, returned to her past position of Speaker of the House. The House is considered the most diverse in history. The Senate gained two new female members, one in each political party, for a total of 25.

Global Pandemic

A new form of coronavirus, known as COVID-19, first appeared in Wuhan, China, in January 2020. Since then, the infectious disease, including several deadly variants, has spread across the world. An epidemic happens in one location, region, community, or even country. A pandemic spreads over multiple countries or continents. COVID-19 became a pandemic. By spring 2022, there were over 82,000,000 cases and over 1,000,000 deaths in the United States, according to the Center for Disease Control (CDC).

As the disease is spread through person-to-person contact, densely populated areas like New York City were especially affected at the beginning of the outbreak. It was an especially difficult time for health care workers as they struggled to keep up with the cases. There were also serious issues with the degree of preparedness and shortages across the states and in the federal government.

At first, only essential businesses, such as grocery stores, pharmacies, gas stations, auto repair shops, and banks were allowed to remain open. Schools were closed and attempted to keep up with students via remote learning. Places of worship were closed to keep people from gathering in large numbers. Small businesses, varying from restaurants to beauty salons and barber shops, suffered since they could not operate. Many restaurants attempted to adjust by offering carry out service or delivery service. Unemployment numbers across the country soared. Americans were encouraged to practice "social distancing," which means staying six feet from other people when in public.

President Trump signed a $2.2 trillion economic relief package called the Coronavirus Aid, Relief and Economic Security Act (CARES). This included direct relief to American families, small businesses, hospitals, and states. For several months, then President Trump conducted almost daily press briefings with a group of medical and business advisors. He was praised for his actions of using government resources to solve problems but was criticized for his unrealistic understanding of the extent and severity of the crisis.

A major effort was begun by the federal government working with pharmaceutical manufacturers to produce an effective vaccine to protect against the virus. After a thorough testing process overseen by the Federal Drug Administration (FDA) and the CDC, two types of vaccines were available on a limited basis by late 2020. By March 2021, the free vaccines were offered to the general public over the age of 15. By October 2021, those over the age of 5 were included as well. As of February 2022, a vaccine for very young children had not been approved.

President Trump tested positive for COVID and was hospitalized for four days in early October 2020. He was well enough to then return to the White House to complete his recovery. President Trump had frequently been questioned and criticized for his failure to wear a mask in public. President and Mrs. Trump received their COVID vaccinations quietly at the White House in January 2021 after the vaccinations had been available to them for about a year. Thousands of his supporters followed his lead by refusing vaccinations and fighting against mask wearing and mandates. While more and more Americans were vaccinated, more and more of the unvaccinated died of COVID. President Biden entered the White House with a major goal of ending the virus. See the section "The COVID-19 Pandemic" in the on page 386 for more on his administration's attempts to fight the pandemic and its effects.

Presidential Election of 2020

Incumbent President Donald J. Trump was nominated by the Republican Party along with his Vice President Mike Pence to run again in 2020. Joseph R. Biden, nominated by the Democratic Party, made history by selecting Kamala Harris, a female Senator of African American and South Asian heritage, to be his running mate. The nomination process for both parties was very different from recent American political history due to the COVID-19 pandemic. Televised speeches replaced huge convention gatherings of thousands of people.

Social Studies Practices
Chronological Reasoning and Causation

Using the Pandemic, identify at least four specific events that caused other Pandemic related events. An example: restaurants lost business and then offered pick up and delivery services.

As a result of the pandemic, there were a record number of ballots cast early and cast by mail. Each state establishes its own procedures for voting. This resulted in some states counting ballots as they received them and other states only beginning to count ballots after the actual election on Tuesday, November 3, 2020. Weeks prior to the election, President Trump expressed and encouraged public suspicion of the security of the election.

The actual results were that President Trump, a Republican, earned 74,216,154 popular votes and 232 electoral votes. Remember that with the Electoral College system (see page 60), the winner of the presidency must win 270 electoral votes. Joe Biden won 81,268,924 popular votes and 306 electoral votes. Due to the factors described above and other issues such as late reporting, it was not possible to declare a winner on the evening of the election. President Trump and many Republicans quickly began to claim that there had been election fraud. By Saturday November 7, Joe Biden was identified as the winner by most media sources. Three states— Georgia, Arizona, and Wisconsin—had results within a margin of 1%. Another five states had results between a 1% and 5% margin. Multiple recounts were conducted. Republicans seeking to overturn the election filed 63 lawsuits in state court, but all were eventually either dismissed by the courts or withdrawn. No state found any errors that would have changed the results of the election. Joseph R. Biden took the oath of office as president of the United States and Kamala Harris as vice president on January 20, 2021.

Congressional Elections of 2020

In the elections of 2020, Democrats in the House of Representatives lost seats but retained their majority party status with 222 seats. Republicans in turn gained seats but remained the minority party with 213 seats.

After the 2020 election, Senate Democrats held 48 seats but counted two Independent Party members, Bernie Sanders (Vermont) and Angus King (Maine) as voting with the Democratic Caucus. With the Republican Party holding the other 50 seats, Democratic Vice President Kamala Harris became especially important as holding the tie breaking vote. The constitution allows for a vice president to preside over the Senate in the case of a tie vote.

The January 6, 2021, Insurrection

January 6, 2021, was the date set by law for the Congress—Senate and House of Representatives—to certify the votes cast in the Electoral College based on the presidential election of November 3, 2020. The vice president presides over this process and announces the results. On the morning of January 6, however, President Trump conducted a rally of thousands of his followers near the White House. He said "We will never give up. We will never concede." He urged them to march to the United States Capitol building. He also told Vice President Mike Pence to go to the Capitol but to reject Biden's win and to send the votes back to the states. Pence, however, released a letter saying that he did not have the unilateral authority (to act by himself) to do what President Trump wanted.

Many rally-goers, however, whipped into a frenzy, stormed the Capitol building, breaking through police barriers. As they entered the building around 2:00 pm, Secret Service agents escorted Vice President Pence and Speaker Nancy Pelosi to secure locations. As the afternoon went on, protesters carrying Confederate, Trump, and American flags swarmed through the Capitol and private offices, destroying anything in their way. Members of Congress and their staffs hid in offices, in the House itself, and anywhere they could secure. Rioters became increasingly dangerous and destructive. Chants of planned violence against government officials could be heard.

Although President Trump was apparently watching on television, he did not go on TV himself but tweeted twice "remain peaceful" and later, "we love you, go home in peace." Biden did speak on television, stating that what was occurring was an "assault on the people's business," accusing Trump of incitement, and calling on him to demand an end to the insurrection.

By 6:00 pm, police were clearing the Capitol of rioters. Later in the evening, the vice president and members of Congress returned to work in the ransacked building and declared Biden the president-elect. The incident, however, had led to several deaths: one rioter shot by Capitol police, one rioter dead of a heart attack, one crushed to death by the mob, and one police officer dead from injuries. Two police officers died by suicide in the immediate aftermath of the event. Additionally, there was more than $1.5 million in damage done. Hundreds of people were arrested on criminal charges, and the FBI called the event an act of domestic terrorism. By early summer, a House Select Committee started a formal investigation into the attack.

Impeachments of Donald J. Trump

President Trump was the first U.S. president to be impeached twice. Remember that impeachment is the process of the House of Representatives making a charge of wrongdoing by the president or other high federal officials. If the president is impeached by the House, then the trial occurs in the Senate. Only if the president is found guilty by the Senate, is the president removed from office. This type of removal has never happened in U.S. history.

President Trump's first impeachment occurred in the summer of 2019. Sources claimed that in a phone call to President Volodymyr Zelensky of Ukraine on July 25, 2019, President Trump asked Zelensky to investigate Joe Biden and his son in exchange for receiving U.S. foreign aid to support Ukraine's war against Russian-backed separatists. In September 2019, Speaker of the House Nancy Pelosi initiated an impeachment inquiry based on this information. At the end of October, the House voted 232 to 196 along partisan lines to establish procedures for public hearings. By December, the House approved two charges of impeachment on the grounds of abuse of power and obstruction of Congress. In the Senate trial in February 2020, President Trump was acquitted (found not guilty) by a vote of 52–48 on abuse of power and 53–47 on obstruction. Both votes had bipartisan support with a few Republicans voting against President Trump.

The second impeachment occurred after President Trump lost the election in November 2020. He and his followers and most of the Republican Party claimed that the election had been rigged in favor of Joe Biden and the Democrats. Trump's supporters called the election "The Big Steal," while Trump's opponents called his claim "The Big Lie." President Trump refused to concede the election and accept the results of the vote tallies. On January 6, 2021, a joint session of Congress was scheduled to meet to officially receive the results of each state's electoral vote. Supporters of Trump who had attended his rally that morning near the White House stormed the Capitol and disrupted proceedings. As a result, a charge of incitement to insurrection was filed against Trump. The House voted to impeach, with the support of all Democrats and 10 Republicans. In February 2021, the Senate trial ended with 57 votes against Trump, which included all 48 Democrats, two Independents, and 7 Republicans. Since a two-thirds majority is required for conviction, Trump was acquitted again.

Unifying Themes
Power, Authority, Governance Origins, Uses and Abuses of Power

Why did some members of Congress accuse President Trump of abuse of power? Identify two other U.S. presidents who were impeached. What were their trial results? What president resigned before he could be impeached?

The Joseph R. Biden Administration

When President Joe Biden was inaugurated on January 20, 2021, with Kamala Harris as his Vice President, it was just two weeks after the January 6 Insurrection. Parts of the United States Capitol building had not been restored, heavy fencing was in place, and security was especially high. Although outgoing President Donald Trump did not attend the ceremony, outgoing Vice President Mike Pence did attend. The country was in the midst of the pandemic and the population was very divided on several major issues.

Domestic Issues

President Biden faced challenging domestic issues when he took office. The COVID-19 pandemic continued to strain the U.S. economy and its people, while the issues of infrastructure and immigration had taken on a new urgency.

The COVID-19 Pandemic The development of a vaccine to prevent COVID-19 was a major goal of the Trump administration. Approval of the first vaccine was granted on an emergency basis shortly before the end of Trump's term. On President Biden's first day in office, less than 1% of the population was fully vaccinated. The new president set high goals for vaccinations for his first 100 days in office. By that time, more than 50% of Americans had at least one shot. A little more than a year later, 63% of eligible Americans were fully vaccinated. More than 526 million doses were administered to Americans free of charge.

President Biden's American Rescue Plan, costing over one trillion dollars, was passed on March 11, 2021. It is one of the largest relief measures in United States history. It included free vaccines and direct financial aid to businesses, individuals, health care facilities, and educational institutions of all levels. Still, the United States has lagged behind other nations for the percentage of citizens vaccinated. This is largely blamed on the misinformation campaign by right-wing politicians.

Infrastructure One of President Biden's primary goals was to convince Congress to pass the Infrastructure Investment and Jobs Act. It was passed with limited partisan support in November 2021 with over one trillion dollars designated for roads, bridges, trains, airports, broadband internet access, and the replacement of every lead pipe in the United States.

The Economy The pandemic has been a major cause of economic concerns for the Biden presidency. In January 2021, unemployment was 6.3%—an undesirable number, but better than it had been in 2020. By December 2021, unemployment had improved to 3.9% and there was a 2.4% increase in wages. Simultaneously, the rate of inflation crept higher, to reach a 40 year high by late winter 2021. During 2020 and 2021, millions of Americans either lost their jobs, began to work full or part time from home, or resigned from their jobs altogether. Some economists called this the Great Resignation. The availability of consumer goods during this time varied greatly as a decreased work force could not keep up with the limits of the supply chain.

Unifying Themes
Economic Systems

During the spring of 2022, Americans continue to experience a high rate of inflation as evidenced by high prices for gasoline, groceries, and rent.

Immigration On his first day in office, President Biden submitted a new immigration act, the Citizenship Act of 2021. It has not become law. His additional goal was to rescind (cancel) several Trump policies related to immigration. These included the resumption of the Diversity/Lottery visa program, prohibiting limits on legal immigration, continuing family-based immigration, and ending the Trump "wait in Mexico" plan. That plan was briefly stopped but restarted due to a Supreme Court decision supporting the plan.

Supreme Court Appointment As a candidate, President Biden had promised that he would appoint an African American woman to the Supreme Court if there should be an opening. When Justice Stephen Breyer announced his retirement effective at the end of the Supreme Court's 2021–2022 session, President Biden fulfilled his promise. At the end of February, he nominated Ketanji Brown Jackson to fill the seat. Since the Supreme Court first met, there have been 115 judges appointed, and 108 have been white men. When confirmed to the Court by the Senate on April 7, 2022, Judge Jackson became the third African American and the first female African American appointed to the highest court in the United States.

Foreign Issues

President Biden campaigned on a plan to return the United States to a more active leadership position in the world. One of his first acts as president was to begin the process of returning the United States to membership in the Paris Climate Agreement. He also met with NATO leaders to assure them that the United States was anxious to return to a working relationship with that organization.

Afghanistan When President Biden took office, Americans had been fighting in Afghanistan since shortly after the terrorist attacks of September 11, 2001. For a time during President Obama's administration, that number was as high as 100,000. A major goal of President Biden was to end the war there and to bring the remaining American troops home. In August 2021, the withdrawal of American troops began with little or no advance public warning. Over 130,000 people were airlifted out of Kabul, the capital, over a few days. The process was not smooth or easily completed, causing severe criticism. Americans and many Afghans who had worked with Americans were airlifted to safe countries in the Middle East, Europe, and the United States—one of the largest evacuations in American history. During this event, an ISIS attack killed 13 American service people and 170 Afghans. American leadership had overestimated the strength of the Afghan army to take over and underestimated the organization and leadership of the Taliban who seized control of the country.

Ukraine When the government of the Soviet Union collapsed in 1991, Ukraine was one of its fifteen republics. It declared its independence in 1991 and formed its own government. Remember that the cause of President Trump's first impeachment in 2019 was the accusation that he asked President Zelensky of Ukraine to do him a political favor in order to receive previously promised military aid during Ukraine's struggle with Russian-backed separatists. In late February 2022, Russia, under the direction of President Vladimir Putin, attacked Ukraine. President Zelensky and Ukraine's army has fought back while thousands of refugees have fled to bordering countries. The United States has joined European nations in placing strong economic sanctions (limits) on Russia in hope of ending the war. Military and humanitarian assistance has also been given.

Unifying Themes
Civic Ideals and Practices

Identify the first two African American Supreme Court Justices. Identify the first female justice who was appointed and the five other female justices who followed. Of the justices you have identified, who are still serving on the court? What does this tell you about how long it has taken to diversify the Supreme Court?

International Terrorism

Although the attacks on New York and Washington, D.C., on September 11, 2001, were aimed at one nation, they mobilized government leaders all over the world. The attacks showed how terrorism has expanded its global reach and has affected the security and stability of all nations. As the war in Iraq fueled anti-Western attitudes in 2004, terrorists caused almost 200 deaths in a railroad bombing in Spain. Other areas of the world heightened their efforts at limiting the ability of terrorist groups to share information, money, weapons, and personnel. Random terrorist attacks have occurred in France, Great Britain, Germany and the Netherlands in recent years all involving loss of lives.

Security Concerns

The global increase in acts of terrorism, especially the attacks on the Pentagon and the World Trade towers, made some Americans fear that they were not safe. In response, the government took a number of measures to help ensure national security. Airport security was tightened, as was security at bridges, tunnels, nuclear power plants, courthouses, and other vulnerable places.

Scarce Energy Sources

Scarce oil supplies have led scientists to research **alternative energy sources,** such as solar power and wind power. There are already communities in New York State that are utilizing and benefiting from wind power. Other communities in the state as well as in the nation are giving serious study to the possibility of developing this natural resource. Recently, horizontal hydraulic fracturing/hydrofracking (fracking), drilling with millions of gallons of pressurized water for natural gas, has become very controversial in New York State. Nuclear power is being used in some parts of the world. However, the hazards associated with nuclear energy, such as the storage of nuclear waste, are also controversial.

Computer Usage

The prevalent use of computers in American homes and businesses since the 1980s has revolutionized record keeping and the storage of information. Advocates of computers praise their ability to process and store large volumes of information. Critics charge that computers have increased the chances for the invasion of privacy as people access private records without permission, particularly as **Internet** use becomes increasingly widespread. The introduction of automation and computers is considered a cause of job losses in manufacturing industries. Social media, such as Facebook®, now connects millions of people globally. The speed at which videos, such as those posted to YouTube®, can be shared with countless numbers of worldwide viewers has introduced the new phrase "going viral" into the language of pop culture.

New Lifestyles and Longer Life Spans

American attitudes toward family size and divorce have changed since the 1950s. Average family size has declined. After years of expansion, many school districts throughout the nation, including in New York, experienced declining school enrollments in the 1980s. Divorce rates first rose and then remained constant. This created the largest number of single-parent households in the nation's history.

At the same time, health care improvements resulting from new technologies, such as laser surgery and organ transplants, have increased average life spans. This has increased the number of older Americans, who in recent years have organized to protect their rights and improve their lives. Social scientists use the term "the graying of America" to describe the aging of the nation's population.

Unifying Themes
Technology

Bill Gates, as founder of Microsoft, became one of the world's richest individuals. Huge fortunes have been made and lost in the computer industry in the last fifteen years. Bill and his wife Melinda administer the charitable Gates Foundation that has given millions of dollars in aid for education and medical research, among other causes.

- Identify three factors that might limit a person's use of technology.

- Why is access to technology important in today's world?

Preparing for the Regents

- How have Americans' lifestyles been influenced by each of the following since the end of World War II?
  – average family size
  – longer life spans
  – expansion of public
  – education

Expansion of Public Education

Access to free public education has helped many Americans improve their standard of living. As individuals complete higher levels of education, they have the chance to secure better-paying jobs and more desirable housing. Thus, education helps further social mobility.

Increasingly Diverse Population

If current trends continue, it is projected that the population of the United States will grow increasingly diverse over the next half century. More of the newest immigrants to the United States come from Asian and Latin American countries, compared with earlier waves of immigration that came from Europe.

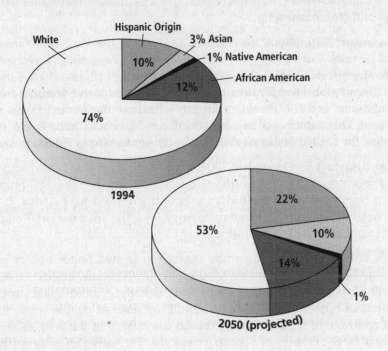

The Changing Ethnic Composition of the United States

White — 74%
Hispanic Origin — 10%
3% Asian
1% Native American
African American — 12%

1994

53%
22%
10%
14%
1%

2050 (projected)

Preparing for the Regents

Stimulus-Based Questions: Pie Graph

Use the chart to answer the following questions.

- Between 1994 and 2050, which group of Americans is expected to grow most rapidly?
- Which group is expected to be a smaller proportion of the U.S. population?
- Which group is expected to remain the same proportion of the overall population?
- What, if any, effect will this have on the nation?

Helping the Homeless

Not everyone enjoyed the prosperity of the post–World War II years. President Johnson's Great Society programs in the 1960s tried to reduce poverty in the United States. However, cuts in social programs and high unemployment have caused a significant rise in the number of Americans living below the poverty line. Local communities and private charitable organizations have tried to provide relief, but homelessness remains a serious concern.

Environmental Concerns

Because of increased interdependence, an environmental problem in one nation frequently raises global concerns. One example is the destruction of the Brazilian tropical rain forests, which some scientists believe has contributed to global climate change.

Environmental Activism Many groups have organized to reduce and clean up pollution on the land, in the water, and in the air. Other activist groups work to save endangered species of animals. Recycling efforts have been organized to reuse paper, glass, plastic, and aluminum. Community organizers have

Preparing for the Regents

Every ten years since 1790 the United States has conducted a census to count all citizens. In 2010, over 134 million forms were sent at the cost of over $14,000,000.

- Given the topics covered in this lesson and elsewhere in this text, what kinds of decisions might the government make based on the statistics it learns from the census?
- The 2010 census indicated that New York State has lost population again since the last census. New York lost two congressional seats and is being redistricted. Will this change impact representation in the Senate?

Unifying Themes
The Environment

The concept of a global community means that the United States cannot isolate itself from problems in other countries. Population growth in developing nations and environmental concerns in nations with essential ecosystems are two issues that affect the entire world.

- Why should the destruction of tropical rain forests be a concern to people in other nations, including the United States?

Social Studies Practices
Gathering Evidence

List two ways that environmental activists have raised public awareness about environmental issues.

1.

2.

Unifying Themes
The Environment

The winter of 2011–2012 brought record breaking warmth. The tornado season of 2013 began with a level 5 tornado (the highest level that is currently recognized) in Moore, Oklahoma, killing 24 people. January through May 2014 was the coldest year in American recorded history. The winter of 2014–15 was colder and snowier in the Northeast than in previous recent winters, but the following winters were milder than normal.

- How do these fluctuations in weather cause problems?

opposed plans to convert vacant lands into dumpsites. Communities have studied the effects of industrial pollution on the groundwater that people drink. In response to public pressure, the federal government has enacted laws requiring automobile manufacturers to put antipollution devices on their cars.

Since the first **Earth Day** celebration in 1970, the American people, along with the rest of the world, have begun to realize their obligation to protect the environment for future generations. The phrase "going green" has come to mean the conscious efforts of Americans to conserve energy in all aspects of daily life. Presidents Clinton, Bush (43), and Obama have all directed efforts within the White House itself to increase energy efficiency. Efforts that extend from the First Family to all American families include activities such as recycling, installation of energy efficient light bulbs, the use of solar power where possible, appropriate conservation of heating and cooling sources, and other individual initiatives. In the 2017 Congress, some members advocated a Green Revolution to focus attention on issues like **climate change** and **global warming.**

In November 2016, about 150 countries agreed to the Paris Agreement of the United Nations Convention on Climate Change. These nations recognized the need to strengthen the global response to the threat of climate change by making efforts to limit global temperature rise. The goal is to limit and decrease greenhouse gas emissions. In 2017, President Trump withdrew the United States from the agreement. This withdrawal became effective in November 2020. Under President Joe Biden, the United States rejoined the Paris Agreement in February 2021.

Natural Disasters In December 2004, a tsunami, or a giant destructive wave, caused more than 200,000 deaths and left as many as 5,000,000 homeless in parts of Southeast Asia, the Indian subcontinent, and East Africa. It was the worst natural disaster in modern history, and the international community joined together in a massive outpouring of financial aid.

In 2005, one of the worst hurricane seasons in United States history occurred. Hurricane Katrina caused major flooding in New Orleans, Louisiana, and along the Gulf Coast states of Mississippi and Alabama. About 2,000 people died, thousands of homes were destroyed, and thousands of people were evacuated. Media coverage of the hurricane exposed the misery in the area, especially the poverty of large numbers of African Americans. The Bush (43) administration had to defend the slow and inadequate response of the federal government led by FEMA, the Federal Emergency Management Agency. In November 2007, Congress passed the $23 billion Water Resource Bill, with $3.5 billion specifically earmarked for areas destroyed by Hurricane Katrina.

In April 2010, a fire and explosion at a British Petroleum oil rig in the Gulf of Mexico off the coast of Louisiana cost eleven workers their lives and began the worst oil spill disaster in United States history. The spill ultimately impacted the coastline and wildlife of Louisiana, Mississippi, Alabama, and parts of Florida. Environmental damage to wetlands, beaches, and wildlife was catastrophic.

The largest hurricane since Katrina occurred in the fall of 2012. Superstorm Sandy caused the deaths of 285 people in seven countries from the Caribbean to Canada and damages were estimated at over $50 billion dollars. At the worst of the storm,

Aerial view of the destruction in Breezy Point, New York, as a result of Superstorm Sandy in 2012

there were an estimated 7,500,000 people without power. Particularly hard hit were the New Jersey and New York shorelines where thousands of homes were damaged and many just washed into the ocean. Congress was criticized for taking weeks to provide federal assistance.

For twenty years, the United States has had a fire assistance agreement with Australia and New Zealand. In 2018, those countries sent assistance to contain wildfires that were out of control in Northern California. Between 2019 and 2020, parts of Australia were devastated by wildfires that caused 34 deaths and destroyed 72,000 square miles of land and 5,900 buildings. The fires caused the deaths of an estimated one billion animals. The United States sent experts in wildfire control, environmental issues, forest restoration, disaster management, and wildlife preservation to assist.

Base your answers to questions 1 through 3 on the speech below and on your knowledge of social studies.

> I've heard some folks try to dodge the evidence by saying they're not scientists; that we don't have enough information to act. Well, I'm not a scientist, either. But you know what, I know a lot of really good scientists at NASA, and at NOAA, and at our major universities. And the best scientists in the world are all telling us that our activities are changing the climate, and if we don't act forcefully, we'll continue to see rising oceans, longer, hotter heat waves, dangerous droughts and floods, and massive disruptions that can trigger greater migration and conflict and hunger around the globe. The Pentagon says that climate change poses immediate risks to our national security. We should act like it. . . .
>
> I am determined to make sure that American leadership drives international action. In Beijing, we made a historic announcement: the United States will double the pace at which we cut carbon pollution. And China committed, for the first time, to limiting their emissions. And because the world's two largest economies came together, other nations are now stepping up, and offering hope that this year the world will finally reach an agreement to protect the one planet we've got.

Source: President Barack Obama, State of the Union, January 21, 2015

1 What change in history is illustrated by this speech?

(1) The threats associated with climate change have become a major concern for our country.

(2) The president is now required to provide scientific evidence for any environmental policy changes.

(3) The United States is resuming a leadership role in the world for the first time since the Cold War.

(4) The differing views on how to deal with environmental problems have led to conflict among nations.

2 President Obama acted on this speech when he

(1) authorized the mission to kill Osama Bin Laden

(2) repealed the policy of "don't ask; don't tell"

(3) authorized the United States to join the Paris Agreement

(4) called on Congress to pass the Affordable Care Act

3 How does President Obama's philosophy on the issue described in this document differ from President Trump's philosophy?

(1) President Trump did not see climate change as a national security threat to the United States.

(2) President Trump argued for more international cooperation to combat climate change.

(3) President Trump did not experience any major climate events during his presidency.

(4) President Trump drastically increased funding to the EPA and NOAA.

Base your answers to questions 4 and 5 on the passage below and on your knowledge of social studies.

> Apple has become one of the best-known, most admired and most imitated companies on earth, in part through an unrelenting mastery of global operations. . . .
>
> Apple employs 43,000 people in the United States and 20,000 overseas, a small fraction of the more than 400,000 U.S. workers at General Motors in the 1950s, or the hundreds of thousands at General Electric in the 1980s. Many more people work for Apple's contractors: An additional 700,000 people engineer, build and assemble ipads, iphones and Apple's other products. But almost none of them work in the United States. Instead, they work for foreign companies in Asia, Europe and elsewhere, at factories that almost every electronics designer relies upon to build their wares.

Source: Charles Duhigg and Keith Bradsher, "In its early days, Apple usually didn't look beyond its own tech backyard for manufacturing solutions. But that changed." *The Mercury News*, 2012

4 This article is most closely associated with

(1) the War on Terror

(2) the Patriot Act

(3) globalization

(4) immigration

5 Which claim is supported by this article?

(1) Multinational corporations regularly violate child labor laws.

(2) Multinational corporations often rely on foreign workers to produce goods.

(3) Multinational corporations have benefited from the U.S.–China trade rivalry.

(4) Multinational corporations believe the U.S. education system has fallen behind.

Base your answers to questions 6 and 7 on the speech below and on your knowledge of social studies.

> Just two hours ago, allied air forces began an attack on military targets in Iraq and Kuwait. . . . This conflict started August 2 when the dictator of Iraq invaded a small and helpless neighbor. Kuwait, a member of the Arab League and a member of the United Nations, was crushed, its people brutalized. Five months ago, Saddam Hussein started this cruel war against Kuwait. Tonight the battle has been joined. This military action, taken in accord with United Nations resolutions and with the consent of the United States Congress, follows months of constant and virtually endless diplomatic activity. . . . Our objectives are clear: Saddam Hussein's forces will leave Kuwait, the legitimate government of Kuwait will be restored to its rightful place, and Kuwait will once again be free. Iraq will eventually comply with all relevant United Nations resolutions, and then . . . it is our hope that Iraq will live as a peaceful and cooperative member of the family of nations.

Source: President George H. W. Bush, Address to the Nation, January 16, 1991

6 Which claim is best supported by this speech?

(1) By 1991, the United States had returned to an isolationist foreign policy.

(2) By 1991, the United States had become a supporter of international collective security.

(3) By 1991, the United States was heavily involved in the War on Terror.

(4) By 1991, the United States had ended its membership in the United Nations.

7 President George W. Bush justified American military action against Iraq in 2003 when he

(1) alleged that Saddam Hussein was developing weapons of mass destruction

(2) claimed that Saddam Hussein was the mastermind behind the September 11th attacks

(3) argued that the United States must protect the sovereignty of its ally Kuwait

(4) pledged support for Iran in the Iran-Iraq War

Base your answers to questions 8 and 9 on the graph below and on your knowledge of social studies.

Unemployment Rate of Select Countries, 2007–2010

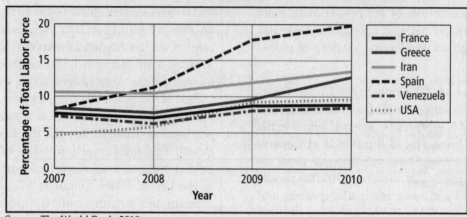

Source: The World Bank, 2019

8 Using the data on this graph, what claim can be made about the recession of the late 2000s?

(1) It affected the Chinese labor force most deeply as it has the largest market.

(2) It affected the United States the least due its multiple international trade agreements.

(3) It affected countries all over the world because of globalization.

(4) It affected more nations with service-based economies than industrialized-based economies.

9 The actions taken by President Obama's administration to deal with the problem illustrated in the graph was similar to

(1) President Roosevelt's policies of government spending during the Great Depression.

(2) President Harding's "return to normalcy" policies following World War I.

(3) President Hoover's laissez-faire policies following the 1929 stock market crash.

(4) President Reagan's "Reaganomics" policies to reduce inflation in the 1980s.

Base your answers to questions 10 and 11 on the timeline below and on your knowledge of social studies.

October 7, 2001
United States invades Afghanistan (Operation Enduring Freedom)

September 11, 2012
U.S. Ambassador to Libya is killed in a terrorist attack in Benghazi

April 7, 2017
United States launches missile strike against Syrian airbase in response to the use of chemical weapons

2000   2004   2008   2012   2016   2020

March 19, 2003
United States launches Operation Iraqi Freedom

June 18, 2004
United States launch a drone strike against al Qaeda in Pakistan

August 8, 2014
United States begins airstrikes against ISIS targets in Iraq

Source: "Instances of Use of United States Armed Forces Abroad, 1798–2018," Congressional Research Services, 2018

10   Which event is the most likely cause to the events shown on this timeline?

(1) September 11th terrorist attacks

(2) Soviet invasion of Afghanistan

(3) Kim Jong Un's testing of ballistic missiles

(4) Human rights abuses in Kosovo

11   Which claim is supported by this timeline?

(1) The United States has returned to a policy of isolation in the 21st century.

(2) The United States relies mostly on drone strikes as its main method of combat.

(3) The United States military has been active in the Middle East in the 21st century.

(4) The United States no longer has a military presence in Europe due to the ending of the Cold War.

Short Essay Questions

Task: Read and analyze the following documents, applying your social studies knowledge and skills to write a short essay of two or three paragraphs in which you:

- Describe the historical context surrounding these documents
- Identify and explain the *relationship* between the events and/or ideas found in these documents (Cause and Effect, *or* Similarity/Difference, *or* Turning Point)

In developing your short essay answer of two or three paragraphs, be sure to keep these explanations in mind:

Describe means "to illustrate something in words or tell about it"

Historical Context refers to "the relevant historical circumstances surrounding or connecting the events, ideas, or developments in these documents"

Identify means "to put a name to or to name"

Explain means "to make plain or understandable; to give reasons for or causes of; to show the logical development or relationship of"

Types of Relationships:

Cause refers to "something that contributes to the occurrence of an event, the rise of an idea, or the bringing about of a development"

Effect refers to "what happens as a consequence (result, impact, outcome) of an event, an idea, or a development"

Similarity tells how "something is alike or the same as something else"

Difference tells how "something is not alike or not the same as something else"

Turning Point is "a major event, idea, or historical development that brings about significant change. It can be local, regional, national, or global"

Document 1

With more than a billion people, China is the largest new market in the world. Our administration has negotiated an agreement which will open China's markets to American products made on American soil, everything from corn to chemicals to computers. . . .

We will be exporting, however, more than our products. By this agreement, we will also export more of one of our most cherished values, economic freedom. Bringing China into the WTO [World Trade Organization] and normalizing trade will strengthen those who fight for the environment, for labor standards, for human rights, for the rule of law. For China, this agreement will clearly increase the benefits of cooperation, and the costs of confrontation. . . .

Though China may be changing, we all know it remains a one-party state, that it still denies people the rights of free speech and religious expression. We know that trade alone will not bring freedom to China or peace to the world. That's why permanent normal trade relations must also signal our commitment to permanent change.

America will keep pressing to protect our security and to advance our values. The vote today is a big boost to both efforts. For the more China liberalizes its economy, the more it will liberate the potential of its people—to work without restraint; to live without fear. . . .

This is a good day for America. And 10 years from now we will look back on this day and be glad we did this. We will see that we have given ourselves a chance to build the kind of future we want. This is a good economic agreement because we get all the economic benefits of lower tariffs and lowered access to the Chinese market.

Source: President Bill Clinton, Remarks on Passage of Permanent Normal Trade Relations With China, May 24, 2000

Document 2

My great friendship with President Xi of China and our country's relationship with China are both very important to me. Trade between our nations, however, has been very unfair, for a very long time. This situation is no longer sustainable. China has, for example, long been engaging in several unfair practices related to the acquisition of American intellectual property and technology. These practices . . . harm our economic and national security and deepen our already massive trade imbalance with China.

In light of China's theft of intellectual property and technology and its other unfair trade practices, the United States will implement a 25 percent tariff on $50 billion of goods from China that contain industrially significant technologies. This includes goods related to China's *Made in China 2025* strategic plan to dominate the emerging high-technology industries that will drive future economic growth for China, but hurt economic growth for the United States and many other countries. The United States can no longer tolerate losing our technology and intellectual property through unfair economic practices.

These tariffs are essential to preventing further unfair transfers of American technology and intellectual property to China, which will protect American jobs. In addition, they will serve as an initial step toward bringing balance to the trade relationship between the United States and China.

Source: President Donald Trump, Statement by the President Regarding Trade With China, June 15, 2018

Document Analysis for Civic Literacy Essay

Historical Context: Right to Privacy

Throughout U.S. history, many constitutional and civic issues have been debated by Americans. These debates have resulted in efforts to address these issues. One of these constitutional and civic issues is the right to privacy.

Task: Read and analyze the documents. Using information from the documents and your knowledge of United States history, write an essay in which you

- Describe the historical circumstances surrounding this constitutional or civic issue
- Explain efforts to address this issue by individuals, groups, and/or governments
- Discuss the extent to which these efforts were successful

Document 1

On September the 11th, enemies of freedom committed an act of war against our country. Americans have known wars—but for the past 136 years, they have been wars on foreign soil, except for one Sunday in 1941. Americans have known the casualties of war—but not at the center of a great city on a peaceful morning. Americans have known surprise attacks—but never before on thousands of civilians. All of this was brought upon us in a single day—and night fell on a different world, a world where freedom itself is under attack. . . .

Tonight, we face new and sudden national challenges. We will come together to improve air safety, to dramatically expand the number of air marshals on domestic flights, and take new measures to prevent hijacking. We will come together to promote stability and keep our airlines flying, with direct assistance during this emergency.

We will come together to give law enforcement the additional tools it needs to track down terror here at home. We will come together to strengthen our intelligence capabilities to know the plans of terrorists before they act, and find them before they strike.

Source: President George W. Bush, Address to the Joint Session of the 107th Congress, September 20, 2001

1. How does President Bush intend to deal with the national security challenge of terrorism?

Document 2

The United States PATRIOT Act was well intentioned, Mr. Chairman, especially during a time of uncertainty and panic. However, now we have had a chance to step back and examine it objectively. . . . While I agree with some of the new powers granted to the Federal law enforcement authorities that may be . . necessary, many more are unjustified and are dangerously undermining our civil liberties. . . .

One provision, section 213, allows delayed notification of the execution of a search warrant. It authorizes no-knock searches of private residences, our homes, either physically or electronically. . . . These ``sneak and peek" searches give the government the power to repeatedly search a private residence without informing the residents that he or she is the target of an investigation. Not only does this provision allow the seizure of personal property and business records without notification, but it also opens the door to nationwide search warrants and allows the CIA and the NSA to operate domestically.

American citizens, whom the government has pledged to protect from terrorist activities, now find themselves the victims of the very weapon designed to uproot their enemies.

Source: Representative C.L. "Butch" Otter (R-ID), Congressional Record, p. H7289, July 22, 2003

2. According to Representative Otter, what constitutional right is being compromised by the USA Patriot Act?

The Preamble states the broad purposes the Constitution is intended to serve—to establish a government that provides for greater cooperation among the States, ensures justice and peace, provides for defense against foreign enemies, promotes the general well-being of the people, and secures liberty now and in the future. The phrase We the People emphasizes the twin concepts of popular sovereignty and representative government.

Legislative Department

Section 1. Legislative power; Congress

Congress, the nation's lawmaking body, is bicameral in form; that is, it is composed of two houses: the Senate and the House of Representatives. The Framers of the Constitution purposely separated the lawmaking power from the power to enforce the laws (Article II, the Executive Branch) and the power to interpret them (Article III, the Judicial Branch). This system of separation of powers is supplemented by a system of checks and balances; that is, the several provisions the Constitution gives to each of the three branches various powers with which it may restrain the actions of the other two branches.

Section 2. House of Representatives

Clause 1. Election Electors means voters. Members of the House of Representatives are elected every two years. Each State must permit the same persons to vote for United States representatives as it permits to vote for the members of the larger house of its own legislature. The 17th Amendment (1913) extends this requirement to the qualification of voters for United States senators.

Clause 2. Qualifications A member of the House of Representatives must be at least 25 years old, an American citizen for seven years, and a resident of the State he or she represents. In addition, political custom requires that a representative also reside in the district from which he or she is elected.

Clause 3. Apportionment The number of representatives each State is entitled to is based on its population, which is counted every 10 years in the census. Congress reapportions the seats among the States after each census. In the Reapportionment Act of 1929, Congress fixed the permanent size of the House at 435 members with each State having at least one representative. Today there is one House seat for approximately every 700,000 persons in the population. The words "three-fifths of all other persons" referred to slaves and reflected the Three-Fifths Compromise reached by the Framers at Philadelphia in 1787; the phrase was made obsolete, was in effect repealed, by the 13th Amendment in 1865.

The gray words indicate portions of the Constitution altered by subsequent amendments to the document.

Clause 4. Vacancies The executive authority refers to the governor of a State. If a member leaves office or dies before the expiration of his or her term, the governor is to call a special election to fill the vacancy.

United States Constitution

PREAMBLE

We the People of the United States, in Order to form a more perfect Union, establish Justice, insure domestic Tranquility, provide for the common defence, promote the general Welfare, and secure the Blessings of Liberty to ourselves and our Posterity, do ordain and establish this Constitution for the United States of America.

Article I

Section 1.

All legislative Powers herein granted shall be vested in a Congress of the United States, which shall consist of a Senate and House of Representatives.

Section 2.

▶ 1. The House of Representatives shall be composed of Members chosen every second Year by the People of the several States, and the Electors in each State shall have the Qualifications requisite for Electors of the most numerous Branch of the State Legislature.

▶ 2. No Person shall be a Representative who shall not have attained to the age of twenty-five Years, and been seven Years a Citizen of the United States, and who shall not, when elected, be an Inhabitant of that State in which he shall be chosen.

▶ 3. Representatives and direct Taxes* shall be apportioned among the several States which may be included within this Union, according to their respective Numbers, which shall be determined by adding to the whole Number of free Persons, including those bound to Service for a Term of Years and excluding Indians not taxed, three fifths of all other Persons. The actual Enumeration shall be made within three Years after the first Meeting of the Congress of the United States, and within every subsequent term of ten Years, in such Manner as they shall by Law direct. The Number of Representatives shall not exceed one for every thirty Thousand, but each State shall have at Least one Representative; and, until such enumeration shall be made, the State of New Hampshire shall be entitled to choose three, Massachusetts eight, Rhode Island and Providence Plantations one, Connecticut five, New York six, New Jersey four, Pennsylvania eight, Delaware one, Maryland six, Virginia ten, North Carolina five, South Carolina five, and Georgia three.

▶ 4. When vacancies happen in the Representation from any State, the Executive Authority thereof shall issue Writs of Election to fill such Vacancies.

5. The House of Representatives shall choose their Speaker and other Officers; and shall have the sole Power of Impeachment.

Section 3.

1. The Senate of the United States shall be composed of two Senators from each State chosen by the Legislature thereof for six Years; and each Senator shall have one Vote.

2. Immediately after they shall be assembled in Consequences of the first Election, they shall be divided, as equally as may be, into three Classes. The Seats of the Senators of the first Class shall be vacated at the Expiration of the second Year; of the second Class, at the Expiration of the fourth Year; and of the third Class, at the Expiration of the sixth Year; so that one-third may be chosen every second Year; and if Vacancies happen by Resignation, or otherwise, during the Recess of the Legislature of any State, the Executive thereof may make temporary Appointments until the next Meeting of the Legislature, which shall then fill such Vacancies.

3. No Person shall be a Senator who shall not have attained to the Age of thirty Years, and been nine Years a Citizen of the United States, and who shall not, when elected, be an Inhabitant of that State for which he shall be chosen.

4. The Vice President of the United States shall be President of the Senate but shall have no Vote, unless they be equally divided.

5. The Senate shall choose their other Officers, and also a President pro tempore, in the Absence of the Vice President, or when he shall exercise the Office of President of the United States.

6. The Senate shall have the sole Power to try all Impeachments. When sitting for that Purpose, they shall be on Oath or Affirmation. When the President of the United States is tried, the Chief Justice shall preside: And no Person shall be convicted without the Concurrence of two thirds of the Members present.

7. Judgment in Cases of Impeachment shall not extend further than to removal from Office, and disqualification to hold and enjoy any Office of honor, Trust, or Profit under the United States: but the Party convicted shall nevertheless be liable and subject to Indictment, Trial, Judgment and Punishment, according to Law.

▶ **Clause 5. Officers; impeachment** The House elects a Speaker, customarily chosen from the majority party in t House. Impeachment means accusation. The House has the exclusive power to impeach, or accuse, civil officers the Senate (Article I, Section 3, Clause 6) has the exclusi power to try those impeached by the House.

Section 3. Senate

▶ **Clause 1. Composition, election, term** Each State has two senators. Each serves for six years and has one vote. Originally, senators were not elected directly by the peopl but by each State's legislature. The 17th Amendment, ad in 1913, provides for the popular election of senators.

▶ **Clause 2. Classification** The senators elected in 1788 were divided into three groups so that the Senate could become a "continuing body." One-third of the Senate's seats are up for election every two years.

The 17th Amendment provides that a Senate vacancy is to be filled at a special election called by the governor State law may also permit the governor to appoint a successor to serve until that election is held.

▶ **Clause 3. Qualifications** A senator must be at least 30 years old, a citizen for at least nine years, and must live the State from which elected.

▶ **Clause 4. Presiding officer** The Vice President presides over the Senate, but may vote only to break a tie.

▶ **Clause 5. Other officers** The Senate chooses its own officers, including a president pro tempore to preside wh the Vice President is not there.

▶ **Clause 6. Impeachment trials** The Senate conducts the trials of those officials impeached by the House. The Vice President presides unless the President is on trial, in which c the Chief Justice of the United States does so. A conviction requires the votes of two-thirds of the senators present.

No President has ever been convicted. In 1868 the House voted eleven articles of impeachment against President And Johnson, but the Senate fell one vote short of convicting hin In 1974 President Richard M. Nixon resigned the presidency in the face of almost certain impeachment by the House. Th House brought two articles of impeachment against Preside Bill Clinton in late 1998. Neither charge was supported by e a simple majority vote in the Senate, on February 12, 1999.

▶ **Clause 7. Penalty on conviction** The punishment of an official convicted in an impeachment case has always be removal from office. The Senate can also bar a convicte person from ever holding any federal office, but it is not required to do so. A convicted person can also be tried punished in a regular court for any crime involved in the impeachment case.

Section 4. Elections and Meetings

Clause 1. Election In 1842 Congress required that representatives be elected from districts within each State with more than one seat in the House. The districts in each state are drawn by that State's legislature. Seven States now have only one seat in the House: Alaska, Delaware, Montana, North Dakota, South Dakota, Vermont, and Wyoming. The 1842 law also directed that representatives be elected in each state on the same day: the Tuesday after the first Monday in November of every even-numbered year. In 1914 Congress also set that same date for the election of senators.

Clause 2. Sessions Congress must meet at least once a year. The 20th Amendment (1933) changed the opening date to January 3.

Section 5. Legislative Proceedings

Clause 1. Admission of members; quorum In 1969 the Supreme Court held that the House cannot exclude any member-elect who satisfies the qualifications set out in Article I, Section 2, Clause 2.

A majority in the House (218 members) or Senate (51) constitutes a quorum. In practice, both houses often proceed with less than a quorum present. However, any member may raise a point of order (demand a "quorum call"). If a roll call then reveals less than a majority of the members present, that chamber must either adjourn or the sergeant at arms must be ordered to round up absent members.

Clause 2. Rules Each house has adopted detailed rules to guide its proceedings. Each house may discipline members for unacceptable conduct; expulsion requires a two-thirds vote.

Clause 3. Record Each house must keep and publish a record of its meetings. The Congressional Record is published for every day that either house of Congress is in session, and provides a written record of all that is said and done on the floor of each house each session.

Clause 4. Adjournment Once in session, neither house may suspend (recess) its work for more than three days without the approval of the other house. Both houses must always meet in the same location.

Section 4.

▶ 1. The Times, Places and Manner of holding Elections for Senators and Representatives, shall be prescribed in each State by the Legislature thereof; but the Congress may at any time by law make or alter such Regulations, except as to the Places of choosing Senators.

▶ 2. The Congress shall assemble at least once in every Year, and such Meeting shall be on the first Monday in December, unless they shall by Law appoint a different Day.

Section 5.

▶ 1. Each House shall be the Judge of the Elections, Returns and Qualifications of its own Members, and a Majority of each shall constitute a Quorum to do Business; but a smaller Number may adjourn from day to day, and may be authorized to compel the Attendance of absent Members, in such Manner, and under such Penalties, as each House may provide.

▶ 2. Each House may determine the Rules of its Proceedings, punish its Members for disorderly Behavior, and, with the Concurrence of two thirds, expel a Member.

▶ 3. Each House shall keep a Journal of its Proceedings, and from time to time publish the same, excepting such Parts as may in their Judgment require Secrecy; and the Yeas and Nays of the Members of either House on any question shall, at the Desire of one fifth of those Present, be entered on the Journal.

▶ 4. Neither House, during the Session of Congress, shall, without the Consent of the other, adjourn for more than three days, nor to any other Place than that in which the two Houses shall be sitting.

Section 6.

▶ 1. The Senators and Representatives shall receive a Compensation for their Services, to be ascertained by Law, and paid out of the Treasury of the United States. They shall in all Cases, except Treason, Felony, and Breach of the Peace, be privileged from Arrest during their Attendance at the Session of their respective Houses, and in going to and returning from the same; and for any Speech or Debate in either House, they shall not be questioned in any other Place.

▶ 2. No Senator or Representative shall, during the Time for which he was elected, be appointed to any civil Office under the Authority of the United States, which shall have been created, or the Emoluments whereof shall have been increased during such time; and no Person holding any Office under the United States, shall be a Member of either House during his Continuance in Office.

Section 7.

▶ 1. All Bills for raising Revenue shall originate in the House of Representatives; but the Senate may propose or concur with amendments as on other Bills.

▶ 2. Every Bill which shall have passed the House of Representatives and the Senate, shall, before it become a law, be presented to the President of the United States: If he approve, he shall sign it, but if not he shall return it, with his Objections to that House in which it shall have originated, who shall enter the Objections at large on their Journal, and proceed to reconsider it. If after such Reconsideration two thirds of the House shall agree to pass the Bill, it shall be sent, together with the Objections, to the other House, by which it shall likewise be reconsidered, and if approved by two thirds of that House, it shall become a Law. But in all such Cases the Votes of both Houses shall be determined by Yeas and Nays, and the Names of the Persons voting for and against the Bill shall be entered on the Journal of each House respectively. If any Bill shall not be returned by the President within ten Days (Sunday excepted) after it shall have been presented to him, the Same shall be a law, in like Manner as if he had signed it, unless the Congress by their Adjournment, prevent its Return, in which Case it shall not be a Law.

▶ 3. Every Order, Resolution, or Vote to which the Concurrence of the Senate and House of Representatives may be necessary (except on a question of adjournment) shall be presented to the President of the United States; and before the Same shall take Effect, shall be approved by him, or, being disapproved by him, shall be repassed by two thirds of the Senate and House of Representatives, according to the Rules and Limitations prescribed in the Case of a Bill.

Section 6. Compensation, Immunities, and Disabilities of Members

▶ Clause 1. **Salaries; immunities** Each house sets its members' salaries, paid by the United States; the 27th Amendment (1992) modified this pay-setting power. This provision establishes "legislative immunity." The purpose of this immunity is to allow members to speak and debate freely in Congress itself. Treason is strictly defined in Article III, Section 3. A felony is any serious crime. A breach of the peace is any indictable offense less than treason or a felony; this exemption from arrest is of little real importance today.

▶ Clause 2. **Restrictions on office holding** No sitting member of either house may be appointed to an office in the executive or in the judicial branch if that position was created or its salary was increased during that member's current elected term. The second part of this clause— forbidding any person serving in either the executive or the judicial branch from also serving in Congress—reinforces the principle of separation of powers.

Section 7. Revenue Bills, President's Veto

▶ Clause 1. **Revenue bills** All bills that raise money must originate in the House. However, the Senate has the power to amend any revenue bill sent to it from the lower house.

▶ Clause 2. **Enactment of laws;** veto Once both houses have passed a bill, it must be sent to the President. The President may (1) sign the bill, thus making it law; (2) veto the bill, whereupon it must be returned to the house in which it originated; or (3) allow the bill to become law without signature, by not acting upon it within 10 days of its receipt from Congress, not counting Sundays. The President has a fourth option at the end of a congressional session: If he does not act on a measure within 10 days, and Congress adjourns during that period, the bill dies; a "pocket veto" has been applied to it. A presidential veto may be overridden by a two-thirds vote in each house.

▶ Clause 3. **Other measures** This clause refers to joint resolutions, measures Congress often passes to deal with unusual, temporary, or ceremonial matters. A joint resolution passed by Congress and signed by the President has the force of law, just as a bill does. As a matter of custom, a joint resolution proposing an amendment to the Constitution is not submitted to the President for signature or veto. Concurrent and simple resolutions do not have the force of law and, therefore, are not submitted to the President.

Section 8. Powers of Congress

Clause 1. The 18 separate clauses in this section set out 27 of the many expressed powers the Constitution grants to Congress. In this clause Congress is given the power to levy and provide for the collection of various kinds of taxes, in order to finance the operations of the government. All federal taxes must be levied at the same rates throughout the country.

Clause 2. Congress has power to borrow money to help finance the government. Federal borrowing is most often done through the sale of bonds on which interest is paid. The Constitution does not limit the amount the government may borrow.

Clause 3. This clause, the Commerce Clause, gives Congress the power to regulate both foreign and interstate trade. Much of what Congress does, it does on the basis of its commerce power.

Clause 4. Congress has the exclusive power to determine how aliens may become citizens of the United States. Congress may also pass laws relating to bankruptcy.

Clause 5. has the power to establish and require the use of uniform gauges of time, distance, weight, volume, area, and the like.

Clause 6. Congress has the power to make it a federal crime to falsify the coins, paper money, bonds, stamps, and the like of the United States.

Clause 7. Congress has the power to provide for and regulate the transportation and delivery of mail; "post offices" are those buildings and other places where mail is deposited for dispatch; "post roads" include all routes over which mail is carried.

Clause 8. Congress has the power to provide for copyrights and patents. A copyright gives an author or composer the exclusive right to control the reproduction, publication, and sale of literary, musical, or other creative work. A patent gives a person the exclusive right to control the manufacture or sale of his or her invention.

Clause 9. Congress has the power to create the lower federal courts, all of the several federal courts that function beneath the Supreme Court.

Clause 10. Congress has the power to prohibit, as a federal crime: (1) certain acts committed outside the territorial jurisdiction of the United States, and (2) the commission within the United States of any wrong against any nation with which we are at peace.

Section 8.

The Congress shall have Power

▶ 1. To lay and collect Taxes; Duties, Imposts and Excises to pay the Debts and provide for the common Defence and general Welfare of the United States; but all Duties, Imposts and Excises, shall be uniform throughout the United States;

▶ 2. To borrow Money on the credit of the United States;

▶ 3. To regulate Commerce with foreign Nations, and among the several States, and with the Indian Tribes;

▶ 4. To establish an uniform Rule of Naturalization, and uniform Laws on the subject of Bankruptcies throughout the United States;

▶ 5. To coin Money, regulate the Value thereof, and of foreign Coin, and fix the Standard of Weights and Measures;

▶ 6. To provide for the Punishment of counterfeiting the Securities and current Coin of the United States;

▶ 7. To establish Post Offices and post Roads;

▶ 8. To promote the Progress of Science and useful Arts, by securing, for limited Times to Authors and Inventors the exclusive Right to their respective Writings and Discoveries;

▶ 9. To constitute Tribunals inferior to the supreme Court;

▶ 10. To define and punish Piracies and Felonies committed on the high Seas, and Offences against the Law of nations;

11. To declare War, grant Letters of Marque and Reprisal, and make Rules concerning Captures on Land and Water;

12. To raise and support Armies; but no Appropriation of Money to that Use shall be for a longer Term than two Years;

13. To provide and maintain a Navy;

14. To make Rules for the Government and Regulation of the land and naval Forces;

15. To provide for calling forth the Militia to execute the Laws of the Union, suppress Insurrections and repel Invasions;

16. To provide for organizing, arming, and disciplining the Militia, and for governing such Part of them as may be employed in the Service of the United States, reserving to the States respectively the Appointment of the Officers, and the Authority of training the Militia according to the discipline prescribed by Congress;

17. To exercise exclusive Legislation in all Cases whatsoever, over such District (not exceeding ten Miles square) as may, by Cession of Particular States, and the Acceptance of Congress, become the Seat of the Government of the United States, and to exercise like Authority over all Places purchased by the Consent of the Legislature of the State in which the Same shall be, for the Erection of Forts, Magazines, Arsenals, Dockyards and other needful Buildings;—And

18. To make all Laws which shall be necessary and proper for carrying into Execution the foregoing Powers and all other Powers vested by this Constitution in the Government of the United States, or in any Department or Officer thereof.

Section 9.

1. The Migration or Importation of such Persons as any of the States now existing shall think proper to admit, shall not be prohibited by the Congress prior to the Year one thousand eight hundred and eight, but a Tax or duty may be imposed on such Importation, not exceeding ten dollars for each Person.

Clause 11. Only Congress can declare war. However, the President, as commander in chief of the armed force (Article II, Section 2, Clause 1), can make war without su a formal declaration. Letters of marque and reprisal are commissions authorizing private persons to outfit vesse (privateers) to capture and destroy enemy ships in time of war; they were forbidden in international law by the Declaration of Paris of 1856, and the United States has honored the ban since the Civil War.

Clauses 12 and 13. Congress has the power to provid for and maintain the nation's armed forces. It establishe the air force as an independent element of the armed forces in 1947, an exercise of its inherent powers in fore relations and national defense. The two-year limit on spending for the army insures civilian control of the milit

Clause 14. Today these rules are set out in three princi statutes: the Uniform Code of Military Justice, passed b Congress in 1950, and the Military Justice Acts of 1958 and 1983.

Clauses 15 and 16. In the National Defense Act of 19 Congress made each State's militia (volunteer army) a p of the National Guard. Today, Congress and the States cooperate in its maintenance. Ordinarily, each State's National Guard is under the command of that State's governor; but Congress has given the President the pow to call any or all of those units into federal service when necessary.

Clause 17. In 1791 Congress accepted land grants from Maryland and Virginia and established the District of Columbia for the nation's capital. Assuming Virginia's grant would never be needed, Congress returned it in 18 Today, the elected government of the District's 69 squar miles operates under the authority of Congress. Congre also has the power to acquire other lands from the State for various federal purposes.

Clause 18. This is the Necessary and Proper Clause, a often called the Elastic Clause. It is the constitutional ba for the many and far-reaching implied powers of the Fed Government.

Section 9. Powers Denied to Congress

Clause 1. The phrase "such persons" referred to slave This provision was part of the Commerce Compromise, one of the bargains struck in the writing of the Constitut Congress outlawed the slave trade in 1808.

Clause 2. A writ of habeas corpus, the "great writ of [lib]erty," is a court order directing a sheriff, warden, or other [p]ublic officer, or a private person, who is detaining another [to] "produce the body" of the one being held in order that [th]e legality of the detention may be determined by the [co]urt.

▶ 2. The Privilege of the Writ of Habeas Corpus shall not be suspended, unless when in Cases of Rebellion or Invasion the public safety may require it.

Clause 3. A bill of attainder is a legislative act that inflicts [p]unishment without a judicial trial. See Article I, Section [9], and Article III, Section 3, Clause 2. An ex post facto [la]w is any criminal law that operates retroactively to the [di]sadvantage of the accused. See Article I, Section 10.

▶ 3. No Bill of Attainder or ex post facto Law shall be passed.

Clause 4. A capitation tax is literally a "head tax," a tax [le]vied on each person in the population. A direct tax is [on]e paid directly to the government by the taxpayer—for [ex]ample, an income or a property tax; an indirect tax is [on]e paid to another private party who then pays it to the [go]vernment—for example, a sales tax. This provision was [m]odified by the 16th Amendment (1913), giving Congress [th]e power to levy "taxes on incomes, from whatever source [de]rived."

▶ 4. No Capitation, or other direct, Tax shall be laid, unless in Proportion to the Census of Enumeration hereinbefore directed to be taken.

Clause 5. This provision was a part of the Commerce [C]ompromise made by the Framers in 1787. Congress has [th]e power to tax imported goods, however.

▶ 5. No Tax or Duty shall be laid on Articles exported from any State.

Clause 6. All ports within the United States must be [tr]eated alike by Congress as it exercises its taxing and [co]mmerce powers. Congress cannot tax goods sent by [w]ater from one State to another, nor may it give the ports of [on]e State any legal advantage over those of another.

▶ 6. No Preference shall be given by any Regulation of Commerce or Revenue to the Ports of one State over those of another: nor shall Vessels bound to, or from, one State, be obliged to enter, clear or pay Duties in another.

Clause 7. This clause gives Congress its vastly important ["p]ower of the purse," a major check on presidential power. [Fe]deral money can be spent only in those amounts and for [th]ose purposes expressly authorized by an act of Congress. [All] federal income and spending must be accounted for, [re]gularly and publicly.

▶ 7. No Money shall be drawn from the Treasury, but in Consequence of Appropriations made by Law; and a regular Statement and Account of the Receipts and Expenditures of all public Money shall be published from time to time.

Clause 8. This provision, preventing the establishment [of] a nobility, reflects the principle that "all men are created [eq]ual." It was also intended to discourage foreign attempts [to] bribe or otherwise corrupt officers of the government.

▶ 8. No Title of Nobility shall be granted by the United States: And no Person holding any Office of Profit or Trust under them, shall, without the Consent of the Congress, accept of any present, Emolument, Office, or Title, of any kind whatever, from any King, Prince, or foreign State.

[Se]ction 10. Powers Denied to the States

Section 10.

Clause 1. The States are not sovereign governments and [c]annot make agreements or otherwise negotiate with [for]eign states; the power to conduct foreign relations is an [ex]clusive power of the National Government. The power [to] coin money is also an exclusive power of the National [Go]vernment. Several powers forbidden to the National [Go]vernment are here also forbidden to the States.

▶ 1. No State shall enter into any Treaty, Alliance, or Confederation; grant Letters of Marque and Reprisal; coin Money; emit Bills of Credit; make any Thing but gold and silver Coin a Tender in Payment of Debts; pass any Bill of Attainder, ex post facto Law, or Law impairing the Obligation of Contracts, or grant any Title of Nobility.

Clause 2. This provision relates to foreign, not interstate, [co]mmerce. Only Congress, not the States, can tax imports; [an]d the States are, like Congress, forbidden the power to [ta]x exports.

▶ 2. No State shall, without the Consent of the Congress, lay any Imposts or Duties on Imports or Exports, except what may be absolutely necessary for executing its inspection Laws; and the net Produce of all Duties and Imposts, laid by any State on Imports or Exports, shall be for the Use of the Treasury of the United States; and all such Laws shall be subject to the Revision and Control of the Congress.

▶ 3. No State shall, without the Consent of Congress, lay any Duty of Tonnage, keep Troops, or Ships of War in time of Peace, enter into any Agreement or Compact with another State, or with a foreign Power, or engage in War, unless actually invaded, or in such imminent Danger as will not admit of delay.

Article II
Section 1.

▶ 1. The executive Power shall be vested in a President of the United States of America. He shall hold his Office during the Term of four Years, and, together with the Vice President, chosen for the same Term, be elected as follows:

▶ 2. Each State shall appoint, in such Manner as the Legislature thereof may direct, a Number of Electors, equal to the whole Number of Senators and Representatives to which the State may be entitled in the Congress: but no Senator or Representative, or Person holding an Office of Trust or Profit, under the United States, shall be appointed an Elector.

▶ 3. The Electors shall meet in their respective States, and vote by Ballot for two Persons, of whom one at least shall not be an Inhabitant of the same State with themselves. And they shall make a List of all the Persons voted for, and of the Number of Votes for each; which List they shall sign and certify, and transmit sealed to the Seat of the Government of the United States, directed to the President of the Senate. The President of the Senate shall, in the Presence of the Senate and House of Representatives, open all the Certificates, and the Votes shall then be counted. The Person having the greatest Number of Votes shall be the President, if such Number be a majority of the whole Number of Electors appointed; and if there be more than one who have such Majority, and have an equal Number of Votes, then, the House of Representatives shall immediately choose by Ballot one of them for President; and if no Person have a Majority, then from the five highest on the List the said House shall in like Manner choose the President. But in choosing the President, the Votes shall be taken by States, the Representatives from each State having one Vote; a quorum for this Purpose shall consist of a Member or Members from two thirds of the States, and a Majority of all the States shall be necessary to a Choice. In every Case, after the Choice of the President, the Person having the greatest Number of Votes of the Electors shall be the Vice President. But if there should remain two or more who have equal Votes, the Senate shall choose from them by Ballot the Vice President.

Executive Department
Section 1. President and Vice President

▶ **Clause 3.** A duty of tonnage is a tax laid on ships according to their cargo capacity. Each State has a constitutional right to provide for and maintain a militia; no State may keep a standing army or navy. The several restrictions here prevent the States from assuming pow that the Constitution elsewhere grants to the National Government.

▶ **Clause 1. Executive power, term** This clause gives to the President the very broad "executive power," the power to enforce the laws and otherwise administer the public policies of the United States. It also sets the leng of the presidential (and vice-presidential) term of office; see the 22nd Amendment (1951), which places a limit c presidential (but not vice-presidential) tenure.

▶ **Clause 2. Electoral college** This clause establishes the "electoral college," although the Constitution does not that term. It is a body of presidential electors chosen in each State, and it selects the President and Vice Presid every four years. The number of electors chosen in eac State equals the number of senators and representative that State has in Congress.

▶ **Clause 3. Election of President and Vice President T** clause was replaced by the 12th Amendment in 1804.

ause 4. Date Congress has set the date for the
posing of electors as the Tuesday after the first Monday
November every fourth year, and for the casting of
ctoral votes as the Monday after the second Wednesday
December of that year.

ause 5. Qualifications The President must have been
rn a citizen of the United States, be at least 35 years old,
d have been a resident of the United States for at least
years.

ause 6. Vacancy This clause was modified by the
th Amendment (1967), which provides expressly for
succession of the Vice President, for the filling of a
cancy in the Vice Presidency, and for the determination
presidential inability.

ause 7. Compensation The President now receives
alary of $400,000 and a taxable expense account
$50,000 a year. Those amounts cannot be changed
ring a presidential term; thus, Congress cannot use the
sident's compensation as a bargaining tool to influence
ecutive decisions. The phrase "any other emolument"
ans, in effect, any valuable gift; it does not mean that the
sident cannot be provided with such benefits of office as
White House, extensive staff assistance, and much else.

ause 8. Oath of office The Chief Justice of the United
tes regularly administers this oath or affirmation, but any
icial officer may do so. Thus, Calvin Coolidge was sworn
o office in 1923 by his father, a justice of the peace in
mont.

ction 2. President's Powers and Duties

ause 1. Military, civil powers The President, a civilian,
ads the nation's armed forces, a key element in the
nstitution's insistence on civilian control of the military.
President's power to "require the opinion, in writing"
vides the constitutional basis for the Cabinet. The
sident's power to grant reprieves and pardons, the
wer of clemency, extends only to federal cases.

▶ 4. The Congress may determine the Time of choosing the
Electors, and the Day on which they shall give their Votes;
which Day shall be the same throughout the United States.

▶ 5. No Person except a natural born Citizen, or a Citizen of the
United States, at the time of the Adoption of this Constitution,
shall be eligible to the Office of President; neither shall any
person be eligible to that Office who shall not have attained
to the Age of thirty-five Years, and been fourteen Years a
Resident within the United States.

▶ 6. In Case of the Removal of the President from Office, or of his
Death, Resignation, or Inability to discharge the Powers and
Duties of the said Office, the Same shall devolve on the Vice
President, and the Congress may by Law provide for the
Case of Removal, Death, Resignation or Inability, both of the
President and Vice President, declaring what Officer shall then
act as President, and such Officer shall act accordingly, until
the Disability be removed, or a President shall be elected.

▶ 7. The President shall, at stated Times, receive for his Services,
a Compensation, which shall neither be increased nor
diminished during the Period for which he shall have been
elected, and he shall not receive within that Period any other
Emolument from the United States, or any of them.

▶ 8. Before he enter on the Execution of his Office, he shall take the
following Oath or Affirmation:
"I do solemnly swear (or affirm) that I will faithfully execute the
Office of President of the United States, and will to the best of
my Ability, preserve, protect and defend the Constitution of
the United States."

Section 2.

▶ 1. The President shall be Commander in Chief of the Army
and Navy of the United States, and of the Militia of the
several States, when called into the actual Service of the
United States; he may require the Opinion, in writing, of the
principal Officer in each of the executive Departments, upon
any Subject relating to the Duties of their respective Offices,
and he shall have Power to Grant Reprieves and Pardons
for Offences against the United States, except in Cases of
Impeachment.

2. He shall have Power, by and with the Advice and Consent of the Senate, to make Treaties, provided two thirds of the Senators present concur; and he shall nominate, and by and with the Advice and Consent of the Senate, shall appoint Ambassadors, other public Ministers and Consuls, Judges of the supreme Court, and all other Officers of the United States, whose Appointments are not herein otherwise provided for, and which shall be established by Law: but the Congress may by Law vest the Appointment of such inferior Officers, as they think proper, in the President alone, in the Courts of Law, or in the Heads of Departments.

3. The President shall have Power to fill up all Vacancies that may happen during the Recess of the Senate, by granting Commissions which shall expire at the End of their next Session.

Section 3.

He shall from time to time give to the Congress Information of the State of the Union, and recommend to their Consideration such Measures as he shall judge necessary and expedient; he may, on extraordinary Occasions, convene both Houses, or either of them, and in Case of Disagreement between them, with Respect to the Time of Adjournment, he may adjourn them to such Time as he shall think proper; he shall receive Ambassadors and other public Ministers; he shall take Care that the Laws be faithfully executed, and shall Commission all the Officers of the United States.

Section 4.

The President, Vice President and all Civil Officers of the United States, shall be removed from Office on Impeachment for and Conviction of, Treason, Bribery, or other high Crimes and Misdemeanors.

Article III
Section 1.

The judicial Power of the United States, shall be vested in one supreme Court, and in such inferior Courts as the Congress may from time to time ordain and establish. The Judges, both of the supreme and inferior Courts, shall hold their Offices during good Behaviour, and shall, at stated Times, receive for their Services, a Compensation, which shall not be diminished during their Continuance in Office.

▶ Clause 2. **Treaties, appointments** The President has the sole power to make treaties; to become effective, a treaty must be approved by a two-thirds vote in the Senate. In practice, the President can also make execu agreements with foreign governments; these pacts, whi are frequently made and usually deal with routine matte do not require Senate consent. The President appoints principal officers of the executive branch and all federal judges; the "inferior officers" are those who hold lesser posts.

▶ Clause 3. **Recess appointments** When the Senate is in session, appointments that require Senate consent c be made by the President on a temporary basis, as "re appointments." Recess appointments are valid only to t end of the congressional term in which they are made.

Section 3. President's Powers and Duties

The President delivers a State of the Union Message to Congress soon after that body convenes each year. Th message is delivered to the nation's lawmakers and, importantly, to the American people, as well. It is short followed by the proposed federal budget and an econo report; and the President may send special messages to Congress at any time. In all of these communication Congress is urged to take those actions the Chief Exec finds to be in the national interest. The President also has the power: to call special sessions of Congress; to adjourn Congress if its two houses cannot agree for th purpose; to receive the diplomatic representatives of o governments; to insure the proper execution of all fede laws; and to empower federal officers to hold their post and perform their duties.

Section 4. Impeachment

The Constitution outlines the impeachment process in Article I, Section 2, Clause 5 and in Section 3, Clauses and 7.

Judicial Department
Section 1. Judicial Power, Courts, Terms of Off

The judicial power conferred here is the power of feder courts to hear and decide cases, disputes between the government and individuals and between private perso (parties). The Constitution creates only the Supreme C of the United States; it gives to Congress the power to establish other, lower federal courts (Article I, Section 8 Clause 9) and to fix the size of the Supreme Court. The words "during good behaviour" mean, in effect, for life.

Section 2. Jurisdiction

Clause 1. Cases to be heard This clause sets out the [juris]diction of the federal courts; that is, it identifies those [cas]es that may be tried in those courts. The federal courts [can] hear and decide—have jurisdiction over—a case [dep]ending on either the subject matter or the parties [invo]lved in that case. The jurisdiction of the federal courts [in c]ases involving States was substantially restricted by the [11th] Amendment in 1795.

Clause 2. Supreme Court jurisdiction Original jurisdiction [refe]rs to the power of a court to hear a case in the first [inst]ance, not on appeal from a lower court. Appellate [juris]diction refers to a court's power to hear a case on [app]eal from a lower court, from the court in which the case [was] originally tried. This clause gives the Supreme Court [both] original and appellate jurisdiction. However, nearly [all o]f the cases the High Court hears are brought to it on [app]eal from the lower federal courts and the highest State [cour]ts.

Clause 3. Jury trial in criminal cases A person accused [of a] federal crime is guaranteed the right to trial by jury in a [fede]ral court in the State where the crime was committed; [see] the 5th and 6th amendments. The right to trial by jury in [seri]ous criminal cases in the State courts is guaranteed by [the] 6th and 14th amendments.

Section 3. Treason

Clause 1. Definition Treason is the only crime defined in [the] Constitution. The Framers intended the very specific [defi]nition here to prevent the loose use of the charge of [trea]son—for example, against persons who criticize the [gov]ernment. Treason can be committed only in time of war [and] only by a citizen or a resident alien.

Clause 2. Punishment Congress has provided that the [pun]ishment that a federal court may impose on a convicted [trait]or may range from a minimum of five years in prison [and/]or a $10,000 fine to a maximum of death; no person [con]victed of treason has ever been executed by the United [Sta]tes. No legal punishment can be imposed on the family [or d]escendants of a convicted traitor. Congress has also [ma]de it a crime for any person (in either peace or wartime) [to c]ommit espionage or sabotage, to attempt to overthrow [the] government by force, or to conspire to do any of these [thin]gs.

Section 2.

▶ 1. The judicial Power shall extend to all Cases, in Law and Equity, arising under this Constitution, the Laws of the United States, and Treaties made, or which shall be made, under their Authority;— to all Cases affecting Ambassadors, other public ministers, and Consuls;— to all Cases of Admiralty and maritime Jurisdiction;— to Controversies to which the United States shall be a Party;— to Controversies between two or more States;— between a State and Citizens of another State;— between Citizens of different States;— between Citizens of the same State claiming Lands under Grants of different States, and between a State, or the Citizens thereof, and foreign States, Citizens, or Subjects.

▶ 2. In all Cases affecting Ambassadors, other public Ministers and Consuls, and those in which a State shall be a Party, the supreme Court shall have original Jurisdiction. In all the other Cases before mentioned, the supreme Court shall have appellate Jurisdiction, both as to Law and Fact, with such Exceptions, and under such Regulations as the Congress shall make.

▶ 3. The trial of all Crimes, except in Cases of Impeachment, shall be by Jury; and such Trial shall be held in the State where the said Crimes shall have been committed; but when not committed within any State, the Trial shall be at such Place or Places as the Congress may by Law have directed.

Section 3.

▶ 1. Treason against the United States shall consist only in levying War against them, or in adhering to their Enemies, giving them Aid and Comfort. No Person shall be convicted of Treason unless on the Testimony of two Witnesses to the same overt Act, or on Confession in open Court.

▶ 2. The Congress shall have Power to declare the Punishment of Treason, but no Attainder of Treason shall work Corruption of Blood, or Forfeiture except during the Life of the Person attainted.

Article IV

Section 1.

Full Faith and Credit shall be given in each State to the public Acts, Records, and judicial Proceedings of every other State. And the Congress may by general Laws prescribe the Manner in which such Acts, Records and Proceedings shall be proved, and the Effect thereof.

Section 2.

▶ 1. The Citizens of each State shall be entitled to all Privileges and Immunities of Citizens in the several States.

▶ 2. A Person charged in any State with Treason, Felony, or other Crime, who shall flee from justice, and be found in another State, shall on Demand of the executive Authority of the State from which he fled, be delivered up, to be removed to the State having Jurisdiction of the Crime.

▶ 3. No Person held to Service or Labor in one State, under the Laws thereof, escaping into another, shall, in Consequence of any Law or Regulation therein, be discharged from Service or Labor, but shall be delivered up on Claim of the Party to whom such Service or Labor may be due.

Section 3.

▶ 1. New States may be admitted by the Congress into this Union; but no new State shall be formed or erected within the Jurisdiction of any other State; nor any State be formed by the Junction of two or more States, or Parts of States, without the Consent of the Legislatures of the States concerned as well as of the Congress.

▶ 2. The Congress shall have Power to dispose of and make all needful Rules and Regulations respecting the Territory or other Property belonging to the United States; and nothing in this Constitution shall be so construed as to Prejudice any Claims of the United States, or of any particular State.

Section 4.

The United States shall guarantee to every State in this Union a Republican Form of Government, and shall protect each of them against Invasion; and on Application of the Legislature, or of the Executive (when the Legislature cannot be convened) against domestic Violence.

Relations Among States

Section 1. Full Faith and Credit

Each State must recognize the validity of the laws, pu[blic] records, and court decisions of every other State.

Section 2. Privileges and Immunities of Citizens

▶ **Clause 1. Residents of other States** In effect, this cla[use] means that no State may discriminate against the resi[dents] of other States; that is, a State's laws cannot draw unreasonable distinctions between its own residents a[nd] those of any of the other States. See Section 1 of the [14th] Amendment.

▶ **Clause 2. Extradition** The process of returning a fugi[tive] to another State is known as "interstate rendition" or, more commonly, "extradition." Usually, that process w[ill] routinely; some extradition requests are contested how ever—especially in cases with racial or political overto[nes.] A governor may refuse to extradite a fugitive; but the f[ederal] courts can compel an unwilling governor to obey this constitutional command.

▶ **Clause 3. Fugitive slaves** This clause was nullified by [the] 13th Amendment, which abolished slavery in 1865.

Section 3. New States; Territories

▶ **Clause 1. New States** Only Congress can admit new [er] States to the Union. A new State may not be created b[y] taking territory from an existing State without the cons[ent] of that State's legislature. Congress has admitted 37 S[tates] since the original 13 formed the Union. Five States— Vermont, Kentucky, Tennessee, Maine, and West Virgi[nia] were created from parts of existing States. Texas was [an] independent republic before admission. California was admitted after being ceded to the United States by Me[xico.] Each of the other 30 States entered the Union only aft[er a] period of time as an organized territory of the United S[tates.]

▶ **Clause 2. Territory, property** Congress has the powe[r to] make laws concerning the territories, other public land[s,] and all other property of the United States.

Section 4. Protection Afforded to States by the Nation

The Constitution does not define "a republican form of government," but the phrase is generally understood to mean a representative government. The Federal Government must also defend each State against atta[ck] from outside its border and, at the request of a State's legislature or its governor, aid its efforts to put down internal disorders.

ovisions for Amendment

section provides for the methods by which formal
ages can be made in the Constitution. An amendment
be proposed in one of two ways: by a two-thirds vote
ach house of Congress, or by a national convention
d by Congress at the request of two-thirds of the State
slatures. A proposed amendment may be ratified in
of two ways: by three-fourths of the State legislatures,
y three-fourths of the States in conventions called for
purpose. Congress has the power to determine the
nod by which a proposed amendment may be ratified.
amendment process cannot be used to deny any State
qual representation in the United States Senate. To this
t, 27 amendments have been adopted. To date, all of the
ndments except the 21st Amendment were proposed by
gress and ratified by the State legislatures. Only the 21st
endment was ratified by the convention method.

tional Debts, Supremacy
National Law, Oath

ction 1. Validity of Debts

gress had borrowed large sums of money during the
olution and later during the Critical Period of the 1780s. This
vision, a pledge that the new government would honor those
ts, did much to create confidence in that government.

ction 2. Supremacy of National Law

section sets out the Supremacy Clause, a specific
aration of the supremacy of federal law over any
all forms of State law. No State, including its local
ernments, may make or enforce any law that conflicts
any provision in the Constitution, an act of Congress, a
ty, or an order, rule, or regulation properly issued by the
sident or his subordinates in the executive branch.

ction 3. Oaths of Office

provision reinforces the Supremacy Clause; all public
cers, at every level in the United States, owe their first
giance to the Constitution of the United States. No
ious qualification can be imposed as a condition for
ling any public office.

tification of Constitution

proposed Constitution was signed by George
shington and 37 of his fellow Framers on September
1787. (George Read of Delaware signed for himself and
for his absent colleague, John Dickinson.)

Article V

The Congress, whenever two thirds of both Houses shall deem
it necessary, shall propose Amendments to this Constitution, or,
on the Application of the Legislatures of two thirds of the several
States, shall call a Convention for proposing Amendments, which,
in either Case, shall be valid to all Intents and Purposes, as Part
of this Constitution, when ratified by the Legislatures of three
fourths of the several States, or by Conventions in three fourths
thereof, as the one or the other Mode of Ratification may be
proposed by the Congress; Provided that no Amendment which
may be made prior to the Year One thousand eight hundred and
eight shall in any Manner affect the first and fourth Clauses in the
Ninth section of the first Article; and that no State, without its
Consent, shall be deprived of its equal Suffrage in the Senate.

Article VI

Section 1.

All Debts contracted and Engagements entered into, before the
Adoption of this Constitution, shall be as valid against the United
States under this Constitution, as under the Confederation.

Section 2.

This Constitution, and the Laws of the United States which shall
be made in Pursuance thereof; and all Treaties made, or which
shall be made, under the Authority of the United States, shall be
the supreme Law of the Land; and the Judges in every State shall
be bound thereby, anything in the constitution or Laws of any
State to the Contrary notwithstanding.

Section 3.

The Senators and Representatives before mentioned, and the
Members of the several State legislatures, and all executive and
judicial Officers, both of the United States and of the several
States, shall be bound by Oath or Affirmation, to support this
Constitution; but no religious Test shall ever be required as a
Qualification to any Office or public Trust under the United States.

Article VII

The ratification of the Conventions of nine States, shall be
sufficient for the Establishment of this Constitution between the
States so ratifying the same.

Done in Convention by the Unanimous Consent of the States present the Seventeenth Day of September in the Year of our Lord one thousand seven hundred and Eighty-seven and of the Independence of the United States of America the twelfth. In witness whereof We have hereunto subscribed our Names.

Attest:
William Jackson,
Secretary
George Washington,
*President and Deputy
from Virginia*

New Hampshire
John Langdon
Nicholas Gilman

Massachusetts
Nathaniel Gorham
Rufus King

Connecticut
William Samuel Johnson
Roger Sherman

New York
Alexander Hamilton

New Jersey
William Livingston
David Brearley
William Paterson
Jonathan Dayton

Pennsylvania
Benjamin Franklin
Thomas Mifflin
Robert Morris
George Clymer
Thomas Fitzsimons
Jared Ingersoll
James Wilson
Gouverneur Morris

Delaware
George Read
Gunning Bedford, Jr.
John Dickinson
Richard Bassett
Jacob Broom

Maryland
James McHenry
Daniel of St. Thomas
Jenifer
Daniel Carroll

Virginia
John Blair
James Madison, Jr.

North Carolina
William Blount
Richard Dobbs Spaight
Hugh Williamson

South Carolina
John Rutledge
Charles Cotesworth
Pinckney
Charles Pinckney
Pierce Butler

Georgia
William Few
Abraham Baldwin

first 10 amendments, the Bill of Rights, were each
posed by Congress on September 25, 1789, and ratified
the necessary three-fourths of the States on December
1791. These amendments were originally intended to
rict the National Government—not the States. However,
Supreme Court has several times held that most of
r provisions also apply to the States, through the 14th
endment's Due Process Clause.

Amendment. Freedom of Religion, Speech, ss, Assembly, and Petition

1st Amendment sets out five basic liberties: The guarantee
reedom of religion is both a protection of religious thought
practice and a command of separation of church and
e. The guarantees of freedom of speech and press assure
ll persons a right to speak, publish, and otherwise express
r views. The guarantees of the rights of assembly and
tion protect the right to join with others in public meetings,
tical parties, interest groups, and other associations to
uss public affairs and influence public policy. None of
se rights is guaranteed in absolute terms, however; like all
er civil rights guarantees, each of them may be exercised
with regard to the rights of all other persons.

Amendment. Bearing Arms

right of the people to keep and bear arms was insured
he 2nd Amendment.

Amendment. Quartering of Troops

s amendment was intended to prevent what had been
mon British practice in the colonial period; see the
laration of Independence. This provision is of virtually no
ortance today.

Amendment. Searches and Seizures

basic rule laid down by the 4th Amendment is this:
ce officers have no general right to search for or seize
dence or seize (arrest) persons. Except in particular
umstances, they must have a proper warrant (a court
er) obtained with probable cause (on reasonable
nds). This guarantee is reinforced by the exclusionary
, developed by the Supreme Court: Evidence gained as
result of an unlawful search or seizure cannot be used at
court trial of the person from whom it was seized.

Amendment. Criminal Proceedings; Due cess; Eminent Domain

erson can be tried for a serious federal crime only if
r she has been indicted (charged, accused of that
e) by a grand jury. No one may be subjected to
ble jeopardy—that is, tried twice for the same crime.
persons are protected against self-incrimination; no
son can be legally compelled to answer any question
ny governmental proceeding if that answer could lead
at person's prosecution. The 5th Amendment's Due
cess Clause prohibits unfair, arbitrary actions by the
eral Government; a like prohibition is set out against
States in the 14th Amendment. Government may take
ate property for a legitimate public purpose; but when it
rcises that power of eminent domain, it must pay a fair
e for the property seized.

1st Amendment

Congress shall make no law respecting an establishment of
religion, or prohibiting the free exercise thereof, or abridging
the freedom of speech, or of the press; or the right of the people
peaceably to assemble, and to petition the Government for a
redress of grievances.

2nd Amendment

A well-regulated Militia being necessary to the security of a free
State, the right of the people to keep and bear Arms, shall not be
infringed.

3rd Amendment

No Soldier shall, in time of peace be quartered in any house,
without the consent of the Owner, nor, in time of war, but in a
manner to be prescribed by law.

4th Amendment

The right of the people to be secure in their persons, houses,
papers, and effects, against unreasonable searches and
seizures, shall not be violated, and no Warrants shall issue, but
upon probable cause, supported by Oath or affirmation, and
particularly describing the place to be searched, and the persons
or things to be seized.

5th Amendment

No person shall be held to answer for a capital, or otherwise
infamous crime, unless on a presentment or indictment of a
Grand Jury, except in cases arising in the land or naval forces,
or in the Militia, when in actual service in time of War, or public
danger; nor shall any person be subject for the same offence to
be twice put in jeopardy of life or limb; nor shall be compelled
in any criminal case to be a witness against himself, nor be
deprived of life, liberty, or property, without due process of law;
nor shall private property be taken for public use, without just
compensation.

6th Amendment

In all criminal prosecutions, the accused shall enjoy the right to a speedy and public trial, by an impartial jury of the State and district wherein the crime shall have been committed, which district shall have been previously ascertained by law, and to be informed of the nature and cause of the accusation; to be confronted with the witnesses against him; to have compulsory process for obtaining witnesses in his favor, and to have the Assistance of Counsel for his defence.

7th Amendment

In Suits at common law, where the value in controversy shall exceed twenty dollars, the right of trial by jury shall be preserved, and no fact tried by a jury, shall be otherwise re-examined in any Court of the United States, than according to the rules of the common law.

8th Amendment

Excessive bail shall not be required, nor excessive fines imposed, nor cruel and unusual punishment inflicted.

9th Amendment

The enumeration in the Constitution, of certain rights, shall not be construed to deny or disparage others retained by the people.

10th Amendment

The powers not delegated to the United States by the Constitution, nor prohibited by it to the States, are reserved to the States respectively, or to the people.

6th Amendment. Criminal Proceedings

A person accused of crime has the right to be tried in c without undue delay and by an impartial jury; see Articl Section 2, Clause 3. The defendant must be informed o the charge upon which he or she is to be tried, has the to cross-examine hostile witnesses, and has the right to require the testimony of favorable witnesses. The defen also has the right to be represented by an attorney at e stage in the criminal process.

7th Amendment. Civil Trials

This amendment applies only to civil cases heard in fed courts. A civil case does not involve criminal matters; it dispute between private parties or between the govern and a private party. The right to trial by jury is guarantee in any civil case in a federal court if the amount of mone involved in that case exceeds $20 (most cases today in a much larger sum); that right may be waived (relinquis put aside) if both parties agree to a bench trial (a trial by judge, without a jury).

8th Amendment. Punishment for Crimes

Bail is the sum of money that a person accused of crime be required to post (deposit with the court) as a guarante that he or she will appear in court at the proper time. The amount of bail required and/or a fine imposed as punishr must bear a reasonable relationship to the seriousness o the crime involved in the case. The prohibition of cruel ar unusual punishment forbids any punishment judged to b harsh, too severe for the crime for which it is imposed.

9th Amendment. Unenumerated Rights

The fact that the Constitution sets out many civil rights guarantees, expressly provides for many protections ag government, does not mean that there are not other rig also held by the people.

10th Amendment. Powers Reserved to the Stat

This amendment identifies the area of power that may b exercised by the States. All of those powers the Constit does not grant to the National Government, and at the s time does not forbid to the States, belong to each of the States, or to the people of each State.

th Amendment. Suits Against States

oosed by Congress March 4, 1794; ratified February 7, 1795,
official announcement of the ratification was delayed until
uary 8, 1798. This amendment repealed part of Article III,
tion 2, Clause 1. No State may be sued in a federal court by
sident of another State or of a foreign country; the Supreme
rt has long held that this provision also means that a State
not be sued in a federal court by a foreign country or, more
ortantly, even by one of its own residents.

th Amendment. Election of President
Vice President

oosed by Congress December 9, 1803; ratified June
1804. This amendment replaced Article II, Section 1,
use 3. Originally, each elector cast two ballots, each
a different person for President. The person with the
est number of electoral votes, provided that number
a majority of the electors, was to become President;
person with the second highest number was to become
President. This arrangement produced an electoral vote
etween Thomas Jefferson and Aaron Burr in 1800; the
se finally chose Jefferson as President in 1801. The 12th
endment separated the balloting for President and Vice
sident; each elector now casts one ballot for someone
resident and a second ballot for another person as
President. Note that the 20th Amendment changed
date set here (March 4) to January 20, and that the 23rd
endment (1961) provides for electors from the District
olumbia. This amendment also provides that the Vice
sident must meet the same qualifications as those set
for the President in Article II, Section 1, Clause 5.

th Amendment. Slavery and
oluntary Servitude

oosed by Congress January 31, 1865; ratified December
865. This amendment forbids slavery in the United States
in any area under its control. It also forbids other forms of
ed labor, except punishments for crime; but some forms of
npulsory service are not prohibited—for example, service
uries or in the armed forces. Section 2 gives to Congress
power to carry out the provisions of Section 1 of this
endment.

11th Amendment

The Judicial power of the United States shall not be construed
to extend to any suit in law or equity, commenced or prosecuted
against one of the United States by Citizens of another State, or
by Citizens or Subjects of any Foreign State.

12th Amendment

The Electors shall meet in their respective States and vote by
ballot for President and Vice President, one of whom, at least,
shall not be an inhabitant of the same State with themselves;
they shall name in their ballots the person voted for as President,
and in distinct ballots the person voted for as Vice President,
and they shall make distinct lists of all persons voted for as
President, and of all persons voted for as Vice President, and
of the number of votes for each, which lists they shall sign and
certify, and transmit sealed to the seat of the government of the
United States, directed to the President of the Senate;— The
President of the Senate shall, in the presence of the Senate and
the House of Representatives, open all the certificates and the
votes shall then be counted;— the person having the greatest
Number of votes for President shall be the President, if such
number be a majority of the whole number of Electors appointed;
and if no person have such a majority, then, from the persons
having the highest numbers not exceeding three on the list of
those voted for as President, the House of Representatives shall
choose immediately, by ballot, the President. But in choosing the
President, the votes shall be taken by States, the representation
from each State having one vote; a quorum for this purpose shall
consist of a member or members from two thirds of the States,
and a majority of all the States shall be necessary to a choice.
And if the House of Representatives shall not choose a President
whenever the right of choice shall devolve upon them, before
the fourth day of March next following, then the Vice President
shall act as President, as in case of death or other constitutional
disability of the President. The person having the greatest
number of votes as Vice President, shall be the Vice President,
if such number be a majority of the whole number of Electors
appointed, and if no person have a majority, then from the two
highest numbers on the list, the Senate shall choose the Vice
President; a quorum for the purpose shall consist of two thirds of
the whole number of Senators, a majority of the whole number
shall be necessary to a choice. But no person constitutionally
ineligible to the office of President shall be eligible to that of
Vice-President of the United States.

13th Amendment

Section 1. Neither slavery nor involuntary servitude, except as
a punishment for crime whereof the party shall have been duly
convicted, shall exist within the United States, or any place
subject to their jurisdiction.

Section 2. Congress shall have power to enforce this article by
appropriate legislation.

14th Amendment

Section 1. All persons born or naturalized in the United States and subject to the jurisdiction thereof, are citizens of the United States and of the State wherein they reside. No State shall make or enforce any law which shall abridge the privileges or immunities of citizens of the United States; nor shall any State deprive any person of life, liberty, or property, without due process of law; nor deny to any person within its jurisdiction the equal protection of the laws.

Section 2. Representatives shall be apportioned among the several States according to their respective numbers, counting the whole number of persons in each State, excluding Indians not taxed. But when the right to vote at any election for the choice of electors for President and Vice President of the United States, Representatives in Congress, the Executive and Judicial officers of a State, or the members of the Legislature thereof, is denied to any of the male inhabitants of such State, being twenty-one years of age and citizens of the United States, or in any way abridged, except for participation in rebellion, or other crime, the basis of representation therein shall be reduced in the proportion which the number of such male citizens shall bear to the whole number of male citizens twenty-one years of age in such State.

Section 3. No person shall be a Senator or Representative in Congress, or elector of President and Vice President, or hold any office, civil or military, under the United States, or under any State, who, having previously taken an oath, as a member of Congress, or as an officer of the United States, or as a member of any State legislature, or as an executive or judicial officer of any State, to support the Constitution of the United States, shall have engaged in insurrection or rebellion against the same, or given aid or comfort to the enemies thereof. But Congress may, by a vote of two thirds of each House, remove such disability.

Section 4. The validity of the public debt of the United States, authorized by law, including debts incurred for payment of pensions and bounties for services in suppressing insurrection or rebellion, shall not be questioned. But neither the United States nor any State shall assume or pay any debt or obligation incurred in aid of insurrection or rebellion against the United States, or any claim for the loss or emancipation of any slave; but all such debts, obligations and claims shall be held illegal and void.

Section 5. The Congress shall have power to enforce, by appropriate legislation, the provisions of this article.

14th Amendment. Rights of Citizens

Proposed by Congress June 13, 1866; ratified July 9, 1[8]
Section 1 defines citizenship. It provides for the acquisi[tion] of United States citizenship by birth or by naturalization. Citizenship at birth is determined according to the princ[iple] of jus soli—"the law of the soil," where born; naturalizat[ion] is the legal process by which one acquires a new citizen[ship] at some time after birth. Under certain circumstances, citizenship can also be gained at birth abroad, accordin[g] to the principle of jus sanguinis—"the law of the blood,"[to] whom born. This section also contains two major civil ri[ghts] provisions: the Due Process Clause forbids a State (and its local governments) to act in any unfair or arbitrary wa[y]; the Equal Protection Clause forbids a State (and its loca[l] governments) to discriminate against, draw unreasonab[le] distinctions between, persons.

Most of the rights set out against the National Government in the first eight amendments have been extended against the States (and their local government[s]) through Supreme Court decisions involving the 14th Amendment's Due Process Clause.

The first sentence here replaced Article I, Section 2, Cla[use] 3, the Three-Fifths Compromise provision. Essentially, a[ll] persons in the United States are counted in each decen[nial] census, the basis for the distribution of House seats. Th[e] balance of this section has never been enforced and is generally thought to be obsolete.

This section limited the President's power to pardon tho[se] persons who had led the Confederacy during the Civil W[ar.] Congress finally removed this disability in 1898.

Section 4 also dealt with matters directly related to the [Civil] War. It reaffirmed the public debt of the United States; b[ut] it invalidated, prohibited payment of, any debt contracte[d] by the Confederate States and also prohibited any compensation of former slave owners.

Amendment. **Right to Vote—**
, Color, Servitude

sed by Congress February 26, 1869; ratified February
'0. The phrase "previous condition of servitude" refers
very. Note that this amendment does not guarantee the
o vote to African Americans, or to anyone else. Instead,
ids the States from discriminating against any person
e grounds of his "race, color, or previous condition of
ude" in the setting of suffrage qualifications.

Amendment. **Income Tax**

sed by Congress July 12, 1909; ratified February 3,
This amendment modified two provisions in Article
tion 2, Clause 3, and Section 9, Clause 4. It gives to
ress the power to levy an income tax, a direct tax,
ut regard to the populations of any of the States.

Amendment. **Popular Election of Senators**

sed by Congress May 13, 1912; ratified April 8,
This amendment repealed those portions of Article
tion 3, Clauses 1 and 2 relating to the election of
ors. Senators are now elected by the voters in each
. If a vacancy occurs, the governor of the State
ved must call an election to fill the seat; the governor
appoint a senator to serve until the next election, if the
's legislature has authorized that step.

Amendment. **Prohibition of Intoxicating Liquors**

osed by Congress December 18, 1917; ratified January
919. This amendment outlawed the making, selling,
porting, importing, or exporting of alcoholic beverages
e United States. It was repealed in its entirety by the
Amendment in 1933.

Amendment. **Equal Suffrage—Sex**

osed by Congress June 4, 1919; ratified August 18,
. No person can be denied the right to vote in any
tion in the United States on account of his or her sex.

15th Amendment

Section 1. The right of citizens of the United States to vote shall
not be denied or abridged by the United States or by any State
on account of race, color, or previous condition of servitude.
Section 2. The Congress shall have power to enforce this article
by appropriate legislation.

16th Amendment

The Congress shall have power to lay and collect taxes on
incomes, from whatever source derived, without apportionment
among the several States, and without regard to any census or
enumeration.

17th Amendment

The Senate of the United States shall be composed of two
Senators from each State, elected by the people thereof, for six
years; and each Senator shall have one vote. The electors in each
State shall have the qualifications requisite for electors of the
most numerous branch of the State legislatures.

When vacancies happen in the representation of any
State in the Senate, the executive authority of such State shall
issue writs of election to fill such vacancies: Provided, That the
legislature of any State may empower the executive thereof to
make temporary appointments until the people fill the vacancies
by election as the legislature may direct.

This amendment shall not be so construed as to affect the
election or term of any Senator chosen before it becomes valid as
part of the Constitution.

18th Amendment.

Section 1. After one year from the ratification of this article
the manufacture, sale, or transportation of intoxicating liquors
within, the importation thereof into, or the exportation thereof
from the United States and all territory subject to the jurisdiction
thereof for beverage purposes is hereby prohibited.

Section 2. The Congress and the several States shall have
concurrent power to enforce this article by appropriate
legislation.

Section 3. This article shall be inoperative unless it shall have
been ratified as an amendment to the Constitution by the
legislatures of the several States, as provided in the Constitution,
within seven years of the date of the submission hereof to the
States by Congress.

19th Amendment

The right of citizens of the United States to vote shall not be
denied or abridged by the United States or by any State on
account of sex.

Congress shall have power to enforce this article by
appropriate legislation.

20th Amendment

Section 1. The terms of the President and Vice President shall end at noon on the 20th day of January, and the terms of Senators and Representatives at noon on the 3d day of January, of the years in which such terms would have ended if this article had not been ratified; and the terms of their successors shall then begin.

Section 2. The Congress shall assemble at least once in every year, and such meeting shall begin at noon on the 3d day of January, unless they shall by law appoint a different day.

Section 3. If, at the time fixed for the beginning of the term of the President, the President elect shall have died, the Vice President elect shall become President. If a President shall not have been chosen before the time fixed for the beginning of his term, or if the President-elect shall have failed to qualify, then the Vice President elect shall act as President until a President shall have qualified; and the Congress may by law provide for the case wherein neither a President elect nor a Vice President elect shall have qualified, declaring who shall then act as President, or the manner in which one who is to act shall be selected, and such person shall act accordingly until a President or Vice President shall have qualified.

Section 4. The Congress may by law provide for the case of the death of any of the persons from whom the House of Representatives may choose a President whenever the right of choice shall have devolved upon them, and for the case of the death of any of the persons from whom the Senate may choose a Vice President whenever the right of choice shall have devolved upon them.

Section 5. Sections 1 and 2 shall take effect on the 15th day of October following the ratification of this article.

Section 6. This article shall be inoperative unless it shall have been ratified as an amendment to the Constitution by the legislatures of three fourths of the several States within seven years from the date of its submission.

21st Amendment

Section 1. The eighteenth article of amendment to the Constitution of the United States is hereby repealed.

Section 2. The transportation or importation into any State, Territory, or possession of the United States for delivery or use therein of intoxicating liquors, in violation of the laws thereof, is hereby prohibited.

Section 3. This article shall be inoperative unless it shall have been ratified as an amendment to the Constitution by conventions in the several States, as provided in the Constitution, within seven years from the date of the submission hereof to the States by the Congress.

20th Amendment. Commencement of Terms; Sessions of Congress; Death or Disqualification President-Elect

Proposed by Congress March 2, 1932; ratified January 23, 1933. The provisions of Sections 1 and 2 relating to Congress modified Article I, Section 4, Clause 2, and the provisions relating to the President, the 12th Amendment. The date on which the President and Vice President now take office was moved from March 4 to January 20. Similarly, the members of Congress now begin their term on January 3. The 20th Amendment is sometimes called the "Lame Duck Amendment" because it shortened the period of time a member of Congress who was defeated reelection (a "lame duck") remains in office.

This section deals with certain possibilities that were no covered by the presidential selection provisions of either Article II or the 12th Amendment. To this point, none of these situations has occurred. Note that there is neither President-elect nor a Vice President-elect until the electo votes have been counted by Congress, or, if the electora college cannot decide the matter, the House has chosen President or the Senate has chosen a Vice President.

Congress has not in fact ever passed such a law. See Section 2 of the 25th Amendment, regarding a vacancy the vice presidency; that provision could some day have impact here.

Section 5 set the date on which this amendment came in force.

Section 6 placed a time limit on the ratification process; note that a similar provision was written into the 18th, 21 and 22nd amendments.

21st Amendment. Repeal of 18th Amendment

Proposed by Congress February 20, 1933; ratified December 5, 1933. This amendment repealed all of the 1 Amendment. Section 2 modifies the scope of the Federa Government's commerce power set out in Article I, Secti 8, Clause 3; it gives to each State the power to regulate transportation or importation and the distribution or use intoxicating liquors in ways that would be unconstitution the case of any other commodity. The 21st Amendment the only amendment Congress has thus far submitted to States for ratification by conventions.

d Amendment. Presidential Tenure

osed by Congress March 21, 1947; ratified February
951. This amendment modified Article II, Section I,
se 1. It stipulates that no President may serve more
two elected terms. But a President who has succeeded
office beyond the midpoint in a term to which another
dent was originally elected may serve for more than
years. In any case, however, a President may not serve
than 10 years. Prior to Franklin Roosevelt, who was
ed to four terms, no President had served more than
ull terms in office.

d Amendment. Presidential Electors for the rict of Columbia

osed by Congress June 16, 1960; ratified March 29,
. This amendment modified Article II, Section I, Clause
d the 12th Amendment. It included the voters of the
ict of Columbia in the presidential electorate; and
des that the District is to have the same number of
ors as the least populous State—three electors—but no
than that number.

n Amendment. Right to Vote in Federal ctions—Tax Payment

osed by Congress August 27, 1962; ratified January 23,
. This amendment outlawed the payment of any tax as
ndition for taking part in the nomination or election of
federal officeholder.

n Amendment. Presidential Succession, Vice sidential Vacancy, Presidential Inability

osed by Congress July 6, 1965; ratified February 10,
. Section 1 revised the imprecise provision on presidential
ession in Article II, Section 1, Clause 6. It affirmed the
edent set by Vice President John Tyler, who became
dent on the death of William Henry Harrison in 1841.
ion 2 provides for the filling of a vacancy in the office of
President. The office had been vacant on 16 occasions
remained unfilled for the rest of each term involved.
n Spiro Agnew resigned the office in 1973, President
n selected Gerald Ford per this provision; and, when
ident Nixon resigned in 1974, Gerald Ford became
ident and chose Nelson Rockefeller as Vice President.

22nd Amendment

Section 1. No person shall be elected to the office of the President
more than twice, and no person who has held the office of
President, or acted as President, for more than two years of a term
to which some other person was elected President shall be elected
to the office of the President more than once. But this Article
shall not apply to any person holding the office of President,
when this Article was proposed by the Congress, and shall not
prevent any person who may be holding the office of President,
or acting as President, during the term within which this Article
becomes operative from holding the office of President or acting
as President during the remainder of such term.

Section 2. This article shall be inoperative unless it shall have
been ratified as an amendment to the Constitution by the
legislatures of three fourths of the several states within seven
years from the date of its submission to the States by the
Congress.

23rd Amendment.

Section 1. The District constituting the seat of Government of
the United States shall appoint in such manner as the Congress
may direct:
   A number of electors of President and Vice President
equal to the whole number of Senators and Representatives in
Congress to which the District would be entitled if it were a
State, but in no event more than the least populous State; they
shall be in addition to those appointed by the States, they shall
be considered, for the purposes of the election of President and
Vice President, to be electors appointed by a State; and they
shall meet in the District and perform such duties as provided by
the twelfth article of amendment.

24th Amendment.

Section 1. The right of citizens of the United States to vote in
any primary or other election for President or Vice President,
for electors for President or Vice President, or for Senator or
Representative in Congress, shall not be denied or abridged by
the United States or any State by reason of failure to pay any poll
tax or other tax.

Section 2. The Congress shall have power to enforce this article
by appropriate legislation.

25th Amendment.

Section 1. In case of the removal of the President from office
or of his death or resignation, the Vice President shall become
President.

Section 2. Whenever there is a vacancy in the office of the Vice
President, the President shall nominate a Vice President who
shall take office upon confirmation by a majority vote of both
Houses of Congress.

Section 3. Whenever the President transmits to the President pro tempore of the Senate and the Speaker of the House of Representatives his written declaration that he is unable to discharge the powers and duties of his office, and until he transmits to them a written declaration to the contrary, such powers and duties shall be discharged by the Vice President as Acting President.

Section 4. Whenever the Vice President and a majority of either the principal officers of the executive departments or of such other body as Congress may by law provide, transmit to the President pro tempore of the Senate and the Speaker of the House of Representatives their written declaration that the President is unable to discharge the powers and duties of his office, the Vice President shall immediately assume the powers and duties of the office as Acting President.

Thereafter, when the President transmits to the President pro tempore of the Senate and the Speaker of the House of Representatives his written declaration that no inability exists, he shall resume the powers and duties of his office unless the Vice President and a majority of either the principal officers of the executive department or of such other body as Congress may by law provide, transmit within four days to the President pro tempore of the Senate and the Speaker of the House of Representatives their written declaration that the President is unable to discharge the powers and duties of his office. Thereupon Congress shall decide the issue, assembling within forty-eight hours for that purpose if not in session. If the Congress, within twenty-one days after receipt of the latter written declaration, or, if Congress is not in session, within twenty-one days after Congress is required to assemble, determines by two-thirds vote of both Houses that the President is unable to discharge the powers and duties of his office, the Vice President shall continue to discharge the same as Acting President; otherwise, the President shall resume the powers and duties of his office.

This section created a procedure for determining if a President is so incapacitated that he cannot perform the powers and duties of his office.

Section 4 deals with the circumstance in which a President will not be able to determine the fact of incapacity. To this point, Congress has not established the "such other body" referred to here. This section contains the only typographic error in the Constitution; in its second paragraph, the word "department" should in fact read "departments."

26th Amendment.

Section 1. The right of citizens of the United States, who are eighteen years of age or older, to vote shall not be denied or abridged by the United States or by any State on account of age.

Section 2. The Congress shall have the power to enforce this article by appropriate legislation.

26th Amendment. Right to Vote—Age

Proposed by Congress March 23, 1971; ratified July 1, 1971. This amendment provides that the minimum age for voting in any election in the United States cannot be more than 18 years. (A State may set a minimum voting age of less than 18, however.)

27th Amendment.

No law varying the compensation for the services of the Senators and Representatives, shall take effect, until an election of Representatives shall have intervened.

27th Amendment. Congressional Pay

Proposed by Congress September 25, 1789; ratified May 7, 1992. This amendment modified Article I, Section 6, Clause 1. It limits Congress's power to fix the salaries of its members—by delaying the effectiveness of any increase in that pay until after the next regular congressional election.

Presidents of the United States

George Washington (1732–1799) Years in office: 1789–1797 Federalist Vice President: John Adams	• Commanded the Continental army during the American Revolution • President of the Constitutional Convention • Set precedents that were followed by other presidents, such as forming a cabinet • Strengthened new government through support of Hamilton's financial policies and use of force against the Whiskey Rebellion • Kept peace through Proclamation of Neutrality and Jay Treaty • Set basis of U.S. foreign policy in his Farewell Address
John Adams (1735–1826) Years in office: 1797–1801 Federalist Vice President: Thomas Jefferson	• American Revolution leader who protested Stamp Act • Helped draft Declaration of Independence • President during times of war in Europe • Alien and Sedition Acts contributed to his unpopularity and the fall of his party
Thomas Jefferson (1743–1826) Years in office: 1801–1809 Democratic-Republican Vice President: Aaron Burr, George Clinton	• Major author of the Declaration of Independence • Opposed Federalists • Favored limited, decentralized government • Opposed Hamilton's financial plan and Alien and Sedition Acts • Negotiated the Louisiana Purchase from France, which doubled the size of the nation
James Madison (1751–1836) Years in office: 1809–1817 Democratic-Republican Vice President: George Clinton, Elbridge Gerry	• Called the "Father of the Constitution" • An author of the Virginia Plan; his journals provide a record of events at the Constitutional Convention • Wrote 29 of *The Federalist Papers* • Proposed the Bill of Rights to Congress • Gained popularity after the War of 1812
James Monroe (1758–1831) Years in office: 1817–1825 Democratic-Republican Vice President: Daniel Tompkins	• Established U.S. foreign policy in the Western Hemisphere with the Monroe Doctrine • Settled boundaries with Canada (1818) • Acquired Florida (1819) • President during this "Era of Good Feelings" • Supported and signed Missouri Compromise (1820)
John Quincy Adams (1767–1848) Years in office: 1825–1829 Democratic-Republican Vice President: John Calhoun	• Became president after election was decided in the House of Representatives • Secretary of State under James Monroe • After leaving office as president, served in House of Representatives; only president to do so

Andrew Jackson (1767–1845) *Years in office: 1829–1837* *Democrat* *Vice President: John Calhoun,* *Martin Van Buren*	• Hero of Battle of New Orleans (War of 1812) • Opposed Calhoun and nullification of 1828 and 1832 tariffs • Vetoed rechartering of Second National Bank • Supported Indian Removal Act • Associated with Jacksonian Democracy—the start of mass politics and nominating conventions • Used "spoils system" to give jobs to supporters
Martin Van Buren (1782–1862) *Years in office: 1837–1841* *Democrat* *Vice President: Richard Johnson*	• First New Yorker to become president • Served as vice president to Jackson • Opposed Texas annexation because slavery issue divided his party • Presidency weakened by economic crisis of the Panic of 1837 • Had major role in creating the Democratic Party from the Democratic-Republicans and the nation's second party system—the Democrats versus the Whigs
William Henry Harrison (1774–1841) *Years in office: 1841* *Whig* *Vice President: John Tyler*	• While governor of Indiana Territory, led military actions against Native Americans in the Battle of Tippecanoe (1811) • Elected as first Whig candidate on the slogan "Tippecanoe and Tyler Too" • First president to die in office; served only one month
John Tyler (1790–1862) *Years in office: 1841–1845* *Whig* *Vice President: none*	• First vice president to come into presidency on death of president, called "His Accidency" • Texas annexed by congressional vote largely because of his influence • His pro South and pro states rights positions resulted in his expulsion from the Whig Party by its pro nationalism leaders
James K. Polk (1795–1849) *Years in office: 1845–1849* *Democrat* *Vice President: George Dallas*	• Foreign policy aimed at fulfilling goal of Manifest Destiny • With slogan "54' 40 or fight!" campaigned for all of Oregon country, settled for Oregon Treaty (1846) with Great Britain, dividing region at 49th parallel • Supported Tyler's annexation of Texas and favored acquisition of California • Led nation in Mexican War, 1846–1848 • The Treaty of Guadalupe Hidalgo gave the United States the Mexican Cession, which included California
Zachary Taylor (1784–1850) *Years in office: 1849–1850* *Whig* *Vice President: Millard Fillmore*	• West Point graduate and military hero of Mexican War, known as "Old Rough and Ready" • A Virginian, a slave owner, and a nationalist—he opposed secession • Died in office after 16 months as president
Millard Fillmore (1800–1874) *Years in office: 1850–1853* *Whig* *Vice President: none*	• New Yorker by birth, became president on death of Taylor • Negotiated passage of the Compromise of 1850 • Supported enforcement of the Fugitive Slave Law and opposed secessionists, angering both Northerners and Southerners • Failure of Compromise of 1850 marked end for Whig Party • In 1856, lost as presidential candidate of the Know-Nothing Party
Franklin Pierce (1804–1869) *Years in office: 1853–1857* *Democrat* *Vice President: William King*	• New Englander who supported Kansas-Nebraska Act • Gadsden Purchase ratified during his presidency • Trade treaty with Japan became effective during his administration, due to the efforts of Commodore Matthew Perry

James Buchanan (1791–1868) *Years in office: 1857–1861* *Democrat* *Vice President: John Breckinridge*	• In office when *Dred Scott* v. *Sanford* decision was issued and John Brown's raid at Harper's Ferry occurred • Took no action in response to the secession of South Carolina and six other states, claiming he lacked the power to act
Abraham Lincoln (1809–1865) *Years in office: 1861–1865* *Republican* *Vice President: Hannibal Hamlin, Andrew Johnson*	• Became nationally known as result of Lincoln-Douglas debates in 1858 • First Republican to be elected president • Used war powers of the presidency during Civil War to achieve his goal of preserving the nation • Issued Emancipation Proclamation; gave Gettysburg Address • Assassinated before he could act on his plans for reconstruction
Andrew Johnson (1808–1875) *Years in office: 1865–1869* *Democrat* *Vice President: none*	• Impeached by House after bitter disagreements with Congress over Reconstruction; acquitted by a single vote in Senate • Thirteenth and Fourteenth Amendments ratified during his presidency
Ulysses S. Grant (1822–1885) *Years in office: 1869–1877* *Republican* *Vice President: Schuyler Colfax, Henry Wilson*	• Civil War military leader who served as General-in-Chief of the Union army • Transcontinental railroad completed and Fifteenth Amendment ratified during his presidency • Crédit Mobilier and the Whiskey Ring scandals marred his presidency
Rutherford B. Hayes (1822–1893) *Years in office: 1877–1881* *Republican* *Vice President: William Wheeler*	• Election decided through compromise, preventing a constitutional crisis after a dispute over electoral votes • Federal troops removed from the South, marking the end of Reconstruction
James A. Garfield (1831–1881) *Years in office: 1881* *Republican* *Vice President: Chester A. Arthur*	• Assassinated after four months in office
Chester A. Arthur (1830–1886) *Years in office: 1881–1885* *Republican* *Vice President: none*	• Vetoed Chinese Exclusion Act (1882) but signed another act reducing the Chinese immigration ban to ten years • Supported Pendleton Act (1883) that enacted civil service reform • Worked to reform American restrictive tariffs
Grover Cleveland (1837–1908) *Years in office: 1885–1889; 1893–1897* *Democrat* *Vice President: Thomas Hendricks, Adlai Stevenson*	• Expanded the civil service • Only president to serve two nonconsecutive terms • Served as governor of New York • In second term, confronted major depression that began with Panic of 1893 • An anti-imperialist, he opposed annexation of Hawaii • In 1894, sent federal troops to end Pullman Strike

Benjamin Harrison (1833–1901) *Years in office: 1889–1893* *Republican* *Vice President: Levi Morton*	• Elected president with most electoral but not popular votes • Supported Sherman Antitrust Act • Encouraged conservation of forest reserves • Favored U.S. expansion in the Pacific Ocean and building of a canal in Central America • Expanded U.S. Navy
William McKinley (1843–1901) *Years in office: 1897–1901* *Republican* *Vice President: Garret Hobart,* *Theodore Roosevelt*	• President during a period of expansionism marked by Spanish-American War • A high tariff and the Gold Standard Act passed during his administration • Annexed Hawaii • Open Door Policy issued by his secretary of state • Assassinated in 1901
Theodore Roosevelt (1858–1919) *Years in office: 1901–1909* *Republican* *Vice President: Charles Fairbanks*	• Progressive governor of New York (1899–1900) • Presidential programs called the Square Deal • Known as a trustbuster, conservationist, reformer, and nationalist • Used the power of presidency to regulate economic affairs of the nation and to expand its role in Asia and the Caribbean • Issued the Roosevelt Corollary to the Monroe Doctrine
William Howard Taft (1857–1930) *Years in office: 1909–1913* *Republican* *Vice President: James Sherman*	• Policy of "dollar diplomacy" gave diplomatic and military support to U.S. business investments in Latin America • Continued Progressive Era policies of business regulation, but his conservative tariff and conservation policies split the party
Woodrow Wilson (1856–1924) *Years in office: 1913–1921* *Democrat* *Vice President: Thomas Marshall*	• Progressive Era president whose program was known as New Freedom • Reform regulation included Clayton Antitrust Act, Federal Reserve System, Federal Trade Commission Act, and Underwood Tariff Act (which lowered rates) • Led the nation during World War I • Supported the Treaty of Versailles and League of Nations, which the Senate failed to approve
Warren G. Harding (1865–1923) *Years in office: 1921–1923* *Republican* *Vice President: Calvin Coolidge*	• Led nation into "Roaring Twenties" on a call for "normalcy" • Administration known for corruption and scandals, including the Teapot Dome Scandal • Opened Washington Conference on Naval Disarmament in 1921, although he opposed internationalism
Calvin Coolidge (1872–1933) *Years in office: 1923–1929* *Republican* *Vice President: Charles Dawes*	• Presidency marked by conservative, laissez-faire attitudes toward business, stating that "after all, the chief business of the American people is business" • Presided over "Coolidge prosperity" • Kellogg-Briand Pact signed during his administration • Immigration Act (1924), setting national quotas, passed during his presidency
Herbert Hoover (1874–1964) *Years in office: 1929–1933* *Republican* *Vice President: Charles Curtis*	• Used government resources against the Great Depression without success • Supported loans through Reconstruction Finance Corporation • Opposed direct relief • Used federal troops against the World War I veterans' "Bonus Army"

Franklin D. Roosevelt (1882–1945) *Years in office: 1933–1945* *Democrat* *Vice President: John Garner, Henry Wallace, Harry S. Truman*	• Led U.S. through Great Depression and World War II from which the nation emerged as world's leading economic, military, and political power • Increased government's role in and responsibility for economic, financial, and general welfare of nation through New Deal policies such as Social Security Act. • Expanded power of federal government with programs of Relief, Recovery, Reform, as well as by military and diplomatic conduct of the war • New Deal programs criticized as both inadequate and too extreme • Issued Japanese-American internment order; proposed "Court-packing" • Only president to serve more than two terms
Harry S. Truman (1884–1972) *Years in office: 1945–1953* *Democrat* *Vice President: Alben Barkley*	• Made decision to drop two atomic bombs on Japan in 1945 to end World War II • Began the policy of containment of communism with the Truman Doctrine • Supported economic recovery in Europe through the Marshall Plan • Continued the New Deal philosophy with his Fair Deal • Entered the Korean War during his presidency
Dwight D. Eisenhower (1890–1969) *Years in office: 1953–1961* *Republican* *Vice President: Richard M. Nixon*	• Commander of Allied forces in Europe during World War II • Issued Eisenhower Doctrine • Approved Saint Lawrence Seaway and 1956 Federal Highway Act • Sent troops to Little Rock, Arkansas, to support school desegregation • In office when Alaska and Hawaii became 49th and 50th states
John F. Kennedy (1917–1963) *Years in office: 1961–1963* *Democrat* *Vice President: Lyndon B. Johnson*	• Promoted the New Frontier program (which centered on containment), the Peace Corps, and the Alliance for Progress • Successfully resolved the Cuban missile crisis • Assassinated in 1963
Lyndon B. Johnson (1908–1973) *Years in office: 1963–1969* *Democrat* *Vice President: Hubert Humphrey*	• Promoted antipoverty programs and civil rights through his Great Society program • Used the Gulf of Tonkin Resolution to expand the Vietnam War • Division over his war policy led to his decision not to seek reelection • President during a period of active civil rights movements for African Americans and women
Richard M. Nixon (1913–1994) *Years in office: 1969–1974* *Republican* *Vice President: Spiro Agnew, Gerald R. Ford*	• Pursued a "Vietnamization" policy and increased bombing followed by a 1973 cease-fire in Vietnam • Relaxed relations with USSR and the People's Republic of China • Resigned as president in order to avoid impeachment for his role in the Watergate scandal
Gerald R. Ford (1913–2006) *Years in office: 1974–1977* *Republican* *Vice President: Nelson Rockefeller*	• Only president not to be elected by the American public; appointed as vice president under Nixon and succeeded to the presidency after Nixon's resignation • Pardoned Nixon, for which he was both criticized and praised • Worked to restore faith in government after Watergate crisis

Jimmy Carter (1924–) *Years in office: 1977–1981* *Democrat* *Vice President: Walter Mondale*	• Domestic problems included inflation and oil shortages • Supported international human rights and Panama Canal treaties • Opposed the Soviet invasion of Afghanistan • Facilitated the Camp David Accords, which led to peace between Egypt and Israel
Ronald Reagan (1911–2004) *Years in office: 1981–1989* *Republican* *Vice President: George H.W. Bush*	• Held conservative viewpoint on issues such as abortion and prayer in school • Based his supply-side economic policy (or "Reaganomics") on the belief that government works against individual initiative • Presidency marked by trade and federal budget deficits • Arms control agreements signed with the USSR in 1985, 1986, and 1987 • Foreign policy aimed at keeping communism out of Latin America • Popularity damaged and foreign policy weakened by Iran-Contra scandal
George H.W. Bush (1924–2018) *Years in office: 1989–1993* *Republican* *Vice President: J. Danforth Quayle*	• Inherited budget deficit, savings and loan scandal, and legacy of Iran-Contra Affair from the Reagan administration • In office when Cold War ended, and communist governments in Eastern Europe and Soviet Union fell • Led the United States in the Persian Gulf War against Iraq
William (Bill) Clinton (1946–) *Years in office: 1993–2001* *Democrat* *Vice President: Albert Gore, Jr.*	• Domestic policies centered on health care and social security reform, as well as economic issues, such as reduction of the national deficit • Secured approval of NAFTA (North American Free Trade Agreement) • Backed NATO intervention against Serbia to stop "ethnic cleansing" • Impeached by the House of Representatives in 1998 on charges of perjury and obstruction of justice, but acquitted by the Senate
George W. Bush (1946–) *Years in office: 2001–2009* *Republican* *Vice President:* *Richard (Dick) B. Cheney*	• Took office after a close election in which a dispute over ballot recounts in Florida was decided by the Supreme Court in *Bush* v. *Gore* (2000) • Conservative domestic agenda included tax cuts, No Child Left Behind, creation of Department of Homeland Security, and attempts to privatize social security • After attacks of September 11, 2001, ordered U.S. forces into Afghanistan to defeat Taliban and al Qaeda extremists and into a war against Iraq • Left office with nation in major recession, and controversy that included Iraq War, treatment of prisoners, and balancing of liberty versus security in a democracy
Barack H. Obama (1961–) *Years in office: 2009–2017* *Democrat* *Vice President:* *Joseph (Joe) R. Biden, Jr.*	• First African American to be elected president; first president since Eisenhower to twice win at least 51 percent of the national popular vote • Led nation during most serious economic crisis since the Great Depression • Withdrew U.S. troops in Iraq and moved those in Afghanistan to a support mission • Legislation passed included Patient Protection and Affordable Health Care Act and American Recovery and Reinvestment Act
Donald J. Trump (1946–) *Years in office: 2017–2021* *Republican* *Vice President: Michael R. Pence*	• First person elected president without either military or government service; won electoral vote but lost popular vote • Signed historic Tax Cuts and Jobs Act of 2017 into law • First and only president to be impeached twice and acquitted twice • Signed $2.2 trillion Coronavirus Aid, Relief, and Economic Security Act (CARES)
Joseph (Joe) R. Biden, Jr. (1942–) *Years in office: 2021–* *Democrat* *Vice President: Kamala Harris*	• First to select a female African American as Vice President and first to nominate a female African American to the Supreme Court • Legislation includes American Plan for Relief from COVID-19 and a trillion dollar American Infrastructure Plan

Landmark Supreme Court Cases

Every Supreme Court case deals with important **constitutional principles.**
Some cases have had such an enduring impact on United States history
and government that they require greater examination. The lasting
significance and central constitutional principles of 37 landmark
Supreme Court cases are outlined briefly in this section. The cases in blue
are in the new Framework and may appear in the Regents exam. For more
information about the meaning of the constitutional principles, review the
Thirteen Basic Constitutional Principles found on pages A-13 through A-17.

Year	Name of Case	Constitutional Principle	Why Decision is Important
1803	*Marbury* v. *Madison*	• Separation of Powers: Checks and Balances • the Judiciary	• Established the Supreme Court's right of *judicial review*—the right to determine the constitutionality of laws • Strengthened the judiciary in relation to other branches of government
1819	*McCulloch* v. *Maryland*	• Federalism: Federal Supremacy • National Power: Necessary and Proper Clause • the Judiciary	• Said no state could tax a federally chartered bank because *the power to tax involves the power to destroy* • Ruling established the principle of national supremacy—that the Constitution and federal laws overrule state laws when the two conflict • Expanded national power by supporting use of *necessary and proper* clause to carry out constitutional powers
1824	*Gibbons* v. *Ogden*	• Federalism: Federal Supremacy • Property Rights/ Economic Policy: Interstate Commerce • the Judiciary	• States may regulate only what is solely intrastate commerce (within a state) • Congress has power to regulate interstate commerce, including commerce that involved intrastate-interstate activity • Ruling established the basis of congressional regulation of interstate commerce
1832	*Worcester* v. *Georgia*	• Federalism • National Power • Separation of Powers • Equality • Rights of Ethnic/ Racial Groups	• The Constitution gives the federal government, not state governments, exclusive jurisdiction over Native American nations • Treaties between the U.S. government and Native American nations are the *Supreme Law of the Land* • Therefore, Georgia laws taking jurisdiction of Cherokee people and land were void • President Andrew Jackson defied the ruling and the national policy of Indian Removal followed

Year	Name of Case	Constitutional Principle	Why Decision is Important
1857	*Dred Scott* v. *Sanford*	• the Judiciary • Equality • Civil Liberties • Rights of Ethnic/Racial Groups	• Ruled that African Americans were not citizens (overturned by 14th Amendment) • Declared enslaved people to be property of owners • As property, protected by 5th Amendment, enslaved people could be taken anywhere; therefore, Missouri Compromise was unconstitutional
1883	Civil Rights Cases	• Equality • National Power: Congress • Rights of Ethnic/Racial Groups: 13th and 14th Amendments	• Declared 1875 Civil Rights Act unconstitutional • 14th Amendment prohibited *states* from discrimination, but not individual actions in the private sector, such as in theaters, hotels, and restaurants • *Private discrimination* was not a violation of the 13th Amendment, prohibition against slavery and *involuntary servitude*
1886	*Wabash, St. Louis & Pacific RR* v. *Illinois*	• Property Rights/Economic Policy: Interstate Commerce • National Power • Federalism	• Invalidated state law setting railroad rates on the part of an interstate trip within state borders • By declaring it a federal power to regulate rates and by limiting state regulations, Court strengthened Constitution's interstate commerce clause • Ruling paved way for creation in 1887 of Interstate Commerce Commission
1895	*United States* v. *E.C. Knight Co.*	• National Power: Anti-Trust • the Judiciary • Federalism • Property Rights/Economic Policy: Interstate Commerce	• While federal government did have the right to regulate some parts of economy, states, under the 10th Amendment, could regulate intrastate economic activities, such as manufacturing • Refineries were *manufacturing operations*, not commerce; therefore, the Sherman Anti-Trust Act could not be applied to American Sugar Refining Co. although company controlled 90% of sugar processing in the nation
1895	*In Re Debs*	• National Power: Commerce Clause • Property Rights/Economic Policy: Commerce Clause and Labor	• Ruled that federal government under commerce clause of Constitution had right to issue an injunction to halt 1894 Pullman strike • Said strike hurt *general welfare* of nation by disrupting commerce and mail delivery
1896	*Plessy* v. *Ferguson*	• Equality • Rights of Ethnic/Racial Groups 14th Amendment Equal Protection Clause • the Judiciary	• Upheld Louisiana law providing for *equal but separate accommodations for white and colored races* • Said law did not conflict with 13th or 14th Amendments, nor with commerce clause • 14th Amendment was not intended to enforce what Court called *social equality* • Provided legal justification for *separate but equal* segregation policy until overturned in 1954 by *Brown* v. *Board of Education*

Year	Name of Case	Constitutional Principle	Why Decision is Important
1904	*Northern Securities Co. v. United States*	• National Power: Anti-Trust, Commerce Clause • Property Rights/ Economic Policy	• Federal suit (part of T. Roosevelt's trust-busting) using Sherman Antitrust Act • Court ruled that the Northern Securities Company was formed only to eliminate competition and ordered it to be dissolved • Congress under commerce clause had authority to regulate any *conspiracy* to eliminate competition
1905	*Lochner v. New York*	• Property Rights/ Economic Policy: Contracts • Civil Liberties: 14th Amendment	• Ruled that a New York law limiting bakers to 10-hour days and 60-hour weeks in order to protect public health was unconstitutional because it violated the 14th Amendment *right and liberty of an individual to contract* • New York law went beyond *legitimate* police powers of a state
1908	*Muller v. Oregon*	• Civil Liberties: 14th Amendment • Federalism: 10th v. 14th Amendments • Equality • Rights of Women	• Upheld an Oregon law that limited women to a 10-hour work day in laundries or factories in order to protect women's health • Cited the physical differences between men and women when ruling that the need to protect women's health outweighed the liberty to make a contract that was upheld in *Lochner v. New York*
1919	*Schenck v. United States*	• Civil Liberties: Limited in Wartime • the Judiciary	• Established limits on free speech; right is not absolute but dependent on circumstances, i.e. person is not protected if falsely shouts fire in a crowded theatre • In this case, Court saw defendants' actions as a *clear and present danger* to security of the nation in wartime
1935	*Schechter Poultry Corporation v. United States*	• Separation of Powers • Property Rights/ Economic Policy: Commerce Clause	• Placed limits on the ability of Congress to delegate legislative powers to president • By narrowly defining interstate commerce, also restricted congressional powers to regulate commerce • Declared the New Deal's National Industrial Act unconstitutional
1944	*Korematsu v. United States*	• Civil Liberties: Equal Protection • Presidential Power in Wartime • Rights of Ethnic/ Racial Groups	• Upheld the power of the president in wartime to limit a group's civil liberties • Ruled that forcible relocation of Japanese Americans to Wartime Relocation Agency Camps during World War II was legal
1954	*Brown v. Board of Education*	• Equality: Equal Protection • Federalism • Rights of Ethnic/ Racial Groups	• In this school segregation case, Court overturned *Plessy v. Ferguson separate but equal* doctrine • Ruled that *separate educational facilities are inherently* (inseparably) *unequal* and violate the 14th Amendment's *equal protection* clause

Year	Name of Case	Constitutional Principle	Why Decision is Important
1957	*Watkins* v. *United States*	• Criminal Procedures: Due Process • National Power: Congressional Investigations • Civil Liberties	• Congressional investigations must spell out their legislative purpose and jurisdiction • The Bill of Rights is applicable to congressional investigations • Watkins was within his rights to refuse to testify to matters beyond scope of House Committee on Un-American Activities
1961	*Mapp* v. *Ohio*	• Criminal Procedures: 4th Amendment • Civil Liberties: 14th Amendment	• Ruled that 4th and 14th Amendments protected citizen from illegal searches • Applied *exclusionary rule* to state courts, i.e. evidence obtained unconstitutionally—in this case without a search warrant—could not be used in federal or state courts
1962	*Baker* v. *Carr*	• Avenues of Representation: Voting Rights; Equal Protection • Federalism	• Court has jurisdiction over apportionment of seats in state legislatures • Overrepresentation of rural voters and under representation of urban voters was a violation of 14th Amendment's *equal protection* clause • Ruling led to other court cases that established *one person-one vote* concept
1962	*Engel* v. *Vitale*	• Civil Liberties: Establishment Clause, 1st and 14th Amendments	• Reciting of an official prayer in the schools violated the 1st Amendment's *establishment of religion* clause, which was applied to the states by the 14th Amendment • Although students were not required to say the non-denominational prayer, its recitation in class put them under pressure. Allowing students to leave room and non-denominational nature of prayer did not make New York law constitutional.
1963	*Gideon* v. *Wainwright*	• Civil Liberties • Criminal Procedures: 6th and 14th Amendments	• Ruled unanimously that the 6th Amendment right to an attorney, which was applied to the states by the 14th Amendment, required that a state provide lawyers for poor people accused of felony crimes, not just in cases of capital crimes
1964	*Heart of Atlanta Motel* v. *United States*	• National Power: Commerce Clause • Civil Liberties: Equal Protection Clause	• Upheld constitutionality of 1964 Civil Rights Act's use of congressional interstate commerce powers to prohibit discrimination in private facilities whose operations affect interstate commerce
1966	*Miranda* v. *Arizona*	• Criminal Procedures: Due Process, Self-Incrimination • Civil Liberties: Equal Protection	• Established the requirement prior to questioning to inform those accused of crimes that they have the right to remain silent, the right to a lawyer, and that what they say can be used against them in court • Evidence obtained without this warning may not be used in court under the *exclusionary rule*

Year	Name of Case	Constitutional Principle	Why Decision is Important
1969	*Tinker* v. *Des Moines Independent Community School District*	• Civil Liberties: 1st Amendment, Student Rights/ Safe School Environment	• While recognizing the authority of schools *to prescribe and control conduct in the schools,* the court ruled that *neither students or teachers shed their constitutional rights to freedom of speech or expression at the schoolhouse gate* • Symbolic, silent expression of opinion in absence of any disorder (wearing of black armbands to protest Vietnam War) is protected under the 1st Amendment
1971	*New York Times Co.* v. *United States*	• Civil Liberties: Freedom of the Press • National Power	• Court, in 6–3 vote, upheld 1st Amendment right to freedom of the press • Ruled that government had not met the *heavy burden of prior restraint* i.e. not made a strong enough case to stop publication of *The Pentagon Papers* on the grounds that national security would be hurt
1973	*Roe* v. *Wade*	• Civil Liberties: Right to Privacy • Rights of Women	• Declared state laws making abortions illegal to be unconstitutional while stating certain limits and conditions • Basis of decision was right to privacy, citing primarily the *due process* clause of 14th Amendment
1974	*United States* v. *Nixon*	• Separation of Powers: Due Process, Executive Power	• By 8-0 vote, Court ruled that Nixon had to turn over the Watergate tapes to the Special Prosecutor. • No president was above the law; *executive privilege* (confidentiality) was not absolute • Separation of powers does not protect a president from judicial review of *executive privilege,* nor from the needs of the judicial process
1985	*New Jersey* v. *T.L.O.*	• Civil Liberties: 4th Amendment, Student Rights/ Safe School Environment	• Affirmed that 4th Amendment prohibition on *unreasonable searches and seizures* applied to school officials • But, necessity of maintaining discipline allowed for searches when there are *reasonable grounds* that the law or school rules have been broken compared to police requirement of *probable cause*
1985	*Oneida Indian Nation of New York State* v. *County of Oneida*	• Equality: Equal Protection, Due Process • Rights of Ethnic and Racial Groups	• American Indian tribes have the right to sue state governments to reclaim their tribal lands
1990	*Cruzan* v. *Director Missouri Department of Health*	• Civil Liberties: Due Process	• Ruled that under *due process* clause, a competent person has the right to refuse life-sustaining treatment • Evidence of the wishes of an incompetent person must be *clear and convincing;* evidence not presented in this case • Cruzan's parents then gathered what Missouri court agreed was *clear and convincing* evidence and the life support system was removed

Year	Name of Case	Constitutional Principle	Why Decision is Important
1992	*Planned Parenthood of Southeastern Pennsylvania et al.* v. *Casey*	• Civil Liberties • Rights of Women	• Upheld *Roe* v. *Wade* decision • Determined that Pennsylvania law with provisions, such as 24-hour waiting period and parental consent to a minor's abortion, did not create *undue burden or substantial obstacles* to abortion • Struck down requirement of husband notification
1995	*Vernonia School District* v. *Acton*	• Civil Liberties: 4th Amendment, Student Rights/Safe School Environment	• Ruled that a school's practice of testing athletes randomly for drug use did not violate their rights under the 4th and 14th Amendments • Cited schools need to maintain student safety and fulfill its educational mission
2000	*Bush* v. *Gore*	• Avenues of Representation • Federalism: Balance Between Nation and State • Equality	• Stopped the recount ordered by Florida Supreme Court in the 2000 presidential election • Ruled that Florida Supreme Court had violated equal protection clause of Constitution
2010	*Citizens United* v. *Federal Election Commission*	• Avenues of Representation • the Judiciary	• Under the First Amendment, political spending is political speech so corporations and unions cannot be prevented from funding independent political advertising for and against candidates in elections. • Defended political speech from a corporation as member of society; not an "artificial entity"
2015	*Obergefell* v. *Hodges*	• 14th Amendment • Due Process Clause • Equal Protection Clause	• Ruled that since states have the right to sanction opposite-sex marriages, they must also sanction same-sex marriages
2015	*King* v. *Burwell*	• Federalism—Balance Between Nation and State	• Decision upheld the Affordable Care Act (ACA), a primary piece of legislation of the Obama administration • Court ruled that under this Act, Congress created the health exchanges and tax credits for federal use if states did not create them for their residents • Internal Revenue Service did not have that authority and did not create the tax credit

The Thirteen Basic Constitutional Principles

Thirteen basic constitutional principles have endured since the ratification of the Constitution. These principles continue to be important to the development of American government and society.

Constitutional Principle 1
National Power—Limits and Potential

The powers of the federal government are limited. The Constitution states the powers held by each branch of government. The powers that are not delegated to the national government are reserved to the states or to the people (Tenth Amendment). The Bill of Rights also limits the government's interference with basic rights.

However, the powers of all three branches of the federal government have grown.
- Has the national government become too powerful?
- Do the limits placed on the national government make it incapable of dealing with the problems of the modern age?

Examples of This Principle as a Recurring Theme in U.S. History

Need for a strong central government: debate over ratification

Loose vs. strict interpretation of the Constitution: Hamilton's financial plan, Louisiana Purchase

Conflict over slavery: Constitutional Convention, 1820–1860

Civil War: establishing federal supremacy over the states

Imperialism: Spanish-American War, acquiring an overseas empire

Progressive movement: Theodore Roosevelt and Woodrow Wilson

Elastic clause: Pure Food and Drug Act, Social Security

Commerce clause: expanding powers of government

New Deal: expanding role of government

Great Society: demand for reform

New Federalism: less government involvement

Constitutional Principle 2
Federalism—Balance Between Nation and State

The Constitution created a new federal government that divided power between the states and the national government. The Constitution reserved certain powers to the states and to the people, but the Constitution and the laws and treaties of the United States are supreme to state laws.

- Is the power still balanced, or has it tilted to the federal government?
- Has the shift of power to the federal government become greater since the New Deal, or did Reagan's New Federalism reverse this trend?

Examples of This Principle as a Recurring Theme in U.S. History

Marshall Supreme Court cases: *McCulloch* v. *Maryland*, *Gibbons* v. *Ogden*

Virginia and Kentucky Resolutions, John C. Calhoun, nullification, states' rights, secession

Conflict over slavery: 1820–1860

Civil War: establishing federal supremacy over the states

Reconstruction: greater federal supremacy; 13th, 14th, and 15th Amendments

Populists and Progressive reform

New Deal legislation

Rights of minorities: *Brown* v. *Board of Education*

Fourteenth Amendment: extends Bill of Rights protections to states

Great Society, mid-1960s

New Federalism, 1980s

King v. *Burwell*

Constitutional Principle 3
The Judiciary—Interpreter of the Constitution or Shaper of Public Policy

The Judiciary interprets the law (Article III) and has the power to declare laws unconstitutional. This power of judicial review dates from Marshall's decision in *Marbury* v. *Madison,* which was based on Article III, and the supremacy clause in Article VI, which states that the Constitution is the "supreme law of the land."

- By acting when Congress has not acted, or by reversing congressional actions to favor the states, have the courts become lawmakers instead of law interpreters?
- If the courts did not have the power to shape public policy, would the Bill of Rights and democracy itself be endangered?

Examples of This Principle as a Recurring Theme in U.S. History

Marbury v. *Madison:* judicial review strengthened judiciary, government, and national unity

Federal vs. state powers: *McCulloch* v. *Maryland, Gibbons* v. *Ogden*

Limiting protections and rights: *Dred Scott* v. *Sanford,* Civil Rights Cases

Reversals of decisions: *Plessy* v. *Ferguson, Brown* v. *Board of Education*

State vs. federal powers: *United States* v. *E.C. Knight Co., Lochner* v. *New York, Schechter Poultry* v. *United States*

Rights of accused: *Miranda* v. *Arizona, Gideon* v. *Wainwright*

First Amendment cases (freedom of speech, press, religion, assembly): *Engel* v. *Vitale, Schenck* v. *United States, New York Times Co.* v. *United States, Tinker* v. *Des Moines Independent Community School District, Citizens United* v. *F.E.C.*

Ninth Amendment privacy cases: *Roe* v. *Wade; Cruzan* v. *Director, MO Dept. of Health; Griswold* v. *CT*

Checks and balances: *Watkins* v. *United States, United States* v. *Nixon*

Constitutional Principle 4
Civil Liberties—Protecting Individual Liberties From Government Abuses; the Balance Between Government and the Individual

A problem unique to a democratic government is how to balance the rights of the individual and the needs of society. The Constitution's Bill of Rights and Fourteenth Amendment guarantee certain basic rights, rights which predate any government. But these rights are not unlimited.

- What are the rights of the individual?
- Should government protect and/or extend the rights of the individual?
- Should government decide where the balance should be between individual and societal rights?

Examples of This Principle as a Recurring Theme in U.S. History

Right to dissent: Alien & Sediton Acts; Virginia & Kentucky Resolutions

Equal protection clause: Fourteenth Amendment—Civil Rights Cases, *Heart of Atlanta Motel* v. *United States*

Freedom of speech v. "clear and present danger": *Schenck* v. *United States*

Relocation of Japanese Americans: *Korematsu* v. *United States*

Red Scare, McCarthyism: fear of subversion, the erosion of liberties *Watkins* v. *United States*

Testing for drug use: *Vernonia School District* v. *Acton*

Rights of individuals: effects of technology

Individual's rights v. security against terrorism: USA PATRIOT Act, Foreign Intelligence Surveillance Act

Constitutional Principle 5
Criminal Procedures—The Balance Between the Rights of the Accused and the Protection of the Community and Victims

This is a question of balancing the rights of individuals accused of crimes and those of citizens to be safe and secure.
- Why does an individual accused of a crime have rights?
- Are those rights easily defined?

- What are the rights of a victim of a crime?
- When do the rights of the accused interfere with society's ability to maintain law and order?

Examples of This Principle as a Recurring Theme in U.S. History

Free press vs. the rights of the accused

Death penalty: individual rights v. rights of society

Writ of *habeas corpus:* purpose

Due process of law, search and seizure: *Mapp* v. *Ohio*

Students' rights and search and seizure: *New Jersey* v. *T.L.O.; Vernonia School District* v. *Acton*

Rights of the accused: *Miranda* v. *Arizona, Gideon* v. *Wainwright*

Constitutional Principle 6
Equality—Its Historic and Present Meaning as a Constitutional Value

This issue involves questions of who is equal and in what ways. When Jefferson wrote that "all men are created equal," he referred to the equality before the law of white, property-owning males. The equal protection clause of the Fourteenth Amendment and the due process clause of the Fifth Amendment were later interpreted to make equal justice more of a reality for all Americans.

- According to the Constitution, who is equal: men and women? All races? Rich and poor? Young and old?
- How has the Constitution expanded equality?
- Has equality been achieved?
- How are people equal: equal in opportunity? Before the law? In entitlements?

Examples of This Principle as a Recurring Theme in U.S. History

Conflict over slavery: Constitutional Convention; 1820–1860
Passage of 13th, 14th, and 15th Amendments
Equal protection clause: 14th Amendment
Jim Crow laws: legal basis for segregation
Plessy v. *Ferguson*
Brown v. *Board of Education*
Martin Luther King, Jr.: Civil Rights Movement
19th-century women's rights movement

19th Amendment
1960s women's rights movement
Treatment of Native Americans: *Worcester* v. *Georgia*
Native American movement
New Deal: relief of human suffering
Great Society: help for less fortunate
Affirmative action: court decisions
LGBT movement: Stonewall Inn, *Obergefell* v. *Hodges*

Constitutional Principle 7
The Rights of Women Under the Constitution

Women are not mentioned in the Constitution except in the Nineteenth Amendment, which protects their right to vote.
- What is the historic and present meaning of equality for women as a constitutional value?

- How were these changes achieved?
- Are federal laws and court rulings sufficiently protective of the rights of women?
- Was there a need for the defeated Equal Rights Amendment?

Examples of This Principle as a Recurring Theme in U.S. History

Elizabeth Cady Stanton and Susan B. Anthony: Women's suffrage movement
Seneca Falls: Women's rights movement
Effects of industrialization on the role of women

1960s women's rights movement
Roe v. *Wade*: Ninth amendment, right to privacy, abortion
Affirmative action and women
Equal Pay Act, Title IX

Constitutional Principle 8
The Rights of Ethnic and Racial Minority Groups Under the Constitution

The Constitution has not always protected ethnic, racial, and other minority groups. When first ratified, in fact, the Constitution contained clauses that protected slavery and the rights of slaveholders.
- Has the Constitution protected the rights of ethnic and racial minority groups?

- Has the Constitution protected the rights of economically powerful groups better than those of minority groups?
- Are the gains that minorities have made secure, or do such groups need more protection of their rights?
- How do we balance minority rights and rule by a majority?

Examples of This Principle as a Recurring Theme in U.S. History

Conflict over slavery: Constitutional Convention; 1820–1860
Frederick Douglass: abolition movement, Fugitive Slave Law
Dred Scott v. *Sanford*
Civil War: Emancipation Proclamation
Reconstruction: 13th, 14th, and 15th Amendments
Jim Crow laws, *Plessy* v. *Ferguson*: legal basis for segregation
Equal protection clause: 14th Amendment

Brown v. *Board of Education*
Martin Luther King, Jr.: Civil Rights Movement of 1960s
Restrictions on immigration: quota system, exclusion of Chinese and Japanese
Relocation of Japanese Americans: *Korematsu* v. *United States*
Native Americans: treaty rights, *Worcester* v. *Georgia*, Dawes Act, citizenship in 1924, American Indian Movement (AIM)

Constitutional Principle 9
Presidential Power in Wartime and in Foreign Affairs

The Constitution gives the president the power to make treaties, as well as other major foreign-policy responsibilities. The president is also the commander in chief of the armed forces. The powers of the president have grown since the early days of the United States government, and they are even greater in wartime.

- Does the president have too much power, particularly since the Civil War?
- Are broad presidential powers necessary to conduct war and foreign affairs?

Examples of This Principle as a Recurring Theme in U.S. History

George Washington: expanded governmental powers, Proclamation of Neutrality

Increase of presidential power during wartime by Lincoln, Wilson, and FDR.: *Schenck* v. *United States*, *Korematsu* v. *United States*

T. Roosevelt: increase of presidential power: Roosevelt Corollary to Monroe Doctrine, Panama Canal

Truman: decision to drop atomic bomb

Korean and Vietnam Wars: expanded presidential wartime powers

Kennedy: Cuban missile crisis

War Powers Act: a check on presidential power

Carter: Camp David Accords

G.H.W. Bush: Persian Gulf Crisis

Clinton: Somalia, Bosnia, Haiti, Yugoslavia

G.W. Bush: Bush Doctrine; presidential powers in wartime: writ of *habeas corpus*, wiretapping

Constitutional Principle 10
The Separation of Powers and the Effectiveness of Government

The Constitution established three branches of government with separate powers, as well as a system of checks and balances among them.

- Has the system of separation of powers and of checks and balances been effective in preventing dominance by one branch?

- Is this system necessary, or has it resulted in a badly-run government that is slow to respond to the needs of the people and the nation?

Examples of This Principle as a Recurring Theme in U.S. History

Checks and balances: presidential veto

Judicial review: *Marbury* v. *Madison*

Reconstruction: powerful Congress, A. Johnson impeachment

Checks and balances: Treaty of Versailles

Checks and balances: FDR and Supreme Court reorganization

Checks and balances: Vietnam War

Checks and balances: *Watkins* v. *United States*, *United States* v. *Nixon*

War Powers Act: check on presidential power

Watergate: government based on laws and not on an individual

Clinton: impeachment and acquittal

Constitutional Principle 11
Avenues of Representation

Since the Constitution was ratified, there has been a continuing expansion of the right to vote. However, while the system has become more democratic and reflective of majority rule, the power of political parties and special interest groups has grown, as has the influence of technology.

- Has the federal government become more or less representative of "we the people"?

Examples of This Principle as a Recurring Theme in U.S. History

Great Compromise: representation in Congress

Electoral college system

Direct election of senators

Passage of 15th, 19th, 24th, and 26th Amendments

19th-century and Progressive reform movements

Populist and Grange movements

Women's suffrage movement

Third parties' effect on the political process

"One man, one vote": effect on representative government

Campaign financing: public v. private, individual rights, rights of lobbyists and other special interests, *Citizens United*

Effects of technology: electronic voting; the Internet

Constitutional Principle 12
Property Rights and Economic Policy

The Constitution gives the government responsibility for promoting the general welfare and Congress the power to regulate commerce and taxes.

- Has government balanced its two roles as the promoter of capitalism and free enterprise and as the protector of the public from the abuses of business?

Examples of This Principle as a Recurring Theme in U.S. History

Hamilton: government encouragement of business, national bank

Andrew Jackson: second national bank

Expanded interstate commerce clause: *Gibbons* v. *Ogden; Wabash, St. Louis & Pacific R.R.* v. *Illinois*

Weakened interstate commerce clause: *United States* v. *E.C. Knight Co., Lochner v. New York, Schechter Poultry* v. *United States*

Interstate commerce clause used against labor: *In Re Debs*

Antitrust activities: Sherman Antitrust Act, T. Roosevelt and W. Wilson, *Northern Securities Co.* v. *United States*, Clayton Antitrust Act

Federal Reserve Act: regulating monetary system

Government environmental and consumer protection, EPA, Consumer Financial Protection Bureau

New Deal: farm price supports, National Labor Relations Act

L. Johnson and R. Reagan: economic policies compared

21st century: globalization, multinational companies, trade wars, tariffs

Constitutional Principle 13
Constitutional Change and Flexibility

The Constitution has adapted to changing circumstances over the years because of certain provisions built into it, such as the necessary and proper clause and the interstate commerce clause.

- Has the Constitution proven adaptable to changing times?

- Should the Constitution be easier to change?
- Has the amendment process, combined with judicial interpretation and the implied powers of the executive and legislative branches, kept the Constitution able to meet the challenges of the modern world?

Examples of This Principle as a Recurring Theme in United States History

Washington: the unwritten constitution

Hamilton's bank plan: implied powers

Commerce clause: expansion of government authority, regulation of business, Federal Reserve System

Amendments and court decisions used to expand rights

Cabinet and congressional committees: custom and precedent

Role of political parties

Important People in United States History and Government

The following list highlights the key people other than presidents who may be tested on the new Framework-based Regents Examinations.

Samuel Adams (1722–1803)	• American Revolutionary War leader who helped to organize the Sons of Liberty and the Massachusetts Committee of Correspondence • Signer of the Declaration of Independence
Jane Addams (1860–1935)	• Progressive Era reformer in the social settlement house movement • Founder of Hull House, a Chicago settlement house • Cofounder of Women's International League for Peace and Freedom • Corecipient of the Nobel Peace Prize (1931) • Involved in organizing of the NAACP
Madeleine K. Albright (1937–2022)	• Sworn in as the 64th and first female secretary of state in January 1997, at the start of President Clinton's second term in office • Previously served as U.S. ambassador to the United Nations
Susan B. Anthony (1820–1906)	• Women's rights leader from 1851 until her death in 1906 • Most active for women's suffrage, but also worked for women's property rights, rights of married women, temperance, and abolition
Yasser Arafat (1929–2004)	• Palestinian leader involved in efforts to negotiate peace in the Middle East during President Clinton's administration • Led Palestinians during a number of violent clashes with Israel
Osama bin Laden (1957–2011)	• Leader of al-Qaeda terrorist network; directed September 11, 2001 attacks against World Trade Center and Pentagon; killed in 2011
John Brown (1800–1859)	• Extreme abolitionist who believed in use of violence to promote his cause • His antislavery group killed proslavery settlers at the Pottawatomie Creek Massacre; his raid of Harper's Ferry resulted in his trial and execution • Immortalized by Ralph Waldo Emerson and Henry David Thoreau
William Jennings Bryan (1860–1925)	• Unsuccessful Democratic presidential candidate in 1896 and 1900 • Populist who supported farmers and free silver • Orator, religious fundamentalist (Scopes Trial), and anti-imperialist
Aaron Burr (1756–1836)	• Elected third vice president of the United States when House of Representatives settled tie between Thomas Jefferson and Burr for president that led to passage of 12th Amendment. • When vice president, killed Alexander Hamilton in a duel. In 1807, found not guilty of treason in a political conspiracy.

John C. Calhoun (1782–1850)	• Outspoken southern leader and advocate of states' rights • Favored nullification and the extension of slavery into the territories • Vice president under Presidents John Quincy Adams and Andrew Jackson; resigned over nullification issue
Stokely Carmichael (1941–1998)	• African American civil rights advocate, part of the civil rights movement of the 1960s, especially associated with the phrase "black power," which he described as meaning that African Americans should be working to control their own economic and political futures
Andrew Carnegie (1835–1919)	• Industrialist and philanthropist who built Carnegie Steel Company • In an article, *The Gospel of Wealth* (1889), he defended Social Darwinism, but also stated that the rich had a duty to help the poor and improve society in areas they deemed important.
Rachel Carson (1907–1964)	• Writer, scientist, and environmentalist whose book, *Silent Spring* (1962), identified the hazards of agricultural pesticides • Inspired the environmental movement and legislation
Fidel Castro (1926–2016)	• Won Cuban revolution against dictator Batista; headed Cuba 1959–2008; limited civil liberties, and nationalized industries • Allied with Soviet Union in 1962 Cuban Missile Crisis • 1962 U.S. trade embargo eased in 2016 but tightened in 2019
Cesar Chavez (1927–1993)	• Latino leader of California farm workers from 1962 until his death in 1993 • Organized the United Farm Workers (UFW) to help migrant farm workers gain better pay and working conditions; used nonviolent tactics, boycotts, hunger strikes
Winston Churchill (1874–1965)	• Prime minister of Great Britain during World War II • Made famous the term "iron curtain" regarding the USSR (1946)
Hillary Rodham Clinton (1947–)	• In 2000, became the first First Lady elected to U.S. Senate and first woman elected to statewide office from New York; reelected in 2006 • In 2008, ran unsuccessfully for Democratic Party presidential nomination • In 2009, became 67th secretary of state • In 2016, first woman from a major party to run for president; lost electoral vote but won popular vote
Eugene V. Debs (1855–1926)	• Union organizer and Socialist presidential candidate in every election from the 1890s until World War I; see Supreme Court case *In Re Debs*
Dorothea Dix (1802–1887)	• Nineteenth-century reformer who revolutionized mental health reform
Stephen Douglas (1813–1861)	• Illinois Senator whose Kansas-Nebraska Act included his idea of popular sovereignty, which increased sectional tensions • Lincoln-Douglas debates (1858) made Lincoln nationally known • Candidate of northern faction of Democratic party in 1860 election
Frederick Douglass (1818–1895)	• Former slave, leading abolitionist, writer, orator; supported women's rights • Wrote his *Autobiography*; founded *The North Star*, an abolitionist newspaper

W.E.B. Du Bois (1868–1963)	• African American civil rights leader, historian, writer, and sociologist • Cofounder of Niagara Movement and of NAACP • A leader of Harlem Renaissance, published writings of African Americans in NAACP paper, *The Crisis*; organized The Silent Protest • Opposed Marcus Garvey's "back to Africa" movement and disagreed with Booker T. Washington by pressing for civil and political, not just economic, equality for African Americans
Edward K. "Duke" Ellington (1899–1974)	• Songwriter, band leader, jazz composer, pianist, and a leading figure of the Harlem Renaissance
Medgar Evers (1925–1963)	• African American activist and NAACP field secretary in Mississippi • Murdered in 1963, murderer was convicted in 1994
F. Scott Fitzgerald (1896–1940)	• Novelist whose works reflect climate of the "Roaring Twenties" • Novels include *The Great Gatsby* and *Tender Is the Night*
Henry Ford (1863–1947)	• Industrialist who headed Ford Motor Company • His innovative production methods reduced the cost of producing cars, making it possible for the average person to own an automobile
Benjamin Franklin (1706–1790)	• Philadelphia statesman, diplomat, scientist, and writer in revolutionary period; drafted the 1754 Albany Plan of Union • Member of Second Continental Congress; served on committee to write the Declaration of Independence, which he signed • Helped persuade France to sign the 1778 Treaty of Alliance against England and helped negotiate the Treaty of Paris of 1783, ending American Revolution; delegate to Constitutional Convention
Betty Friedan (1921–2006)	• Women's rights activist whose book, *The Feminine Mystique* (1963), encouraged women to find their own identity outside marriage • Helped found National Organization for Women (1966) and National Women's Political Caucus (1971)
William Lloyd Garrison (1805–1879)	• Abolitionist editor of *The Liberator,* published 1831–1865 demanding immediate end to slavery; a leader of American Anti-Slavery Society
Marcus Garvey (1887–1940)	• Jamaican-born publisher, businessman, and orator; leader in Harlem Renaissance; promoted Black Nationalism, separatism and Pan-Africanism • Advocated racial pride and self-help as a means of empowerment; founded Universal Negro Improvement Association; led a "back to Africa" movement • Influenced Nation of Islam, Malcolm X, and African nationalist leaders
Samuel Gompers (1850–1924)	• Organizer and president of American Federation of Labor, a craft union for skilled workers; stressed issues such as wages and hours

Albert A. Gore, Jr. (1948–)	• Vice President of the United States (1993–2001); won popular vote but lost electoral vote in 2000 election that went to Supreme Court in *Bush* v. *Gore* • Shared 2007 Nobel Peace Prize with U.N. Intergovernmental Panel on Climate Change. His film on global warming, *An Inconvenient Truth*, won an Academy Award.
Sarah and Angelina Grimké (1792–1873) and (1805–1879)	• Antislavery sisters who left their South Carolinian slaveholding family, came North, became Quakers, in 1830s were speaking and writing for abolition and women's rights
Fannie Lou Hamer (1917–1977)	• African American civil rights leader and early advocate for African American voting rights especially in the state of Mississippi
Alexander Hamilton (1757–1804)	• New York delegate at Constitutional Convention who worked for a strong central government • Wrote 51 of *The Federalist Papers* supporting ratifying the Constitution • First secretary of the treasury; promoted U.S. economic development
William Randolph Hearst (1863–1951)	• Newspaper publisher whose yellow journalism style helped create public pressure for the Spanish-American War
Ernest Hemingway (1899–1961)	• Novelist whose writings expressed conflict and concern created by changing American values in the 1920s and 1930s; won 1954 Nobel Prize for Literature
Patrick Henry (1736–1799)	• Leader in the American Revolution in Virginia • Member of Continental Congress; supporter of independence • Led movement for addition of the Bill of Rights to the Constitution
Langston Hughes (1902–1967)	• An influential poet, playwright, and novelist of the Harlem Renaissance • Works celebrated hope, pride, and cultural heritage of working class African Americans while protesting Jim Crow and segregation.
Saddam Hussein (1937–2006)	• Long-time Iraqi dictator who invaded Kuwait causing Persian Gulf War • Removed from power in 2003 during Iraq War and hanged in 2006
Robert Jackson (1892–1954)	• Supreme Court Justice who represented the United States at the Nuremberg War Crimes Trials at the end of World War II; associated with the principle that leaders could be tried with crimes against humanity
Robert Kennedy (1925–1968)	• U.S. Attorney General (1961–1963); assassinated in 1968 while seeking Democratic presidential nomination

Martin Luther King, Jr. (1929–1968)	• Civil rights leader who advocated civil disobedience and nonviolent demonstrations to achieve change • Founded Southern Christian Leadership Conference, led Montgomery, Alabama bus boycott, and Selma to Mongomery voting rights march • Gave "I Have a Dream" speech; won Nobel Peace Prize • Assassinated in 1968
Henry Kissinger (1923–)	• Secretary of state under Presidents Nixon and Ford • Deeply involved in foreign policy in Vietnam, China, the Soviet Union, and the Middle East
Robert La Follette (1855–1925)	• Governor of Wisconsin whose program, the "Wisconsin Idea," became the model for progressive reform • Served as United States senator and Progressive leader • Ran for president as the Progressive Party candidate in 1924
Meriwether Lewis and William Clark (1774–1809) and (1770–1838)	• Explorers who led the 1804–1806 expedition to survey lands included in the Louisiana Purchase; documented the land, plants, animals, and other natural resources from Missouri to Oregon
John Locke (1632–1704)	• British Enlightenment writer whose ideas influenced the Declaration of Independence, state constitutions, and the United States Constitution • Believed that people are born free with certain natural rights, including the rights to life, liberty, and property, and must consent to be governed
Henry Cabot Lodge (1850–1924)	• Massachusetts Republican senator whose support of American imperialism and of a powerful navy strongly influenced Theodore Roosevelt • Led successful fight against ratification of the Treaty of Versailles and entry of the United States into the League of Nations • Served as a U.S. representative to Washington Conference
Huey Long (1893–1935)	• Populist governor of Louisiana and U.S. senator • Proposed that income and inheritance taxes on the wealthy be used to give each American a $2,500 income, a car, and a college education • Planned to challenge FDR for president, but was assassinated in 1935
Douglas MacArthur (1880–1964)	• Led U.S. troops in the Pacific in World War II • Commander of U.S. occupation forces in Japan after World War II • Relieved of command by Truman after publicly disagreeing with him about the conduct of the Korean War
Malcolm X (1925–1965)	• Leader of the 1960s Black Power movement; assassinated in 1965
Horace Mann (1796–1859)	• Nineteenth-century educator; helped create tax-based, nonsectarian public schools as well as better teacher-training institutions
George C. Marshall (1880–1959)	• Army chief of staff during World War II and secretary of state under President Truman; promoted the Marshall Plan, which assisted the economic recovery of Europe after World War II

John Marshall (1755–1835)	• Chief Justice of the United States (1801–1835) • Established authority of the Supreme Court and strengthened power of federal government in cases such as *Marbury* v. *Madison* (1803), *McCulloch* v. *Maryland* (1819), and *Gibbons* v. *Ogden* (1824) • First stated the right of judicial review in *Marbury* v. *Madison* (1803)
Thurgood Marshall (1908–1993)	• African American attorney who argued *Brown* v. *Board of Education* before the Supreme Court in 1954 • Appointed in 1967, was first African American to serve on Supreme Court
Joseph R. McCarthy (1908–1957)	• Republican senator of the late 1940s and early 1950s who led a campaign to root out suspected communists in American life • The term *McCarthyism* came to be associated with an era of government investigation of the private lives of many in public service and in the entertainment industry
Russell Means (1939–2012)	• member of the Oglala Lakota Native American tribe, first president of the American Indian Movement (AIM) • Participant in 1973 Native American civil rights seige at Wounded Knee
Baron de Montesquieu (1689–1755)	• French Enlightenment philosopher whose influence is seen in separation of powers and checks and balances provisions of U.S. Constitution
John Pierpont Morgan (1837–1913)	• late 19th- and early 20th-century industrialist and financier, owner of railroads, steel mills, banks
Lucretia Mott (1793–1880)	• Quaker minister, abolitionist, advocate for women's rights; with Elizabeth Cady Stanton, an organizer of Seneca Falls Convention
John Muir (1838–1914)	• Naturalist, conservationist, and writer; influenced President Theodore Roosevelt to protect more land; founded the Sierra Club
Ralph Nader (1934–)	• Consumer rights crusader; wrote *Unsafe at Any Speed* (1965) to expose the lack of safety standards for cars • Third-party presidential candidate (1996, 2000, 2004, 2008)
Robert Oppenheimer (1904–1967)	• Physicist who led the American effort to build the first atomic bomb
Thomas Paine (1737–1809)	• English-born writer and political philosopher whose influential pamphlet *Common Sense* (1776) pressed for independence from Great Britain
Rosa Parks (1913–2005)	• African American civil rights activist whose 1955 refusal to give up her seat to a white person led to the Montgomery, Alabama, bus boycott and helped launch the civil rights movement

Frances Perkins (1880–1965)	• Named secretary of labor under President Franklin D. Roosevelt in 1933, becoming the first woman to serve in a cabinet position
Matthew Perry (1794–1858)	• Led 1853–1854 naval mission to open Japan to world trade and negotiated U.S. trading rights with Japan (Treaty of Kanagawa)
Gifford Pinchot (1865–1946)	• Conservationist and politician who led the Division of Forestry of the Department of Agriculture under President Theodore Roosevelt • Dismissed by Taft after attacking the secretary of the interior for removing from federal protection about a million acres of land
Joseph Pulitzer (1847–1911)	• Publisher of the *New York Journal*, whose "yellow journalism" helped provoke the Spanish-American War
Condoleezza Rice (1954–)	• Second secretary of state under President George W. Bush; first female African American to hold that position
Jacob Riis (1849–1914)	• Journalist, photographer, and social reformer of the Progressive Era • Used writings and photographs to show the need for better housing for the poor, such as in his 1890 book *How the Other Half Lives*
Jackie Robinson (1919–1972)	• Became the first African American to play in major league baseball when he joined the Brooklyn Dodgers in 1947
John D. Rockefeller (1839–1937)	• Industrialist and philanthropist • Founder of the Standard Oil Company
Nelson A. Rockefeller (1908–1979)	• Former governor of New York who was appointed vice president by President Gerald Ford in 1974 • Only nonelected vice president to serve with a nonelected president
Eleanor Roosevelt (1884–1962)	• Early and long-time activist for rights for African Americans and women during the New Deal as First Lady and as political activist on her own • Played a key role in creation of United Nations Declaration on Human Rights (1948) and heading the UN Commission on Human Rights (1961) • Chaired the Presidential Commission on the Status of Women during the Kennedy Administration
Julius and Ethel Rosenberg (1918–1953) and (1915–1953)	• Convicted and executed for espionage in 1953 during the era of McCarthyism
Jean-Jacques Rousseau (1712–1778)	• French Enlightenment philosopher • Influenced the Declaration of Independence with his arguments in support of government by the consent of the governed

Nicola Sacco and Bartolomeo Vanzetti (1891–1927) and (1888–1927)	• Italian immigrants and anarchists executed for armed robbery and murder at the height of the antiradical, anti-immigrant feelings of the 1920s • Cleared by the Massachusetts governor in 1977, some 50 years later
Margaret Sanger (1879–1966)	• Pioneering advocate of birth control • Organized first American birth control conference in 1921 • Founder of a birth-control lobbying group that became Planned Parenthood in 1942
Upton Sinclair (1878–1968)	• Muckraking journalist of the Progressive Era • Influenced the passage of the 1906 Meat Inspection Act with his novel *The Jungle*, which deals with the exploitation of the poor and the factory conditions that led to contaminated meat
Adam Smith (1723–1790)	• In *The Wealth of Nations* (1776), this Scottish political economist rejected mercantilism and advocated a free enterprise system, the basis of modern capitalism. • Saw free trade, division of labor, competition, individual freedom, supply and demand, and *laissez-faire* as necessary for sound economy
Alfred E. Smith (1873–1944)	• Reform governor of New York and first Catholic to run for president • Lost to Hoover in the 1928 election, because voters did not want a Catholic president and Smith favored repeal of the Eighteenth Amendment • In 1930s, was conservative Democrat who helped organize American Liberty League (1934) and opposed New Deal
Bessie Smith (1894–1937)	• Harlem Renaissance blues singer known as the "Empress of the Blues" • Recorded with prominent jazz musicians, such as Louis Armstrong and Benny Goodman
Elizabeth Cady Stanton (1815–1902)	• Leading crusader for women's rights; also for abolition and temperance • Began women's rights movement with Seneca Falls Convention in New York in 1848; wrote Declaration of Sentiments (1848) • With Susan B. Anthony, cofounded the National Woman Suffrage Association and coedited *Revolution*, a women's rights journal
John Steinbeck (1902–1968)	• Author whose novels often deal with problems of the working class during the Great Depression • *The Grapes of Wrath* (Pulitzer Prize, 1939) describes the effect of the drought that created the Dust Bowl on a group of farmers forced to leave Oklahoma and work as migrant laborers in California
Harriet Beecher Stowe (1811–1896)	• Writer whose emotional, best-selling novel, *Uncle Tom's Cabin* (1852), focused attention on slavery and contributed to start of the Civil War
Ida Tarbell (1857–1944)	• Muckraking journalist whose *History of Standard Oil Company* exposed Rockefeller's unfair and often ruthless business practices

Nat Turner (1800–1831)	• Enslaved African American who led consequential slave rebellion in 1831, killing 55 Virginians; resulted in 200 African Americans killed by vigilante mobs and stricter slave codes
Voltaire (1694–1778)	• French Enlightenment philosopher who influenced framers of the Constitution • Wrote against religious intolerance and persecution
Earl Warren (1891–1974)	• Chief Justice of the United States (1953–1969) • Landmark cases such as *Brown* v. *Board of Education* (1954) and *Miranda* v. *Arizona* (1966) marked his tenure
Booker T. Washington (1856–1915)	• African American educator, author, and leader • Founded Tuskegee Institute (1881) and wrote *Up from Slavery* (1901) • Urged vocational education and self-improvement rather than confrontation as the way for African Americans to gain racial equality
Ida Wells-Barnett (1862–1931)	• African American journalist, suffragist, and reformer • Launched a national crusade against lynching in the 1890s • Cofounder of the NAACP and of the National Association of Colored Women
Mao Zedong (1893–1976)	• Leader of the communist Chinese government from 1949 until 1976 • Met with President Nixon on Nixon's historic trip to China in 1972
John Peter Zenger (1697–1746)	• German immigrant, printer and journalist • Tried for criminal libel for criticizing New York governor in his paper; jury found him not guilty on the grounds that he had printed the truth • His case was an early step in establishing freedom of the press

Glossary

A

abolitionist movement 19th-century movement that sought an end to slavery

acquit to be found not guilty in a trial

"advise and consent" an informal process in which the president can acquire guidance from the Senate in policies and decision-making

affirmative action steps taken to increase the representation of women and minorities, especially in jobs and higher education

AFL/CIO influential labor union resulting from a merger between the American Federation of Labor and the Congress of Industrial Organizations in 1955

agrarian protest demands by farmers for improvements in areas affecting agriculture, especially in the late 1800s

Agricultural Revolution introduction of new farming methods in the 19th century that improved the quality and quantity of farm products and led to the Industrial Revolution

al Qaeda world terrorist organization responsible for the September 11, 2001, attacks on the World Trade Center and the Pentagon; led by Osama bin Laden

alien a citizen of a foreign country

alliance a group of nations mutually allied by treaty

Allied Powers coalition made up of Great Britain, France, Russia, Italy, and the United States that fought against the Central Powers in World War I

Allies the World War I alliance of Great Britain, France, Russia, and later the United States; also, the World War II alliance of Great Britain, the United States, the Soviet Union, and other nations

alternative energy sources sources of energy that are not based on fossil fuels, such as solar, wind, and biofuels

amendment a change in or addition to a legal document, motion, bylaw, law, or constitution

American Anti-Imperialist League organization formed in 1898 in opposition of the annexation of the Philippines and American imperialism

American Anti-Slavery Society abolitionist organization formed in 1833 to develop and support a plan for immediate rather than gradual abolition of slavery

American Colonization Society organization formed in 1817 to send free African Americans to Africa

American Expeditionary Force U.S. Army force, under the command of General John Pershing, that fought with the Allies during World War I

American Federation of Labor labor union that organized skilled workers in a specific trade and made specific demands rather than seeking broad changes

American System a plan offered by Henry Clay for internal improvements

anarchy lawlessness; disorder caused by lack or absence of government authority

annex to attach new territory to an existing area, such as a country

annexation the act of taking over or adding new territory to a larger state or country

Anti-Federalist a person opposed to the Constitution during the ratification debate of 1787

anti-Semitism prejudice against Jews

antitrust opposed to practices and agreements that restrict trade, such as monopolies, price-fixing, and trusts

appeasement the policy of giving in to an aggressor's demands in order to keep the peace

appellate jurisdiction the authority of a court to review the decisions of inferior (lower) courts

Articles of Confederation the first American constitution

assassination the murder of a public figure

assembly line arrangement of equipment and workers in which work passes from operation to operation in direct line until the product is assembled

assimilation the process of becoming part of another culture

assumption plan part of Hamilton's financial plan; called for the new federal government to take over and pay off American Revolution war debts of Continental Congress and states

atomic age a term used to describe period begun by the explosion of the first atomic bomb in 1945

atomic bomb powerful nuclear weapon developed by the United States and dropped on Japan to end World War II

Axis Powers the group of countries led by Germany, Italy, and Japan that fought the Allies in World War II

B

"baby boom" the rapid growth in the population of the United States between 1945 and 1964

Back to Africa movement advocating the return of African Americans to their ancestral homelands in Africa

balance of power distribution of political and economic power that prevents any one nation from becoming too strong

balance of terror a balance of power achieved when opposing sides possess nuclear weapons

balance of trade the difference in value between a nation's imports and its exports

bank holiday 1933 banking act that closed banks to prevent collapse of banking system; sound banks then reopened

bankruptcy a court action to release a person or corporation from unpaid debts

belligerents nations fighting a war, usually after a declaration of war

Berlin Wall dividing wall built by East Germany in 1961 to isolate West Berlin from communist-controlled East Berlin

bicameral legislature a lawmaking body composed of two houses

big business corporations or monopolies seen as having too much control over a society and its economy

Big Stick diplomacy foreign policy of President Theodore Roosevelt threatening intervention in Latin American nations to insure their stability

bill a proposal presented to a legislative body for possible enactment as law

bill of attainder an act of a legislature that finds a person guilty without a trial; prohibited by the Constitution

Bill of Rights the first ten amendments to the U.S. Constitution, dealing mostly with civil rights

bipartisan supported by two political parties

black codes laws passed, especially by Southern states after the Civil War, to control the actions and limit the rights of African Americans

Black Nationalism movement advocating the unity and political self-determination of African Americans and the formation of a separate black nation

blacklist a list, circulated among employers, of people who will not be hired because of their views, beliefs, or actions

blitzkrieg a sudden invasion or "lightning war," first practiced by Germany in World War II

blockade the shutting off of a port to keep people or supplies from moving in or out

blue-collar worker someone who holds an industrial or factory job

border states during the Civil War, the states that allowed slavery but remained in the Union

boycott an organized refusal to buy or use a product or service, or to deal with a company or group of companies, as a protest or as a means to force them to take some action

brain trust term given to the group of academic and political advisors of Franklin D. Roosevelt

brinkmanship the policy of being willing to go "to the brink" of war to preserve peace

bureaucracy a collective term for all of the workers who run the agencies that do the everyday business of government

cabinet the group of officials who head government departments and advise the president

capital money or wealth used to invest in business or enterprise

capitalism economic system based on private initiative, competition, profit, and the private ownership of the means of producing goods and services

carpetbagger pejorative name for a Northerner who went to the South during Reconstruction

"cash and carry" U.S. policy during World War II by which goods could be sold to warring nations as long as those nations paid for them in cash and transported them with their own ships

cash crops crops grown for sale rather than for family consumption

census gathering information on the nation's population; required by the U.S. Constitution every ten years to determine number of votes a state has in the House of Representatives and the Electoral College

Central Powers coalition made up of Germany, Austria-Hungary, the Ottoman Empire, and Bulgaria that fought against the Allied Powers in World War I

charter legal document giving certain rights to a person or company

checks and balances the system set up by the U.S. Constitution in which each branch of the federal government has the power to limit the actions of the other branches

Chicano movement movement that focused on raising Mexican American consciousness

citizen a person who by birth or naturalization owes loyalty to, and receives the protection of, a nation's government

civic virtue the belief that citizens should take an active role in society for the public good

civil disobedience nonviolent protest against unjust laws

civil liberties certain rights guaranteed to all citizens of a nation

civil rights rights guaranteed to citizens by the U.S. Constitution and laws of the nation

civil service government jobs for which appointments and promotions are now based on merit rather than on political patronage

civil service reform efforts to transform the civil service system from one based on the spoils system to one based on a system of merit

"clear and present danger" phrase used in the Supreme Court decision in *Schenck* v. *United States* that defines when freedom of speech can be limited

climate change any measurable long-term change in climate

closed shop a workplace in which employees must be labor union members in order to be hired

cloture procedure that may be used to limit or end floor debate in a legislative body

coalition an alliance of political groups

Code Talker a member of the Navajo nation who used his tribe's language as a code to send military messages during World War II

Cold War the state of tension between the United States and the Soviet Union after World War II

collective bargaining the process by which a union negotiates with management for a contract

collective security a system in which member nations agree to take joint action to meet any threat or breach of international peace

colonialism the practice under which a nation takes control of other lands for its economic, military, or other use

colony a settlement of people in a distant land who are ruled by a government of their native land

Columbian Exchange the global exchange of goods and ideas between Europe, Africa, and the Americas after Columbus made his first transatlantic voyage in 1492

command economy an economic system in which the government makes all decisions on the three key economic questions

commerce the buying and selling of goods and services

commerce clause Article I, Section 8, Clause 3 of the U.S. Constitution, which gives Congress the power to regulate interstate and foreign trade

committee system method under which members of the legislative branch form into smaller groups to facilitate such business as considering proposed legislation and holding investigations

common law an unwritten law made by a judge that has developed over centuries from those generally accepted ideas of right and wrong that have gained judicial recognition

communism the economic system based on the collective ownership of property and the means of production, with all individuals expected to contribute to society according to their abilities and to receive from it according to their needs

company town community whose residents rely upon one company for jobs, housing, and shopping

compromise the resolution of conflict in which concessions are made by all parties to achieve a common goal

concentration camps a place where political opponents or other "enemies" of a nation are forcibly confined, especially those established by Nazi Germany before and during World War II

concurrent powers powers shared by the national and state governments

confederacy a league or alliance among people or states formed for a specific purpose

Confederate States of America government of 11 Southern states that seceded from the United States and fought against the Union in the Civil War

confederation an alliance of independent states

conference committee a temporary joint committee of both houses of a legislature, created to reconcile differences between the two houses' version of a bill

conglomerate a corporation that owns many different, unrelated businesses

Congress the legislative, or lawmaking, branch of the United States government, made up of the Senate and the House of Representatives

congressional representation a key issue of the Constitutional Convention that was resolved by the Great Compromise, creating a bicameral legislature with an upper house based on equal representation and a lower house based on population

conquistador Spanish conqueror

conservation the careful use or preserving of natural resources

conspicuous consumption public enjoyment of costly possessions done in such a way as to emphasize the fact that one can afford such possessions

constitution body of fundamental law, setting out the basic principles, structures, processes, and functions of a government and placing limits on its actions; the supreme law of the United States

constitutional permissible under the Constitution

Constitutional Convention formal meeting of state delegates in Philadelphia in 1787 at which the Constitution was written

constitutional principles the several fundamental and enduring ideals set down in the United States Constitution

consumer person who spends money on goods and services

consumer goods items bought and used by consumers

consumer-oriented economy economy that is propelled by consumer spending

consumer protection measures to shield buyers of goods and services from unsafe products and unfair or illegal sales practices

consumerism the practice of protecting consumers; also theory that increased consumption of goods is economically and personally beneficial

containment U.S. policy after World War II of trying to keep the Soviet Union from expanding its area of influence and dominance

contraband goods captured from an enemy during wartime

convict to be found guilty in a trial

corporation business owned by many investors that raises money by selling stocks or shares to those investors

cotton gin machine invented in 1793 to separate the cotton fiber from its hard shell

"court-packing" Franklin Roosevelt's 1937 plan to add justices to the Supreme Court

credit delayed payment for goods or services

creditor nation a nation that is owed money by other nations

Crisis (The) magazine published by the NAACP

Critical Period period of time after independence when the new American government was struggling to maintain control under the Articles of Confederation

cultural diversity many cultures existing in the same society

cultural pluralism the idea that different cultures can exist side by side in the same society, all contributing to the society without losing their identities

culture the way of life of a given people

custom a habit or practice so established that it strongly influences social behavior

debtor nation a nation that owes money to another nation or nations

Declaration of Independence the 1776 document that stated Great Britain's North American colonies had become free and independent of the parent country

deficit the amount by which money spent is greater than money received

deficit spending government practice of spending more money than it takes in from taxes and other revenues

delegated powers powers given by the Constitution to the national government and denied to state governments

demagogue a person who gains political power by rousing the passions of the people

demobilization the process by which a nation reconverts to peacetime status after a war or the threat of war

democracy system of government in which supreme authority rests with the people, either directly or through elected representatives

Democratic Party one of the modern political parties, descended from Jefferson's Democratic-Republican Party

Democratic-Republican member of one of the first political parties in the United States, led by Jefferson and other leaders who were opposed to the Federalists

demography the study of populations through statistics

denied powers certain powers that are specifically denied to the national and/or state governments by the Constitution

depression a long and severe decline in economic activity

détente the easing of tension between nations

dictatorship form of government in which the power to govern is held by one person or a small group

direct democracy system of government in which the people participate directly in decision-making through the voting process

direct election of senators system put into practice under the Seventeenth Amendment whereby the voters rather than the state legislatures elect members of the U.S. Senate

direct primary an election held within a party to pick that party's candidates for the general election

direct tax type of tax in which an individual taxpayer or organization pays a levied tax directly to the government

disarmament reduction of a nation's armed forces or weapons of war

discrimination policy or attitude that denies rights to people based on race, religion, sex, or other characteristics

disestablishment depriving a state church of official support from the government, or never allowing a state church to be founded

distribution of wealth the way in which wealth is spread out among a nation's population

diversity variety

division of powers basic principle of federalism; the constitutional provisions by which governmental powers are divided between the national and the state governments

dollar diplomacy President Taft's policy of encouraging U.S. investment in Latin America

domestic policy everything a nation's government says and does in relation to internal matters

domino theory the idea, prevalent during the Vietnam War, that if one Asian nation became communist, neighboring nations would as well

dove a person who opposed U.S. involvement in the Vietnam War

due process clause part of the 14th Amendment which guarantees that no state deny basic rights to its people

Dust Bowl term used for the central and southern Great Plains during the 1930s when the region suffered from drought and dust storms

Earth Day annual event of environmental activism and protest, begun in 1970

ecomienda system a system in which areas of land were granted to Spanish settlers with the legal permission to demand labor or taxes from Native Americans

economic pertaining to production, distribution, and use of wealth

economic nationalism policies focused on improving the economy of one's own nation

economic programs any policies set forward by a government that relate to the workings of its economy

elastic clause Article I, Section 8, Clause 18 of the Constitution, which is the basis for the implied powers of Congress

Electoral College an assembly elected by the voters that meets every four years to formally elect the president of the United States

Electoral College system process of electing the president of the United States in which voters cast their ballots for electors who then cast the actual votes for president and vice president

electoral votes number of votes each state and the District of Columbia can cast for president, equal to the number of senators plus representatives of each state, with 270 electoral votes needed to be elected president

electorate all the persons entitled to vote in a given election

emancipation the act of setting a person or people free

embargo government prohibition of trade with another nation or nations; also prohibition of ships leaving home ports

empathy the process of sharing and understanding the feelings or thoughts of another person

English Bill of Rights 1689 agreement between Parliament and William and Mary which established that representative government and the rule of law outweighed the power of any monarch

Enlightenment 18th-century movement that emphasized science and reason as key to improving society

entrepreneur person who organizes, operates, and assumes the risks of a business enterprise

environment natural surroundings and all the things that make them up; also the social, cultural, and physical surroundings that affect behavior in a society

equal protection clause a clause in the 14th Amendment requiring that states apply due process equally, without preference to an individual or group

espionage spying

ethnic cleansing systematic effort to purge an area or society of an ethnic group through murder or deportation

ethnic group people of foreign birth or descent living in another country

eugenics movement movement that supported the idea that the human race can be improved by controlling which people have children

European Union the economic organization of European nations designed to increase the economic power of Europe in the world economy

excise tax tax levied on the production, transportation, sale, or consumption of goods and services

executive branch part of a government that carries out its laws

executive power the powers of the head of an executive branch of government to carry out the laws

executive privilege the right claimed by presidents to withhold information from the legislative or judicial branches

expatriate a person who leaves his or her own country and takes up residence in a foreign land

expressed powers those delegated powers of the national government that are given to it in so many words by the Constitution

extermination the killing of an entire group or race of people

F

factory system manufacturing system based on using machinery rather than hand tools

Fair Deal President Truman's program to expand New Deal reforms

farm output total value of products produced by a nation's farms

fascism political philosophy that calls for glorification of the state, a single party system with a strong ruler, and aggressive nationalism

federal government the central or national government

Federal Reserve System the nation's central banking system, established in 1913; a system of 12 regional banks overseen by a central board

federalism a system of government in which authority is divided between national and state governments

Federalist member of one of the first political parties in the United States, organized by those who favored ratification of the Constitution

feminist movement the struggle of women for equality

filibuster various tactics, usually long speeches, aimed at defeating a bill in a legislative body by preventing a final vote

Final Solution (The) Nazi policy to eliminate all Jewish people throughout Germany-controlled territories during World War II

First Continental Congress a group of delegates that met in 1774 and represented all the American colonies, except Georgia

fiscal policy policies relating to a nation's finances

flapper nickname for a young woman in the 1920s who declared her independence from traditional rules

forced assimilation process by which a group of people is made to take on the language, dress, and culture of another community by the government

foreign policy the actions and stands that every nation takes in every aspect of its relationships with other countries; everything a nation's government says and does in world affairs

Fourteen Points President Woodrow Wilson's proposal in 1918 for a postwar European peace

free enterprise system an economic system based on private ownership, individual enterprise, and competition

free silver major 19th-century economic issue in which Populist advocates pushed for the free coinage of silver

Freedmen's Bureau federal agency designed to aid freed slaves and poor white farmers in the South after the Civil War

freedom of speech the right of freedom of expression guaranteed to Americans by the First Amendment

freedom of the seas the right of merchant ships and ships of neutral countries to move freely on the seas during peace or war

frontier the border of a country; as defined by the U.S. Bureau of the Census, the edge of settlement beyond which the land was occupied by two or fewer people per square mile

frontier thesis idea set forth by historian Frederick Jackson Turner that the nation's frontier regions shaped its character and institutions

fundamentalist one who believes that the Bible is the literal word of God

G

gag rule rule lasting from 1836 to 1844 that banned debate about slavery in Congress

Gay Rights movement movement advocating for the equal rights of homosexuals

genocide the systematic destruction of a race of people

Gettysburg Address famous speech by President Abraham Lincoln on the meaning of the Civil War, given in November 1863 at the dedication of a national cemetery on the site of the Battle of Gettysburg

ghetto area in which many members of some minority group live, to which they are restricted by economic pressure or social discrimination

Gilded Age term used to describe the period from 1865 to 1900

glasnost a period of "openness" in relations between the United States and the Soviet Union that began in the late 1980s

global interdependence the idea that the nations of the world must rely on each other in many different ways, including trade, transportation, and communication

global warming the increase in Earth's average surface temperature over time

globalization process by which national economies, politics, cultures, and societies mix with those of other nations around the world

Glorious Revolution the bloodless revolution in 1689 in which the English Parliament overthrew James II and replaced him with William and Mary

gold standard a system in which a nation's currency is based on the value of gold

Good Neighbor Policy Franklin D. Roosevelt's policy toward Latin America intended to strengthen relations with the nations of that region

government the complex of offices, personnel, and processes by which a state is ruled, and by which its public policies are made and enforced

"Government Issue" (G.I.) slang term for American soldier

graduated income tax method of taxation in which individuals with larger incomes are taxed at a higher rate than people with lower incomes

Grand Alliance military alliance made up of the United States, United Kingdom, and the Soviet Union during World War II

grandfather clause laws passed in Southern states giving the right to vote only to people who had that right on January 1, 1867, and their descendants; intended to keep African Americans from voting

Grange (The) organization of farmers founded for social reasons in 1867, which later campaigned for state regulation of railroads and other reforms

Granger Movement coalition of farmers that pressed for political changes in order to limit the power of the railroad

grassroots the ordinary individuals or citizens that make up an organization

Great Awakening religious movement in the English colonies during the 1730s and 1740s, which was heavily inspired by evangelical preachers

Great Compromise the plan for a two-house legislature adopted at the Constitutional Convention in 1787 that settled differences between large and small states over representation in Congress; also known as the Connecticut Plan

Great Depression period from 1929 to 1941 of severe worldwide economic downturn

Great Migration migration of African Americans from the South to the North in the early 20th century

Great Society the name given to President Johnson's domestic program in the 1960s

gross national product (GNP) the total value of all the goods and services produced in a nation in a year

guerilla war fighting by stealth and with small bands, which make surprise raids against stronger forces

H

Harlem Renaissance an African American cultural movement centered in New York City from the 1920s to the mid-1930s; focused on African American identity and pride through literature, art, music, dance, and philosophy

hawk a person who supported U.S. involvement in the Vietnam War

hemisphere half of the Earth's surface

holding company a company that gains control of other companies by buying their stock

Holocaust name given to Nazi Germany's persecution of Jews before and during World War II; in this time, more than six million Jews died

Hoovervilles term used to describe makeshift shantytowns set up by homeless people during the Great Depression

House of Representatives lower house of the U.S. Congress in which states are represented according to the size of their populations

House Un-American Activities Committee (HUAC) congressional committee that investigated possible subversive activities within the United States

Hull House settlement house founded by Progressive reformer Jane Addams in Chicago in 1889

human rights basic rights that should belong to all people including freedom of speech, religion, and the press

humanitarian one who is concerned with the welfare of all people

"hyphenated Americans" negative term used for Americans whose ancestors are foreign-born

I

immigration the movement of people into another nation in order to make a permanent home there

immigration laws laws controlling the movement of people into a country

immigration quota sets limits on numbers of people and/or their nation of origin to limit immigration from those nations

impeachment the process by which the House of Representatives makes an accusation of wrongdoing against the president or other high federal officials

imperialism policy by which one country takes control of another either directly or through economic or political dominance

implied powers those delegated powers of the national government implied by (inferred from) the expressed powers; those powers "necessary and proper" to carry out the expressed powers

impressing seizing people or property for military or public service

indentured servant person who worked in the colonies for period of three to seven years in exchange for passage, food, housing, clothing; system resulting from labor shortage in colonies

Indian Removal Policy under President Andrew Jackson, the policy of moving all Native Americans to lands west of the Mississippi River in the 1830s

indigenous original or native inhabitants of a country or region

individual rights basic rights that belong to each person

industrialization change from an agricultural society to one based on machine-made goods

inflation an economic condition in which prices rise substantially over a significant period of time

initiative a process in which a certain number of qualified voters sign petitions in favor of a proposed statute or constitutional amendment, which then goes directly to the ballot

injunction a court order prohibiting a given action; used frequently against workers in 19th-century labor-management disputes

interchangeable parts parts made exactly like each other, making the mass production of products on an assembly line possible

interdependence a condition in which parties are reliant on each other

internal affairs public or business matters within the boundaries of a country

internal improvements roads, bridges, canals, and other similar projects funded by the national government

internationalism the belief, held by some Americans in the 1930s, that the United States should aid the victims of international aggression

international law the norms of behavior generally agreed to and followed by the nations of the world in their dealings with each other

Internet computer network that links people around the world

internment camps places of confinement, especially in wartime

interstate commerce trade among the states

intervention interference by one nation in the affairs of another

Intifada a Palestinian campaign of violent resistance against Israeli control

intrastate commerce trade within the borders of a state

"iron curtain" the line between Soviet-dominated Eastern Europe and the West, so-called because the Soviets and their satellite nations prevent the free passage of people, information, and ideas across their borders

Iroquois Confederacy confederation made up of five Iroquois peoples: the Mohawks, Oneidas, Onondagas, Cayugas, and Senecas

irreconcilables isolationist senators who opposed any treaty ending World War I that had a League of Nations folded into it

isolationism a policy of avoiding alliances and other types of involvement in the affairs of other nations

isolationist a person favoring a policy of staying out of world affairs

isthmus a narrow trip or neck of land running from one larger land area to another

J

Japanese-American relocation policy under which Americans of Japanese ancestry were confined during World War II

Jazz Age a name for the 1920s when the jazz style of music became widely known and popular

Jim Crow laws laws in the Southern states in the 19th and 20th centuries that forced the segregation of the races

jingoism aggressive nationalism

joint resolution legislative measure which must be passed by both houses and approved by the chief executive to become effective; similar to a bill, with the force of law, and often used for unusual or temporary circumstances

joint-stock company a company run by a group of investors who share the company's profits and losses

judicial activism broad interpretation of the Constitution leading to court-directed change

judicial branch part of the government that decides if laws are carried out fairly

judicial independence the idea that the judicial branch should be independent from the legislative and executive branches of government and their influence

judicial restraint narrow interpretation of the Constitution

judicial review power of the Supreme Court to determine the constitutionality of acts of the legislative and executive branches of the government

judiciary judicial branch of a government, its system of courts

jurisdiction power of a court to hear (to try and decide) a case

jury a group of people who hear evidence in a legal case and give a decision based on that evidence

justice fairness; trial and judgment according to established process of the law

 K

"Know Nothings" a common name for the American Party, a nativist political organization formed in 1849

Korean War conflict over the future of the Korean peninsula, fought between 1950 and 1953 and ending in a stalemate

Ku Klux Klan secret society first formed in the South during Reconstruction to ensure white supremacy over blacks; reformed in the 1920s to express opposition to Jews, Catholics, Bolsheviks, and others considered "un-American"

 L

labor union workers organized as a group to seek higher wages, improve working conditions, and obtain other benefits

labor-intensive crop a type of crop that requires a number of people to plant, tend, and harvest to its final saleable state

laissez faire noninterference; has come to mean a policy by which the government minimizes its regulation of industry and the economy

landslide election an election in which a victorious candidate gathers an overwhelming percentage of the total votes cast

law rule recognized by a nation, state, or community as binding on its members

League of Nations association of nations to protect the independence of member nations proposed by President Wilson in his Fourteen Points and formed after World War I

legislative branch the lawmaking agencies of a government

legislature group of people with the power of making laws for a nation or state

less developed nations nations that have not fully industrialized, usually Third World nations

LGBT movement social movement advocating for equality and acceptance of lesbians, gays, bisexuals, and transgender people

lifespan the lifetime of an individual

limited government basic principle of the American system of government; belief that government is not all-powerful, and may only do those things the people have given it the power to do

limited liability corporation a type of business in which the owners are not responsible for the company's debts or financial obligations

literacy the ability to read and write

literacy test test of a potential voter's ability to read and write; once used in several states to prevent African Americans and other minorities from voting; provision of the 1917 Immigration Act that barred all immigrants who could not read from entering the United States

Little Rock Nine group of nine African American students chosen to integrate a high school in Little Rock, Arkansas, in 1957 but were barred from entering

lobby to attempt to influence legislation; also, group that attempts to do so

lockout during a labor dispute, the closing of a business (by locking the gates) to keep employees from entering

loose constructionists one who argues a broad interpretation of the provisions of the Constitution

"Lost Generation" term for American writers of the 1920s marked by disillusion with World War I and a search for a new sense of meaning

Louisiana Purchase purchase by the United States of the Louisiana Territory from France in 1803

Lowell mill textile mills in Lowell, Massachusetts, that used machinery to manufacture its goods

lynching executing someone illegally, by hanging, burning, or other means

 M

Magna Carta English document from 1215 that limited the power of the king and provided basic rights for citizens

majority at least one more than half (e.g., over 50 percent of the votes in an election)

majority rule a system in which the majority of a group has the power to make decisions for the entire group

Manhattan Project secret American program during World War II to develop an atomic bomb

Manifest Destiny a belief held in the first half of the 19th century that the United States had a mission to expand its borders to incorporate all land between the Atlantic and Pacific oceans

margin a small part of the total price of a stock purchase deposited with a broker at the time of purchase with the promise to pay the full sum at a later date

marital law law administered by the military by order of the government in times of emergency

market economy economic system in which decisions on the three key economic questions are based on voluntary exchange in markets

Marshall Court the Supreme Court during the tenure of John Marshall as chief justice in which key decisions were made that strengthened the federal government's role in the nation's economic business

mass consumption the large-scale demand for goods

mass production production of goods in large numbers through the use of machinery and assembly lines

McCarthyism the use of indiscriminate and unfounded accusations and sensationalist investigative methods to suppress political opponents portrayed as subversive; term taken from the name of Senator Joseph McCarthy, who carried out such practices

Medicaid federal program created in 1965 to provide low-cost health insurance to poor Americans of any age

Medicare federal program created in 1965 to provide basic hospital insurance to most Americans over the age of sixty-five.

melting pot theory the idea that different immigrant groups in the United States will lose their old identities and that a new American identity will emerge from the blending of cultures

mercantilism economic theory that a nation's strength came from building up its gold supplies and expanding its trade

merger a combining of two or more companies into a larger company

Middle Passage transportation by force to European colonies in Western Hemisphere of Africans to be sold as enslaved people; name refers to second of three-part transatlantic trade called Triangular Trade

migration historically, a regular, deliberate movement of a group of people to specific locations

militarism policy of building up strong military forces to prepare for war

militia a military force made up of citizen volunteers

minimum wage the lowest wage that can be paid to certain workers as set by national or state law

minor party one of the less widely supported political parties in a governmental system

minority less than half

minority group group within a nation that differs from most of the population in race, religion, national origin, and so on

missionary one who attempts to spread the religious ideas of a faith in a foreign land

mobilization the call-up of military forces, usually in preparation for war

monarchy government headed by a single ruler, usually a king or queen

monetary policy actions and positions taken by a government in regard to its system of money

monopoly dominance in or control of a market for certain goods or services by a single company or combination of companies

Monroe Doctrine policy statement of President James Monroe in 1823 warning nations of western Europe not to interfere with the newly independent nations of Latin America

moral diplomacy a term describing President Woodrow Wilson's approach to foreign policy, which emphasized the use of negotiation and arbitration rather than force to settle international disputes

Mormons members of the Church of Jesus Christ of Latter-day Saints; in the 1840s, thousands moved to Utah seeking freedom from religious persecution

Morrill Land Grant Act act pass in 1862 that provided public land for agricultural, mechanical arts, and military science colleges

muckraker early 20th-century American journalist who tried to improve society by exposing political corruption, health hazards, and other social problems

multilateral action joint action taken by three or more nations

multinational corporations companies that produce and sell their goods and services all over the world

municipal government the government of a city, town, or village

nation-states a type of political organization in which a group of people who share traditions and history live in a region under one government

National Association for the Advancement of Colored People (NAACP) an organization founded in 1909 to fight for the rights of African Americans

National Association of Colored Women federation of African American women's clubs that advocated for the rights of women and children and social reforms

national bank bank chartered by the federal government

national government in the United States, the federal government

National Organization for Women (NOW) founded in 1966 to work for equal rights for women

national self interest aim of all foreign policy

nationalism pride in or devotion to one's country

nativism a belief in the superiority of the way of life of one's home country; in the United States, this was often associated with a desire to limit immigration

natural rights rights that all people are entitled to from birth

naturalization the process by which a citizen of one country becomes a citizen of another

Navigation Acts British trade laws enacted by Parliament during the mid-1800s that regulated colonial commerce

"necessary and proper" clause another name for the elastic clause, which is the basis of the implied powers of Congress

negotiation talking over an issue by two or more parties with the aim of reaching a mutually agreeable settlement

neutrality the policy of not taking sides in a dispute or a war

Neutrality Acts a series of acts passed by Congress in the 1930s aimed at keeping the United States out of World War II

New Deal a name given to the programs of President Franklin D. Roosevelt

New Deal coalition political force formed by diverse groups who united to support Franklin D. Roosevelt and his New Deal

New England Anti-Slavery Society abolitionist organization formed by William Lloyd Garrison in 1831

New Federalism name given to the attempt to lessen the federal government's role in its dealings with states during the presidencies of Nixon and Reagan

New Freedom name given to the programs of President Woodrow Wilson

New Nationalism plan under which Theodore Roosevelt ran for president in 1912

Nisei a person born in the United States of Japanese parents who are first generation immigrants

nominating convention political gathering at which a party names candidates for office

non-intervention the practice of not become involved in the affairs of other nations

noncombatant a civilian or member of the military who does not take part in the fighting of a war

nonimportation agreement colonial consumer boycott of British exports as a response to taxes passed by Parliament

nonrecognition refusal to establish formal diplomatic relations with the new government of a nation

normalcy President Warren G. Harding's term for the return to peace after World War I

North American Free Trade Agreement (NAFTA) agreement calling for the removal of trade restrictions between the United States, Canada, and Mexico

North Atlantic Treaty Organization (NATO) alliance formed for mutual defense in 1949 under the North Atlantic Treaty, and now made up of 15 nations stretching from Canada to Turkey

Northwest Passage a sea route sought by early explorers believed to connect the Atlantic to the Pacific Ocean along the northern coast of North America

nuclear arms race the development and stockpiling of nuclear and nonnuclear weapons by the United States and Soviet Union during the Cold War

nuclear freeze a halt in the manufacture and deployment of nuclear weapons

nuclear power energy produced from a controlled atomic reaction

nuclear waste the byproducts of the production of nuclear power

nullification a state's refusal to recognize a federal law

Nullification Crisis 1832–1833 sectional political conflict in which South Carolina claimed it had the authority to nullify federal actions that the state deemed unconstitutional

nullify to determine something has no legal force

Nuremberg Trials post–World War II trials in which German government and military figures were tried for crimes committed during the war

 O

on margin system of buying stocks in which a buyer pays a small percentage of the purchase price while the broker advances the rest

one hundred percent Americanism belief in everything American while condemning foreign ideas and people

Open Door Policy policy toward China set out by Secretary of State John Hay allowing any nation to trade in any other nation's sphere of influence

Ordinance of Nullification South Carolina law declaring the federal tariffs of 1828 and 1832 null and void within the state

original jurisdiction the court in which a case is heard firsthand

overproduction a condition that exists when the supply of a product exceeds the demand for that product

 P

pacifist a person who is opposed to war and refuses to fight under any circumstances

Paleo-Indians pre-historic ancestors of Native Americans

Palestine Liberation Organization a terrorist group dedicated to the destruction of Israel; later an official organization representing Palestinians in negotiations with Israel

Pan-Africanism movement which began in the 1920s that emphasized the unity and strength of Africans and people of African descent around the world

Pan-Indian Movement 19th-century movement promoted by Shawnee leaders Prophet and Tecumseh, encouraging a united resistance against the U.S. government

pandemic spread of a disease across a large area, country, continent, or the entire world

pardon a release from the punishment or legal consequences of a crime granted by a president or governor

parliament the legislature of Great Britain

partition a division into pieces

patent and copyright laws laws giving rights to inventions, literary, musical, and artistic works to their creators

patriotism love and support of one's nation

patroonship an estate granted to a Dutch proprietor in New Netherland in the 17th century

peaceful coexistence phrase describing the aim of U.S.–Soviet relations during a time of improved relations between those nations in the 1950s

per capita income income per person

perestroika the restructuring of the Soviet Union's economy under Mikhail Gorbachev that began a move toward free enterprise

philanthropist a person who donates generous amounts of money for the benefit of others and society

Pilgrims English Puritans who sought religious freedom and founded Plymouth Colony in 1620

plantation system a system of large-scale agriculture based on the cultivation of cash crops

political action committee (PAC) the political extension of special-interest groups which have a major stake in public policy

political machines a political party's organization that wins voter loyalty and guarantees power to a small group of leaders, who often abuse it for their own gain

political party organized group that seeks to control government through the winning of elections and the holding of public office

political system the way a nation is governed

poll tax a tax that must be paid before one can vote, often used in Southern states to discourage or prevent blacks from voting and now banned in national elections by the Twenty-fourth Amendment

pool method of ending competition used by railroads in the late 1800s in which they divided up business in given areas and fixed prices

popular sovereignty basic principle of the American system of government that the people are the only source of any and all governmental power; political policy that permitted the residents of federal territories to decide on whether to enter the union as free or slave states

Populist Party political party formed in 1891 to advocate a larger money supply and other economic reforms

power control, authority, right

Preamble an introduction to a speech or piece of writing

prejudice unfavorable opinion about people who are of different religion, race, or nationality

Presidency Compromise compromise reached at the Constitutional Convention of 1787 whereby the president would serve a four-year term and be elected through an indirect election by the Electoral College

president the chief executive of a modern republic, especially of the United States

primary election held before a general election in which voters choose their party's candidates for office

Progressive Era the period from 1900–1920 that saw the greatest action by Progressive reformers

Progressive movement reform movement that worked to correct abuses in American society

prohibition outlawing the manufacture and sale of alcoholic beverages

Prohibition the period of 1920–1933 when the making and sale of liquor was illegal in the United States

propaganda spreading of ideas or beliefs that help a particular cause and hurt an opposing cause

proprietary colony English colony granted to an individual or group by the monarch

protectionism belief in policies that favor the protection of domestically produced goods

protective tariff tax on imports designed to discourage their sale and to favor the development of domestic industry

protectorate a country under the protection and partial control of a stronger country

public opinion those attitudes held by a significant number of persons on matters of government and politics; expressed group attitudes

purchasing power the ability to buy goods and services; the value of what money could buy at one time compared to what the same amount could buy at another time

Puritan work ethic the belief that hard work builds character and is its own reward

Puritans English Protestants who believed in strict religious discipline and the simplification of worship; setters of the Massachusetts Bay Colony

push-pull factors factors that motivate people to leave their home countries or attract people to a new location

Q

quota system arrangement that limited the number of immigrants who could enter the United States from specific countries

R

race-based slavery system of slavery based on a specific race of people

racial equality a condition in which people are treated in the same manner by law and society regardless of their race

racism belief that one race is superior to another

Radical Reconstruction period following the Civil War in which congressional Radical Republicans dictated the terms of the reconstruction of the South

Radical Republicans group of Republicans in Congress who wanted to protect the rights of people freed from slavery in the South and keep rich Southern planters from regaining political power

ratify to give formal approval; to give final consent to the effectiveness of a constitution, constitutional amendment, or treaty

raw materials natural substances before processing that will in some way increase their value or usefulness

Reaganomics President Reagan's economic program that cut taxes, spending on social programs, and regulations affecting businesses

recall a petition procedure by which voters may remove an elected official from office before the completion of his or her regular term

recession a decline in economic activity usually shorter and less severe than a depression

Reconstruction the period of 1867–1877 when the federal government or local republican governments ruled the Southern states that had seceded

recovery a restoring to a normal condition; one of the aims of FDR's New Deal

Red Scare term used to describe periods in the 1920s and 1950s when American fear and suspicion of communism was at its height

referendum a process by which a legislative measure is referred to the state's voters for final approval or rejection

reform change for the better; one of the goals of FDR's New Deal

Reformation 16th-century movement encouraging reforms in the Roman Catholic Church

regulatory agencies parts of the federal bureaucracy charged with overseeing different aspects of the nation's economy

religious freedom the ability to worship as one chooses, guaranteed in this nation by the First Amendment

Renaissance a time of creativity and change in Europe ranging from the 14th century through the 17th century

reparations payments for losses a nation has suffered during a war

representation condition of being acted and spoken for in government

representative democracy a type of democracy in which voters elect government officials who make laws and run the government in their stead

representative government system of government in which voters elect representatives to make laws for them

representative legislature a lawmaking body in which the delegates are elected by the people and authorized to act as their representatives

republic nation in which voters choose representatives to govern them

republican government a form of government in which political authority comes from the people

Republican Party one of the modern political parties, founded in 1854 in opposition to slavery

republican principles basic principles of a republican form of government, such as limited government and consent of the governed

reservation limited area set aside for Native Americans by the U.S. government

reservationists a group of senators who opposed the Treaty of Versailles to end World War I, unless specific changes were included

reserved powers those powers held by the state in the American federal system

"return to normalcy" phrase used by Warren G. Harding for Americans' desire to return to peace after World War I

revenue income

right of petition the right to seek redress or assistance from government without fear of punishment or reprisal

robber baron terms used to describe large-scale entrepreneurs of the late 1800s

Rosie the Riveter popular name for women who worked in war industries during World War II

royal colony English colony that was under direct control of the monarch

"rugged individualism" belief that people can overcome hardships on their own without government assistance

rule of law concept that government and its officers are always subject to the law

rural in or of the country

salad bowl theory idea that people of different backgrounds can exist side by side in the United States, maintaining their identities while still contributing to the overall society

salutary neglect manner in which England governed the American colonies in the late 1600s and early 1700s, marked by weak enforcement of laws regulating colonial trade

scalawag white Southerner who supported Radical Republicans during Reconstruction

scarcity too small a supply

school desegregation process through which the United States ended race-based segregation in schools

Scopes Trial 1925 trial of a Tennessee schoolteacher for teaching Darwin's theory of evolution

secede to withdraw formally from a membership in a group or an organization

secession the act of formally withdrawing from membership in a group or organization; in the United States, the withdrawing of 11 Southern states from the Union in 1861

secret ballot a voting method in which a voter's selections made on a ballot are anonymous

sectionalism strong sense of loyalty to a state or section instead of to the whole country

seditious libel communication, written or oral, that incites the overthrow of the government by force or unlawful means

segregation separation of people of different races

self-determination right of national groups to their own territories and their own forms of government

Senate upper house of the U.S. Congress in which each state has two members

separate but equal principle upheld in *Plessy* v. *Ferguson* (1896) in which the Supreme Court ruled that segregation of public facilities was legal

separation of church and state principle set out in the First Amendment that the government shall take no actions to establish or interfere with the practice of religion

separation of powers the principle that gives the powers of making, enforcing, and interpreting laws to separate legislative, executive, and judicial branches of government

settlement house movement a reformist social movement of the 1800s focused on creating community centers that offered services to the poor

sharecropper farmer who works land owned by another and gives the landowner part of the harvest

sit-down strike work stoppage in which employees refuse to leave the workplace and occupy it in an attempt to force their employer to come to terms

slavery condition in which one person is the property of another; banned in this country by the 13th Amendment

social contract idea promoted by Enlightenment philosopher, John Locke, in which the people of a society agree to give up some of their freedoms in order to establish a government for their benefit

Social Darwinism the belief that the evolutionary idea of "survival of the fittest" applied to societies and businesses

Social Gospel reform movement that emerged in the late 19th century that sought to improve society by applying Christian principles

social reform efforts to better conditions within a society

social safety net a set of government programs that protect people who face unfavorable economic conditions

Social Security programs of the federal government to provide economic assistance to the disabled, unemployed, poor, and aged

social welfare programs to promote public well-being

socialism economic and political system based on the public ownership of the means by which goods and services are produced, distributed, and exchanged

solid South term used for the stance of the Southern states as a solid voting bloc supporting the Democratic Party following the Civil War

Sons of Liberty organization of colonists formed in opposition to the Stamp Act and other British laws and taxes

Southeast Asia Treaty Organization (SEATO) defensive alliance aimed at preventing communist aggression in Asia

Southern Christian Leadership Conference (SCLC) an organization of clergy founded by Martin Luther King, Jr., and others in 1957 that played a major role in the civil rights movement of the 1960s

sovereign having supreme power within one's own territory; neither subordinate nor responsible to any other authority

soviet elected assembly in the Soviet Union; when capitalized, pertaining to the Soviet Union

space race the competition between the United States and the Soviet Union to develop the technology to successfully land on the moon

specialization the concentration of the productive efforts of individuals and businesses on a limited number of activities

speculation practice of making high-risk investments in hopes of obtaining large profits

sphere of influence a region dominated and controlled by an outside power

spoils system system or practice of giving appointed offices as rewards from the successful party in an election; name for the patronage system under President Andrew Jackson

Sputnik the first ever manmade satellite launched into space, developed by the Soviet Union in 1957

Square Deal President Theodore Roosevelt's program of reforms to keep the wealthy and powerful from taking advantage of small business owners and the poor

stagflation an economic condition characterized by both inflation and recession

standardization process of making parts of a product uniform in order to speed up production

state compact theory belief that since United States was formed by a compact of the states the states have final authority on determining the constitutionality of acts of the federal government

states' rights idea that individual states had the right to limit the power of the federal government

stereotype a fixed, oversimplified idea about a person or group

stock market place where shares in corporations are traded

Stonewall Inn riots a series of riots that occurred as a result of police raid of a gay bar; helped inspire the Gay Rights movement

strategic having value in order to achieve a plan, especially related to military tactics

strict constructionist one who argues a narrow interpretation of the Constitution's provisions

strike the refusal to work by a group of employees as a form of protest

Student Non-Violent Coordinating Committee (SNCC) grass-roots movement founded in 1960 by young civil rights activists

suburbs residential areas surrounding a city

suffrage the right to vote

suffragists people who campaigned for women's right to vote

supply-side economics the theory that the government can best stimulate the economy by cutting taxes and encouraging investment in business

Supreme Court the highest federal court and the final interpreter of the Constitution

supreme law of the land clause in the U.S. Constitution that establishes that the Constitution, federal laws, and treaties are above all other laws of the United States

surplus goods extra goods

swing state in a presidential election year, a state that is not clearly for either a Democratic or Republican candidate; the popular vote of the state that determines the electoral vote may be a major factor in the outcome of an election

Taliban a reactionary, extremist Islamic group that imposed strict conservative laws when it controlled the Afghan government in the 1990s and remains an opponent to westernization

tariff tax placed on goods brought into a country

taxation without representation the act of being taxed without elected legislative representation; a phrase used to gain support for the American rebellion against the British government

technology practical application of knowledge

temperance movement campaign against the sale or drinking of alcohol

tenant farming system of farming in which a farmer rents land to farm from a landowner

tenement multistory building divided into apartments to house as many families as possible

territorial integrity condition in which a nation's borders are guaranteed against disturbance by other nations

terrorism the use of violence, intimidation, and coercion to achieve an end, to gain publicity for a cause, or to disrupt the normal functioning of society

third party a political party formed in addition to the Democratic and Republican parties, which usually promotes a limited platform; historically, the two major parties have adopted some aspects of third parties' platforms

Third World during the Cold War, nations in the modern world that professed not to be allied with the Soviet Union and its allies or the United States and its allies, especially the developing nations of Asia, Africa, and Latin America

38th parallel dividing line between North and South Korea

three branches of government the division of the powers of government into legislative, executive, and judicial functions

Three-Fifths Compromise compromise reached at the Constitutional Convention of 1787 whereby three fifths of a state's population of enslaved people would be counted for both representation and taxation

Title IX portion of the Educational Amendments Act of 1972 that forbids gender discrimination in federally funded education programs and activities

Tory colonist who remained loyal to Britain during the Revolution

totalitarian form of government in which the power to rule embraces all matters of human concern

town meeting a form of direct democracy in which all voting members of a town meet and decide public policy for local government

Townshend Acts series of laws passed by Parliament in 1767 in which new import duties were levied on everyday items, such as glass, lead, tea, paper, and paint

tradition the handing down of beliefs, customs, and practices from generation to generation

Trail of Tears the forced movement of the Cherokee in 1838–1839 to land west of the Mississippi River

transatlantic slave trade the transportation of enslaved Africans to the Americas from the 16th to the 19th century

transcontinental railroad railway extending from coast to coast; completed in 1869

transportation revolution a time of major developments in transportation, including canals, steamboats, and railroads, that connected the nation and created a national economy

treaty a formal agreement concluded between two or more countries

triangular trade trans-Atlantic trade among three regions; in particular in the 17th, 18th, and early 19th centuries with cash crops from colonies, manufactured goods from Europe, and enslaved people from West Africa

Triple Alliance name of the alliance of Germany, Austria-Hungry, and Italy before World War I

Triple Entente name of the alliance of Great Britain, France, and Russia before World War I

Truman Doctrine President Truman's promise to help nations struggling against communist movements

trust group of corporations run by a single board of directors

trustbuster person who wanted to break up some or all trusts

trust-busting the act of breaking up some or all trusts

two-party system political system in which the candidates of only two major parties have a reasonable chance of winning elections

two-way trade under mercantilism, a system of trade between a mother country and its colonies

tyranny cruel and oppressive abuse of power by a government

U.S.S. _Maine_ American battleship that exploded and sank in Cuba in 1868, a leading cause of the Spanish-American War

unconstitutional not permitted by the constitution of a nation

underconsumption when people buy fewer goods than are produced

Underground Railroad system that existed before the Civil War, in which black and white abolitionists helped escaped slaves travel to safe areas

unicameral legislature lawmaking body made up of a single house

unilateral action an action taken by one nation only

unitary government form of government in which all of the powers are held in a single agency

United Nations international organization founded in 1945 to promote peace

universal suffrage the right to vote is extended to all adults

unrestricted submarine warfare naval warfare in which submarines attack merchant ships without warning

unwritten constitution a combination of executive and legislative actions and interpretations and judicial decisions, especially judicial review, as well as customs and traditions such as development of political parties

urban in or of the city

urbanization process by which more of a nation's population becomes concentrated in its cities

venture capital money invested in a new corporation or other business enterprise

veto chief executive's power to reject a bill passed by a legislature

Vietnam Syndrome term used to describe American unwillingness to commit the U.S. military anywhere in the world unless necessary to protect national interests

Vietnamization President Nixon's plan for gradual withdrawal of U.S. forces as South Vietnamese troops assumed more combat duties

Virginia House of Burgesses the first democratically elected lawmaking body in the British colonies of North America

Virginia Plan James Madison's proposal for a bicameral legislature with representation based upon population

War on Terror international military campaign promoted by President George W. Bush in response to the 9/11 terrorist attacks

Warsaw Pact military alliance of the Soviet Union and its satellite states

Watergate scandal political scandal involving illegal activities that ultimately led to the resignation of President Nixon in 1974

weapons of mass destruction devices used for large scale and total destruction, i.e. nuclear bombs, nerve gas, chemical warfare

westward expansion the movement of people into the western frontier of the United States that led to the growth of the nation's territory from coast to coast

Whigs one of the first political parties, standing for the limitation of executive power and the defense of liberty

white-collar worker someone holding a job in business or in a profession

women's Rights Convention the first women's rights convention, organized by Elizabeth Cady Stanton and others in Seneca Falls, New York in 1848

women's rights movement the struggle of women for equality

work ethic a belief that hard work is a virtuous end in itself

writ of assistance blanket search warrant with which British customs officials had invaded private homes to search for smuggled goods

writ of *habeas corpus* a court order which prevents unjust arrests and imprisonments

xenophobia fear or dislike of foreigners or anything strange or unfamiliar

yellow dog contracts a contract between an employer and an employee in which the employee agrees not to join a union while employed; this is no longer legal

yellow journalism sensational style of reporting used by some newspapers in the late 1800s

yellow peril derogatory term implying that Asian peoples threatened the ways of life of white Americans

Index

Acknowledgments

Photographs:
Every effort has been made to secure permission and provide appropriate credit for photographic material. The publisher deeply regrets any omission and pledges to correct errors called to its attention in subsequent editions. Unless otherwise acknowledged, all photographs are the property of Savvas Learning Company LLC. Photo locators denoted as follows: Top (T), Center (C), Bottom (B), Left (L), Right (R), Background (Bkgd)

Cover f11photo/Shutterstock; **title page** f11photo/Shutterstock; **xxvii** Library of Congress Prints and Photographs Division [LC-USZC4-2158]; **xxx** Pictorial Press Ltd/Alamy Stock Photo; **xxxix** Library of Congress, Books and Printed Material Division; [http://hdl.loc.gov/loc.rbc/rbpe.06002200]; **lii:** Victor Gillam, Judge, 1899 (adapted); **lxxi** Granger/Granger—All rights reserved. **7** Dominick Miserandino/Alamy Stock Photo; **20** Historic Images/Alamy Stock Photo; **26** GL Archive/Alamy Stock Photo; **37** Library of Congress Prints and Photographs division [LC-USZC4-5315]; **43** John Parrot/Stocktrek Images/Alamy Stock Photo; **46** 2733991/Shutterstock; **50** Architect of the Capitol; **68** (C) IanDagnall Computing/Alamy Stock Photo; **68** (T) IanDagnall Computing/Alamy Stock Photo; **99** Pictures Now/Alamy Stock Photo; **101** GL Archive/Alamy Stock Photo; **103** Pictorial Press Ltd/Alamy Stock Photo; **111** GL Archive/Alamy Stock Photo; **115** Brian Jannsen/Alamy Stock Photo; **117** World History Archive/Alamy Stock Photo; **131** (B) Carl Michelle/Alamy Stock Photo; **131** (T) PictureLux/The Hollywood Archive/Alamy Stock Photo; **133** Library of Congress Prints and Photographs Division [LC-DIG-ppmsca-39879]; **136** Fotosearch/Archive Photos/Getty Images; **138** Sandra Opdycke, *The Routledge Historical Atlas of Women in America,* Routledge; **139** Everett Historical/Shutterstock; **141** (L) John N. Choate/MPI/Archive Photos/Getty Images; **141** (R) John N. Choate/MPI/Archive Photos/Getty Images; **147** (B) Everett Historical/Shutterstock; **147** (T) John Parrot/Stocktrek Images/Getty Images; **150** Nawrocki/ClassicStock/Alamy Stock Photo; **152** Library of Congress Prints and Photographs Division [LC-USZ62-68344]; **158** (B) Bettmann/Getty Images; **158** (T) Pictorial Press Ltd/Alamy Stock Photo; **160** North Wind Picture Archives/Alamy Stock Photo; **163** Science History Images/Photo Researchers/Alamy Stock Photo; **166** Sandra Opdycke, *The Routledge Historical Atlas of Women in America,* Routledge; **173** Everett Collection Historical/Alamy Stock Photo; **184** Bettmann/Getty Images; **185** Hulton Archive/Getty Images; **187** Photo Researchers/Science History Images/Alamy Stock Photo; **189** The Picture Art Collection/Alamy Stock Photo; **192** JT Vintage/Glasshouse Images/Alamy Stock Photo; **196** IanDagnall Computing/Alamy Stock Photo; **197** Everett Collection Historical/Alamy Stock Photo; **198** *Allies Day, May 1917,* 1917, Childe Hassam. Oil on canvas, overall: 92.7 x 76.8 cm (36 1/2 x 30 1/4 in.). Gift of Ethelyn McKinney in memory of her brother, Glenn Ford McKinney (1943.9.1). National Gallery of Art, Washington, DC. Art Resource, NY; **200** Stock Montage/Archive Photos/Getty Images; **201** WorldPhotos/Alamy Stock Photo; **204** Photo Researchers/Science History Images/Alamy Stock Photo; **206** Photo Researchers/Science History Images/Alamy Stock Photo; **208** Hum Images/Alamy Stock Photo; **210** Everett Collection Historical/Alamy Stock Photo; **213** Photo Researchers/Science History Images/Alamy Stock Photo; **220** Archive Pics/Alamy Stock Photo; **224** (B) Everett Collection Historical/Alamy Stock Photo; **224** (T) Detroit Publishing Company photograph collection/Library of Congress Prints and Photographs Division Washington, D.C. [LC-DIG-det-4a25712]; **228** Historica Graphica Collection/Heritage Image Partnership Ltd/Alamy Stock Photo; **230** Everett Collection Historical/Alamy Stock Photo; **234** Pictorial Press Ltd/Alamy Stock Photo; **235** (B) Pictorial Press Ltd/Alamy Stock Photo; **235** (T) Photo Researchers/Science History Images/Alamy Stock Photo; **236** (B) Everett Collection Historical/Alamy Stock Photo; **236** (T) Everett Collection Historical/Alamy Stock Photo; **245** Library of Congress, Prints & Photographs Division, FSA/OWI Collection, [LC-DIG-fsa-8b27287]; **247** GL Archive/Alamy Stock Photo; **248** Fotosearch/Archive Photos/Getty Images; **250** Underwood Archives/Alamy Stock Photo; **254** Fotosearch/Getty Images; **257** Glasshouse Images/Alamy Stock Photo; **258** Granger/Granger—All rights reserved.; **261** Granger/Granger—All rights reserved.; **274** Everett Collection Inc/Alamy Stock Photo; **276** High school recess period, Manzanar Relocation Center, California/Ansel Adams/Library of Congress Prints and Photographs Division Washington, D.C. [LC-DIG-ppprs-00338]; **277** Joe Rosenthal/Pictorial Press Ltd/Alamy Stock Photo; **279** Ralph Crane/The LIFE Picture Collection/Getty Images; **284** (L) The Advertising Archives/Alamy Stock Photo; **284** (R) Shawshots/Alamy Stock Photo; **286** JT Vintage/Glasshouse Images/Alamy Stock Photo; **288** Universal Images Group/Getty Images; **292** D.R. Fitzpatrick (1947)/The Granger Collection, NY; **296** Corbis Historical/Getty Images; **308** Everett Collection Inc/Alamy Stock Photo; **310** Everett Collection Inc/Alamy Stock Photo; **312** Bettmann/Getty Images; **315** Bob Daugherty/AP Images; **319** INTERFOTO/Alamy Stock Photo; **321** 1973 Herblock cartoon, copyright The Herb Block Foundation; **322** (L) Lionel Cironneau/AP Images; **322** (R) Leslie Gilbert Illingworth/Solo Syndication; **325** Military Collection/Alamy Stock Photo; **326** Charles Dixon/*The Boston Globe*/Getty Images; **331** World History Archive/Alamy Stock Photo; **333** Keystone-France/Gamma-Keystone/Getty Images; **339** Dana Fradon/The New Yorker Collection/The Cartoon Bank; **341** Rick Diamond/Archive Photos/Getty Images; **343** AP Images; **344** (B) Matt York/AP Images; **344** (T) Archive PL/Alamy Stock Photo; **353** Bettmann/Getty Images; **355** Bloomberg/Getty Images; **356** Library of Congress Prints and Photographs Division [LC-DIG-yan-1a38165]; **357** (L) Elliott Erwitt/Magnum Photos; **357** (R) Clay Bennett Editorial Cartoon used with the permission of Clay Bennett, the Washington Post Writers Group and the Cartoonist Group. All rights reserved.; **365** Corbis Historical/Getty Images; **366** GL Archive/Alamy Stock Photo; **368** Steve Sack/Cagle Cartoons; **370** Everett Collection Inc/Alamy Stock Photo; **375** GL Archive/Alamy Stock Photo; **376** 506 collection/Alamy Stock Photo; **379** George Frey/Getty Images News/Getty Images; **382:** Erik Pendzich/Alamy Stock Photo; **386:** Richard Ellis/UPI/Alamy Stock Photo; **391:** DOD Photo/Alamy Stock Photo; **E-11** Bettmann/Getty Images

Acknowledgments

Text:

xxiii Current Population Reports Consumer Income: Income of Persons in the United States 1955. United States Bureau of the Census, November 1956.; **xxiv** U.S. Census Bureau; **xxv** Neil A. Armstrong, as he stepped on the moon, July 20, 1969. Footage from the Apollo 11 moonwalk. https://www.nasa.gov/wav/62284main_onesmall2.wav; **xxv** Sanders Lamont, "Man Walks on Moon: Neil, Buzz Prepare for Return Trip," *The Democrat Chronicle,* July 21, 1969; **xxvi** Justice John Marshall, opinion in *McCulloch* v. *Maryland,* 1819.; **xxxiii** Upton Sinclair, March 10, 1906. Letter from Upton Sinclair to President Theodore Roosevelt. Department of Agriculture. Office of the Secretary. 1889. Series: Letters Received, 1893–1906. Record Group 16: Records of the Office of the Secretary of Agriculture, 1794–ca. 2003; **xxxiv** Andrei Cherry, April 17, 2008., *The Candy Bombers: The Untold Story of the Berlin Aircraft and America's Finest Hour.* Penguin Random House.; **xxxvii** President Dwight D. Eisenhower, Press Conference, April 7, 1954; **xxxvii** Tonkin Gulf Resolution, August 7, 1964. National Archives and Records Administration. **xxxix** United States (1854)., "The Constitution of the United States, with the acts of Congress, relating to slavery, embracing, the Constitution, the Fugitive slave act of 1793, the Missouri compromise act of 1820, the Fugitive slave law of 1850, and the Nebraska and Kansas bill, carefully compiled," Rochester: Published by D. M. Dewey.; **li:** Howard Jones, Crucible of Power: A History of American Foreign Relations to 1913, Scholarly Resources, Inc., 2002; **liii:** Albert Beveridge, "The March of the Flag" speech, September 16, 1898; **liv:** Carl Schurz, Address at the Anti-Imperialistic Conference in Chicago, October 17, 1899; **liv:** Democratic Party Platform, July 4, 1900; **lv:** Republican Party Platform, June 19, 1900; **lvii:** Stephen Kinzer, The True Flag: Theodore Roosevelt, Mark Twain and the Birth of an American Empire, 2017; **xlii** Eric Foner, June 26, 2013. *Forever Free: The Story of Emancipation and Reconstruction.* Knopf Doubleday Publishing Group.; **lxix** Adam Fairclough, *Better Day Coming: Blacks and Equality, 1890–2000,* (2001). New York: Viking.; **lxix** Glenda Elizabeth Gilmore & Thomas J. Sugrue, *These United States: A Nation in the Making 1890 to the Present, 2015.* W.W. Norton.; **lxx** Beth Bailey, et al, *The Fifties Chronicles,* 2008. Publications International, Ltd.; **lxxi** Henry Louis Gates, Jr., *Life Upon These Shores: Looking at African American History 1513–2008,* 2011, pp. 355 & 356; **lxxi** Peter Braunstein, 2004. *The Sixties Chronicle.* Legacy.; **lxxii** Robin D. G. Kelley and Earl Lewis, eds. *To Make Our World Anew: Vol. Two: A History of African Americans Since 1880,* 2000; **7** Don Antonio de Otermín, governor of New Mexico, letter on the Pueblo Revolt, 1680; **8** Russell Thornton, (1987) *American Indian Holocaust and Survival: A Population History Since 1492,* University of Oklahoma Press.; **10** Chief Powhatan, 1609; Source: *History of the Early Discovery of America and Landing of the Pilgrims* by Samuel Gardner Drake, 1854, p. 353; **18** Robert Beverley, *The History and Present State of Virginia,* 1705; **19** Olaudah Equiano, *The Interesting Narrative of the Life of Olaudah Equiano;* **22** Magna Carta, Clause 39, 1250; **24** John Locke, *Two Treatises on Government,* 1690; *The Works of John Locke,* 1751, p. 194; **27** Mayflower Compact, 1620; **28** John Reid Jr.'s Indenture of apprenticeship with Robert Livingston Jr., November 1, 1742. (Gilder Lehrman Collection); **28** William Cathcart, (1883) *The Baptist Encyclopædia: A Dictionary of the Doctrines, Ordinances, Usages, Confessions of Faith, Sufferings, Labors, and Successes, and of the General History of the Baptist Denomination in All Lands: with Numerous Biographical Sketches of Distinguished American and Foreign Baptists, and a Supplement,* Volume 2, L. H. Everts; **29** (1878) "The Pennsylvania Magazine of History and Biography," Historical Society of Pennsylvania; **29** William Byrd (1841) *The Westover Manuscripts: containing The History of the Dividing Line betwixt Virginia and North Carolina; A Journey to the Land of Eden, A.D. 1733;* **31** Audrey Smedley, (November 1997) "Origin of the Idea of Race" from Anthropology Newsletter," California Newsreel; **31** Charles de Secondat baron de Montesquieu (1793) *The Spirit of Laws,* Volume 1. Publisher: David Niven; **34** Chief Minavanana, statement to English fur trader Alexander Henry, 1761; published in *Indian Biography; or, An Historical Account of Those Individuals Who Have Been Distinguished Among the North American Natives as Orators, Warriors, Statesmen, and Other Remarkable Characters* by B.B. Thatcher, Esq. Harper & Brothers pp. 76 and 77, 1848; **34** Reverend Solomon Stoddard, *An Answer to Some Cases of Conscience Respecting the Country,* Boston, 1722; published in the Magazine of History with Notes and Queries, pp. 204–205, 1917; **39** Patrick Henry speech, 1765; **41** John Adams letter to Hezekiah Niles Quincy, 1818; **42** Thomas Paine, *Common Sense,* 1776; *Common Sense,* p. 21 and 36.; **45** From a petition of a group of slaves to the Massachusetts legislature, 1777; *The Colored Patriots of the American Revolution,* 1855, p. 47; **49** Northwest Ordinance, 1787; **52** Article IV, Section 2, U.S. Constitution; **55** Brutus (Robert Yates), Antifederalist Essay I, October 18, 1787; *Founding the Republic: A Documentary History,* 1995, pp. 203–206; **55** James Madison, Federalist Paper No. 10, November 23, 1787; **55** Preamble of the U.S. Constitution; **57** James Madison, Federalist Paper No. 51; **63** Alexander Hamilton, *The Federalist Papers,* #84, July 16–August 9, 1788; **63** Patrick Henry, speech, June 5, 1788; Source: American Eloquence: A Collection of Speeches and Addresses, 1858, p. 14 and 15.; **68** Article I, Section 8, Clause 18, U.S. Constitution; **69** George Washington's Farewell Address, 1796; **73** concession speech, December 2000 by Al Gore. Copyright © 2000 by Albert Gore, used by permission of The Wylie Agency LLC.; **73** From Supreme Court decision in *Bush* v. *Gore,* 2000; **73** Justice John Paul Stevens, dissenting opinion, *Bush* v. *Gore,* 2000; **75** "The Constitution of the State of New York". **75** Article I, Section 1, US Constitution; **75** Letter of Archibald Hinshelwood to Joshua Mauger (August 19, 1765). Found online at Gilder Lehrman Collection.; **77** George Washington letter to James McHenry, 1785; **77** Thomas Jefferson, letter to James Madison, January 30, 1787. In *Thomas Jefferson, The Works of Thomas Jefferson, vol. 5 (Correspondence 1786–1789)* [1905]. G.P. Putnam's Sons; **79** Source: U.S. Department of Justice; **80** Declaration of Independence, July 4, 1776; **81** From Africans in America, "Colin Powell on the Declaration of Independence and how it applied to black people," (https://www.pbs.org/wgbh/aia/part2/2i1601.html) © 1998, 1999 WGBH Educational Foundation. Other than the foregoing, neither WGBH nor any WGBH program or series will be identified in any way as the supplier of the Materials without WGBH's express prior written permission.; **82** (1856) Debates and proceedings in the Convention of the commonwealth of Massachusetts, held in the year 1788, and which finally ratified the Constitution of the United

Acknowledgments

States; **82** Bryan, S., (1787) "Centinel, no. II : To the people of Pennsylvania. Friends, countrymen, and fellow-citizens, as long as the liberty of the press continues unviolated...," Library of Congress.; **86** President Thomas Jefferson, letter to Robert R. Livingston, U.S. Minister to France, April 18, 1802. In *Thomas Benton Edgington* (1905) Little, Brown & Co.; **87** (1970) "Historical Statistics of the United States, Colonial Times to 1970, Part 2," Bureau of the Census.; **91** Source: U.S. Census Bureau; **95** C. B. Taylor (1839) "President Andrew Jackson, 1st Annual Message to Congress, December 1829." *A Universal History of the United States of America: Embracing the Whole Period, from the Earliest Discoveries, Down to the Present Time*. New York: E. Strong; **96** Cherokee Address, July 17, 1830. In (1830) Niles' Weekly Register, Volume 38. H. Niles & Son; **101** Frederick Douglass, July 5, 1852, The meaning of July Fourth for the Negro. In Frederick Douglass, Philip Sheldon Foner (1975) *The Life and Writings of Frederick Douglass*. International Publishers; **101** William Lloyd Garrison (January 1, 1831) *The Liberator,* Vol. 1; **103** Declaration of Sentiments, 1848; **105** The National Archives and Records Administration; **107** Abraham Lincoln, acceptance speech, 1858; **107** *Dred Scott* v. *Sanford,* 60 U.S. (19 How.) 393 (1857); **111** U.S. Constitution, Article I, Section 9; **114** American War and Military Operations Casualties: Lists and Statistics: Congressional Research Service, September 14, 2018.; **115** Abraham Lincoln, Draft of the Gettysburg Address: Nicolay Copy. Transcribed and annotated by the Lincoln Studies Center, Knox College, Galesburg, Illinois. Available at Abraham Lincoln Papers at the Library of Congress, Manuscript Division (Washington, D.C.: American Memory Project, [2000-02]), http://memory.loc.gov/ammem/alhtml/malhome.html.; **116** (1845), "The United States Magazine and Democratic Review, Volume 17," Lagtree and O'Sullivan.; **116** President Monroe, James., "Transcript of Monroe Doctrine (1823)," Our Documents (9, May 2019); **119** Excerpt from "Uncle Tom's Cabin, A Moral Battle Cry for Freedom?," Harriet Beecher Stowe Center, Hartford, CT.; **119** The Erie Canal and its Impact: Erie Canalway National Heritage Corridor, 2019.; **120** *Dred Scott* v. *Sanford,* Chief Justice Roger B. Taney for the Supreme Court, 1857. In (1885) Reports of Cases Argued and Decided in the Supreme Court of the United States: 1-351 U.S; 1790 October term, 1955, Book 27.; **121** Barrett, J. H., (1864) *Life of Abraham Lincoln: Presenting His Early History, Political Career, and Speeches in and Out of Congress; Also a General View of His Policy as President of the United States; with His Messages, Proclamations, Letters, Etc., and a Concise History of the War,* Moore, Wilstach & Baldwin.; **122** (1865) *The Political History of the United States of America, During the Great Rebellion, from November 6, 1860, to July 4, 1864,* Philp & Solomons.; **122** Salmon Portland Chase, (1866) "U.S. Reports: Ex parte Milligan, 71 U.S. (4 Wall.) 2," The Library of Congress. **137** General Philip Sheridan speech to the Texas Legislature, 1873; cited in *The Border and the Buffalo: An Untold Story of the Southwest Plains* by John R. Cook, p. 113.; **140** T. J. Morgan, The Present Phase of the Indian Question, 1891, cited in Source-*Book of American History*, Albert Bushnell Hart, ed., 1903, p. 367; **142** U.S. Constitution, 15th Amendment; **149** Roosevelt, T., (1906) *A Square Deal and The Dignity of Labor*, Best Books, p. 23.; **156** (1949) "Historical statistics of the United States, 1789–1945: a supplement to the Statistical abstract of the United States, Part 1," U.S. Government Publishing Office.; **163** Supreme Court decision in *Lochner* v. *New York* (1905). State of New York Department of Labor.; **166** 19th Amendment to the US Constitution; **167** Booker T. Washington, Atlanta Exposition address, 1895; **167** W.E.B. Du Bois, editorial in *The Crisis,* 1912; **172** Emma Goldman, *Living My Life*, 1931, pp. 84 and 86; **172** Riis, J. A. (1890) *How The Other Half Lives*, University of Michigan Library.; **174** Historical Census Statistics On Population Totals by Race, 1790 to 1990, and by Hispanic Origin, 1970 to 1990, For Large Cities And Other Urban Places In The United States: United States Bureau of the Census, February, 2005.; **174** Population: 1790 to 1990. United States Urban and Rural: United States Bureau of the Census, August 26, 1993.; **175** Andrew Carnegie, "Wealth," *North American Review,* June 1889; **175** William Jennings Bryan, "Cross of Gold" speech at the Democratic National Convention, July 9, 1896; **176** Booker T. Washington, speech at the Atlanta Exposition, 1895; **177** W.E.B. Du Bois, "The Talented Tenth," *The Negro Problem,* 1903; **178** Source: Let's Sing!, Educational Department, International Ladies' Garment Workers' Union, New York City; **182** Bicentennial Edition: Historical Statistics of the United States, Colonial Times to 1970: United States Bureau of the Census, September 1975.; **184** Josiah Strong, *Our Country: Its Possible Future and its Present Crisis*, 1885, p. 175; **186** U.S. Secretary of State Gresham report to President Cleveland, 1894 (found in *A Digest of International Law*, published 1906); **187** "We Don't Want to Fight" (aka McDermotts' War Song), 1877; **188** Senator Albert J. Beveridge, speech to the Senate, 1900 (found in *The Pacific Monthly,* vol. III, November 1899-April 1900, published 1900).; **190** Secretary of State John Hay, 1898; **197** German foreign secretary Arthur Zimmermann, 1917 (Zimmerman note/telegram); **198** President Woodrow Wilson's Fourteen Points, speech to joint session of Congress, January 8, 1919; **199** Vincent Joseph Esposito, (1962) *A Concise History of World War I*, Praeger Publishers.; **207** The Sedition Act of 1918. United States, Statutes at Large, Washington, D.C., 1918, Vol. XL, pp 553 ff.; **208** Justice Oliver Wendall Holmes, majority opinion in *Schenck* v. *United States,* March 3, 1919; **210** President Woodrow Wilson's Fourteen Points; **211** Bartolomeo Vanzetti, statement to the court, April 9, 1927, pp. 141 and 144. In Fraekel, O. K., (1931) *The Sacco-Vanzetti case.* George Routledge & Sons, Ltd.; **211** W. E. B. Du Bois, "The Migration of Negroes," *The Crisis,* June 1917, pp. 65 & 66; **212** Thomas G. Paterson et al., (1991) "American Foreign Policy: A History 1900 to Present," D. C. Heath and Company.; **213** World War I and the American Red Cross, 2019.; **214** Senator Albert J. Beveridge, "The March of the Flag" campaign speech, 1898; **215** Mark Twain, *New York Herald,* 1900; **216** Justice Oliver Wendell Holmes, Jr., dissenting opinion in *Abrams* v. *United States,* 1919; **216** Justice Oliver Wendell Holmes, Jr., majority opinion in *Schenck* v. *United States* (1919). U.S. Reports: *Schenck* v. *United States,* 249 U.S. 47 (1919), Supreme Court of the United States; **219** Warren G. Harding, campaign address in Boston, MA, May 14, 1920; **228** Supreme Court majority opinion in *Epperson* v. *Arkansas,* 1968; **228** *The Klansman's Manual,* 1925; **229** Source: U.S. Census Bureau; **233** Langston Hughes, "The Negro Artist and the Racial Mountain," *The Nation,* June 23, 1926; **241** (1975) Historical Statistics of the United States, Colonial Times to 1970, Part 1, U.S. Department of Commerce, Bureau of the Census.; **247** Herbert Hoover, *The Memoirs of Herbert Hoover Volume 3*, 1952; **249** from Franklin D. Roosevelt's acceptance speech, Democratic National Convention,

Acknowledgments

July 2, 1932; **249** President Herbert Hoover, 1932; **251** National Labor Relations Act (Wagner Act) July 5, 1935; **251** U.S. Social Security Act, 1935; **256** Ossie Davis, interview for The Great Depression, August 29, 1992. Washington University Digital Gateway; **256** Paul F. Brissenden, Earnings of Factory Workers 1899 To 1927: United States Bureau of the Census.; **256** Statistical Brief: How Consumers Spend Their Money: United States Bureau of the Census, June 09, 1992.; **258** Statistical Abstract of the United States: United States Bureau of the Census, 1929.; **261** United States presidential election of 1928: Encyclopedia Britannica, 1928. Retrieved from https://www.britannica.com/event/United-States-presidential-election-of-1928.; **262** Marcus Garvey, "Declaration of Rights of the Negro Peoples of the World," August 1920; **268** Quote by President Franklin Delano Roosevelt; **276** Walter Lippmann, "The Fifth Column," *Los Angeles Times,* February 13, 1942; **283** President Franklin D. Roosevelt, "Arsenal of Democracy" fireside chat, December 29, 1940; **283** President Truman, radio address of Sept 1, 1945, announcing the surrender of Japan.; **285** President Franklin D. Roosevelt, Address to Congress, December 8, 1941; **287** Letter of apology from President George H.W. Bush to Japanese internees, October 1990; **293** American diplomat George Kennan, July 1947, from telegram to the State Department but also printed as an article in Foreign Affairs. Council on Foreign Relations, Inc.; **320** (1988) "United States Code: War Powers Resolution, 50 U.S.C. §§ 1541–1548," Library of Congress.; **320** Letter from a group of nine U.S. Senators to President Jimmy Carter, June 28, 1977; **323** (June 5, 1947) "The Marshall Plan Speech," The George C. Marshall Foundation.; **323** North Atlantic Treaty, April 4, 1949; **325** President John F. Kennedy, speech before a Joint Session of Congress, May 25, 1961; **337** Current Population Reports Consumer Income: Income of Persons in the United States 1955. United States Bureau of the Census, November 1956.; **338** Ariane Hegewisch, M. Phil., On 2018. *The Gender Wage Gap: 2017; Earnings Differences by Gender, Race, and Ethnicity.* Institute for Women's Policy Research; **352** U.S. Social Security Act, 1935; **356** Student Nonviolent Coordinating Committee, statement of purpose, April 1960; **358** Majority Opinion by Anthony Kennedy, (2015) "Obergefell v. Hodges," Supreme Court of the United States.; **358** Ronald Reagan Question and Answer Session, Feb 19, 1981; **359** Mary Beth Norton, et al., 2014. *A People and a Nation, Volume II: Since 1865.* Cengage Learning.; **361** Civil Rights Act of 1964; **361** Excerpt from JFK's Report to the American People on Civil Rights, 11 June 1963; **362** Rachel Carson, *Silent Spring,* 1962; **386** from President Barack Obama's State of the Union Address, 2015.; **387** Charles Duhigg and Keith Bradsher, "In its early days, Apple usually didn't look beyond its own tech backyard for manufacturing solutions. But that changed." *The Mercury News,* 2012; **387** President George H.W. Bush, Address to the Nation, January 16, 1991; **388** Unemployment, total (% of total labor force) (modeled ILO estimate), April 2019. World Bank Group.; **389** Instances of Use of United States Armed Forces Abroad, 1798-2018, December 28, 2018. Congressional Research Service.; **391** President Bill Clinton, speech to House of Representatives on Permanent Normal Trade Relations with China, May 24, 2000; **391** President Donald Trump, statement on Trade with China, June 15, 2018; **392** from a speech by George W. Bush, The White House Archives; **392** Representative C.L. "Butch" Otter (R-ID), Congressional Record, p. H7289, July 22, 2003. **E-2** Jonathan Earle, 2016. *The Routledge Atlas of African American History.* Routledge.; **E-3** Secretary of the Treasury Alexander Hamilton, Report on a National Bank, December 13, 1790; published in Reports of the Secretary of Treasury of the United States, 1828; **E-3** Thomas Jefferson, letter to George Washington on the Constitutionality of a National Bank, February 15, 1791; found at Library of Congress; **E-4** United States Presidential Election Results, Encyclopedia Britannica.; **E-5** President Andrew Jackson, Nullification Proclamation, December 10, 1832; **E-6** Henry William Revenal, a plantation owner from South Carolina, diary entry, May 25, 1865; **E-6** laws of Mississippi, November 25, 1865; published in *Index to the Executive Documents of the Senate of the United States, 1866-67;* **E-7** Henry Ford, "My Life and Work," *McClure's Magazine,* July 1922; **E-8** Secretary of State John Hay, First Open Door Note, September 6, 1899; **E-9** Lorena Oropeza, Latino Heritage Initiatives Fighting on Two Fronts: Latinos in the Military, National Park Services, 2012; **E-9** Senator Joseph McCarthy, speech to Women's Republican Club in Wheeling, West Virginia, February 1950; **E-10** 2017 Yearbook of Immigration Statistics Office of Immigration Statistics, July 2019. Department of Homeland Security. **E-11** Supreme Court Justice Abraham Fortas, majority opinion, *Tinker* v. *Des Moines Independent Community School District,* 1969; **E-12** President George W. Bush, State of the Union Address, January 29, 2002; **E-14** King Philip, Metacom (Wampanoag), 1676; **E-14** Population in the Colonial and Continental Periods; Census procedure in colonial and continental periods prior to 1790—recent estimates of early population, population of cities, changes in urban population 1710 to 1900: United States Bureau of the Census.; **E-16** "The Crime Wave," *Time,* June 30, 1975; **E-16** Richard A. Leo, "The Impact of Miranda Revisited," *The Journal of Criminal Law and Criminology,* Vol. 86, Spring, 1996, p. 671; **E-18** U.S. Constitution; **E-19** U.S. Constitution; **E-20** President Lyndon B. Johnson, Special Message to the Congress: The American Promise, March 15, 1965; **E-20** Seth C. Mckee, 2018. *The Dynamics of Southern Politics: Causes and Consequences,* CQ Press.; **E-21** Elizabeth Cady Stanton, The Declaration of Sentiments, Seneca Falls Conference, 1848; **E-21** Senator Robert L. Owen (D-OK), speech at the American Academy of Political and Social Science, 1910; **E-22** Declaration of Principles of the National Progressive Republican League, January 21, 1911, *La Follette's Weekly Magazine;* **E-22** President Richard Nixon, Statement About the Ratification of the 26th Amendment to the Constitution, June 30, 1971

Note: Every effort has been made to locate the copyright owner of material reproduced in this component. Omissions brought to our attention will be corrected in subsequent editions.

This section contains a simulated Regents Examination in United States History and Government that is similar to the examination you will take in June 2020.

This examination has three parts. You are to answer **all** questions in all parts. Use black or dark-blue ink to write your answers to Parts II and III.

Be sure to refer to the test-taking strategies in the front of this book as you prepare to answer the test questions.

Part I contains 28 stimulus-based multiple-choice questions. Circle your answers for the multiple-choice questions in Part I.

Part II contains two short essay questions.

Part III is a Civic Literacy Essay based on several documents. Each document or document set is followed by a question. Write your answer to each question on the lines following that question. Then answer the essay.

Although you can write your answers to the questions for the Civic Literacy documents on the lines provided, you should write your responses to the Short Essay Questions and the Civic Literacy Essay in Parts II and III on separate sheets of paper.

Part I

Answer all questions in this part.

Directions (1–28): For each statement or question, record on your separate answer sheet the *number* of the word or expression that, of those given, best completes the statement or answers the question.

Base your answers to questions 1 and 2 on the map below and on your knowledge of social studies.

African Americans in the 13 Colonies, 1680 and 1740

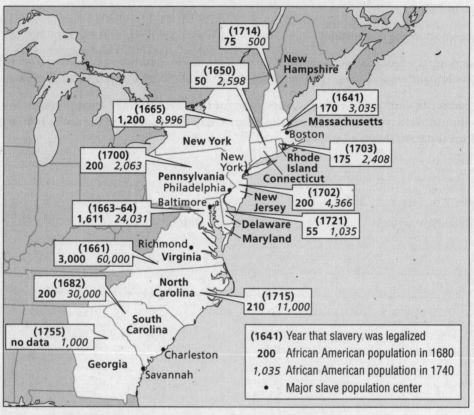

Source: Jonathan Earle, *The Routledge Atlas of African American History,* 2000

1 Which claim is best supported by this map?

  (1) African Americans resided primarily in states producing tobacco and rice.

  (2) By 1740, northern colonies no longer had an African American population.

  (3) Pennsylvania's African American population was mostly free.

  (4) African Americans tended to settle in large cities.

2 What is the primary cause of the change in African American populations between 1680 and 1740?

  (1) The expansion of indentured servitude in the colonies.

  (2) The transition to the factory system in the northern colonies.

  (3) The reliance on a slave-based economy in some of the colonies.

  (4) The changes in British policy towards immigration in the colonies.

Base your answers to questions 3 and 4 on the passages below and on your knowledge of social studies.

In obedience to the order . . . requiring the Secretary of the Treasury to prepare and report . . . such further provision as may, in his opinion, be necessary for establishing the Public Credit; the said Secretary further respectfully reports . . . that a National Bank is an institution of primary importance to the prosperous administration of the Finances, and would be of the greatest utility in the operations connected with the support of the Public Credit . . . .

Source: Secretary of the Treasury Alexander Hamilton, Report on a National Bank, December 13, 1790

The incorporation of a bank, and the powers assumed by this bill, have not, in my opinion, been delegated to the United States, by the Constitution.

I. They are not among the powers specially enumerated: for these are: 1st. A power to lay taxes for the purpose of paying the debts of the United States; but no debt is paid by this bill, nor any tax laid. Were it a bill to raise money, its origination in the Senate would condemn it by the Constitution. . . .

Source: Thomas Jefferson, letter to George Washington on the Bill for Establishing a National Bank, February 15, 1791

3   What problem does Jefferson identify in Hamilton's recommendation of establishing a National Bank?

(1) The federal government does not have the authority to levy a national income tax.

(2) A National Bank would undermine the power of Senate.

(3) The federal government does not have the authority to create a National Bank.

(4) A National Bank would undermine the power of the states.

4   The differing opinions of Hamilton and Jefferson regarding the formation of a National Bank was one of the issues that eventually led to

(1) the formation of two political parties

(2) a broad interpretation of the elastic clause

(3) the establishment of judicial review

(4) a new economic policy on interstate trade

Base your answers to questions 5 and 6 on the table below and on your knowledge of social studies.

Final Election Returns for Select Presidential Elections

Election of 1876	Popular Vote		Electoral College Vote
	Total	Percentage	
Hayes*	4,036,298	47.98	185
Tilden	4,300,590	51.12	184
Cooper	75,973	0.90	—
Election of 1888	Popular Vote		Electoral College Vote
	Total	Percentage	
Harrision*	5,439,853	47.82	233
Cleveland	5,540,309	48.70	168
Fisk	249,819	2.20	—
Street	146,602	1.29	—
Election of 2000	Popular Vote		Electoral College Vote
	Total	Percentage	
Bush*	50,456,002	47.87	271
Gore	50,999,897	48.38	266
Nader	2,882,955	2.74	—

*Elected by Electoral College

Source: Encyclopaedia Britannica; Federal Election Commission

5 Which conclusion can be drawn from the data on the chart?

(1) The Electoral College was created to officially select the president according to the popular vote.

(2) Third-party candidates have had little affect on the results of presidential elections since the 1800s.

(3) A presidential candidate does not need to win the popular vote in order to be elected president.

(4) The United States has a complicated system of counting the popular vote in presidential elections.

6 Based on the information provided in this table, which claim is most accurate?

(1) As more people participate in elections, the need for an Electoral College is decreasing in today's presidential elections.

(2) Despite conflicting results in the popular and Electoral College votes, the U.S. election process ensures a peaceful transfer of power.

(3) Although its vote can differ from the popular vote, the Electoral College ensures the most qualified candidate is elected president.

(4) As extremely close popular votes are infrequent, the Electoral College is not called upon to vote for the president that often.

Base your answers to questions 7 and 8 on the passage below and on your knowledge of social studies.

Whereas a convention assembled in the State of South Carolina, have passed an ordinance, by which they declare that the several acts and parts of acts of the Congress of the United States, purporting [making a false claim] to be laws for the imposing of duties and imposts on the importation of foreign commodities, and now having actual operation and effect within the United States, and more especially "two acts for the same purposes, passed on the 29th of May, 1828, and on the 14th of July, 1832, are unauthorized by the Constitution of the United States, and violate the true meaning and intent thereof, and are null and void, and no law". . . .

The Constitution of the United States . . . forms a government, not a league, and whether it be formed by compact between the States, or in any other manner, its character is the same. It is a government in which all the people are represented, which operates directly on the people individually, not upon the States; they retained all the power they did not grant. But each State having expressly parted with so many powers as to constitute jointly with the other States a single nation, cannot from that period possess any right to secede [break away], because such secession does not break a league, but destroys the unity of a nation, and any injury to that unity is not only a breach which would result from the contravention [disobeying] of a compact, but it is an offense against the whole Union. To say that any State may at pleasure secede from the Union, is to say that the United States are not a nation.

Source: President Andrew Jackson, Nullification Proclamation, December 10, 1832

7   What problem is Andrew Jackson addressing in his remarks?

   (1) South Carolina's state government wants to continue the charter for the National Bank.

   (2) South Carolina's state government is refusing to follow federal law.

   (3) South Carolina is forcing Native Americans off of their homelands.

   (4) South Carolina is attempting to impose tariffs on neighboring states.

8   Which constitutional principle is addressed in Jackson's proclamation?

   (1) rights of the individual

   (2) checks and balances

   (3) federalism

   (4) separation of powers

Base your answers to questions 9 and 10 on the passage below and on your knowledge of social studies.

> We still remain in doubt as to the emancipation policy. No official announcement except President Lincoln's amnesty proclamation has been published. . . . The party in power now are radical abolitionists and will do all in their power to urge it forward. Both policy and humanity would dictate that it should be gradual, so that both parties at the South may accommodate themselves to so radical a change in social and political economy. . . . My Negroes have made no change in their behavior, and are going on as they have always hitherto done. Until I know that they are legally free, I shall let them continue. If they become free by law then the whole system must be changed. If the means which I now possess of supporting the old and the young are taken away, they must then necessarily look for their support to their own exertions. How they can support themselves at present, I cannot see. . . . If Emancipation prevails, the negro must become a laborer in the field, as the whites will soon occupy all the domestic and mechanic employments.

Source: Henry William Revenal, a plantation owner from South Carolina, diary entry, May 25, 1865

9 Which generalization is best supported by this document?

(1) The economies of many of the Southern states remained mostly intact at the end of the Civil War.

(2) At the end of the Civil War, the resolutions of key issues were unclear to some Southerners.

(3) The Southern farmers resented having to compete with freedmen for land that they once owned.

(4) After the Civil War, most Southerners strongly supported the reconstruction plans of the Radical Republicans.

10 At the time of the writing of this document, which major turning point in history has yet to occur?

(1) surrender at Appomattox

(2) delivery of the Gettysburg Address

(3) secession of South Carolina

(4) ratification of the 13th Amendment

Base your answers to questions 11 and 12 on the laws below and on your knowledge of social studies.

> **Section 5** . . . Every freedman, free negro, and mulatto shall, on the second Monday of January, 1866 and annually thereafter, have a lawful home or employment, and shall have written evidence thereof. . . .
>
> **Section 6** . . . All contracts for labor made with freedmen, free negroes, and mulattoes for a longer period than one month shall be in writing, and a duplicate, attested and read to said freedman, free negro, or mulatto by a beat, city or county officer . . . and if the laborer shall quit the service of the employer before the expiration of his term of service, without good cause, he shall forfeit his wages for that year up to the time of quitting.
>
> **Section 7** . . . Every civil officer shall, and every person may, arrest and carry back to his or her legal employer any freedman, free negro, or mulatto who shall have quit the service of his or her employer before the expiration of his or her term of service without good cause. . . .

Source: Laws of Mississippi, enacted November 25, 1865

11 The authors of these laws were reacting to the expected ratification of the 13th Amendment by

(1) expanding the rights of former slaves

(2) attempting to create a political and economic system similar to slavery

(3) punishing slave owners for their treatment of slaves

(4) supporting programs to provide job training to former slaves

12 Which economic system is most closely associated with these laws?

(1) sharecropping

(2) mercantilism

(3) communism

(4) free market

Base your answers to questions 13 and 14 on the passage below and on your knowledge of social studies.

A Ford car contains about five thousand parts—that is counting screws, nuts and all. Some of the parts are fairly bulky and others are almost watch parts. In our first assembling we simply started to put a car together at a spot on the floor and workmen brought to it the parts as they were needed in exactly the same way as one builds a house. When we started to make parts it was natural to create a single department of the factory to make that part, but usually one workman performed all of the operations necessary on a small part. The rapid press of production made it necessary to devise plans of production that would avoid having the workers falling over one another. . . .

The first step forward in assembly came when we began taking the work to the men instead of the men to the work. We now have two general principles in all operations—that a man shall never have to take more than one step, if possibly it can be avoided, and that no man need ever stoop over. . . .

. . .In short, the result is this: by the aid of scientific study one man is now able to do somewhat more than four did only a comparatively few years ago. That line established the efficiency of the method and we now use it everywhere. The assembling of the motor, formerly done by one man, is now divided into eighty-four operations—those men do the work that three times their number formerly did.

Source: Henry Ford, "My Life and Work," *McClure's Magazine,* July 1922

13 A historian could best use this passage to study which topic?

   (1) philanthropic activities of industrialists
   (2) the use of trusts and monopolies to limit competition in business
   (3) technological innovation during the period of industrialization
   (4) the impact of nativists on the United States

14 This type of production created a need for

   (1) funding in math and science education
   (2) unskilled factory workers in cities
   (3) strict immigration laws
   (4) the Federal Highway Act

Simulated Regents Examination

Base your answers to questions 15 and 16 on the passage below and on your knowledge of social studies.

> Earnestly desirous to remove any cause of irritation and to insure at the same time to the commerce of all nations in China the undoubted benefits which should accrue [increase] from a formal recognition by the various powers claiming "spheres of interest" that they shall enjoy perfect equality of treatment for their commerce and navigation within such "spheres," the Government of the United States would be pleased to see His German Majesty's Government give formal assurances, and lend its cooperation in securing like assurances from the other interested powers. . . .

Source: Secretary of State John Hay, First Open Door Note, September 6, 1899

15 What problem does John Hay hope to resolve?

(1) China and Germany's strong military alliance that is posing a threat to the United States.

(2) The United States need for Pacific territories to act as coaling stations along its trade routes to China.

(3) China's prevention of the annexation of Hawaii by the United States.

(4) The United States lack of the same trade opportunities in China as other nations.

16 This document helps support the claim that

(1) the United States sought to expand its economic influence into the Pacific at the turn of the 20th century

(2) the United States invoked the Monroe Doctrine to stake a claim in Chinese markets

(3) the United States supported spheres of influence in China as opposed to an Open Door Policy

(4) the United States sought to return to isolationism after the Spanish American War

Base your answers to questions 17 and 18 on the timeline below and on your knowledge of social studies.

The Harlem Renaissance

1909
The NAACP is founded in New York City

1924
Louis Armstrong comes to New York to play with the first big band jazz orchestra

1927
Duke Ellington's orchestra begins its run as the house band at the Cotton Club

1929
Louis Armstrong returns to New York, plays at Connie's Inn in Harlem

1905 | 1910 | 1915 | 1920 | 1925 | 1930 | 1935

1921
Langston Hughes' poem "A Negro Speaks of Rivers" appears in *The Crisis* magazine

1925
Alain Locke publishes *The New Negro*

1928
Claude McKay publishes his novel *Home to Harlem*

1935
The Harlem Arts Guild is formed

17 Which claim is best supported by this timeline?

(1) Harlem became a cultural center during the 1920s.

(2) The Great Depression impacted Harlem more than other cities.

(3) Much of Harlem remained segregated in the beginning of the 20th century.

(4) African American artists were not well known outside of Harlem.

18 The events on this timeline were in part a result of the

(1) prohibition of alcohol

(2) Great Migration

(3) 19th Amendment

(4) New Deal

Base your answers to questions 19 and 20 on the passage below and on your knowledge of social studies.

> The massive mobilization effort that [World War II] required, moreover, ensured widespread participation from non-combatants. Countless Latinas joined the Army's WACS, the Navy's WAVES, or similar all-female auxiliary units associated with the U.S. Air Force. Just 19, Maria Sally Salazar of Laredo, Texas, for example, was so eager to join the Army's Women Army Corps that she borrowed her sister's birth certificate so that she could pass for 21, the minimum age requirement for women. After basic training, she spent 18 months in the Philippine jungle working out of an administrative building but also tending the wounded when needed. In addition, thousands of Mexican American men and women found jobs in defense industries, an opportunity that was almost denied them because anti-Mexican prejudice remained so high. Although President Franklin Roosevelt had issued an executive order in 1941 banning discrimination in defense industry hiring, the war's seemingly ceaseless demand for labor soon proved more effective in trouncing employer reluctance to hire Latino workers.

Source: Lorena Oropeza, *Fighting on Two Fronts: Latinos in the Military*, National Park Services, 2012

19 According to this document, what was the primary motivation for banning discrimination in defense industry hiring?

(1) the desire to end racial injustice in America

(2) the need for workers to keep wartime production high

(3) the loss of Japanese workers due to Executive Order 9066

(4) the desire of so many women to help in the war effort

20 Which group of Americans faced a similar experience as those described in this document?

(1) African Americans

(2) German Americans

(3) Italian Americans

(4) Chinese Americans

Base your answers to questions 21 and 22 on the passage below and on your knowledge of social studies.

> The reason why we find ourselves in a position of impotency [weakness] is not because our only powerful potential enemy has sent men to invade our shores, but rather because of the traitorous actions of those who have been treated so well by this Nation. It has not been the less fortunate or members of minority groups who have been selling this Nation out, but rather those who have had all the benefits that the wealthiest nation on earth has had to offer—the finest homes, the finest college education and the finest jobs in Government we can give. This is glaringly true in the State Department. There the bright young men who are born with silver spoons in their mouths are the ones who have been worst. . . . I have here in my hand 57 cases of individuals who would appear to be either card carrying members or certainly loyal to the Communist Party, but who nevertheless are still helping to shape our foreign policy.

Source: Senator Joseph McCarthy, speech to Women's Republican Club in Wheeling, West Virginia, February 1950

21 A historian would best use this quote to study

(1) immigration policy after World War II

(2) the domestic impact of the Cold War

(3) the impact of the Cuban missile crisis on Soviet-American relations

(4) policies leading to the fall of the Berlin Wall

22 Which congressional action is most closely associated with this speech?

(1) passage of the Patriot Act

(2) support for the Marshall Plan

(3) increase of federal funding for the development of nuclear weapons

(4) investigations of the film industry by the House Un-American Activities Committee

Base your answers to questions 23 and 24 on the graph below and on your knowledge of social studies.

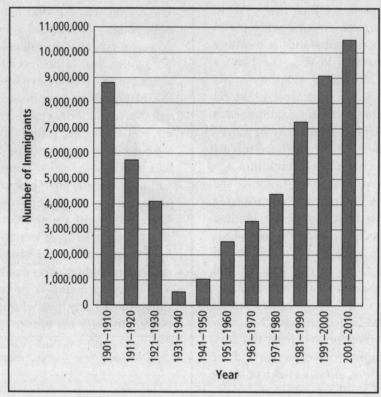

United States Immigration, 1901–2010

Source: Department of Homeland Security, 2017 Yearbook of Immigration Statistics, July 2019

23 What is a primary cause for the increase in the number of immigrants after 1980?

(1) the end of international tensions due to the Cold War

(2) the passage of laws reducing immigration restrictions

(3) the outsourcing of factory jobs overseas

(4) the collapse of the Soviet Union

24 A similarity between immigration in the first decade of the 1900s and the first decade of the 2000s is that

(1) immigrants continue to come primarily from Southern and Eastern Europe

(2) immigrants tend to settle in cities due to available jobs in the service industry

(3) immigrants come to the United States for economic opportunity

(4) immigration levels decreased from the prior decade

Base your answers to questions 25 and 26 on the image and passage below and on your knowledge of social studies.

Mary Beth Tinker and John Tinker display the armbands that led to the landmark Supreme Court case on student rights

First Amendment rights, applied in light of the special characteristics of the school environment, are available to teachers and students. It can hardly be argued that either students or teachers shed their constitutional rights to freedom of speech or expression at the schoolhouse gate.

Source: Supreme Court Justice Abraham Fortas, majority opinion, *Tinker v. Des Moines Independent Community School District*, 1969

25 The armbands shown in this image were worn by students
   (1) in protest of the Vietnam War
   (2) to support prayer in school
   (3) to advocate for the freedom of the press
   (4) in response to Bloody Sunday in Selma, Alabama

26 A lawyer researching students' rights would best compare the *Tinker* case to
   (1) *Marbury* v. *Madison*
   (2) *Worcester* v. *Georgia*
   (3) *Miranda* v. *Arizona*
   (4) *New Jersey* v. *TLO*

Simulated Regents Examination

Base your answers to questions 27 and 28 on the speech below and on your knowledge of social studies.

> Our second goal is to prevent regimes that sponsor terror from threatening America or our friends and allies with weapons of mass destruction. Some of these regimes have been pretty quiet since September the 11th. But we know their true nature. North Korea is a regime arming with missiles and weapons of mass destruction, while starving its citizens.
>
> Iran aggressively pursues these weapons and exports terror, while an unelected few repress the Iranian people's hope for freedom.
>
> Iraq continues to flaunt [display] its hostility toward America and to support terror. The Iraqi regime has plotted to develop anthrax, and nerve gas, and nuclear weapons for over a decade. This is a regime that has already used poison gas to murder thousands of its own citizens—leaving the bodies of mothers huddled over their dead children. This is a regime that agreed to international inspections—then kicked out the inspectors. This is a regime that has something to hide from the civilized world.
>
> States like these, and their terrorist allies, constitute an axis of evil, arming to threaten the peace of the world. By seeking weapons of mass destruction, these regimes pose a grave and growing danger. They could provide these arms to terrorists, giving them the means to match their hatred. They could attack our allies or attempt to blackmail the United States. In any of these cases, the price of indifference would be catastrophic.
>
> We will work closely with our coalition to deny terrorists and their state sponsors the materials, technology, and expertise to make and deliver weapons of mass destruction. We will develop and deploy effective missile defenses to protect America and our allies from sudden attack. And all nations should know: America will do what is necessary to ensure our nation's security.

Source: President George W. Bush, State of the Union Address, January 29, 2002

27 President George W. Bush acted upon these stated goals when he

    (1) ordered an invasion of Afghanistan

    (2) supported No Child Left Behind

    (3) established a detention camp in Guantanamo Bay

    (4) authorized the use of military force in Iraq

28 How did President Obama's actions to address the conflict with Iran differ from those taken by President Bush in the Middle East?

    (1) Obama asked Congress for a declaration of war against Iran.

    (2) Obama negotiated a nuclear arms agreement with Iran.

    (3) Obama used drone strikes in Iran to target nuclear sites.

    (4) Obama increased tariffs on Iranian goods sold in the United States.

Part II

SHORT ESSAY QUESTION–SET # 1

This Short Essay Question is based on the accompanying documents and is designed to test your ability to work with historical documents. Each Short Essay Question set will consist of two documents. Some of these documents have been edited for the purposes of this question. Keep in mind that the language and images used in a document may reflect the historical context of the time in which it was created.

Task: Read and analyze the following documents, applying your social studies knowledge and skills to write a short essay of two or three paragraphs in which you:

- Describe the historical context surrounding these documents
- Identify and explain the *relationship* between the events and/or ideas found in these documents (Cause and Effect, *or* Similarity/Difference, *or* Turning Point)

In developing your short essay answer of two or three paragraphs, be sure to keep these explanations in mind:

Describe means "to illustrate something in words or tell about it"

Historical Context refers to "the relevant historical circumstances surrounding or connecting the events, ideas, or developments in these documents"

Identify means "to put a name to or to name"

Explain means "to make plain or understandable; to give reasons for or causes of; to show the logical development or relationship of"

<u>Types of Relationships:</u>

Cause refers to "something that contributes to the occurrence of an event, the rise of an idea, or the bringing about of a development"

Effect refers to "what happens as a consequence (result, impact, outcome) of an event, an idea, or a development"

Similarity tells how "something is alike or the same as something else"

Difference tells how "something is not alike or not the same as something else"

Turning Point is "a major event, idea, or historical development that brings about significant change. It can be local, regional, national, or global"

Document 1

Population Growth in New England Colonies, 1620–1750

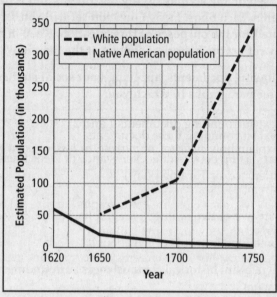

Source: U.S. Census Bureau; New England Historical Society

Document 2

The English who came first to this country were but a handful of people, forlorn, poor and distressed. My father was then sachem [chief]. He relieved their distresses in the most kind and hospitable manner. He gave them land to build and plant upon. He did all in his power to serve them. Others of their countrymen came and joined them. Their numbers rapidly increased. My father's counselors became uneasy and alarmed lest, as they were possessed of firearms, which was not the case of the Indians, they should finally undertake to give law to the Indians, and take from them their country. They therefore advised him to destroy them before they should become too strong, and it should be too late. My father was also the father of the English. He represented to his counselors and warriors that the English knew many sciences which the Indians did not, that they improved and cultivated the earth, and raised cattle and fruits, and that there was sufficient room for both the English and the Indians. His advice prevailed. They concluded to give victuals [supplies] to the English. They flourished and increased.

Experience taught that the advice of my father's counselors was right. By various means they got possessed of a great part of his territory. But he still remained their friend till he died. My elder brother became sachem. They pretended to suspect him of evil designs against them. He was seized and confined, and thereby thrown into sickness and died. Soon after I became sachem they disarmed all my people. They tried my people by their own laws, and assessed damages against them which they could not pay. Their land was taken. . . . Sometimes the cattle of the English would come into the cornfields of my people, for they did not make fences like the English. I must then be seized and confined till I sold another tract of my country for satisfaction of all damages and costs. Thus tract after tract is gone. But a small part of the dominion of my ancestors remains. I am determined not to live till I have no country.

Source: King Philip (Metacom), Wampanoag chief, 1676

SHORT ESSAY QUESTION–SET # 2

This Short Essay Question is based on the accompanying documents and is designed to test your ability to work with historical documents. Each Short Essay Question set will consist of two documents. Some of these documents have been edited for the purposes of this question. Keep in mind that the language and images used in a document may reflect the historical context of the time in which it was created.

Task: Read and analyze the following documents, applying your social studies knowledge and skills to write a short essay of two or three paragraphs in which you:

- Describe the historical context surrounding documents 1 and 2

- Analyze **Document 2** and explain how *audience*, **or** *purpose*, **or** *bias*, **or** *point of view* affects this document's use as a reliable source of evidence

In developing your short essay answer of two or three paragraphs, be sure to keep these explanations in mind:

Describe means "to illustrate something in words or tell about it"

Historical Context refers to "the relevant historical circumstances surrounding or connecting the events, ideas, or developments in these documents"

Analyze means "to examine a document and determine its elements and its relationships"

Explain means "to make plain or understandable; to give reasons for or causes of; to show the logical development or relationship of"

Reliability is determined by how accurate and useful the information found in a source is for a specific purpose

Document 1

[A]long with other Warren Court decisions, *Miranda* has increased public awareness of constitutional rights. The *Miranda* warnings may be the most famous words ever written by the United States Supreme Court. With the widespread dissemination [broadcasting] of *Miranda* warnings in innumerable [many] television shows as well as in the movies and contemporary fiction, the reading of the *Miranda* rights has become a familiar sight and sound to most Americans; *Miranda* has become a household word. As Samuel Walker writes, "[e]very junior high school student knows that suspects are entitled to their '*Miranda* rights.' They often have the details wrong, but the principle that there are limits on police officer behavior, and penalties for breaking those rules, is firmly established." As we have seen, a national poll in 1984 revealed that 93% of those surveyed knew that they had a right to an attorney if arrested, and a national poll in 1991 found that 80% of those surveyed knew that they had a right to remain silent if arrested. Perhaps it should not be surprising that, as many of my research subjects told me, some suspects assert their rights prior to the *Miranda* admonition [warning] or in situations where police warnings are not legally required. Indeed, in the last thirty years, the *Miranda* rights have been so entrenched [deeply rooted] in American popular folklore as to become an indelible [permanent] part of our collective heritage and consciousness.

Source: Richard A. Leo, "The Impact of Miranda Revisited,"*Journal of Criminal Law and Criminology,* Vol. 86, Spring, 1996

Document 2

The familiar fact is that the vastly troubled criminal-justice system often exacts no price at all for crime. An adult burglar has only one chance in 412 of going to jail for any single job, according to Gregory Krohm of the Virginia Polytechnic Institute's Center for the Study of Public Choice. For juveniles under 17, the figure is one in 659 burglaries, with a likelihood of only a nine-month term if the 659-to-1 shot comes in. Many critics are convinced that such odds were created in large part by those constitutional-law rulings of the Warren Court that expanded the rights of criminal defendants. Mapp, Escobedo, Miranda and Wade are still names that enrage law-and-order advocates. But despite all the years of talk and four Nixon appointments, the court has so far been willing only to trim some of the rules, not reverse them. The new rulings obviously add to the work of the courts, and some experts believe that they have hampered the criminal-justice system's capacity to convict guilty offenders, though as yet there have been no studies demonstrating any such significant damage.

Source: "The Crime Wave," *Time* magazine, June 30, 1975

PART III

CIVIC LITERACY ESSAY

This Civic Literacy essay is based on the accompanying documents. The question is designed to test your ability to work with historical documents. Some of these documents have been edited for the purpose of this question. As you analyze the documents, take into account the source of each document and any point of view that may be presented in the document. Keep in mind that the language and images used in a document may reflect the historical context of the time in which it was created.

Historical Context: Representation and Voting in a Democracy

Throughout United States history, many constitutional and civic issues have been debated by Americans. These debates have resulted in efforts by individuals, groups, and governments to address these issues. These efforts have achieved varying degrees of success. One of these constitutional and civic issues is representation and voting in a democracy.

Task: Read and analyze the documents. Using information from the documents and your knowledge of United States history, write an essay in which you

- Describe the historical circumstances surrounding this constitutional or civic issue
- Explain efforts to address this constitutional or civic issue by individuals, groups, and/or governments
- Discuss the extent to which these efforts were successful

Describe means "to illustrate something in words or tell about it"

Explain means "to make plain or understandable; to give reasons for or causes of; to show the logical development or relationship of"

Discuss means "to make observations about something using facts, reasoning, and argument; to present in some detail"

Document 1

We the People of the United States . . .

Article I, Section 2

The House of Representatives shall be composed of Members chosen every second Year by the People of the several States. . . .

Article I, Section 3

The Senate of the United States shall be composed of two Senators from each State, chosen by the Legislature thereof. . . .

Article II, Section 1

The executive Power shall be vested in a President of the United States of America. He shall hold his Office during the Term of four Years, and, together with the Vice President, chosen for the same Term, be elected, as follows

Each State shall appoint, in such Manner as the Legislature thereof may direct, a Number of Electors, equal to the whole Number of Senators and Representatives to which the State may be entitled in the Congress: but no Senator or Representative, or Person holding an Office of Trust or Profit under the United States, shall be appointed an Elector.

The Electors shall meet in their respective States, and vote by Ballot for two Persons. . . .

Source: United States Constitution, 1787

1. According to the U. S. Constitution, what is one group that has the power to elect federal officials? [1]

_____

_____

Document 2

Amendments to the U.S. Constitution

Amendment 15 (1870)

The right of citizens of the United States to vote shall not be denied or abridged by the United States or by any State on account of race, color, or previous condition of servitude.

Amendment 17 (1913)

The Senate of the United States shall be composed of two Senators from each State, elected by the people thereof. . . .

Amendment 19 (1920)

The right of citizens of the United States to vote shall not be denied or abridged by the United States or by any State on account of sex.

Amendment 24 (1964)

The right of citizens of the United States to vote in any primary or other election for President or Vice President, for electors for President or Vice President, or for Senator or Representative in Congress, shall not be denied or abridged by the United States or any State by reason of failure to pay any poll tax or other tax.

Amendment 26 (1971)

The right of citizens of the United States, who are eighteen years of age or older, to vote shall not be denied or abridged by the United States or by any State on account of age.

Source: United States Constitution

2. According to the Constitution, who are two groups who have had increased representation in government based on constitutional amendments? [1]

_____

_____

Document 3a

Voting Restrictions in Southern States, 1899–1908

Year	Poll Tax	Literacy Test	Property Test	Grandfather Clause	Other*
1889	Florida				Florida Tennessee
1890	Mississippi Tennessee	Mississippi			Mississippi
1891					Arkansas
1892	Arkansas				
1893					Alabama
1894					South Carolina Virginia
1895	South Carolina	South Carolina			South Carolina
1896					
1897					Louisiana
1898	Louisiana	Louisiana	Louisiana	Louisiana	
1899					North Carolina
1900	North Carolina	North Carolina	North Carolina	North Carolina	
1901	Alabama	Alabama	Alabama	Alabama	
1902	Virginia Texas	Virginia	Virginia		Virginia
1903					
1904					
1905					
1906					
1907					
1908		Georgia	Georgia	Georgia	Georgia

* Registration, multiple-box, secret ballot, understanding clause

Source: State constitutions

Document 3b

Our fathers believed that if this noble view of the rights of man was to flourish, it must be rooted in democracy. The most basic right of all was the right to choose your own leaders. The history of this country, in large measure, is the history of the expansion of that right to all of our people. Many of the issues of civil rights are very complex and most difficult. But about this there can and should be no argument. Every American citizen must have an equal right to vote. There is no reason which can excuse the denial of that right. There is no duty which weighs more heavily on us than the duty we have to ensure that right. Yet the harsh fact is that in many places in this country men and women are kept from voting simply because they are Negroes. . . . This bill will strike down restrictions to voting in all elections—Federal, State, and local—which have been used to deny Negroes the right to vote. . . . To those who seek to avoid action by their National Government in their own communities; who want to and who seek to maintain purely local control over elections, the answer is simple: Open your polling places to all your people. Allow men and women to register and vote whatever the color of their skin. Extend the rights of citizenship to every citizen of this land.

Source: President Lyndon B. Johnson, Special Message to the Congress: The American Promise, March 15, 1965

3. Based on these documents, state one way in which limitations were placed on who had the right to vote? [1]

_____

_____

Document 4a

The history of mankind is a history of repeated injuries and usurpations [seizures] on the part of man toward woman, having in direct object the establishment of an absolute tyranny over her. To prove this, let facts be submitted to a candid world.

He has never permitted her to exercise her inalienable right to the elective franchise.

He has compelled her to submit to laws, in the formation of which she had no voice.

Source: Elizabeth Cady Stanton, The Declaration of Sentiments, Seneca Falls Conference, 1848

Document 4b

The great doctrine of the American Republic that "all governments derive their just powers from the consent of the governed," justifies the plea of one-half of the people, the women, to exercise the suffrage. The doctrine of the American Revolutionary War that taxation without representation is unendurable, justifies women in exercising the suffrage.

Source: Senator Robert L. Owen (D-OK), speech at the American Academy of Political and Social Science, 1910

4. What problem is described in these documents? [1]

_____

_____

Document 5

Popular [democratic] government in America has been thwarted and progressive legislation strangled by the special interests, which control caucuses, delegates, conventions, and party organizations; and, through this control of the machinery of government, dictate nominations and platforms, elect administrations, legislatures, representatives in Congress, United States Senators, and control cabinet officers. . . .

The Progressive Republican League believes that popular government is fundamental to all other questions. To this end it advocates:

(1) The election of United States Senators by direct vote of the people.

(2) Direct primaries for the nomination of elective officials.

(3) The direct election of delegates to national conventions with opportunity for the voter to express his choice for President and Vice-President.

(4) Amendment to state constitutions providing for the Initiative, Referendum and Recall.

Source: Declaration of Principles of the National Progressive Republican League, January 21, 1911, *La Follette's Weekly Magazine*

5. What is one way in which the National Progressive Republican League sought to expand democracy in America? [1]

_____

_____

Document 6

Tonight Ohio's Legislature ratified the 26th Amendment to the Constitution. This Amendment guarantees the right of 18-year-old persons to vote in State and local, as well as Federal, elections. It appears that 38 States have now ratified the Amendment that will now become a part of the law of the land.

Some 11 million young men and women who have participated in the life of our Nation through their work, their studies, and their sacrifices for its defense, are now to be fully included in the electoral process of our country.

For more than 20 years, I have advocated the 18-year-old vote. I heartily congratulate our young citizens on having gained this right.

The ratification of this Amendment has been accomplished in the shortest time of any amendment in American history. This fact affirms our Nation's confidence in its youth and its trust in their responsibility. It also reinforces our young people's dedication to a system of government whose Constitution permits ordered change.

I urge them to honor this right by exercising it—by registering and voting in each election.

Source: President Richard Nixon, Statement About the Ratification of the 26th Amendment to the Constitution, June 30, 1971

6. According to Richard Nixon, why was the 26th Amendment important? [1]

_____

_____